Project
Management
Pathways

Project
Management
Pathways

Edited by Martin Stevens

Project Sponsor: Bill Johnson

The Association for
Project Management

Thornton House 150 West Wycombe Road High Wycombe Buckinghamshire HP12 3AE

The Association for Project Management Limited.
Thornton House.
150 West Wycombe Road,
High Wycombe,
Buckinghamshire,
HP12 3AE.

Tel: +44 (0) 1494 440 090
Fax: +44 (0) 1494 528 937

Website: www.apm.org.uk

First published in Great Britain in 2002

© The Association for Project Management Limited 2002.

ISBN 1-903494-01-X

British Library Cataloguing in Publication Data:
A CIP catalogue record for this book can be obtained from the British Library.

Typeset Frutiger Light and Helvetica Rounded
Printed and bound in Great Britain by Michael Heath Limited, Reigate.

"A thing which cannot be accomplished should never be undertaken"

Anonymous. African (Yoruba) Proverb

Project Management Pathways

CONTENTS

Contents

LIST OF FIGURES AND ILLUSTRATIONS

Contents

Section 3   Control

Section 4   Technical

Section 5   Commercial

Section 6   Organisational

Section 7   People

FORWARD

Bill Johnson

"Think like a man of action, act like a man of thought."
Henri Bergson.

In the summer of 2000 with the support of Don Heath, I announced a new initiative in the Association's Journal "Project": - 'The Association is going to publish a book to support The Body of Knowledge'. This book is the result of that initiative.

Like all professions, project management has a Body of Knowledge (BoK) (Dixon, 2000) that resides with those practitioners and academics that apply and advance it. The BoK describes both the skill set and knowledge that those individuals who profess or aspire to be practitioners in the field of project management are expected to possess. It is central to our profession and provides the academic references for candidates preparing for examination at APMP or developing their knowledge through CPD and on to Certification. Recognition of this was one of the driving forces behind Pathways and it was logical to develop topic texts and references and combine them in a single book that could become a cornerstone of our educational programme.

This is particularly relevant as, increasingly, public and private sector organisations depend upon management by project. Dedicated project teams working within the larger organisation develop new initiatives, new working methods and new products or services. Thus it is that project management has evolved and, as Robert Heller observes, (in Buttrick, 2000) many managers "spend as much of their time in interdisciplinary, cross functional, interdepartmental project teams as they do in their normal posts."

Project Management Pathways was designed to call on the expertise of our members, both individual and corporate drawn from many business sectors, with the intention of reflecting the broad church that sits upon the core skills.

Briefs for each topic chapter were developed from the BoK baselines and the membership trawled for individuals willing to both write and review the texts. A core review panel was established to oversee the whole process and provide consistency across the completed work.

Prospective authors were invited to submit synopses for each chapter and, meanwhile, topic reviewers were asked to prepare coverage checklists against which each synopsis would be reviewed. Synopses were adjudicated and amended in consultation with authors and reviewers to provide an agreed basis for each chapter following which authors were formally commissioned.

Final drafts of each chapter text were again subjected to peer group review on a stand-alone basis by experienced topic reviewers and were also reviewed by the core review panel in the context of the book as a whole.

This is a book written and reviewed by practitioners for practitioners. In this way it is hoped that it will be truly representative of both current thinking and practice in daily use by practitioners themselves. We believe this approach adds real value to both other practitioners and those seeking to improve their skills and understanding and truly differentiates this book.

The science or art of project management is dynamic. The state of knowledge of professionals and the tools they need to practice successfully is ever changing. Organisations, be they large, small, public or private, strive to improve the ways in which they conduct business. The link between successful projects and successful businesses has now been firmly established and as business becomes more project oriented the particular skills of the project manager have become recognised and sought after. The project management Body of Knowledge is the project managers map of the practice methodologies required for project management success. Project Management Pathways is the guidebook.

Bill Johnson
APM Hon. Treasurer.
Little Shoesmiths August 2002.

THE PATHWAYS CONCEPT AND BOK

Bill Johnson, Bob Saunders, Martin Stevens

"Knowledge is little; to know the right context is much, to know the right spot is everything."
Hugo von Hofmannsthal.

Introduction

"Body of Knowledge" (BoK) is an inclusive term describing the sum of knowledge within the project and programme management profession. As with other professions, such as law, medicine and accounting, the BoK rests with those practitioners and academics who apply and advance it.

APM began developing a BoK in the late eighties, publishing the first edition in 1992. Whilst it has been updated since then, the 4th Edition, published in 2000, (Dixon, 2000) was the first fundamental revision that the Association had undertaken and forms the baseline for Project Management Pathways.

Continental Experience / Influence

The two most significant BoK's are those published by APM and PMI (Project Management Institute).

Broadly speaking other National Associations or groupings use one or other of these as the basis for their own BoK's: The Dutch, French, Swiss and German project management Associations have BoK's that substantially reflect the APM Model, whilst the Australian Association uses PMI's but as a basis of competence rather than knowledge. (APM like other IPMA members, introduces competency assessment via an examination and certification programme).

The International Project Management Association, is working to harmonise the BoK's of its member Associations seeking to provide an international baseline for certifying competency and benchmarking best practice and performance in project management and has published its own competence baseline (Caupin et. al., 1999).

A Universal BoK

In creating a valid (universal) BoK, there are a number of challenges:

- What should the elements be,
- What is a proper definition of each of these elements, and
- How should the elements be structured.

Deciding what to include is important. Different languages, which connote different ways of doing (or thinking about) things, increases the difficulty as does language variation between industries. (Some industries have different conceptions, for example, of what words like systems engineering, configuration management, procurement, mobilisation, and logistics mean).

The challenge is, therefore, to strike a balance between creating a genuinely useful general language of project management and putting people off with unfamiliar terms.

Content

The 2000 edition BoK was commissioned because project and programme management is changing, and the body of knowledge needed to reflect this. The primary input was a research project undertaken by the Centre for Research into the Management of Projects at the University of Manchester's Institute of Science and Technology, led by Professor Peter Morris. (Morris, 2000). The importance of this research was that it carried out an independent survey of the practice of project management in relation to the elements of knowledge that project management professionals in a range of industries felt they needed.

Thus the BoK represents the topics that practitioners and experts consider professionals in project management should be knowledgeable of and competent in.

Pathways therefore incorporates not only inwardly focused project management topics, such as planning and control tools and techniques, but also those broader topics essential to the effective management of projects. These cover the context in which the project is being managed, such as the social and ecological environment, as well as a number of specific areas, such as technology, economics and finance, organisation, procurement, and people, as well as general management.

Throughout Pathways we have chosen to refer to topics as "Sessions". They are grouped into seven sections (Figure 1). The first section deals with a number of *General* and introductory items. The remaining six sections comprise sessions to do with managing: the project's *Strategic* framework, including its basic objectives; *Control* issues that should be employed; the definition of the project's *Technical* characteristics; the *Commercial* features of its proposed implementation; the *Organisational* structure that should fit the above; and issues to do with managing the *People* that will work on the project.

Though there is nothing fixed about this sequence, it is logical insofar as a strategic framework should be put in place first. Processes, practices and systems required for effective control - in the sense of planning, reporting and taking corrective action - should be established from the outset. The project's technical definition should then be determined and developed in parallel with consideration of commercial matters (which may sometimes slightly lag behind the technical definitional work) and then finally, the organisational and people issues need to be factored in. These last two are by no means the least important. Many consider, quite properly, that people issues are at the very heart of successful project management.

Many of the sessions in each of these sections are closely linked or are interdependent. They are treated separately here however due to their individual significance. Teamwork and leadership, for example, although they could be treated as a part of communications, are independently addressed due to their inherent importance in project management. In reality, many of the sessions fit in more than one section. Remember therefore that the categorisation is not intended to be too limiting.

1	General						
10	Project Managment	11	Programme Managment	12	Project Context	10	Cultural Influences

2	Strategic				
20	Project Success Criteria	22	Value Management	24	Quality Management
21	Strategy / Project Management Plan	23	Risk Management	25	Health, Safety and Environment

3 Control	4 Technical	5 Commercial	6 Organisational	7 People
30 Work Content and Scope Management	40 Design, Implementation and Hand-Over Management	50 Business Case	60 Project Success Criteria	70 Communication
31 Time Scheduling / Phasing	41 Requirements Management	51 Marketing and Sales	61 Opportunity	71 Teamwork
32 Resource Management	42 Estimating	52 Financial Management	62 Design and Development	72 Leadership
33 Budget and Cost Management	43 Technology Management	53 Procurement	63 Implementation	73 Conflict Management
34 Change Management	44 Value Engineering	54 Legal Awareness	64 Hand-Over	74 Negotiation
35 Earned Value Management	45 Modelling and Testing		65 (Post) Project Evaluation Review	75 Human Resource Management
36 Information Management	46 Configuration Management		66 Organisation Structure	
			67 Organisation Rôles	

Figure 1: Grouping of Pathways Sessions.

Importance

Almost all practitioners (not to mention their employers and clients) are interested in knowing what knowledge they should have to be considered a competent project management professional. Further, they also seek a "sign-posted" route for career development. They look to APM and other professional bodies to advise them and, typically, they value a certificate or qualification that says they have attained a required standard.

The Association therefore uses its BoK for baselining competencies in project management and for benchmarking project management best practice and performance. Additionally, APM has developed a competency "ladder" that benchmarks the stages of knowledge and experience through which an aspirant project manager will pass on the way to becoming an "expert" (Figure 2).

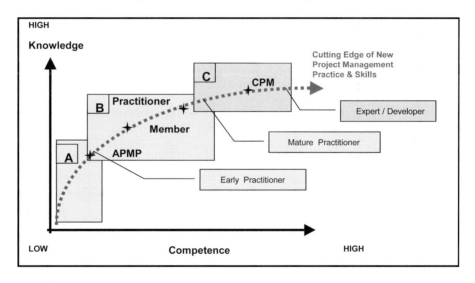

Figure 2: *Project Management Maturity Model.*

The ladder starts with the foundation qualification "Project Management Professional" (APMP) and progresses through "Member" and "Practitioner" status to "Certificated Project Manager" which is a Pan-European recognised, peer group adjudicated acknowledgement of competence (knowledge plus experience).

Thus the Body of Knowledge and Project Management Pathways together form the basis for the benchmarks and the means to focus continuing professional development programmes that will guide and enable practitioners to attain "expert" status.

Conclusion

Understanding what factors have to be managed to deliver successful projects is important, because it exposes the issue of the professional remit - the ethos - of project and programme management. Is it to deliver projects "on time, within budget, to scope", or is it to deliver projects that meet the requirements of the project customer / sponsor?

It must be the latter. If not, project management is an introverted profession that, long-term, few serious managers are going to get very excited about.

Decision makers in government, business and elsewhere require that their projects are managed effectively and efficiently; that they represent value-for-money and meet or exceed their strategic objectives. Defining the scope, cost, and time targets properly is only half the battle; ensuring that the technical, commercial, business, environmental, and other factors are effectively aligned with organisational objectives is the other.

Contributing to a better understanding of project and programme management processes and developing the skills of project management professionals is the raison d'être of Project Management Pathways.

Section 1

General

10 PROJECT MANAGEMENT

Michael Holton

"Managing is getting paid for home runs someone else hits."
Attributed to: Casey Stengel (1890?-1975), U.S. baseball manager.

Introduction

This session is presented as an overview of the nature of project management. Other sessions will provide detailed information and guidelines about the tools, techniques, disciplines, competencies and skills that are part of the art and science of Project Management.

Project Management, A Definition

Project Management is defined by British Standard 6079 - 1: 2000 as the:

"Planning, monitoring and control of all aspects of a project and the motivation of all those involved in it to achieve the project objectives on time and to the specified cost, quality and performance".

An alternative definition is: "The controlled implementation of defined change".

Project Management is widely regarded as the most efficient way of introducing unique change. Essentially, project management achieves this by:

- defining what has to be accomplished, generally in terms of time, cost, and various technical and quality performance parameters;
- developing a plan to achieve these and then working this plan, ensuring that progress is maintained in line with these objectives;
- using appropriate project management techniques and tools to plan, monitor and maintain progress;
- employing persons skilled in project management - including normally a project manager - who are given responsibility for introducing the change and are

accountable for its successful accomplishment.

Project Management can and should be applied throughout the project lifecycle, from the earliest stages of concept definition through delivery and on into operations and maintenance.

Projects, A Definition

Similarly, BS 6079 -1 : 2002 defines a project as a:

"Unique process, consisting of a set of co-ordinated and controlled activities, with start and finish dates, undertaken to achieve an objective conforming to specific requirements, including the constraints of time, cost and resources."

An alternative definition is: "An endeavour in which human, material and financial resources are organised in a novel way to deliver a unique scope of work of given specification, often within constraints of cost and time, and to achieve beneficial change defined by quantitative and qualitative objectives".

Historic Context

It can be conjectured that the history of project management goes back to the time of the pharaohs and the construction of the pyramids at Giza (2600-2500 BC.) or to the Qin dynasty and the Great Wall of China (221-210 BC.)

Contemporary project management has its roots in the 1950's and 60's although Henry Gantt, widely recognised as the "father" of planning and control techniques and his eponymous bar chart first published his ideas in the early 1900's and as Burke (1999) notes Gantt charts were used during World War 1 to reduce the build-time of cargo ships.

Many of the project management tools used today including precedence diagrams, critical path analyses, PERT (Project Evaluation and Review Technique), work breakdown structures, earned value and configuration management were largely developed by the American defense and aerospace industries between 1950 and 1965.

Through the 70's and 80's tools and techniques were refined with increasing integration and acceptance into practice methodologies. Early focus on the tools and techniques concentrated on the implementation and delivery phase of the project life-cycle. As the 80's progressed however, attention turned to more careful consideration of a project's "front end" wherein lay the greatest opportunity to add value by careful analysis of the objectives, definition of a client's needs, undertaking of feasibility studies and assessment of risk.

With the advent of the new millennium, project management is increasingly seen as part of the general management toolkit and its techniques are deployed across all sectors of business and all types of project.

The Nature and Scope of Project Management

Projects are, by definition, unique and time limited. Accordingly the project management task is to create, sustain and motivate a temporary organisation (team) to deliver the client's objectives and, on completion, disband it.

Fundamentally the change(s) to be delivered by the project highlight the nature of project management which is to:

- Bring order, structure and discipline to a unique and non-repeatable undertaking.
- Reduce the risk of failure from poor investment decision-making, scope creep, inadequate specification, over-stated benefits, under-stated costs etc.
- Create and lead a cross- functional, multi disciplinary team focused on a super -ordinate goal.

Implicit in this is the objective scope of project management set out in Figure 10 - 1.

> - Define the purpose & objectives of the project and plan what has to be done, who will do it, how it will done & to what standard to achieve the objectives.
> - Create the temporary organisation required to deliver the project, ensuring it has the right people, skills, experience, tools, processes, governance & facilities to do the job.
> - Monitor & control all aspects of a project and the motivation of those involved in it.
> - Ensure the project objectives are achieved on time to specified cost, quality and performance or acceptance criteria.
> - Provide the single point of responsibility needed to ensure that every aspect of the project is managed effectively to ensure success.
> - Ensure there are repeatable processes to manage further changes in the future.
> - Ensure there are re-usable skills and experience to manage further changes in the future.

Figure 10 - 1:   The Scope of Project Management

Life Cycles

The project manager's role and the functionality of the tasks to be undertaken by the manager and team are necessarily linked to the business (and other) life cycles, namely:

- The company cycle of strategy formulation and strategic planning having regard to corporate policies and approach to project management
- The Project life cycle from the capturing the strategic need, through investigation, design, development and implementation to the realisation of benefits
- The Project team life cycle of creating, motivating and ultimately dissolving the temporary organisation required to deliver the project
- The learning cycle - What can we learn from the specific project to improve organisational capability for the future?

The relationship between the cycles is illustrated in Figure 10 - 2.

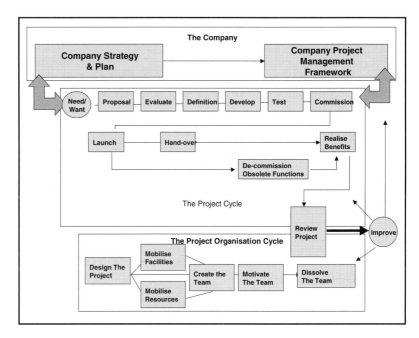

Figure 10 - 2:   The Project Cycle.

The Process of Project Management

The project management process is concerned with satisfying a business need or requirement for change that arises from a unique problem or opportunity. It is not concerned with satisfying the day-to -day or routine needs of an organisation.

It achieves this by bringing structure and discipline 'Project Management' to a non - routine or one-off requirement.

Through the Project Management process business needs and requirements are transformed into the deliverables or outputs that the project will provide to meet those needs. The transformation process is made up of the application of constraints such as time, cost, quality, the motivation of people, the deployment of skills and expertise and the application of project management tools and techniques (Figure 10 - 3).

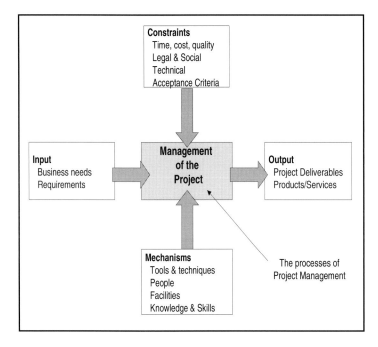

Figure 10 - 3: The Project Management Process

The Processes of Project Management

The successful delivery of a project requires that participants, lead by the project manager, undertake a number of processes which cover 7 key areas:

1 Processes that define what needs to be achieved.

- Business Case (Session 50)
- Strategy/Project Management Plan (Session 21)
- Requirement Management (Session 41)

2 Processes that plan work to achieve what needs to be done.

- Work Content & Scope Management (Session 30)
- Time Scheduling & Phasing (Session 31)

3   Processes that monitor the work to ensure it will be done as planned.

- Resource Management (Session 32)
- Budget and Cost Management (Session 33)
- Earned Value Management (Session 35)

4   Processes that control change within the project environment.

- Work Content and Scope Management (Session 30)
- Change Control (Session 34)
- Risk Management (Session 23)

5   Processes that ensure the outputs of the project are fit for purpose.

- Quality Management (Session 24)
- Modelling & Testing (Session 45)

6   Processes that ensure the outputs of the project are successfully launched in the business /customer environment.

- Implementation (Session 63)
- Hand -over (Session 64)
- Configuration Management (Session 46)

7   Processes that engage and motivate the stakeholders of the project.

- Marketing & Sales (Session 51)
- Communication (Session 70)
- Configuration Management (Session 46)

Some of these processes can be considered as project phases in their own right e.g. testing, whilst others need to be enacted for the duration of the project, although the emphasis or priority may change as the project moves through its life-cycle.

The Project Delivery Model (Project Life-cycle)

The end- to- end process of project delivery is generally broken down into a distinct set of process steps or phases. A phased approach:

- Allows for the insertion of decision gateways between each phase which permits the project manager and the project sponsor to review not only the progress of the project but the business environment in which project is being conducted and to test whether the project is still viable. This helps reduce the risk to the organisation
- Makes planning, resourcing, monitoring and control easier
- Makes key aspects of the project more visible
- Makes progress toward the end goal much more obvious

Figure 10 - 4 illustrates the major generic project process stages or steps and decision gateways that will be common to most projects in most environments. The table focuses on the purpose of each process stage or step, although it should be recognised that nomenclature will vary between business sectors and organisations.

The model is a four step one:

Decide Stage

An idea or need is developed into a proposal that an organisation can make a decision to proceed or abort without the risk of loss being too high. The aim is to be sure about why the project is required.

Define Stage

This stage refines the initial proposal into a fully defined, scoped and planned project. This phase should include the business case on which an appraisal and investment decision can be made to proceed with the development stage. In this stage what you want or need to do becomes what you are going to do, how you are going to do it and who is going to do it by when.

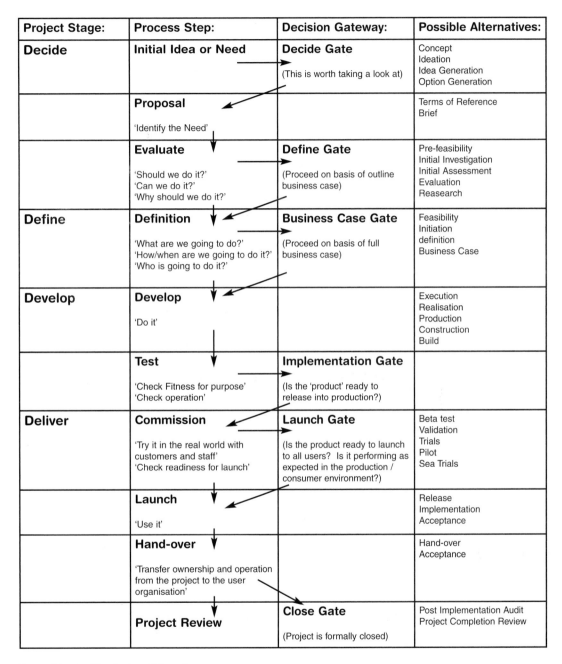

Project Stage:	Process Step:	Decision Gateway:	Possible Alternatives:
Decide	**Initial Idea or Need**	**Decide Gate** (This is worth taking a look at)	Concept Ideation Idea Generation Option Generation
	Proposal 'Identify the Need'		Terms of Reference Brief
	Evaluate 'Should we do it?' 'Can we do it?' 'Why should we do it?'	**Define Gate** (Proceed on basis of outline business case)	Pre-feasibility Initial Investigation Initial Assessment Evaluation Reasearch
Define	**Definition** 'What are we going to do?' 'How/when are we going to do it?' 'Who is going to do it?'	**Business Case Gate** (Proceed on basis of full business case)	Feasibility Initiation definition Business Case
Develop	**Develop** 'Do it'		Execution Realisation Production Construction Build
	Test 'Check Fitness for purpose' 'Check operation'	**Implementation Gate** (Is the 'product' ready to release into production?)	
Deliver	**Commission** 'Try it in the real world with customers and staff' 'Check readiness for launch'	**Launch Gate** (Is the product ready to launch to all users? Is it performing as expected in the production / consumer environment?)	Beta test Validation Trials Pilot Sea Trials
	Launch 'Use it'		Release Implementation Acceptance
	Hand-over 'Transfer ownership and operation from the project to the user organisation'		Hand-over Acceptance
	Project Review	**Close Gate** (Project is formally closed)	Post Implementation Audit Project Completion Review

Figure 10 - 4: The Project Lifecycle
(after Robert Butterick, The Interactive Project Workout - The Project Framework)

Development Stage

Here the solution is built and tested to ensure it meets the originally defined business needs and operates as expected, at this point the project can move into the Delivery Stage.

Delivery Stage

The Delivery stage is concerned with the transfer of the deliverables of a project from the project environment into the operational environment and consists of commissioning, a closed trial of the project deliverables in the users and customers operational and working environments to prove that the 'products' work in normal operating conditions. The Launch step, the release of the project deliverables into the working environment, the point at which the change defined by the project occurs. This is closely coupled with the Hand-over step, where the operational part of a business takes responsibility for that which the project has delivered to it. Once this has happened the project can be regarded as complete and can be formally closed following a Project Review that determines whether the project has achieved all its objectives, its outputs are performing as expected, ownership for any outstanding work or issues has been ascribed and accepted elsewhere in the organisation and responsibility for benefits delivery is clear.

The delivery model represents the project processes used to break down the 'transformation' into time/cost/quality bounded 'chunks'. Alongside it are the management and control, activities that span the whole of the life-cycle. Figure 10 - 5 provides a view of the total project process lifecycle, linking the transformation phases and management activities together.

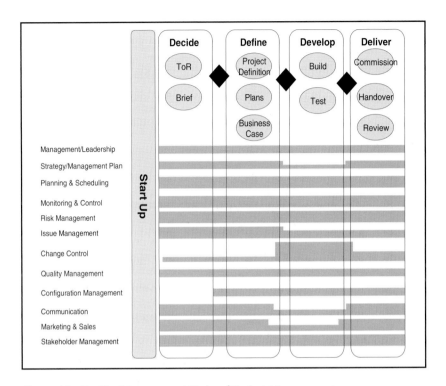

Figure 10 - 5: The Management Tasks of Project Management

What The Project Manager Does

The aim of the project manager is to successfully deliver projects that meet the objectives set for them. To do this the Project Manager must be able to:

- Create the conditions and environment for the project to be successful.
- Employ processes, tools and techniques appropriately to ensure the success of the project.
- Develop and lead the project team.
- Manage the interests of the stakeholders of the project.

The basic context of what the project manager does is bound in the key parameters of: Time, Cost and Quality (or specification). All projects are bound by the time by which the project must be delivered, the cost at which it should be delivered and the quality required of the project deliverables. What the project manager does is to manage the tensions between these three elements to ensure project success. Equally and increasingly the project manager also has to manage the tensions between 3 other elements, Cost, Risk and Benefit (Figure 10 - 6).

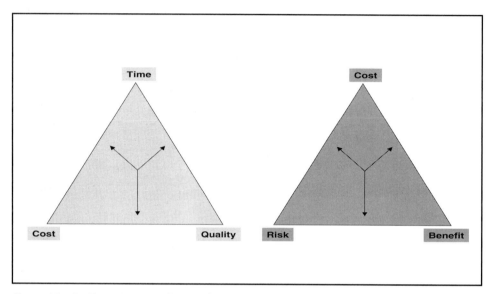

Figure 10 - 6: Time, Cost, Quality v Risk, Cost, Benefit

In seeking to achieve a balance between these conflicting elements, the project manager:

Plans
Directs
Co-ordinates
Controls

The project manager organises the project into a plan comprising logical steps, phases, work-packages, tasks, activities, resources, budget etc.

S/he creates and directs the project organisation that is needed to deliver the project and ensures that the right roles and responsibilities are included and that the right people with the right skills are deployed to the project, assigned to roles and made responsible for the deliverables of the project.

The Project Manager establishes the project control framework, decides what processes will be used, how documents will be written, how and when status reports will be provided etc.

The Project Manager manages the process of project management, the project manager leads the team, the Project Manager ensures the sponsor or client is aware of and/or happy with the ways things are going.

These things are the visible elements of project management which are, in many respects 'clerical'. However, they only represent the base level of project management. In truth the project manager can employ technical experts for these tasks or set up a Project Support Office for them.

The key thing a project manager does is manage not do and a vital thing that Project Managers do is to manage the 'white space', the area between and around the documented processes, procedures and work.

The project manager is the agent of change and the catalyst within the project process. The Project Manager has to create the reaction within the process that makes things happen. Having excellent project definitions, an outstanding plan, an exemplary team, and a good project approach and control framework doesn't mean that the project will be successful. Something needs to happen to breathe life into the enterprise; this is what the Project Manager does.

The Project Manager, therefore, has to be managerial and entrepreneurial in spirit and approach rather than clerical. This means:

- Being a leader and displaying/employing the qualities of leadership (Dynamic, Flexible, Creative, Persistent, Patient, Assertive, Persuasive, Confident, Imaginative, Analytic, Decisive, Organised, Goal Driven, Humble)
- Having a clear vision of the desired end result and communicating it
- Keeping the big picture in mind at all times
- Motivating people in the project team both individually and at team level

- Empowering the project team to be creative, solve problems, deliver
- Use peoples skills, expertise and experience effectively
- Ensuring all work is purposeful, with clear end results that the team can see contributes value to the whole
- Recognising and celebrating success (however small)
- Making sure that the processes, tools and techniques used add value to both the project and the people in the project team. Ensuring that the project is not a bureaucratic exercise or a 'text book' project
- Using the project management process as a tool, rather than being driven or constrained by the process
- Anticipating problems, issues, risks and fixing them. Negotiating directly with clients, sponsors, stakeholders and suppliers to ensure the project gets what it needs to be successful

There are some other aspects to what the project manager does that are also important or becoming increasingly important.

Benefits Management

Increasingly there is much more explicit focus on what benefits a project will deliver and on the establishment of mechanisms for planning and tracking the benefits from a project. Often business projects are being defined in terms of benefits. It is, therefore, important that the Project Manager ensures that benefit management processes and techniques are used within the project.

Change Management

Change Management (not be confused with Change Control) is often separated from Project Management and is seen to be the approach or process by which organisational change is delivered. However, change management and project management are related and can/should be used together. If project management is about creating a change then change management is about creating the right environment/culture/conditions for the project change to be successful in a sustainable way. Thus the project manager should consider 'change management' as one of the techniques or approaches used to ensure project success at least as part of the stakeholder management approach. Figure 10 - 7 suggests a nine- step change management approach, wherein the connections to Project Management are immediately clear.

Change Step	Purpose / Outcome
Diagnose	◆ What is the problem to be solved or opportunity to be exploited?
Align	◆ Ensure stakeholders are aware of the problem or opportunity and understand it.
Prepare	◆ Design a workable approach to solving the problem/exploiting the opportunity
Commit	◆ Seek active stakeholder/user involvement ◆ Secure a champion of the change to assure alignment.
Mobilise	◆ Mobilise resources/teams to tackle the issue ◆ Commission early wins to build confidence and commitment
Enable	◆ Commission enabling changes that lay the ground for principal changes in future.
Action	◆ Implement the change, drive the benefits
Measure	◆ Ensure systems are in place for ongoing measurement and review ◆ Does the solution deliver the benefits ◆ Are the benefits flowing, will they continue to flow
Institutionalise	◆ Ensure that belief and reward systems underpin the changes delivered to assure use, sustainability and improvement ◆ Encourage 'leveraging' activities that engage users in consolidating that change as part of the fabric of the operation/organisation

Figure 10 - 7: The Nine Step Change Management Process

Marketing and Sales

This is, in some part, a method of stakeholder management, but project managers need to realise the critical importance of 'marketing and selling' the project to sponsors, clients, customers, stakeholders and users as part of the effort required to make the project a success.

Applying marketing and selling approaches to stakeholder management, including communication, tends to make it more purposeful and targeted, thus consequentially more successful.

Roles & Responsibilities In Project Management

The project manager is normally the single point of integrative responsibility for the project, but the project manager is not responsible for everything. The responsibilities within a project management environment are wider than the responsibilities of the project manager alone.

Responsibility for the aims and objectives of a project fall to a number of key players in the project management organisation. Most projects will or should have these roles defined within in them.

The Project Sponsor or Owner

Responsible for ensuring a real business need is being addressed by the project and that the benefits of the project are realised. The project sponsor or owner is also responsible for:

- Appointing the project manager
- Ensuring the project is and continues to be a viable business proposition
- Signing off /accepting the outputs of the project
- Resolving issues outside the mandate of the Project Manager
- Chairing the Project Board or Steering Committee if there is one

The Project Board, Steering Committee or Champion

The role of the board or committee or champion (if required) is to enable the sponsor or owner to deliver the project benefits by:

- Ensuring the best interests of the organisation as a

whole are served by the project.
- Being a forum or facilitator for taking cross- functional decisions, resolving cross-functional issues and removing obstacles in the path of the project.

The Project Team

The project team has two dimensions the core team, directly responsible to the project manager and the extended or wider project team who report to direct team members or who the project draws on from time to time to assist in the delivery of the project. Often the wider or extended team will be drawn from the operational areas affected by the project or will be experts whose advice is required on an ad-hoc basis. The Project Team (or the managers or team leaders within it) is accountable to the project manager and responsible for:

- Delivery of the work allocated to them, to Cost, Time and Quality parameters
- Monitoring and managing the work delegated to them
- Managing and motivating the resources allocated to them to deliver the delegated activities

The Project Manager

The project manager is the appointee of the project sponsor or owner and is accountable to that person for the day- to -day management of the project involving the project team across all the functions. Whilst the project sponsor or owner is benefits focussed, the project manager is delivery or output or action oriented. The key responsibility of the project manager is to ensure that the outputs or deliverables of the project are presented on time, on budget and to the right quality (performance/functionality etc.) To do this the project manager must make projects and the results of projects more predictable by:

- Being benefit focused
- Building in quality
- Managing risks and issues
- Exploiting enablers and removing blockers

- Exploiting the resources and facilities of the organisation to the project's ends.

The key responsibilities of the Project Manager are:

- Provide the single point of responsibility needed to ensure that every aspect of the project is managed effectively to ensure success
- Define the project and plan what has to be done, who will do it, how it will done and to what standard to achieve the objectives
- Create the temporary organisation required to deliver the project, ensuring it has the right people, skills, experience, tools, processes, governance & facilities to do the job
- Monitor & control all aspects of a project including risk, opportunities, issues, scope change, benefits, etc.
- Ensure the project objectives are achieved on time to specified cost, quality and performance or acceptance criteria
- Manage the stakeholders of the project making sure they are involved and informed as necessary
- Manage the hand-over of the project deliverables into the operational environment
- Close the project down

Using the Tools of Project Management

There are many tools and techniques at the disposal of the project manager (described in other sessions of this book) all of which aim to increase the chances of success for a project. However, it is important that the project manager uses judgement in employing these tools and techniques to ensure they are appropriate for the project in question. There are four aspects to be taken into consideration that will influence what tools are used and how they are used.

- The skill and experience of the Project Manager
- The skills and experience of the Project Team
- The project management maturity of the organisation sponsoring the project

◆ The 'size' of the project in terms of complexity of the problem or opportunity, budget, timescale, risk/benefit profile etc.

The point is to use tools and techniques that are right for the job in hand. Too simple or too few in a large or complex project in a mature environment will not enhance the chances of success. Neither will over sophisticated approaches in a small or short duration project where there is a low level of maturity in the organisation or within the project team.

Project Managers should understand that projects are unique but it is not necessary to have a unique approach to each project. If the job of project management is to reduce risk by bringing order and structure to uncertain undertakings, then it is sensible for the management approach to be a tried and tested one. The job of the Project Manager is to apply and/or adapt the method, the tools and techniques to the specific nature of the particular project (Figure 10 - 8).

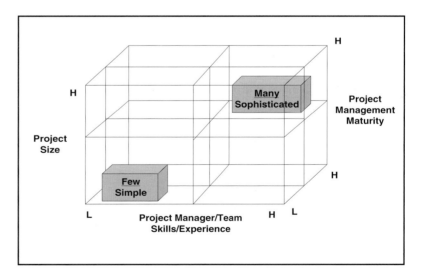

Figure 10 - 8: Application of Project Management Tools.

As a rule all projects should employ tools that allow for adequate:

- Planning and scheduling of work (e.g. product based planning, work breakdown, cost breakdown, organisational break down, critical path analysis)
- Identification, analysis and mitigation of risks
- Resolution of issues
- Identification, tracking and management of dependencies
- Estimating tools for cost, resource, duration, benefits etc.
- Monitoring and controlling cost, completion of work, quality of work, use of time, benefits etc.
- Tracking stakeholder 'reaction' to the project.

All of these tools should allow the project manager to 'project forward' and predict or anticipate the likely end position of the project and take corrective action rather than merely look back on passed events.

Project Management in the Business/Organisational Context

This section looks at project management in the organisational context and explores different approaches to project management that are driven by the business context of the project.

Projects and project management operate in an environment wider that that of the project itself. Project Managers need to understand this wider context. Managing just the day-to-day activities of a project are not always enough to ensure success:

- Project Management will be influenced by the organisation it is being undertaken within and how that organisation is set up to deliver projects.
- Organisational culture and style will have a direct influence on project management.
- Socio- economic conditions and changes will also have an influence on how project management operates in any organisation.

Where do Projects Come From

Projects arise as a need for a change, change may be desired from two standpoints; a problem needs to be solved or an opportunity needs to be exploited.

Within the strategic or business planning cycle of an organisation, projects will arise as a means of problem solving or opportunity exploitation. Such projects will probably already be structurally "framed" and planned. In such cases the project management approach will be to (a) confirm/affirm the estimate of time, cost, quality and resources provided in the corporate business plan from the assumptions made in the corporate strategic plan and (b) precisely define and plan the deliverables to meet the stated strategic aims. (Figure 10 - 9).

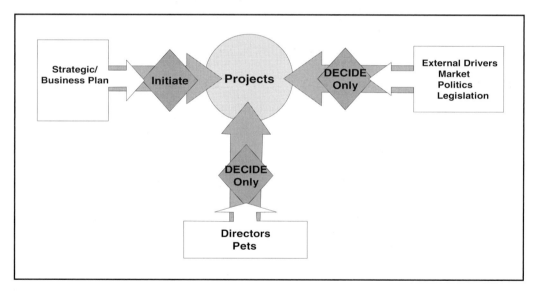

Figure 10 - 9: The Sources of Projects.

Outside of the normal planning cycle, however, events will occur which will drive the need for a project to deal with an unpredicted or planned for problem or opportunity. This may be driven by market or political changes or by changes to legislation.

In many organisations there is also the 'phenomenon' of the 'directors pet'. A project idea developed outside of the main stream of the business cycle by an executive or a director.

Dealing with the first type of project is relatively straight -forward.

The second case is more problematic in that what needs to be done or how it needs to be done may be unclear. All that is certain is that 'something must be done'. The organisation will need to decide how much effort/resource it is going to divert from planned projects or if it is going to cancel planned projects to accommodate this sort of change. One of the key aspects of decision making will be determining how real or long term the threat is, whilst realising that the decision time-frame might well be short. Normally large organisations can absorb one or two projects like this before there is a serious knock-on effect to planned/ or on-going operations.

The third type of project is potentially most difficult to deal with as there could be many 'ideas' being generated and many 'great opportunities' to be had. The key issue here is the diversion of resource from planned activity into unplanned/uncertain activity.

With 'something must be done' and 'directors pet' projects. It may be wise to limit the risk to planned projects by limiting the commitment or diversion of resources from elsewhere. The best way to deal with these is to only commit to the 'decide' stage of the project to determine whether something needs to be done, can be done and will deliver benefits. The next stage would then be to re-plan at the business level by including 'new' projects and cancelling existing ones that are either lesser opportunities (in terms of cost/benefit/risk) or have been superseded by changes to external factors.

Different Approaches to Project Management in Different Organisations

Fundamentally, the approach to Project Management is remarkably similar within many organisations, differences tending to occur in the following areas:

- The emphasis placed on one aspect of project management as opposed to others.
- The emphasis placed on project management as a specific skill or professional discipline.
- How projects are organised
- The language of project management
- The use of specific tools & techniques etc.

These differences are driven by the level of change going on in the organisation; the sector the business organisation is in; the culture of that organisation and the organisation's project management maturity. Organisational size is also a contributing factor to differences between companies. The fewer and shorter communication chains often influence the approach in smaller organisations, which reduces some of the formality in the project management approach.

Organisational Culture and Style

Organisational cultures will be reflected in shared values, norms, beliefs and expectations. Often the culture of an organisation will be reflected in its policies and procedures. This is likely to have a direct influence on project management and projects. For example a high- risk project or a high- risk approach is more likely to gain approval in an aggressive or entrepreneurial organisation than a conservative one. A project manager with an open, participative style is likely to experience difficulties in a strictly hierarchical organisation. Equally a project manager with an autocratic or authoritarian approach is unlikely to succeed in an organisation that promotes openness and participation.

Organisational Structure

The way a company is structured will have an impact on the way project management and project managers function. Organisations range from functionally aligned to project aligned.

In functionally aligned organisations, the organisation is divided into clear hierarchical towers built around a particular specialism or function and where a single superior ultimately manages all the staff.

A project- aligned organisation is organised around projects with staff co-located in pools (based on skills/experience etc.) Most of the organisations work is project based and staff will be allocated to one or more projects working for one or more project managers. In these organisations, project managers are the dominant managerial force and have a great deal of influence and power. In functional organisations by contrast, the line or functional managers are dominant and the project manager has little influence or power.

Between these two points is a hybrid organisational style, the matrix organisation. In matrix organisations there is a mix of functional and project based structures. Within this type of organisation, the influence/power of line vs. project managers varies. In a 'weak' matrix organisation where there is no defined project management function, the role of project management and project managers can be reduced to merely co-ordinating activity across functional boundaries. In more projectised matrices, the role of project management and project managers is stronger where either a functional manager has project managers working within his division or dept. and/or the organisation has a project management function that ranks along-side the other functional departments and takes responsibility for project management and managing projects across the organisation.

Figure 10 - 10 illustrates the impact on Project Management of various types of organisational structure.

Organisation Type	Functional Aligned	Weak Matrix	Strong Matrix	Project Aligned
Project Characteristics				
Project Managers Authority	Little to None (Line Manager Dominant)	Limited (Line Manager Dominant)	Moderate to High (Equal to Line Manager)	High to Total (Project Manager Dominant)
% of Organisation's workforce dedicated to projects	Virtually none	0 - 25%	50 - 95%	80 - 100%
Project Manager's role	Part-time	Part-time	Full-time	Full-time
Common titles for Project Manager's role	Co-ordinator Project Leader	Co-ordinator Project Leader	Project Manager	Project Manager Programme Manager Portfolio Manager
Project Support Staff	Part-time	Part-time	Full-time	Full-time

Figure 10 - 10: Role of Project Management/Manager in Different Organisation Types
(After PMI - Project Management Body of Knowledge - Organisational Structure Influences on Projects)

There are three other organisational characteristics that will influence the way in which project management is carried out. These are: size, culture and the project management maturity of the organisation. Figure 10 - 11 illustrates the impact of these characteristics.

Doing the Right Things Right - Some Lessons For Project Management

The aim of Project Management is to deliver successful projects by doing the right things right. Doing the right things right is within the total scope of project management not just the scope of the project manager in the context of a specific project (Figure 10 - 12).

Approach to Project Management

Small Organisation or Entrepreneurial	Medium Organisation	Large Organisation or Conservative
Informal ⟶		Formal
No specific process / framework	Recommended process / framework	Mandatory process / framework

Project Management Maturity

Immature	Normal	Mature ⟶
Line Management Dominant	Matrix Management Dominant	Project Management Dominant
Stand-alone Projects	Mix of Stand-alone and strategic plan led initiatives	Project closely coupled with Business Strategy Projects organised into Programmes and Portfolios
Line Managers do Projects. No formal training or qualification	Professional Project Managers Dedicated resource pools	Organisation is managed by Projects. All managers are project managers
Simple processes, tools and techniques	Mix of simple and complex approaches	Sophisticated processes, tools and techniques
Intuitive Project Managers	Process Dominated Project Managers	Judgemental Project Managers
Task Oriented	Product Oriented	Output Oriented
Deliverable Driven		Benefits Driven

Figure 10 - 11: Organisational Influences on Project Management

Cause of failure	Rules for success
Organisations initiate too much change: • Avoid tough decisions on priorities • Make decisions based on horse-trading rather than the merits of each case • Allow executive pet projects • Believe staff will always rise to meet challenge of whatever is thrown at them	Only those projects are implemented which have a direct link to the achievement of business strategy and will deliver benefits. The capacity of managers and staff to implement change is used as a basis for selecting new change projects. Experience of previous projects is used to influence the choice of future projects
Senior Executive sponsorship is weak: • Concentrate top management discussions on today's business and not on tomorrow's • Assume that a good general manager will have all the skills, experience and motivation to be an effective sponsor • Sponsors 'disappear' or change often • Delegate responsibility for benefits delivery to the Project Manager	Senior executives actively and visibly sponsor major change projects and their accountability is clear and enforced.
Projects take too long to deliver benefits: • Design large-scale transformation projects that take years to deliver • Forget what the project was/is for • Start implementing immediately to 'save' the time consumed by planning • Get locked into analysis phases for too long • Adopt a 'big bang' approach which delays all benefits until after the end of the project	Projects are as short as possible and broken down into chunks designed to deliver benefits within six months
Projects are not focused on delivering benefits: • Tell users you understand their requirements better than they do • Decide projects on basis of narrow financial criteria • Never question the validity of the original business case and estimates of benefit • Manage only to time, cost and quality	The focus of project management is delivering benefits within time and cost constraints. Projects are kept under review and are stopped if conditions make them no longer a priority or the benefits are not being delivered.
Projects over-emphasise technology: • Focus on completing the technical deliverables and let the benefits look after themselves • Get technology right first an sort out the people and processes later on • Buy the most leading-edge technology you can afford as the best way of winning competitively	Benefits come from people changing their behaviour. Technology, process, people and place deliverables are balanced within projects. Stakeholders have a major influence over the design of a project and throughout its life
Managers lack the required skills: • Assume that general management experience is all that is required to manage your biggest projects • Assign your best people to business as usual activities and staff projects with 'failed' line managers • Signal to managers that taking responsibility for a tough, challenging project will put their future careers at risk	Project Managers have the deep business understanding and change management skills to influence stakeholders
Organisation gets in the way: • Frequent re-organisations • Functional thinking and functional motives	Take the helicopter, organisation wide view The project is the benefit of the organisation Isolate the project from re-organisations (see sponsors)
Ignorance is bliss: • Untested assumptions • Ignoring the risks	All assumptions are risks treat them as such Make decisions based on risk analysis

Figure 10 - 12: Key lessons for Project Management
(After Doing the Right Things Right - Some lessons for organisations wrestling with change: The Organisational Consulting Partnership, 80 Cannon Street, London, EC4N 6 HL, Jan 2000.

A Universally Applicable Project Model

There are many project management models and approaches in the world today. Some are proprietary products; others have been developed by organisations and individuals to meet the specific needs of that business or the individual. However, fundamentally they are similar, the core components or building blocks are the same. Where they differ is:

- Language.
- Granularity in breaking down the steps or phases.
- Emphasis /priority placed on each step or phase.
- The order of each step of each phase.

The fundamental major steps of Project Management are, in all cases, as follows:

1   Define the project
2   Design the project
3   Develop / build the solution
4   Test the solution
5   Implement the solution
6   Review the project
7   Close the project

Figure 10 - 13 expands on this model and explains the purpose and outcome from each of these steps:

Phase	Purpose	Practice
Start Up	**DECIDE** Determine the objectives of the project	**PURPOSE** Why the results are needed: Diagnose the business problem or opportunity Benefits to be gained Who will benefit & why **END RESULTS** Vision of the final result - What do we want to end up with? Deliverables - What the product or service will look like **SUCCESS CRITERIA** Performance (time, cost, quality, process etc.)Risks to be managedBenefits to be realisedSponsor, stakeholder, user satisfaction **INFORMATION** Known Needed Ideas/Options
Plan	**DEFINE** Specify what needs to be done	**PLAN and SCHEDULE** Workplan to achieve end results/success criteria (Product Based Planning) Resource allocation to workplan (time, skills, money, people) Set Monitoring Points - milestones Project Design to ensure success - Implementation strategy/tactics - who, what, when, where, how **PREPARE** Design a workable solution - that satisfies purpose (People, Process, Technology, Place, Product, Organisation, Operation) ALIGN - engage stakeholders (WIIFM) Awareness - Communication Plan Understanding - engage in dialogue, ensure concerns are answered **REINFORCE** Identify who will operate the process/solution and how they will do it Obtain commitment to operational ownership of the process/solution **COMMIT** Seek active stakeholder/user involvement (WIIFM) Secure champions of change to assure alignment.
	DEVELOP Execute the Change	**BUILD THE SOLUTIONTEST THE SOLUTIONMOBILISE** Commission early wins to build confidence and commitment **ENABLE** Commission 'enabling' works that lay the foundations for principal changes
Execute	**DELIVER** Implement the Change	**ACTION** Implement the change Drive the benefits **MONITOR and REVIEW** Review against Definition and Design Review the process Troubleshoot -anticipate barriers, barriers/problems/issues, take remedial action **OPERATIONAL HANDOVER** Ensure process/solution owners formally take ownership of project deliverables Ensure process/solution owners take responsibility for continuous improvement Ensure process/solution owners take responsibility for benefits delivery
Close	**COMPLETE and REVIEW** Learn for future success	**MEASURE** Does the solution meet the purpose of the project, has the opportunity been leveraged or problem resolved Ensure systems are established for ongoing measurement and review Are the benefits flowing, will they continue to flow **REVIEW** Project success/failure Effectiveness of project systems and processes Team performance Capture learnings for the future **INSTITUTIONALISE** Ensure belief and reward systems underpin the changes delivered by the project to assure use, sustainability and improvement Encourage 'leveraging' activities that engage users in consolidating the change as part of the fabric of the operation. e.g. Benefits leveraging

Figure 10 - 13: A Project Guide.

11   PROGRAMME MANAGEMENT

Michel Thiry

"Too bad all the people who know how to run the country are busy driving cabs and cutting hair."
Attributed to: George Burns (1896-1996), U.S. comedian and actor.

Links to other BOK Topics

It would take a whole book to properly address programme management. In this session, we have tried to outline the main elements of the management of programmes; especially those that are of interest to project managers. Programme Management is directly linked to the topics in the Strategic Section of Pathways; specifically Project Success Criteria (20); Strategy/Project Management Plan (21); Value Management (22) Risk Management (23) and Quality Management (24). Programme Management is also closely linked to Control topics, in particular: Work Content and Scope Management (30) and Change Control (34) as well as Organisational topics such as: Life-Cycle Design and Management (60); Opportunity (61); Hand-Over (64) and Post-Project Evaluation Review (65) because they all relate to the delivery of benefits which is key to programme management. Finally, issues in the People Section are mostly relevant in terms of communications between the project level and the programme level; specifically Communications (70); Leadership (72); Conflict Management (73) and Negotiation (74).

Programmes and Programme Management

The APM Body of Knowledge (BoK) states: "There is widespread variation in the use of the term Programme Management. The most common - and cogent - definition is that a programme is a collection of projects related to some extent to a common objective". The CCTA (1999) has offered the following definition: "Programme management is the co-ordinated management of a portfolio of projects that change organisations to achieve benefits that are of strategic importance". The CCTA has taken a view of programmes that is associated with large IT change programmes or, by the use of 'portfolio', to multi-project management. From a more generic organisational point of view, programmes can also include, in addition to projects, on-going operations or support to projects. Murray-Webster and Thiry (2000) have suggested the following definition: "A programme is a collection of change actions (projects and operational activities) purposefully grouped together to realise strategic and/or tactical benefits". This last definition is broader in scope than the two previous ones in that it includes on-going operations in support of programmes and specifies that, either strategic or tactical benefits, or both, should be considered. This means that one of the key differences between projects and programmes is that the programme will deliver benefits that could not have been achieved if the projects had been managed independently of each other. Additionally, the concept of purposefulness is central to this definition; it is a key element of programmes that they should be a deliberate strategy and that expected benefits should be clearly outlined.

Once a definition of programmes is accepted, organisations need to ask themselves the following questions: "Why do programmes need to be managed? Why should an organisation adopt a programme management approach? What business conditions or drivers should inform the decision to establish programme management?"

The Strategic Link

The answer lies in the fact that one of the major problems of strategic management lies with the controlled implementation of strategic decisions and the measure of their successful delivery (see Session 20). Currently, strategic decisions are seldom evaluated on their actual measured results, but rather on the conformity of the decision process, or on the satisfaction of the managers with their own decision. Recently, a number of management authors (Senge, Argyris, Weick, Porter, Kaplan & Norton and others) have called for a more systemic view of organisations and a learning organisation perspective. What this means is that strategic decisions cannot be seen in isolation anymore, but that their quality must be assessed with regard to their influence on organisational effectiveness, which includes economic factors, customer satisfaction, human resources development and sustainability.

Recently the BS EN ISO 9000: 2000 suite of standards and the EFQM Excellence Model® (European Foundation for Quality Management) have provided a framework which clearly demonstrates the link between business results and the successful implementation of strategic decisions. If we agree that programmes are collections of actions by which strategies and policies are delivered, then programme management is the management of the process that will effectively achieve expected strategic benefits. As for tactical benefits, they are related to the sustainability of the factors outlined above through the integration of change and day-to-day operations. This is specifically why programmes require to be implemented in cycles with periods of stability where benefits can be assessed.

In conclusion; any organisation that wishes to increase the rate of success of strategic decision implementation, or reap the benefits of integrated organisational initiatives, should seriously think of using programme management for, as Tsuchiya (1997) has stated it: "Unaligned organization is a waste of energy, whereas commonality of direction develops resonance and synergy."

Difference Between Programmes and Projects

The most frequent mistake organisations make is to treat programmes as large projects; there are a number of differences between programmes and projects. The main one is that, whereas in projects, the goal is to achieve clear and well-defined objectives with the least possible resources, programme management also includes the identification and understanding of stakeholders' needs and expectations and reduction of ambiguity through negotiation. Winch et al. (1998) have associated project management with an 'uncertainty-reduction' process; a number of authors (Wijnen & Kor, Görög and Smith, Partington, Murray-Webster and Thiry) have recently taken a strategic perspective, where programmes are more associated to an 'ambiguity-reduction' process.

One other major difference is that project management is a process focused on the delivery of specific outcomes, whereas programme management aims to create interfaces between projects, a framework, by which those deliverables are combined to deliver overall business benefits. Other differences are outlined in the table below:

Projects	Programmes
Fixed duration Predefined objectives Focused on tasks Process life-cycle Project manager as an overseer Single deliverable	Undetermined duration Negotiated objectives Focused on goals Product life-cycle Programme manager as a creative thinker Multiple interrelated deliverables

Figure 11 - 1: Major differences between programmes and projects

Programme Support Office

One of the most recent organisational structures instituted to support the management of programmes is the Programme (or project) Support Office (PSO). Initially created to support the migration of organisations towards a more project-oriented management style, including the establishment of processes and procedures, it has become in recent years the favoured framework for the management of programmes. Because it has been used to develop, implement and monitor the consistent application of project management methodology across the organisation and the management of resources across projects, and therefore sits above projects, it offers the ideal framework to manage projects' interactions and interdependencies. There is a danger though that it becomes only a project co-ordination structure and neglects the strategic link of programmes.

The Programme Management Process

As explained above, the rationale for programme management lies in strategic management. Strategic management is typically divided into three areas: analysis, choice and implementation. Analysis seeks to understand the strategic position of the organisation (environment, capability and purpose); choice is the formulation of possible courses of action and implementation is the planning and management of those actions . These three areas are interlinked in an iterative and cyclic process. Typically, programme management follows strategic analysis, although some authors have suggested that programme management includes a 'sensemaking' process, which can be considered an analysis process.

There are two characteristics that make programme management the most suitable methodology to ensure successful implementation of strategies; they are:

- An emphasis on the 'interdependability' of projects, which ensures strategic alignment;
- The concept of periods of stability, which enable regular assessment of benefits, overall management of 'net benefits' and pacing of the process.

The Programme Life Cycle

Programme management can be divided into four major processes which, when iterated within a series of 'cycles', constitute its whole life cycle; they are:

- Formulation (sensemaking, seeking of alternatives, evaluation of options, and choice)
- Planning (strategy planning and selection of actions)
- Implementation (execution of actions? projects and support operational activities, and control)
- Appraisal (assessment of benefits, review of purpose and capability, and repacing, if required)

The formulation process is a learning process, as is the appraisal process; they are mainly aimed at ambiguity reduction; value management is the methodology of choice

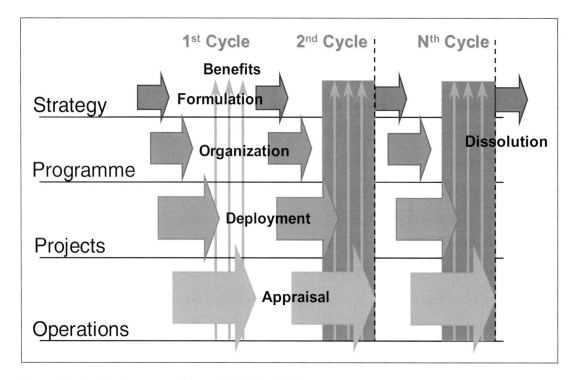

Figure 11 - 2: The Programme Life-cycle (© Thiry, 2000)

here (see Session 22). The planning and implementation processes are performance processes aimed at uncertainty reduction, project management provides the main elements of the methodology in this case (see Session 10).

The Formulation Phase

"The need to change is triggered by an unsatisfactory condition, which requires to be addressed. There are two major sources of pressures to change which influence organizations. Those are the external pressures and the internal pressures" (see Session 12). The formulation phase aims to identify those pressures to change and determine the best way to address them to add value for the stakeholders (see Session 20: Project Success Criteria).

As seen above, strategy formulation seeks to understand the environment of the organisation, its capability and the purpose to be achieved. In programmes, it is crucial to take a value perspective to formulation, seeking the best balance between the purpose and the capability. In the model in Figure 11 - 2, the formulation process, which is a learning loop ,is divided into sensemaking, seeking, evaluation and decision, which are described in detail in Session 22 (Value Management). This model shows the relationship between value and project management in a programme framework.

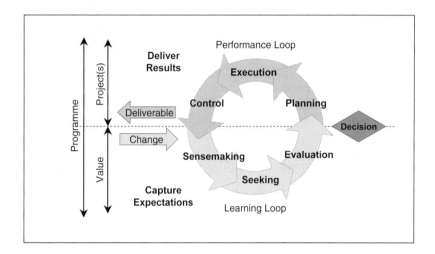

Figure 11 - 3: Model of the Programme Process Cycle

During formulation, benefits management includes the identification of the expected benefits and the assessment of their achievability. This means that both opportunities and threats, created by the pressure to change, must be identified. Opportunities must be sought to increase organizational effectiveness or competitiveness for, as Peter Drucker once wrote: "Effective management should focus on maximizing opportunities, rather than on minimizing risks". Recently, management frameworks like the 'Balanced Scorecard', the 'Learning Organisation' and the 'Value Chain' concepts or the 'EFQM® Business Excellence Model', which have been adopted by a number of organisations, have all outlined the importance of learning and of a systemic view of effectiveness and competitiveness; this is why formulation must rely on a learning process.

The sensemaking process is well described in Session 22, let's just say that, in order to achieve maximum benefits, the stakeholders, and especially those directly concerned with the outcomes of the programme, must have a clear understanding of the pressures to change and on the purpose of the programme. Critical success factors must be identified and expected benefits agreed before any action can be initiated (see Sessions 20 and 21). The key point in the sensemaking process is to allow the necessary time for all the stakeholders to understand all the issues involved and to agree on a shared definition of the needs and expectations.

Once those have been agreed, the programme management process should actively and creatively seek alternative courses of actions. Creativity is crucial in this part of the process as demonstrated by the management frameworks identified above. They all include a feedback-innovation-learning loop as part of the management process. Innovation and continuous improvement are key elements of today's organisational success. Creativity techniques, which support this process, are described in Session 22.

The programme team must then evaluate options, by looking at alternatives, or combinations of alternatives, which have been identified in the seeking stage, in order to identify the most promising ones. The evaluation stage of the process involves selecting those alternatives for which suitability (fit with overall strategy), achievability (expected long term benefits) and feasibility (availability and capability of resources) are most promising whilst unacceptable ones are rejected. Alternatives which cannot be clearly rejected or accepted, should be looked at in more detail and further options may be developed by combining alternatives or developing risk responses (see Session 23); which can then be re-evaluated. Following this process, all those alternatives that are clearly acceptable are ranked in order of their contribution to the critical success factors of the programme. The best tool for this is probably the weighted matrix, where options are assessed against weighted success criteria. At this stage of the process; value, risks and quality need to be considered; they are all crucial to the sound evaluation of programme alternatives.

Deciding the best course (or courses) of action is the last step of this phase; management will make a decision on the purpose, critical success factors and key performance indicators of the programme, as well as on its expected benefits. It is also the stage where 'fit' with the strategy is confirmed; priorities are set between different programmes within the organisation and 'business cases' are compiled. The decision will be based on the evaluation of alternatives and will seek to secure approval and support for the programme and allocation of funding and authority to undertake it. This whole process should be applied as well to 'strategic', 'portfolio' or 'incremental' programmes (see Gower Handbook of Project Management, Chapter 3 for a definition of each programme configuration).

The Organisation Phase

Once funds are allocated to a programme, or the first 'cycle' of a programme, and the authority of the programme manager is acquired, the programme's planning phase can begin. In programmes, the planning phase essentially consists of a strategic level planning for the programme; the strategic plan; and of the selection of actions, which will constitute it.

Strategic Plan

The first step is to create and plan the organisation that will be put in place to implement the programme; this consists essentially of the allocation of roles and responsibilities and the control of interactions between the projects within the programme as well as the communication systems to be put in place. The programme manager should ensure that a responsible party is appointed to manage each critical success factor of the programme, if a function breakdown structure (FBS) has been developed (see Session 22), the programme organisation should be based on it. The FBS is a simple way to assign roles and responsibilities as each 'function' is expressed in terms of a task (active verb + measurable noun) and lower levels detail each upper level in the same way as a WBS (see Session 30). The FBS can be to the programme what the WBS is to the projects.

The programme organisation structure should also identify the communication channels for the programme; how information should be filtered and sorted to suit different organisational levels and how access to systems should be allowed or restricted. The programme manager needs to act as a buffer between senior management, or the customer's representatives, and the project managers in order to allow them to concentrate on the delivery of outcomes. This specifically needs to be considered in the context of large groups, international projects and multi-national corporations. In the next section we will also examine how interactions between actions should be controlled.

The efficient management of resources across the organisation is a key component of programme management; but this process must also foster the effective use of resources in each project (see Session 32). Knowledge resource planning (KRP) essentially consists of matching demand with supply; it is a value-based concept. Demand consists of the prioritisation of the workload required to implement the programme; supply consists of the evaluation of the capacity, capability and availability of resources to match the demand. Matching the two allows for use of the best resources for the most significant assignments; enhanced flexibility through regular re-prioritisation and re-evaluation, as well as proactive, rather that reactive resource allocation. Concepts of the Critical Chain, like the holistic view, sequential tasking and use of buffers, must also be applied to programme planning.

Another major issue of planning is the pacing of the programme; the initial CCTA document (1994) defined the concept of islands of stability, periods where benefits were allowed to become positive, which should be spread significantly throughout the programme to pace it.

Their distribution depends on benefits sought and the significance of those benefits for the business. This is a period during which the programme "catches its breath".

The key concept behind the duration of cycles and the interval between periods of stability is based on a minimum acceptable level of performance, which cannot be crossed (see Figure 11 - 4). Financial issues such as cash-flow and funding, and human resource issues like the organisation's culture (e.g. risk seeking or risk averse), resistance to / acceptance of change, determine this minimum level. Programme planning must focus on early benefits, positive cash flow and maintenance of the motivation of stakeholders. The programme appraisal process is also build around the programme 'cycles' (see Figure 11 - 3).

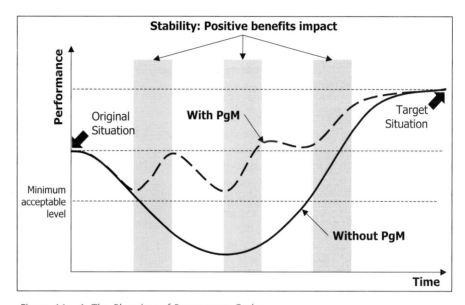

Figure 11 - 4: The Planning of Programme Cycles

Major project changes and benefits appraisal, both of which involve the sponsor(s), are usually combined around the approval gateways; which must be significantly spread to correspond both to actual project deliverables and to expected benefits delivery for the programme. They are not related to the programme cycles, but rather to project milestones.

The last element of the programme's strategic plan is the change management system. In programmes, the change process must be value-based. This signifies that, because the programme's critical success factors and objectives are very likely to be modified as it progresses, opportunities and threats are to be evaluated on a regular basis, as well as the capacity and capability of the programme organisation to respond to them. Regular 'learning loops' must be planned into the programme's strategic plan, as part of the appraisal process and any pressure to change must be addressed with it (see Figure 11 - 2).

Selection of Actions

The selection of actions consists of identifying and prioritising projects and operational actions required to support it; and of developing the strategic project management plans (see Session 21) in collaboration with the project managers. During this process, the programme manager acts as the sponsor of the projects.

The selection of actions will take into account the 'interdependability' of projects, in terms of effects on each other, and in terms of their combined contribution to the benefits sought by the organisation. They have been defined by Reiss as: direct; synergistic; enabling or passenger. The programme team must undertake a thorough analysis of the interactions or interfaces between the project and other actions that are part of the programme. The decision to implement must not be made solely on the individual value of each project, but also on their capability to contribute to the programme as a whole, and to align with the strategy. The programme team must assess their achievability, suitability and feasibility.

The prioritisation of actions in the overall programme ensures that synergies between projects are sought out, that there are no overlapping or conflicting projects and that benefit delivery is maximised and measured against the key performance indicators. Again, the weighted matrix is the best tool to prioritise projects and other actions. The criteria against which projects will be prioritised should include the critical success factors of the programme, but also take into account elements discussed in the pacing. Financial factors include payback period, cash flow, cost-benefit and risk elements; the objective being to make early gains to 'fund' the rest of the programme and reassure stakeholders, especially investors. Concerning human resources issues, the programme team must take into account the responsiveness to change of the organisation in which the programme is being implemented; the demonstration of benefits for the users; the assessment of expectations of those affected by the change; and the measures put in place to support smooth transition from the original situation to the target situation. Interdependability issues should also be part of the prioritisation of projects. Finally, the prioritisation plan should be flexible enough to allow regular re-prioritisation as the programme progresses and priorities or objectives change. If the initial plan has been well documented, this should pose no problem.

The last point requires the identification of constraints and assumptions and their documentation. It is crucial that the constraints and other factors on which the assumptions have been based are well identified, because they will evolve and change as the programme progresses and will need to be re-assessed regularly. This should be an integral part of the risk management process (see Session 23) of the programme.

The Deployment Phase

In the case of programmes, the implementation phase includes the continuous re-assessment of project benefits and priorities; resource management and prioritisation across projects; and a responsive, flexible control style. The theory of constraints is very much in line with principles of programme implementation; it states that one must:

1   Identify the system's constraints
2   Prioritise constraints according to their impact on goal achievement
3   Concentrate resources on areas of high constraints
4   Reduce the constraints' limiting impact by taking a higher level view
5   Reiterate continually

The implementation process itself essentially consists of the execution of actions and of their control.

Execution of Actions

During this phase of the programme, the main task of the programme manager is to act as the sponsor of projects and allocate or re-allocate funds and other resources according to priorities. In developing and approving project management plans, the programme manager will authorise or confirm the allocation of resources to undertake the detailed planning of projects and the 'working' of this plan

The programme manager's role is also to continually assess and manage the programme environment; particularly stakeholders' needs and expectations, and their controlled communication to project managers, as well as senior management's direct influence the projects. The identification of emergent (unplanned) inputs to the programme, which could trigger the need for changes, also needs to be monitored and managed in an orderly way. This is where the use of risk and value management techniques becomes essential. It is not reasonable to expect project managers and project teams to, at the same time, focus on delivering specific project objectives; and develop effective responses to emergent change; the latter is the role of the programme team.

This role requires the programme manager to concentrate on project interdependencies, rather than on project activities; even in terms of the project product, the programme level intervention should only consist of assessing benefits of major project deliverables and output-input relationships between projects; not solving the technical or operational level problems. Programme management requires that the projects' review/approval process be put in place to regularly assess benefits and deliverables of projects at the major milestones; these correspond to the 'gates' or 'gateways' of the project management process.

Control

In programmes, control is not only a simple deductive (based on set parameters) and 'summative' (assessment) type of control, based on performance parameters, but rather a continuous re-evaluation or 're-formulation' of the programme, in regards of the achievement of organisational benefits, an inductive (based on emergent inputs) and 'formative' (improvement) type of control. This means that programme level control of projects concentrates on the impact of deliverables on the overall programme benefits and strategic alignment; the need to adjust the programme to respond to results that do not correspond to the plan, rather than a simple assessment of cost and schedule; or even earned value. All these measures become valid only as a means to make the necessary adjustments to achieve overall objectives.

One of the roles of the programme manager is to assess the need for project plan reviews or readjustment; propose or implement changes in projects and assess their impact on the critical success factors. The programme manager will consider project deliverables against key performance indicators and analyse project outputs, like schedule, budget or earned value results, specifically with a view to the reallocation or reprioritisation of resources amongst projects, as well as the decision to continue, realign or stop the individual projects. Because of this, a sound information management system, including project reporting, should be put in place, both at project level and at programme level. The programme level information management will address both the information between project and programme level stakeholders, but also all the information circulating between projects that need to be managed at programme level (see Session 36).

The Appraisal Phase

The periods of stability, which mark the end of each cycle, are the ideal period to appraise the programme. This is the period when the organisation, whether the programme is internal or undertaken for an external customer, must evaluate the need to carry on with the programme, review its purpose, or stop it. The programme team should ask itself a number of questions like:

- Have the expected benefits for this cycle been achieved?
- Have stakeholders' needs or expectations changed?

◆ Should the programme be stopped; should it be reviewed?

The appraisal process itself requires the programme team to loop back to the formulation and plan of the programme, in order to reassess the validity of the original business needs with regards to developments since the programme was started, or since the end of the preceding cycle; any changes in the critical success factors must be identified and examined to understand how they could modify the expected benefits of the programme. Following that exercise, the actual benefits of the cycle are evaluated against the expected benefits and a gap analysis is performed. Once the gaps have been identified, the team needs to identify how the programme plan should be modified to take them into account; alternatives are examined and options evaluated. Finally a decision is made on how to modify the plan for the next cycle. This is again a learning loop where value and risks must be assessed. If everything has gone as planned and nothing has changed in the expected benefits, then the decision is made to carry on according to the original plan.

When assessing the delivery of benefits from a programme management point of view, the team must have a broad perspective and look at two different levels:

At the organisational level, the team needs to feedback against critical success factors; specifically it must assess the continuous and effective management of:

◆ Changing corporate or client objectives.
◆ Shared and/or limited resources.
◆ Interface between function and project managers clear definition of roles & responsibilities and mutual support to achieve corporate goals.
◆ Project review and approval process.
◆ Project managers' focus on key business issues.

At the project level, the programme team needs to:

◆ Assess overall performance of projects against business benefits, including emergent factors.
◆ Identify new threats and opportunities and implement

changes, if required.

- Re-plan work and relative priorities, at business level, for subsequent projects or phases of projects.
- Loop back to project definition and readjust, if required (learning loop).
- Ensure information is recycled into a feedback loop, for subsequent phases or future programmes.

Some projects, which are part of an overall programme, will span over a number of cycles, these are the ones that will need to be reviewed in the light of the programme appraisal outcomes.

In summary, this learning/improvement process needs to outline and feedback the programme team's response to emergent change in business environment, including changing needs and to bottom-up initiatives; the overall performance against CSFs, including identification of threats and opportunities; the management of resources in general and of line and project manager's complementary roles, in particular; and finally, knowledge management. It is on these elements that the justification for continuation will be built.

Programme Dissolution

A programme typically extends over a period of many months, (IT supported change programmes, Business Process Re-engineering, etc.) or many years (Drug development, transportation, infrastructure, refurbishment, etc.). Some programmes - typically portfolio or incremental - (account management, continuous improvement, etc.) are even on-going. Even with on-going programmes, the appraisal process must be carried out on a regular basis and, every time the programme team must ask itself: "Should the programme be stopped?"

A programme should be stopped if the rationale for its existence is no longer defensible; when the initial benefits have been achieved; when the cost of the programme is greater than the benefits it is bringing to the organisation; but also, when the environment or context have changed and the benefits that the programme was seeking to achieve are no longer required, or when the implementation of the first cycle(s) has demonstrated that the programme's ultimate purpose cannot be achieved. The first two are typical examples of performance-based decisions; the latter two, of learning or value based decisions.

As for projects, the closing, or dissolution, of the programme is not an easy task. When a decision to stop a programme is made, a number of people and funds will be re-allocated to other ventures and therefore there is likely to be resistance from the team to 'let go'. For this reason, some organisations even choose to involve a team external to the programme in the closing phase, to make it more efficient. Whoever actually carries out the dissolution though, there will always be some uncompleted work that needs to be either completed within a reasonable period of time, or re-allocated to other programmes, which are then re-formulated as required. All the documentation must be updated and filed and a post programme review conducted. These are then fed back into the organisation through a learning/innovation loop such as the one recommended in the EFQM® Business Excellence Model.

Once all this has been accomplished, the programme dissolution team is disbanded and re-assigned.

Competencies

The main difference between project management and programme management is that the former is first and foremost a performance process, using uncertainty-reduction tools and techniques, whereas the latter is both a learning and performance process, using a mix of ambiguity and uncertainty reduction tools and techniques. The competencies of a programme manager are therefore different from those of a project manager, and the latter does not necessarily lead to the former. In this section, we will examine the main differences between the two (see Figure 11 - 5). Note that we have outlined the two extremes of a continuum from pure project to pure programme; individual responsibilities can be anywhere on this continuum and both personality, style and organisational/business constraints can dictate the specific skills required.

Some of the specific skills required by a programme manager are:

Project Manager Mindset	Programme Manager Mindset
Application of specific performance-based skills in clearly defined role.	Improvisation from a repertoire of learning and performance-based skills and approaches.
Aiming to clearly define requirements and objectives of stakeholders.	Continually aiming to identify emerging needs and expectations from stakeholders.
Resistant to changes with adverse effects on project objectives; threat-based risk approach.	Open to new ideas and welcoming ambiguity and change; value-based risk approach.
Single-focused on project deliverables and stated benefits.	Focus on increasing organisational effectiveness and strategic advantage.
Visible, direct, decisive management style.	Political, negotiation-based, facilitation style.

Figure 11 - 5: Programme Manager vs Project Manager Mindset

- Strategic - Systemic thinking
- Financial acumen
- Cultural awareness
- Lateral thinking - Flexibility
- Facilitating approach
- Negotiation and motivation skills
- Intuitive decision-making

Specifically, in terms of leadership and motivation, the programme manager will use a transformational style of leadership , which changes or transforms values, beliefs and behaviours, whereas the project manager will favour a transactional leadership style, where the objective is to influence team members in pursuit of defined, rational goals. The motivation style of the project manager will be 'task-oriented', whereas the motivation style of the programme manager will be more 'goal-oriented'.

Conclusions

Whereas the exact definition of "programme" is still the subject of debate, a consensus is slowly being reached that they are of a wider scope than "project" and have a more strategic perspective. The major new developments are the fact that programmes are related to a learning perspective of organisations and that they are not only an uncertainty-reduction process, but also an ambiguity-reduction process.

The benefits of programme management are numerous; the CCTA outlines a number of them in "Managing Successful Programmes" (1999, p.3), but the major benefit of programme management lies in its capacity to link business strategy with its implementation through projects. The CCTA (1999, p.5) also outlines some of the circumstances when programme management should be favoured: where the complexity of the situation is too great for project management; when there is a need to manage interfaces and/or resources across projects; when outcomes are not clearly defined, therefore increasing the likelihood of change, amongst the more important.

But the future of programmes and programme management lies with the concepts put forward by models like the EFQM® Business Excellence Model, the 'Value Chain' or the 'Balanced Scorecard' through which organisations have understood that strategic decisions cannot be made in isolation, solely on financial grounds, without taking into account their impact on the workforce, the customers and the community. Programme management is the ideal methodology to ensure that strategic decisions will be implemented successfully and, if it relies on value concepts, that the results will satisfy a wide range of stakeholders.

References and Further Reading

Central Computer and Telecommunications Agency (CCTA) (1999) Managing Successful Programmes. Stationery Office, London. (Note: CCTA is now part of The Office for Government Commerce)

Murray-Webster, R. and Thiry, M. (2000). 'Managing Programmes of Projects' 'Gower Handbook of Project Management, 3rd edition' Chapter 03

Partington, D. (2000) 'Implementing strategy through programmes of projects' 'Gower Handbook of Project Management, 3rd edition' Chapter 02

Central Computer and Telecommunications Agency (CCTA) (1994) Programme Management Case Studies: Volume 1, ISBN: 0 11 330666 0

Drucker, P. (1989) Managing for Results. Heinemann Professional

Görög, M. and Smith, N. (1999) 'Project Management for Managers', Project Management Institute, Sylva, NC

Hershey, P. (1997) The Situational Leader. Center for Leadership Studies, Escondido, CA.

Johnson, G. and Scholes, K. (1997). Exploring Corporate Strategy, 4th ed. Hemel Hempstead: Prentice Hall Europe.

Kerzner, H. (1998) Project Management: A Systems Approach to Planning, Scheduling and Controlling. John Wiley and Son, New-York, NY (Specifically Ch1, 2, 3, 4, and 10)

Locke, E. A. and Latham, G. (1990) A Theory of Goal Setting and Task Performance, London: Prentice-Hall (Specifically, Ch 14 "Macro vs Micro Goal Setting Research", pp.320-336)

Rea, P.J. and Kerzner, H. (1997) Strategic Planning: A Practical Guide. Van Nostrand Reinhold, New-York, NY

Reiss, G. (1996) Programme Management Demystified, Spon Press

Stacey, R.D. (1993) Strategic Management and Organizational Dynamics. London, Pitman.

Thiry, M. (1997) Value Management Practice. Sylva NC, Project Management Institute Inc.

Turner, J.R. (1999) The Handbook of Project-Based Management, 2nd edition. McGraw-Hill Publishing Co., Maidenhead.

Turner, J.R. and Simister, S.J., (2000). Gower Handbook of Project Management, 3rd edition Gower Publishing.

Becker, M. (1999) "Project or Program Management?, PM Network, PMI Communications, Drexel Hill, PA, Vol.13- No.10, pp. 78-79

Grundy, T. (1997) "Strategy implementation and project management", International Journal of Project Management, Eslsevier Science Ltd. and IPMA. 16, 43-50.

Hobbs, B., Ménard, P., Laliberté, M. and Coulombe, R (1999) "A Project Office Maturity Model", Project Management Institute 30th Annual Seminars & Symposium Proceedings, PMI Communications, Drexel Hill, PA

Kaplan, R.S. and Norton, D.P. (1996) "Using the Balanced Scorecard as a Strategic Management System", Harvard Business Review, Harvard College, Jan.-Feb. 1996, pp.75-85

Levy, D., (1994) Chaos Theory and Strategy: Theory, Management and Managerial Implications. Strategic Management Journal, 15, 167-178.

Marion, E.D. and Remine, E.W. (1997) "Natural Networks-A different approach." Project Management Institute 28th Annual Seminars & Symposium Proceedings, PMI Communications, Drexel Hill, PA

Mintzberg, H. and Waters, J.A. (1985). 'Of strategies, deliberate and emergent'. Strategic Management Journal, 6-3, 257-272

Nevis, E., DiBella, A. and Gould, J. (1997) "Understanding Organizations as Learning Systems", The Society for Organizational Learning, Massachusetts Institute of Technology, http://learning.mit.edu/

O'Neil, J. (1999) "Short-Staffed? Maximise Scarce Resources with Knowledge Resource Planning." PM Network, Project Management Institute, February, pp.37-41

Pellegrinelli, S. and Bowman, C. (1994) "Implementing Strategy Through Projects' "Long Range Planning' Vol 27, No.4, pp125-132

Pellegrinelli, S. (1997) "Programme management: organising project-based change", International Journal of Project Management, Elsevier Science Ltd. and IPMA. 15, 141-149.

Quinn, J. B. (1978). 'Strategic change: logical incrementalism'. Sloane Management Review, 1-20, 7-21

Thiry, M. (1999) "Would you tell me please which way I ought to go from here?" Is Change a Threat or an Opportunity?" Project Management Institute 30th Annual Seminars & Symposium Proceedings, PMI Communications, Drexel Hill, PA

Thiry, M. (2000) "The Emergent Organisation", Proceedings of the 3rd PMI Europe Conference, Jerusalem,

Thiry. M. (2000) "A Learning Loop for Successful Program Management", Proceedings of the 31st PMI Seminars and Symposium, PMI, Newton Square, PA

Thiry, M. (2000) "Successfully integrating value & project management into a complete strategic decision making-implementing cycle", Proceedings of the 'International Business and Corporate Planning and Strategy Congress 2000', Amsterdam.Tsuchiya, S. (1997) "Simulation/Gaming, An Effective Tool for Project Management", Project Management Institute 28th Annual Seminars & Symposium Proceedings, PMI Communications, Drexel Hill, PA

Ward, J., Murray, P. (1997). Benefits Management: Best Practice Guidelines. The Information Systems Research Centre, Cranfield School of Management.

Winch, G., Usmani, A. and Edkins, A. (1998) "Towards total project quality: a gap analysis approach", Construction Management and Economics, Vol 16, pp. 193-207

12   PROJECT CONTEXT

Martin Stevens

"Great men make history, but only such history as it is possible for them to make. Their freedom of achievement is limited by the necessities of their environment."
C. L. R. James (1901-1989), Trinidadian writer, political theorist, and educator.
The Black Jacobins (1938).

Introduction

The successful accomplishment of a project generally requires a sensitivity to, and appreciation of, the context in which it is being undertaken.

Some commentators use the term "environment" i.e. "the project environment" to mean this context. APM prefers to use the term "context" and hence "project context" since this avoids the potential confusion with the use of the term "environment" to mean the physical surroundings of the project.

Projects and their management both affect and are affected by their context, often significantly. A project's context comprises both the internal and external influences that have a bearing on the way in which the project is carried out and managed.

The mnemonic PESTLE may be used as an aide-memoire for these influences:

Political
Economic
Social
Technical
Legal
Environmental

Together they shape the issues that project management has to deal with and may assist or restrict the attainment of the project's objective(s). Thus it is that project managers, together with the management team, sponsors and other interested parties need to give careful consideration to each of these and develop appropriate strategies to deal with them.

Clearly, not all projects will be influenced by all factors, but nevertheless, from an audit perspective they should all be thought about even if the outcome is to record that the matter is "not applicable". Indeed, depending on the nature of the project, its geographic location, sector, purpose and objectives, as well as its owner/sponsor and the project strategy chosen, the impact of each of these contexts will vary. For example, not all projects will have a political context in the geo-political sense. Some, including those involving public funding or having an impact on the local society or ecology such as a new airport or highway clearly will.

The main contributors to the successful outcome of any project - the sponsor, the project manager and the end-user each have a different set of project success criteria (Session 20) and accordingly may take a different view of the impact of these diverse contexts. Ultimately the responsibility for monitoring the project contexts, any changes therein and their likely impact on the project outcome (and hence its success or failure), rests with the project sponsor; since it is the sponsor who is accountable to the project owning organisation for the investment deployed. Clearly other players - the project manager and the user/operator amongst others - have a duty of care for the project to support the sponsor in this role.

Political

Small 'p' and big 'P'.

As Harpham (in Turner, 2000) observes, the political context covers two areas: Firstly, Politics (capital P) surrounding the project from the outside including the impact on the project of all the major external stakeholders, including national and international ones and secondly politics (little p) within the project, created by 'local' stakeholders not acting in concert.

Big 'P' Politics

The project team must consider the following:

- Politics of the host nation
- Politics of foreign suppliers and their governments
- Local politics including regional and sub-regional politics especially if these are at variance with the national political view
- Interest and lobby groups, both international, national and local
- The media

Also, the team need to be alert to these influences varying over time with changes in balances of power or public perceptions. This will be especially true of long duration projects or volatile political regimes.

Small 'p' Politics

Small 'p' politics involve the views of the various stakeholders and other project participants. Stakeholders may be either inside or outside the core project team, but their "politics" may come into play in the interactions between any participant, at any time and with regard to any topic. Small 'p' players therefore include the:

- Client organisation
- Funding organisation
- Project management team
- Sub-consultant teams
- Contracting and supplier teams
- Regulatory bodies

Politics at this level may affect behaviour, attitude, performance, interactions, information flow, decision-making and so on. A further complication is that the various groups of participants may also play politics amongst themselves either to finesse a particular position or for reasons outside the project itself.

The project manager will need not only to manage the project team and all of the interfaces that result, but importantly, will need to manage the expectations of all participants. Harpham offers sage advice: "This involves proper communication with them, listening to their concerns, being open about the project plans and seeking to accommodate changes within the plan to reduce their concerns to an acceptable level. Thus the 'interpersonal skills' of the sponsor and project manager and their ability to manage the 'softer' tasks within the project are of increasing importance" (see Section 7).

Economic

A project's economic context also exists at several levels: Micro-economic, macro economic and supra-macro economic.

Micro-economic

The micro-economic context exists at the project's business case level and concerns the economics of the project proposition itself, the financial capability and performance of the client and the financial "environment" of the business sector within which the client business is operating.

These are factors that will be capable of a degree of management by both the project management team and the sponsor's management team. They can therefore be fully explored, evaluated and considered as part of the project life-cycle. The Business Case (Session 50) will model the project within the economic circumstances of the client's business and within the sector of operation. Accept/reject decisions for proceeding with the project will be made in the light of the client's payback criteria, internal rates of return or net present value considerations (or any other chosen criteria). Sensitivity analyses may be conducted to establish the range of values for which a "Go" decision will or can still be made.

In parallel with these appraisals, risk management techniques (Session 23) can be deployed to assess the likelihood of occurrence of any particular out-turn. Further, the project manager and sponsor can identify those "levers" available to the project team to increase the probability of advantageous economic circumstances prevailing whilst minimising disadvantageous ones.

Macro-economic

The macro-economic level exists largely outside the control of the project management and sponsor's team. It occurs at a national fiscal policy level and the effects of movement in the project's context will be manifested in inflation rates, interest rates, exchange rates and the commodity and equity markets.

Whilst such factors are outside the team's control, this does not mean they should be ignored. Here too, the business case and project success criteria (Session 20) can be re-considered in the light of any changes in macro-economic circumstances. The impacts of such changes can be determined, together with their probability of occurrence. (see Session 23).

Supra-macro Economics

These are those influences that occur between States at the geo-political level. Matters for consideration here may include tariff barriers; agreements on extent of "local content" in a project; licenses, bonds and guarantees.

For the majority of projects, financial influences at the macro and supra-macro level will be outside of the project manager's and sponsor's control. The exception, of course, being those projects for which a Government Agency is either a participant or sponsor, wherein Ministers and Civil Servants may be able to exert influence.

Social

Historically, many projects, particularly major publicly funded ones for infrastructure, health care or defence have been initiated by sponsors on a patrician "we know best" basis.

Today "consultation" and "partnership" are the watch words and project sponsors and managers are not only expected but required to consult with "interested parties".

Projects involving public funding, whether from European or National Government levels including Single Regeneration Budgets or Lottery sources will have to demonstrate "buy-in" and support from the beneficiary community. Effective consultation with the local community through exhibitions, workshops, public meetings, mail drops and surveys can all be used to mobilise support (and clarify opposition) from local sources. In the author's experience, there are two key factors to be considered here if the consultation process is to be viewed as successful. Firstly, the local community must perceive the consultation to be valuable. Which means that the project team need to listen to the feedback. Secondly, it is almost inevitable that some of the local community's aspirations will be unfulfilled, so it is vital to inform them why this is so.

For some types of project; consultation may be mandatory as part of an environmental impact assessment. This is considered later in the session.

Technical

A project's technical content goes beyond the "nuts and bolts" of project delivery itself. Most of the sessions of this book deal with a "technical" aspect of the management process whether it is at a strategic, control, technical or commercial level.

At a higher level, the project management and sponsorship team will need to consider the following:

- Is the project technically feasible?
- Where does the technical expertise reside? (Inside or outside the organisation)
- Is the expertise available?
- Does the technical expertise rest with competitors?
- Is the project itself intended to develop new technology, knowledge, etc? (i.e. is it a research project?)
- Does the project need to develop new technology to succeed? (i.e. will some aspects of the project need to break new ground?)

Once conclusions about these issues have been drawn, in principal, they can be "fed into" the technical management processes described throughout Pathways.

Legal

The legal context of the project will include the following:

- The nature of the legal vehicle(s) to implement the project itself
- The legal status and relationships between project participants
- Consideration of any legal drivers behind the project (for example to comply with regulatory or other imperatives)
- The regulatory environment itself (which may inform the way in which the project has to be managed and or implemented)
- Consideration of the arrangements with foreign suppliers or service providers
- Determination of applicable law under which contractual relationships will be created, executed and (if necessary) adjudicated by the courts. i.e. will the legal process of the host territory (or otherwise) be adopted?

Once the sponsor and project manager has considered the legal context, it may be necessary for the team to obtain specific legal advice on any or all of the above matters. This will hold especially true for projects involving overseas suppliers and for those projects being undertaken beyond the domestic national boundaries of the sponsor and/or main contractor.

Environmental

In this session, the Environmental context is taken to mean the physical surroundings of the project.

Environment for Project Implementation

The project manager will need to carefully consider where the project is to be implemented:

- Is the project on-shore?
- Is the project off-shore?
- Is the project sub-terranean?
- Is the project extra-terrestrial?
- Is the project site contaminated?
- Are there special climatic circumstances on site?
- Are there times when the site is too hot or too cold for site work to proceed?
- Does the project use or produce hazardous materials?

Environmental Impact of the Project

Some types of project will have an impact on their surroundings during their implementation and/or their operation.

EC Directive 85/337/EEC: Assessment of the effects of Certain Public and Private Projects on the Environment makes an Environmental Impact Assessment (EIA) mandatory for certain classes of project including: nuclear power stations, oil refineries, airport runways and motorways. Additionally, it requires that an EIA be undertaken for projects including agriculture, mining, waste material and chemicals where "there is likely to be a significant impact on the environment".

Subsequently, EC Directive 97/11/EEC amended this directive by giving guidance on when environmental impact is "significant" and making it mandatory to consider alternative sites. This Directive also defines the scope of the EIA to prevent developers supplying minimal material only.

Managing Stakeholders

To promote a project's successful outcome, the project manager needs to develop and maintain a continuous relationship with all stakeholders. This will be a two-way process of listening and negotiation. The process of stakeholder management has seven steps and the project manager and sponsor should:

- Identify all the project success criteria and the resources needed
- Identify and critically analyse all the stakeholder groups and their likely levels of interest
- Link the stakeholder analysis to the project risk analysis

- Identify strategies for each stage of the project, for each stakeholder group - the communication plan. These strategies should focus on the desired stakeholder response. For example, if you need the full support of a group, don't just write a letter, go and see them, talk to them, listen and respond
- Monitor external and internal influences on the project and particularly any changes
- Monitor the factors that affect the stakeholder disposition towards the project and their levels of satisfaction with it
- Repeat this process formally and informally throughout the life of the project. It is important to be prepared to alter the strategy in response to changes to the project or its context

Public Relations

Medium and Message

The media are not averse to making the news rather than reporting it. Communication channels deliver "news" more quickly than ever before. Broadcast and other media have become a fantastic agent for change, but can also destroy projects and project teams very quickly. Effective management of the media may be a critical success factor for today's projects in the political and social arena.

For example, Shell proposed the best technical solution to de-commission their Brent Spar platform, but was out-played by Greenpeace who orchestrated a more successful media campaign. It was only after Greenpeace had "won" the argument that they subsequently admitted that the outcome was not the optimal solution and conceded that Shell's original plan was a better one.

Both the sponsor and project management team should adopt a positive and pro-active approach towards the media. They should endeavour to ensure that the right message is promulgated through the most appropriate medium at all times. For certain types of project it may be appropriate to appoint a public relations specialist to the project team.

Good Messaging

The following are ways in which good messaging can be promoted:

1   Mobilise and involve senior management support
2   Maintain internal communications (for example through newspapers, company magazines, notice boards and intranets)
3   Use the marketing, finance and human resource management functions within the sponsor's, project manager's and contractors' organisation to support positive messages. Co-ordinate their efforts
4   Meet regularly with interest groups
5   Network with people in other organisations.
6   Involve the local community.

Project Management Approaches for Different Types of Project

Projects are unique undertakings. The purpose of project management is to bring order and structure to the uncertain and risky business of delivering projects. Thus, in reality it is the project context that is unique and not the project management methodology applied to each project. To apply a unique and untested or untried approach to an uncertain, risky and transitory enterprise such as a project would be to compound the risk and uncertainty. The project management approach for different types of project is therefore one of judgement that the Project Manager applies in determining how to proceed.

The project context may be summarised as:

◆   What type of change is proposed or needed.
◆   How much is known about the problem/opportunity and what is known about how it will be solved or exploited.

Change may be:

◆   Evolutionary: Improving existing business operations or leveraging existing capabilities or

♦ Revolutionary: Actively exploring outside current operations and/or ways of working or solving problems/exploiting opportunities by changing current operations and/or ways of working

And, the context or nature of the change project can, be described Obeng (1996) in the following four ways:

1 Painting by Numbers: This covers 'traditional' projects, projects with clear goals and clearly defined activities. The organisation and project manager will know what is required and how it will be achieved. This type of project is often referred to as a closed project.

2 Going on a Quest: In this type of project, what has to be done is clear, but how the results will be achieved is unknown. In this project, therefore, the aim is to explore and explore again all the possible solutions to the problem or opportunity until there is sufficient visibility and certainty on how the project objectives can be satisfied. This type of project is often referred to as a semi -closed project.

3 Making a Movie: Here the organisation and project manager are sure of how something will be done but not what to do. Typically an organisation has built up competence or expertise and is looking for ways to exploit it. This type of project is often referred to as a semi - open project.

4 Walking in the Fog: In this type of project neither what has to be done nor how it will be achieved is clear. What is certain is that something has to be done. Changes to economic, market, regulatory and social circumstances often drive this type of project. In these cases, organisations have to act rapidly. This type of project is often referred to as an open project.

In terms of the project management approach, each of these project contexts presents different project management challenges and the project manager will need to focus on particular elements of the project management process in each case.

The challenge for Quests, Movies and Fog projects is to

move them into the Paint by Numbers 'space' as the Project moves through the project life-cycle. The aim of the project manager should be to close uncertainty and risk down around Quests, Movies and Fog projects before moving into the development stage. As a consequence these types of project may need a longer decide stage (see Session 10). Figure 12 - 1 highlights the different characteristics of the main project types and the project management approaches that might be taken in each case.

Project Type	Type of Change	Application	Project Management Challenges
Paint by Numbers	Evolutionary	Improving continuing business operation	Traditional Project Management Approach
Going on a Quest	Revolutionary	Actively exploring outside current operations and/or ways of working	**Problems** Overruns on time and costDelivering nothing of benefit **Action** Tight control needs to be maintained over cost and timescales without constraining scope **Approach** Extended Decide Phase Strict time-box and budget for each exploration work-stream but unconstrained scope Focus on benefits of solutions
Making a Movie	Evolutionary	Leveraging existing capabilities	**Problems** Can become aimless and meandering. Markets and benefits marginal Needs organisational commitment to methods to be used **Action** Tight control needs to be maintained over cost and timescales Stakeholder management & communication emphasis **Approach** Extended Decide Stage Focus on benefits of solutions Focus on gaining stakeholder buy in
Walking in the Fog	Revolutionary	Solving problems/exploiting opportunities by changing current operations and/or ways of working	Problems Time imperative to act Do nothing is not an option Action Tight control needs to be maintained over cost and timescales Parallel investigation of options and solutions. Approach Short Decide Stage Strict time-box and budget for each exploration work-stream but unconstrained scope

Figure 12 - 1: Project Type and Project Management Challenge.
(After Eddie Obeng/Secret Project Leaders Handbook & Robert Butterick/The Interactive Project Workout)

Time-constrained Projects

Speed of delivery is the other key characteristic of a project that warrants further exploration, especially given the time to market imperatives surrounding product development and e-commerce in particular.

First, it is worth remembering that time is a constraint in all projects, along with cost, quality, risk and benefits. The project management approach, therefore, has been developed over-time to cope specifically with the time constraint element of projects and it is clear that the project management process or framework should be used in all circumstances. Thus, in terms of fast projects the question is not one of how much of the process or discipline of project management can be discarded or ignored but rather what emphasis is placed on the elements of the process where time to market becomes the absolute constraint and the project lifecycle has to be contained within a short period of time, perhaps 6 to 12 weeks.

Secondly it is also worth pointing out that a number of tools and techniques have been developed including Rapid Application Development (RAD) to accelerate the production of deliverables. These, however, are not replacements or alternatives to project management, but tools and techniques to use within the project management framework. Rather than less structure and discipline, it could be argued that tightly time constrained projects require more discipline and structure.

The key to managing tightly time- constrained projects is managing the trade off with cost and risk this can be accomplished by:

- A higher frequency of releases or launches.
- Smaller scope of change in each release or launch.
- Iterative change - incremental 'feature' updates onto base products and services.
- Smaller teams focused on specific changes or deliverables.
- Shorter approval/sign off routes.
- Greater direct end user (customer) involvement in acceptance and testing of new products and services. A greater emphasis on commissioning rather than testing

The focus of the project manager needs to be on four key elements of project management:

Schedule Management

Each development/release must have a defined, unbreakable time-box for delivery. Major releases should be planned in full, feature releases can be planned in outline.

Scope Management

Scope must be ruthlessly managed to ensure timescales can be met. Moving 'outside scope' features and opportunities to future development and release slots is an option for managing scope creep for a particular release without loosing the creativity and potential benefit of de-scoped requirements.

Quality Management

The aim will be to ensure that all major faults and risks are eliminated and controlled. Risk based decisions can be made to release products and services not completely bug-free on the basis that the rolling/multiple release approach will allow rapid discovery and correction of faults. In this type of project using real end-users (customers) as testers in the live environment should be considered.

Release Management

Traditional projects have major releases every three or six months with more frequent fix or patch releases. In rapid projects a more frequent release cycle is desirable perhaps down to a daily level. However, this makes back-out difficult and when associated with the risk based approach to testing adds more risk/complexity into the release management process. Thus, releases still need to be strictly controlled and managed. Good configuration management is paramount and defining the characteristics of each release is vital e.g. New Construction - a new product or service, Re-modelling - updating something that already exists, Feature Release - adding functionality to an existing product or service and

Maintenance Release - fault fixing, housekeeping etc.

In summary the key considerations for rapid project developments, especially in e-commerce are:

- Streamline don't abandon process
- Plan ahead for next 3 to 4 iterations
- Implement an iterative release cycle process
- Make planning effort only 10% (maximum 20%) of total project effort
- Plan testing based on risk
- Use automated tools wherever possible
- Use end-users as testers

Figure 12 - 2 outlines the differences between a traditional project and a significantly time constrained one - based on e-commerce products.

	Traditional Project	E- Project
Requirement Gathering	Rigorous	Descriptive Overview
Technical Specification	Robust	Descriptive Overview
Project Duration	Months & Years	Days, Weeks and Months
Testing & QA	Focused on quality targets	Focused on risk control
Risk Management	Explicit	Inherent
Half Life of Deliverables	18 months +	3 to 6 months
Release Process	Rigorous	Expedited
Post -release Customer Feedback	Requires pro-active effort	Automatically obtained from user interaction

Figure 12 - 2: Traditional vs. e-Commerce Project Approaches
(After Peter Kulik and Robert Samuelson; e- Project Management for the new e- Reality: PMI Network, March 2001)

Conclusion

Understanding the context within which a project is undertaken is therefore crucial to its success. Project management as a discipline must have regard to all of the factors discussed here. Importantly the appointed project manager must also understand these factors and the dynamics between them if s/he is to deliver successful projects.

Bibliography and Further Reading

British Standards Institution., BS : 6046.

Buttrick R, The Interactive Project Workout, 2nd edition, Prentice Hall, 2000.

Cleland D & King W., Project Management Handbook, 2nd edition, Van Nostrand Reinhold, 1988.

Field M & Keller L, Project Management, The Open University, 1998.

Harpham, A., 2000, "Political, economic, social and technical influences - PEST", in Morris P W G, Hough G H., The Anatomy of Major Projects, Wiley, 1987.

Obeng E., Putting Strategy to Work. The blueprint for transforming ideas into action, Pitman, London, 1996.

Pinto J K (ed)., The Project Management Institute: Project Management Handbook, Jossey Bass, 1998.

Turner J R., The Commercial Project Manger, McGraw Hill, 1995.

Turner J R., The Handbook of Project - Based Management, 2nd edition, McGraw Hill, 1999.

Turner J R and Simister S J, (eds), 2000, The Gower Handbook of Project Management, 3rd edition, Gower, Aldershot.

13   CULTURAL INFLUENCES

Martin Stevens

"Cultures are maps of meaning through which the world is made intelligible."
Peter Jackson

Introduction

What could "culture" possibly have to do with project management? The impact of culture upon the practice of project and programme management is something about which APM's Body of Knowledge is silent. Nevertheless, as discussed in the previous session, the successful accomplishment of a project and the attainment of its objectives are influenced by the context within which it is carried out. Culture is one such context and the purpose of this session is to present an overview of the cultural issues that may help or hinder the successful delivery of a project or programme.

What is Culture?

Culture is a word that has a range of meanings. Consulting dictionaries gives us a selection:

"The act of tilling; husbandry; farming; breeding and rearing"
"A set of microscopic organisms produced by artificial development"
"The development and use of artefacts and symbols in the advancement of a society"
"Enlightenment and sophistication acquired through education and exposure to the arts"
"The beliefs, customs, practices, and social behaviour of a particular nation or people"
"A group of people whose shared beliefs and practices identify the particular place, class, or time to which they belong"
"A particular set of attitudes that characterises a group of people"

Hofstede (1994) offers:

"Culture is the collective programming of the mind, which distinguishes the member of one group or society from those of another".

Culture influences the behaviour of all members of an organisation, including the project team and affects issues such as how decisions are made, who makes them, how the group responds to outside stimuli, how people are treated, what is important and so on.

To understand another culture we need to analyse it. According to Harris and Moran (1996), there are three ways to analyse a culture, either: by its components (e.g. human nature, relationship to others, relationship to nature, spatial conception and temporal focus); by its characteristics (e.g. communications and language, beliefs and attitudes, mental processes and learning, relationships, sense of self and space, time and time consciousness); or by its systems (e.g. kinship, political, associational, educational, religious and health).

The Project Environment

Many different kinds of group can be identified that may have an involvement in a project thereby contributing to the project context and therefore shaping the issues that the project manager has to deal with. They may assist or restrict the attainment of the project objectives.

Handy (1985) describes project oriented businesses as a form of task culture. The culture brings together appropriate resources and enables the project manager and the team to deliver as best they know how.

When setting up a project, the Project Manager needs to spend some time establishing the true objectives for the project, who the stakeholders are and whether or not they have their own objectives or hidden agenda which may conflict with those true objectives. Understanding the stakeholders is one of the major ways of identifying and understanding the critical success factors for the project and it may also lead to a clearer view of the risks to be faced by the project which the project manager may need to mitigate or promote (see Session 23).

Stakeholder Analysis

Self evidently, successful projects are the result of effective alliances between participating stakeholders. Harbison and Pekar (1998) note that cultural differences are one of the key implementation issues that requires evaluation and management during alliance formation. Consequently, consideration of the nature of an organisation's culture should be a factor when forming the project team and when undertaking due diligence of prospective partners, suppliers, contractors and consultants.

For any project, the list of stakeholders involved and the questions to be considered by the sponsor and project manager may start to look like those in Figure 13 - 1.

Stakeholder	Prospective Questions
Project Organisation	Why is this Company undertaking this project?
Project Manager and the Project Team	What do they expect from the project?
Sub-Contractors and Suppliers	What do they expect from the project? What are their relationships to the other parties?
The Customer	Why are they paying for this? What do they expect from their investment?
The End Users	What do they want as a result of this activity?
Financiers	Why are they funding this project? Is the funding project specific?
Local Authorities	Are the LA involved? What is their role? (Regulatory or partner?)
Regulatory Bodies	Who are they? What are they interested in?
Opinion Formers	Who are they? Are they supporters or oponents?
Pressure / Lobby Groups	Who are they? Are they supporters or oponents?
Landowners	What are their views?
The Media	What are they interested in? Are they supporters or oponents?
Anyone Else?	

Figure 13 - 1: Project Stakeholders and Questions arising.

Each of these stakeholders will have their own organisational culture, which may be different to that of other participants (especially so when the project has an international dimension). The project manager therefore has a significant task in understanding the nature of the project's contributors before starting to deal with the project itself!

Ethnic Culture

Ethnicity and the racial heritage of project participants will provide variations in their expectations and behaviour throughout the project. The project manager must be aware of and understand the reasons for these variations and moderate both his leadership style and communication methodology as required to accommodate it. (see Sessions 72 and 70). Further, it may also be necessary to adjust project programmes, working time, and milestone dates to accommodate the ethnic and cultural sensibilities of contributors. Examples here include noon devotions by Muslims or Hindus, observance of the Sabbath etc.

Turner (1999) tabled a country ranking table for 'fitness for project management' (Figure 13 - 2) derived from fieldwork be Jessen. The basis for the analysis was to assess respondent's attitudes towards initiation, planning, execution and termination throughout the project life-cycle. The conclusion was that project management sits more easily in western, rather than eastern cultures. Once again therefore, it is important for the project manager to be cognisant of these distinctions.

1	Germany	10	Sweden
2	Italy	11	Denmark
3	France	12	Japan
4	USA	13	Thailand
5	Netherlands	14	West Africa
6	Norway	15	Philippines
7	Great Britain	16	Yugoslavia
8	Arab Countries	17	Malaysia
9	East Africa		

Figure 13 - 2: "Fitness" for Project Management by Country

Gender

Gender may also have an impact. Women project participants may be viewed with less credibility when working in some middle or far eastern territories where the societal norms of the host nation ascribe the female with a subservient position or status. Similarly, male executives and suppliers from such territories or backgrounds may be reluctant to accept the authority of female participants when working on projects being implemented in Europe or the Americas.

Corporate or Organisational Culture

Organisational culture is studied by a number of social science specialities including anthropologists, sociologists, psychologists, political scientists and economists.

Anthropology informs us about the physiological development of the human species, its rituals, myths and beliefs. Sociology concerns man as a social creature, societal evolution and the formation of communities. Psychologists examine behaviour and cognitive processes of an individual and the impact of the individual's behaviour on others. Political scientists study control structures, power and authority within the boundaries of social groups and territories. Economists seek to develop an understanding of exchange systems and how they can be utilised by and between human groupings.

The value of such studies is two-fold. Firstly, they improve understanding of management behaviour and secondly, they inform consideration of those factors that improve business (and hence project) performance.

As Rees (2000) points out: Business success becomes a function of the degree to which we understand the effects of human behaviour and are able to act on such knowledge.

Harrison and Stokes devised a methodology that enables an assessment of organisational culture to be made. Their thesis is that there are four types of organisational culture:

1. Power Culture: Based on survival and valuing strength, decisiveness and determination. The leader in a power culture is strong and charismatic.
2. Support Culture: Based on community and valuing mutuality, value, service and integration. People in a support culture go out of their way to co-operate and trust that they are viewed as worthwhile human beings by the organisation.
3. Achievement Culture: Based on self-expression and valuing growth, success and distinction. People manage themselves and share a sense of urgency in attaining goals and values.
4. Role Culture: Based on security and valuing order, stability, control and profit. In this culture, performance is judged against written descriptions and as long as you meet requirements you are safe.

Each type of culture has strengths and weaknesses and often an organisation may exhibit more than one cultural type. Understanding each contributing organisation's culture is important if the project team is to use these strengths and weaknesses to promote successful project delivery.

In the US, Hagberg Consulting Group have developed a "Cultural Assessment Tool" that identifies 40 elements of an organisation's culture extending from underlying beliefs and assumptions to explicit practices and artefacts.

Among the elements examined are:

- Accountability
- Commitment to Core Values
- Competitor Awareness
- Confronting Conflict
- Creativity and Innovation
- Customer Driven
- Nimbleness
- Risk-taking
- Supporting Employee Growth
- Teamwork
- Trust

Shaping and Communicating Culture

The basis for an organisation's culture are the assumptions, values and attitudes of its founders and/or senior management; the qualities and characteristics of the people who join it and the way the organisation responds to events and challenges. i.e. the way it conducts its business.

Culture is perpetuated and communicated by:

- The formal statements of philosophy and values of the organisation
- The organisation's design and structure
- The organisation's performance and promotion systems
- The organisations internal systems and procedures (i.e. how things get done)
- The criteria used for recruitment, selection and termination

In all of these areas, leadership is a key factor. Leaders shape the organisation by the way in which they perform: how they control, how they measure performance, what they pay attention to and the way they react to critical events.

Culture is also communicated by the informal "history" of the organisation. The anecdotes, stories and legends about important events or key people that have "shaped" the past will 'colour' the way in which current members conduct themselves and their expectations about the conduct of their colleagues.

Team and Project Culture

Successful teams and organisations are constantly responding to changing business events. Such "change events" include:

- New projects and challenges
- Attracting and retaining new talent
- New tools and technolgies
- Staff turnover
- Succession planning

- Growth
- Formation and disbandment

Change demands adaptation and consequently cultural change. Organisations need to modify their culture to respond to internal and external events and challenges. What has worked previously, may no longer be effective. Accordingly, the unique nature of any project will necessitate a cultural shift in the project team assembled to deliver it. The constituent parts of the team will bring with them the culture and behavioural norms of their 'parent' team or organisation, but as the project team passes through the forming and storming phases (see Session 71 on Teamwork and 72 on Leadership), the team will develop its own culture, style and behavioural norms.

Managing Cultural Differences

Managing cultural differences involves asking lots of questions about the culture of participants and team members; generating the answers and examining the collective understanding of the answers. By so doing, the team and its members will be better prepared to work in the emerging new culture, be more able to work together and better able to manage the project in context.

These team building processes can be promoted by the project manager and, if required, supported by external facilitators as part of the "team building" process. Particular issues that are likely to require managerial sensitivity are authority, communications, 'face' or loss of it, motivation, risk-taking, pace of work, politics, ethical understandings and religion.

In addition to the cultural differences arising from ethnic, racial and parent company, the project manager, sponsor and their respective teams should also be aware that there are cultural differences between the professions that comprise the project team.

Good and Bad Culture

There is no such thing as 'good' or 'bad' culture. All there is, is "reality". That is the way one group or race behaves normally compared to the behaviour of another group or race. It follows, therefore, that members of a group or race will perceive individuals from another group or race as exhibiting odd behaviour when such behaviour is out with the norms of the peer group.

Conclusion

Understanding the cultural influences that overlay the project and its participants will assist the project manager is achieving the desired project outcomes. Remember, however, that project management is itself a culture-bound concept (Rees, 2000). Some organisations embrace projects as a way of conducting business itself and a "project approach" is, no doubt, better suited to some sectors than others. Further, the principles of project management are more readily assimilated into some cultures than others.

As mentioned earlier in this session, there are many stakeholders to a project, each with their own culture. The greatest danger of cultural analysis, however, is stereotyping - assuming that everyone from that culture will behave the same way. They will not. The successful project manager must not stereotype!

I hope, therefore, that armed with an understanding of the discussion above, project managers will be better equipped for their project roles and this will lead them to more successful projects.

References and Further Reading

Handy, C. (1985), Understanding Organisations, 3rd Edition, Penguin, London.

Harbison, J. and Pekar, P (1998), Smart Alliances, Jossey-Bass, San Francisco.

Harpham, A. (2000), "Political, economic, social and technical influences - PEST", in JR Turner and SJ Simister, (eds), 2000, The Gower Handbook of Project Management, 3rd edition, Gower, Aldershot.

Harris, P. R and Moran, R. T (1996), Managing Cultural Differences, Gulf Publishing.

Hofstede, G (1994), Cultures and Organisations, Harper Collins, London.

Rees, D. (2000), "Managing Culture" inJR Turner and SJ Simister, (eds), 2000, The Gower Handbook of Project Management, 3rd edition, Gower, Aldershot.

Section 2

Strategic

20 PROJECT SUCCESS CRITERIA

Rodney Turner

"There is every excuse for failure but no reason for success"
Joe Hyman, Industrialist.

Introduction

The question of project success is a critical issue for project managers. Based on the work of John Wateridge (1995), I have said elsewhere, (Turner, 1999, 2000), that there is one factor which determines project success above all others. Don't do this and you are bound to fail. Do it and you have a much greater chance of success, (though unfortunately something else may cause you to fail). So what is this critical success factor. It is to: *agree the success criteria with all the stakeholders before you start*

There are three key elements to this statement:

A   Knowing where you are going
B   Knowing which road will take you there
C   Having agreement of the project team to A and B so everyone is going in the same direction along the same road

In his book, Alice in Wonderland, Lewis Carrol has a conversation between Alice and the Cheshire Cat. Alice asks the Cat, "Which road should I take from here," to which the Cat replies, "That all depends where you want to get to." "I don't much care where," says Alice. "Then it doesn't matter which road you take," says the Cat.
If you don't know where you are going, any road will take you there. If the project team members don't know where they are going, then they may all be travelling along different roads.
So before the project starts its is important to agree:

◆   What the project will deliver and when, (the project deliverables or outcomes)
◆   How achievement of those deliverables will be judged to be successful, (success criteria)

- What project delivery techniques increase the chances of successfully delivering those project outcomes
- That you have the support of all the project team members to these decisions

The title of this topic area is Project Success Criteria, yet the content as described in the Body of Knowledge covers both success criteria and success factors. This is unfortunate, because it adds to the confusion between success criteria and factors. Lynn Crawford (2001) has said that writers on project success divide into three types:

1   Those who write about success criteria
2   Those who write about success factors
3   Those who don't understand the difference

In this session, I write about project success. I start with definitions from my books and the APM Body of Knowledge, to set the terminology, and make it clear how I will be using the terms. Then I discuss what we mean by project success. A specific form of success criteria are Key Performance Indicators, KPI's; measures of the critical success factors which can be tracked throughout the project. I discuss the need to build these indicators into the control mechanisms for the project. I then describe some of the initial research into success factors, and two models for the strategic management of projects. I finish by discussing methods for obtaining the agreement of the team to the chosen success criteria and success factors.

Definitions

I start by recalling some definitions. In what follows, words in italics are definitions from my own books, especially Turner (1999). Words in bold are also contained in the APM Pathways Glossary of Terms. Words denoted by an asterisk are further defined in British Standard BS6079.

Purpose: A project is undertaken to achieve a purpose; that is solve a problem or exploit an opportunity for the owner or sponsoring organisation. The solution of that problem or opportunity will be of benefit to the owner or sponsor, and if that benefit has greater value than the cost to them of the project (the price), the project will make a profit for the owner or sponsor. (Please note, I have carefully avoided talk of monetary or qualitative values here. Benefits, values or profits can be qualitative in nature).

Facility: The project itself is work that delivers a facility. The facility is the final result, outcome or deliverable of the project. The facility will be operated throughout its life to solve the problem and provide the benefit. In what follows, I assume the end of the project is the time at which the facility is commissioned and handed over to the owner and users for beneficial operation. The facility can be a new factory, a new product, a computer system, a new organisation structure, a design.

Functionality: In order to solve the problem and deliver benefit, the facility is required to fulfil certain functions. The ability to perform these functions is known as the functionality of the project's outputs.

Owner and **Sponsor***: The sponsor is the person or group that takes the main economic risk for the project. They are usually, but not always the owner. The owner is the person or group with beneficial ownership of the facility. They get the value or benefit from the operation of the facility to repay their investment in it. Sometimes the sponsor will be the owner's bankers or shareholders, sometimes they will be a property developer who sells the facility on to the owner on completion of the project.

Champion: The champion is an advocate of the project proposal, and is usually a senior user, who sells the idea to the parent organisation, particularly the owner and sponsor, and thereby win resources for the project, particularly money. The champion does not figure as strongly in the story of success that follows as does the owner and sponsor. I mention the champion mainly to draw the distinction from the role of the sponsor. I have defined the roles in accordance with BS6079. Some people use the word sponsor to describe what I have called the champion. That is not necessarily wrong, but I want to make it clear that I am using the words as above, in accordance with BS6079 and the APM Body of Knowledge.

Users: The users operate the facility on behalf of the owner to fulfil the functions. (I have shown users in italics and not bold, because this is not the definition of users as given in the APM Pathways Glossary. There **users** are defined to mean what I have called the owner. I am afraid I so fundamentally disagree with this use of the word users that I will continue to use my definition).

Consumers: Sometimes the function of the facility is to deliver a product or services, which the owner sells on to consumers. The owner's benefit comes from a revenue stream paid by the consumers for that product or service.

Project team*: The project team are the group that do the work to deliver the facility. If the price they receive from the owner or sponsor is greater than the cost to them of doing the work, they make a profit. The project team are sometimes known as the contractor, and their profit is known as the contractor's profit.

Success criteria: These are qualitative or quantitative measures by which the success of the project is judged. If the value achieved for the measure during or after the project exceeds a predefined hurdle rate, the project can be judged to be a success against that criterion.

Key performance indicators: These are success criteria the value of which can be measured during the project in such a way that it can be assessed whether or not they will achieve the hurdle rate by the end of the project. They can therefore be used as measures of the likely success of the project while the project is progressing. It has been suggested these should be called key success indicators or key requirements indicators.

Success factors: These are elements of the work of the project, or the management process, that can be controlled by the project manager or the project team so as to increase the chance of achieving a successful outcome. They are levers that the project manager can pull to increase the chance of achieving the hurdle rate of the success criteria. (It is worth saying at this point that those two statements are not the same thing. There is no guarantee that even if the project team achieve the hurdle rates defined ex ante for the success criteria that the project will be perceived by the stakeholders ex post to be successful.)

Please note that in the definitions above, I avoided the use of the word "goals", a term which I think is used confusingly on projects. What we need to be clear about is that there are (at least) two levels of objectives for a project:

1   The Purpose: this is the owner's business objectives, the long term benefit that they want from the operation of the facility

2   The Facility: this is the short term objective of the project itself, the desired outcome of the work or endeavour that is the project. The owner has a short term objective of buying the facility, in order to be able achieve their long term objective of satisfying the purpose. The project team have a short term objective of successfully delivering the facility, in order to make a profit from doing the work and to satisfy the owner.

See Figure 1.10 of my book The Handbook of Project-based Management (Turner 1999) for a cascade of six objectives of which the above two are the first and second combined and the third and fourth combined respectively.

Success Criteria

So what are the criteria by which a project is judged to be successful? The conventional view, but now widely discredited, is that the project is a success if it is delivered:

◆   Within budget
◆   On time
◆   To the defined level of quality or functionality

This is a perspective very much from the point of view of the project team, and very much on the last day of the project. It is now widely accepted that there is a basket of success criteria, reflecting different people's interests, and judged over different time scales. Some success criteria will be judged on the last day of the project, some months later, some years later. Further, these criteria may not necessarily be compatible. They are usually not mutually exclusive, but some effort is required to make them aligned. It is part of the development of the project organisation to ensure that the various stakeholders' objectives are aligned, (Turner and Simister, 2001).

John Wateridge (1995) asked participants on information systems projects to think of projects on which they had worked, to consider whether they were a success or failure, and against what criteria they were making that judgement. He also asked them their role: sponsor, user, designer, or project manager. On successful projects, all four groups were looking for the project to provide value for the sponsor. On unsuccessful projects:

1   The sponsors were looking for value
2   The users were looking for good functionality
3   The designers wanted to produce the best design
4   The project managers wanted to finish on cost and time

What is sad about this is what the various parties were focusing on in unsuccessful projects are important. To be successful, to produce value for the sponsor, the project must deliver good functionality, through a good design, completed at or near cost and time. However, there seems to be a way in which the parties' focus on what is important to them to the exclusion of everyone else, which results in the team being torn apart. Or there is a way in which the team members can focus on what is important to them, but oriented to the common good. This may require the team members to sub-optimise what is important to them, to achieve the overall global optimum.

This is a feature of projects which is starkly different from routine operations, (Turner and Keegan, 2001). In routine operations, the parts of the system are disconnected, and so the overall optimum is obtained by optimising the parts separately. In a project, the parts of the system are all integrated, one affects the other, so the system must be optimised as a whole, and that may not optimise the parts separately. So the project team must determine in advance what the overall optimum required is, what the success criteria for the project are, and what that means for their individual parts of it. The project manager must agree the success criteria with all the stakeholders before the project starts. It is impossible to pull the project into the optimum at the end if it has not been the target from the start. It would seem that the overriding aim should be to produce value for the sponsor, to achieve the project's purpose. All the other project team members goals should be aligned with that overall aim. As I said above, achieving goal alignment should be the main aim of project organization.

Figure 20 - 1 shows a basket of success criteria, the stakeholders to whom each of the criterion is the main concern, and the timescale over which the assessment is made. Note that the criteria that are of importance to the project team, (time, cost and quality), are perceived at the end of the project. Good functionality, which is of importance to the users is perceived over the coming months. Whether or not the project achieved its purpose, and owner made a profit, is sometimes only perceived over a period of years. This leads to an initial focus on time, cost and quality, the conventional, but discredited, criteria. Research done in Australia showed that projects finishing on cost and time were less likely to be perceived to be successful over the long term than those delivering good functionality. Research done in the US showed that on product development projects, achieving good functionality was the most important outcome. Finishing on time was reasonably important, but money could be thrown at the project to achieve the other two parameters, (Turner, 1999).

Success Criterion	Interested Stakeholders	Timescale
Increases shareholder value	Shareholders	End + years
Makes a profit for the owner	Owner	End + years
Satisfies owner and sponsor	Sponsor, owner	End + years
Satisfies consumers	Consumers	End + years
Satisfies users and champion	Users, champion	End + years
Achieves purpose	Users, champion, owner	End + months
Meets specification	Users, champion, team	End + weeks
• Functionality		
• Availability, reliability, maintainability		
• Flexibility, updatibility		
Time, cost, quality	Project team, users	End
Satisfies project team	Project team	End
Makes a profit for the contractor	Project team	End

Figure 20 - 1: Success Criteria for Projects

Finally, in this section, when presenting the above ideas on courses, some project managers have said to me that in their annual appraisal they are judged by how many of their projects finish on cost and time, not how many make a profit for the sponsor, so what should they focus on. My answer is they should focus on changing the appraisal system, so that it is oriented towards the successful delivery of projects.

Key Performance Indicators and Project Control

Key performance indicators, KPI's, are measures of the success criteria that can be judged throughout the project, to ensure that the project is progressing towards the successful achievement of the success criteria. It is no good waiting to the end of the project and saying, "How did we do?" and finding that the project has failed. The project team need to track progress throughout the project against measures of the success criteria, and take action early on to counter any shortfall.

Now we come to another frequently made mistake by project managers. The success criteria as defined are good functionality, good quality, within budget, or makes a profit for the owner, but the project progress reports track time only, because that is all Microsoft Project tracks. The project team must chose their control methods (methodology) and their key performance indicators to reflect the success criteria. That is if the key success criteria is to:

1   Make a profit for the owner: the team need to track net present value throughout the project, as calculated on the first day of the project, and from this point forward

2   Make a profit for the contractor: they need to perform earned value analysis to calculate the forecast cost to completion, and compare that to the price to be paid for the project

3   Deliver appropriate functionality: configuration management needs to be used

4   Deliver the facility within the defined time-scale: then the schedule needs to be tracked using bar charts, milestone tracker charts or critical path networks

The project team may need to track a basket of these key performance indicators, but they need to agree in advance what their relative importance is when faced with a critical decision during the project; do you give priority to net present value, functionality, cost or time. I have shown that to maximise net present value, functionality should almost always take precedence, (Turner, 1999). The relative importance of time and cost will depend on the circumstance. However, there are some projects where if they are not done by a certain date they have no value; the Olympic games for instance.

Success Factors

The earliest research on project success was done into success factors, identifying project success factors, the elements of project managers and their teams can influence to increase the chance of a successful outcome. The first work was done in Norway by Kristoffer Grude while working as managing director of an information systems supplier, (Andersen et al, 1987). However, he looked more at pitfalls, things that cause projects to go wrong. However, I have recast these as success factors, Figure 20 - 2, (Turner, 1999). Peter Morris (1988) conducted the first study in the UK. He identified success factors at four stages of the project life cycle, Formation, Build-up, Execution, and Close-out, Figure 20 - 3. His factors are mainly behavioural, but technical expertise, technological advantage and financial support also figure. Morris also identified inhibitors to successful implementation, also in Figure 20 - 3. These all tend to be behavioural in nature. Baker, Murphy and Fisher (1988) conducted the first study into success factors in the US. They surveyed over 650 projects and derived the list of success factors in Figure 20 - 4. The definitive study was done by Jeffrey Pinto and Dennis Slevin, (1988). They identified ten critical success factors from a survey of 400 projects, Figure 20 - 5.

Please note that in Figures 20 - 3, 20 - 4 and 20 - 5, the factors are in decreasing order of significance; the factors with the highest impact are first. In Figure 20 - 2 the order relates to the project management life-cycle. Kristoffer Grude's work was qualitative. He identified recurring themes that caused projects to fail in his company.

Project stage	Success factors
Foundation	Align the project with the business Gain commitment of involved managers Create a shared vision
Planning	Use multiple levels Use simple friendly tools Encourage creativity Estimate realistically
Implementation	Negotiate resource availability Agree co-operation Define management responsibility Gain commitment of resource providers Define channels of communication Project manager as manager not chief technologist

Control	Integrate plans and progress reports
	Formalize the review process through
	   • defined intervals
	   • defined criteria
	   • controlled attendance
	Use sources of authority

Figure 20 - 2: Grude's Success Factors for Projects

Stage	Success factors	Barriers
Formation	Personal ambition Top management support Team motivation Clear objectives Technological advantage	Unmotivated team Poor leadership Technical limitations Money
Build-up	Team motivation Personal motivation Top management support Technological expertise	Unmotivated team Conflict in objectives Poor leadership Poor top management support Technical problems
Execution	Team motivation Personal motivation Client support Top management support	Unmotivated team Poor top management support Deficient procedures
Close-out	Personal motivation Team motivation Top management support Financial support	Poor control Poor financial support Ill-defined objectives Poor leadership

Figure 20 - 3: Morris's Success Factors for Projects

Success factors
Coordination and team-client relations
Adequacy of team structure and control
System uniqueness, importance and public exposure
Success criteria salience and consensus
Competitive and budgetary pressure
Initial over-optimism and conceptual difficulty
Internal capabilities build-up

Figure 20 - 4: Baker Murphy and Fisher's success factors

Success factor		Description
1.	Project mission	Clearly defined goals and direction
2.	Top management support	Resources, authority and power for implementation
3.	Schedule and plans	Detailed specification of implementation process
4.	Client consultation	Communication with and consultation of all stakeholders
5.	Personnel	Recruitment, selection and training of competent personnel
6.	Technical tasks	Ability of the required technology and expertise
7.	Client acceptance	Selling of the final product to the end users
8.	Monitoring and feed back	Timely and comprehensive control
9.	Communication	Provision of timely data to key players
10.	Trouble-shooting	Ability to handle unexpected problems

Figure 20 - 5: Pinto and Slevin's Success Factors

On the one hand there is little in common between the four lists; on the other hand I think common themes can be identified; the first five items on Pinto and Slevin's list provide a guide to the most significant success factors:

1   Project mission: agree clear goals and objectives, agree the success criteria with the stakeholders before you start.
2   Top management support: don't proceed without political support.
3   Schedule/plans: have good clear plans.
4   Client consultation: agree the specification, the plans and the success criteria with the client before you start. The client is a multi-headed beast, consisting of the sponsor, the users and the consumers.
5   Project team: gather a competent, motivated team to undertake the project.

These five things are all necessary conditions for success, but unfortunately they are not sufficient conditions. They must be there for the project to be a success, but if they are there, it does not guarantee success, other things can go wrong. However. their absence is a sufficient condition for failure. If they are not there the project will fail.

Project Strategy

Several authors have tried to formalise the success criteria and success factors into model's of project strategy. I discuss two.

The Strategic Management of Projects

Peter Morris developed a model for project strategy following his work investigating the performance of major projects in the UK from the 1960's, 1970's and 1980's, (Morris and Hough, 1987). I have converted his model into a seven forces model for project success, Figure 20 - 6, (Turner, 1999, 2000). The seven forces are:

Two forces external to the parent organisation:

I   The drivers arising from the sponsorship of the organisation's financiers, the benefit they expect, and the urgency that creates
II   The resistance arising from political, economic, social, technical, legal and environmental influences in the project's context

Two forces internal to the parent organisation, but external to the project:

III The drivers arising from the definition of the project required to deliver the returns to the financiers
IV   The resistance arising from the attitudes of people within the organisation

Three drivers from within the project, the people, systems and organisation of project management:

V   The people working on the project, their knowledge and skills, needs for careers, team working, leadership and industrial relations

VI   The management systems to be used to manage functionality, configuration, work, organisation, quality, cost, time, risk and safety, and the life-cycle to be followed

VII   The organisation of the project, the roles and responsibilities of the people working on the project, the numbers required, and the need to procure additional skills from outside the parent organisation where they don't exist internally.

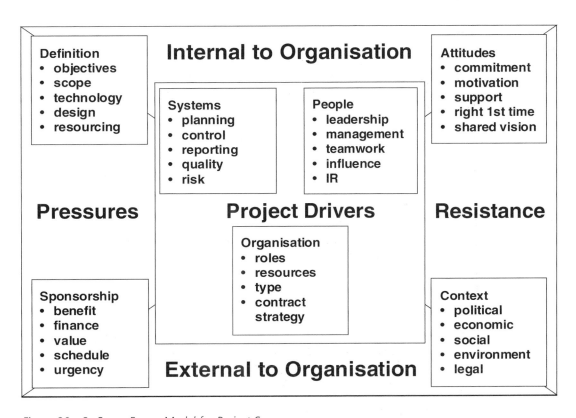

Figure 20 - 6: Seven Forces Model for Project Success

The Project Excellence Model

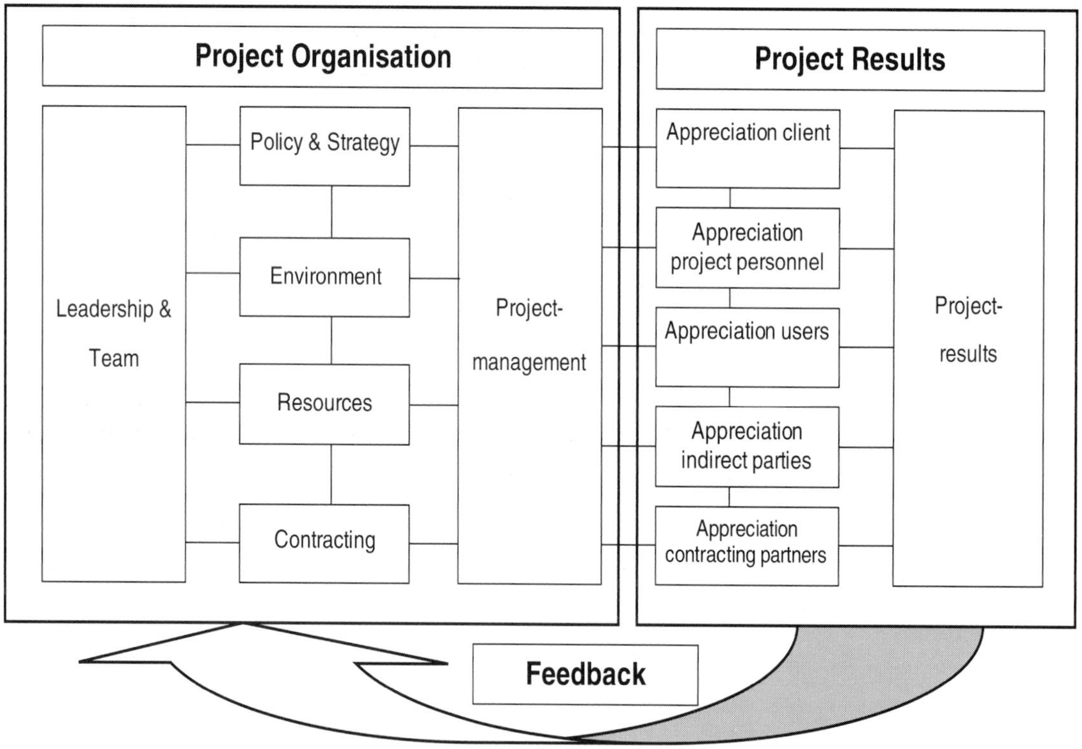

Figure 20 - 7: EFQM Project Excellence Model

Eddy Westerveld (Westerveld and Walters, 2001) has developed the project excellence model (PEM), adapted from the EFQM model for total quality, Figure 20 - 7. This model combines success criteria and success factors into one model. It shows expected outcomes for projects and the inputs likely to deliver those outcomes. The right-hand side shows the desired outcomes for the project, but it also shows that those outcomes are perceived and appreciated in different ways by different stakeholders. These stakeholders include all those that we have met above. The left hand-side shows the elements of project organisation (success factors) required to deliver the desired results. These elements are similar to those in the seven forces model in Figure 20 - 1. Thus, this Project Excellence Model combines all the previous work into success factors and success criteria into a single coherent model.

Further, Eddy Westerveld has developed versions of the model for different sizes and types of project giving guidance to a wide range of project managers. The model therefore provides a consistent picture of success criteria and success factors for a project, how to judge a project to be successful, and how to achieve that in different project scenarios.

Obtaining Agreement of the Team

I started this session by saying that the main factor for project success was to agree the success criteria with the stakeholders before the project starts. I close by describing methods of obtaining agreement of the team. The main way of doing it is through the start-up process and particularly the use of start-up workshops, (Turner, 1999; Simister, 2000; Gareis, 2000). Project definition reports and project manuals can also be used to communicate the agreed decisions to the team, (Turner, 1999; Gareis, 2000). Here I briefly describe an agenda for the project start-up process, and describe two things that can be used as part of the start-up process to help obtain agreement. These are:

- The three questions suggested by Francis Hartman
- The use of succcess / failure diagnostics

Project Start-up Workshops

Figure 20 - 8 presents a suggested agenda for a project start-up workshop. The early stages set the success criteria, the later stages the success factors:

Project definition: The team agree the project's purpose, the definition and specification of the facility, and the work to deliver it. At this stage the definition of the work is high level, and includes what is to be done by this project, by other projects and operations and the necessary interfaces. Here the project participants agree what the

Time (hours)	Agenda item
1.5	Project definition, purpose, facility, scope
1.5	Project success criteria and mission
3.0	Milestone plan
2.0	Responsibility chart
1.0	Milestone schedule
1.0	Stakeholder analysis
1.0	Risk analysis
2.0	Plan early milestones
1.0	Control process

Figure 20 - 8: Agenda for a Project Start-up Workshop

project does and does not entail. The interfaces may also be key success factors and need careful definition.   The interfaces may also influence the success criteria of this and other projects.

Agree the success criteria and mission: Now the quantitative and qualitative measures of success are defined. These include key performance indicators, and measures made on the last day of the project, one months later, six months later, one year later and five years later.

The project is now planned and the success factors identified. Decisions at these stages should be influenced by those taken at the first two steps.

Milestone plan and responsibility chart: It is critical to agree a strategy for delivering the project, and who takes responsibility for elements of that strategy.   It is also important to agree the schedule to co-ordinate the input of the various participants and stakeholders.

Stakeholder analysis: The idea is to get the agreement of the stakeholders to the success criteria. The project team identify the stakeholders, and to identify their objectives. From this the team should try to derive an appropriate influence strategy, (McElroy and Mills, 2000).

Risk analysis: Uncertainties in the definition or delivery of the purpose, facility, work, success criteria and factors, and key performance indicators should be identified This will help identify threats to the successful delivery of each of these, and thus of the overall project. A positive approach will also identify opportunities for a more successful outcome.

The results can be captured in a project definition report, (Turner, 1999).

Hartman's Three Questions

Francis Hartman has suggested three questions to help in several steps in this process. If the team members (or attendees at the start-up workshop) are asked to complete these questions separately, then it can help identify differences of opinion within the team. The three questions to ask the team are:

Q1: On the last day of the project, what will the project team hand over to operations?
Q2: How will success of the project be judged?
Q3: Who has an opinion on questions 1 and 2?

Question 1 defines the facility, question 2 the success criteria and question 3 the stakeholders, and so contribute to three steps of the start-up workshop. It is important to get the team to complete the questions on their own initially to tease out differences of opinion. Francis Hartman gives examples of teams whose members are all working to the same end date giving answers ranging from completion of acceptance testing to successful operation for a year to question 1.

Project Success Diagnostic

Finally, formal diagnostics and questionnaires can help fulfil a similar role. John Wateridge (2000) has developed a questionnaire to help identify the success criteria and success factors for a project. This too can be given to the members of the project team separately to help tease out differences of opinion to be worked on in the start-up process.

References and Further Reading

ES Andersen, KV Grude, T Haug and JR Turner, 1987, Goal Directed Project Management, Kogan Page/Coopers & Lybrand, London, 196ppg, ISBN: 1-85091-315-3, Hardback, & ISBN: 1-85091-734-5, Paperback.

BN Baker, PC Murphey, and D Fisher, 1988, "Factors affecting project success", in DI Cleland and WR King, (eds), Project Management Handbook, 2nd edition, Van Nostrand Reinhold, New York, ISBN: 0-442-22114-2, Hardback.

L Crawford, 2001, Project Management Competence: the value of standards, DBA Thesis, Henley Management College, Henley-on-Thames.

R Gareis, "Managing the project start", in JR Turner and SJ Simister, (eds), 2000, The Gower Handbook of Project Management, 3rd edition, Gower, Aldershot, ISBN: 0-566-08138-5, Hardback, & ISBN: 0-566-08397-3, CD-ROM.

W McElroy and C Mills, "Managing stakeholders", in JR Turner and SJ Simister, (eds), 2000, The Gower Handbook of Project Management, 3rd edition, Gower, Aldershot, ISBN: 0-566-08138-5, Hardback, & ISBN: 0-566-08397-3, CD-ROM.

PWG Morris, 1988, "Managing project interfaces", in DI Cleland and WR King, (eds), Project Management Handbook, 2nd edition, Van Nostrand Reinhold, New York, ISBN: 0-442-22114-2, Hardback.

PWG Morris and G Hough, The Anatomy of Major Projects: a study of the reality of project management, Wiley, Cichester, ISBN: 0-471-91551-3, Hardback.

JK Pinto, and DP Slevin, 1988, "Critical success factors in effective project implementation", in DI Cleland and WR King, (eds), Project Management Handbook, 2nd edition, Van Nostrand Reinhold, New York, ISBN: 0-442-22114-2, Hardback.

SJ Simister, "Managing scope - functionality and value", in JR Turner and SJ Simister, (eds), 2000, The Gower Handbook of Project Management, 3rd edition, Gower, Aldershot, ISBN: 0-566-08138-5, Hardback, & ISBN: 0-566-08397-3, CD-ROM.

JR Turner, 1999, The Handbook of Project Based Management, 2nd edition, McGraw-Hill, London, ISBN: 0-07-709161-2, Hardback.

JR Turner, 2000, "Project success and strategy", in JR Turner and SJ Simister, (eds), 2000, The Gower Handbook of Project Management, 3rd edition, Gower, Aldershot, ISBN: 0-566-08138-5, Hardback, & ISBN: 0-566-08397-3, CD-ROM.

JR Turner and AE Keegan, 2001, "Mechanisms of Governance in the Project-based Organization: a transaction cost perspective", European Management Journal, 19(3).

JR Turner and SJ Simister, 2001, "Project contract management: a transaction cost perspective", in Proceedings of PMI Europe 2001, A Project Management Odyssey, London, ed TM Williams, Marlow Events, Marlow, UK, June.

JF Wateridge, 1995, "IT projects: a basis for success", International Journal of Project Management, 13(3).

JF Wateridge, 2000, "Project health checks", in JR Turner and SJ Simister, (eds), 2000, The Gower Handbook of Project Management, 3rd edition, Gower, Aldershot, ISBN: 0-566-08138-5, Hardback, & ISBN: 0-566-08397-3, CD-ROM.

E Westerveld and DG Walters, 2001, Op weg naar project excellence, Samson/Kluwer, to appear.

21   STRATEGY / PROJECT MANAGEMENT PLAN

Rob Blanden

"Strategy is buying a bottle of fine wine when you take a lady out for dinner. Tactics is getting her to drink it"
Attributed to: Frank Muir (1920-1998), British writer and broadcaster.

Introduction

This session introduces the concepts of strategy, strategic management and strategic decision-making and develops the 'planning view' of strategic development. These concepts of corporate strategy are then applied to best practice project management techniques to define the process of strategic project planning. The resulting framework provides an understanding of how the strategic project planning process can used to convert an organisation's strategy into specific deliverables through project planning.

For the purposes of this chapter, organisation is used as a generic term for firm, business, enterprise or company. Corporate strategy is used as a generic term for organisational strategy and business strategy. Efficiency is a term used for doing things right and effectiveness is a term for doing the right things.

The main focus of this session is the effective implementation and delivery of specific change initiatives, programmes or projects using a framework for strategic project planning. This framework is based on the strategic management processes that, over time, result in the implementation of an organisation's corporate strategy. Strategy is a deliberate search for a plan of action that will develop an organisation's competitive advantage and compound it for the future. For any organisation, the search is an iterative process that begins with recognition of where you are and what you have now.

This session considers a generic approach to strategic project planning based on the premise of best practice project management, without attempting to differentiate between client or contractor organisations, or between the numerous ways that project management services are delivered within organisations, e.g. as a specific line managed department or business unit, or as a centrally resourced corporate support function.

The aim is to provide project managers with an understanding of how 'projects' are planned strategically and describe the tools that can be used to facilitate the process. There are four sections in this chapter on strategic project planning. Each addresses a key aspect of the process; from definition to result.

What is Strategy?

The 'planning view' of strategic management (Ansoff, 1988) has re-emerged as the process of strategic project planning, since project management is playing more and more of an essential and crucial role in the development of organisations' corporate strategy and the management of change processes.

However, the fact that a planned, intended strategy does not materialise, does not mean that an organisation has no strategy at all. If strategy is regarded as the direction of an organisation, which develops over time, then it can also be conceived as an emergent process (Mintzberg, 1985).

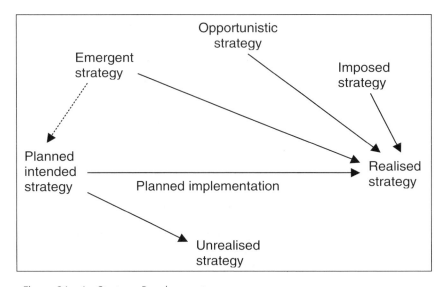

Figure 21 - 1: Strategy Development

Figure 21 - 1 shows the routes by which strategy is developed in organisations and how strategy can be conceived as a deliberate, systematic process of development and implementation, i.e. intended, planned and realised.

Strategic management is the responsibility of all managers and, what is more, a responsibility that is becoming more and more important. Modern organisations exist in a complex environment with an increasing demand for fast and effective strategic responses, as well as accelerated project implementation timescales, for example in the IT industry.

There is also a growing expectation that managers will be able to take decisions about change and implement change with a great deal more assurance and skill than hitherto.

Johnson and Scholes (1993) provided a definition of strategy:

"Strategy is the direction and scope of an organisation over the long-term; ideally, which matches its resources to its changing environment, and in particular its markets, customers or clients so as to meet stakeholder expectations".

Strategies can exists at a number of levels in an organisation. First, there is the corporate level: the main issues are about the overall scope of the organisation; how it is to be run in structural and financial terms; and how resources are to be allocated throughout the organisation. All of these are likely to be influenced by the vision and mission of the organisation.

The second level can be thought of in terms of competitive or business strategy. Here strategy is about how to compete in a market: the concerns are therefore which products or services should be developed and offered to which markets; and the extent to which these meet customers needs in such a way as to achieve the objectives and goals of the organisation.

The third level of strategy is the operating end of the organisation. Here there are operational strategies which are concerned with how the different functions of the enterprise contribute to the other levels of strategy. Such contributions are important in terms of how an organisation seeks to be competitive. Indeed, in most businesses, successful business strategies depend to a large extent on decisions which are taken, or activities which occur, at the operational level. The integration of strategy and operations is therefore of great importance and it is the process of strategic project planning that facilitates the conversion of a strategy into operational deliverables through a plan.

Corporate Strategic Management

The strategic management process is not only concerned with taking decisions about major issues facing the organisation, it is also concerned with ensuring that the strategy is put into effect. It consists of:

- Strategic analysis - context.
- Strategic choice - content.
- Strategy implementation - process.

Strategic analysis is concerned with understanding the strategic position of the organisation in order to form a view of the key influences on the present and future well-being of the organisation and therefore on the choice of strategy. Together, a consideration of the environment, the resources, the expectations and the objectives within the cultural and political framework of the organisation provide the basis for strategic analysis.

Strategic analysis provides a basis for strategic choice. This aspect of the strategic management process has three parts:

1   Generation of strategic options, i.e. the identification of what courses of action are available.
2   Evaluation of strategic options, i.e. the examination of strategic options in the context of the strategic analysis to assess their relative merits.
3   Selection of strategy, i.e. the strategy or strategies which the organisation will pursue

Strategy implementation is concerned with the translation of strategy into action and planning how the choice of strategy can be put into affect and managing the changes required.

Corporate Strategic Planning

Strategic planning is perhaps the most traditional view of how strategic decisions are made in organisations. This process includes strategic decision-making elements, such as:

- The setting of objectives and goals.
- The analysis of the environment and the resources of the organisation, so as to match environmental opportunities and threats with resourced-based strengths and weaknesses.
- The generation of strategic options and their evaluation.
- The planning of implementation through resource allocation processes, the structuring of the organisation and the design of control systems.

The proponents of such a planning view of strategy implementation emphasise the need for a highly systematic approach, perhaps through what used to be termed a corporate planning function, but which is more commonly termed a project or programme support office (PSO), together with a structured set of procedures.

Typical functional management processes have been described as logical incrementalism by Quinn (1980). This means that senior managers have an adaptive view of where they want the organisation to be in years to come and they try to move towards this position in an evolutionary way.

The benefits of such a process include improved quality of information for decision making and better sequencing of elements of major decisions. There is also a stimulation of managerial flexibility and creativity, and, since change will be gradual, the possibility of gaining a commitment to change throughout the organisation is increased.

Effective strategic planning is necessary to achieve and maintain excellence in project management. Many companies recognise the strategic importance of their project management acumen and there is a clear focus on senior manager's understanding what project management capabilities exist in the environment in which they operate.

The key to progress in the 21st Century will be the ability of managers to think and act strategically. Strategy formulation and development has long been perceived as a responsibility of senior management; survival and growth will depend on middle and lower management's perception of, and commitment to, the organisation's strategy. No longer can these roles be concerned solely with day-to-day issues. Middle and lower level managers must have a commitment to the goals, direction and strategy of their organisation.

Individual project managers and project management departments need to be the driving force behind the effectiveness of an organisation, since it is the cross-functional (horizontal) and line management (vertical) influence that they exert that allows them to facilitate the organisation-wide process of strategic project planning.

Identifying Strategic Project Variables

Strategic project planning is performed at the horizontal hierarchy level, with final approval by senior management. For a project to be successful, all members of the horizontal team must be aware of those strategic variables that can influence the success or failure of the project plan.

The project manager must be able to identify and evaluate strategic variables, in terms of the objectives of the organisation with regards to constraints on existing resources. The analysis begins with the environment, subdivided into internal, external and competitive, as shown in Figure 21 - 2.

Once the environmental variables are defined, the strategic planning process continues with the following:

1   Identification of organisational strengths and weaknesses.
2   Understanding personal values of senior management
3   Identification of opportunities.
4   Definition of product market.
5   Identification of competitive edge/unique selling points.
6   Establishment of goals, objectives and standards.
7   Identification of resource deployment.

Environment	Analysis of:
Internal	Management skills & capabilities Required & available resources Budgets & forecasts Policies & procedures
External	Political Economic Social Technical Legal
Competitive	Industry characteristics Corporate goals & objectives Market share & product mix Resources

Figure 21 - 2: Evironmental Analysis

Senior management support must be available for identification of strategic planning variables so that effective decision making can occur at the operational level.

Identification and classification of the strategic variables are necessary to establish relative emphasis, priorities and selectivity amongst the alternatives, to anticipate the unexpected, and to determine the restraints and limitations that face projects and programmes.

Strategic Project Selection

A primary output of the strategic project planning process is the actual selection of projects. This tends to be the responsibility of senior management, or in some cases, project sponsors. Most organisations have established selection criteria, which can be subjective, objective, quantitative or qualitative.

From a financial perspective, project selection is basically a two-part process. First, organisations tend to conduct a feasibility study to determine whether the project can be done. The second part is to perform a cost-benefit analysis to establish whether the company should do it.

The purpose of the feasibility study is to validate that the project meets cost, technological, safety, marketability and ease of execution criteria. Historically, project managers were not assigned until the feasibility study has been performed; however, project managers are more and more often being assigned to projects at the 'pre-contract' phase in the life-cycle of best practice project management.

It is the project manager's responsibility to ensure that all known constraints and assumptions are carefully documented at this stage. Unrealistic or unrecognised assumptions are often the cause of unrealistic benefits. The go or no-go decision to continue with a project into the initiation phase could very well rest upon the validity of the assumptions.

Strategic Project Planning 1 - An Introduction

As a process, strategic project planning is more than simply a linear combination of strategic planning and project planning. It is the synergy between a best practice culture of project management in an organisation and the effective implementation of corporate strategy, goals and objectives at all levels within the organisation.

Every organisation's strategy should consist of an 'envisioned future' (the inflexible 'What'), in terms of long-term, clearly articulated objectives and compelling translations of the organisational goals; and a mission (the flexible 'How'), in terms of core purpose, core values and behaviour guidelines for action.

Strategic project planning is the iterative process that project managers use to implement corporate strategy frameworks by developing project strategy plans that deliver success based on the mission of the organisation.

The goal of strategic project planning is not just to produce a project initiation document or even a complex Gantt chart, but to ensure that all the project stakeholders have a common understanding of the reasons why a project exists and its main objectives.

Project managers tend to be concerned with the immediate execution of an operational plan. Therefore, they are operational planners. However, because of the company-wide knowledge that the project managers obtain from functional operations and integration, they become invaluable assets to senior managers during the formal corporate strategic planning process.

"Project managers are not known for their corporate strategic planning posture, but for their strategic planning capability" (Kerzner, 1998a).

Senior managers and executives, therefore, should expect to work closely with project managers and take an active sponsorship role during the initial conceptualisation and detailed planning stages of a project, but then step back during the implementation phase to focus on priority-setting and conflict resolution.

Project Objectives

The first step in strategic project planning is to understand the project objectives. These objectives are generally not independent, but tend to be interrelated, both implicitly and explicitly. Sometimes it is not possible to satisfy all objectives and project managers have to prioritise strategic objectives ahead of those which are not.

Typical problems with developing objectives include:

1   Project objectives/goals are not agreeable to all stakeholders.
2   Project objectives are too rigid to accommodate changing priorities.
3   Insufficient time exists to define objectives.
4   Objectives are not adequately quantified.
5   Objectives are not documented well enough.
6   Efforts of active stakeholders in a project are not co-ordinated.

Once the project objectives have been clearly defined, four questions must be considered:

1   What are the major elements of work required to satisfy the objectives, and how are those elements interrelated?
2   Which functional divisions will assume responsibility for accomplishing these objectives and the major work-element requirements?
3   Are the required corporate and organisational resources available when required?
4   What are the expected information flow requirements

of the project, i.e. communications plan?

If a project is large and complex, then careful planning and analysis must be carried out. Work plans and schedules must be established so that maximum utilisation and optimum allocation of resources can be made. Effective strategic project planning cannot be accomplished unless all of the relevant and required information becomes available at the project definition phase.

Project Definition

Too many projects are started without sufficient definition or direction, with project managers having to hope that matters will clarify as the project progresses. In many cases, this results in a significant amount of re-work, pushing the project beyond time and budget targets.

The aim of best practice project management is to establish strategic project planning processes that should, at each stage of the project definition phase, highlight the need to establish how the project affects and benefits the whole organisation and how it fits within the corporate strategy framework.

To deliver a project well, project managers must understand, from each stakeholder's perspective, why it is needed at the start of the planning process. There is often a temptation to move away quickly from the 'big picture' thinking process to 'how' something can be done - before the 'why' and 'what' are properly understood. (Refer to Figure 21 - 3).

The thoughts of 'why' should be tested for their reasoning in the 'what'. The logic from the 'what' should be tested for viability and do-ability by answering the questions about 'how' it can be done and 'who' is going to do it.

The iterative process of strategic project planning is defined in Figure 21 - 3, in terms of the project context, the processes that will be used and the tasks and roles that are required to successfully implement the project.

Predicting Project Success

One of the most difficult project management tasks is predicting whether a project will be successful. Most goal-orientated managers focus on time, cost and performance criteria. If an out-of-tolerance condition exists, then additional analysis is required to identify the cause of the problem.

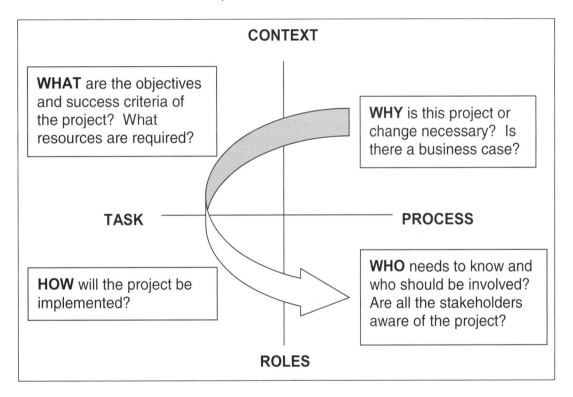

Figure 21 - 3: The Basis of Strategic Project Planning

Project success is often measured by the 'actions' of three groups: the project manager and team, the parent/sponsoring organisation and the client's organisation. A project cannot be successful unless it is recognised as a project and has the support of senior management. Senior management must be willing to commit resources and provide the necessary administrative support.

For a project manager to be effective in the successful delivery of a project, then from an organisational perspective, adequate authority must be delegated from senior management. Moreover, from a personal perspective, project managers themselves must establish a suitable power-base from which to manage a project. To achieve this project managers must utilise their expertise (technical or managerial), their credibility (both within the organisation and with clients) and their leadership and decision-making skills.

Strategic Project Planning 2 - The Process

Strategic project planning breaks the project down into life-cycle phases. The life-cycle phase approach is not an attempt to put the handcuffs on the project manager, but to provide a methodology for uniformity in project planning. Most companies tend to prepare checklists of activities that should be considered in each phase. Project managers are still expected to exercise their own initiative within each phase, so that this approach is consistently applied to the relative context of every project.

A second benefit of using life-cycle phases is control. At the start of a project the 'exit' and 'entry' criteria for each phase are documented. At the end of each phase there is a meeting between the project stakeholders to review and assess the stage plan for that phase and approve the stage plan for the next phase. Typical stage plans contain details about the risks, issues, change controls and lessons learnt for each phase, prior to the start of subsequent phases. Therefore, the structuring of projects into life-cycle phases provides senior management with control of major decision points, or 'review gates' in order to:

- Avoid committing key resources too early.
- Preserve future options.
- Maximise the benefit of each project in relation to all other projects.
- Assess risks

Strategic project planning is determining what needs to be done, by whom, and by when; in order to fulfil one's assigned responsibility. Strategic project planning should clearly establish why a particular project is being undertaken. The logic of strategic project planning requires answers to several questions in order for the alternative scenarios and activity constraints to be fully understood.

Action	Question
Prepare environmental analysis	Where are we? How and why did we get here?
Set objectives	Is this where we want to be? Where would we like to be? In a year? In five years?
List alternative strategies	Where will we go if we continue as before? Is that where we want to go? How could we get to where we want to go?
List threats and opportunities	What might prevent us getting there? What might help is get there?
Prepare forecasts	Where are we capable of going? What do we need to take us where we are going?
Select strategy portfolio	What is the best course for us to take? What are the potential benefits & risks?
Prepare action programmes	What do we need to do? How will we do it? Who will do it?
Monitor and control	Are we on course? If not, why not? What do we need to do to be on course? Can we do it?

Figure 21 - 4: Strategic Project Planning Questions

An outline of the types of questions that should be posed by project managers during the definition stage of a project is shown in Figure 21 - 4.

Strategic Project Planning 3 - The Tools

The successful accomplishment of both project and corporate objectives requires a plan that:

- Defines all effort to be expended.
- Assigns responsibility to a specially assigned

organisational element.

 ◆ Establishes schedules and budgets for the accomplishment of the work.

Development of a Work Breakdown Structure (WBS) for a project is the first major step in the strategic planning process following the definition of project objectives. A WBS is a product/deliverable-orientated family tree sub-division of materials, services and data required to deliver the project.

The WBS acts as a vehicle for breaking the work down into smaller, more manageable elements, thus providing a greater probability that every activity will be accounted for. Figure 21 - 5 shows the six common elements of a WBS:

Level	Element	Role	Type
1	Total programme	Senior	Managerial
2	Projects	Cross functional	
3	Work packages	Operational & functional	Technical
4	Tasks	Managerial	
5	Sub-tasks	Team leaders	
6	Level of effort	Development & implementation	

Figure 21 - 5: WBS Elements

Project managers tend to provide the summary and status reports to management based on the upper three levels. The lower levels are generated for the control of work. Each level serves a specific purpose: level one is generally used for the authorisation and release of all work, budgets are prepared at level two and detailed schedules are prepared at level three.

Together with the other project planning tools shown in Figure 21 - 6, the WBS acts as a communications tool, providing detailed information to different levels of management that are used to validate project assumptions.

Progress Monitoring

The difficulty with monitoring the progress of projects at regular intervals in the life-cycle is the estimation of completion at that point in time. Several methods exist for

Basis of Evaluation	Validation of:
Interlocked objective networks major corporate objectives divisional objectives departmental sub-objectives sectional feeder objectives	Organisational structure Management co-ordination Project performance
WBS	Work packages Tasks
Roles & responsibilities matrix	Work methods Accountability
Network scheduling	Timescales Schedules
Decision Trees	Risks Constraints Assumptions Impact of decision-making
Cost Breakdown Structure (CBS)	Total costs Cost structure Budget structure

Figure 21 - 6: Project Planning Tools

Method	Description
50/50 Rule	50% of time or costs are allocated at the time work is scheduled to begin; the remaining 50% is allocated when the work is scheduled to be completed.
Bulk Monitoring (0/100 Rule)	No time or costs are allocated until the work package or task is completed.
Milestones	No time or costs are allocated until the milestone has been achieved.
Percentage Completion	A judgement of the percentage of work completed at that point in time.

Figure 21 - 7: Monitoring Tools

measuring progress (time) or expenditure (cost) as shown in Figure 21 - 7.

These methods of progress measurement are important for monitoring the financial commitment using the accruals concept and also for monitoring project performance using the earned value concept through the life-cycle of a project.

Variance Analysis

A variance is defined as any schedule, technical performance, quality, or cost deviation from a specific plan. The establishment of variance measurement and analysis procedures is integral to the strategic project planning process. Variances are almost always identified as critical items and tend to be reported at all organisational levels.

Not all companies have a uniform methodology for variance thresholds and permitted variances may be dependent on such factors as the length of a project, it's life-cycle phases and the type and accuracy of estimates.

For many programmes and projects, variances are permitted to change over the duration of the programme. Five questions must be addressed as part of variance analysis:

1   What is the problem causing the variance?
2   What is the impact on time, cost and performance?
3   What is the impact on other efforts?
4   What corrective action is planned?
5   What are the expected results of the corrective action?

Strategic Project Planning 4 - The Result

The output from the strategic project planning process is a Strategy Plan or a Project Initiation Document (PID), which provides the specific context for a project in terms of objectives, scope and success/acceptance criteria.

Documentation termed a Project Management Plan (PMP) or Project Execution Plan (PEP) is sometimes produced during the initiation phase of a project, but they are not relevant in the context of this session. The inference is that this type document is best suited to define exactly 'how' a project will be carried out, once the project objectives have been defined as part of the strategic project planning process.

In many of today's high technology companies, the short cycle time project is down to a matter of weeks. Stakeholders expect performance to be accelerated and they expect to see deliverables earlier. Therefore, Strategy Plans have to be 'fit-for-purpose' and cannot be all-encompassing. Together with product and or solution technical documentation, Strategy Plans are most effective when they are template and checklist based, such that key project initiation milestones can be achieved in the near term.

The Strategy Plan is the most important document in the overall planning of a project, but not for the monitoring and implementation phases of a project. Monitoring is most effectively performed using planning tools (e.g. MSP2000), Quality Control Plans for deliverable items, Bulk Monitoring checklists and graphs, Document Submission Schedules, etc. An up-front Technical Plan or Solution Specification should define the technical implementation of a project.

Since project environments are becoming more and more turbulent and since customer service and effectiveness of delivery are now the key differentiators for competing organisations in similar industries, the clear definition of an organisation's approach to a project or programme is critical and strategic project planning is the process by which this can be achieved.

Moreover, project management has to be established as a core discipline to work alongside the functional management disciplines, such as operations, sales or finance, for the successful management of projects in a continuously changing environment.

Planning For Excellence - Best Practice Project Management

This concluding section has been derived from the conclusions and recommendations of Kerzner (1998a), who defines excellence and maturity in best practice project management as "a continuous stream of successfully managed [planned and delivered] projects".

This session should provide project managers with an aide memoir that will assist them in understanding the context within which they have to perform their duties as project management professionals.

Executives must define the meaning of 'project success' in terms of both project and corporate parameters.

- Project managers to participate in non-project activities, such as corporate strategic planning and administrative control.
- Encourage 'dialogue' between project managers.
- Question whether decisions are in the interest of the company and not just the project.

Any project management organisational structure can be made to work efficiently and effectively through multi-directional communication, co-operation and trust.

- Encourage a peer-to-peer relationship between project managers and functional managers.
- Encourage multi-directional communications.
- Foster a culture of trust.
- Do not delegate authority to individuals simply because of the information they possess.

Project managers should negotiate for the commitment of functional managers to meet time, cost and performance criteria, rather than for specific people.

- Maintain a balance of authority between project managers and functional managers.
- Functional managers should provide the technical direction of their staff.
- Functional managers should be encouraged to provide realistic estimates and then be held responsible for delivery against those estimates.
- Functional managers should be kept fully informed of project progress throughout the life-cycle.

Executive project sponsorship must exist and be visible, so that the project-functional management interface is kept in balance.

- Educate senior managers as to the business benefits of project management.

- Convince executives of the necessity for on-going, visible support to project managers.
- Convince executives that they do not need to know all the details.

Many organisations are committed to life-cycle planning, life-cycle cost estimating, life-cycle decision-making and life-cycle auditing of project performance.

- Develop a life-cycle phase approach to planning, scheduling and controlling.
- Encourage project management through the whole life-cycle.
- Insist that project managers have well-defined audit trails.

References and Further Reading

Ansoff, H.I., 1988. Corporate Strategy. Pelican.

Dixon, M., 2000. Project Management Body of Knowledge (BoK). 4th Ed. Association for Project Management.

Johnson, G. & Scholes, K., 1993. Exploring Corporate Strategy: Text and Cases. 3rd Edition. Prentice Hall.

Kerzner, H., 1998a. Project Management: A Systems Approach to Planning, Scheduling and Controlling. 6th Edition. Van Nostrand Reinhold.

Kerzner, H., 1998b. In Search of Excellence in Project Management: Successful Practices in High Performance Organisations. Van Nostrand Reinhold.

Mintzberg, H. & Waters, J.A., 1985. Of Strategies, Deliberate and Emergent. Strategic Management Journal, Vol. 6, No. 3, pp. 257-272.

Quinn, J.B., 1980. Strategies for Change. Irwin.

22   VALUE MANAGEMENT

Michel Thiry

"What we must decide is perhaps how we are valuable, rather than how valuable we are."

F. Scott Fitzgerald (1896-1940), U.S. writer. The Crack-Up (1936)

Links to Other Topics

Value Management is directly linked to Value Engineering (44). The latter is a subset of the former. Value Management sits in the Strategic Section of the Body of Knowledge (BoK), it is therefore also linked to Project Success Criteria (20); Strategy/Project Management Plan (21); Risk Management (23) and Quality Management (24). Finally, because of its focus on the delivery of value to stakeholders, it is one of the key elements of Programme Management (11) and, directly linked to Change Control (34).

Value and Value Management

The success of projects does not lie in the simple delivery of the outcome anymore. In a continually changing context, project managers are required to deliver a product, service or process which will satisfy or exceed stakeholders' needs and expectations at the time of delivery. Value management focuses on the definition and iterative assessment of stakeholders' needs and expectations, which will increase stakeholders' buy-in and project team understanding of their changing needs and expectations.

The BoK states that: "Value lies in achieving a balance between the satisfaction of many differing needs and the resources used in doing so. The fewer resources used or the greater the satisfaction of the need, the greater is the value". At a strategic level, it can be expressed in terms of cost vs benefits, parameters vs objectives, expenditure vs needs, or investment vs outcome." At project level, it concerns the ratio between scope and quality on one side and cost and time, on the other side. At the technical or operational level, it represents the level of functionality of the goods or services provided, against the resources expended to achieve them.

The BoK also states that: "Value Management is a structured means of improving "business decisions; increase effectiveness and enhance competitiveness". It refers to the overall process of identifying key issues and setting targets in terms of success criteria; identifying the teams and processes necessary to achieve them; and reviewing these throughout the project to obtain successful results". In this Session, we will examine how these are achieved and what methods can be used to deliver value to stakeholders during the course of programmes or projects.

There is currently debate between value societies around the world as to what Value and Value Management (VM) mean; more specifically, the US-based SAVE International uses the term 'value management' to define the management of value proposals generated through value engineering (VE) (SAVE, 1997) and value is defined as a traditional function/cost ratio. In Europe though, a number of value societies have collaborated on the definition of value management and of its components. This effort has resulted in the BS-EN 12973:2000 European Standard on Value Management (VM Standard), which was issued in April 2000. This is the first Standard specifically on Value Management, worldwide, and it is the one that both the APM and IPMA would acknowledge.

Within this VM Standard, the terms Value Engineering (VE) and Value Analysis (VA) are used as equivalents and those represent one of the techniques used to support the management of value (see Session 44).

VM as "A Style of Management"

In its foreword, the VM Standard defines value management as "a style of management that has evolved out of previous methods based on the concept of value and functional approach". The VM Standard claims that VM uniquely brings together:

- Management style
- Positive human dynamics
- Consideration of external and internal environment
- Effective use of methods and tools

It also introduces concepts such as:

- Transverse approach
- Better business decisions
- Increased effectiveness or enhanced competitiveness
- Value culture and VM programmes in organisations

The positive human dynamics and transverse approach have always been at the core of VM. VM is first and foremost a group process; a number of VM writers even claim it is a Group Decision Support Methodology. Since its inception in the late forties, value analysis, and the other techniques derived from it, have been linked to cross-functional team workshops; although some steps of the process can be done individually, the foundation has always been the group; what we would call today: 'the stakeholders' plus the assurance that it covers all perspectives of the situation being addressed. Furthermore, the innovative approach of VM encourages participation of contributors external to the core VM team. All participants are treated equally and given the opportunity to actively participate in the making of the decisions, in many situations, senior participants' ideas are not the ones which finally prevail.

Because of its broad focus, VM is ideally suited to consider both the external and internal environment of programmes and projects. The definition of value as a ratio enables VM to comfortably integrate techniques such as 'SWOT Analysis', 'Balanced Scorecard', 'Cost-Benefit Analysis' and other management tools into its framework. The VM Standard mentions that, not only 'core' VM methods and tools, but "all of the available methods should be considered for use [...], they should be combined to create the most suitable approach to the proposed study". This means that VM should not be based on specific tools and techniques, but rather on achievement of results and satisfaction of needs; it is the right combination of tools and techniques, which will create success.

Although it does not renounce traditional value approaches, the VM Standard definitely promotes a more 'managerial' approach of the management of value. As a management style, it is more in line with recent quality concepts like the 'Business Excellence Model' (EFQM®) and the new ISO 2000 series of standards, which view organisational effectiveness as a whole system supported by strong 'learning and innovation' principles. This is also the view promoted by most current management writers as a means to increase effectiveness and enhance competitiveness. When set in this framework, the decision-making process leading to programmes and projects is directly linked to business results and tied in with leadership and organisational policies; it considers people, processes and partners, including customers, as part of the whole equation and thus ensures that the solutions delivered address the 'right' issue wholistically.

The Players

Whereas VA and VE specifically focus on the function/cost issues of the project, and therefore interest more those members of the project team who have to deal with those issues, VM has a wider scope and therefore has a broader range of players.

- Project Sponsors, in particular Senior Executives, will use VM in decision-making, and to generally improve organisational effectiveness. They use project management to make sure the strategies and policies they have developed are implemented with the highest possible efficiency, but they require a methodology that will ensure the right benefits are being provided. VM can help them render the strategic decision and development process more effective by ensuring that the right issues are addressed; that achievable success criteria are set and that the most resource effective solutions are chosen, combining TQM (see Session 24), Risk (see Session 23) and VM within a Programme Management (see Session 11) framework.
- Project managers, need to understand the way VM is used to understand stakeholder needs and expectations and improve delivery, in order to apply it effectively to the delivery of project outcomes. VA and VE specifically apply to resource management, once the objectives are well defined (see Session 44); it is first and foremost a problem solving methodology. VM, on the other hand,

is a decision-making process and is aimed at both 'setting' and achieving the project objectives. It will therefore be used as an overall framework and is a sponsor-led process. More specifically, during the course of the project, it will be the framework for 'gateway reviews' to assess deliverables, with regard to the expected business or programme level benefits.

- Value Management specialists, will often be involved in the formal application of VM within specific projects. There is now a recognised European Certification and Training System, leading to the Professional Value Manager (PVM) certification, which will ensure that Value practitioners have the required qualifications to carry out their task.

Recent developments of VM include a greater focus on the community, specifically the environment and a greater sustainability of the solution(s) as part of the value equation.

The Process

Change is concerned with the modification of an existing situation, either to adapt to new circumstances, dissatisfaction with the current state or the need to correct a deviation. It is therefore crucial to define the expectations, the current unsatisfactory situation and the means to achieve the successful change. The value system developed through value management is refined into more specific value criteria, which determine the success factors for the project or change process' deliverable. These value criteria have gained stakeholders' agreement through the VM process and will become the basis for change management and delivery.

The BoK states that: "Value Management is concerned with the broader optimisation of strategic issues, generation of alternative courses of action and assessment of options. Generally Value Management consists of a series of structured workshops, facilitated by a value management specialist." Below is the outline of the VM process. It does not include the VE process, which is described in Session 44. It is a 'soft', high-level process that is aimed at ambiguity-reduction, rather than uncertainty-reduction, which is the purpose of Planning, Risk Management and Quality Management (see Sessions 21, 23, 24) in particular, and of project management in general. This decision-making process is firmly grounded in strategic choice and is undertaken at a number of decision levels, in order to create a consistent, well-supported decision framework leading to increased effectiveness.

The VM Process Specifically Involves a Focus on Outcomes. It Includes:

- Sensemaking - the need to make sense and construct a shared model of complex situations
- Seeking of solutions - the creative and innovative, function-based approach to alternative generation
- Evaluation of options - the qualitative and quantitative assessment of opportunities
- Decision/Recommendation - the choice of solutions, in line with success criteria
- Follow-up and project review - the processes put in place to ensure achievement of the benefits and effective response to emergent inputs

Sensemaking

"Sensemaking is triggered by the need for individuals to make sense of the world around them. It is set in motion by ambiguity and uncertainty. For groups, it involves a constructivist interaction, which is characterised by effective communication based on co-operation and the development of a shared frame of reference. The sensemaking process can lead to either positive or negative results that are influenced by the way information is communicated. The confidence of achieving desired goals also affects the sensemaking process." It is based on the concept that people, when their beliefs or routines are challenged, will have a tendency to revert to known, tested methods and therefore resist change and that, in order to succeed, this behaviour needs to be understood and managed.

Obviously, a constructive sensemaking process is key to any successful change process where paradigms are challenged and, based on the fact that programmes and projects are about change (see Sessions 10 and 11), it is essential that a sensemaking process take place in the early stages of programme formulation or project definition.

Making Sense of an Ambiguous Situation

Sensemaking requires stakeholders to let go of their old ways and accept 'new ways of doing things'. This situation applies, not only in change implementation, but also during the decision process. It has been demonstrated, by a number of authors, that managers will mostly rely on judgement or intuition to make strategic decisions; they do so even more when a situation is ambiguous, meaning that there are many possible solutions because of the number of factors and combinations involved. This is especially true of strategies, where a number of actors, each with their own perspective, are involved in the decision.

Because one of the keys to successful project management is the ability to "ensure a successful project deliverable", it is essential that ambiguity be reduced and objectives clearly defined in measurable terms (see Session 20).

There are many ways in which VM can address the sensemaking process to make its outcome positive.

The first requirement in the sensemaking process, is to perform a stakeholder analysis, which will enable the team to identify all the possible stakeholders of a programme, or project; taking into consideration both external and internal environments. Stakeholder analysis also involves the classification of stakeholders and an acknowledgement of their significance for the project. There are a few factors that define stakeholders' impact on programmes or projects and enable them to be grouped: a) decision-making level; b) type of functional role c) type of need; d) type of influence; e) organisational influence. Stakeholder analysis is not, strictly speaking, a VM technique, but it is essential in any kind of decision-making process aiming to achieve outcomes. Once stakeholders have been identified and their significance agreed, the most significant are invited to participate in the next step of the sensemaking process. Function(al) analysis is one of the core elements of VM. It is based on the principle that most decision-makers, under pressure, will choose the first acceptable, or least objectionable, solution without really examining all the possible alternatives and even, without making sure the solution addresses the true needs. It is Peter Drucker who said: "I would much prefer to arrive at the wrong solution to the right problem, than find the right solution to the wrong problem." Functional analysis assures the team that they are 'solving the right problem' or making a decision about the right issues.

Traditionally, functional analysis has consisted of identifying the functions of a product that are really essential as compared to those which are only 'nice-to-have'; the purpose of VM has been to make sure that the essentials are achieved before any resources are invested in the 'nice-to-have'. At the strategic level, those functions are called benefits, success criteria or objectives (see Sessions 10 and 20); they are the requirements of the programme or project by which the needs of the stakeholders will be satisfied.

Essentially, functional analysis consists of identifying the needs and requirements of the significant stakeholders and expressing them in simple terms - typically an active verb and a noun - which, at a later stage, could be expressed as a high level work package to be fulfilled and thus, help define the work content and scope of the programme or project (see Session 30) and allocate resources (see Session 32). Once this is achieved, the list of functions is organised into a model, which VM practitioners call a function model or function diagram, but which has also been called Function Breakdown Structure (FBS) . The logic of the FBS consists of comparing the functions between them by asking the question why? and how? as shown in Figure 22 - 1.

The FBS enables the team, not only to identify the functions and model them, but also to identify the right levels for the success criteria of the programme or project. Having participated in the elaboration of the FBS, the whole team 'makes sense' of its conclusions. Additionally, it is easy for project team members to make sense of the FBS, as it basically follows the same rules as a WBS. It is also a very logical step to go from a programme FBS to a number of project FBS's and further down to work packages, all the while ensuring that all actions are logically interconnected to support the strategy.

Stuart Green, researcher from Reading University, recommends the use of Soft Systems Methodology (SSM) to

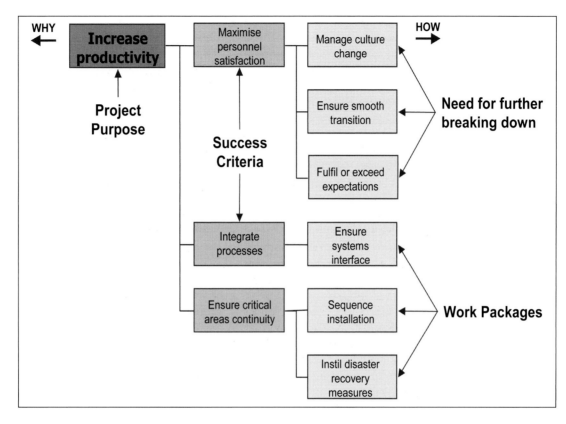

Figure 22 - 1: Example of Function Breakdown Structure

do the equivalent of function analysis. This method is lessfamiliar to programme and project managers and requires more practice to lead to precise results.

The following step is to prioritise the success criteria of the programme or project. This is usually done simply using a weighted matrix, where criteria are compared in pairs and given a relative weight. Other methods are also available to achieve this, like simple 1-10 weighting, or subjective ordering.

Once the success criteria are set, they must be translated into measurable objectives, usually called key performance indicators (KPI's) (see Session 20). VM offers a basis for this through characterisation . Characterisation consists of quantifying the expected levels of performance required by the stakeholders for each identified function, in order to be able to control its achievement. Typically it is expressed in terms of a measuring criterion; a level of required performance; and a range, or tolerance.

For example, in the case of: "Minimum disruption to ongoing operations", which could be a success criteria in the above FBS example, KPI's could be:

1   Measuring criterion as: Availability of systems - Time - Reduction of performance
2   Required level of performance in: % of availability - Y minutes - X units per day
3   Tolerance as: ± % - ± y minutes - ± x units

Once all these steps have been fulfilled, the resulting data can be put into a document that comprises a needs statement and business case. If the sensemaking process has been well managed, this document constitutes the shared definition of the programme, or the project, by its significant stakeholders and ensures that the programme or project manager will have a clear understanding of the needs and requirements they must fulfil and of the fundamental success criteria, which are both measurable and achievable.

Seeking of Solutions

Following the identification of stakeholders' needs and expectations and the prioritisation of expected benefits, the team needs to find a number of potential alternatives to choose from, in order to make the best possible decision.

One of the most recognised features of VM is its ability to foster innovativeness. The VM process is based on the creative thinking concept that alternatively uses lateral (imaginative) and vertical (analytical) thinking; the seeking of solutions is a lateral thinking process; the evaluation of options is a vertical thinking process.

Using Creativity to Generate Alternative Solutions

Project management is a performance process (see Session 11); it is based on vertical thinking and aims to achieve the best results with the least resources. It is difficult for project managers to both: "focus on delivering specific project objectives and develop effective responses to emergent change". VM is therefore a method of choice to find effective alternatives or respond to changes which are affecting the project objectives.

VM uses a number of creativity techniques to generate ideas; the best known are brainstorming and forced comparison, but there is a whole range of other techniques available to generate innovative solutions to implement a strategy, a programme, or a project. Whereas in later stages, hundreds of ideas can be expected from a value workshop (see Session 44), at the early, more strategic stages, a dozen ideas can be considered a good number. The reason is that ideas are at a more abstract level and therefore broader-based.

The best environment for a group to be creative is a facilitated workshop where ideas are exchanged and nurtured in a team environment. There are some basic rules to any creativity process; they are to:

1   Write down all ideas and comments
2   Target quantity rather than quality
3   Exclude criticism; assume that each idea will work
4   Hold judgement until the evaluation phase
5   Eliminate the word "Impossible" from your vocabulary
6   Let your imagination roam free (the craziest ideas are often the most important)
7   Use piggybacking (build on other ideas and comments).
8   Cross-fertilise ideas (associate or modify ideas and comments)
9   Let everybody talk, do not interrupt!

There are also known roadblocks to creativity and innovation; some of them are:

◆   Rigid and unbending rules
◆   Unwritten guidelines
◆   Fear of failure, fear of ridicule
◆   Contentment with status quo
◆   Negative comments, judgement
◆   Bureaucratic processes, red tape
◆   Intimidating superiors or colleagues

These roadblocks must be taken into account and eliminated for an innovation and creativity process to be successful. Although creativity and innovativeness are traditionally thought of as a 'free for all', the success of a creativity workshop rests on the ability of the programme, project, or value manager, to effectively manage the process. This includes having a facilitator, external to the team, to run any significant workshop; choosing the participants so that none of them will be dominating the group; establishing clear rules from the start and sticking to them throughout; following up the creativity session with an evaluation; and focusing the creativity process on the objectives.

This last statement may seem contradictory but, if the group is not regularly refocused on the decision-making process objectives, the creativity process will lose its power by diluting the results and wasting time of the participants and of the organisation. Focusing creativity also means that, at different stages of the project, the group will be looking for different types of solutions.

At the programme formulation phase, the team will use creativity to identify stakeholders, as well as their needs and expectations, which will be translated into success criteria; it will also look for project alternatives that will fulfil those criteria. During the project definition phase, it will aim to identify the objectives of the project and functions of its outcome, as well as list the criteria by which the options will be judged. During the planning phase, the purpose will be to generate implementation options, with their advantages and disadvantages. During the execution phase, the goal will be to find the easiest implementation paths and to identify alternatives when faced with the need to implement change. This phase is an instance where VM and risk management should be combined (see Session 23) to identify risks for each of those options.

Specifically, when using brainstorming, keep the group relatively small; state the issue in an open way; use a facilitator; note every idea and limit the time. If there is a possibility that the workshop participants might not feel at ease to explore new ideas, it may be a good idea to use the 'step-ladder' technique, where each group member is given time to think about the issue before the workshop (sensemaking); participants are then asked to discuss their preliminary ideas in pairs; groups of four are then formed, and so on until the whole group considers the solutions presented to make the final decision(s). This technique allows for active participation of all the members of the team and makes sure to tap into all the participants' knowledge and skills.

For forced comparison, define the subject of study; identify any other concept; brainstorm on second concept; associate the brainstorming ideas to first subject and evaluate. For example, when addressing a team problem, the group could brainstorm on ducks. One idea could be that ducks, when flying south, relay each other at the head of the formation. When reapplied to the team, it could flag up the fact that the leader has to delegate more and trust others to take the lead from time to time.

Evaluation of Options

One of the key points of VM is to match intent to capabilities, whilst aiming for the best balance of all factors underlying the decision. Alternatives generated in the prior process therefore need to be assessed and evaluated to ensure that the ones which are put forward will truly be beneficial to the programme or project. Evaluation can take two views: a) the comparison of a number of options between them, to prioritise resources, or b) the analysis of a proposed option to assess its suitability, acceptability and feasibility. These three strategic criteria are described as follows by Johnson & Scholes (1997) :

- Suitability - alignment with strategy (KPI's, CSF's, fit in context, qualitative assessment)
- Acceptability - outcomes assessment (likely benefits vs expectations, return on investment, etc.)
- Feasibility - capability assessment (required resources vs capability; probability of success, quantitative assessment)

Although, traditionally, VM has been more concerned with the comparison of options, it is more and more used in combination with other methods like risk analysis and strategic analysis techniques to evaluate single strategic options, mostly in regards of the VM standard's perspective.

Evaluating Ideas Generated Against KPI's

As mentioned above, the evaluation phase of the VM process is the area of choice to combine risk and value analysis. All the options generated during the seeking process are evaluated to their merit. Evaluation criteria should first and foremost include the KPIs of the programme or project; but they should also include the analysis of risks (both threats and opportunities, or as usually called in VM: advantages and disadvantages) and any other consideration which might be important.

Because the creativity process will have generated a large number of ideas, the first step of the evaluation process is to eliminate all the options that are not suitable, acceptable or feasible. As in Risk management, it is important to use programme or project specific measures to assess options and, although generic factors can be transferred from historic data sources, they should always be re-evaluated against the new situation.

Once the number of options to be evaluated has reached an acceptable level, which will be levelled against the available resources, they need to be classified into categories and prioritised, in a similar way as risks are classified in terms of probability and impact. Alternatives can be classified in terms of achievability and benefits; those which score high on both counts will be recommended; those who have a mixed score would be re-examined to see if they can be improved to be recommended and those which score low on both points are eliminated. This is a qualitative analysis, which can be supported by a quantitative financial, resource or risk analysis. If the value criteria have been quantified and metrics have been agreed (KPI's), they would also be used.

Ranking and prioritising can also involve the classification of ideas in order of importance, so that the ones that are the most beneficial to the programme or project objectives can be identified and available resources allocated accordingly. VM uses a number of prioritisation techniques, from simple ranking (e.g. numerical scoring or paired comparison) to more complicated weighted matrices (ideas scored against a number of pre-weighted factors). This is an area where the use of concepts such as the Balanced Scorecard, CBA or SWOT analysis can be useful, but a number of other methods exist in the literature and value managers should not fear to use the ones they, and the team, feel the most comfortable with.

Decision / Recommendation

There are two major components in the decision/recommendation process; the first one is to actually develop options to a level sufficient to make a well-documented decision; the second is to agree a choice between the stakeholders.

Developing the best options is an extension of the work undertaken in the evaluation phase when options have been prioritised. The same criteria can be used, but options need to be developed further, enough to persuade sponsors to support them. Benefits must be outlined, advantages and disadvantages stated and contingency plans drawn. In a VM process the main argument will be value-based, which means that benefits are always presented against resources required to achieve them, and that all the options are evaluated on a similar basis.

In terms of the actual choice, VM has always promoted consensus, but consensus takes time as it "refers to a unanimous agreement about a decision". Compromise, on the other hand, "alludes to a settlement reached by mutual concessions". Consensus requires discussion, deliberation and presentation of contrasting viewpoints. Therefore compromise is usually the route chosen having regard to the limited resources of projects. In programmes, on the other hand, consensus is a more acceptable option.

Following these, there are a series of techniques which are also acceptable with regards to circumstances, time or resources available. They are, in democratic order: a) voting with discussion; b) majority decision; c) leader decision with discussion and; d) leader decision.

The last step of this process consists in presenting the selected solutions to stakeholders for approval or funding. If the VM process has been followed throughout, if options are well documented and based on value principles, the stakeholders will find it difficult not to approve them, except if the needs and expectations have changed and these have not been properly assessed.

Follow-up and Project Review

VM would not succeed in managing value if the process were not iterative and, like project management, "applied throughout" (see Session 10). Once the projects are underway, the VM process becomes key to the control processes, and in particular, to change control (see Session 34).

One of the tasks of the programme or project manager consists in developing the life cycle of the project (see Session 60); this includes defining the evaluation and approval points; the 'gates' or 'gateways', which usually correspond to milestones. These gates generally represent the boundary between phases of the programme or project and correspond to deliverables whose successful delivery will prompt the next phase or the closing of the project.

By applying VM to gates or project reviews, stakeholders will be assured that their needs and expectations are constantly taken into account and that the success criteria, set at the beginning, are fulfilled. Additionally, VM applied to the change control process will ensure that the 'real' issues are addressed and that changes are made for the good of the project and in line with the success factors and the expected benefits. VM also acts as a regular review of stakeholders' needs and expectations and will alert programme and project managers early enough to identify the most resource-effective alternatives for the project and evaluate them on a rational basis. Obviously the focus of VM would vary from a strategic level to a tactical and technical/operational level as the project progresses towards its outcome (see Thiry, 1998 for more detail).

Traditionally, control has been based on measurement (quantitative evaluation), description (qualitative evaluation) or judgement (subjective evaluation). Recently, with increasing complexity of situation and continually changing environmental concerns; evaluation, based on an iterated negotiation of the evaluation criteria, has become more and more popular. In the framework of an organisation-based VM programme or project-integrated VM; responsive evaluation becomes possible and cost-effective.

The 'summative' approach to control, is based on pre-set standards which consist of comparing the actual situation with the expected standard and is predicated on the achievement of set and well defined objectives and deliverables. It is ideal for assessing performance against a baseline, as long as changes are within the set project criteria of scope, time, cost and quality. The problem lies where it is these parameters that need to change. VM enables programme and project managers to evolve from a summative to a 'formative' evaluation, necessary when the relationship between means and ends is not well defined. This is the type of approach to control that is required when there is a need to improve a situation beyond the set parameters of the project.

By using the stakeholders' needs and success criteria as a basis for decision-making, a value-based change control process ensures both stakeholders and project manager that only changes that are necessary and useful are implemented and that those which are have an effective resource/benefit ratio.

Conclusions

Value management, because of its focus on sensemaking and functions, is a learning process; it is also a performance improvement process, because it continually challenges the established order and requires the team to think beyond their boundaries. In the highly competitive, fast moving world in which we currently live, value management should be part of every organisation's culture; even more so where managers are judged on their ability to deliver results. Neither managers, nor programme and project managers can afford to ignore VM as an integral part of programme and project management.

Additionally, it is essential that VM becomes part of the training portfolio of programme and project managers in order for them to be able to manage it so that it really makes a difference.

Below are outlined some of the most obvious benefits of VM, which are both hard and soft.

Hard Benefits of VM Include:

- Balance between expected performance (scope, quality) and available resources (time, cost)
- Identification of best revenue opportunities
- Improvement of capital productivity
- Avoidance of unnecessary costs and over-specification
- Consideration of both capital and life cycle costs
- Optimal development/design solutions
- Effective management of change

A VM Strategy will Also Achieve Softer Benefits:

- Increased problem understanding
- Clear scope definition
- Sharing of objectives and purpose
- Development of team spirit
- Flexibility of solutions
- Heedfulness of team
- Resolution of complex problems

References and Further Reading

Hamilton, A., Managing for Value: Achieving high quality at low cost, Oak Tree Press, Dublin, 1999

Kaufman, J. J., Value Management: Creating Competitive Advantage, Crisp Publications, 1998

Thiry, M., Value Management Practice, Sylva NC., Project Management Institute, 1997

Technical Committee DS/1 (BSI), PD 6663: Guidelines to BS EN 12973: Value management- Practical guidance to its use and intent, British Standards Institution, Chiswick, June 2000

Technical Committee CEN/TC 279, Value Management, BS EN 12973:2000, European Committee for Standardization (CEN)- British Standards Institution (BSI) Technical Committee DS/1, Apr. 2000

Technical Committee CEN/TC 279, Value Management, value analysis, functional analysis vocabulary BS EN 1325-1:1997, European Committee for Standardization (CEN)- British Standards Institution (BSI) Technical Committee DS/1, Jan. 1997

CUP Central Unit on Procurement, CUP Guidance Note 54, H M Treasury, 1996

CIRIA, Value Management in Construction: A Client's Guide, Special Publication 129, (CIRIA), 1996

ASTM Subcommittee E-06.81 on Building Economics, Standard Practice for Performing Value Analysis (VA) of Buildings and Building Systems, Standard Designation: E 1699-95, ASTM, Philadelphia, Pa, July 1995

SAVE International, Value Methodology Standard, Save International, 1997.

Kaufman J. J., Value Engineering for the Practitioner, NCS University, NC, 1985

Kelly, J., Male, S. Value Management in design and construction (The economic management of projects), London, U.K., E & FN Spon, Chapman and Hall, 1993.

Male, S.; Kelly, J.; Fernie, S.; Grönqvist, M. and Bowles, G., The value management benchmark: A good practice framework for clients and practitioners, London: Thomas Telford Publishing, 1998

Miles, L. D., Techniques of Value Analysis and Engineering, McGraw-Hill Book Company, New-York, NY, Third Edition, 1972

Murray-Webster, R. and Thiry, M., 'Managing Programmes of Projects' in Gower Handbook of Project Management, J. Turner and S. Simister Eds., 3rd edition' Chapter 03, 2000

Simister, S.J., 'Managing scope - functionality and value' in Gower Handbook of Project Management, J. Turner and S. Simister Eds., 3rd edition' Chapter 14, 2000

Zimmerman L. W., Hart G. D., Value engineering (A practical approach for owners, designers and contractors), New York, NY, Van Nostrand Reinhold Ltd., 1982

Articles

Green, S. D. (1993) "A Reinterpretation of Value Management", CIB W-65, Organisation and Management of Construction - The Way forward, (ed. Lewis, T. M.), Trinidad, W. I.

Green, S. D. (1997). 'A Kuhnian crisis in value management?' Value World. Vol. 20 (3), pp. 19-24.

Thiry. M. (1998) "The benefits of value management through the project life cycle". Projects the Magazine of the Association for Project Management, Vol.10-9, pp. 12-15.

Thiry. M. (1999) "Would you tell me please which way I ought to go from here?" Is Change a Threat or an Opportunity? Proceedings of the 30th PMI Seminars and Symposium, Philadelphia, PA.

Thiry. M. (2001a) "Sensemaking in Value Management Practice" International Journal of Project Management, Elseveir Science, Oxford.

Thiry. M. (2001b) "Combining value and project management into an effective programme management model." Proceedings of the 4th Annual PMI-Europe Conference, London.

Thiry. M. (2001c) "The European VM Standard; will it change the way we practice VM?" Proceedings of the 4th Annual PMI-Europe Conference, London.

23 RISK MANAGEMENT

Karl Davey

"Whenever you see a successful business, someone once made a courageous decision."
Attributed to: Peter F. Drucker (1909-), Austrian-born U.S. management consultant.

Risk should be defined as "An uncertain event that, should it occur, would have an effect (positive or negative) on the project or business objectives).

Risk Management is an integral part of project and business management techniques. Risk management relates to the formal process of 'Identification', 'Assessment' and subsequent 'Management' of the 'Threats' and 'Opportunities' which face any endeavour.

Related Topics:

20   Project Success Criteria
22   Value Management
31   Time Scheduling and Phasing
33   Budget and Cost Management
35   Earned Value Management
50   Business Case
70   Communication

Introduction and Concepts

Risk Management is an integral feature of business and organisational culture and procedures. It must involve all levels of responsibility within an organisation, and be applied in a continuous and consistent manner, constantly moving forward as the project or business evolves. To succeed the risk management process must be treated with respect within an organisation and has to be implemented early to achieve the greatest effectiveness. The risk management process outlined in this session is a flexible process that can be tailored to reflect any type of endeavour equally applicable, to a project, programme, business assessment or management audit.

Risk Management - Just a Part of Project Management

Risk management is an integral part of good project management. It is an iterative process enabling continual improvement in rational decision-making. Risk management comprises methods of identifying, analysing, assessing, managing, controlling and communicating risks associated with any activity, or operation in a way to minimise threats and maximise opportunities. It must always be remembered that risk management is as much about identifying and maximising opportunities as avoiding or mitigating threats.

Within the project management process, risks can be identified against work packages, requirement definitions, cost breakdowns, programme activities, and operations. Once risks have been assessed and appropriate risk management actions have been agreed, then these actions should be incorporated within the programme as specific packages of work and treated with the same priorities as other work packages.

The Process

Risk Management is the process of the identification of risk, its causes, effects and its ownership with a view to increasing overall understanding; in order to manage, reduce, transfer or eliminate threats and then to manage, maximise, enhance or develop opportunities.

The objectives of the risk process can be defined as:

- Definition of the key objectives and scope of the risk process and Risk Management Plan
- Identify risk issues through structured brainstorms, data gathering exercises and interviews
- Allocate responsibilities for each identified risk, to provide further details of background, consequence and management information
- Assess each risk against an agreed consistent scale for likelihood and potential consequence on project milestones, objectives and budgets
- Compare risk significance to identify the top risks

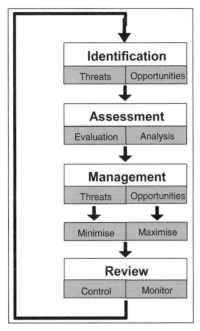

Figure 23 - 1: Basic Risk Process

requiring urgent management attention

♦ Examine the distribution of risk to reveal common causes or areas of the project under particular threat or leading to opportunity

♦ Develop detailed management action plans and responses for each risk

♦ To provide a framework to Implement actions and monitor their effectiveness

♦ To provide a baseline for the risk process, allowing the risks to be re-evaluate and further threats and opportunities to be identified.

The whole process is usually repeated on a periodic basis to determine the effectiveness of the risk reduction measures and to re-assess the level of risk which remains in the project. The frequency of this review process depends on the size of project, and can be monthly, quarterly etc. However, there should be a continuous exposure of risk information to the project team during meetings, briefings and project progress reviews.

The output of the process should include the Risk Management Implementation Plan, the risk register, conclusions and of course the identified risk management actions. A full formal risk management process is outlined in Figure 23 - 2.

The Risk Management Implementation Plan

The first step in implementing risk management is to develop a risk management plan, this is done in much the same way as the development of a quality or work plan.

The risk management plan identifies the procedures that the project or business will adopt to manage risk. It includes the activities to be carried out by the project management team and key stakeholders and their timescales throughout all phases of the project. It covers the identification, assessment, analysis, management and control of risk and provides a basis for defining the risk management roles and responsibilities for each of the team members. The document can also list the software tools and techniques to be used to support the risk process and how the process will be integrated into theproject management culture.

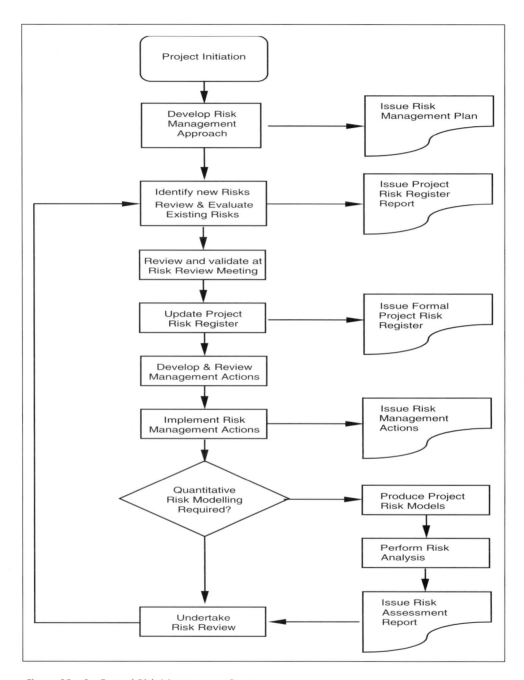

Figure 23 - 2: Formal Risk Management Process

Risk Identification and Assessment

Full risk management involves a comprehensive identification of all sources of risk, an objective assessment of their significance, planning of responses to the risks and management of the responses in order to achieve the desired outcome.

Identifying Risks

Good risk identification provides the starting point for effective Risk Management, key to this is to ensure that the risk identification is conducted accurately and consistently. At each stage of the project, risks to the timely and effective completion of each milestone should be identified. To aid risk identification a number processes and methods can be used, these include the use of:

- Project Documentation
- Brainstorms
- Structured interviews
- Assumptions
- Historic information and lessons learnt

Ideally as a bare minimum the information shown in Figure 23 - 3 should be recorded during the risk identification process.

Each risk must be assigned to a Risk Owner. The risk owner will be responsible for ensuring that the risk reduction and mitigation actions identified are performed in a timely and effective manner, and progress reported within the project team and as appropriate. This person should have the appropriate subject matter background, sufficient authority to ensure risk management actions will be pursued, and the necessary awareness of the project objectives.

Depending on the maturity of the risk process supplemental information can be recorded which may aid the definition of the risk. This can include triggers, those events which would lead to the risk occurring, dates of possible risk occurrence and strategy windows and possible secondary risks resulting from management actions.

A Short Title -	This briefly outlines the name of the risk and can be used as a reference in indexes.
High Level Description of Risk -	This should be no more than two sentences and concisely define the risks nature (often defined as cause and effect).
Background Information -	This can be used to define links to related documentation or further information pertaining to the nature of the risk.
Consequence / Benefit -	A high level effect of the risk should be recorded to enable an understanding of whether the risk is a threat or opportunity and its impact to the project in terms of time, cost or performance etc, to aid the later qualitative assessment of the risk.
High level Strategy -	A defined strategy for the management of the risk, outlining the management objective and resource requirement.
Fallback Position -	A contingency response to address the risk should it occur, which aims to limit or control the consequence of the risk consequence.

Figure 23 - 3: Minimum Data for Risk Identification Process

Methods of Identifying Risks

Documentation Reviews

Performing a structured and detailed review of the key project documentation provide an invaluable source of risk information. Documentation can include Work Breakdown Structures, cost plans, work instructions, business plans, project plan and tender documentation. Any documentation which is key to the project or sets the objectives should always be reviewed as a must.

Brainstorms

Brainstorming is a common risk identification technique and one of the most effective. The purpose of this technique is to obtain a comprehensive and high level list of risks which can be used as the starting point for the risk identification process.

When brainstorming, a meeting should be organised

with key project stakeholders. The attendees are requested to identify the key threats, their concerns and possible opportunities. Sources of risks must be identified from as wide a scope as possible and posted for all to see and comment on. Brainstorming can be more effective if participants prepare in advance, the risk co-ordinator should develop a breakdown based on either project phase, scope, deliverables or risk categories. This documentation describing the goals of the brainstorming meeting should be issued at least a week prior to the meeting.

Interviews

Risks can be identified using interview sessions held with the project stakeholders. These individuals should be drawn from all levels of the organisation and from all areas of the project, i.e. senior management, marketing, sales, development, design, etc. to ensure the knowledge base is as wide as possible.

As the experience of individuals within any organisation provides a wealth of knowledge relating to possible risks, it is important for all to contribute. This also demonstrates that individual perceptions and opinions are valued and will form a significant part of risk management activities. If individuals see that their involvement is included in the process they will be prepared to contribute in the future and thereby buy-in to the risk management process.

Assumptions Analysis

During the initial stages of a project, the requirements and any specifications are reviewed in order to identify areas of uncertainty. These are addressed by making assumptions (i.e. statements of belief concerning the outcome of future events) which will be recorded in a formal assumption list. Assumptions may cover such issues as provision of resources, information, equipment availability, functionality, or facilities. These assumptions, if proved false, may lead to risks and therefore must be addressed or at least considered. Assumptions can be made at any stage in the project life-cycle and at any level within the project team.

Assumption management must therefore be undertaken continuously if all potential risks are to be identified.

Historic Information and Lessons Learned

Information or performance on prior projects, history and lessons learned from previous endeavours provide an extensive source of risk information. By recording the problems and benefits which were gained on previous projects, the data can be used as a starting point or a prompt list to ensure similar or future projects gain from this experience.

Other Identification Methods

Other methods which can be used to aid the process of risk identification can include undertaking SWOT (Strength and Weakness, Opportunity and Threat) analyses. This presents a structured approach in breaking down a project by questioning understanding. Inputs from other project management processes can also be used as risk source information. These can include HAZOP, safety studies, configuration documentation or change requests. Common risk prompt lists or generic risk listings can also be used to ensure all sources of risk are covered.

Risk Assessment

♦ Risk Assessment is a qualitative process, concerned with identifying significant risks, through evaluation of the likelihood and consequence, in terms of time, cost and performance, and determining the causes of the risk, and establishing the timing of the risk.

♦ The goal of Risk Assessment is to capture judgmental perceptions of risk in a structured way to obtain the most objective assessment possible. The key to a successful assessment is good communication, achieved by employing proven consistent techiques applied in a flexible and clear manner.

Assessing Risks Consistently

Risks should be assessed qualitatively to allow a consistent evaluation and prioritisation of the risk to be undertaken. This ensures that management attention is focussed on those risks that are most significant to the success of the project. To ensure a consistent approach, it is essential that a common basis for determining risk probability and impact is defined.

These assessment criteria can be developed for any size or scope of project. In general these criteria reflect a range of boundary values that can be used to consistently assess different perceptions of risk significance. An example of which is shown in Figure 23 - 4, but actual values must be developed to the actual size and scope of the project.

The example in Figure 23 - 4 employs 5 bands for Threat and Opportunity, this ensures that significant risks can be easily discriminated from those risks identified.

		Prob.	Timescale Impact	Cost Impact	Performance Impact	
Threat (loss)	VHI	70%- 100%	8 24 weeks	50K 1M (£)	70%- 100%	**Reduction in performance**
	HI	50% - 70%	4 8 weeks	25 50 K (£)	50% - 70%	
	MED	30% -50%	2 4 weeks	10 25 K (£)	30% -50%	
	LO	10% - 30%	1 2 weeks	5 10 K(£)	10% - 30%	
	VLO	0% - 10%	0 - 1 week	0 5 K(£)	0% - 10%	
	Nil	0%	0	0	0%	
Opportunity (saving)	VLO	0% - 10%	0 - 1 week	0 5 K(£)	0% - 10%	**Increase in Performance**
	LO	10% - 30%	1 2 weeks	5 10 K(£)	10% - 30%	
	MED	30% -50%	2 3 weeks	10 25 K (£)	30% -50%	
	HI	50% - 70%	3 4 weeks	25 50 K (£)	50% - 70%	
	VHI	70%- 100%	4 10 weeks	50K 1M (£)	70%- 100%	

Figure 23 - 4: Example Risk Assessment Criteria

The assessment criteria used to assess the risk in terms of their probability of occurrence and likely impact then needs to be developed into a weighting system to allow the comparison of the risks (Figure 23 - 5). The score generated is in itself a dimensionless number, but it can then be used to identify the relative severity of the risk for the Project. Any weighting number can be used, however, it is recommended that the numbering system used places an emphasis on the impact of a risk rather that on its frequency. This ensures that those risks with a significant impact rate higher than those minimal impact risks with a greater frequency of occurrence.

0.72	0.36	0.18	0.09	0.05	VHI		VHI	0.05	0.09	0.18	0.36	0.72	HI >0.2
0.56	0.28	0.14	0.07	0.04	HI		HI	0.04	0.07	0.14	0.28	0.56	
0.40	0.20	0.10	0.05	0.03	MED		MED	0.03	0.05	0.10	0.20	0.40	MED 0.1-0.2
0.24	0.12	0.06	0.03	0.02	LO		LO	0.02	0.03	0.06	0.12	0.24	
0.10	0.08	0.04	0.02	0.01	VLO		VLO	0.01	0.02	0.04	0.08	0.10	LO <0.1
VHI	HI	MED	LO	VLO				VLO	LO	MED	HI	VHI	

Probability (vertical axis label)

Opportunity   **Impact**   **Threat**

Figure 23 - 5: Example Probability - Impact weighting scales.

It is important to ensure that assessments gained from individuals are as accurate and unbiased as possible. The assessment criteria should be always available at brainstorms or interview for reference. Schedule Impact is assessed as potential movement to key milestones dates. Cost Impact is based upon values of total project cost, and performance impact is based upon relevant technical parameters or objectives.

Understanding Results

The Project Risk Register

The Risk Register is a result of the risk assessment methodology adopted by project team. The overall purpose of the Risk Register is to present a statement of the risks and their subsequent management actions to be faced during the course of the project or programme. The risk register serves four main functions:

- Identifies risks and their likely impact upon the programme
- Records the results of the risk assessment process and supporting discussions
- Provides a basis for the management review of risks to the project
- Documents proposed Risk Management action plans to be used to mitigate risks, and provides a basis for monitoring the progress of Risk Management action

Risk Register Format

Risks which are perceived to be facing the project are contained within the register as individual risk records. The risk records themselves usually consist of two parts. Part One provides details of the risk and Part Two describes the management response to the risk.

The register is also supported by an index which precedes the register records. The risk register index identifies the Project and its current status, outlines the risk records held within the register and dictates the order in which they appear. The index details a short title to give a brief description of the risk as well as the status, significance and timescale information.

The format of the risk register should be tailored to reflect the reporting structure used within the project. It is however recommended that the register reflect's the information outlined in Figure 23 - 6.

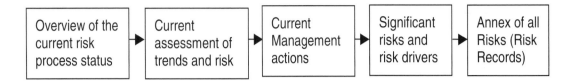

Figure 23 - 6: Risk Register Data

Management of Risk

The objective of risk management is to manage those risks associated with the project in advance of their occurrence. Risk Management may require that some risks be avoided completely by changing the project approach, absorbing some risks within financial or scheduled float and preparing fall-back plans for those critical areas which cannot be resolved in advance. In addition, management activities will be required to ensure risk opportunities are realised.

Risk management planning must to be carried out regularly throughout the course of the project and reviewed to ensure validity and effectiveness. Risk planning enhancements should then be undertaken following these reviews if either the current risk management strategy is deemed to be ineffective or the situation has evolved.

The Risk Owner will be responsible for ensuring that the risk reduction and management actions identified are performed in a timely and effective manner by their Actionee's, and progress reported to the Risk Manager and Project Manager as appropriate.

Methods of Managing Risk (Threats)

There are four basic methods of mitigating Threats:

Risk Avoidance - Eliminate the cause of uncertainty that first introduced the risk.

Risk Reduction - Target key areas or drivers in order to reduce the severity of the impact. Alternatively, apply a contingency budget or slack in the programme. The aims is to reduce a risk to an 'acceptable' level.

Risk Transfer - Seek to place liability onto a third party should the risk occur.

Risk Acceptance - The process of managing a risk by making a judgement that the risk is at an acceptable level. It may be that the benefits of attempting to reduce the risk further are outweighed by the costs of implementing mitigation actions. The risk is then continually monitored to ensure that any escalation is captured and appropriate strategies are then implemented. It is vital that all accepted risks have a viable fall-back plan.

Methods of Managing Risk (Opportunity)

There are four basic methods of managing Opportunities:

Risk Develop - Clarify the cause of uncertainty that first introduced the risk to ensure the risk is realised.

Risk Enhance - Targets key areas or drivers in order to increase the severity of the impact.

Risk Share - Seek to share the benefit with a third party should the risk occur and use the realised benefits to give incentives to partners.

Risk Ignore - The process of managing a risk by making the judgement that the risk is at a level where the return on the risk management investment does not make it cost effective to pursue. The risk is then continually monitored to ensure that if in the future it becomes viable, appropriate strategies are implemented.

Developing Effective Strategies

(Smart Risk Management)

It is important that we develop appropriate management actions. This means developing actions that are neither too detailed or too general to be of use. A risk management action has to be a task that is both measurable and realistic to achieve. Known as SMART risk management an action must be *Specific* to the issue we seek to address. *Measurable* in terms of the perceived goal, *Achievable* and *Realistic*, not impossible to achieve and will have tangible results. Finally, the action must be Timebound, a predefined window of opportunity in which the risk can be addressed.

SMART Risk Management

Specific

Measurable

Achievable

Realistic

Timebound

'The entire management process needs to be proactive. In addition the results and benefits of successful management actions need to be seen by all'

Figure 23 - 7: SMART Risk Management

Fall-back Planning

Contingency plans and fall-back scenarios are those strategies which are implemented when a risk has or is about to occur. These strategies are kept as contingencies and fall-backs in the event that the primary risk mitigation strategies fail to produce the desired reduction in risk exposure. Contingency plans represent viable alternatives and fall-back measures usually accept some degree of loss.

Risk Analysis

Quantitative Risk Analysis is aimed at evaluating the effects which the identified risks could have on the project cost or timescale. Such analyses will expose uncertainties in schedule or cost estimates caused by risk, and can be used to test the extent to which project plans might meet programme milestones or commercial targets.

Monte-Carlo type analysis provides the mechanism for this by conducting many thousands of simulated project outcomes using the identified uncertainty, incorporating the risks assigned from the Risk Register and further uncertainty estimates applied to network activities and cost items. Risk should, in practice be modelled outside the baseline estimate. Giving a risk a likelihood of occurrence and then modelling it as a discrete event will lead to a more realistic and optimistic analysis.

The results of these analyses can be presented in various ways. For example, total cost or time estimates can be plotted against probability of achievement; criticality indices can be produced for each activity showing the probability that each will be on the critical path and show when risks are most likely to impact. The benefit of using Monte Carlo analysis when assessing risk and uncertainty is that it allows for the consideration of all potential project outcomes. This includes consideration of all issues and comparisons of alternative solutions. Therefore, the effect of project alternatives on the overall level of risk and project uncertainty can be fully understood. In addition, the analysis may direct the project team to uncertain areas of a project, and lead to the firming of requirements.

Monte Carlo Analysis

Monte Carlo analysis refers to the technique for using random or pseudo-random numbers to sample from a probability distribution. Traditionally, analyses combine single 'point' estimates of a model's uncertainty to predict a single result. In reality however, things often just don't turn out the way they are planned.

Monte Carlo sampling techniques are entirely random, ie; any given sample may fall within the uncertainty range of the given input distribution. Monte Carlo sampling will 'recreate' the input distribution using this sampling'

Consider an activity that is most likely to cost £1.1 million but could cost as little as £1 million or as much as £1.5 million, this uncertainty could be represented by the frequency density function shown in Figure 23 - 8. Monte Carlo analysis would then represent this function as a cumulative probability function and generate a random number between 0 and 1 (0% to 100%). For each random number or sample a corresponding cost will be returned eg; sample 1 returns £1.35 million and sample 2 returns £1.25million. All these samples are possible activity costs. This process allows the recreation of thousands of potential

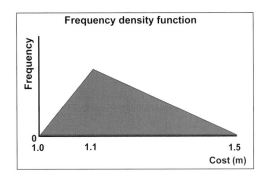
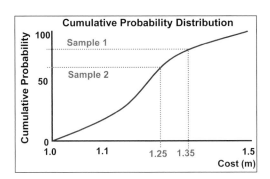

Figure 23 - 8: Frequency Density Function and Cumulative Probability Distribution

project outcomes to be analysed. These results can then be combined together for all activities to produce an overall Cumulative Probability Distribution (S-Curve) for the entire project. From this the results and confidence levels can be predicted. Software tools which perform Monte Carlo analysis are now available which allow a project to be analysed thousands of times within a couple of minutes. These tools use probability distributions to describe uncertainty values. There are many forms and types of probability distributions, each of which describes a range of possible values and their likelihood of occurrence. Most people have heard of normal or triangular distributions, but there are a wide variety of distribution types. These "distribution" functions can be placed in worksheet cells as formulae. Once placed, analysis results such as profit, turnover and baseline cost can then be generated in the form of S-Curves and probability distributions.

The results from this type of Risk Analysis, the output probability distributions, give the user a complete picture of all the possible project outcomes. This is a tremendous improvement on the "worst-expected-best" case analysis commonly used. The resulting probability distribution (S-Curve) does in fact provide more than just filling in the gaps between the best case - worse case:

They determine a "correct" Range of outcomes because the uncertainty associated with every cost element has been more rigorously. They show a "Probability of Occurrence", a probability distribution showing the relative likelihood of occurrence for each possible project outcome in the predicted range and the confidence level of achieving it.

Cost Risk Analysis

All projects have a budget, and most have some form of cost breakdown structure detailing the breakdown of the cost items that make up the budgetary figure. However these costs are very rarely fixed costs and are subject to some form of inherent uncertainty. In addition to this are the risks identified in the Risk Register, some of which may have an identified cost consequence. The undertaking of a cost risk analysis permits uncertainty in the baseline cost estimates to be modelled whilst taking account of the potential consequence of these cost risks.

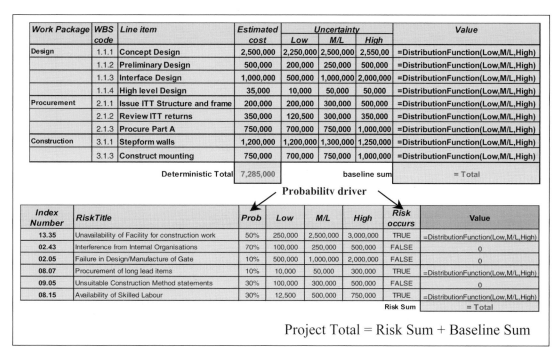

Work Package	WBS code	Line item	Estimated cost	Uncertainty Low	Uncertainty M/L	Uncertainty High	Value
Design	1.1.1	Concept Design	2,500,000	2,250,000	2,500,000	2,550,00	=DistributionFunction(Low,M/L,High)
	1.1.2	Preliminary Design	500,000	200,000	250,000	500,000	=DistributionFunction(Low,M/L,High)
	1.1.3	Interface Design	1,000,000	500,000	1,000,000	2,000,000	=DistributionFunction(Low,M/L,High)
	1.1.4	High level Design	35,000	10,000	50,000	50,000	=DistributionFunction(Low,M/L,High)
Procurement	2.1.1	Issue ITT Structure and frame	200,000	200,000	300,000	500,000	=DistributionFunction(Low,M/L,High)
	2.1.2	Review ITT returns	350,000	120,500	300,000	350,000	=DistributionFunction(Low,M/L,High)
	2.1.3	Procure Part A	750,000	700,000	750,000	1,000,000	=DistributionFunction(Low,M/L,High)
Construction	3.1.1	Stepform walls	1,200,000	1,200,000	1,300,000	1,250,000	=DistributionFunction(Low,M/L,High)
	3.1.3	Construct mounting	750,000	700,000	750,000	1,000,000	=DistributionFunction(Low,M/L,High)
Deterministic Total			7,285,000		baseline sum		= Total

Probability driver

Index Number	Risk Title	Prob	Low	M/L	High	Risk occurs	Value
13.35	Unavailability of Facility for construction work	50%	250,000	2,500,000	3,000,000	TRUE	=DistributionFunction(Low,M/L,High)
02.43	Interference from Internal Organisations	70%	100,000	250,000	500,000	FALSE	0
02.05	Failure in Design/Manufacture of Gate	10%	500,000	1,000,000	2,000,000	FALSE	0
08.07	Procurement of long lead items	10%	10,000	50,000	300,000	TRUE	=DistributionFunction(Low,M/L,High)
09.05	Unsuitable Construction Method statements	30%	100,000	300,000	500,000	FALSE	0
08.15	Availability of Skilled Labour	30%	12,500	500,000	750,000	TRUE	=DistributionFunction(Low,M/L,High)
						Risk Sum	= Total

Project Total = Risk Sum + Baseline Sum

Figure 23 - 9: Example of Cost Risk Model

Uncertainty in the estimates is incorporated by representing the cost estimates in the cost breakdown structure by a spread of values rather than by a single figure and modelled by a distribution function. In the same way the cost impact of each risk can be modelled as a distribution with a separate probability of occurrence. This information is compiled into a cost risk model. The model undergoes a simulation which is a series of recalculations or iterations, each time sampling different values from the various distributions, see Figure 23 - 9.

A picture of all the possible total costs is created by summing up the individual items in the cost breakdown structure during each iteration. This information can then be used to see if particular total cost has occurred, and hence estimate the likelihood of this cost occurring in reality. See Figure 23 - 10.

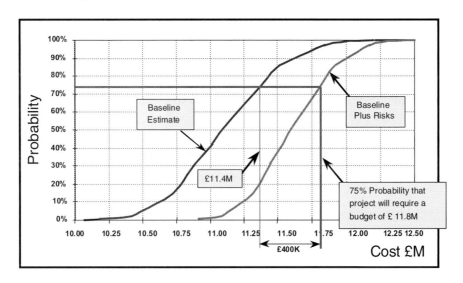

Figure 23 - 10: Cost Risk Analysis Results

The information resulting from this type of analysis can then be used to generate the 'Risk Provision' fund and assist project cost understanding and substantiate bid prices or budgetary requirements.

Schedule Risk Analysis

A schedule risk analysis is a quantitative analysis of the variability of project schedules including the effects of identified risks and variation in planning data. It indicates the spread and likelihood of possible project milestone dates. Every project is subject to deadlines and time constraints. To enable these deadlines to be met, projects normally have some form of programme or plan, indicating the inter-relationships between the various tasks of a project and the duration of each task. Milestones will be incorporated in the plan at strategic points, indicating dates that are of interest, deadlines etc. Activity durations are rarely fixed, as there is normally some uncertainty about how long each activity will take. Further uncertainty is added by the risks identified in the Risk Register, each of which may have a possible time impact. A schedule risk analysis permits uncertainty in the baseline duration figures and task relationships to be modelled whilst taking account of the potential impact of the risks. Uncertainty in the estimates is incorporated by representing the duration figures in the project plan by using a spread of values. The information is compiled into a schedule risk model, (Figure 23 - 11).

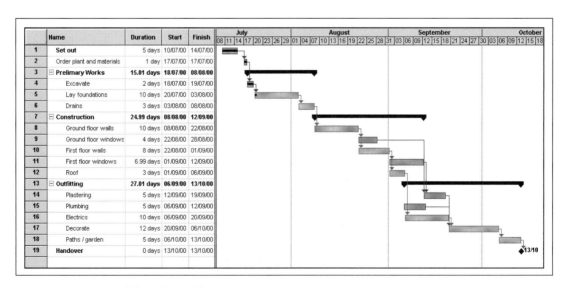

	Name	Duration	Start	Finish
1	**Set out**	5 days	10/07/00	14/07/00
2	Order plant and materials	1 day	17/07/00	17/07/00
3	Prelimary Works	15.01 days	18/07/00	08/08/00
4	Excavate	2 days	18/07/00	19/07/00
5	Lay foundations	10 days	20/07/00	03/08/00
6	Drains	3 days	03/08/00	08/08/00
7	Construction	24.99 days	08/08/00	12/09/00
8	Ground floor walls	10 days	08/08/00	22/08/00
9	Ground floor windows	4 days	22/08/00	28/08/00
10	First floor walls	8 days	22/08/00	01/09/00
11	First floor windows	6.99 days	01/09/00	12/09/00
12	Roof	3 days	01/09/00	06/09/00
13	Outfitting	27.01 days	06/09/00	13/10/00
14	Plastering	5 days	12/09/00	19/09/00
15	Plumbing	5 days	06/09/00	12/09/00
16	Electrics	10 days	06/09/00	20/09/00
17	Decorate	12 days	20/09/00	06/10/00
18	Paths / garden	5 days	06/10/00	13/10/00
19	**Handover**	0 days	13/10/00	13/10/00

Figure 23 - 11: Schedule Risk Model

This model then undergoes a simulation; each time sampling different values from the various duration distributions. As the durations of the tasks in the plan change, each milestone date in the plan is re-calculated. This information can then be used to see if a particular date has occurred, and hence the likelihood of this date occurring estimated (Figure 23 - 12).

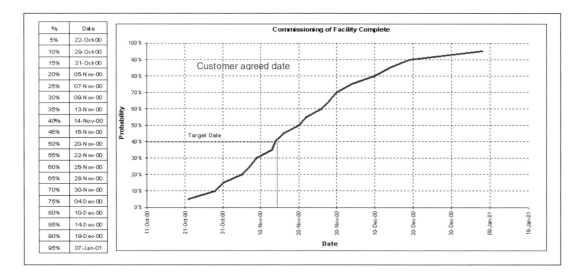

Figure 23 - 12: Schedule Risk Analysis Results

Promoting Buy-in and Encouraging Commitment

Risk management is not just about processes and methodologies, its about people, their perceptions and their involvement. The key to successful risk management and in fact any process is commitment and communication. It is therefore necessary to ensure that the project manager either develops or enhances a risk management process that encourages contribution from all involved in the project or business endeavour.

People, The Risk Process and its Shortfalls

Some risk management processes which on paper appear to be well thought out often fail due to a lack of commitment by stakeholders. 'Involvement' is key when it comes to developing a successful process. It is essential to talk to stakeholders right from the start, and at all stages of the project. Encouraging contribution demonstrates that everyone's perceptions and opinions are valued and will form a significant part of the project management activities.

Techniques to Gain Involvement

Highlighting the benefits of involvement is core to the risk process, this means naming successful individuals in Board meetings, management team reviews and in dispatches. Increasing the visibility of risk management within the work place is also crucial. This highlights that risk management is taken seriously and is important. Improvement in risk can be seen by placing 'Risk Posters' around the project office. These posters are simple, they list the key risks, both the threats and opportunities and highlight their owner and management activity. This acts as a reminder to the issues driving the project. Successes such as risks avoided, opportunities realised and management activities completed should be highlighted.

Corporate Governance

The Turnbull Guidance on internal controls for companies listed on the London stock exchange states that the board should conduct a review of the risks facing their organisation. In general terms the report states that:

- A company should be aware of the risks they face
- Be aware of the extent and likelihood of these risks
- Have identified the appropriate management strategies
- Ensure management actions are implemented and evaluated

This re-iterates the risk management process. Acordingly, the results of the risk identification, assessment and management activity can be used to help satisfy the corporate governance requirements.

Conclusion and Summary

It is important that risk management is applied early in a project's life-cycle and an appropriate process implemented to allow risk to be identified, assessed, mitigated and monitored. As the project evolves risk management should be used to anticipate how decisions affect the project. The risk management process needs to be supported at all levels within the project team. Actionees must be encouraged to pursue mitigation actions within required timescales. Risk owners must be aware of their risks and have the forum to raise these issues so that the project team gains visibility of any potential problems or opportunities. Managers and management must be proactive and have the necessary authority to respond rapidly to risk. If decisions cannot be made in a timely manner then opportunities will be missed and the affect of delays will cascade throughout the project. Therefore the benefits of risk management include:

- Greater understanding of project or business objects or goals
- More realistic business and project planning
- Improved management of project and business costs
- More effective communication within an organisation

It must always be remembered that the key to risk management is Management! The process will fail if commitment and contribution is lacking and risks are not efficiently identified, assessed and pursued to their conclusion.

References and Further Reading

Internal Control - A Guidance for Directors on the Combined Code, The Institute of Chartered Accountants in England & Wales (www.icaew.co.uk/internalcontrol), September 1999

British Standard 6079-1:2000, 6079-2:2000, 6079-3:2000 Project Management, British Standard institute, 15 January 2001

Project Risk Analysis & Management Guide, Association of Project Managers, 1997

24   QUALITY MANAGEMENT

Terry Brennand

"The great society is a place where men are more concerned with the quality of their goods than the quantity of their goods."
Lyndon Baines Johnson (1908-1973), U.S. president.

Introduction

In this session reference is made to the EFQM Excellence model, to provide a rationale for the process of self-assessment, review and refinement cycles; as part of an overall management strategy. It aids the quest for completeness of coverage and for an integrated approach to Project and Programme Management. A prerequisite to putting this approach to work will be for the reader to have spent time understanding the EFQM Excellence Model, its concepts and evaluation tools.

The model is a non-prescriptive framework recognising that there may be many approaches to achieving excellence on a sustainable basis. Underpinning the model are a number of fundamental concepts giving rise to nine criteria. Using the nomenclature of the model, nine of the criteria are known as *Enablers* and four are referred to as *Results*. *Enabler* criteria concern what an organisation does and *result* criteria cover what an organisation achieves.

"Excellent results with respect to Performance, Customers, People and Society are achieved through Leadership driving Policy and Strategy, People, Partnerships and Resources and Processes". (EFQM 1)

Figure 24 - 1 illustrates the model and also shows the weighting assigned to each criterion. This paper advocates an approach whereby a thought process and an appropriate balance in the use and drawing together of other BoK elements may be established within the EFQM framework. The purpose of this exercise from a project excellence point of view being, not only to meet requirements but to exceed the expectations, of all parties involved and affected by project activities.

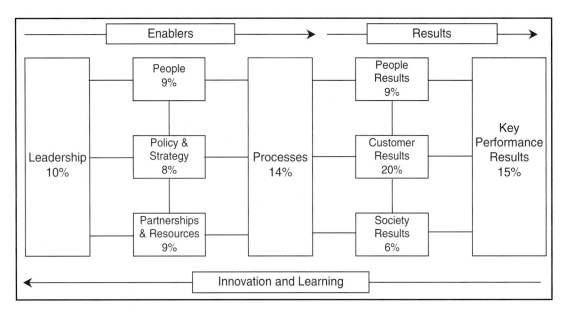

Figure 24 - 1: The EFQM Excellence Model

The excellence model seeks a clear rationale when describing how things are done and looks for completeness of coverage in what is to be achieved - and that these achievements are compared with targets and benchmarks.

It encourages that each and every improvement initiative be implemented throughout all relevant project areas and that this is done in a systematic way. It requires that lessons are learnt, that findings are used to continually improve performance via routine analysis of results and the application of improvement actions.

Challenging our Mindset

The challenge is to use the excellence model as the outline thought structure and checklist with which to prompt issues to be addressed, whilst developing the project plan. Benefit from using the model will be maximised if the project business case and activity plans are merged within this format.

Each project phase is assessed and reviewed to establish

the appropriateness and completeness of arrangements in place. The most important phases to be dealt with in this way, being those of project inception through design and development. When preparing for each subsequent phase this review will enable the identification, clarification and validation of further Key Outcomes, related in-process predictors and the processes for their delivery.

It is the ongoing development of all relevant processes and their integration to form routine day to day activities, that distinguishes an excellent project.

The Positioning of Other Standards

For some time now there has been a recognition of a progressive dovetailing of the standards, Quality Management ISO 9000:2000, Investors in People (IIP), Environmental and Health and Safety standards. This fits neatly with the Excellence Model in that all relevant matters covered by these standards would be identified under policy and strategy as being appropriate and the processes section would embrace the elemental processes for their achievement.

Investors in People plays a significant role in preparing company ethos to be more flexible and as a consequence is often put in place prior to embracing the Excellence Model as part of a Continuous Improvement programme.

The changes that have taken place in moving from ISO 9000 to ISO 9000:2000 has resulted in a near fit with the excellence model in terms of coverage. However, the model prompts the user more fully on the "what?" and the "how?" of activities in order to achieve the desired results.

The Formative Phases.

Prior to inception and throughout the opportunity identification phase where an organisation has recognised the need for a project, whether it be to deliver or improve internal facilities generally, or to develop the provision of products and services for the market place, some notional ideas of a way forward will have been tabled. Often, key outcomes will have been proposed, if not ratified and a probable outline of an organisational structure, appropriate to address these outcomes, both in keeping with the way in which the organisation works and its capabilities, will be emerging.

It is useful at this time to outline the first project plan intentions and, where known, the means of their achievement in this new format. Clearly there are often many matters still to be resolved but an outline assessment at this stage serves to clarify the completeness of coverage of intentions and thereby helps with the specifying of further actions and in ranking their priorities. These matters, together with technical and commercial success criteria, need to be rigorously addressed during the design and development phase for their appropriateness at this and indeed other subsequent stages. Such matters have often featured strongly in discussions with prospective project or programme managers at their appointment or selection interviews.

In particular early output from the design and development phase will be providing those involved in sponsoring the project with a feel for the extent to which the success of the project will depend upon the mix and experience of the project management team and upon the extent to which the project manager needs to have the use of resources which are independent of existing departmental heads.

An understanding between the project manager and the sponsor, often informally, on some of the more significant matters relating to the projects importance, urgency and style of operation - is established quite early and has a considerable bearing on the standing of the project.

Key intentions and provisions usually become clear and can be documented as the design and development stage advances. Their assessment and evaluation in terms of the excellence model will provide a feel for completeness of coverage and a valuable predictor from which to judge the likely quality of project performance.

The description of the model's criteria and sub criteria, prompt those involved to think their way through a proper balance and an appropriate mix of BoK elements. This assessment provides a structured opportunity to clarify what is intended and to examine the best way to do things in a realistic, integrated and harmonious way. The designing, testing and refining of management systems should flow smoothly from these assessment findings.

The fuller the involvement of team members in this project assessment exercise and in the writing of the project plan, the greater will be the commitment to succeed. Equally important, is the enthusiasm with which line managers, who have reports assigned part time on project activities are encouraged to observe and opine on implications. The more effective these contributions are perceived to be, the more robust will be the integration of working practices and sharing of goals. Improved 'buy-in' and alignment of purpose is the aim.

Clearly, this is an iterative process in that the model's enablers and results criteria should be developed and refined along with other technical elements. In particular the project's success criteria should be carefully explored for the extent of coverage occurring across the enablers within the excellence model.

Developing A Project Plan in EFQM Excellence Model Format

Understanding What is Needed

The EFQM Excellence Model comprises nine criteria, the first five criteria are those which enable the project to deliver its desired results and the remaining four criteria describe the results themselves (as shown in the excellence model diagram). In its simplest form the documentation needed by the self-assessment process, comprises statements crafted from thoughts on how you intend to do things and on what you intend to achieve - stimulated by reading each of the models criterion descriptions (see EFQM a).

The five enabling criteria cover Leadership, Policy and Strategy, People, Partnerships and Resources and Processes. Each criterion is defined and is supported by several sub criteria which deal more fully with an aspect of this definition and are described in terms of possible examples of project activities. For example, the first sub criterion level under leadership suggests that the pre-assessment document may include a description of how leaders develop the organisation's mission and vision and how these intentions are to be further developed, managed and deployed.

The four results criteria cover Customer, People, Society and Key Performance. Each result criterion is defined and supported by two sub criteria which deal more fully with an aspect of this definition, one dealing with perception and the other dealing with performance indicators predicting perception outcomes. For example, under the definition for customer result, at the sub criterion level, a possible customer perception measure may include responsiveness and the performance indicators predicting these outcomes may include time to market measures.

For all results criteria, there would be comparisons between plan and actual, comparisons with targets and with benchmarks wherever possible. However, since outcomes are closely related to project purpose, there can be a considerable variation in those chosen as relevant from one project to another.

Writing the Plan

At this initial stage and when refining target results and approaches the model uses a review process referred to as RADAR logic.

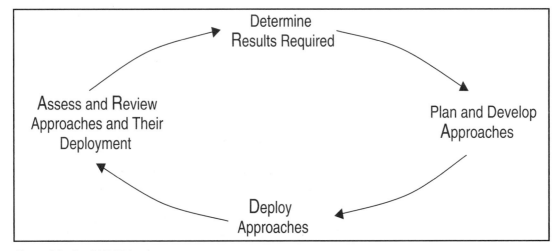

Figure 24 - 2: RADAR Logic

The following generic example illustrates some of the thought processes associated with grouping project intentions under the model's criteria headings and applying the model's guidance.

Leadership

Prior to the design and development phase the setting down of principles and values underpinning a clearly stated mission and vision for the project is vital to its conduct and success. The project manager often benefits at this early stage from the creation of a personal activity list describing his intended personal involvement in project activities and in ensuring the projects management systems are developed and in place.

Policy and Strategy

Although top level strategies and policy are often clearly evident the necessary rationale to review and refine their ongoing relevance to meeting the projects business case can often benefit from clarification at this early assessment stage. This assessment could also help in seeing that arrangements are in place to ensure the mission and vision is implemented via a clear stakeholder focused strategy and that arrangements are also in place to ensure that any decisions are based on relevant performance measurements, research and learning. All project outcomes should be perceived as clear, measurable and targeted (and as few as possible in number) and that internal performance predictors of project outcomes are fully justified, clearly identified and have appropriate targets set.

Key processes needed to deliver project policy and strategy and to achieve the project outcomes should be clearly identified at this stage and wherever possible draw attention to the linkage between policy and strategy, processes and key project outcomes. Many of the building blocks addressed by this assessment will have been developed using other Pathways topic areas, in particular the Business Case (Session 50), Project Success Criteria (Session 20), Requirements Management (Session 41) and Financial Management (Session 52). The intention here being to develop an appropriate balance of approach across these matters and to achieve a clear stakeholder focus.

People

Having clarified what is wanted, together with the key processes for its achievement, a strategic view will be developing on the sourcing of project personnel and on the extent to which external partnerships and other resourceswill be used. Before final decisions are made on these matters it is often beneficial to address the continuum between appointing a self contained project team and utilising various numbers of part time staff controlled by other departmental heads. On the one hand a self contained project team would have high salary costs but be essentially free of external priority conflicts and on the other hand, total dependency on other departmental staff would significantly increase the complexity of project management and carry a higher risk of failing to achieve the desired project outcomes.

The likely duration of the project is also significant in this matter since part time or short duration contributions to a project are not usually perceived as having a significant effect on promotion prospects and may create situations where team motivation can become significantly more difficult. A careful and proper balance of the sources from which project staff is drawn pays dividends in both the creation of an enjoyable working environment, where people know where they stand from the start and by clarifying the interface requirements for the projects internal people management systems.

The development of detailed arrangements describing how the project will adopt or vary existing personnel policy and how the opportunities provided by the project for the development of those involved, in terms of knowledge, capability and promotional opportunities, is key to success. Recognition and rewards are particularly important where staff are seconded full time since they could perceive themselves as separated from their parent department.

Partnerships and Resources

Equally important as the management of internal project staff is the management of external partnerships. This brings with it a different set of matters to be managed. These include the identification of appropriate parties, the structuring of the relationships, the establishing of their added value, the management of cultural differences and of the sharing of knowledge - all of which feature highly in terms of project success.

At this stage where people and resources are being put in place the number and needs of information streams from other internal departments, from external partnerships, from other stakeholders and from the market place are becoming known.

Clearly the collecting, structuring and managing of information and knowledge in support of policy and strategy, throughout the life-cycle of the project, are central to its success. It is very easy at this stage to be overwhelmed by the sheer volume and to lose sight of the key management criteria. A useful approach is to continually ask the question, what effect would there be to achieving the projects key outcomes and to the usefulness of the in-process performance predictors, if this information/data were not available? A careful review of the information systems currently offered to clarify their benefit, simplify their use and minimise keyboard input could also be useful.

Processes

Process assessment provides an opportunity to review the inputs and feedback from other model criteria, for their completeness of coverage and appropriateness, and to ensure that processes are in place to address all project outcomes and their predictors.

Many processes will need input from more than one line management department and in some cases external partners also. The involvement of these bodies in the review and refinement of those processes will be crucial and the extent to which the full set of processes integrates into smooth day to day project working, will also be indicative of the effectiveness of their design.

The knowledge and tools from other topic areas in particular those covering strategic, Technical, Commercial and Organisational will be drawn upon when developing balanced and detailed process designs, necessary to deliver project outcomes.

Results

The results arising from the various enablers described are measured and provide outcomes describing what the project is achieving in relation to: Customers; People; Society, both local and international and its Key Performance Indicators - compared with its planned performance and trend.   In each case the intention is to compare results with targets, with best in class and to benchmark with world class wherever possible.

Review Assess and Refine

An assessment review often benefits from awarding a score to each criterion so that comparisons can be made as the project progresses through its various phases and as an aid to benchmarking significant aspects of the project. Scores may be awarded using the RADAR scoring matrix as the evaluation tool. Practice is needed to become consistent in the use of this tool and further reading to support this need is mentioned at the end of this session.

Following completion of each assessment and evaluation exercise its review and refinement cycle will normally result in the document being revised for use in a subsequent phase. Otherwise, periodic assessments take place dependent upon project duration and on the rate of change of circumstances.

Review exercises offer a tremendous benefit to the well being of a project in that a newly formed team can become involved in setting out the way in which they work, at a time when change is welcomed and custom and practice has not taken root. Subsequent excellence assessments provide an opportunity for the team to be involved in the continual improvement of their projects effectiveness.

The general focus of these reviews should be to examine the project's processes for their appropriateness and continuing capability to continue to deliver policy and strategy and in particular to deliver key project outcomes. The first assessment is often a 'desk top' exercise only, since there are usually no results to consider but subsequent exercises may include focus groups, walkabouts and individual interviews to glean information, on what is actually perceived and what is actually being done, by all those involved and affected.

Particularly important within this assessment exercise is the need to address the interface issues, for example, the tensions that will arise in project resourcing, where a project team member is subject to matrix working and where external partners are subjected to rapidly changing commercial priorities. Such matters can intervene in smooth working relationships and often put outcomes at risk.

Relationships are a general issue which benefits from being addressed during review cycles. Dialog with customers and other stakeholders at this time helps to align understanding and to enhance the relationship.

Breaking New Ground - Innovative Application

This section deals largely with innovatively applying the EFQM Excellence Model to Project and Programme Management within the setting provided by the Body of Knowledge. A mapping of the attributes of BoK elements to the main criteria descriptions in the EFQM model has been developed. A mapping diagram is included for reference in Figure 24 - 3.

To test the validity of this notion the diagram shows Excellence Model Criteria, together with their associated definitions and shows how the Body of Knowledge (BoK) topic areas map for completeness.

Initially this mapping suggests a strong correlation between the emphasis BoK elements place on the Model's enabler criteria of Policy and Strategy, and Resources and Partnerships; with a somewhat lesser correlation in the cases of Leadership and People. The strength of linkages between the enabling criteria, as expressed in terms of BoK elements and Results criteria, will emerge as projects develop and will be dependent on the type and purpose of each project.

Excellence Model Enablers	BoK Elements	Model Links	Model Links Summary
Leadership How leaders develop and facilitate the achievement of the mission, develop values required for long term success and implement these via appropriate actions and behaviours, and are personally involved in ensuring that the organisations management system is developed and implemented.	Project Success Strategy PM Plan Value Management Risk Management Health, Safety and Environment Work Content and Scope Management Change Control Design, Implementation and Hand-over Configuration Management Business Case Marketing and Sales Opportunity Project Evaluation Review Organisation Structure Leadership Conflict Management	facilitate/behaviour facilitate/behaviour develop values facilitate facilitate/values facilitate/values facilitate facilitate facilitate champion/values/facilitate facilitate/behaviour facilitate/champion facilitate/behaviour facilitate facilitate/behaviour facilitate	• Champion • Value development • Facilitating involvement • Behavioural role
Policy and Strategy How the organisation implements its mission and vision via a clear stakeholder strategy, supported by relevant policies, plans, objectives, targets and processes.	Project Management Programme Management Project Context Project Success Factors Strategy PM Plan Value Management Risk Management Health, Safety and Environment Work Content and Scope Management Budgets and Cost Management Change Control Earned Value Management Information Management Design, Implementation and Hand-over Management Requirements Management Estimating Technology Management Value Engineering Modelling and Testing Business Case Marketing and Sales Financial Management Procurement Legal Awareness Life-cycle Design and Management Opportunity Design and Development (Post) Project Evaluation Review Organisation Structure Organisation Roles Communication	policies/plans/key processes/targets policy/plans/key processes/targets policies policies/targets/key processes/targets vision/mission/stakeholder/policies policies/key processes policies/key processes policies/objectives/key processes policies/key processes/targets policies/key processes/targets policies/key processes policies/key processes policies/objectives/key processes policies/objectives/key processes/targets policies key processes policies policies/key processes/targets policies/key processes vision/mission/stakeholder/policies/key processes/targets policy/plans and targets policy/objectives/stakeholder policy/key processes/targets policies policies/key processes policies/key processes policies/key processes/targets policies/objectives/key processes/targets policy/objectives/key processes policy/objectives/key processes policy/objectives/key processes/stakeholders	• Vision • Mission • Stakeholders • Policies • Objectives • Key Processes • Targets • Plans

Figure 24 - 3 & (Opposite) : Body of Knowledge Elements Mapped to Excellence Model Enablers

Excellence Model Enablers	BoK Elements	Model Links	Model Links Summary
People How the organisation manages, develops and releases the knowledge and full potential of its people at an individual, team based, and organisation wide level, and plans these activities in order to support its policy and strategy and effective operation of its processes.	Project Management Project Context Strategy PM Plan Health, Safety and Environment Work Content/Scope Management Marketing and Sales Organisation Roles Communication Team Work Conflict Management Negotiation Personnel Management	release potential/supports policy develops knowledge/supports policy develops knowledge/supports policy develops knowledge/supports policy supports policy develops knowledge/supports policy develops potential/supports effective processes support P&S/ supports effective processes release potential/develops knowledge/ supports processes supports effective processes operation supports effective processes operation support P&S/supports effective processes operation	• Supports P & S • Develops knowledge • Releases potential • Supports processes
Partnerships and Resources How the organisation plans and manages its external partnerships and internal resources in order to support policy and strategy and the effective operation of its processes.	Project Management Programme Management Strategy PM Plan Work Content/Scope Management Time Scheduling and Phasing Resource Management Budgeting and Cost Management Information Management Estimating Technology Management Modelling and Testing Financial Management Procurement Life-cycle Design and Management Implementation Hand-over Organisation	supports P&S/manage partnerships & resources supports P&S/manage partnerships & resources support effective operation & processes supports P&S & effective processes supports P&S & effective processes supports P&S/manage partnerships & resources supports internal resources & processes supports P&S/manage partnerships & resources supports effective processes supports P&S & internal resources supports P&S/supports effective processes supports P&S/supports effective processes supports P&S/supports effective processes supports P&S/supports effective processes supports P&S / & effective processes supports P&S & effective operation supports P&S	• Supports P & S • Manages partnerships • Manages resources • Supports processes
Processes How the organisation designs, manages and improves its processes in order to support its policy and strategy and fully satisfy and generate increasing value for; customers and other stakeholders.	Project Management Programme Management Project Context Project Success Criteria Value Management Risk Management Health, Safety and Environment Work Content/Scope Management Time Scheduling & Phasing Resource Management Budget & Cost Management Change Control Earned Value Management Information Management Design, Implementation and Hand-over Management Requirements Management Estimating Technology Management Value Engineering Modelling and Testing Configuration Management Business Case Marketing and Sales Financial Management Procurement Life-cycle Design and Management Opportunity Design and Development Hand-over Post Project Evaluation Review Organisation Structure Communication	fully satisfy/P&S/manages fully satisfy/P&S/manages P&S fully satisfy/increasing value fully satisfy/increasing value designs/fully satisfy/P&S /stakeholders designs/fully satisfy support P&S/fully satisfy fully satisfy/P&S fully satisfy/P&S fully satisfy/P&S/increasing value support P&S support P&S/stakeholders fully satisfy/P&S /stakeholders fully satisfy/P&S supports P&S/stakeholders fully satisfy/increasing value supports P&S/fully satisfy supports P&S supports P&S/fully satisfy supports P&S/fully satisfy fully satisfy/P&S /stakeholders supports P&S/increasing value supports P&S/increasing value support P&S/fully satisfy fully satisfy/P&S /stakeholders support P&S fully satisfy/P&S /stakeholders fully satisfy/P&S fully satisfy/P&S /stakeholders support P&S fully satisfy/P&S/increasing value	• Supports P & S • Supports Design • Aids Management • Supports satisfaction • Addresses all Stakeholders • Aids increasing value

Practitioners should be aware that the extent of correlation may change significantly dependent upon the way in which the BoK elements are developed and applied to each project.

Issues of Debate Amongst Practitioners

The systemic nature of the excellence model's approach, and its emphasis on strengthening causal linkages between results and the actions taken to achieve them has currently emerged as central to the model's own improvement. Strengthening the contribution of leadership to the achievement of excellence is also seen to be crucial and in need of further development.

Practical Tips for Novices

A Practical Approach to an Excellence Assessment

It is perfectly feasible to obtain training material available from the British Quality Foundation and to set about a self assessment programme using project or other in house staff. However, to avoid time spent on learning how to apply the assessment process and to use this time to best effect, it is often helpful for some staff to receive external training or alternatively for an external facilitator trained and practised in using the model to be used.

Assessment Team Roles and Arrangements

Ideally the assessment team will comprise a lead assessor who has considerable experience of managing an assessment team and a group of four to six assessors. Whenever possible this team will train together and have a pre-assessment meeting at which the team leader will describe the way in which he or she wishes to work and, by agreement, team members will adopt the role of criterion leaders for the exercise. Over the next period the team will individually assess the arrangements as described in the current version of the project plan, by comparing the extent to which these arrangements are aligned with the model and they will assign a score to each criterion.

The consensus process requires careful preparation by each criterion leader. Findings from each of the other team members relating to his criterion responsibility are merging into what he perceives will be a collective team view on strengths and areas for improvement. At the consensus meeting each criterion leader presents his set of merged statements and explains his reasons for the choice and how he has taken differing views into account. Following debate and appropriate changes to the wording of each strength and area for improvement, a new score is agreed upon and together these form the consensus statement and score for that criterion. When a consensus statement and score has been agreed for all nine criterion points this group of findings represents the full 'desk top' consensus from which a project visit to clarify and validate understanding can be planned.

The project visit is concluded by a short meeting where the criterion leaders present the now validated findings. Where necessary agreement will be reached on changes to the description of strengths and areas for improvement and the most significant of these matters to be included in a summary. The score is again addressed and varied as appropriate. This consensus group of validated findings represents the source of feed back to the project team and provides the detail from which the excellence assessment report can be produced.

It is for the project management team to decide on the extent to which they will take action to align their activities more closely with the model. When determining and implementing corrective actions there is a tendency to identify a need for further measurements to be made and to add these to those already being made.

Predictors are often chosen for this purpose. An essential requirement of any predictor is that it should draw attention to any lessening in the likelihood of achieving a satisfactory project outcome, and that it is chosen such that there will be sufficient time and opportunity for corrective action to take effect and for the unsatisfactory outcome to be avoided. However, the use of too many or unjustifiable predictors will use resources unnecessarily and will tend to move the team's focus away from meeting project outcomes. The general rule being, if it can't be justified don't do it.

A Practical Approach to Data Use and Management

These days computing capability to process and present data is readily available and the sales literature encourages us to use them more and more. Just as we have attempted to minimise the number of predictors to be measured to those proven necessary for project purpose, it is equally important to minimise the number of reports to those that are as simple as possible and easily comprehended by those who need to use them and to minimise the amount of data input, particularly keyboard input. In general the use of data which is not already available to the project should be challenged and unless a business case can be made to show that project control will significantly benefit, then one should think very hard before giving approval. In come cases approximations or alternative groupings of existing data could serve the purpose just as well.

Variations Across Sectors of Industry

The difference in emphasis between the application of the excellence model within the public, private and voluntary sectors, flows largely from the external legislative requirements placed upon them.   When these differences arise they are expressed in terms of what and how things are done. For example, there is often a greater need to emphasise 'soft' results in the voluntary sector and to put in place 'hard-nosed' financial targets in the private sector.

Cultural Influences that Might Moderate or Impact the Application of These Skills

Experience to date suggests that cultural differences have little overall impact on the application of the Excellence Model with the exception of the "what?" and "how?" within leadership style.

The results required may vary from culture to culture but are always dependent on the perception of the customer.

References and Further Reading

Since quality approaches are being continually improved, booklets available from the British Quality Foundation will provide a sound and current source of further study. In particular, the latest version of the RADAR scoring matrix can be seen in the most recent edition of The EFQM Excellence Model booklet.

EFQM (a): The EFQM Excellence Model, EFQM Publications, Brussels, 1999.
EFQM: Assessing for Excellence - A Practical Guide for Self-Assessment, EFQM Publications, Brussels, 1999.
British Standards Institution., Quality management - Guidelines for Quality Plans, BS : 10005, 1995.
British Standards Institution., Quality management - Guidelines to Quality in Project Management, BS : 10006, 1997.

25   HEALTH, SAFETY AND ENVIRONMENT

Rob Blanden

"When a man throws an empty cigarette packet from an automobile, he is liable to a fine of $50. When a man throws a billboard across a view he is richly rewarded."
Pat Brown, U.S. former Governor of California. Ogilvy on Advertising (1985)

Introduction

The aim of this session is to capture all of the high level detail required for project managers to understand their responsibilities in terms of the relatively complex United Kingdom Law covering Health, Safety and Environment (HS&E). A further aim is to provide project managers with some tools and guidance on the effective management of health, safety and environmental issues, such that the risks of incidents occurring are minimised.

The principle of HS&E is widely accepted as applicable to all sectors of industry (APM BoK, 2000) and the UK has laws which are designed to regulate the safety of people at work. In recent years, the welfare of people at work has become both a moral and an economic issue (please refer to other sessions on organisation roles and structure, project context and cultural issues).

Legal Framework

The principal legislative statute under UK Law concerning industrial health and safety is the Health and Safety at Work etc. Act 1974 (HSWA) and Regulations and Approved Codes of Practice (ACOP's) made thereunder. The law is strengthened by a system of inspection and by legal proceedings against those who transgress. Clearly, the effectiveness of legislation must depend to a large extent on how stringently the law is enforced.

Statutes are amplified by UK Regulations (i.e. Statutory Instruments or SI's) which may also implement EU Directives, including, for example, the Control of Substances Hazardous to Health Regulations (COSHH) 1994.

Of particular importance to best practice project management are the Management of Health and Safety at Work Regulations and associated Approved Code of Practice (1992).

Duties

The legislation places duties on both employers and employees (including the self-employed) to ensure, so far as is reasonably practicable, the safety and health of those both at work and those who might be affected by work activities. For example, Section 6 of the HSWA places general duties on designers, manufacturers, installers, importers or suppliers of articles for use at work to ensure, so far as is reasonably practicable, that articles are designed, manufactured and installed so that they are safe and without risk to health.

Goal Setting

The HSWA is an example of so-called 'goal-setting' legislation. That is, it specifies what the end result should be - safety - not how to achieve it. The term 'so far as is reasonably practicable' implies that as much has to be done as is necessary, taking into account cost, time and effort in a balance against the risks involved. What is considered to be 'reasonably practicable' in any situation will depend to some extent on what is accepted practice, but the 'state-of-the-art' is also an important factor in law. If technology advances to allow risks to be reduced further at reasonable cost, then it would be expected that the new technology would be adopted. In this way, risks are reduced to a level which is considered to be 'as low as is reasonably practicable' (ALARP).

Technical standards can form an important benchmark as to what is likely to be considered 'reasonably practicable'. In this overall context, the use of most standards is voluntary (e.g. IEC 61508, discussed later). However, the effective use of a standard which has wide acceptance is likely to be viewed, by either a court of law or a regulator, as an acceptable way of achieving what is 'reasonably practicable'

Industry Specific Legislation

Some industry-specific legislation includes the Reporting of Injuries Diseases and Dangerous Occurrences Regulations (RIDDOR) 1995; Safety Signs and Signals Regulations 1996; and Consultation with Employees Regulations 1996.

Despite the widely publicised Construction (Design and Management) Regulations (CDM), a great deal of the project management profession consider they have no safety responsibilities under this act because of the word 'construction' without realising the broadness of its definition in law. This applies especially to those engaged in IT and telecommunications projects.

For the purposes of the Regulations "construction" includes:

"the installation, commissioning, maintenace, repair or removal of mechanical, electrical, gas, compressed air, hydraulic, telecommunications, computer or similar services which are normally fixed within or to a structure."

It is instructive to note that CDM provides an excellent template for good project safety management regardless of industry or legal requirements.

Regulatory Control

The 1996 Memorandum of Understanding (MoU) between the Environment Agency and the Health and Safety Executive establishes an overarching framework between the two government bodies to ensure the effective co-ordination of the regulation of plant, processes, substances and measures to protect people and the environment.

In terms of Environmental Regulations, the initial question to be addressed is whether a certain activity is prescribed for regulatory control, either by the Environment Agency or the Local Government Environmental Health Department.

Health and Safety Commission (HSC)

The Health and Safety Commission (HSC) is responsible to the Secretary of State for the Environment, Transport and the Regions and to other Secretaries of State for the administration of the HSWA. Its functions are:

- To secure the health, safety and welfare of persons at work
- To protect the public generally against risks to health or safety arising out of work activities and to control the keeping and use of explosives, highly flammable and other dangerous substances
- To conduct and sponsor research; promote training and provide an information and advisory service
- To review the adequacy of health and safety legislation and submit to Government proposals for new or revised regulations and approved codes of practice

The Commission has general oversight of the work of the Health and Safety Executive (HSE) and has power to delegate to the Executive any of its functions.

Health and Safety Executive (HSE)

The Health and Safety Executive (HSE) ensures that risks to people's health and safety from work activities are properly controlled. The law states that:

- Employers have to look after the health and safety of their employees
- Employees and the self-employed have to look after their own health and safety
- All have to take care of the health and safety of others, for example, members of the public who may be affected by their work activity

It is the HSE's responsibility to see that everyone does this. The HSE is also interested in the health and safety of people at work - that includes people who may be harmed by the way work is done (for example because they live near a factory, or are passengers on a train). In some situations, the HSE is also concerned with the way work affects the environment. The HSE develops new health and safety laws and standards, and plays a full part in international developments, especially in the European Union. Additionally it:

- Inspects workplaces
- Investigates accidents and cases of ill health
- Enforces good standards, usually by advising people how to comply with the law, but sometimes by ordering them to make improvements and, if necessary, by prosecuting them
- Publishes guidance and advice and provides an information service
- Carries out research and various related activities such as nuclear site licensing and accepting off shore installation safety cases

The HSE is structured into divisions called Directorates, which include functional Inspectorates, as shown in Figure 25 - 1.

Responsibility:	Division:
Director General	Resources & Planning Directorate
	Safety Policy Directorate
	Health Directorate
Deputy Director General	Strategy & Analytical Support Directorate
	Health & Safety Laboratory
	Field Operations Directorate
	Railway Inspectorate
	Nuclear Safety Directorate
	Nuclear Installations Inspectorate
	Hazardous Installations Directorate
	Offshore Division
	Land Division
	Mines Inspectorate
	Technology Division
	Chief Scientist

Figure 25 - 1: Health and Safety Executive (HSE) Structure

Relevant UK Health and Safety Law

The Employer's General Duty of Care (Consultation with Employees) Regulations 1996; the Health and Safety at Work etc. Act 1974 (amended 1977) and the Safety Signs and Signals Regulations (1996) are very relevant to how project managers perform their duties.

As part of this legislation there is a clear requirement for project managers to:

- Develop organisational HS&E Policy
- Facilitate HS&E Training & Briefing
- Provide HS&E reporting, review and improvement

The HSWA provides the legislative framework to promote, stimulate and encourage high standards of health and safety at work. Duties are assigned to employers, manufacturers and suppliers, and employees. H&S inspectors have certain powers, which for example, include the right to enter the premises of a company at any reasonable time to investigate and question. Inspectors also have the power to serve prohibition or improvement notices and they can even prosecute companies that contravene relevant statutory provisions. The HSWA legislation that is relevant to the management of projects includes the Management of Health and Safety at Work Regulations (1992).

Statutory Requirements

Statutory requirements relevant to project management and the responsibilities of project personnel, include the Construction Design and Management (CDM) Regulations 1994; the Reporting of Injuries Diseases and Dangerous Occurrences Regulations (RIDDOR) 1995 and the Control of Substances Hazardous to Health Regulations (COSHH) 1994.

The Construction (Design and Management) Regulations 1994

The Construction (Design and Management) Regulations 1994 (abbreviated to CDM, formerly CONDAM) implement EC Directive 57/92. These Regulations are prescriptive with regard to the duties of various parties involved in a (construction) project and additionally create the roles of "planning supervisor" and "principal contractor" and a requirement for a "health and safety plan" and a "health and safety file".

Under the Regulations project participants including designers and contractors have to be selected on the basis that they are aware of their health and safety duties and will allocate adequate resources to discharge them.

Moreover, the Regulations impose on the client the duty to select and appoint a 'planning supervisor' and a 'principal contractor' for the project. The client has the legal duty not to permit construction to start until the principal contractor has prepared a satisfactory health and safety plan.

The key responsibilities of the three main parties defined by the Regulations are shown in Figure 25 - 2.

Under the Regulations:

- The person appointed as the planning supervisor must be competent and have adequate resources. The client may appoint the project manager, a consultant or any other person as the planning supervisor. Similarly a member of the client's staff may be appointed
- The principal contractor appointed must also be competent and have adequate resources. It can be the main contractor for constructing the project, a management contractor or a specialist in Health and Safety
- The client has a duty to appoint designers who have the competency and resources needed for their duties

Main Party:	Duties
Planning Supervisor	Ensuring that the H&S requirements are met in design.
	Ensuring that the particulars of the project are notified to the H&S authorities.
	Preparation of the H&S Plan for the project.
Principal Contractor	Maintaining the H&S Plan.
	Ensuring co-operation between all contractors on H&S.
	Ensuring that everybody on site complies with the rules of the H&S Plan.
Designer	Consider during the design the hazards & risks which may arise to those who will construct & maintain the works.
	Design to avoid HS&E risks throughout the lifecycle of the project.
	Reduce risks at source if avoidance is not possible.
	Consider measures which will protect all workers if neither avoidance or reduction to a safe level are possible.
	Ensure that drawings, specifications, operations and maintenance (O&M) instructions, etc. include adequate information on H&S.
	Pass this information to the Planning Supervisor, so that it can be included in the H&S Plan.
	Co-operate with the Planning Supervisor and where necessary other Designers on the project.

Figure 25 - 2: Key Responsibilities under the CDM Regulations

The Reporting of Injuries, Diseases and Dangerous Occurrences Regulations 1995

These regulations abbreviated to RIDDOR require employers, self-employed people or people in control of work to report incidents of some work-related accidents, diseases and dangerous occurrences. Reporting accidents and ill health at work is a legal requirement. The information enables the Health and Safety Executive (HSE) and local authorities to identify where and how risks arise and to investigate serious accidents.

All of the following must be reported:

- A death or major injury
- An over-three-day injury (that is when an employee or self-employed person has an accident at work and is unable to work for over three days, but does not have a major injury)
- A work-related disease
- A dangerous occurrence (this is when something happens that does not result in a reportable injury, but which clearly could have done)

The reporting procedures which had been in place since 1996 have now been simplified and offer a facility to report all cases to a single point, the Incident Contact Centre (ICC), based at Caerphilly in Wales. The new centre will mean that you no longer need to be concerned about which office and which enforcing authority you should report incidents to.

The Control of Substances Hazardous to Health Regulations 1994

COSHH Regulations obligate the employer, under UK law, to undertake a comprehensive risk assessment of the substances to which its employees, and others on its site, are exposed. Only competent persons should undertake COSHH assessments and records should be kept. The assessments must be regularly updated.

Environmental Management

The Environmental Protection Act 1990 gives high priority to the options available regarding releases to the environment, with particular reference to Best Available Techniques Not Entailing Excessive Costs (BATNEEC) and Best Practicable Environmental Option (BPEO). These well-known acronyms are the basis for regulatory thinking.

For example, in process industries, the nature of regulatory control can be determined by reference to SI 472 1991, the Environmental Protection (Prescribed Processes and Substances) Regulations (as amended). Each section in SI 472 1991 is subdivided into Part A (Environment Agency control) and Part B (processes prescribed for air pollution control by Local Authorities). Applications are typically made to the Environment Agency for an Integrated Pollution Control (IPC) Authorisation to perform a particular activity or process. Recent changes (1996) to IPC Regulations means that all EC member states are required to implement the requirements of the IPPC Directive 96/61/EC concerning Integrated Pollution Prevention and Control.

In developing an Environmental Management regime manager should therefore consider:

- The environmental impact of the project
- Environmental policy, planning and manuals
- Environmental reporting requirements

ISO 14001

ISO 14001: 1996 is the only Standard in the ISO 14000 series to which an organisation can become registered. It provides a structured basis for environmental management control and is based on the process of plan, implement, audit and review.

ISO 14001 includes 21 specific requirements for areas of environmental management control, with the aim of supporting environmental protection and prevention of pollution in balance with socio-economic needs. ISO 14001 requires organisations to commit to legal compliance, pollution prevention and continuous improvement, as well as maintaining documented procedures regarding the organisation's operations and activities.

This section presents an overview of the ISO 14001 Environmental Management System Standard, discusses keys to success and the benefits of implementing ISO 14001, and provides contacts for obtaining the standard.

ISO 14001 is a voluntary international standard that establishes the requirements for an Environmental Management System (EMS). The objective of the standard is for an organisation to establish an EMS that is integrated with the overall business management process. Elements of the EMS include Environmental Policy, Planning, Implementation and Operation, Checking and Corrective Action, and Management Review.

These elements are discussed further below. Integral to the model is the concept of Continual Improvement of the EMS. This improvement can take many forms, such as improved communications and employee awareness, improved environmental performance, and improved emergency planning and response programs. It is not necessary for all elements of the EMS to be improved simultaneously.

Environmental Policy

An organisation's environmental policy establishes the foundation for an organisation to build its EMS. The following requirements apply:

- Top management shall define the policy
- The policy must be relevant to the activities, products, and services of the organisation
- The policy must show commitment to continual improvement of the EMS and prevention of pollution
- The policy must be documented, communicated to all employees and available to the public

For example, IBM's Environmental Policy covers the corporation's activities, products, and services worldwide, and includes a commitment to environmental leadership and continual improvement of it's EMS and performance.

Planning

An organisation must identify and plan for those elements of its business that could interact with the environment. Actions necessary to meet this element of the ISO 14001 standard include:

Identifying the significant environmental aspects and impacts of its activities, products, and services. Depending on the organisation's business, significant aspects could include matters such as air emissions, water discharges, chemical consumption, and energy consumption.

Identifying and having access to applicable legal and other requirements that apply to the organisation. This includes understanding legal and permit requirements and ensuring that employees whose jobs could impact these requirements understand permit parameters.

Setting and documenting environmental objectives and targets. Objectives and targets are not required for every significant aspect. In some cases, the significant aspect may be under operational control.

Establishing environmental management programs for achieving these objectives and targets. The environmental management program should detail who is responsible for achieving the objectives and targets, the time frame, and the means.

Implementation and Operation

Implementation and operation are the next steps in putting together an effective EMS. ISO 14001 requires the following:

- Define and communicate roles, responsibility, and authorities necessary to establish, implement, and maintain the EMS. There must be an appointed management representative who, irrespective of other duties, is responsible for establishing, implementing, and maintaining the EMS

- Communicate the environmental policy, objectives and targets, and other elements of the EMS to employees and contractors. Communication can take several forms such as training, poster campaigns, and/or bulletin board announcements

- Ensure that those employees whose job can have a significant impact on the environment are appropriately trained. These employees must be informed of the potential environmental consequences of their actions and must be competent to do their jobs

- Establish procedures to handle environmental inquiries from interested parties. These inquiries could be about the EMS; the organisation's significant aspects, objectives, and targets; environmental performance; or other environmental issues

- Identify and describe the core elements of the EMS. These could include the environmental policy, operating procedures, and instructions

- Control EMS documents and procedures. Ensure they are current, reviewed by the authorized person(s), and available at point of use
- Maintain documented procedures to control operations that could impact the environment. These include work instructions, preventive maintenance procedures, and other operational control procedures
- Have an effective emergency preparedness and response plan. Test it periodically, as appropriate, and update it, as necessary after the occurrence of environmental incidents

Checking and Corrective Action

To ensure effective implementation of the EMS it must be periodically checked and corrective/preventive action taken when needed by performing the following:

- Monitor and measure key characteristics of its operations and activities that can have a significant impact on the environment, such as energy use, chemical use, and waste, air, and water emissions
- Handle non-conformances to the EMS efficiently by investigating root cause(s) and ensuring corrective and preventive action is taken
- Identify and maintain environmental records such as permits, calibration records, training records, and monitoring and measuring data
- Periodically conduct audits of the EMS, which include the whole EMS and not just compliance with regulations

Management Review

Management must regularly review the EMS in order to:

- Ensure its continuing suitability, adequacy and effectiveness
- Address possible needs for changes to the environmental policy, objectives and targets, and other elements of the EMS
- Identify opportunities for continual improvement

Keys to Success

Keys to Success of the implementation process for ISO 14001 include:

- Top management commitment
- Adequate resources to establish, implement, and maintain the EMS
- Assigned roles, responsibility, and authorities
- Buy in from all levels
- A structured and documented implementation plan
- Adequate education, awareness, and training with respect to the EMS
- Appropriate procedures and documentation
- An effective audit program

Benefits of Implementing ISO 14001

There are numerous benefits of implementing ISO 14001. These include:

- Providing a framework for a systematic and integrated approach for environmental management which allows the EMS to become part of the fabric of the organisation's business
- Making the EMS "system" dependent and not "person" dependent
- Promoting sound environmental management which becomes a means of doing business and not an end in and of itself
- Positioning the organisation as an environmental leader and providing a framework by which to respond to environmental inquiries from customers, stockholders, and other interested parties

Industry-Specific Issues

Major hazard accidents, quite apart from deaths and injuries, tend also to attract bad publicity, uninsurable losses, damage to share values and long-term damage to corporate reputations. Organisations that are complacent about or pursue a policy of minimal compliance to the HS&E legislation in their particular industry are increasingly likely to be forced to adopt a more diligent and ethical stance by stakeholder scrutiny. This section discusses the approach to regulatory compliance of several different industries.

Nuclear Industry

Several of the companies that operate in this high profile mature industry are currently decommissioning some of their older power stations. There are clearly major HS&E implications of such an exercise due to the criticality of the process and the possible effects on stakeholders. In this context, HS&E procedures have to be applied for the long-term, not just in terms of day-to-day reviews and monthly/quarterly audits, but setting policies and procedures that will be effective and in place for tens of years, long after the current management team have retired. This approach includes Long Term Safety Reviews (LTSR) and Periodic Safety Reviews (PSR).

The long-term approach to HS&E in safety-critical industries is embodied in standards such as the International Electrotechnical Commission (IEC) 61508 entitled 'Functional Safety of Electrical/Electronic/Programmable Electronic Safety-related Systems. This standard in particular sets out a generic approach for all safety life-cycle activities for electrical / electronic / programmable electronic systems (E/E/PES's) that are used to perform safety functions. Whilst the scope of this, and similar standards is wide-ranging, the focus is on the adoption of more rational and consistent technical policies for safety-related systems.

Hazardous Installations - COMAH

The European Communities (Control of Major Accident Hazards Involving Dangerous Substances) Regulations, 2000 (S.I. No. 476 of 2000), were signed into law by the Tanaiste and Minister for Enterprise, Trade and Employment on, 21st December, 2000 and came into effect from that date. These regulations give effect to European Directive 96/82/EC on the control of major accident hazards involving dangerous substances, also known as the Seveso II Directive. The regulations apply to companies where dangerous substances are present in quantities equal to or above specified thresholds.

The focus of this legislation is on the duty of hazardous site operators to implement a Safety Management System (SMS). Moreover, operators are required to have an effective Major Accident Prevention Policy (MAPP), goals and objectives, and to ensure that all employees are aware of these. The safety report requirements, with their emphasis on demonstrating that risks are reduced to as low as reasonably practicable (ALARP), are similar to the 'safety case' justification model that is well established for offshore installations, nuclear sites and railway activities.

Safety management systems are used to facilitate compliance with a company's HS&E policies and procedures and tend to be based on the HSE guidelines, termed POPMAR, which stands for:

- Policy
- Organisation
- Planning and implementation
- Measuring performance
- Auditing
- Review of performance

Quarries and Mines

Mining and quarrying is a good example of a mature industry that has invested heavily in research into health and safety issues. The reason for this investment is due to the potential serious impact of hazardous occurrences.

Mining health and safety can be categorised into catastrophic and insidious problems. Catastrophic problems include the classic mine hazards such as roof falls, fires, explosions, and transport accidents. The word 'catastrophic' is used in the dual sense to mean an event which occurs with little or no prior warning and one which may cause major loss of life. Insidious problems are those whose effects are only noticed over considerable periods of time; they include dust, noise, radiation and vibration. Catastrophic and insidious problems are usually, but not always, related to safety and health, respectively.

In terms of legislation, the mining and quarrying industry, like other hazardous industries, tends to be subject to European HS&E Directives that are ratified and then implemented in the UK and for which the DTI has the primary enforcement responsibility of the statutory regulations and approved codes of practices (ACOPs).

However, since other EU member states tend to retain their right to produce their own national legislation and enforcement policies, there can be widely differing interpretations of HS&E Directives, such that global mining companies have to address multiple, differing requirements to ensure that they operate within the boundaries of legislation in a particular territory.

A Safety Culture - The Way Forward

In high reliability industries, there has been an increasing recognition of the importance of cultural and behavioural aspects of HS&E management. Investigations into major disasters (e.g. Piper Alpha, Zeebrugge, Clapham Junction) have revealed that complex systems broke down disastrously, despite the adoption of a full range of engineering and technical safeguards, because people failed to do what they were supposed to do. These were not just cases of simple, individual errors, but malpractices that corrupted large parts of the social make-up of these organisations.

The Confederation of British Industry (CBI) defines a 'safety culture' as the way we do things around here. The Advisory Committee for Safety in Nuclear Installations describes a safety culture as the product of individual and group values, attitudes, perceptions, competencies and patterns of behaviour that determine commitment to, and the style and proficiency of, an organisation's HS&E management.

Organisations with a positive safety culture are characterised by communications founded on mutual trust, by shared perceptions of the importance of safety and by the efficacy of preventative measures.

Human Factors

As the frequency of technological failures in industry has diminished over recent years, the role of human behaviour has become more apparent, and safety experts now estimate that 80-90% of all industrial accidents are attributable to human factors. It is now widely accepted that the most effective way to further reduce accident rates is to address the social and organisational factors that influence HS&E performance, in particular the responsibilities that are delegated to project managers by senior managers. Within a legal framework, corporate strategy should direct the managerial decision making processes. Individual social responsibility defines the ethics of the decision made. Decision-maker's responsibilities are outlined in Figure 25 - 3.

Definition	Detail
Holding accountabler	Responsibility for the outcomes of past actions or the causes of events.
Rule following	Responsibility in the context of externally imposed norms associated with social roles.
Decision-making	Responsibility in terms of judgement, reliability and independent thought processes.

Figure 25 - 3: Decision-maker's Responsibilities

Human failure modes are defined in Figure 25 - 4 (Reason, 1990). The term error type relates to the presumed origin of an error within the stages involved in conceiving and then carrying out an action sequence. Planning refers to the processes concerned with identifying a goal and then deciding upon the means to achieve it. Since plans are not usually acted upon immediately, it is likely that a storage phase of some variable duration will intervene between formulating the intended actions and running them off.

An execution stage covers the processes involved in actually implementing the stored plan. Unsafe acts can be split into unintended (slips & lapses) and intended (mistakes, plus violations) actions.

Performance Level	Error Type	Failure Modes
Skill-based	Slips & lapses	Inattention
		Overattention
Rule-based	Mistakes (failure of expertise)	Misapplication of good rules
		Application of bad rules
Knowledge-based	Mistakes (lack of expertise)	Selectivity
		Overconfidence
		Bounded rationality
		Incomplete or incorrect knowledge

Figure 25 - 4: Human Failure Modes

Any productive system can be broken down into a number of elements and the trajectory of accident/incident causation through these elements is shown in Figure 25 - 5. Fallible decisions are an inevitable part of the managerial process. The question is not so much how to prevent them from occurring, as how to ensure that their adverse consequences are speedily detected and recovered.

All organisations have to allocate resources to two distinct goals: production and safety. In the long term, these are clearly compatible goals. But, given that all resources are finite, there are likely to be many occasions on which there are short-term conflicts of interest. Resources allocated in the pursuit of production could diminish those available for safety; the converse is also true.

These dilemmas are exacerbated by two factors:

1. Certainty of outcome. Resources directed at improving productivity have relatively certain outcomes; those aimed at enhancing safety do not, at least in the short term

2. Nature of the feedback. The feedback generated in the pursuit of production goals is generally unambiguous, rapid, compelling and (when the news is good) highly reinforcing. That associated with the pursuit of safety

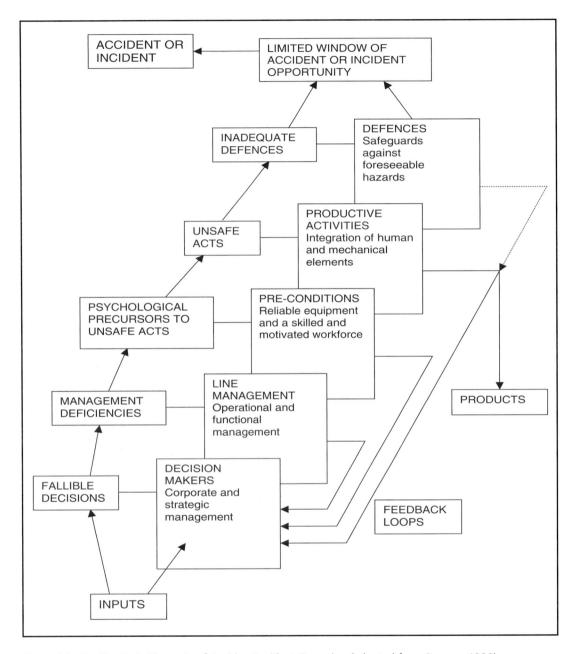

Figure 25 - 5: The Basic Elements of Accident/Incident Causation (adapted from Reason, 1990).

goals is largely negative, intermittent, often deceptive and perhaps only compelling after a major accident or string of incidents. Production feedback will, except on those rare occasions, always speak louder than safety feedback. That makes managerial control of safety extremely difficult

Techniques and Tools

Project managers often utilise the following techniques to ensure safe working practices:

- Risk Assessments
- Safety audits
- Safe systems of work
- Permit to work system
- Safety Training

Contracting organisations tend to take guidance from clients in terms of relevant statutory regulations that apply and the procedures that sub-contractors must abide by, in specific project circumstances. However, as mentioned previously, it is the responsibility of all parties to ensure that adequate HS&E plans are implemented.

The degree (type & duration) of on-site work on a project will likely determine the scope and depth of HS&E responsibilities that project managers will have to address. Similarly the industry type will play a role in determining the specific regulations which will have to be addressed.

Research (Sawacha, Naoum & Fong, 1999) has shown that the top five important issues found to be associated with site safety performance were:

1 Management talks on safety
2 Provision of safety booklets
3 Provision of safety equipment
4 Provision of a safe and tidy environment
5 Appointment of a trained safety representative

Areas of Innovation

HS&E management is breaking new ground in the modern business environment where homeworking is becoming commonplace. With home working and tele-working the traditional HS&E lines of responsibilities of employers are becoming blurred as more and more people set up home offices away from the corporate premises. Teleworking refers specifically to any employee that regularly works remotely from the organisation using IT and communications equipment. The employer is still responsible and liable for the health and safety of the employee.

In the case of teleworking, the actual work, the remote workplace and the equipment used must be suitable. Management style may have to change in these circumstances due to lack of direct supervision, from 'management by attendance' to 'management by results'. Both the employer and employee will have to address the insurance requirements of such a scenario.

Also 'hot-desking' is becoming more common in organisations that are working in dynamic environments. Work space for employees has to be consistent and uniform, so that they are able to work effectively at any of the designated areas within the company (which may be multi-site).

In terms of environmental regulations, a planned revision of ISO 14001 is scheduled and should increase the appeal to smaller organisations, require external reporting of performance, link to the principles of sustainability and improve the harmonisation with ISO 9000.

References and Further Reading

Dixon, M., 2000. Project Management Body of Knowledge (BoK). 4th Ed. Association for Project Management.

BS EN ISO 14001:1996 Environmental Management Systmes - Specification with guidance for use.

Holt, A., 1999. Principles of Health and Safety at Work. 4th Edition, IOSH Publishing.

IEC 61508 Symposium Proceedings, 1999. IEC 61508 Explained. The Institute of Measurement and Control.

Lawson, G., Wearne, S. & Iles-Smith, P. (Eds.), 1999. Project Management for the Process Industries. The Institution of Chemical Engineers.

Reason, J., 1990. Human Error. Cambridge University Press.

Sawacha, E., Naoum, S. & Fong, D., 1999. Factors Affecting Safety Performance on Construction Sites. International Journal of Project Management, Vol. 17, No. 5, pp.309-315.

Section 3

Control

30   WORK CONTENT AND SCOPE MANAGEMENT

Paul Vollans

"Candidates should not attempt more than six of these."

Hilaire Belloc (1870-1953, French-born British writer. Suggested addition to the Ten Commandments.

Intoduction - A Structured Approach

Planning a project involves many variables (such as work, duration, resources and costs) and to attempt to juggle them all at the same time is likely to introduce inaccuracy and error. Furthermore, trying to fit a project between given start and finish dates may well compound the problem if the given completion date is unrealistic. The result is a plan that may appear to do what is required but in fact is unrealistic, unachievable and is quickly forgotten as fire-fighting mode takes over.

To overcome these problems, a good planning process should:

◆   Adopt a structured step by step approach so that variables are dealt with logically, one at a time
◆   Initially, allow the end date to float (ie: it will be determined by the plan)

The initial aim should be to produce a credible and realistic plan in which some confidence can be placed. It can then be used as a tool to help identify and resolve problems of timescale and resource.

The structured step-by-step approach is described in the following paragraphs and summarised as follows:

1   Define Objectives
2   Develop the Work Breakdown Structure
3   Develop the Organisation Breakdown Structure
4   Decide who will undertake which tasks (Responsibility Matrix)
5   Decide on the sequence of tasks (Dependencies)
6   Assess task durations

7   Calculate the Critical Path and project duration (Network Analysis)
8   Carry out a resource analysis
9   Resolve any problems of timescale and resource hi-lighted in steps 7 & 8

In planning the project, it is important to implement the steps in the order shown and generally focus on one step at a time. It should be noted that the level of management for a given project will depend on the nature of the project. Thus a small, low risk project will require less management "weight" than one of high value and risk. Not all the steps, therefore, will necessarily be applied to the same extent in all projects.

Step 1 - Project Definition

Project Scope - High Level

Clear objectives is an obvious requirement for any project. It is surprising, though, how many projects have unclear, ill-defined objectives and fail as a consequence of this. Each project should have a written document, or Requirements Definition, describing the scope. This must define user/customer requirements. Some of the characteristics that it should embody are as follows:

- Requirements should have clear deliverables ie: measurable events with a clear definition of when they have been successfully achieved
- There should be an emphasis on what is required, rather than how it will be achieved
- It should use clear, unambiguous English without jargon and with all acronyms explained
- Bullet points are easier to understand than lengthy descriptive paragraphs
- Division into logical sections will make the document easier to read and use

All project stakeholders should buy into the scope definition document and for this reason there should be a formal approval and sign-off procedure.

Project Deliverables - Product Breakdown Structure (PBS)

To help with the development of the project scope, a Product Breakdown Structure (PBS) can be developed. This identifies in a hierarchical manner the products that the project will produce. A simple example is given in Figure 30 - 1.

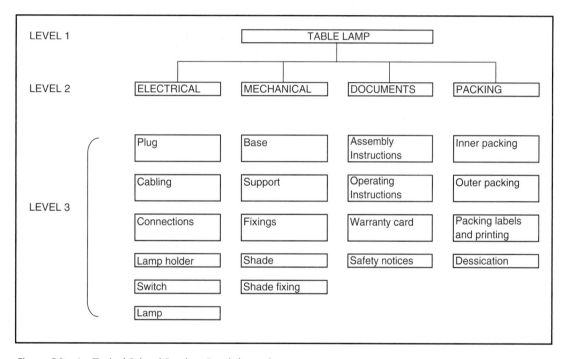

Figure 30 - 1: Typical 3-level Product Breakdown Structure

Developing the Requirements Definition

Based on the high level definition of the project, detail can be added so that implementation of the project can be undertaken. For example, at high level, the project definition may require a marshalling area to be illuminated to a defined level. This can then be developed further by the project team to include design requirements, determination of mounting details and types of luminaires etc. so that the work can actually be undertaken.

Check lists can be used to help ensure that no relevant details are omitted. Typically, such a list might include:

- Ergonomics
- Legal issues
- Insurance
- Pollution
- Customer training
- Energy consumption
- Disposal
- Political
- Packing
- Transport / shipping
- Patents
- Maintenance
- Size
- Life-span
- Warranty

Similarly, a library of standard specifications can save time and ensure consistency within an organisation. For example, a company involved in process control may need to purchase pumps on many of its projects. A standard pump specification could be developed so that purchased pumps are always to the required standard across all projects.

Changes to the Project Scope - Change Control

Any changes made to the scope definition after sign-off must be subject to a change control procedure. This should include:

- An assessment of the change in terms of cost, time, quality, risk, commercial benefit etc.
- A decision making process - is the change to be formally adopted or discarded?
- A formal sign-off/authorisation

♦ A process to communicate details of authorised changes to all stakeholders
♦ A formal record of the change

Step 2 - Work Breakdown Structure (WBS)

Definition

The WBS breaks down the overall project into a hierarchical set of tasks and sub-tasks which facilitate the planning and control of the project. It is important to appreciate that in general the WBS is a structured list of tasks and that sequencing (the dependencies) of those tasks is not important at this stage. An example of a simple WBS is shown in Fig 30 - 2.

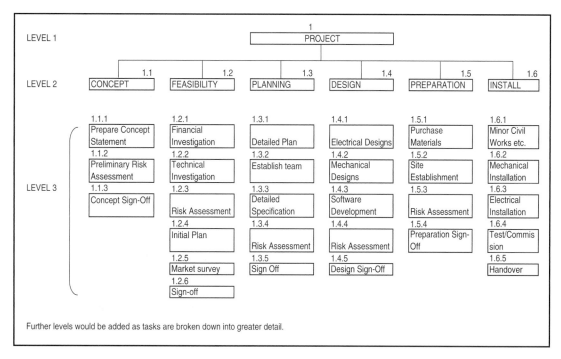

Figure 30 - 2: Typical 3-level Work Breakdown Structure

Types

At the highest level (level 1), will be a single task representing the whole project. The next level (level 2) will be based on phase, product or organisation.

Phase - Level 2 is based on the broad sequential phases that the project may pass through eg: Concept, Feasibility, Development, Design etc.

Product - Level 2 is based on the tangible deliverables that will be evident upon completion of the project eg: Hardware, Software, Documentation, Training etc.

Organisation - Level 2 is based on the groups or departments that will be undertaking the project eg: Engineering, Systems, Quality, Manufacturing, Finance etc.

Combinations of these techniques can be used as required. In practice phase is probably the easiest and most common approach.

Although the WBS is essentially just a structured list of tasks, without any information concerning the sequence in which those tasks are completed. The use of phases for the development of level 2, though, is a slight anomaly.

Parent-Child Relationship

Tasks in a work breakdown structure are organised into parents and children. For example in Figure 30 - 2, task 1.1 is a parent of tasks 1.1.1 and 1.1.2 because they are directly linked. Conversely, 1.1.1 and 1.1.2 are child tasks of 1.1. Another name for parent tasks is summary tasks.

By definition, parent tasks will only be complete when all associated child tasks are complete. Completion of all child tasks means that the corresponding parent task is finished. By virtue of the parent/child relationship, completing the lowest level of tasks completes the whole project. It should also be clear from the parent/child principle that no parent will have only one child - it would be pointless as both tasks would be identical!

Deliverables

Each task must have at least one clearly defined deliverable so that there is no doubt when the task has been completed (very often some sort of approval or sign-off). Such deliverables should be measurable, thus "drawings finished" is not really measurable as it could be subjective. "Drawing signed off by the customer" is measurable and there is little scope for doubt.

Include all Work

The WBS will be used in due course to develop the cost and timescale of the project. To avoid inaccuracy, therefore, It must include all aspects of work that require resource or materials. Thus less obvious elements such as meetings, safety procedures, QA requirements, administration needs and reporting must all be included.

Risk Actions in the WBS

Risk Management is covered in Session 23 - "Risk Management". As part of the process, it is likely that a number of tasks will be identified to mitigate risk or take advantage of opportunity. Such tasks must be incorporated within the WBS.

Rolling Wave Effect

At the outset of a project, in the planning stages, it is unlikely that all tasks can be fully defined. Consider a new product development project as an example. At level 2 in the WBS, based on phases, we might have tasks such as Feasibility, Development, Design, Prototype, and Test. The precise nature of Testing will be defined at least to some extent by the Development and Design stages. Thus it will not be possible to fully define testing until these earlier stages are complete. In effect, the level 2 task, Testing, may not be fully broken down into all its children until a later stage in the project is reached.

Stated more generally, the full development of tasks in the WBS may occur as the project proceeds rather than right at the start. This can be thought of as a wave of detail that surges forwards through the project as time elapses. It is referred to as the "Rolling Wave Effect". It is worth noting in the light of this that the WBS should not be viewed as fixed, but as an organic, developing tool that has detail added as the completion of earlier tasks provides new information.

Creating a WBS

Top-Down Approach

In this approach, start with level 1 (the whole project) and break the work down into levels 2, 3 and so on. To do this, it can help to think of the deliverables of a given task: Suppose a level 2 task is "Feasibility". The deliverables may include a financial appraisal, technical feasibility, a risk assessment, market investigation, a summary report and so on. These deliverables become, in effect, the child (level 3) tasks of which "Feasibility" is the parent.

Bottom-Up Approach

Here, by using brainstorming or other techniques, the aim is to write down all the tasks that can be thought of. Their order, importance and size are irrelevant at this stage, the emphasis being on making sure that all work has been included. When the list is complete, the raw list of tasks can be assembled into a WBS.

Practical Tips

1   The WBS is best developed using small self-adhesive "post-it" stickers on a large sheet of paper (or, for larger projects, a wall). This has the advantages of being easily changed, easily viewed by the whole project team, and giving the "big picture" (ie - the ability to see the whole project at once). When finalised, it can readily be transferred to computer. It is inadvisable to try creating the WBS straight onto a computer as with most software only a limited number of tasks can be seen on the screen at any one time.

2   It is important to avoid the trap of going into too much detail (ie: too many levels). This will make the plan unwieldy and too sensitive to change. Further detail can always be added selectively later.

3   Remember that the WBS is essentially just a structured list of tasks. When designing a WBS, avoid getting involved in the sequence of tasks, resources, timing etc. - this all comes later in the planning process (see below).

A Generic WBS

Companies frequently develop 3-level work breakdown structures that can be applied to most of their projects. This ensures consistency and best practice across projects, reduces the risk of work being omitted, and forms the basis of a standard in-company project management procedure. A simple example is given in Figure 30 - 2.

Task Coding in the WBS

Each task in the structure can be allocated a reference number for time sheet coding, purchase order coding etc, thereby enabling costs to be allocated to specific tasks. The numbering system is commonly based on level - see Figure 30 - 2.

Program Management and the WBS

In programme management, where a group of individual but related projects is being managed, the overall programme becomes the level 1 task, with individual projects making up level 2, and so on.

Step 3 - Organisation Breakdown Structure (OBS)

Definition

The OBS is about the people who will be doing the project and is the hierarchical way in which management levels and groups are set up for planning and control purposes. It should be a definitive project document in its own right, covering team structure, operation and characteristics as described in the following sections:

Company Structure

Any project-orientated organisation should consider how it should best be structured in order to facilitate effective project management. A widely used approach here is a matrix structure, as shown in Figure 30 - 3. Departments within the organisation (represented in Figure 30 - 3 by columns) are made up of staff with corresponding skills and are managed on a day-to-day basis by a departmental head, to whom the departmental staff report. Project teams (represented by rows in Figure 30 - 3) are made up of a project leader together with a selection of staff from the various departments as dictated by the skills required for the project. As the projects are completed and new projects start, the project teams will be continually changing.

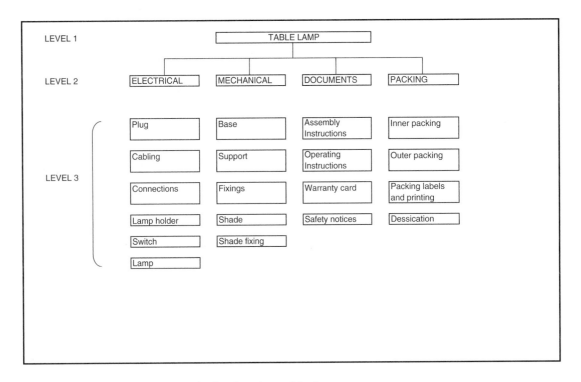

Figure 30 - 3: Project Team Organisation Based on a Matrix.

The potential benefits of a matrix approach are:

- Good communication between departments
- Good communication within projects
- Direct communication between the project leader and the team
- Good project prioritisation and resource management if departmental heads and project leaders work together constructively and effectively

Potential problems, however, are:

- Departmental staff report to more than one person
- Work allocation to a given individual by more than one person may lead to exploitation and conflict
- Poor working relations between departmental heads and project leaders may result in conflict and poor resource control
- If the project leader is selected from within a department, lack of authority and departmental bias may be an issue
- Inherent flexibility dilutes single project responsibility & planning

In moving from a traditional hierarchical organisation structure to a matrix based approach, cultural and other issues are likely to be significant, the change requiring considerable time to reach effective and stable operation.

Project Team Structure

Determination of the project team structure will address issues such as:

- Who will lead the team?
- Who will be in the team? - (Remember it may include people from the end-users' organisation, sub-contractors and external specialists)?
- How will the team be structured? - (who will be responsible to whom)
- Who will be the Project Champion? - (ie: the member of senior management supporting the project so that it is completed successfully)

In answering such questions, it will be necessary to take into account the nature of the project and therefore the skills and experience required. In deciding skill levels, reference must be made to the tasks in the WBS. Indeed, skill is probably the key link between the WBS and the OBS - if the former comprises tasks likely to need an electrician, there will be little point in having a project team made up largely of carpenters! A skill matrix can help assess whether or not the skill levels on a project are about right. This compares quantitatively team members' skill/experience against the skill required. An example is shown in Figure 30 - 4. Care should be exercised as it can be quite subjective and run the risk of causing offence. It is, however, a useful device to high-light and report on the situation where serious under or over-skilling is believed to exist.

Project Team:	John	Helen	Peter
Skills Available/Required:			
Software Writing	2/4	1/0	1/3
Electronic Circuit Design	2/3	4/3	2/3
Test/Commission	3/3	2/3	2/2

Skill Level

0	No knowledge
1	Basic skill level, simple tasks, supervised
2	Intermediate skill level, moderate tasks, some unsupervised work
3	Considerable skill level, complex tasks, much unsupervised work
4	Recognised expert

A matrix like this can help show quantitatively whether or not skill levels on a project are adequate. The numerator of each fraction gives the skill available and the denominator gives the skill level required. The numbers represent skill level in accordance with the simple scale shown.
This example would suggest that insufficient software writing skill is available to the project. In the case of Peter, a skill level 3 is required but his skill has been assessed as 1. Similarly John is assessed as level 2 but level 4 is required.

Figure 30 - 4: A Simple Skills Matrix.

Reporting Structures

The main objective of the project reporting structure is to agree in advance who will report what, to whom, when and in what format. It will cover reporting both with in the team (ie: information that the project leader and others may require in order to effectively manage the project) and outside the team (eg: reporting to senior management, customer reports etc). The requirements can be defined in the form of a reporting matrix as shown in Fig 5. One of the key aims is to ensure as far as practicable the right people get the right information when they need it.

Report Title:	Prepared by:	Information From:	Copied To:	Dates of Issue: Feb	Mar	Apr	May	June
Weekly Summary (Internal)	Project Leader	Team	Eng. Manager	7,14, 21,28	6,13,20,27	3,10,17,24	1,8,15,22,29	5,12
Weekly Summary (External)	Project Leader	Team Sales/Marketing	Customer Sales/Marketing	7,14, 21,28	6,13,20,27	3,10,17,24	1,8,15,22,29	5,12
Monthly Progress	Project Leader	Team	MD., Board Eng. Manager Prod. Manager	25	31	28	26	30

This example shows how a reporting matrix can be used to define what reports are required, when, who will produce them and to whom they are issued. The exact content of each report (format, data etc.), and medium (e-mail, fax, verbal etc.) should also be defined in order to complete the picture

Figure 30 - 5: Reporting Matrix.

It is likely that part of the reporting process will require regular review or progress meetings. A matrix similar to Figure 30 - 5 can be used to define the meeting requirements in detail, including such information as dates, who should attend, to whom minutes are circulated, the standard agenda for the meeting, location, time and so on.

Team Authority

The authority of the project team and team members will be dictated by the level of delegation that exists within the organisation. On the basis that only chaos would ensue if everybody could authorise, for example, any change or expenditure as they saw fit, delegated authority will address questions such as:

- ◆ Who is empowered to authorise expenditure?
- ◆ Who is empowered to authorise change?
- ◆ What limits of expenditure and change does the authorisation extend to?
- ◆ What other limits on authority apply eg: staff recruitment, design approval etc.
- ◆ How will the authorisation process be implemented and documented?
- ◆ How will matters outside the team's delegated authority be authorised?

Communication

A communication matrix can be used to show who issues and receives project documents and information. A typical example is given in Figure 30 - 6.

	Project Manager	Engineering Manager	Project Team	Purchasing Dept.	MD	File	Customer
Specification	P	R	P/R		A/R	R	R
Variations	A	(R)	P/R			R	P
Purchase Orders	A		P	R		R	
Work Breakdown Structure	A		P			R	
Gantt Chart	A/R	R	P	R		R	R
Customer Correspondence	P/R		(R)			R	R/P
etc...							

Relevant project documents are written down the left, and all project stakeholders are written across the top. Letters in the matrix indicate who authorises, sends and recieves the various documents.

Key:	A	Authorise
	P	Prepare/Send
	R	Receive
	(R)	Receive as appropriate

Figure 30 - 6: Typical Communication Matrix.

Resource Costs

The individual labour costs must be established and the following should be included in the OBS as appropriate:

♦ Standard rates
♦ Overtime rates - there may be more than one. For example, some companies will have a normal rate, evening/Saturday rate, and a third Sunday/Bank-Holiday rate
♦ Future resource rate changes (eg: pay rises that will take place during the project duration)
♦ Multiple resource rates, for example one resource might have a certain cost rate for working in the office but a higher rate for working on the Customer's site

Clearly there are practical difficulties of knowing the actual resource cost of each team member - salary details can be potential dynamite! To avoid this problem, grade rates are sometimes used ie: staff are allocated to a certain grade that broadly reflects their cost to the company, and are costed to a project on the basis of their grade rate, their actual cost rate remaining confidential. Company Accounts Departments should be able to provide this sort of information.

Step 4 - Responsibility Matrix

Essentially, this will be a grid with the WBS down the left hand side and the resources (from the OBS) across the top. Ticks in the appropriate squares of the grid will indicate who is doing what. This approach can be taken further and the RACI idea is one such development. Here the letters R (Responsible), A (Accountable), C (Consult) and I (Inform) are used in place of ticks. "Accountable" means the person who must ensure that the task is completed successfully. "Responsible" means the person - or people - who will actually do the work. Only one person can be accountable for a given task, but many can be responsible. The person accountable can also be one of the people responsible (ie: can actually do it). It should be noted that by virtue of the parent/child relationship (see WBS above), it is only necessary to allocate resources to the lowest level of tasks in the WBS.

By definition, when these are completed their parents are completed and so on up the WBS structure to the top most level ie: the whole project is completed.

The responsibility matrix is limited in that it only shows who will do each task and not how much time (and therefore cost is incurred). If cost is important, the responsibility matrix must be developed further into a full Cost Breakdown Structure or Cost Account (see Session 33 - Budget and Cost Management).

Steps 5, 6 & 7 - Task Dependencise, Durations and Network Analysis

The dependencies of tasks in the Work Breakdown Structure should now be determined, that is, the sequence in which they are to be completed. Then, by determining the duration of individual tasks, the critical path and therefore the overall project duration can be calculated. (See Session 31 - Time Scheduling and Phasing for full details). Figure 30 - 7 shows an example of a simple network diagram, with dependencies, task durations and the critical path shown. Traditionally (before computers!), a network analysis would be carried out manually, the data then being used to create a gantt chart which is generally easier to use on an everyday basis. With the advent of computers, the network anaysis is completed automatically and it is possible to work entirely in the Gantt chart mode.

Step 8 - Resource Analysis

The Gantt chart gives the periods of time over which tasks are active and the responsibility matrix and cost account give the resource assigned to each task. It is therefore possible to use this information to determine what resource is required when. This could be presented as a histogram or in spread sheet form. Details of resource availability can then be added and by comparing the two, periods of resource over and underloading become evident. This topic is covered in more detail in Session 32 - Resource Management.

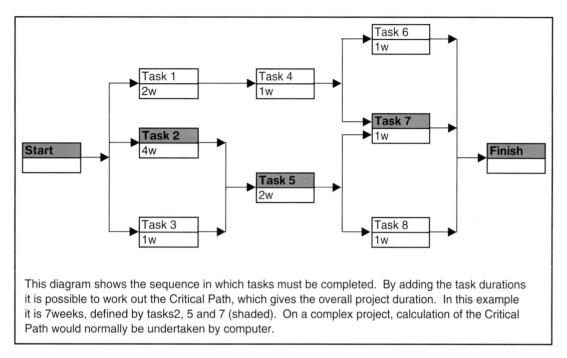

This diagram shows the sequence in which tasks must be completed. By adding the task durations it is possible to work out the Critical Path, which gives the overall project duration. In this example it is 7weeks, defined by tasks2, 5 and 7 (shaded). On a complex project, calculation of the Critical Path would normally be undertaken by computer.

Figure 30 - 7: Dependency Diagram or Network Diagram.

Step 9 - Problem Solving

As was seen in the introduction to this section, the completion date determined from the network diagram may not agree with the required date. Also, the resource analysis may have high lighted resource problems. Adjustments must therefore be made. There are broadly speaking four categories of change that can be made. These are listed as follows, with examples given:

1   Change Resources

♦   Overtime
♦   More people
♦   Different skills
♦   Training

2   Change Method - ie: How tasks are carried out

+   Automate a process
+   Sub-contract
+   Uprate equipment

3   Change Objectives - ie: The overall project goals

+   Omit features
+   Change the required end date
+   Change quality
+   Increase the budget

4   Change the Logic of the Plan

+   Use slack to release resources that can then be applied to expedite critical tasks
+   Overlap tasks where possible (introduce negative lag)
+   Review the sequence of tasks - can any be carried out simultaneously?

A few guidelines to bear in mind:

The categories are not mutually exclusive and frequently a corrective action will drop into more than one (eg: automating a process to change method may require an increased budget, thereby changing objectives).

By constructing the plan carefully and in the structured manner described, it has credibility and accuracy. It is important not to weaken or destroy this by introducing unjustified optimism or error at this stage. To avoid this, every action to resolve problems must have a clear rationale and justification. For example, arbitrarily halving a task duration may achieve a desired end date, but without a sound reason for the decision, it will simply not be achieved.

The longest duration tasks on the critical path will be the first ones to look at with a view to reducing timescale. The non-critical tasks with large resource assignments or significant total float will probably be the first ones to consider when resolving resource overloads

The problem solving process should involve the whole project team in order to capture their knowledge and experience.

Risk should be considered. For example, a timescale problem may be reduced by digging a trench with a JCB, rather than hand-digging, but this may increase the risk of damage to buried cables.

The Four-Fields Diagram

The WBS, OBS, Responsibility Matrix and Dependency Diagram can all be brought together into a single diagram. An example is shown in Figure 30 - 8. The WBS (to two levels) is shown on the left, the OBS across the top, the level three tasks and their dependencies are shown in the main body of the chart, and the horizontal position of each task indicates the people in the OBS responsible for that task. Generic diagrams of this nature are often developed and tailored by companies to represent their standard procedure for management of a project (ie: it will apply to most if not all of their projects). Back-up procedures describe in more detail the exact nature of each of the level three tasks shown (eg: Objectives, deliverables, standard documentation required etc.)

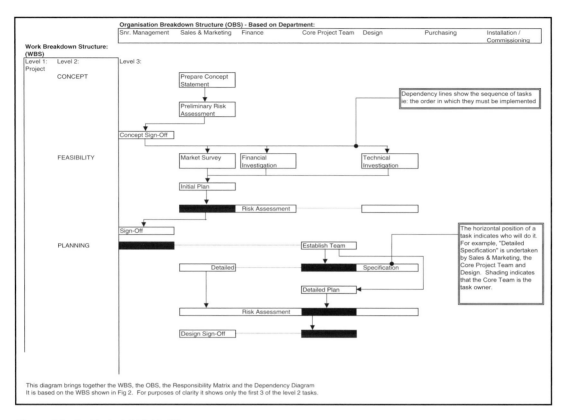

Figure 30 - 8: Typical 4-Fields Diagram.

31 TIME SCHEDULING AND PHASING

Dennis Lock

"Three o'clock is always too late or too early for anything you want to do."
Jean-Paul Sartre (1905-1980), French philosopher, playwright, and novelist. Nausea (1938).

This session deals with schedules that specify when project activities should be performed. We have to assume that those activities have already been identified, preferably in a comprehensive work breakdown structure (see Session 30). Although there are exceptions (particularly for work delegated to subcontractors), schedules cannot usually be made without regard to resources. Resource management therefore completes the scheduling process and is dealt with in Session 32. The need for carefully prepared schedules is apparent if projects are to finish on time but scheduling and subsequent control are important for other reasons. This applies particularly to costs. Projects that finish late are also likely to exceed their planned cost.

What Makes a Good Schedule?

Scheduling usually needs specialised techniques. Before discussing some of these it is necessary to consider the characteristics by which any schedule can be judged as effective or otherwise. A good schedule should:

- Contain all significant tasks or activities needed to complete the project
- Place tasks in a logical, feasible sequence
- Obey and display interdependencies between different tasks
- Be sufficiently detailed to provide reference points for frequent progress checks
- Be flexible, so that it can be updated to accommodate progress results or approved changes in the project's scope or strategy
- Highlight priorities so that management attention and scarce resources can be directed to the most critical activities

   ♦   Be visually effective: a schedule must communicate well
       to all project participants including those without
       specialist training

Milestone Planning

Milestone planning is the simplest method of project scheduling but is of limited use. It consists of identifying key events in a project and then declaring the dates by which each of those events should be achieved. This can also be called 'diary planning'.

Milestone dates are often seen on project authorisation forms, or on contract documents where milestone events are associated with stage payments. The nature of milestone events must depend on the type of project but might typically include the initial contract signing, issue of design drawings for client approval, first delivery of materials to a project site, beginning of commissioning and final handover to the client. Whether or not the milestone dates set are achievable will, of course, depend on the experience of the person who sets them.

Milestone plans are useful in setting the overall project timescale and are sometimes regarded as project master plans. Subsequent detailed planning will, however, have to be undertaken to underwrite the milestone target dates. Milestone plans by themselves cannot provide the level of detail needed for day-to-day measurement and control of progress.

There is another form of milestone analysis, described in Chapter 23 of Lock (2000), which should not be confused with the simple milestone planning just described. Milestone analysis is a form of achievement assessment that can be used as a simpler alternative to earned value analysis (Session 35).

Bar Charts

Bar charts, often called Gantt charts after the American engineer Henry Gantt (1861-1919), are a useful and much employed method for calculating and displaying project schedules. They are always set out according to a suitable horizontal timescale. Bar charts are easily understood with no need for any special training. They can display schedule data very clearly but their visual effectiveness decreases as the amount of detail increases.

Practical limits depend on the method of presentation but visual effectiveness begins to fall off when there are more than about 50 tasks. A bar chart also becomes unwieldy if a long project duration has to be split into a large number of short periods. It might be possible, for example, to divide a project into 200 weeks (200 columns on the chart) but those weeks could not easily be further divided into days.

Simple Bar Charts

Figure 31 - 1 shows a very simple bar chart schedule for a project to strip and refurbish a kitchen in an empty house. This chart is better in many respects than a milestone plan because it can show more clearly the complete schedule and the timings of individual tasks. The level of detail included is, however, barely sufficient for control purposes and will need expansion if the chart is to become a fully effective control tool.

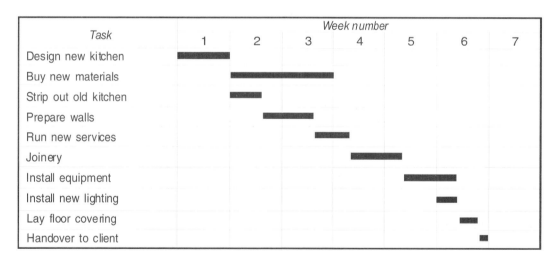

Figure 31 - 1: Kitchen Refurbishment Project: A Simple Bar Chart

Some Extended Bar Chart Applications

Wall Chart Displays

At one time the principal way of displaying bar charts was on wall-mounted panels. Proprietary kits allowed these to be adjustable and capable of most of the extended applications about to be described. The main problem with wall-mounted charts was that they could not easily be communicated outside the project management or departmental office except by photographing them. Wall-mounted chart boards are still used but most project bar charts are now produced on paper from computer driven printers or plotters. Even the worst project management software can plot reasonable charts.

Colour Codes

Bars can be coloured to convey specific information about individual tasks. Bars for tasks with the highest priority (critical tasks) might be made bright red for example. Whatever the reason for using colour codes, there is always a practical limit to the number of different colours that can be used before a chart becomes too difficult to interpret.

Where colour facilities are not available, bars can be coded by filling them with different shading patterns. The number of different patterns that can be used before confusion sets in is probably fewer even than the number of different colours that might have been used.

Simple Resource Scheduling

One application of colour is to code task bars according to the department responsible or type of resource that the task requires. Simple resource scheduling might then become possible if an adjustable chart is used. If, for instance, blue is used for all tasks needing a design engineer, the number of design engineers needed in any period can be found by counting the number of blue bars that traverse the relevant column. This method becomes difficult or impossible when there are individual tasks that need more than one unit of a resource or several different resource types.

Time-now Cursor

When the project is in progress, a vertical line can be drawn on the chart to correspond with the relevant progress review date (the 'time-now' date). With simple manual planning time-now will probably be today's date because progress will be under continuous daily review. On adjustable wall charts the dateline cursor is usually formed by a moveable elastic cord or ribbon, typically coloured red.

Bars on chart boards should be removed from the chart when the tasks are finished. Paper charts should be replotted regularly so that completed tasks are either removed or suitably coded as finished. If everything is going to plan, work to the left of the cursor (work scheduled for completion before time-now) should have been done. Any jobs remaining on the chart before time-now will stand out as late work, demanding some corrective action.

Linked Bar Charts

The more complex a hand-drawn or board-mounted bar chart becomes, the easier it is for the planner to schedule by mistake one or more tasks at times before they can logically take place. For instance, in a bar chart for a big construction project the planner might mistakenly schedule the building of a wall before the foundations have been finished. Such mistakes can be prevented by grouping work-related tasks on the chart and by placing vertical connecting link lines to show which tasks must be finished before other tasks can begin. The problem with this method is that complex charts become too cluttered and the link paths are very difficult to follow. Another method of notation is needed. That need (plus many others) is met by critical path networks.

Critical Path Networks

All critical path network techniques can be traced back to a number of separate mid-20th Century sources in Europe and the US but their application, assisted by project management computer software, became common from the 1960's. Morris (1997) gives a well-researched account of the history.

The kitchen refurbishment project can be used here to explain the critical path method but the schedule must first be presented in slightly more detail than that used in the simple bar chart of Figure 31 - 1. This enhanced detail is provided in the task list of Figure 31 - 2. In addition to the name of each task, this list shows the estimated task durations (of which more will be said later) and immediately preceding task or tasks that must be finished before each new task can start.

Task number	Task description	Task duration (half-days)	Tasks immediately preceding
01	Design	10	None
02	Remove all fixtures and equipment	4	None
03	Remove old water pipes	2	None
04	Disconnect and remove old wiring	2	None
05	Disconnect and remove gas pipes	1	None
06	Replaster walls	8	02, 03, 04, 05
07	Rewire	4	01, 06
08	Buy wall tiles	10	01
09	Tile walls	6	07, 08
10	Order joinery and built-in units	1	01
11	Deliver timber and built-in units	30	10
12	Order electrical appliances and lighting	1	01
13	Deliver electrical appliances and lighting	20	12
14	Install lighting	4	07, 13
15	Order floor covering	1	01
16	Deliver floor covering	10	15
17	Install plumbing	2	09, 11
18	Install all timber units (includes sinks)	8	09, 11
19	Install appliances (refrigerator, hobs, oven etc.)	4	17, 18, 20
20	Lay floor covering	2	14, 16, 19

Figure 31 - 2: Kitchen Refurbishment Project: Preliminary Task List

Logic Diagrams (Networks)

Every critical path method is based on a logic diagram. All logic diagrams comprise a network of arcs (arrows) which intersect at nodes. Depending on the notation system chosen (see below) project tasks are represented either by the arrows or the nodes. The project action always progresses from left to right and allows the constituent activities of a project to be displayed in their logical, practical sequence. Links (constraints) between interdependent activities are clearly shown.

Logic diagrams concentrate on the intended work sequence and pattern. They do not need to be drawn to any timescale. Ideally there should be only one start and one finish node in a network.

Networks are usually best when they are constructed at brainstorming sessions by key project people. Listing the significant activities often starts from the work breakdown structure (see Session 30). The process of identifying all the activities, placing them in their preferred sequence on the network diagram and defining all the inter-activity constraints is always a valuable project management endeavour. The result, even if no other use is made of the diagram, will be a logical process map or flowchart for the efficient execution of the project.

Two Basic Notation Systems

Activity-on-Arrow Networks

Figure 31 - 3 shows the kitchen refurbishment project schedule as an activity-on-arrow network diagram, based on the task list of Figure 31 - 2. These diagrams are called activity-on-arrow networks or, more simply, arrow diagrams (often abbreviated to ADM).

Each node in an arrow diagram is drawn as a circle and represents a project event, such as the start or finish of an activity or the achievement of a milestone. Events are numbered for identification. Arrows joining events denote the activity needed to progress from one event to the next. Activity descriptions, and their estimated durations, are written along the arrows. No activity can start until the event

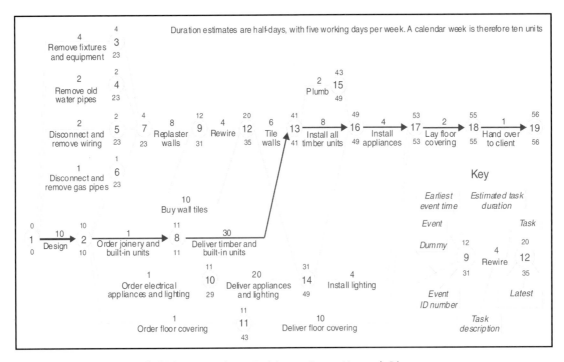

Figure 31 - 3: Kitchen Refurbishment Project: Activity-on-Arrow Network Diagram

at the tail of its arrow has been achieved. Thus activity 7-9, replaster walls, cannot be started until event 7 has been achieved. Another way of putting this is that activity 7-9 cannot start before activities 1-3, 1-4, 1-5 and 1-6 have all been finished.

The dotted arrows linking events 12 to 14 and 14 to16 do not indicate real activity. They are called dummies, and simply indicate constraining links. Thus, for example, the start of activity 14-17, install lighting, depends not only on completion of rewiring but also on the delivery of lighting equipment. Dummies have zero duration by default.

The dummies leading into event 7 are not strictly necessary and the real activities could all have been shown leading directly into event 7. If that were done, however, all four activities would be coded identically as 1-7. This used to be completely unacceptable for computer applications. It is less important now that practically all computer applications can deal only with activity-on-node networks.

The number written above each event circle shows the calculated earliest possible time when the event can be achieved and the number below shows the latest permissible time for event completion if the earliest project completion date is not to be delayed. These numbers are calculated by time analysis, described later in this chapter.

Activity-on-Node Networks

Figure 31 - 4 shows the kitchen refurbishment project using activity-on-node notation (more commonly known as a precedence diagram or PDM). This network contains the same data shown in Figure 31 - 3 and shows exactly the same project schedule.

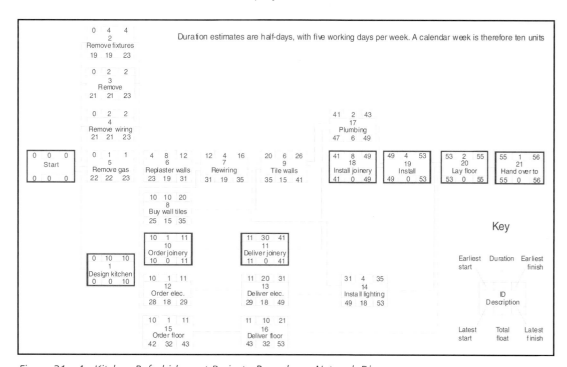

Figure 31 - 4: Kitchen Refurbishment Project: Precedence Network Diagram

With the activities placed at the nodes, and with the links indicating only the flow pattern and constraints, these diagrams resemble engineering flow charts and are considered easier to understand. Remembering that all networks flow from left to right, there is no need to give further explanation of this precedence network. The key in Figure 31 - 4 explains the various numbers written in the activity boxes.

In arrow networks the relationship between consecutive activities is that the earlier activities must be completely finished before their immediate successors can begin. This is known as a finish-start constraint. Variations are possible but difficult to incorporate in arrow notation. In precedence networks it is also likely that most, if not all, constraints will also be finish-start and this is the default assumption of computer software applications. However precedence notation allows the planner to specify and show more complex constraints, as demonstrated in Figure 31 - 5.

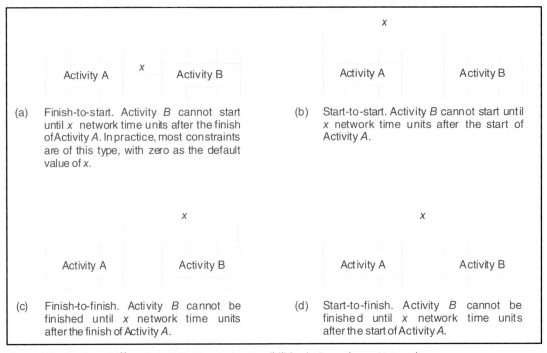

Figure 31 - 5: Four Different Activity Constraint Possibilities in Precedence Networks

Project Management Pathways

Figure 31 - 5 (a) shows that even the usual finish-start constraint can be modified by introducing a time delay, so that the start of activity B will lag behind the finish of activity A. This would be useful, for example, in allowing time for paint to dry or for concrete to cure.

The start-start constraint illustrated in Figure 31 - 5 (b) allows activities A and B to overlap. This is used, for example, when a purchasing activity can start a few days or weeks after design has started, because the design engineers will be expected to release advance information on purchased items that have long delivery times. It would probably be necessary to complement this constraint with a finish-finish link of the kind shown in Figure 31 - 5 (c), indicating that purchasing of all materials for the activity could not be completely finished until time x after design completion.

In most networks complex relationships are either not used or are well outnumbered by the default finish-start constraints. The start-finish relationship shown in Figure 31 - 5 (d) is very rarely used. Burke (1999) gives the example of a crane hired for two consecutive lifting activities (A and B in our case) where the crane is available for only six days. Activity B must, therefore, finish not later than six days after the start of activity A. Devaux (1999) also deals well with complex precedence constraints.

Choosing Between Arrow and Precedence Diagramming

Arrow diagrams are easier to sketch freehand than precedence networks and are ideal for simple planning where no computer is to be used. They are particularly valuable in brainstorming planning sessions because of the ease and speed with which an experienced planner can transfer the ideas of the contributing group to paper. A large sheet or roll of paper, soft pencil, eraser, ruler and stencil for the circles are recommended for this process.

Precedence networks require more careful drawing and are less suited to brainstorming sessions, although in some cases this problem can be overcome using a self-adhesive Post-it note for every activity box. Precedence networks are relatively easy to understand without need for special training and have the technical advantage of being able to deal with complex constraints.

Almost without exception, modern computer software applications allow no choice but demand input as activity-on-node. Those who prefer using arrow diagrams in the early brainstorming stages must therefore convert their networks to precedence diagrams before computer processing (this conversion is a simple procedure for experienced planners).

Estimating Activity Durations

Choice of Time Units

In the kitchen refurbishment project each time unit is half of one working weekday. This choice was made because ten units then represent a working week of five days and we can specify durations of only half of one day without resorting to fractions or decimals. It is always best to choose time units that can be used as integers throughout the plan if possible.

In most real-life cases the planner will choose either days or weeks as the time units, but some modern software will allow a tremendous choice, ranging from minutes to years. The units should be small enough to avoid the need for fractions but not so small that numbers become large when long periods are considered. Although some software will allow different units to be mixed in the same plan, it is wiser and will lead to more elegant reports if the same time units are used throughout.

Responsibility for Estimating

The best task duration estimates are probably those which result from debate (and eventual agreement) at planning meetings. Ideally all estimates should be made by people who have managed similar tasks in the past. These people should be sufficiently experienced to judge the time (and, where necessary, resources) needed in each case. If the estimators happen to be the same people who will ultimately be responsible for managing the work, so much the better. They can then more reasonably be expected to accept responsibility for achieving work on time.

Accuracy and Uncertainty

Accuracy in estimating is a flawed concept. Estimates are best judgments: they are prophecies, not hard indisputable facts. Estimates that are proved correct after the event might give cause for congratulation but the result will have been partly chance. In most, projects it is possible to predict all the task durations sufficiently well to accommodate this element of chance (obviously depending on the complexity and novelty of the project and the skills and experience of the estimators).

If estimating is found to be particularly difficult, giving rise to unacceptable uncertainty, deterministic planning can be abandoned in favour of a probabilistic method such as PERT. With suitable computer software this can be coupled with Monte Carlo analysis.

Unwanted Influences or Threats

It has been said that activity durations should be estimated at random across a network rather than in sequence along any path. The argument here is that sequential treatment could reveal overlong or critical paths while estimating is still in progress, which might tempt the estimators to make unrealistically short estimates for the remaining activities.

There is often a risk that pressure from a customer or senior manager to expedite completion will result in plans that are impossible to achieve. Estimators and planners should always try to resist pressure to reduce any estimate unless there is practical justification. The proper way to deal with such pressure is to attempt one or more of the fast tracking methods described later in this chapter.

Effect of Resources

For critical path network purposes every time estimate predicts the duration of an activity. This is the time expected to elapse between the start and finish of the activity. It is not, directly, an estimate of the cost or amount of human effort required. If, however, the duration of an activity is likely to be affected by the level of resources used, the planner must take the intended resource usage into account.

In anything but the tiniest network, several activities are likely to be competing for common, scarce resources (particularly for people with special skills). How does the planner know the number of resources that will be available for each activity? Fortunately this problem can be solved using commonsense. This is best explained by a simple example.

Suppose that a project organisation has a total of four skilled pipefitters available for project work. The maximum number of pipefitters that could be assigned to any single activity is, therefore, four. The planner should obviously not anticipate or specify the use of more than four pipefitters for any activity.

Now suppose further that the duration of a particular activity could be estimated as follows:

(a)   24 days if only one pipefitter is assigned
      (24 person days total work content)
(b)   10 days using two pipefitters
      (20 person days total work content)
(c)   6 days using four pipefitters
      (24 person days total work content).

Option (b) has the least daily work content and appears to be the most efficient way of completing this activity. The activity duration should therefore be estimated as 10 days, with two pipefitters entered as the planned rate of resource usage. Whether these two fitters will be needed for simultaneous activities on this or other projects is certainly important but need not be considered at this early estimating stage. Resource scheduling (Session 32) is a separate process that depends on, but is subsequent to, network planning and time analysis.

Normal working hours should always be assumed when estimating activity durations. Overtime at evenings or weekends should be regarded as a reserve level of resource, to be called upon only in times of emergency.

Time Analysis

When all activity durations have been estimated it is necessary to calculate the expected duration of the project. Time analysis will also produce valuable data about the timing and priority of every activity in the network.

Forward Pass

The estimated project duration is found by summing duration estimates from left to right through all the paths in the network. This process can be followed in the precedence diagram, Figure 31 - 4. The earliest possible start time for each activity is determined by its longest preceding path. The activity's earliest finish time will be its earliest start time plus its estimated duration. The earliest possible finish time for the whole project must be the earliest finish time for the final activity.

Backward Pass

The forward pass has determined the earliest possible finish time for the final activity in the network. The question that must now be asked is 'What is the latest permissible time for the project to finish?'' In most cases completion will be wanted as soon as possible so that the earliest possible finish and latest permissible finish times for the final activity will be the same. Having made this assumption, a backward pass through the network will reveal the latest permissible start and finish times for every activity.

The backward pass process is similar to the forward pass, except that the results are arrived at by subtraction from right to left. Where an activity leads into two or more paths, the longest of those paths will determine the latest permissible finish for the task.

The latest permissible start for an activity is found by subtracting the estimated activity duration from its latest permissible finish.

The procedure for arrow diagrams is similar, except that the earliest and latest times are calculated to give the earliest and latest times for achieving each event rather than the starts and finishes of activities. Activity times can, however, be derived easily from the event times.

Float (Slack)

Figures 31 - 3 and 31 - 4 both show that the earliest and latest completion times for the kitchen refurbishment project are identical or, in other words, the difference between these times is zero. This difference is known as the float or slack.

Total float is the amount by which any activity in a network can be delayed without affecting the estimated project end time, provided that all its preceding activities have been finished by their earliest dates. In any network there will always be at least one path where the total float is zero. Activities with zero total float are critical to project completion on time and the path (or paths) linking them is known as the critical path.

Float is a quantity that denotes the priority of a task, the highest priorities naturally being given to those tasks which have the least float. This prioritisation allows project management attention and action to be directed to the most critical activities.

Float also plays a big part in resource scheduling. Any activity having total float can be deliberately delayed during subsequent resource scheduling if that should be necessary to remove resource overloads, provided that the imposed delay lies within the total float available.

Because project activities lie along defined paths, it is apparent that total float exhausted early in the project will reduce the amount of total float available for later activities (like robbing Peter to pay Paul). However a few activities can often be found in a network that retain some or all of their total float even when preceding activities are delayed to their latest times. This is called free float. The free float of an activity can be defined as the float available when preceding activities have been delayed to their latest permissible times but following activities can still take place at their earliest times.

Tabulating Time Analysis Results

Figure 31 - 6 tables the time analysis data calculated from Figures 31 - 3 and 31 - 4. Both networks give the same results, except that arrow and precedence diagrams use different systems for their activity ID codes. Figure 31 - 6 includes both sets of codes.

Task No	Arrow network ID	Task description	Task duration (half days)	Earliest start	Latest start	Earliest finish	Latest finish	Total float	Free float
01	1 - 2	Design	10	0	0	10	10	0	0
02	1 - 3	Remove all fixtures and equipment	4	0	19	4	23	19	0
03	1 - 4	Remove old water pipes	2	0	21	2	23	21	2
04	1 - 5	Disconnect and remove old wiring	2	0	21	2	23	21	2
05	1 - 6	Disconnect and remove gas pipes	1	0	22	1	23	22	3
06	7 - 9	Replaster walls	8	4	23	12	31	19	0
07	9 -12	Rewire	4	12	31	16	35	19	4
08	2 -12	Buy wall tiles	10	10	25	20	35	15	0
09	12 -13	Tile walls	6	20	35	26	41	15	15
10	2 - 8	Order joinery and built-in units	1	10	10	11	11	0	0
11	8 -13	Deliver timber and built-in units	30	11	11	41	41	0	0
12	2 -10	Order electrical appliances and lighting	1	10	28	11	29	18	0
13	10 -14	Deliver electrical appliances and lighting	20	11	29	31	49	18	0
14	14 -15	Install lighting	4	31	49	35	53	18	18
15	2 -11	Order floor covering	1	10	42	11	43	32	0
16	11 -17	Deliver floor covering	10	11	43	21	53	32	32
17	13 -15	Install plumbing	2	41	47	43	49	6	6
18	13 -16	Install all timber units (includes sinks)	8	41	41	49	49	0	0
19	16 -17	Install appliances (refrigerator, hobs, oven etc.)	4	49	49	53	53	0	0
20	17 -18	Lay floor covering	2	53	53	55	55	0	0

Figure 31 - 6: Kitchen Refurbishment Project: Time Analysis

Calendar Considerations

Converting Numbers to Dates

So far all time data in this chapter have been expressed as simple numbers. This is usual in practice when schedules are made before the project start date is known. There is nothing then to relate the numbers to the calendar. As soon as the project start date is announced it is necessary to convert all times to calendar dates, taking account of non-working days such as weekends and public holidays.

This process is tedious when performed mentally but essential if the schedules are to be used for issuing and progressing work. It must be assumed that a computer will be used.

Most software allows customization of date formats. It is well known that different formats are preferred in various countries. A date expressed as 10.12.02 in Britain means 10 December 2002 but an American project manager would interpret this as12 October 2002. Confusion can be avoided by adopting the form 10Dec02.

Working Calendars

The default calendar in most software will assume that weekends are non-working days and will allow the planner to identify and exclude all other expected non-working days (such as public holidays). The computer will assign this default calendar to every activity unless given specific instructions to the contrary when the data for the activity record are entered.

Cultural differences in international projects have to be taken into account. Local customs and religious beliefs mean that different countries have public holidays on different dates. In project scheduling this difficulty is easily overcome by setting up a different calendar file in the computer for each case, and then assigning each activity to its appropriate calendar.

Different calendars can also be used when there is a mix of five and seven day working in the same project, or to accommodate some shift working. Some activities, such as concrete curing and paint drying span non-working days and these should strictly be assigned to a seven-day calendar.

Imposed Dates

Time-now

All computer scheduling takes place with reference to a time-now date. In the beginning this is most likely to be the start date of the first project activity, which must be specified as a start milestone for this purpose. Later in the project, the time-now date will probably be the reference point for schedule revisions resulting from scope changes or progress information.

Target Finish Dates

It is often necessary to impose fixed dates on one or two milestone events or activities. A common case is a target finish date on the final project activity. If the critical path is longer than the time available before the target date, time analysis will generate negative float, indicating that the plan cannot be achieved without revision.

Probabalistic Scheduling

When the outcome of a plan is in doubt owing to lack of confidence in the estimates or other risk, a statistical approach may be necessary. Two of the possible methods are described here.

PERT

Program evaluation and review technique (PERT) gives an opportunity for estimating three different durations for each activity. These are:

- Optimistic time, t_o
- Most likely time, t_m
- Pessimistic time, t_p

Assuming a statistically normal distribution of results, the expected time t_e for each activity is calculated from the following formula:

$$\frac{t_o + 4t_m + t_p}{6}$$

Some feel that more pessimism is justified, and it is true that plans usually tend to be optimistic. The following variation on the formula has been used to meet this argument:

$$\frac{t\,o + 3\,t\,m + 2t\,p}{6}$$

Monte Carlo Analysis

Project management software applications often include risk packages that allow probability forecasting. One of these is OPERA, part of the OPEN PLAN Professional suite from WST. Three estimates can be made for activities (the PERT method) and the program will carry out time analysis many times, picking optimistic, most likely or pessimistic durations at random across the network. The planner must select the milestone for which the forecast is required (usually the final activity) and can specify hundreds or thousands of time analysis reiterations. Processing is rapid and results in a time-scaled distribution histogram and cumulative curve that predict the probability of the milestone being achieved across the range of possible dates.

Timesaving Schedules

The results of initial time analysis often predict a completion date that is unacceptable. Perhaps there is a promised delivery date to a customer, or a company wishes to achieve the fastest possible 'time to market' for a new product.

The first step is to revisit the logic diagram and examine which activities might be overlapped, delayed (perhaps until after delivery of the main project) or even deleted. The complex constraints of precedence diagrams are particularly useful in these circumstances. If these measures fail, then some further possibilities are outlined below.

Crashing and Time / Cost Optimisation

The time/cost optimisation method described here began as CPA (critical path analysis) which was one of the significant historic routes to current network scheduling methods. It assumes that the estimated duration of some activities can be reduced (crashed) by injecting more resources or different working methods, usually at increased cost. Theoretically, a table can list a cost/time relationship for crashing every task, since it will be cheaper to shorten the duration of some activities than others. An example is given in Figure 31 - 7. The final column of this table indicates activities which can be shortened for least cost. Although this is expressed as the cost in pounds per time unit saved this cannot, of course, imply a linear relationship between cost and time for every activity.

Task ID	Task description	Normal duration (half days)	Total float	Possible action	Time units saved	Extra cost £	Cost per unit saved
01	Design	10	0	Use two designers	4	600	150
02	Remove all fixtures and equipment	4	19	Work overtime	1	100	100
03	Remove old water pipes	2	21	Crash action not feasible	-	-	-
04	Disconnect and remove old wiring	2	21	Crash action not needed	-	-	-
05	Disconnect and remove gas pipes	1	22	Crash action not needed	-	-	-
06	Replaster walls	8	19	Use faster setting plaster	2	20	10
07	Rewire	4	19	Work overtime	1	100	100
08	Buy wall tiles	10	15	Collect tiles from supplier	8	120	15
09	Tile walls	6	15	Work overtime	2	150	75
10	Order joinery and built-in units	1	0	Crash action not possible	-	-	-
11	Deliver timber and built-in units	30	0	Collect from different supplier	25	500	20
12	Order elec. appliances and lighting	1	18	Crash action not possible	-	-	-
13	Deliver elec. appliances and lighting	20	18	Collect from warehouse	18	36	2
14	Install lighting	4	18	Work overtime	2	100	50
15	Order floor covering	1	32	Crash action not needed	-	-	-
16	Deliver floor covering	10	32	Crash action not needed	-	-	-
17	Install plumbing	2	6	Crash action not possible	-	-	-
18	Install all timber units (includes sinks)	8	0	More workmen and overtime	4	600	150
19	Install appliances	4	0	Work overtime	1	100	100
20	Lay floor covering	2	0	Crash action not possible	-	-	-

Figure 31 - 7: Kitchen Refurbishment Project: Cost/Time Analysis of Possible Task Crash Options

Critical activities must be considered first, because attempting to shorten activities with considerable float will not expedite project completion. In Figure 31 - 7, activity 11 stands out as an obvious first choice for crash action because it has a long duration, is on the critical path and costs only £20 per time unit saved. The action needed is to find a different supplier who has existing stocks and then collect the goods rather than await delivery. The new supplier is unfortunately £500 more expensive but 25 time units can be saved.

Other methods for crashing the times of critical activities include planning for the use of overtime, using different materials such as faster drying paint or rapid curing concrete, engaging additional labour or using more expensive hired machinery. Many options will suggest themselves to the imaginative project manager.

When the critical path has been shortened to the extent that it is no longer critical, other paths through the network will have become critical instead and their activities, too, can be considered for crash action. By concentrating effort on critical activities in a number of reiterations, a theoretical condition could be reached where every activity in the network has been crashed until all are critical.

When taken to these extreme limits of optimisation the schedule aims to complete the project in the shortest possible time. But, with no float available anywhere, risk of failure is increased because there is no float in the system at all to cushion the effects of work problems and delays.

Fast Tracking

Fast tracking is an approach that throws aside the traditional concept of passing work from one department to another in sequence but instead requires a great deal of parallel working. In a manufacturing project, for example, this could mean starting purchasing before designs are assured and beginning production before final assembly drawings have been made. Good communications and co-operation between the groups is essential. The price paid is in the risk of having to back track and carry out re-work. The fastest possible results can be scheduled by combining fast tracking and CPA crashing.

Concurrent Engineering

Also known as simultaneous engineering, concurrent engineering is, like fast tracking, a method of working that requires parallel working and co-operation between different departments, project groups or other stakeholders. The emphasis is not so much on reducing the scheduled time as working together in co-operation, aiming for common 'win-win' technical and cost benefits and seeking holistic rather than personal or parochial advantage.

In the simplest case, the project design leader will meet those responsible for constructing or manufacturing the project and together work out a design strategy that gives maximum benefit to the organisation. This co-operation must continue throughout the life of the project in harmony rather than by confrontation. The chosen strategy might mean accepting increased design effort and costs if the extra design effort produces a greater reduction in the effort and costs needed to execute the project.

An American machine tool company makes heavy machines that are purpose-designed for machining its customers' components (often for automobile engines and gearboxes). The customer's engineers and the tool company's engineers work together to achieve the optimum combined design of the component and the machine in an advanced, mature form of concurrent engineering.

Keeping Schedules up to Date

Updating Need and Frequency

If a project runs from start to finish exactly as its scheduler intended there should be no need to change the schedule in any way. That exceptional condition can occasionally be achieved with a project that is properly scheduled and managed in a very low risk environment.

Most projects do not run according to plan and suffer changes in scope and progress setbacks. Where such changes are very infrequent the project schedule will only need to be updated on correspondingly infrequent occasions. All schedules must be kept up to date, however, so that they remain valid tools from which to issue and progress work.

In large projects and multi-project resource scheduled models frequent changes are the norm. Here, schedules must be updated regularly if they are to remain valid. Updating intervals will depend on several factors, but particularly on the frequency with which scope changes or progress setbacks occur. The project manager should be the best person to judge the frequency of regular updates but monthly is a popular choice, sometimes carried out as part of a process that includes the issue of progress reports to stakeholders outside the project team.

An alternative option to regular updating is continuous updating, with progress information and changes being fed to the computer as soon as the data become known. This method is fine provided that project participants can be relied upon to supply the data on time and in the correct format for the software being used. Staff feeding individual timesheet information to the computer can be asked to include progress assessments for each relevant activity, provided that job coding and other factors are compatible.

If continuous updating is used, there are two options for running file updates in the computer and these depend on the software being used. Microsoft Project will carry out time analysis automatically and update its files every time a piece of data is changed. Other software requires entry to the tools menu and definite commands to carry out fresh time analysis and, where appropriate, resource scheduling.

The method by which updated schedules are made known to departmental managers and other project staff is important. It is usually found that people cannot be relied upon to seek schedule information for themselves but need the stimulus of periodic reports.

Baseline Schedules

When a schedule is updated the previous version will be lost, saved as hard copy, or written to an electronic file. Some managers like to keep the original project schedule so that they can compare the latest updated version with the plan originally intended. Most software allows the planner to save such a baseline schedule.

Progress Reporting Method

Much collection and processing of progress information is somewhat mechanistic. The person reporting progress will be expected to declare work for which he or she is responsible as being not started, in progress or completed. For work in progress an assessment of progress achieved will be needed and that can usually be given in one of the following forms:

- Assessed percentage completion
  (anything from zero to 100 per cent)
- Estimated time remaining to completion
- A code indicating that the activity has been completed

Any special difficulty causing delays must of course be reported urgently and separately (exception reporting) so that appropriate corrective action can be taken if possible.

Progress reports must always be given along with the date on which the progress measurement was taken. If the schedule is to be updated at regular intervals, each re-run will be made with respect to a dateline (time-now) and all progress reporting must be arranged relative to the relevant time-now date. Time-now can, paradoxically, lie a few days in the future and this might entail an element of forecasting in a progress report.

The Supporting Role of Higher Management

Scheduling will inevitably fail in its purpose if support is not forthcoming from senior management in the organisation.

Initial senior management support will be needed for the purchase of effective computer equipment and software. The amount of money required might not be significant in proportion to project costs but the most effective software is by no means the cheapest. Buying cheap software that is not fit for its purpose wastes not only the purchase cost but also time and goodwill when implementation fails. There might be a difference of opinion between what the project management expert specifies and what the senior management perceive as the requirement, especially when a company within a group is expected to use software that is used in other group companies but which is inappropriate for the local organisation. The management support needed cannot be taken for granted and the project manager must be able to make and prove the case for any exceptional purchase. There is information on the choice of project management software in Lock (2000).

Staff may have to be specially trained, perhaps even recruited, to staff the scheduling process. With proper safeguards and the use of appropriate techniques this staff requirement can be kept down to a very small number, in some cases needing only one person plus one or two nominated (and trained) reserves. While the staff quantity might not have to be great, the quality certainly cannot be skimped. The most successful candidates combine experience, qualifications and a special aptitude for the job. They must be logical thinkers and have plenty of drive. Senior management must be willing to pay for finding and engaging the right people.

It may be necessary to provide training for the more senior project participants, so that they can appreciate how scheduling works and understand how they should interpret data and provide input. Time off for training is another expense that will probably need senior management sanction.

Project Management Pathways

Schedules will be useless if they are ignored by the project participants. Enforcement procedures might be needed to ensure that schedules are taken seriously and followed as closely as possible. When they deviate from or ignore schedules, individual supervisors and managers might not always be aware of the wider implications for other departments and other projects.

One of the biggest problems in maintaining a scheduling and control system is in obtaining feedback on progress from the various participants. Here, again, is the need for enforcement and that must be reinforced by the authority and support of higher management.

So, why should higher management give this degree of support? The potential rewards for achieving a successful scheduling and control system are far greater that the associated costs. There are cases where, for the expenditure of not more than one or two per cent of project costs on scheduling and control, projects have been completed not only ahead of time but as much as 30 per cent below their cost budgets. In one organisation, it was found that regular progress meetings were no longer needed because people simply worked to the schedules and any difficulties were found and dealt with by routine monitoring.

References and Further Reading

Backhouse, Chris J. and Brookes, Naomi, (eds), (1996), Concurrent Engineering, Aldershot, Gower

Burke, Rory, (1999), Project Management: Planning and Control, 3rd edn. Wiley, Chichester

Devaux, Stephen, A., (1999), Total Project Control, New York, Wiley

Gray, C. F. and Larson, E. W., (2000), Project Management: the Managerial Process, Singapore, Irwin/ McGraw-Hill

Lock, Dennis, (2000), Project Management, 7th edn, Aldershot, Gower

Lockyer, Keith and Gordon, James, (1996), Project Management and Project Network Techniques, 6th edn, London, Financial Times/Pitman Publishing

Meredith, Jack R. and Mantel, Samuel J. Jr., (2000), Project Management: A Managerial Approach, 4th edn, New York, Wiley

Morris, P. W. G., (1997), The Management of Projects, Thomas Telford, London

Reiss, G., (1995), Project Management Demystified: Today's Tools and Techniques, 2nd edn,
Spon, London

Turner, J. R., (1999), The Handbook of Project-Based Management, Maidenhead, 2nd edn, McGraw-Hill.

Information on OPEN PLAN and OPERA is obtainable from Welcom Software Technology International (WST), South Bank Technopark, 90 London Road, London, SE1 6LN.

32   RESOURCE MANAGEMENT

Dennis Lock

"Your most precious possession is not your financial assets. Your most precious possession is the people you have working there, and what they carry around in their heads, and their ability to work together."
Robert Reich (b. 1946), American economist and politician.

Introduction and Definition

Most, if not all, projects use resources in one form or another but the nature of those resources and the manner in which they are managed varies greatly from one organisation to another. This session examines some of the possibilities.

Resource management means ensuring that resources are in place when they are needed and that they are used efficiently. This session concentrates on resource scheduling, which attempts to match the timing of work with available resources, so that overload peaks or idle periods can be avoided. The use of simple Gantt charts will be described, because this method demonstrates the principles well. It is assumed, however, that one of the many available project management software packages will be used in practice.

Which Resources can be Scheduled?

If scarce resources are needed for a project they must be scheduled to ensure that they are deployed to best effect but some resources can be scheduled far more easily than others. In general, any chosen resource that can be quantified by simple one-dimensional units can be scheduled using project management software.

Solving the Problem of Complexity

Resource scheduling is a complex process involving a large number of possible variables. The way to deal with any such problem is to solve the variables in a logical sequence, one at a time. Seven logical steps can be identified in this process, starting from project definition and ending with the allocation of resources to individual tasks. This process is described at greater length in Lock (2000) but Figure 32 - 1 provides an adequate summary. Although some of the steps can involve the use of fairly sophisticated techniques, the final step of allocating people to individual tasks must be entrusted to the personal skills and judgment of managers and supervisors. The mechanistic aspects of resource scheduling should be seen as a process that allocates work at a rate commensurate with the capacity of each resource group or department. That should prevent departmental overloads. The final allocation of jobs to individual people must remain the responsibility of the relevant supervisors and managers, who know the different characteristics and capabilities of the people who report to them.

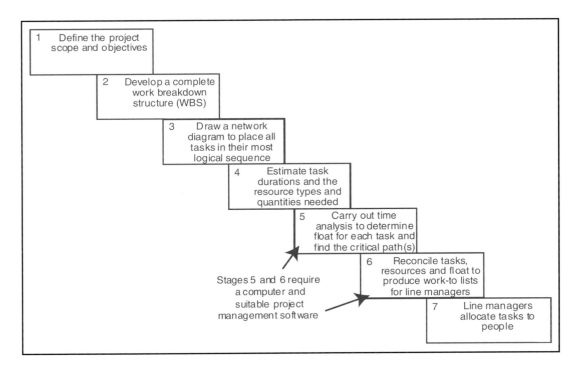

Figure 32 - 1: Seven Logical Stages Leading to a Practicable Resource Schedule.

Who Needs to Schedule Resources?

Any project manager working for an organization that owns resources or employs project personnel will be involved in resource management. A project manager who, on the other hand, employs a main contractor or otherwise outsources project activities will be interested in managing only those resources for which he or she is directly responsible (which might be only a handful of head office design staff). It is clear, therefore, that the need for resource management is determined largely by the operating arrangements of the project organisation.

Resource Categories

Project resources can be any people, objects or commodities that are used to achieve the project deliverables. Resources are classified as storable or non-storable in the Pathways Glossary but I find it useful to identify three main categories of resource, as follows:

1 Exhaustible
2 Replenishable
3 Re-usable.

Exhaustible Resources

Exhaustible resources are those resources that are consumed by a project and which are drawn from a non-renewable source.

Natural Mineral Deposits

Familiar examples of exhaustible resources are mineral deposits and fossil fuels. When an ore body, a coal mine or an oil well ceases to be commercially viable, the mineral resource has effectively been exhausted. It is irreplaceable. Once gone, it has gone for ever. Most exhaustible resources do not concern the manager of an active project but estimates of the amount of resource available will, of course, play a big part in pre-project feasibility studies and financial appraisals.

Time

There is one exhaustible resource that must concern every project manager and that is time. Every second of time that passes is lost for ever and can never be reclaimed. Managing this key resource is one of the most important project management functions. However, this has its unique methods, dealt with elsewhere throughout this book (for example in Sessions 11, 31, 35 and 60).

Replenishable Resources

Replenishable resources are those resources that are consumed entirely by the project but for which new supplies can be obtained.

Materials: Special Purchases of Components and Equipment

Project materials are indisputably project resources but most purchases need no special resource scheduling techniques. If, for instance, a locomotive is required for a new mine, then the specification and purchase of that locomotive can be included as activities on the project network diagram. The resulting critical path analysis should provide all the schedule data necessary for obtaining that resource and delivering it to the project site at the right time.

Management of material resources includes handling and storage, and the project manager responsible for equipment purchases must ensure that suitable facilities will be available for off-loading and handling the goods when they are scheduled to arrive at the project site or factory gates. If the hire of special lifting gear is necessary, this should probably feature as an activity on the project network.

Materials: Bulk Purchases

Some project tasks might use bulk materials throughout their duration and require continuous deliveries of those materials during the process. Building materials are a common example. Delivering all the materials to site before such an activity starts is not usually practicable and the project manager might need the materials to arrive on a just-in-time basis. Ready-mixed concrete is an obvious example. Time analysis of the network will predict only the start and finish times of the activity but subsequent resource scheduling can, given a degree of planning ingenuity and skill, predict the estimated daily delivery requirements. The method and software are the same as those used to schedule human resources: only the units of quantity are different.

Money

Money is usually a replenishable resource. Even when a project is in danger of going far over budget and exhausting its initial funds, the project sponsors might feel obliged to raise further funds rather than see their original investment sink without trace in an abandoned project.

Cash outflow schedules can be produced using the standard time analysis and resource scheduling facilities of project management software. The process will, however, test the planner's skills because it depends on allocating each cost item to the relevant activity record. This can be done by specifying a cost for an activity or by setting a cost rate for each unit of resource to be scheduled. The technique might involve adding special activities to the network on which to place the costs. It might be necessary, for example, to add an activity (with little or no duration) for each expected payment of a significant supplier's or subcontractor's invoice.

Re-usable Resources

Re-usable resources are employed in the course of project activities but they themselves remain substantially unchanged by the work (like catalysts in a chemical reaction). When an activity finishes, its reusable resources are freed for use elsewhere.

People

People, designated by their specialist skills, are the most commonly considered form of re-usable project resource.

Plant and Machinery

Plant and machinery are re-usable resources. Their allocation to project tasks can be scheduled using the same methods as those used to schedule human resources.

Accommodation Space

Accommodation is a re-usable resource for most projects. Accommodation can be defined here as any space needed to house project participants and their work during the active project life-cycle. When, however, a second dimension is introduced (for example in accommodation floor areas) solutions produced from project management software are less likely to be satisfactory because area shape is not taken into account.

There are companies that use space in complex ways for which standard project management scheduling techniques can provide no answer. A heavy machine tool company assembles its giant special purpose machines in an assembly bay where space use is maximised by allowing parts of some machines to overhang other machines and where machines over a certain height can only be assembled in a particular part of the bay. Although scheduling the people working on these activities should be no problem, three-dimensional accommodation problems are best left to production engineers who can use purpose-designed software or physical models.

Scheduling Using Charts

By far the most common chart still in use for scheduling people is the ubiquitous annual holiday chart. Charts remain useful today for the short-term allocation of work to people in departments or small groups. Until the advent of project management software in the 1960's, managers had to rely solely on charts for all their resource scheduling. Charts were often built up using proprietary kits, which were wall-mounted and made adjustable to allow for relatively easy re-scheduling. The physical problems of adjustability were solved by a number of different methods including placing job cards in slots, strips plugged into holes arranged in a grid pattern (in one case using coloured plastic pieces closely resembling Lego bricks) and magnetic strips on steel backboards. Many managers used simple blackboards and chalk for applications such as allocating jobs to machines in small workshops.

When compiling a bar chart for matching resources to project tasks without using a computer an adjustable proprietary kit is essential. Over 100 tasks can be scheduled by such charts. Figure 32 - 2 shows the principle. The planner can use different coloured strips for the tasks, each colour depicting a different type of resource or human skill. For simplicity, only one resource type (coded black) is shown in Figure 32 - 2.

Resource Aggregation

Referring to the bar chart in Figure 32 - 2, the number of people of the skill coded black needed in any period can be found by counting the black strips occurring in the period column. Bar charts are usually drawn with every task shown at its earliest possible time, and that is the case for Figure 32 - 2. The resource pattern here, therefore, represents the resources needed if every task were to be carried out at its earliest date, without taking advantage of any float that might be available. This type of schedule is known as resource aggregation.

Some of the very earliest software systems could only carry out resource aggregation. There are still project managers who eschew resource scheduling altogether in

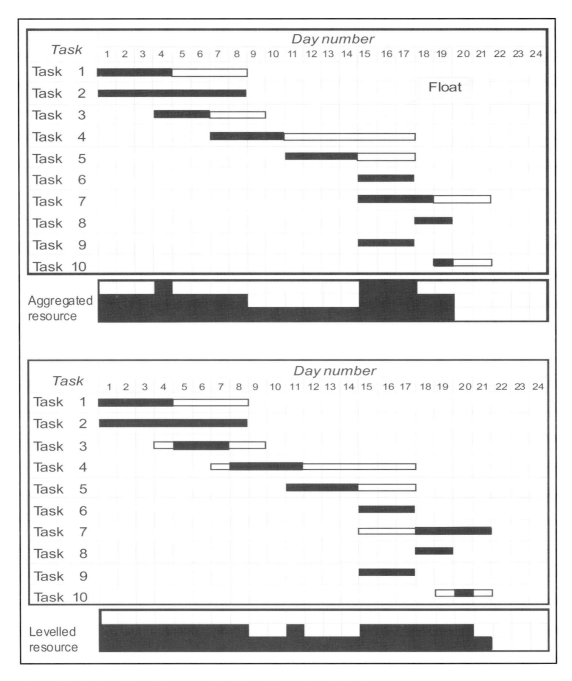

Figure 32 - 2: Principles of Resource Scheduling Using a Gantt Chart.

favour of attempting to try to perform each task at its earliest possible date (as predicted from network time analysis). Resource aggregation almost always results in a schedule that demands uneven use of resources. At times there will be peak overloads while at other times resources will be underutilised. This is apparent in the upper half of Figure 32 - 2.

It is possible to experiment, producing alternative schedules using the latest permissible task times instead of the earliest times. This will delay the peak overloads and change their pattern. However, the use of modern software should remove the need for such experimentation because it allows resource scheduling to be based on more effective task priority rules.

Resource Scheduling

A smoother pattern of resource usage can usually be obtained by delaying one or more non-critical activities. This has been done in the lower half of Figure 32 - 2, where the planner has moved some tasks to the right (delaying the tasks) until the planned usage is brought back within availability limits and made as smooth as possible. Float, in this example, is shown by dotted lines. It is apparent that the planner has been able to achieve a more level resource usage pattern in the lower half of Figure 32 - 2 without having to extend any activity beyond its available float.

Chart Limitations

Resource scheduling with charts is practicable only in relatively simple cases. Charts can, for example, be used with benefit by managers or supervisors to allocate tasks across small groups of people under their direct command (step 7 in Figure 32 - 1). This application is particularly valuable because only these managers can know all the individual skills and characteristics of the people reporting to them. Charts are, however, of far less practical use in the wider resource scheduling context, where the scheduling requirements are more complex and the number of tasks and amount of detail is far greater than at local departmental or group level.

In Figure 32 - 2 each task needs only one unit of one resource type (coded black in our example), but that is hardly typical of most projects. Charting problems arise where some tasks each need more than one unit of a resource or more than one type of resource. Although some of these problems can be solved, chart construction and interpretation then become very tedious and complicated. Different colour coded strips can be used to indicate more than one resource category or skill, for instance, but there is a low practical limit to the number of different categories that can be scheduled in this way.

A great disadvantage of chart boards is that, while it might take only a few hours to set up a new schedule, re-scheduling can be extremely difficult and time consuming. It is also highly likely that interdependencies between activities, easily seen on a network diagram, will be overlooked during manual re-scheduling of a large chart. Vertical links can be placed on the chart to indicate these interdependencies but this is not feasible for charts of any significant size.

Resource Scheduling Using Project Management Software

Most modern project management software is capable of scheduling project resources, although some packages are far more successful than others. Generally speaking, the high-end software must be preferred in all but the simplest cases. The additional investment in higher purchase price and greater need for training will be repaid through better performance and system reliability.

Preliminary Preparation and Decisions

Software Purchase

A number of questions must be answered before embarking on the purchase and application of software for project resource management. Some suppliers make extravagant claims for their systems. The most widely sold software cannot be taken for granted as the most suitable for resource management. Some software, in spite of claiming to be 'powerful', will not be able to meet the requirements of every organisation.

The first step is to decide on the system capabilities and capacity needed. This can be started by compiling a checklist that can be used at first for determining requirements and, later, as a basis of a questionnaire to be sent to all identified prospective software suppliers. A fairly detailed checklist is given in Chapter 12 of Lock (2000). The suppliers' responses can be entered on a comparison matrix chart and subjected first to a go or no-go scrutiny. Analysis and comparison can then be conducted in the same way that a bid comparison should be used for any purchase of expensive project equipment.

In one survey which I conducted for a client, 18 possible suppliers were invited to complete questionnaires, 14 responded, of whom 10 were eliminated for technical reasons. Each of the four remaining candidates was sent a trial project network diagram and invited to attend a separate one-day workshop in the purchaser's offices. Each supplier was given facilities to make a formal sales presentation to relevant managers in the morning session. The afternoons were devoted to system testing and demonstrations based on the trial project network, with detailed questioning by the purchaser's special steering committee. The suppliers were asked to perform a set trial that tested their software at the higher limits of the required system capacities. Only one candidate (not the highest priced) passed all these tests.

Choice of Resource Categories for Scheduling

A common mistake in resource scheduling is to attempt to schedule every conceivable kind of resource used by a project. The result might be some fifty different resource categories, requiring complex input data and producing a vast amount of report material. But it is not usually necessary to schedule every resource in the organisation. For example, if work is being scheduled through a sheet metal department it might not be necessary to schedule the paint shop. If scheduling successfully produces a smooth work pattern in the sheet metal department, the paint shop should automatically receive its work as a smooth flow. In a special-purpose machine tool manufacturing company it was found unnecessary to schedule a small group of control and lubrication engineers, who worked at a rate determined by the release of drawings from the mainstream mechanical engineers (who were scheduled). If in doubt, start by including only a few key resource categories. The range can be extended later if necessary.

These arguments apply only to resource scheduling. They are not valid, of course, for the network planning that must precede resource scheduling (Session 31). Thus the tasks of the paint shop and of the control and lubrication engineers in the above examples must still appear in project networks because, even if their resource usage can be ignored, their work occupies project time so that their tasks add to network path durations.

Coding

Each resource category will require a description and a code. Short codes are used on the network diagram and in project data input. Thus BK might be used as a code for bricklayers, EL for electricians, FT for fitters and so on.

Availability

The computer program will prompt for the number of resource units normally available. So if, for instance, 15 electricians are available in the organisation, 15 would seem to be the appropriate number to enter. However, prudence dictates that a lower level should be declared to allow for sickness, other absences and unplanned work (such as rework or miscellaneous jobs that could not be foreseen and planned). I have typically used 85 per cent of the total resource strength as being available for new project work schedules.

The computer will also prompt for start and finish dates for the availability of each resource. This gives the planner the opportunity to allow for expected future recruitment or staff depletion. This is typically done by entering the expected resource availability number for an appropriate number of future periods. For example, the planner might declare an availability of 12 designers between 1 January 2004 and 30 June 2004, 14 designers from 1 July 2004 to 30 April 2005, and so on according to the expected changes in staffing levels. Naturally these entries must cover at least the total life cycle period of the project or projects being scheduled.

Threshold Availability

Some programs allow the planner to specify a threshold availability level for each resource category, a reserve amount to be drawn upon in times of crisis. If the computer is instructed (say) that the normal level of a resource is ten units, it will attempt to schedule all work using no more than ten units at any time. If, however, additional resources are needed to prevent critical activities being delayed, the computer can call upon the threshold resources. One source of threshold resource might be to allow overtime (a reserve resource that should never be built into normal plans). Other options might be to outsource work or to engage temporary workers.

Resource Cost Rates

The planner will be invited to specify a cost rate for every category of resource. A common method is to express the cost rate in terms of currency units per unit of resource per unit of time. If, for example, activity duration estimates are in days, the cost of assembly fitters might be given as £75, meaning £75 for each fitter per day. Other methods are possible. Costs can usually be given as a total cost for an activity, a method particularly applicable to materials and equipment purchases.

Higher cost rates will usually have to be given for threshold labour resource levels, recognising that these additional resources must be obtained by the temporary employment of people from an external agency or by extending normal working hours into overtime which is paid at premium rates.

Resource Calendars

Some programs will allow resources to be allocated according to different calendars. This can be useful, for example, when some resources work three shifts over seven days and others work only one day shift over five weekdays. This problem can usually be solved, however, by allocating special calendars to the relevant activities rather than to the resource files (see Session 31).

Single Project or Multi-project?

There is little point in attempting to schedule the resources for a new project if the number of resources likely to be available cannot be predicted with a fair degree of certainty. If the project is to occupy all the resources of the organisation, the solution should be simple. If other projects in the organisation are to use the same resources simultaneously, then those other projects must be taken into account if any schedule is to have practical meaning. However, it is best to start by learning how to schedule one project before going to the more complex step of multi-project scheduling.

Scheduling the First Project

Resource scheduling means that data in addition to those required for network time analysis will be required when the project network is fed to the computer. These extra data should also be shown on the network diagram and usually comprise the resource codes and resource amounts applicable to each network activity (see Activity records, below).

Priority Rules

The computer will operate resource scheduling under one or more priority rules, and the planner will probably be given some choice in the application of these. The most fundamental rule is whether the schedule is to be time-limited or resource-limited (Figure 32 - 3).

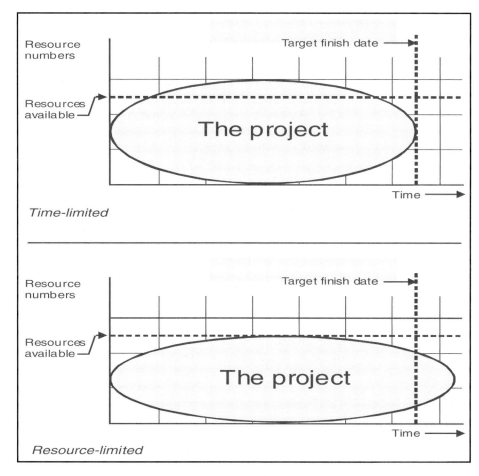

Figure 32 - 3: Time-limited Versus Resource-limited Scheduling

In time-limited scheduling the computer will not allow critical activities to be delayed, so that the project will be scheduled to finish on time even if this means planning for resource levels that exceed the stated normal and threshold levels. The computer should, nonetheless, still attempt to keep overloads to a minimum.

In resource-limited scheduling the computer will never plan for resource usage that exceeds the stated maximum levels, even if this means the project finishing later than the time predicted by the critical path.

The term 'resource levelling' is sometimes used in connection with this process.

The computer applies other priority rules when deciding which activity should be scheduled first when two or more activities compete for the same scarce resource. A common solution is to give priority to activities with least remaining float. However a range of different priority rules might be offered and these can, if considered necessary, be tried to attempt smoother patterns.

Activity Records

When a project is to be resource scheduled, it is necessary first to write the estimated resource usage for every activity on the project network diagram. Thus an activity estimated to need two bricklayers plus two labourers continuously for 20 days might have the network legend 20d 2BK 2LB, where BK and LB have been allocated as the codes for bricklayers and labourers respectively. These data will be input to the computer against prompts on the relevant activity record page on the screen.

The planner might be asked to state whether or not an activity is splittable or non-splittable. A splittable activity may be interrupted to allow temporary diversion of its resources to another more critical activity. Activities are usually assumed to be non-splittable by default.

Rate Constant Resource Usage

The usual default condition is that resources are considered to be rate constant. This means that if (say) four fitters are specified to work on an assembly activity that has an estimated duration of ten days, then that is taken to mean four fitters working full time on the activity, at a constant rate, for ten days. This requirement might be shown on the network diagram in the style shown at Network A in Figure 32 - 4.

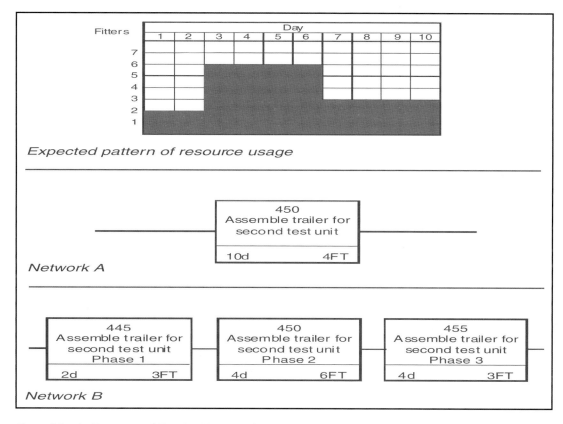

Figure 32 - 4: Two ways of Treating Non-rate Constant Resources.

Non-rate Constant Resource Usage

The better programs allow planners to specify different levels of usage for an activity as it proceeds. In the ten-day assembly example just given, the planner might wish to specify two fitters for the first two days, followed by six fitters for four days, with three fitters taking a further four days to finish the task. This usage pattern is shown at the top of Figure 32 - 4. This information can be entered as a complex resource usage estimate on the computer activity record. It is more difficult to show this condition on the network diagram.

Another way of specifying non-rate constant resources would be to adopt the solution shown in Network B of Figure

32 - 4. Here the activity has been split into three. This makes the intention clearer and easier to denote on the network diagram but, unless the activities can be tied together, there is some risk that the computer will introduce delays between them. This problem can be overcome by tying the activities together using complex precedence constraints: Devaux (1999) gives practical advice on the use of such constraints.

Scheduling by Total Activity Work Content

It is also possible to consider each activity in terms of its total work content rather than by its duration and day-by-day resource usage rate. One very popular program, when presented with an activity such as that shown in Network A of Figure 32 - 4, uses constant work content as its default scheduling condition. In the assembly activity just quoted it is apparent that, whatever the resource usage pattern, the planner is predicting a total work content of 40 fitter days and an activity duration of ten days. If scheduling takes place under total content rules, the computer might decide (apparently arbitrarily) that, if only 3 fitters are available, the duration must be extended to 53.333 days. This is probably not what the planner wants, and can lead to some unexpected, unwanted and very peculiar results in work-to lists and other reports containing times and dates.

Using Common Sense

It should always be remembered that network activity durations and predicted resource usage rates are only estimates, often made subjectively and liable to considerable inaccuracy. Most activities will experience some fluctuation in the use of resources during their progress but these individual variations become insignificant when considered in the context of a complete computer model. Small variations in the day-to-day resource usage of individual activities tend to cancel out or become lost in a project or multi-project model containing more than a few hundred activities. This usually allows the planner to ignore complex resource patterns and adopt the far simpler rate constant option throughout (represented by Network A in Figure 32 - 4). Higher degrees of sophistication are not usually justified.

The Scheduling Process

Time Analysis

The resource scheduling calculation begins with time analysis (see Session 31) because the amount of float possessed by each activity determines priorities and is therefore a vital parameter in resource allocation decisions.

Effect of Target Dates

The specification of target dates (sometimes called scheduled dates) which the planner might impose on one or more activities will affect time analysis. The most obvious candidates for this purpose are the project start and finish activities but target dates can be placed on any milestone activity. If impossible target dates are set, time analysis will be driven into negative float.

Resource Allocation Decisions

The scheduling process varies from one system to another but a common arrangement is that the computer will attempt to schedule every activity at its earliest possible start date, beginning with activities having least float. When there are insufficient resources, the computer will delay the starts of non-critical activities until resources are released by the completion of other activities.

When it is not possible to schedule an activity on or before its latest permissible times without exceeding the resource limit, the computer will determine whether to exceed the limit or delay the activity until resources become available. This decision will be governed according to whether the planner has specified the time-limited or the resource-limited rule.

Remaining Float

The total float of many activities will be eroded as their scheduled times are delayed during resource scheduling. This gives rise to an important category of float known as remaining float. Unfortunately not many programs are capable of reporting remaining float.

Smoothing or Levelling Performance

For a very small project the computer is unlikely to produce schedules as smooth as those which could be produced mentally. In fact the computer process is usually one of resource allocation rather than resource smoothing or levelling. However, this problem becomes less serious as the number of activities being scheduled increases.

However, it must be remembered that a perfectly smooth solution is unlikely to be possible for all resources. That ideal pre-supposes the unlikely suggestion that resource availability and resource requirements can be exactly matched throughout the organisation for every resource at all times.

Computer Reports

Depending on the printer or plotter available, most software programs contain templates that allow a wide range of graphic and text reports to be produced. Because this chapter is concerned with resource management, only reports having particular relevance to resource scheduling will be mentioned here.

Resource Usage Histograms and Tabulations

All competent software can produce a histogram for each category of resource showing the number of units required on the y axis against a timescale along the x axis. Such reports can be attractive in appearance and are often ideal for inclusion in reports to senior management. They are also good for revealing resource usage patterns (including significant overloads and underloads) at a glance.

Histograms primarily show patterns rather than numbers. When actual numbers are wanted, these have to be found by comparing each column on the chart against the vertical scale. This is especially difficult if three-dimensional histograms are plotted, although these can look particularly impressive.

Tabulations are generally of more use for serious analysis of predicted resource usage. The predicted resource quantities can either be set out with the dates running horizontally or (as shown in Figure 32 - 5) vertically. The vertical option will often be found more convenient, and this arrangement usually results in a more compact and easily handled format.

ABC COMPANY RESOURCE SCHEDULE

	DE: Design engineers				DM: Draughtsmen				
Date	Avail	Used	Free	Day cost	Avail	Used	Free	Day cost	Cumulative cost
13May02	70	70	-	7000	45	40	5	3200	10200
14May02	70	70	-	7000	45	40	5	3200	20400
15May02	70	70	-	7000	45	40	5	3200	30600
16May02	70	70	-	7000	45	40	5	3200	40800
17May02	70	70	-	7000	45	40	5	3200	51000
20May02	70	69	1	6900	45	41	4	3280	61180
21May02	70	70	-	7000	45	42	3	3360	71540
22May02	70	70	-	7000	45	44	1	3520	82060
23May02	70	70	-	7000	45	44	1	3520	92580
24May02	70	70	-	7000	45	45	-	3600	103180
27May02	70	70	-	7000	45	45	-	3600	113780
28May02	70	68	2	6800	45	45	-	3600	124180
29May02	70	68	2	6800	45	45	-	3600	134580
30May02	70	70	-	7000	45	45	-	3600	145180
31May02	70	70	-	7000	45	45	-	3600	155780
03Jun02	70	70	-	7000	43	43	-	3440	166220
04Jun02	70	70	-	7000	43	43	-	3440	176660
05Jun02	70	70	-	7000	43	43	-	3440	187100
06Jun02	70	68	2	6800	43	43	-	3440	197340
07Jun02	70	68	2	6800	43	43	-	3440	207580
10Jun02	70	68	2	6800	43	43	-	3440	217820
11Jun02	70	66	4	6600	43	43	-	3440	227860
12Jun02	70	66	4	6600	43	43	-	3440	237900
13Jun02	70	65	5	6500	43	40	3	3200	247600
14Jun02	70	64	6	6400	43	40	3	3200	257200
17Jun02	70	64	6	6400	43	40	3	3200	266800
18Jun02	70	60	10	6000	43	40	3	3200	276000
19Jun02	70	55	15	5500	43	39	4	3120	284620
20Jun02	70	55	15	5500	43	39	4	3120	293240
21Jun02	70	52	18	5200	43	38	5	3040	301480
24Jun02	70	50	20	5000	43	38	5	3040	309520
25Jun02	70	45	25	4500	43	37	6	2960	316980
26Jun02	70	45	25	4500	43	36	7	2880	324360
27Jun02	70	44	26	4400	43	35	8	2800	331560
28Jun02	70	40	30	4000	43	35	8	2800	338360
01Jul02	68	40	28	4000	40	33	7	2640	345000
02Jul02	68	40	28	4000	40	31	9	2480	351480
03Jul02	68	34	34	3400	40	31	9	2480	357360
04Jul02	68	34	34	3400	40	30	10	2400	363160
05Jul02	68	34	34	3400	40	28	12	2240	368800
08Jul02	68	30	38	3000	40	28	12	2240	374040
09Jul02	68	30	38	3000	40	25	15	2000	379040

Figure 32 - 5: Project Resource Usage and Cost Tabulation.

The arrangement in Figure 32 - 5 may not be available in the range of standard reports offered, so that some software customisation might be needed. The results, however, are worth the additional effort. If the data are filtered to include only one project, the cumulative cost column will eventually end in an estimate of project costs for the resources included.

When all projects are included in the tabulation, the 'free' column gives a good indication of when more work must be obtained if people are not to become idle or redundant. Time-limited scheduling will produce negative figures in the 'free' column to indicate periods when additional resources must be provided to maintain the overall delivery programme.

Note that, in the two availability columns shown in Figure 32 - 5, numbers have been reduced at some month-end dates. These allow for staff who have given (or have been given) advance notice of terminating their employment with the organisation.

Work-to Lists

Managers who choose not to schedule resources use the tables derived from time analysis to control work and attempt (at first) to issue all tasks for action at their earliest possible dates. The table columns will probably be headed as follows:

- Activity ID
- Activity description
- Estimated duration
- Earliest start date
- Latest start date
- Earliest finish date
- Latest finish date
- Free float
- Total float

After resource scheduling, two more date columns assume greater importance. These are the scheduled start and finish dates. When these are included in the tabulation, the report becomes a 'work-to' list. The manager responsible for each task is prompted to issue and control work according to the scheduled dates, in the knowledge that this is likely to result in smooth and effective use of the manager's resources. However, if spare resources become available earlier than expected, the manager can scan the work-to list for jobs that can be brought forward to their earliest dates. Conversely, if a task seems likely to run later than its scheduled finish date, the manager can decide whether or not emergency action will be needed depending on the amount of float available.

Filtering

Filtering allows reports to contain data relevant only to the person intended to receive the report. This can be particularly useful, for example, in producing departmental work-to lists. Filtering can be driven by various coding methods. For example, reports can be filtered by the resource codes. Alternatively, codes can be allocated to activity records, using codes that represent different managers.

Sorting

Sorting determines the sequence in which data are presented. For the planner wishing to check data files against hard copy network drawings, unfiltered reports printed in ascending order of activity ID numbers are likely to be most useful. For departmental work-to lists most managers should receive their reports in order of scheduled start dates. A purchasing expeditor might find it useful to receive reports sorted by the expected delivery dates (that is, the completion dates of purchasing activities).

Multi-project Scheduling

The step from single project scheduling to multi-project scheduling is not nearly as great as might be expected. It is simply a matter of adding all the organisation's projects to the computer model and instructing the computer to schedule resources from the net amounts of resources available in total. Care has to be taken in the allocation of activity ID codes and project codes to ensure than no duplication occurs but the method for achieving this will depend on the requirements and capabilities of the particular software.

When all projects are scheduled together an effective model is built up in the computer that represents the total organisation workload. The results have benefits well beyond those enjoyed by individual projects. Forward usage reports (such as that shown in Figure 32 - 5) provide valuable data for resource planning (particularly for manpower planning).

Running what-if? trials can test new project opportunities to predict their effect on projects and resources. Such tests can be run using skeleton or summary networks of the new projects, and should be tested on a second copy of the multi-project model (not on the mainstream working file).

Multi-project scheduling can solve the problem of projects with apparently conflicting priorities. If all projects in the model are given scheduled start and finish dates, time analysis will determine the available float for all tasks in the model and these data will, in turn, drive the resource scheduling. Thus, priority decisions will be made automatically in the system.

Some safeguards are necessary, all aimed at preventing corruption of the main model. With several project managers asking for their projects to be scheduled, and for subsequent updating of those schedules, many people will need access to the system for adding or deleting projects and for reporting progress and timesheet information. One solution to this problem is to set up a small group of people who are specially trained in the use of the software, who can act as a buffer and support group between the users and the system. This group might only need to comprise one person plus one reserve co-ordinator. Managers can be allowed free access to the system, subject to passwords, to obtain information or to report progress. But system changes, logic changes to networks, the input of new projects and re-scheduling must be left to the expert section. One such arrangement, which has been proved in practice, is depicted in Figure 32 - 6.

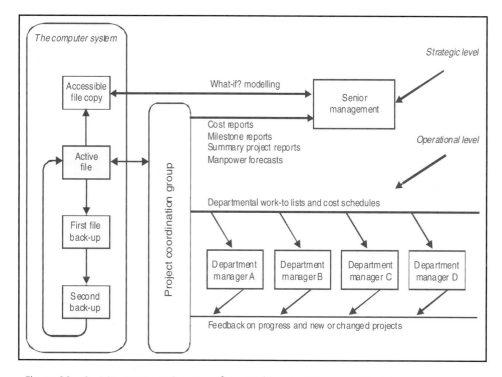

Figure 32 - 6: Management Structure for a Multi-project Resource Model.

The effectiveness of the multi-project model depends on maintaining its integrity at all times. This means ensuring that all project managers in the organisation participate, so that the model does contain all project work. Support and understanding from higher management are crucial factors. Support is needed in providing facilities and ensuring that all relevant staff work with the system to provide input and work to the schedules. Understanding is necessary so that senior managers do not attempt to distort the model by demanding special priority for this project or that. The ideal multi-project schedule should be driven only by delivery promises made to all project customers.

References and Further Reading

Devaux, S. A. (1999), Total Project Control: a Manager's Guide to Integrated Project Planning, Measurement and Tracking, New York, Wiley

Field, M. and Keller, L.. (1998), Project Management, Milton Keynes, The Open University

Lester, A. (1991), Project Planning and Control, 2nd edition, Oxford, Butterworth-Heinemann

Lock, D. (2000), Project Management, 7th edn, Aldershot, Gower

Lockyer, K. G. and Gordon, J. (1996), Project Management and Project Network Techniques, 6th edition, London, Financial Times/Pitman Publising

Reiss, G. (1996), Programme Management Demystified: Managing Multiple Projects Successfully, London, Spon

33   BUDGET AND COST MANAGEMENT

Paul Vollans

"A budget is a method of worrying before you spend instead of afterwards."

Anon.

Introduction

On most projects, derivation of the budget and control of costs are important components of project management. This session covers these topics and also looks at the relevance of cash flow and terms of payment

What is the Project Budget?

The budget can be defined as the authorised money allocated to the completion of the project. Thus if the budget is set at £100,000, then it is expected that the project will be completed for this amount. Even if it becomes evident that the project will cost more or less than this, the budget remains at £100,000 until a revised budget is authorised.

Frequently the total budget is broken down, for planning purposes, into anticipated month by month spend. The total of all such monthly budgets is equal to the total budget for the project.

Budget Derivation

At the outset of a project, a budget will probably be known, but the accuracy may be open to question as it may have been derived without in-depth planning. How can this given budget, lacking in detail as it probably is, be correlated with implementation of all the tasks that detailed planning may present? The answer is to create a Cost Account, as part of the planning process. The relatively accurate project cost that this determines can then be compared with the given budget and adjustments or other actions taken as necessary.

The Cost Account

A simple cost account is shown in Figure 33 - 1. The tasks from the Work Breakdown Structure (see Session 30 - Work Content & Scope Management) are written down the left-hand side. The resources are listed across the top. The numbers in the matrix then indicate how many hours of work will be spent on each task by each resource. It is important to realise that work is not the same as task duration. Writing a report for a customer may require 4 hours of work (ie: time actually spent writing it) but may take 2 weeks to complete because delays by the customer in supplying information mean that the work is interrupted and cannot run continuously. The work dictates the cost of the task and it is for this reason that it appears on the cost account.

WBS	Resource: Jim (Hrs)	Fred (Hrs)	Mary (Hrs)	Alice (Hrs)	Total Lab. (Hrs)	Materials (£)	Expenses (£)
Task 1	10	45		5	60	1500	75
Task 2				20	20		
Task 3	23				23		
Task 4		35			35		
Task 5			35		35	2300	50
Task 6			5	15	20		
Task 7	15	45			60		95
Task 8	12				12		
Task 9				10	10	950	
Task 10	5	35			40		
Totals:	65	160	40	50	315	4750	220
Contingency for risk	10	20	5	0		250	0
Totals (Including contingency)	75	180	45	50			
Labour Rate (£/hr)	15	13	15	19			
Sub-Totals:	1125	2340	675	950		5000	220

Total Project Cost (£): 10310

This simple Cost Account gives a detailed breakdown of the project cost.
Note that a risk contingency has been included as a separately identified item.
This ensures that it is visible, in proportion to real risks, and under the control of the Project Leader.

Figure 33 - 1: Project Cost Account

By adding up the work required of each resource across all tasks and multiplying by the cost rates of the resources, total resource cost on the project can be calculated (see Figure 33 - 1). Furthermore, additional columns can be added to include material costs, expenses and indeed anything else that will contribute to the overall cost of the project. In this way, the cost account builds up a project cost that can be compared with the allocated budget.

Just as the Work Breakdown Structure must include all work associated with a project, the cost account must include all costs. Less obvious examples of these might be transport, warranty, instruction manuals, safety costs etc.

It is helpful to involve each task owner in estimating the work required for their tasks. This draws on their skill and experience in the matter and ensures their buy-in to the agreed target (ie: their budget for the task). Should disagreement arise over the numbers, they can be checked in a variety of ways:

- Check that the task definition is clear
- Break the task down further (Work Breakdown Structure)
- Compare the task with a similar activity on a previous project
- Obtain a second opinion

Risk Provision in the Cost Account

It will be natural for task owners to include their own contingencies within the individual allocations of work shown on the cost account. For example, an estimate of fifty hours of work may be entered as sixty to cover for unforeseen circumstances etc. The ten hours contingency included in this example may give problems for two reasons:

- It is not visible. The budget on the cost account is agreed at sixty hours so this becomes the target and there is little real incentive to achieve anything less than this.
- It has been included to cover for unforseen circumstances that require more hours than planned. Statistically, it is unlikely that all tasks will experience

difficulties and indeed some will require less work than anticipated. Bearing this in mind, it will be seen that the principle of having a contingency for every task, individually, will result in far too many surplus hours of work being built into the job.

One way of addressing these problems is simply to recognise that there are probably more labour-hours in the cost account than are actually required and therefore arbitrarily reduce the total by, say, 10%. This approach, however, is crude and inaccurate (albeit a favourite trick of senior management!). A better way is to encourage a culture in which people give realistic hours for their tasks (ie: no hidden contingency) but also flag up any specific risks they foresee that could jeopardise the completion of the task within budget. By taking an overview of all such risks, across all tasks, a contingency of hours can be introduced by the Project Leader that has some relationship to the overall anticipated risk. This contingency should then be shown on the cost account as a separate budget, to be allocated and managed as necessary by the Project Leader.

Adjusting the Budget

The cost account gives a total project cost that, by virtue of its detail, is likely to be more accurate than any previous budgets. The problem arises if the budget derived from the cost account exceeds any earlier budget set for the project. The following are examples of things that can be done to address the matter:

Change the Objectives of the Project:

- Reduce quality
- Increase the available budget
- Reduce the scope of the project
- Look for variations/extras that the customer will accept

Review the way in which tasks are carried out

- Look for cheaper methods
- Shop around (competitive tendering) for lower cost

materials etc.

- Employ lower cost resources where possible
  Use an alternative approach (eg: a different technology)

Involvement of the project team is desirable when looking at ways to reduce costs. This captures their experience and knowledge but also secures their buy-in to any action decided upon. The exercise, however, should be commercially driven by the Project Leader so that both realism and the desire to achieve the key project goals maintain a high priority.

Once the total cost shown by the cost account has been accepted by senior management, then it should be signed off as the agreed and authorised budget for the project (it might or might not be the same as the original budget).

- Obtaining commitment
  - Contracts/Orders
  - Purchase Orders
  - Sub-Contracts

Uses of the Cost Account

The cost account has many uses:

- It gives the total cost of the project
- It gives budgets for each resource to work to on each task
- It can indicate areas of risk - for example, resources that carry a disproportionately large amount of the total work
- By tracking actual work as the project proceeds and comparing the numbers with those in the cost account, early warning of potential problems becomes evident
- It gives total labour hours which, assuming that at least the approximate duration of the project is known, can be used to give a rough estimation of overall resource requirements

The Timing of Expenditure - The 'S' Curve

The cost account builds up a total project cost, but it does not provide any information about when in time those costs will be incurred. To do this, the project planning process must be carried forward by developing a dependency diagram and estimating task durations. This will enable a gantt chart to be created, showing clearly the periods in time for which each task is active (and therefore incurring cost). Thus a cost account will show the cost of each task and a Gantt chart will show when in time that cost will be incurred. It is then possible to construct a curve showing the cumulative project cost at any point in time. An example is shown in Figure 33 - 2. Other ways of looking at it are that it shows the rate of spend on the project, and shows the target cumulative budget per month (or other period).

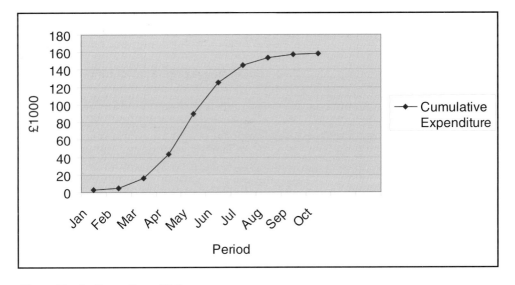

Figure 33 - 2: Expenditure 'S' Curve.

Cash Flow

Definition

The cash flow is the difference between expenditure and income in a given period. For example, if a project for a certain customer incurs a cost in one month of £100,000, but in the same month, the customer is invoiced for £120,000, then the project cash flow in that month is £20,000. Clearly, the cost incurred and the amount invoiced must relate to the same project.

Not all projects will necessarily have a direct income (for example: capital improvement projects), in which case the cash flow will always be negative.

The cumulative cash flow is the sum of the cash flows per period up to the current period.

Determining Cash Flow

The 'S' Curve (see above) gives both the expenditure per period and the cumulative expenditure. A second line can be drawn representing the income (revenue) to the project. A third line, representing the difference between the first two, is the cash flow. An example is given in Figure 33 - 3.

The cash flow will depend very much on the nature of the project. For example, on capital projects with no revenue, it will always be negative. For a construction project undertaken for a paying customer, the cash flow should, ideally, rapidly become positive. This is considered in more detail below.

The Importance of Cash Flow

Cash flow is important for a number of reasons:

- Project Tracking - By tracking actual expenditure and income, the period and cumulative cash flows can be calculated and compared with the planned cash flow. Any discrepancy may indicate a problem (or opportunity!)

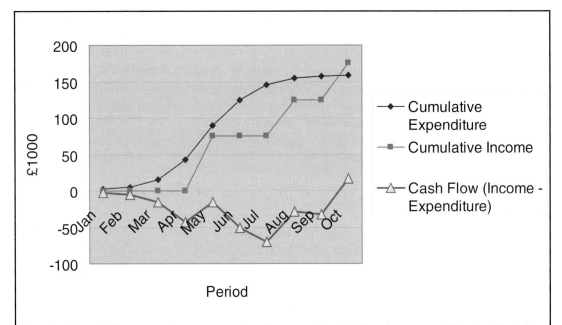

Note: In this cash-flow example, payments have been received in May, August and October. Cash-flow is negative for most of the project, July being the worst month when it is -£75k. The project achieves a positive cash-flow in early October when the third payment is received.

Figure 33 - 3: Cash Flow

- ◆ Funding Level - The planned cash-flow will give an indication of the largest negative expenditure on the project and when this will occur. Thus funding for the project (eg: a bank loan) must be at least equal to this sum. More generally, funding arrangements (in terms of both timing and amount) must cover any planned occurrence of negative cash flow.
- ◆ Overall Profit and Loss - The final cumulative cash flow on a project can be viewed as the profit.
- ◆ Establishing Terms of Payment - The project leader often has at least some control over cash flow. One method is to give close attention to the terms of payment (how much is paid and when) associated with the order from the customers and any orders placed on sub-suppliers. In essence, the customer should be paying as much as possible as early as possible, the reverse being the case

with suppliers. As an example, consider a contract with a customer wherein the customer pays 30 days after delivery of certain goods. If these are being obtained from a sub-supplier then it would be worth trying to negotiate, say, a 60 day payment period with the sub-supplier. In this way, payment is received from the customer before the supplier is paid. Certainly payments to the sub-supplier in less than 30 days should be resisted as this will result in a negative cash flow.

- Company Cash-Flow - By adding up the cash-flows across all projects and bringing any other income or expenditure into the frame, the total cash flow for the company can be found. Clearly it is preferable that this is always positive, or only negative for relatively short periods. Any prolonged instances of negative cash flow will ultimately drive the company into liquidation. It is worth noting that overall company cash flow can cause apparent problems at individual project level. For example, a keen and able project team driving a project ahead of schedule may be prevented from buying an expensive item of equipment earlier than the time originally planned simply because to do so, whilst good for the project, would severely dent company cash flow. Another example may be where senior management insist that certain equipment is delivered to site in an unfinished condition (for instance: not fully tested). From the project point of view this can cause all manner of problems but if delivery of the equipment is a payment milestone, then the problems are offset by benefits to company cash flow.

Forecasting

The Need for Forecasting

As we have seen, the cost account gives a budget for the total project. Whatever this total cost is, it would be remarkable indeed if the final actual cost was exactly equal to the budget! In reality, there is likely to be at least some deviation (hopefully small or downward). At any point in the life of a project, the Project Leader may be required to assess what the projected final cost may be. This figure is called the Estimate at Completion (EAC). At the outset of the project, it will be the same as the budget, but as the project proceeds, it may or may not be the same. The methods of determining the EAC are generally referred to as forecasting.

Forecasting Techniques

1 Actual plus remaining budget - A relatively simple way of estimating the EAC, that can be used at any time during the project, is to simply add together the actual cost of work performed to date (ACWP) and whatever remains of the original budget. An example will illustrate the idea: Suppose a 12 month project has a budget of £12,000, the budget spend per month being £1,000. If at the end of month 7 the actual spend to date is found to be £7,500 (ie: £500 more than it should have been), then the EAC at that point in time would be actual to date (£7,500) plus the remaining budget (5 months at £1,000, ie: £5000) giving an EAC of £12,500.

2 Actual plus re-estimate of remainder - In this approach, the EAC is determined by re-estimating the cost of remaining work on the project (Estimate to Completion, or ETC) and adding it to the ACWP. This technique is frequently used towards the end of the project, where the ETC is relatively straightforward to re-estimate. To use it in the early stages of the project may involve much work in implementing the re-estimate.

3   Trend - The EAC is determined by extrapolating the S curve showing actual spend to date. The method can only be used around mid-project onwards, when sufficient historical data has been collected for meaningful extrapolation to be carried out.

4   Using the Cost Account - As we have seen, the cost account gives the total project budget. By regularly updating it with both actual data and any projected future amendments and changes, then it will give the EAC. The original cost account, giving the original budget, should be retained for record purposes. Whilst keeping the cost account updated in this way can take time, it is the most accurate way of forecasting and gives the EAC at any time during the project.

With all these forecasting techniques, it is important to realise that the EAC does not replace the budget. The budget is the authorised spend on the project at the outset and it does not change until a revised budget is formally authorised.

Monitoring and Controlling Project Costs

Cost Reporting

It is a truism to say that on most projects, costs must be controlled and failure to do this successfully on high-profile projects is frequently a national news item! How, though, can costs be controlled successfully? A number of key factors are involved in the process:

- Clear Goals - The project must be well-defined, with clear, measurable deliverables
- Realistic Budget - The project budget must be realistic, based on sound planning that includes formal risk assessment
- Good Reporting Systems - reporting systems must be set up so that accurate, necessary data is collected at the right times and used in the right ways to identify problems at an early stage

♦ Good Change Control System - Any change on the project must be carefully assessed and tightly controlled

♦ Good Leadership - To instil a desire to work within the budget and seek solutions that are commercially and financially sound

♦ Good Sub-Contract Management - Including clear definition and good reporting and monitoring

Cost Data Collection

Data relating to the original budget should already be available. This should include a detailed cost account and an S Curve giving monthly and cumulative budget. As the project proceeds it will be necessary to collect additional data. This should be done on a task by task basis and typical information collected for each task could include the following:

♦ Time spent by each resource on the task (timesheet data)

♦ Percentage of work completed

♦ Materials purchased, with actual costs

♦ Other costs incurred on the task (eg: expenses)

♦ Current EAC for the task

♦ Risk issues on the task (particularly those involving costs)

For each item of data, the following should also be defined:

♦ Who will collect and format the required data (usually the Task Owner)

♦ At what intervals is the data required? (This will usually be monthly)

♦ What is the required accuracy and format of the data?

♦ Why is the data required? - Collecting unnecessary data should be avoided

♦ Who receives and uses the data?

A matrix can be developed to indicate who reports what and when.

Cost Collection Systems

Cost collection systems are many and varied and almost invariably computer based. They will generally include some or all of the following elements:

- Timesheet system
- Purchase Order control system
- Expenses tracking system
- Customer invoicing system
- Supplier invoice system

Change Control

Change can occur on a project for many reasons. It may be client or market driven, may arise from technological development, or may simply be inspired by an over-zealous member of the project team! If this is allowed to happen in an uncontrolled way the impact on cost (as well as other aspects of the project) can be considerable. Any change control process, therefore, must ensure, first of all, that any proposed change is critically and quantitatively assessed. A complete change control procedure includes:

- Definition
- Analysis
- Authorisation
- Re-planning
- Communication

Analysing the change

Analysis of a proposed change is best implemented using a Change Request Form. In this way, information is presented consistently and the right questions are asked. An example of such a form is shown in Figure 33 - 4. (Also see Session 34).

Change Request Form

Date:	Project Name:		Project No:
Project Manager:			Change Request No:

Description of proposed change:

Approx. Cost (£):	Critical Path:	Yes/No

Reasons for proposed change:

Consequences of NOT implementing the change:

WBS Tasks effected:

Effect on Project Objectives:

Effect on project commercial justification:

Effect on project timescales:

Effect on project cost:

Risk assessment results:

Other comments:

Authorised:	Yes/No	Signed:	Date:

Figure 33 - 4: Change Request Form

Authorisation

Any proposed change should be formally authorised before it becomes an integral part of the project. Such authorisation may depend on the value or other characteristic of the change. For example, the Project Leader may be empowered to authorise changes up to a certain value, after which the endorsement of a Director is required. Each authorised change can be transferred to a Change Register - a document summarising all authorised changes to date. It should be noted that the original project definition together with the Change Register will define exactly the current extent of the project.

Some authorised changes may require a formal increase or decrease in the project budget.

Re-Plan

The authorised change may have significant impact on the plan, which must be updated as necessary after each change is authorised

Communication

Once the change has been authorised, all stakeholders in the project should be advised as appropriate.

Claims

Claims can form an important part of any project that involves a customer/supplier relationship (usually a contract). Essentially a claim is a request by either the customer or the supplier for compensation (usually cost or time) arising from a perceived change or variation. Such a claim may be rigorously resisted by the other party! An example will illustrate the idea: A supplier may be contracted by the customer to carry out certain work on the customer's premises. The supplier may, however, through no fault of his own, waste much time and effort trying to gain entry to the site. In consequence, the supplier may claim extra costs and/or time delays arising from the problem.

Justification of Claims

Any claim must be justified as fully as possible using documentary and other evidence as appropriate. Thus for best results in claims management, good record keeping is essential.

Conditions of Contract and Claims

In processing claims, a good knowledge and understanding of the applicable terms and conditions is essential. The reason for this is that the terms and conditions may specify what claims are permissible and how the claims should be dealt with. For instance, the Terms and Conditions may require a contractor or supplier to notify the customer in writing, within thirty days, of any claim he may be intending to make. Thus if the claim is submitted six months after the event it will not be contractually valid.

Liquidated Damages

A purchaser placing an order with a contractor or supplier may require liquidated damages to be incorporated into the contract. They are intended, in principle, to give the purchaser some financial compensation in the event of late delivery of the goods or services and are usually expressed in the form "X% of the Contract Value to be paid by the supplier to the purchaser for each week, up to a maximum of Y weeks, for which the goods or services are late. X and Y would be specified in the contract and might typically be 0.5% and 10 weeks respectively. It will be clear from this that where liquidated damages apply, it is very much in the suppliers interests to claim for any delays he believes have been caused by the customer or are otherwise outside the scope of his contract.

Time and Cost Aspect of Claims

Claims will usually be for cash, extension of time, or both. Generally, any claim for an extension of time is likely to have a cost implication. Time can be particularly important where liquidated damages are concerned (see above).

Unresolved Claims and Budgeting

A supplier may incur a cost for what is believed to be extra work and submit a claim to that effect. Some considerable time may then elapse before the claim is actually resolved and the supplier finds out for sure what payment (if any) he will receive. Thus there exists a situation where a supplier has incurred additional cost but does not know how much or when he will be paid. This situation can be incorporated into the project income/expenditure profile by allowing for the actual cost of the extra work and also including an assumed income (yet to be agreed). This sum is referred to as an Unagreed Variation and can be shown in the project cash-flow as such. As there is no guarantee that the supplier will receive any income for his claim, it is usual for a percentage of the claim value to be allowed for in the project accounting. For example, if the claim is seen as highly justified, 50% of its value may be used, whereas only 10% of the value of a speculative or poorly justified claim may be included.

Claim Control

Any project should incorporate a claim control procedure. This will be closely linked with the Change Control procedures described above. A Schedule of Unagreed Variations (see above) can be included to give an on-going summary of outstanding claims and an estimate of their value.

Dealing With Claims

This requires good negotiating skills and a sound understanding of the terms and conditions of the contract. It is frequently helpful to resolve several claims together (rather than dealing with them one at a time) as this allows movement onto other issues if an impasse is temporarily encountered on one item.

Measurement of Cost and Work

Tracking costs on a project and comparing actual spend at any point in time with forecast budget at that point is useful but does not in itself give the full picture. It is quite possible, for example, that a project spending on plan is actually behind in terms of work completed. Thus for full knowledge of the state of a project it is necessary to track both spend and work in a way which can relate the two. This concept, called Earned value Analysis, is detailed in Session 35.

Methods of Payment (Terms of Payment)

Definition

The Terms of Payment in a contract define how much is paid by whom and to whom, and when such payments will be made. They will generally be an integral part of the Terms and Conditions of the contract. They may include other relevant requirements such as currency and how eligibility for such payments will in practice be authorised. The nature of the terms and conditions will depend on the nature of the contract (value, risk, timescale, location, complexity etc.)

Typical Types

Terms of Payment come in all sorts of forms, some of which are of low risk to the purchaser (eg: payment against results) and some of which are of low risk to the supplier (eg: payment in advance). A few common approaches are described as follows:

- Payment in advance - The customer pays all or some of the contract value before any work is undertaken by the supplier
- Payment against results/milestones - Payment (or part payment) is made at the satisfactory achievement of identified events eg: 10% of the contract value upon production of approved drawings and 50% upon delivery of equipment to site
- Staged payments - Payment based upon satisfactory completion of identified stages eg: 20% of contract value when pump 1 is put into service, 20% when pump 2 is put into service
- Retentions - Payments withheld by a purchaser, usually for a period of 1 year after completion of a contract, to cover warranty or similar issues. If, for example, the retention was 5% for 12 months, then 5% would be deducted from each payment that became due to the supplier and the money so retained would be paid 12 months after completion of the contract (subject to any deduction for poor performance, warranty issues etc.)

As has been considered already in this section (see above), terms of payment, with both customers and suppliers, are vitally important to cash flow.

Payment Protection - Bank / Parent Company Guarantees

When placing work with a supplier it is possible to gain some financial protection against the supplier's failure to perform by requiring, as part of the contract, a legally binding guarantee from either a bank or, if appropriate, the supplier's parent company. The terms of such a guarantee would require the guarantor to pay compensation to the purchaser in the event of failure on the part of the supplier.

34   CHANGE CONTROL

Dennis Lock

"Where there are changes, there are always business opportunities."
Minoru Makihara (b. 1930), Japanese executive.

The project started as scheduled on 1 June and work progressed unchanged and without interruption for two years. It culminated in delivery one month ahead of schedule, £100,000 below budget, to the customer's original specification and complete satisfaction of all the other stakeholders. This tale should, of course, have been prefixed 'Once upon a time' because it is a fairy story. No project of any significant size and complexity can be expected to run smoothly from start to finish without change. Changes come in all sizes and from all directions. They can produce welcome additions to profitable work or waste time and money. The purpose of this session is to discuss how changes can be recognised and managed to best advantage.

It would be possible to list many Pathways topics that are either affected by changes or which could cause change but by far the most significant is Session 30, which covers work content and scope management. If a project is not adequately defined and managed in these respects from the outset project management will, at least, be difficult and any hope of effective change management can be abandoned.

Introduction to Change Control

How to Recognise a Project Change

A change might be defined as an event or process that alters the intentions of the project customer or contractor as stated in the project definition. The most obvious meaning of project definition in this context is the project scope or nature as defined in a formal contract between the customer and the contractor. However, changes can also arise from sources insider the project organisation, often without the customer's intention or knowledge and not necessarily altering the agreed project deliverables. Changes can also arise after the project has been delivered, as a result of the project customer's experience in operating the product or delivered system.

Some apparent changes do not really change the project definition and lie outside the scope of this chapter. Here is an example: An engineer has been given a complex task to design an electromechanical sub-assembly as a small part of a large project. After working for four weeks, the engineer realises that her approach to the difficult problem is wrong. She clears her computer files and sets out again to achieve the desired solution. The project definition has not changed. This is simply the sort of error that can happen to any competent engineer working on a high technology project. Four weeks' time and money have been wasted, but there has been no change to the project definition. Although some re-scheduling and progress action might be needed to make up the lost time, formal change control action would be inappropriate and unnecessary.

Now suppose that the same engineer has issued her specifications and drawings and that steps have been put in hand to implement her design. Purchase orders have been issued for components and work has started on the manufacture of some parts. If, now, the engineer wishes to change and re-issue her drawings, the work of others in the project organisation will be affected with more serious consequences for time and costs. Although re-issuing the drawings would not change the project scope, it would change the project definition if we regard definition as meaning the content of the project as specified in issued documents, including drawings and specifications.

So, one convenient way of identifying a change, is to say that it is any event that causes a significant change in any formally issued project contract document, drawing or specification. This might not work on all occasions but it is a useful rule of thumb.

Figure 34 - 1 illustrates possible sources of changes (and a range of possible associated documents) for manufacturing and large construction or petrochemical projects. With a little imagination, this diagram can be adapted so that it applies to most kinds of projects involving the design, fulfilment and supply of a project to a paying customer.

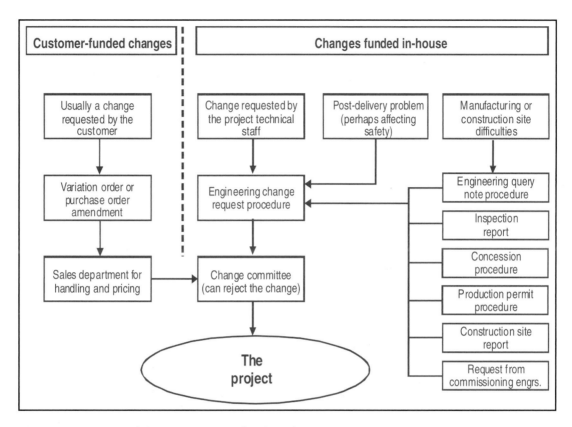

Figure 34 - 1: Some of the Many Sources of Project Changes.

The Need for Change Control

The best way to appreciate the need for change control is to consider what might happen with no control at all. Imagine that any interested stakeholder inside or outside the project organisation could be allowed to introduce a project change without let or hindrance at any stage of the active project life cycle. There is no need to describe the possibilities for waste, technical failure and general mayhem that might result. Chaos would reign. Accepting, therefore, that some degree of change authorisation and control is needed, it is time to consider some appropriate procedures.

A Framework of Procedures for Change Control

A convenient method for describing change control procedures is to follow the various sequences by which a proposed project change might travel through an organisation from the initial request to its final fate. A fairly typical route is depicted in Figure 34 - 2.

Sources of Change Requests

Strictly speaking, any person regardless of seniority or position inside or outside the project organisation should be allowed to request a change. There is no harm in asking. The control point occurs when the change is considered for rejection or approval. Some procedural rules must, however, be imposed.

Any request for a change should be made formally, in writing, using an appropriate form. The nature of this form will depend on the source, as explained in the following paragraphs. The minimum requirement for any such request is that the proposed change should be described in unambiguous detail. Other requirements will depend on whether the change is requested by a paying customer or by some other originator. The origination of any change request is represented by step 1 in Figure 34 - 2.

Changes Requested by a Paying Customer

Changes required by a client or customer obviously claim special priority. The contractor has little choice other than to accept and implement the change, unless it can be shown that the change would adversely affect safety, reliability or some other vital project deliverable. The contractual relationship between customer and contractor should have been established at the beginning of the project by a purchase order or some other form of contract document. The appropriate document for requesting a change should therefore be either a contract variation order or a purchase order amendment.

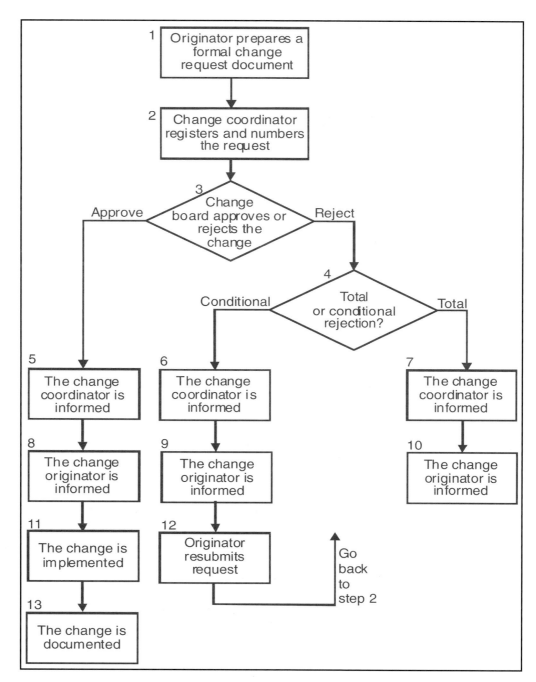

Figure 34 - 2: A Typical Change Control Sequence.

Unless the project is being carried out internally or on some form of cost reimbursement basis (that is, not for a firm price), any customer-requested change will probably qualify for a change to the total price. Although some changes might result in a price reduction, a price increase is usually far more likely.

When the original contract was made the customer no doubt exercised commercial prudence and offered the project to a number of competitors. It is well known that genuine competition can keep prices down. This situation changes dramatically when a contractor quotes or negotiates a price increase resulting from a customer-requested change to an existing contract. The competitors have left the scene now and the contractor has a one-to-one monopoly with the customer. There is, therefore (to put it politely) no need to exercise price restraint. Indeed, some contractors have claimed that they make little or no profit on the original contract but gain their most significant profits from subsequent changes. Any change, nonetheless, can disrupt project work and delay completion. Even profitable customer changes can, therefore, be a decided nuisance.

Dayworks Orders

Dayworks orders are a special category of project change typically found in construction projects. An example would be on a fixed-price refurbishment contract where the customer asks the site foreman 'While your people are working in that corridor do you think they might be asked to paint the walls inside the cupboards too? This is work not allowed for in the original contract price and a typical arrangement is that the contractor performs the work on a cost-plus basis against day-works sheets (torn from a duplicate, serially numbered pad) which the customer signs as required, on the spot. The contractor and the customer each keep a copy of every dayworks sheet until the day of reckoning arrives.

Dayworks orders are not used to change fundamental design, so that only the cost of the additional work needs to be taken into account. Control of dayworks is therefore a special case, not usually requiring all the formality of the change control procedures shown in Figure 34 - 2 and about to be described in this chapter. Unfortunately, however, the number of dayworks sheets on a contract of long duration can build up alarmingly, leading to great difficulty when the time eventually comes to reconcile costs and work done at the time of final invoicing. Standard commonsense commercial practice is essential. This rests on two conditions:

1   Dayworks should only be authorised by a nominated, suitably senior member of the customer's management.
2   All copies of dayworks sheets must be logged and securely kept by the customer against the time when costs and work have to be reconciled against the contractor's final invoice.

Engineering Design Changes from Within the Project Organization

Internally generated changes can arise for a number of reasons. Perhaps an engineer or designer wishes to re-issue a drawing, specification or work instruction to correct a mistake or to effect a perceived improvement of some kind. If the proposed change is going to affect work already put in hand, then control must be exercised. In most organisations the originator will be expected to document the request using an engineering change request (ECR), engineering modification request (EMR) or some similarly named form. A typical form will allow space for the following entries:

- Serial number, by which the change can be identified
- Name and department of the originator
- Drawing and specification numbers that would be affected by the change
- Brief description of the proposed change
- Reason for the request
- Estimated effect on project time and costs
- Authorisation or rejection decision and signature
- Reason, if rejected
- Any special conditions attached to the approval or rejection.

Examples of forms associated with change control can be found in Lock (2000).

Changes Arising from Project Implementation

Implementation in this section means the activities needed to change the designers' intentions into the completely finished project.

Suppose, for example, that a manufacturing department finds that a bonded assembly collapses into its constituent parts as soon as the clamps are removed even though instructions in the relevant drawing and specification have been followed faithfully. There might be a request to bolt or rivet the components together or to use a different adhesive. In an organisation where quality is taken seriously, any such request to deviate from the relevant drawing or specification would have to be submitted to the engineering department on a request form called a production permit. After obtaining approval from the relevant engineer, the production permit becomes part of the official project documentation. It might be used subsequently as the basis of a change request so that the drawings and specifications could be changed permanently.

A different but related case occurs when a product component fails to pass an inspection or test stage. Technically the component exhibits a non-conformance that must be documented on an inspection report by the inspecting authority. If the non-conformance is marginal, a request might be made to the relevant design engineer to allow the component to pass. If the engineer agrees, the inspection report becomes a manufacturing concession document, which must be countersigned by the responsible design authority and kept on record. It might be decided that the original inspection or test tolerances were too close, and that they can be relaxed. This, also, could lead to a formal engineering change request to allow a permanent change of the drawings and specifications.

Design Freeze

Changes made at the beginning of project design usually have less serious consequences than changes made when most design is complete. Many organisations recognise this by having a project milestone called a 'design freeze' or 'stable design condition'. Such milestones act as a watershed, with any request for a design change after the design freeze being refused unless the originator can make an essential case.

Change Co-ordination

Not only can a change introduce additional time and costs into a project but, the change control process itself can add to those delays. To ensure that each change request is dealt with expeditiously throughout its journey, some form of progressing is needed. In other words, the change control process itself needs a control procedure. This is best effected by appointing a change control clerk, often called a change co-ordinator or change co-ordination clerk. This can usually be a part-time appointment, so that an existing technical clerk or person of similar status can undertake the work with no need to recruit an additional person.

The change co-ordinator's duties can be seen clearly by reference to Figure 34 - 2. The co-ordination process starts when the originator of each engineering change request, production permit, concession or similar document passes the form to the co-ordinator for action. The first duty of the co-ordinator is to record summary details of the request in a change register, from which a serial number is allocated. The co-ordinator must then see that all subsequent stages leading to implementation or rejection of the request take place with no undue delay, and that all interested stakeholders are kept informed.

The change register should have, at least, the following fields for each change:

- Serial number
- Name of originator
- Department or other contact details for the originator
- A reference to the part of the project affected by the change
- A brief, descriptive title of the change
- Columns allowing the state of progress to be added
- A final sign-off column to be used when the change is either implemented or rejected.

Approval or Rejection

Factors Governing Change Approval or Rejection

A project stakeholder requesting a change cannot always be expected to foresee or comprehend all the consequences of the proposed change on the project or other stakeholders. Every change request must, therefore be considered carefully against a number of factors before it can be approved or rejected. Some of these factors are listed below:

- Has the paying customer requested the change? (If so, there is usually little doubt that the change will be approved, subject to reliability and safety considerations)
- How much, if anything, would the proposed change add to project costs? If so, how can these costs be recovered, if at all?
- Will the proposed change extend the duration of the project? If so, by how much? Is this acceptable?
- Would the change affect health and safety issues in any way at any stage of the project life cycle?
- Would the operational reliability of the finished project be affected?
- Would the change cause scrap and re-work?
- Would the change render any two or more components of the project non-interchangeable. (A firm rule here is that non-interchangeable parts must have different part

numbers. If a change does make a component non-interchangeable with previously made components, the revised drawing must be given a completely new number - not just a new revision number.)

♦ If the change is likely to affect a number of similar items currently undergoing construction or manufacture, should the change be made retrospective or should it apply only to future items. If the latter, at what stage should the change be introduced (known as the point of embodiment).

Change Committee or Change Board

From the above list of relevant factors governing whether or not a change should be allowed, it is apparent that more than one person in an organisation will normally be required to decide the fate of each change request. In many organisations a change committee or change board is formed to carry out this task. A change board should contain at least one senior member from the design and quality assurance departments, together with a representative of the departments responsible for project implementation (manufacture or construction, for example). The following are key roles:

1   The design authority. This is a person, such as an architect or chief engineer, who is competent to consider the effect that a proposed change might have on the performance of the delivered project.

2   The inspecting or quality authority. This person, together with the design authority, will be interested in how the proposed change might affect reliability, safety and other quality aspects.

3   The manufacturing or construction department. One or more representatives from these implementation departments will be interested in the effect of a change on work already completed, on work in progress and on work still to come.

4   Purchasing manager. The buying department should be involved if a proposed change is likely to affect one or more outstanding purchase orders.

5   Commercial or legal manager. It might be necessary to involve a commercial manager who can advise on the contractual or other legal aspects of some changes.

6   Planning and cost engineers. These engineers will be expected to estimate the effect of a change on project costs and timescale.

The nature and frequency of change board meetings will, naturally, depend on the size and complexity of the project or projects being undertaken by the organisation. It is not suggested that all those listed above will need to attend every meeting but the first three named will probably constitute the quorum.

Change board meetings can be avoided by circulating change requests to the board members. This saves the time of busy individuals but at the expense of the discussion and full consideration that can only be achieved at face-to-face communications in meetings.

The Approval or Rejection Decision

The change board might make one of several possible decisions when considering each change. The following list includes most, if not all, of the options:

1   Approve the change and authorise its implementation on new project work.

2   Approve the change and authorise retrospective implementation, causing scrapping or modification of parts already made.

3   Approve the change and authorise total implementation, which might involve recalling parts of the project already delivered to the customer.

4   Approve the change but impose limitations on its implementation.

5   Reject the change provisionally, but ask the originator to supply more information and/or re-submit the request.

6   Reject the change outright, giving reasons.

Change Implementation

If a change has been rejected (items 5 and 6 above) the co-ordinator must inform the originator and sign the change off in the register. For approved changes the co-ordinator must ensure that the change board's instructions are conveyed to those responsible for taking action.

Documentation

It is important for many reasons that the true as-built condition of a project should be recorded when the project is closed down. This is important for several reasons. Here are some of them:

- The contractor will have some obligation to provide post-project services to the customer. This might be difficult or impossible if there is no record of the project in its finished, as-built state.
- Many companies use design information from previous projects to assist in designing future projects. This is sometimes called using retained engineering. In addition to the obvious cost-saving benefit of this approach, the design engineers should be encouraged by the knowledge that the previous designs have been used successfully, and that the relevant drawings and specifications are free from errors. This, of course, demands that those documents have been fully corrected or otherwise amended to include all changes.
- The as-built condition of a project might become an issue in any post-project investigation, particularly where the professional competence or liability of the contractor is questioned.
- In some industries where reliability is particularly important (such as defence or aerospace) traceability becomes an important factor whenever a technical failure of some kind occurs in the delivered project. Suppose, for example, that an aircraft crashes. The accident investigators should have access to any

changes, concessions or production permits (identifiable from their serial numbers) relating to the particular aircraft. Properly managed documentation is essential to satisfy this requirement.

The co-ordinator should be responsible for following up every approved changed to make sure that it is implemented in all respects, especially including its documentation. The change register can be used as the control tool.

Effect on Time and Costs

When a change will affect costs and timescale, the project budgets and schedules must be updated so that they remain as accurate as possible and useful as control tools. As Devaux (1999) rightly stresses, all change management has to take place with the framework of the work breakdown structure in mind, and this will influence particularly how budgets are updated.

Updating the Project Budget: for Customer-funded Changes

The original project budget should have been spread over all items of the work breakdown structure. There should also be a reserve, unallocated budget related to contingencies and other below-the-line items from the original estimates.

When a change is approved, if the customer can be asked to pay, the relevant part of the budget can be increased accordingly.

It is not always agreed how changes should affect earned value analysis calculations. When the customer is paying, however, the earned value (BCWP) of the changed tasks (including work to be scrapped) can be left intact because the customer has paid for the work. Rework must be added to the schedule of new work, balanced by adding the new funding to the budget.

The Budget for Changes not Funded by the Customer

If the customer cannot be asked to pay for a change, it might still be possible to increase the relevant budget by 'drawing down' the appropriate sum from the reserve budget.

When earned value analysis is being performed, the earned value of any changed task must be judged afresh. For scrapped work the earned value reverts to zero.

Schedule Updating

Every project schedule must be updated at suitable intervals so that it keeps in step with progress. Changes, of course, affect the state of progress. The project planner must, therefore, take every change into account at each schedule update.

Conclusion

No project manager or creative worker likes their work to be interrupted by a change. However, changes can help to improve the final delivered quality of a project. Where changes are requested by a paying customer, they can rack up the selling price and increase profits. It might not always be necessary to include all the formalities described in this session but it is always essential to exercise some form of restraint in allowing changes and to make sure that every change is properly recorded for its effects on project documentation and charges for work done.

References and Further Reading

Devaux, S.A., (1999), Total Project Control, New York, Wiley

Hamilton, A. (1997), Management by Projects: Achieving Success in a Changing World, London, Thomas Telford

Harrison, F.L., (1992), Advanced Project Management: A Structured Approach, Aldershot, Gower

Lock, D., (2000), Project Management, 7th edn, Aldershot, Gower

35   EARNED VALUE MANAGEMENT

Steve Wake

"Any general statement is like a check drawn on a bank. Its value depends on what is there to meet it".
Ezra Pound (1885-1972), U.S. poet and critic. ABC of Reading (1934)

Introduction

Earned Value Management is a system of project control that is based on a structured approach to planning, cost collection and performance measurement. It is a proven process that provides strong benefits for project control. It facilitates the integration of project scope, schedule and cost objectives and the establishment of a baseline plan for performance measurement during the execution of a project. Furthermore, it provides a sound basis for problem identification, corrective actions and management re-planning as required.

History

Earned Value has its origins in the 'scientific management' methods of the late Industrial Revolution. When factories were run by engineers not business graduates. Its roots lie in the comparison of what it actually cost against what it was planned to cost.

Leaping forward to 1962 the US Navy developed Project Evaluation Review Technique (PERT) and then married it to cost. Hence PERT/Cost which included a 'cost of work' report amongst its outputs.

In 1967 the US Airforce created the Cost Schedule Control System Criteria (C/SCSC). A set of 35 criteria that described the characteristics that a supplier's system had to have in order for it to do business with the US Department of Defense. Firmly embedded within these criteria was the concept of Earned Value. It was mandated and a huge support industry grew around it. Projects still failed and went way over budget. It was perceived by many to be a bureaucratic and expensive reporting over-head as well as a ready source of easy income by suppliers who incorporated the costs of their Earned Value Systems back into their projects whilst running their own organisation on an entirely separate system.

In order to halt this notion that Earned Value was all about contractual compliance rather than best practice project management it was decided in 1996 to revisit the criteria. But now, under the ownership of industry rather than government. The result was a not particularly radical overhaul of the criteria but which crucially resulted in the creation of the Earned Value Management Systems (EVMS) guideline. This in turn became the American National Standard Institute/Electronic Industry Association Guide to Earned Value ANSI/EIA 748 in 1998. The document contains the text of the revised criteria but no implementation guidance. Shifting the emphasis to improved business process and extending its use to the wider non-defence community is proving to be a slow and arduous task. A great idea hampered by the legacy of its defence origins.

Elsewhere in the world other countries have devised their own national versions of the criteria. In most instances an attempt to ensure reciprocity of these criteria has been made. If a system has local approval it is also acceptable to another country with its own system.

Countries with fully developed Earned Value Systems are the USA, Canada, Australia and Sweden.

Countries developing systems are the UK and Japan. In mid 2001 Brazil and Germany also joined this expanding community.

The UK has not favoured a mandated approach and consequently its progress has been slower but possibly surer. Industry rather than government has been left to convince itself of the benefits of Earned Value helped by the odd nod of encouragement from the powers that be. In 2000 this slow progress had grown sufficiently for the Association for Project Management to authorise the formation of an Earned Value Specific Interest Group. The first task of the group being the creation of an Earned Value Guideline for the UK, which was published in mid 2002. A first in the UK. Meanwhile, BAeSystems and Rolls-Royce implemented Earned Value in order to be able to bid for international business.

Now they continue to use it because it is a valuable business process. Their use and championship of earned value resulted in an explosion of interest from the Ministry of Defence. Interest also sprang up in a wide variety of other business sectors. Information Technology and Construction being of particular note.

The UK guidelines aim to provide implementation advice as well as a common language. Three levels of earned value are described ranging from Simple, through Integrated, to Criteria based. It is not envisaged that UK specific criteria will ever be created. Rather reference will be made to existing sets with particular emphasis on the originating US criteria.

A Definition

Earned Value is the amount of budget you can claim, representing completed work, without reference to completed costs. This information is then used to derive variance calculations which demonstrate the health of the project and also permit projections about the future to be made.

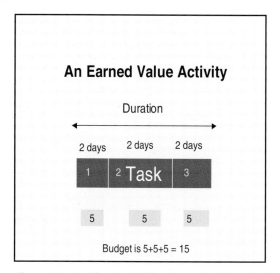

Figure 35 - 1: The Task is The Project Building Block.

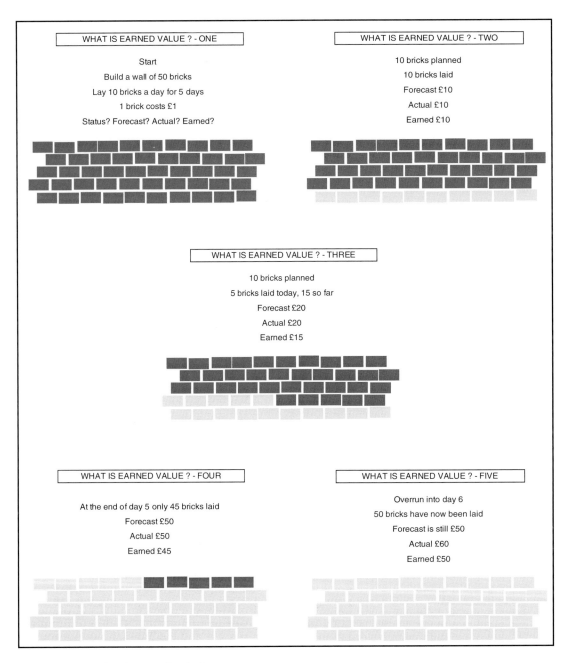

WHAT IS EARNED VALUE ? - ONE

Start

Build a wall of 50 bricks

Lay 10 bricks a day for 5 days

1 brick costs £1

Status? Forecast? Actual? Earned?

WHAT IS EARNED VALUE ? - TWO

10 bricks planned

10 bricks laid

Forecast £10

Actual £10

Earned £10

WHAT IS EARNED VALUE ? - THREE

10 bricks planned

5 bricks laid today, 15 so far

Forecast £20

Actual £20

Earned £15

WHAT IS EARNED VALUE ? - FOUR

At the end of day 5 only 45 bricks laid

Forecast £50

Actual £50

Earned £45

WHAT IS EARNED VALUE ? - FIVE

Overrun into day 6

50 bricks have now been laid

Forecast is still £50

Actual £60

Earned £50

Figure 35 - 2: What is Earned Value?

Figure 35 - 1 depicts the task as a project building block for consideration of earned value and Figure 35 - 2 illustrates how earned value is calculated as work on a task proceeds.

Remember the most you can earn is the forecast but that it can actually cost you a great deal more. This is the key focus of Earned Value.

The Difference between Earned Value Project Management and Ordinary Project Management

The basic building block of a project is a task. A thing that has to be done.

1   Describe the task
2   Estimate how long the task will take
3   Estimate how much it will cost
4   Give it to someone
5   Find out how they're getting on

Right. That's project management.

Earned Value is project management with one extra bit. An earning method.

1   Look at the cost estimate
2   Decide how you are going to earn it
    (Evenly throughout the time of the task; when you reach certain points; unevenly; more at the beginning, less at the end.)
3   Decide which earning method best suits and fairly reflects what you're doing

At the end of each week find out:

◆   How much you've done
◆   How much of the forecast you've done
◆   How much the forecast said you should have done
◆   What it really cost

4   Do the analysis
5   Start managing

It should be noted that whilst it is possible to do Project Management without Earned Value. It is not possible to do Earned Value without Project Management. However the step from Project Management to Earned Value requires little further effort to set up.

The Crucial Earned Value Difference

Earning Methods

A budget is associated with the task and is then distributed across the duration of the task to reflect how quickly it will be earned.

0-100 means that the budget is earned only when the task is completed.

100-0 means that the budget is earned upon commencement of the task.

50-50 means half at the start, half at the end.

Units complete would pay an agreed amount for every item.

There are many variations. The trick is to choose the method that most accurately reflects how value is added to the task.

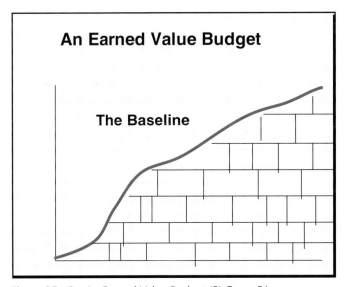

Figure 35 - 3: An Earned Value Budget 'S' Curve Diagram.

Units Employed

Any unit of measure can be used so long as it is applied consistently. Money, hours and units are all equally valid.

Some Benefits of Earned Value

- EVA protects shareholder value
- Use of E.V.A. in some countries is obligatory. Use of it might win you that contract. You've got to be in the game to play
- E.V.A. is now in use at the MOD and it is spreading fast.
- Improved profitability. Companies who use E.V.A. are in charge of their costs which as we all know affects the bottom line
- E.V.A. shows customers and suppliers whether they're getting Value For Money
- E.V.A. proves to internal management and to external parties, such as auditors, that the right information is available to manage the project
- EV.A. allows project information to be consolidated to give an overall Company/Programme/Department view.
- E.V.A. provides information that can allow the objective early cancellation of a project, potentially saving billions

E.V.A. is currently the best way to determine the real status of a project. As well as telling you how much you have spent it shows you how much you have achieved. Further, it tells you how much you still need to do and provides a good indication of final costs and dates.

Earned Value Terminology

A conundrum of language is that the more precise it gets the more puzzled a listener becomes. Professional jargon tends to exclude rather than include. For those of you who don't know, these lists will help you join the gang. When you're in the gang try and get rid of the jargon. The audience that needs to understand E.V.A. will be easier to convince if you tell them in plain English.

ACWP	Actual Cost of Work Performed	What you've really done.
AE	Apportioned Effort	Work that is related to a task and cannot take place without the task e.g. quality control.
BAC	Budget at Completion	The one 'they' never let you forget!
BCWP	Budgeted Cost for Work Performed	The Earned Value.
BCWS	Budgeted Cost for Work Scheduled	The Budget. The Plan. Planned Costs
CA	Cost Account	Also called a Control Account. The place where Cost and Schedule data is amassed so that E.V.A. can take place. To define a CA you need to know what piece of work is being done and which part of the organisation is doing it.
CAM	Cost Account Manager	The person responsible for managing Cost Accounts. Likely to be a cross-functional role and far easier said than done.
CBB	Contract Budget Base	The negotiated contract cost plus the estimated cost of authorised unpriced work.
C/SCSC	Cost/Schedule Control Systems Criteria	
CV	Cost Variance	If the variance is negative you're in trouble.
CPR	Cost Performance Report	A defined standard in those countries using C/CSCS based systems.
CTC	Contract Target Cost	
CWBS	Contract Work Breakdown Structure	Work Breakdown Structures look like family trees and show how all the sub-elements of a project relate to each other in order to produce the finished product.
EAC	Estimate at Completion	An objective formally arrived at figure. The one for public consumption.
EV	Earned Value (BCWP)	
FM	Functional Manager	
LOE	Level of Effort	Effort that doesn't produce definite products but is nevertheless essential e.g. project management.
LRE	Latest (Suppliers) Revised Estimate	The Gut Feel. What you tell your real friends.
MR	Management Reserve	The Contingency Fund.
OTB	Over Target Baseline	You've replanned your work and you haven't got enough money to do it.
PCS	Project Control System	Scapegoat's scapegoat
PM	Programme Manager	Scapegoat
PMB	Performance Measurement Baseline	The time phased budget less Management Reserve. The planned expenditure.
PMO	Programme Management Office	Mission Control
PP	Planning Package	Things that have been identified to do but not yet planned in detail.
RAM	Responsibility Assignment Matrix	A two-dimensional grid where role responsibilities and task elements of the WBS are shown.
SOW	Statement Of Work	
SV	Schedule Variance	A negative means that you haven't done as much as you planned.
AB	Total Allocated Budget	The sum of all the contract budgets.
UB	Undistributed Budget	What you still have left to give out. Not Management Reserve.
VAC	Variance At Completion	
VAR	Variance Analysis Report	
WP	Work Package	Discrete bundles of work.

Figure 35 - 4: Earned Value Acronyms.

Cost Variance	CV	= BCWP - ACWP
Cost Variance in %	CV%	= (CV / BCWP) x 100
Cost Performance Index	CPI	= BCWP / ACWP
To Complete Performance Index	TCPI	= (BAC - BCWP (cum)) / (EAC - ACWP (cum)) or Work Left / Funds Left
Schedule Variance	SV	= BCWP - BCWS
Schedule Variance in %	SV%	= (SV / BCWS) x 100
Schedule Performance Index	SPI	= BCWP / BCWS
Schedule Variance in Months	SV(months)	= SV (cum) / Average Monthly BCWP
Percentage Spent	% Spent	= (ACWP (cum) / BAC) x 100
Percentage Complete	% Complete	= BCWP (cum) / BAC

Independent EAC:

Statistical Examples

Basic Formula	EAC	= ACWP (cum) + PF (BAC - BCWP (cum)) where PF = Performance Factor and popular PF is = ACWP / BCWP or 1 / CPI
	EAC2	= ACWP (cum) + (BAC - BCWP (cum))
	IEAC	= ACWP + ETC
	IEAC 1	= BAC / CPI
	IEAC 2	= ACWP (cum) + BAC - BCWP (cum) / 0.8CPI + 0.2 x SPI
	IEAC 3	= ACWP (cum) + (BAC - BCWP (cum)) x 3 / (CPI - 1 + CPI - 2 + CP1 - 3)
	IEAC 4	= ACWP (cum) + (BAC - BCWP (cum)) / CPI x SPI

It's always a good idea to use more than one IEAC. You'll get a range of answers. If nothing else it will remind you that this is more art than science. Never forget that. The numbers are to help you manage. They are not there to replace management.

Variance At Completion	VAC	= BAC - EAC
Variance At Completion in %	VAC%	= (VAC / BAC) x 100
Budget/Earned Rate	B/E Rate	= BCWP (£) / BCWP (hours)
Actual Rate	Actual Rate	= ACWP (£) / ACWP (hours)
Rate Variance	Rate VAR	= (B/E Rate - Actual Rate) x (Actual Hours)
Price Variance	PV	= (B/E Price - Actual Price) x (Actual Quantity)
Usage Variance	UV	= (Earned Quantity - Actual Quantity) x (Earned Price)
To-Go Rate	To-Go Rate	= ETC (£) / ETC (hours)
Efficiency Variance	Eff VAR	= (BCWP Hours - ACWP Hours) x (B/E Rate)

Figure 35 - 5: Earned Value Formulae.

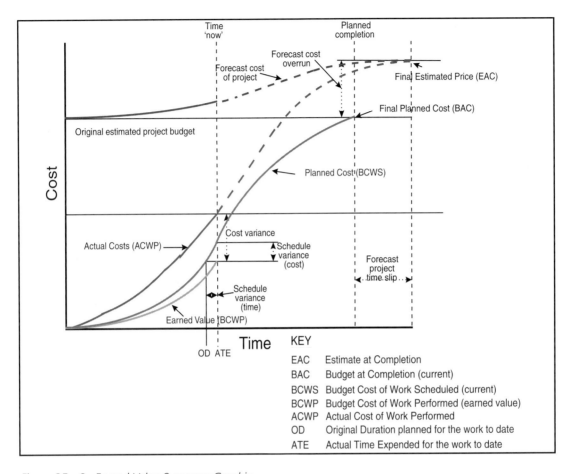

Figure 35 - 6: Earned Value Summary Graphic.

Implementation Guidelines

Do's and Don'ts

There is no simple recipe for success. What works this time will fail utterly another for no apparent reason. This is art not science. However there are areas to watch. Which, if left untended will certainly contribute to problems.

Sponsor

Implementing earned value often involves major organisational change. These kinds of change require champions. People who have a vision of what they think the benefits will be. People who will protect and persevere with an idea in its early days when hostile reaction could easily result in failure and cancellation. It is vital that as senior a person as possible actively supports this kind of change.

Work Breakdown Structure

The WBS defines what the project is making. It shows how the thing is put together. It provides a common description of what is being made to all the participants. This way the project is fully integrated and there is no risk of duplication of effort . When drawn it looks like a family tree. However, if the WBS is wrong then the project will be wrong. Time must be taken to ensure that what is being done is correct. In environments where time is not an apparent luxury a series of template WBS can be used to speed up the launch of projects. A template WBS also helps to standardise data so that comparative analysis with other projects can be carried out.

It cannot be emphasised enough that to ignore or rush the definition of what is to be produced is to rush headlong over a precipice into error. The IT departments of large organisations in particular seem, to be particular victims of 'time-to-market' frenzy at the expense of planned undertaking. Unfortunately the resolution of this syndrome lies as much with the customers as it does with the producers. And as long as a hard-nosed adversarial approach to project delivery is adhered to then the problem is likely to continue. The sharing of common project information that is a feature of earned value management good practice can help promote a collaborative win/win approach but the levels of trust and maturity required are currently beyond the majority of organisations. There are, nevertheless, pockets of significant change with some major organisations in the UK defence and construction industries taking courageous steps to change their contractual practices through the use of earned value.

Data

Data is the lifeblood of any management system. If it is not accurate or cannot be gathered then a system will fail. Rubbish in rubbish out. Quite often earned value is introduced as a means of enforcing new better disciplines. But these initiatives often fail despite often discovering the poor data early on. A common feature of any new change to working practices is that the new way is often perceived as a threat to be fought off or destroyed at the earliest opportunity. The poor data scenario is often used to discredit the earned value process. Consequently it is often the case that earned value is tried on one unsuccessful project and is not then used on further projects as a result. Poor data is therefore to be watched for and remedied before proceeding. Forewarned is forearmed.

Having earned value is not a 'silver bullet'. Better to halt the earned value project and focus on getting the correct data supplied.

Communication

People are suspicious of change and the arrival of earned value is no different. It is highly likely that it will change the way people work. Awareness campaigns, posters talks training should encourage its arrival - and continue after its arrival.

Persist

Give earned value a chance to work. The benefits often take a few months to start working. Allow at least three short-term reporting cycles to happen before worrying. People will be looking for an excuse to blame it on even in the very short-term.

Blame Culture

Many companies suffer from 'blame culture'. This breeds a punitive risk-averse kind of environment.

The point of earned value is that it gives clear and accurate results which can in the wrong hands be used to punish people.

If the data is used to punish rather than for constructive dialogue any trust will disappear rapidly. People don't normally co-operate if they know they are going to get beaten-up.

Miracles

These won't happen with earned value. A project in trouble will not make a remarkable recovery by having earned value introduced. In fact this is another way to quickly get earned value discredited. It should have been there at the start. A project that starts with earned value is not going to be a guaranteed success either. But the information that earned value provides will provide an unparalleled advantage to those individuals and groups that believe that projects need to be managed. Not just reported upon.

Appropriate

Common sense must prevail when defining the type of earned value management system. First and foremost it must be realised that earned value can be used on almost any project. Most of the current available guidance is for large government defence oriented programmes. Unsurprisingly it would be absurd to attempt to implement this model into a small e-business start-up. Equally unsurprisingly this is precisely what people do. They quickly fail and give up because they have tried to implement a model without thinking about it. It is possible to implement a simple form of earned value control using spreadsheets with task lists. For more formal guidelines refer to APM's Earned Value Management Guidline for the UK.

Do It Yourself

Books. Conferences. Training courses. Consultants. Other departments. Other organisations. They can all tell you about earned value. But for earned value to become a way of life, a business process, you have to do it yourself.

Otherwise you end up paying someone else and adding to cost. And you're paying someone to do your job.

There's More to Life Than EV

Earned value is not the be all and end all of project management. It should be one of several tools in use by an intelligent empowered and above all pragmatic project manager. Try and marry risk management to the Work Breakdown Structure. Keep an eye on the Critical Path, earned value doesn't. A low value item will not register any alarm within earned value calculations but could in fact be hindering the progress of the rest of the project.

Lies, Damned Lies and Statistics

In the same vein, overall project performance measures could mask trouble at the lower levels of the project. Remove large static material elements when measuring performance. It will make the measures more sensitive and therefore better able to provide useful management information.

Different Industries

No audit of the UK has been carried out to date. This would be useful research.

An interesting aside. The APM Specific Interest Group for earned value has representatives from different industries. Each came expecting significant differences but in fact through this networking found significant similarities.

The MOD and its major suppliers are now moving into widespread use of earned value.

Non-defence government departments are also using earned value. With the creation of the Office of Government Commerce it is anticipated that the take-up of best practice methods like earned value will increase rapidly.

Many of the public utilities are using earned value. The rail industry in particular.

The construction industry is also using earned value. Of note is the new Heathrow Terminal 5 Project which is using earned value to provide the best possible visibility of information from its suppliers. In return for this visibility and in a ground-breaking move it has taken all the risk away from those suppliers.

In the private sector earned value has captured the imagination of IT software development organisations. Their pragmatic focus on the process benefits rather than the set-up rule book is likely to be the greatest growth area for earned value over the next ten years.

Different Countries

Earned value is used across the world to varying degrees.

In the first row is the USA and Australia with developed mandated systems both of which were under revision in 2001. These systems do not cater for small fast IT type projects.

In the second row are Canada, New Zealand, Sweden and the UK. Each at different stages of growth.

The UK system is not mandated and is unlikely to become so with reliance being placed currently on Standard guidance. Of key interest will be guidance for small systems as well as large ones.

In the third row are new entrants Japan, Germany, Brazil and France. All seeking to participate in the international dialogue.

Whilst the American criteria remain supreme in underpinning the other national systems and, rightly so, it still remains for each country to discover and define for itself just how earned value is going to work within its national boundaries. It would therefore seem likely that we can look forward to an international standard for earned value definitions. A global implementation standard, however, is an entirely different matter and likely to be a labour of several years.

Levels of Implementation Maturity

Maturity models attempt to locate the level of implementation required for a particular project or organisation within a defined framework. The above model equates the level with risk to the level of requirement. There are many other proprietary models in existence normally wrapped up in expensive consultancy methodology.

One assumption that must be debunked. Most maturity models suggest that some kind of evolution must take place and that the 'maturer' the organisation the more complex and consequently better will be the earned value system. This is wrong. The implementation must be a pragmatic combination of what is appropriate and what is achievable. A 'simple' implementation may be all that can be achieved but may still represent a quantum leap in management effectiveness. The UK guidelines under APM development are attempting to reflect this point.

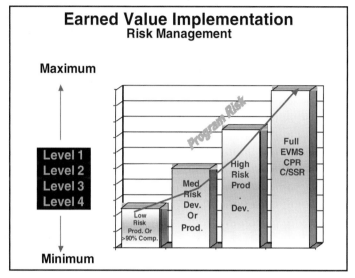

Figure 35 - 7: Earned Value - Levels of Implementation Maturity (Reproduced with the kind permission of Tom Woodling, Northrop Grumman)

Conclusions

Earned value provides simple but powerful answers to many questions such as:

- Are we getting value for money?
- How much is it really costing us to earn each unit of forecast value?
- How much is going to cost by the finish?
- When is it going to finish?
- Where are we now? Exactly!
- Where are our problem areas?
- How does this compare with other projects?

Earned Value is not a' silver bullet'. It will not guarantee a successful project. Only people can do that.

References and Further Reading

Earned Value Manangement APM Guideline for the UK, First Edition, APM, 2002
Earned Value Project Management, Second Edition. Fleming & Koppelman 2000
E.V.A. in the UK, Fifth Edition Steve Wake 2001
BS6079 Guide to Project Management BSI 2001

36   INFORMATION MANAGEMENT

Bob Wiggins

"Don't panic. It's the first helpful or intelligible thing anybody's said to me all day."
Douglas Adams (1952-2001), writer and producer.

Related Topics

The following Body of Knowledge topics are related, or relevant to the subject of Information Management:

66   Organisational structure
70   Communication

Information in the Project Context

Before delving into the details of this Session's topic it is necessary to provide a firm foundation by considering what is meant by information in the context of a project and, furthermore, what does a project constitute.

The Project as an Organisation

A project is defined as a "unique process consisting of a set of co-ordinated and controlled activities with start and finish dates, undertaken to achieve an objective conforming to specific requirements including constraints of time, cost and resources".

Although a project has a defined life span, in all other respects it has the characteristics of an organisation being comprised of the constituent elements of 'structure', 'process', 'people' and 'tools' as depicted in Figure 36 - 1.

The structural element comprises the project strategy framework and associated policies. This will typically draw on some form of project management methodology to provide the basis for its development. In turn, the framework governs the project processes that deliver the various outputs, the human resources necessary to undertake the tasks and activities, and the tools that support the people in undertaking their work.

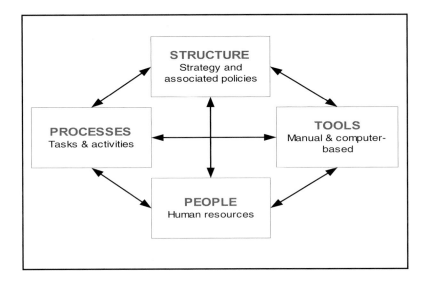

Figure 36 - 1: Project Organisational Elements

Types of Projects

In general, projects are ways of effecting change. However projects can range from those that have highly technical outputs, such as the introduction of a new telecommunication system within a company, to those that have more of a social and political impact as exemplified by educational projects in developing countries funded by aid organisations.

Despite this variety, projects have similar attributes and all have information as an important asset that must be effectively and efficiently managed. The good practice covered in this session is therefore applicable in all cases.

Information is the Glue

Information, and the knowledge of those people involved in the project, is the glue that binds together and inter-connects the project's organisational elements.

The concepts of knowledge management and information management are often ill-defined (if at all). Here knowledge means information (tacit knowledge) that an individual knows and holds in their brain; information (explicit knowledge) is that which is available in recorded form independent of humans.

In this context Project Knowledge Management (PKM) embraces both information and knowledge in the project context as depicted in Fig. 2.

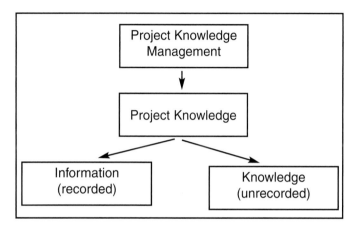

Figure 36 - 2: Project Knowledge Management

The focus in this session is on managing recorded knowledge, i.e. information, although consideration will be given to ways of encouraging the sharing and capturing of tacit knowledge.

The Information Life Cycle

Throughout the phases of a project, a wide range of information is utilised and in doing so it moves through various life cycle activities. The particular activities undertaken will depend on such factors as the type of information involved (for example the revision of a drawing will need to be approved before release) and the stage at which the project is in its life cycle (thus at project termination, some documentation can be weeded out for formal destruction, while some needs to be handed over to the client).

A conceptual representation of the information life cycle is provided in Figure 36 -.3.

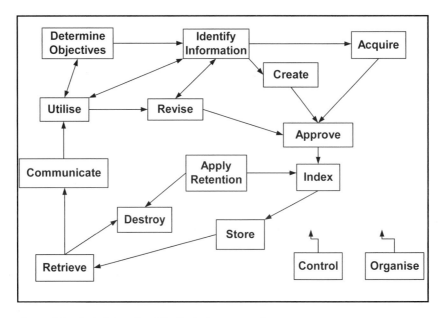

Figure 36 - 3: Information Life Cycle (conceptual)

A summary of the information life cycle activities is provided in Figure 36 - 4.

A Strategic Approach to Information Management

Projects are a necessary component of the activities for delivering business strategies. As part of this process, information management within a project context, needs to be planned strategically.

A strategy is the process of setting overall goals. Goals are long term objectives. The development of an information management strategy and the associated policies for a project involves a planning process as shown in Figure 36 - 5.

It is important to note at this point, that information management within the project context does not per se determine the appropriateness of the project's deliverables. In a similar vein, certification to ISO 9000 - the Quality Management Standard - is not a guarantee of product quality. It merely demonstrates that the company has well

Activity	Scope
Determine objectives	The project objectives that give rise to the need for information are determined
Identify information	Information that is relevant to achieving the determined objectives is identified, e.g. project initiation documents
Acquire	Relevant information already exists elsewhere and is acquired from available sources, e.g. the client organisational structure
Create	The required information does not exist and has to be generated or created by some intellectual and/or automated means, e.g. the project plan with tasks and assigned resources
Approve	Various forms of approval procedures are required, e.g. to sanction a draft report, the release of a design drawing to a client or the destruction of a superseded document
Index	Depending on the type of document and the need for subsequent retrieval, indexing, cataloguing and referencing data is recorded, e.g. for design drawings
Apply retention	The extent to which particular documents, project files or other classes of documents need to be retained is recorded in retention schedules, e.g. documents required for handover must be retained until that stage is reached
Store	Acquired or created information is stored using suitable media and storage systems, e.g. design documents are held electronically for shared access
Retrieve	Retrieval mechanisms appropriate to the particular requirement extract information using the indexes provided, e.g. a drawing register managed by computer-aided-design (CAD) software
Communicate	Information is communicated to inform or initiate action; e.g. copies of key documents, such as standards and specifications are placed on CD-ROMs for distribution under transmittal to contractors
Utilise	Information is utilised as part of a project activity to generate the required output
Revise	Information that has become out-of-date or in need of expansion or correction is revised, e.g. a project plan, or an acceptance test specification
Destroy	Redundant or ephemeral information, and that which has been identified for disposal according to retention schedules is destroyed; e.g. minutes of project teams may not need to be kept after the project's deliverables have been accepted by the client
Organise	The total life cycle of project information is organised efficiently and effectively as regards the people, support tools, policies, and activities and their inter-relationship, e.g. a regularly reviewed and updated project initiation document lays down how a project team is structured and what team members' responsibilities are
Control	Information management within the project is monitored and controlled to ensure it supports the achievement of the project's objectives and protects the integrity of the information, e.g. there is an agreed information life cycle audit and review procedure in place

Figure 36 - 4: Information Life Cycle Activities

documented business processes that it adheres to consistently.

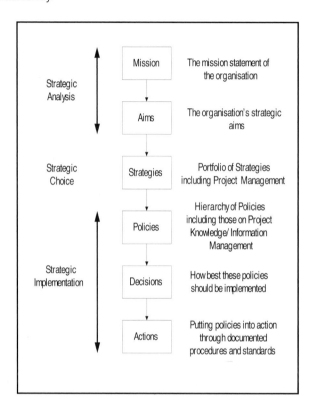

Figure 36 - 5: The Strategic Planning Process

Information Management Policy

The Information Management Policy that emerges from the strategic planning process provides the basis for developing the detailed procedures for handling information needed by the project. It thus forms part of the hierarchy of documentation as indicated in the strategic planning process.

The Policy Document should be formally approved by the appropriate authority, and also be subject to regular reviews to ensure that it reflects the current needs of the project. Where the approval authority lies depends on how the project is viewed and structured by the organisation.

Policy Hierarchy

The Information Management Policy document should include the following:

- Assignment of roles and responsibilities for information management (i.e. covering the life cycle activities)
- Definition of, and reference to the detailed information management scope, procedures, standards and guidelines to be followed
- Specification of the required and allowable supporting systems and tools (for example the types and version levels of computer software to be used)
- Reference to the overall project management structure into which the above is embedded

The standards and guidelines should include such matters as information security, and definition of document types and retention schedules (see later sections).

The project management structure covers the project team, users or clients (those who will benefit from or be affected by the project's outputs) and suppliers (those delivering or assisting the delivery of the solution), as all these must be assigned information management responsibilities.

Where elements of the policy may be subject to periodic amendment, for example relating to document types, retention schedules, security, working procedures and supporting systems, these may best be produced as separate annexes or cross-referenced documents that can be updated independently of the main policy document. Thus the hierarchy of information management documents will appear as in Figure 36 - 6.

Document Types

Most information handled by projects is in the form of documents covering such topics as project progress, risk management, committee meetings, change requests and pictorial representations as exemplified by architectural drawings.

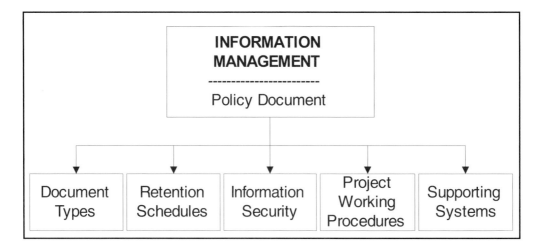

Figure 36 - 6: Information Management Policy Document

Based on such document content, a range of mutually exclusive document types can be defined. The precise choice will depend on the nature of the project and the information handled. The benefit of defining document types is that indexing attributes (i.e. metadata - information about information) can be related to them to facilitate subsequent retrieval, particularly when using computerised systems.

The matrix in Figure 36 - 7 contains examples of document types and associated indexing attributes and is merely illustrative of the approach to be taken. Such a matrix can be used in a requirements specification when tendering for a document management or document control system, for example. The matrix shows where an attribute must be applied ('M'), where it is optional ('O'), and where it is not appropriate ('N') for individual document types. Thus a drawing may comprise several sheets, but have the same drawing number. As no other document types needs to be indexed by sheet number, the document type 'Drawing' is the only one allowed to use the attribute 'Sheet No.'.

Document Type Attribute	Book	Drawing	Report	Correspondence	Meeting Minutes	Standard
Document Type	M	M	M	M	M	M
Title	M	M	M	M	M	M
Author	M	O	M	M	M	O
Originating organisation or publisher	M	M	M	M	M	M
Document No. or Ref.	O	M	M	O	O	M
Date of Document	M	M	M	M	M	M
Revision or Version	O	M	M	N	O	M
Sheet No.	N	O	N	N	N	N
Keywords	O	O	O	O	O	O
Handover	M	M	M	M	M	M
Retention Period	N	M	M	M	M	M
Destruction Date	N	M	M	M	M	M
Destruction Authorisation	N	M	M	M	M	M

Figure 36 - 7: Indexing Attributes for Specific Document Types (Examples only)

Note that 'Document Type' is itself an attribute, thereby enabling an enquirer who is only interested in schematic information to select document type 'drawings' when retrieving information, thereby eliminating other document types not relevant to the query.

Two other attributes of note are 'Keywords' and 'Handover'. 'Keywords' allow users to enter 'free text' terms that can help subsequent retrieval, for example trade names. The 'Handover' attribute can be used to flag documents that are candidates for passing onto the client or end-user on completion of the project.

Defining document types can also help to automate the capture of newly created documents into a retrieval system - a topic covered in the later section on Information Systems.

Retention Schedules

Although Figure 36 - 7 shows 'Retention Period' as an attribute to be applied to particular types of document, such a concept can also pertain to categories or groups of documents, often held in files or folders (whether physical paper or electronic). This 'records management' approach, which is the subject of an International Standard (BS ISO 15489-1:2001) involves grouping documents by a classification scheme which each business needs to formulate based on a hierarchy from its top level business functions through business activities to lower level business transactions.

Retention schedules based on such criteria as legal and regulatory requirements as well as operational needs are applied to groups of 'records'. These groupings will often correspond directly or closely to categories of business activity in the business activity classification.

Where an organisation already has such a classification scheme, it is likely that projects and project management will have already been included, thereby allowing project information to be readily embedded in it for the purpose of retention scheduling.

It is not uncommon to align the conceptual filing of project information to the work breakdown structure in the project plan. This has the advantage of familiarity for those involved in the project.

Information Security

Information handled by, or relating to the project needs to be protected from malicious or inadvertent change or loss. However, those with rights to access information must not be unduly impeded in so doing. A balance therefore needs to be struck to ensure that the protective measures put in place are appropriate to the level of risk posed to the information's integrity.

Risk management in the context of information has been defined (BS 7799-1:1999) as the "process of identifying, controlling and minimising or eliminating security risks that may affect information systems, for an acceptable cost". Separate guidance on the topic of risk assessment and risk management in the context of information security is available (DISC PD 0008:1999).

Although the emphasis now is more on computer-stored information, the same levels of security must apply to paper and microfilmed records, and furthermore, to portable computer storage media such as back-up tapes, CD-ROMs and 'floppy disks'.

It may be that the organisation undertaking a project already has an information management security policy in place, in which case this is likely to cover the needs of the project manager. If such a policy is lacking, or is considered inadequate, guidance is available in the form of a British Standard Code of Practice. It includes aspects of access control, the use of network services and an outline of an information security policy.

Project Working Procedures

Information management procedures need to be embedded in the life-cycle structure of the project. As noted in BS 6079 "Organisations and sectors of industry tend to develop project life cycles that are phased to enable the use of an agreed (project management) methodology between interested parties".

Having phases helps the incorporation of review and decision points (often called gateways) at which problems, progress and plans are considered and approval has to be sought before further work is undertaken. It is vital to have the necessary documentation and project data finalised and accessible to all the relevant decisions makers at these points.

Categorising Project Information

The names given to the supporting project information will vary from organisation to organisation and from one project management methodology to another. Usefully, PRINCE 2, the project management method adopted by the

UK Government identifies three categories of information products :

- ◆ Management information (for the organisation and control of the project)
- ◆ Specialist information (identifies the major products or results which will satisfy the business needs)
- ◆ Quality information (necessary to ensure the quality of project deliverables - deliverables are defined as hardware, software, services, processes, documents or any combination of these)

The extent of mainly management information products that may be required is shown in Figure 36 - 8 in relation to the process viewpoint to project management taken by PRINCE 2.

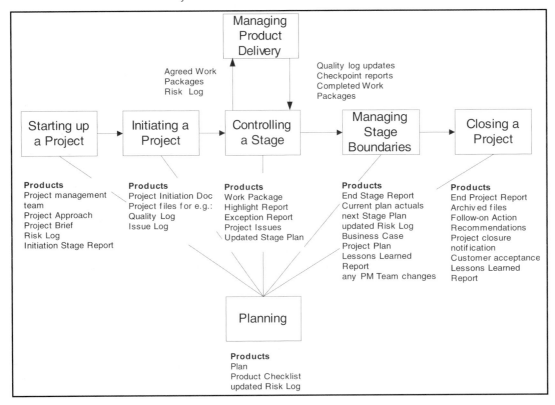

Figure 36 - 8: Documentation Products Associated with PRINCE 2 Processes

The project manager must ensure that the range of project documentation adopted within these categories is commensurate with the type and complexity of the project. Without this balance, the bureaucracy of managing information may endanger the successful delivery of the intended business benefits. Thus a project to procure off-the-shelf commercial software to meet the needs of a standard business function, such as personnel management within a small organisation, will be less complex to manage, and require less documentation, than one where the software is newly written to provide a bespoke solution for a multi-national company.

Similarly, support or enhancement projects will place more emphasis on the revision of existing documentation, and hence require less effort to be expended on documentation than new developments where documents have to be created from scratch.

Ensuring Compliance

Putting an information management policy in place is not enough in itself. It should be adhered to over the life of the project and such adherence should be demonstrated periodically through some form of independent audit.

As a means of assessing a broad range of information management policies and procedures and helping to ensure the legal admissibility of electronically stored information, the Code of Practice DISC PD 0008:1999 together with its Compliance Workbook are recommended. The workbook takes the assessor step-by-step through DISC PD 0008 and provides a set of quantitative parameters for determining compliance. It aims to assist in the demonstration of the integrity of the compliance audit trail as well as an organisation's commitment to fulfil its responsibility of Duty of Care. Despite its title, it is equally valid for assessing paper-based information management practices.

For judging the state of information security the Guide to BS 7799 Auditing includes the definitive requirements that external auditors must address when certifying organisations to BS 7799-2 'Information Security Management'. It can, however, be used less formally by internal staff such as a project manager.

Information Management Support Systems

Managing the information needed to run a project requires a range of supporting systems, and these are increasingly computerised. The systems must provide the necessary functionality including the ability to:

- Receive and acquire information from external sources (e.g. suppliers, clients and consultants)
- Create documents, drawings, plans and databases within the project
- Retrieve required information in a timely fashion
- Distribute information to team members, project board and others who need it
- Support standardised business processes such as document review and approval
- Implement retention scheduling of project records
- Ensure version control over documentation
- Protect information from unauthorised access and change

A diagram showing the relationships between the main information functions is presented in Figure 36 - 9. It is a distillation of the generalised information life cycle activities from Figure 36 - 3 to a form that relates more directly to the reality of project life.

Typical ways in which technology based information systems can deliver this functionality is covered in the following sections.

Document Repository

Increasingly all documentation required by a project is held in some form of computerised storage repository, typically stored on the hard disks of a workstation or server. Specialised software provides the means to index the documents and exercise version and configuration control so

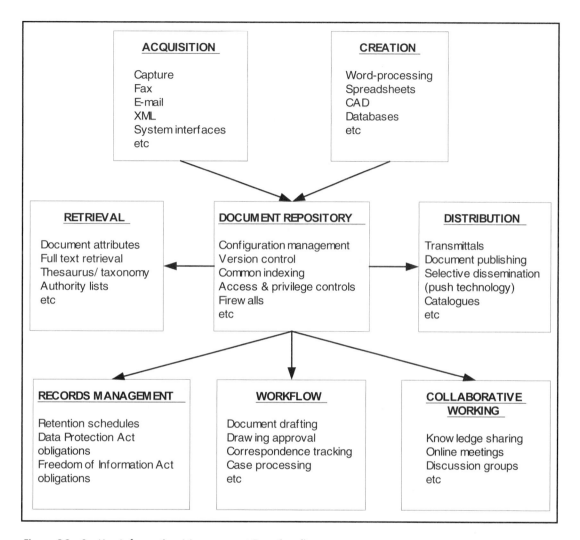

Figure 36 - 9: Key Information Management Functionality

that, for example, users can be made aware of changes to documentation as it is authorised. Standard features provided by operating system software ensure that users or groups of users (such as project teams) are provided with the appropriate rights of access to documentation, including privileges for making changes to specific documents.

Project documentation will normally be arranged according to some form of filing structure within the repository. This structure may be related to a corporate business activity classification, which reflects the functions undertaken by the organisation, a work breakdown structure for the project, or an organisational breakdown structure.

Work breakdown structures provide a high level view of the project by grouping activities under summary headings. Information from these individual activities can be combined to provide summary project information at the higher level. Organisational breakdown structures enable responsibility for activities to be assigned to departments, functions or workgroups, whether in the client or contractor organisation, for example. This enables parts of an organisation to concentrate on its own activities and project information requirements. Increasingly computer-based project support systems are able selectively to provide any of these views depending on the user's requirements at the time.

Acquisition

Acquisition involves a range of approaches for acquiring documents external to the project and converting them so that they are able to be readily incorporated into the system. Information may arrive, for example as faxes, e-mails, in word-processed or spreadsheet form, or as structured data possibly by direct inter-connection between computer systems. Paper can never be completely eliminated, so may need to be converted into electronic form using a scanner.

Increasing use is being made of documents in the formats used on the world-wide-web (www), that is HTML and more recently XML. This latter format enables key data embedded in a document to be made dynamically available, rather than remaining embedded in discursive text.

Creation

Projects can generate considerable amounts of information. Its management can be greatly eased by standardising on the choice of creation software, be it word-processing, spreadsheet, database or CAD. Furthermore by devising suitable standard templates for the range of document types to be created, it is possible to capture automatically much of the indexing information attributes (e.g. title, document reference, author, creation date) required to facilitate subsequent retrieval of the documents.

Retrieval

Success in retrieving required information will rely mainly on effective indexing at the outset. Provided this has been thought of at the document creation stage, as noted above, the chances of successfully retrieving what is sought are much enhanced. Such structured indexing of attributes provides highly specific means of searching for required information.

If the documents are in electronic and editable form, the use of full text indexing software enables the complete content of a document to be searched thereby providing another avenue for finding that elusive piece of project information.

Use can also be made of thesauri or taxonomies, which are typically hierarchical lists of subject terms where the relationships between concepts are made explicit. These terms can then be applied to index the contents of documents and assist with the creation of a filing structure. Thesauri can help find required information while reducing the amount of irrelevant information retrieved. However as projects have a limited life, the effort needed to create thesauri is rarely justified. Of more value are authority lists for controlling the indexing of, for example, company names or more specialised topics such as product components.

The ability successfully and easily to retrieve required information is usually the earliest and most valuable benefit that emerges after implementing a document management system.

Distribution

The ability to distribute the right project documentation to the right places at the right time - and to be able to prove it - is a key contributor to successful project management. It encompasses how requests for distribution are initiated, how lists of recipients are determined, how packages of documentation are made up, what format (paper or electronic) are to be used and what form of transmittal notes (if any) are sent and how the replies are requested and eventually logged to complete the audit trail.

Distribution can also be activated by users pre-registering their interest in specific documents (e.g. project plans) or types of document. When these documents are authorised for distribution, the system automatically sends them to the user, or notifies the user of their existence and where they can access them. This selective dissemination of information (or 'push technology') saves time and administrative effort.

Records Management

The control and management of an integrated series of project records showing how project decisions were made and the consequences that arose, is an important project management function. The topic of retention schedules in this context was covered earlier. Additionally, project managers will need to ensure they meet their obligations under the Data Protection Act 1998 (DPA) which came into force on 1 March 2000 and sets rules for processing personal information. It applies to some paper records as well as all those held on computer.

If the project is one undertaken by a public authority, there may be obligations to be met under the Freedom of Information Act 2000 (FoIA) which was passed on 30th November 2000 and must be brought fully into effect by 30th November 2005.

Both the DPA and the FoIA come under the responsibility of the Information Commissioner.

Collaborative Working

Conducting a project will involve teams and individuals working together. Information technology can facilitate this by creating the means for exchanging ideas and conducting meetings in real time and online. The aspect of 'communication' is covered by a separate Session and is not considered further here.

Workflow

Collaborative working can be ad hoc and informal at one extreme, or highly structured at the other. There are two main approaches to the implementation of workflow systems. The ad hoc casual workflow tools use e-mail, forms and messages as the system infrastructure where information and work is sent out to people whether they need it or not. The higher-end workflow systems are concerned with the proactive management of the flow of work between co-operating individuals and groups of people based on defined procedures and tasks. These systems are usually referred to as engine-based, where the workflow engine handles the management of the actual process and calls other applications and facilities as and when required. They provide significant advantages where close integration is needed and where more sophisticated models of work matching are appropriate.

The coming of the Web and the increasing use being made by business of the Internet, intranets and extranets, has added another dimension to considerations when planning to adopt collaborative working or workflow. Many of the new workflow products are entirely Web-based. While offering rapid and less-expensive deployment than non-Web-based services, other issues emerge. These include security and the need for improved document management to ensure the underlying document base is up-to-date, approved and has appropriate access controls. In this dynamic environment it is also more difficult to provide an effective audit trail. For example one may wish to prove at what time, and by whom, key information was accessed over the web service.

Document and Information Formats

One of the main problems facing recipients and users of computer-generated information is the ability to view and read that information if it has been generated using application software which the recipient does not possess.

Despite the fact that Microsoft software is the de facto standard for most users, it can be difficult or impossible to ensure that a document that has been created on one type of platform using one type of application software will be viewable and appear exactly the same when received by someone using a different platform or application software. When it comes to reading information stored in graphic formats such as those produced by computer-aided design software the problem is compounded further.

Software products usually have in-built conversion utilities, and third party software is also available to address this specific problem. However, 100% conversion accuracy cannot necessarily be assured, hence the popularity of viewing software.

Two main categories of viewers are file format recognition viewers and viewers for documents converted into a single format (e.g. Adobe Acrobat). The former approach has the advantage that given the viewing software, the user can quickly display information that has been created with application software they do not possess. The drawback is that the producer of the viewer has usually to re-program the software to deal with any new applications or upgrades to existing applications.

The latter approach used by Adobe for its Acrobat product, is aimed at a somewhat different market with a particular focus on document distribution. The Adobe Acrobat family of software provides facilities for converting most computer-generated documents and file formats to a Portable Document Format (PDF) in which format the document retains all the look and feel of the original. Adobe provides a royalty-free reader.

With the increasing use of Internet technologies, documentation can, as mentioned earlier, be created or converted into web-based renditions using the hypertext mark-up language HTML or its more recent incarnation XML (extensible mark-up language).

Choice of Information System

Faced with suppliers offering systems to support 'document management', 'content management', 'document control' etc, the project manager must be clear as to what their requirements really are. Is the emphasis, for example on:

◆ Enterprise project management tools with repositories for storing documents as attachments to projects, possibly with the ability for version control

◆ Requirements management tools to help obtain a clear understanding of the problem space (business opportunities, user needs etc) and then define the system to solve that problem

◆ Document management providing document check-in and check-out, version control and controlled distribution or

◆ Workflow to support standardised document life cycle processes?

The choice is therefore extensive, and many products are now web-based. Although this can ease the management of information within the organisation and beyond with clients and suppliers, care needs to be taken when selecting and implementing such systems. Questions of inter-operability with existing systems and the choice of standards have to be addressed, and guidance needs to be sought in these areas.

The Computing Suppliers Federation web site is a useful place to start a search for likely products. It has a forum including vendors of document management, workflow, imaging and scanning systems. The forum also includes suppliers of storage products and other technologies that drive e-business.

References and Further Reading

BS 6079-2:2000 Project Management - Part 2: Vocabulary

BS 6079-1:2000 Project Management - Part 1: Guide to Project Management

BS ISO 15489-1:2001 Information and Documentation - Records Management - Part 1: General

ISO/TR 15489-2:2001(E) Technical Report. Information and Documentation - Records Management - Part 2: Guidelines.

BS 7799-1:1999 Information Security Management - Part 1: Code of Practice for Information Security Management

DISC PD 3002:1998 Guide to BS 7799 risk assessment and risk management

Managing Successful Projects with PRINCE 2. HMSO 1998 ISBN 0 11 330685 7

DISC PD 0008:1999 Code of Practice for Legal Admissibility and Evidential Weight of Information Stored Electronically

DISC PD 0009:1999 Compliance workbook for use with PD 0008:1999. Code of practice for legal admissibility and evidential weight of information stored electronically

DISC PD 3004:1999 Guide to BS 7799 auditing

BS 7799-2:1999 Information Security Management - Part 2: Specification for Information Security Management Systems

http://www.dataprotection.gov.uk/

AIIM ARP1-2001 - Implementation Guidelines and Standards for Web-Based Document Management Systems. Association for Information and Image Management International (USA). 9th March 2001.

http://www.martex.co.uk/computing-suppliers/

Section 4

Technical

40 DESIGN, IMPLEMENTATION AND HAND-OVER MANAGEMENT

Akin Oluwatudimu

"Every people should be the originators of their own designs, the projector of their own schemes, and creators of the events that lead to their destiny; the consummation of their desires."
Martin Robinson Delany (1812-1885), U.S. physician, abolitionist, and newspaper editor.

Closely Related Topics in the Body of Knowledge

Although it primarily addresses the technical characteristics of a project, Design, Implementation & Hand-over Management cuts across other sections of the APM Body of Knowledge. The topic covers a substantial proportion of the life-cycle of a project and many of the processes and activities referred to are closely linked or interrelated to other topics. Some of which include:

21 Strategy/Project Management Plan
30 Work Content and Scope Management
41 Requirements Management
45 Modelling and Testing
60 Lifecycle Design and Management
62 Design and Development
63 Implementation
64 Hand-over

Introduction

Projects are unique undertakings, which generally involve a series of activities or tasks intended to deliver a defined product or service within agreed parameters of performance (or quality), time and costs among others. A project sponsor or client may initiate a project following the establishment of a valid 'business case' for such an undertaking. Projects always involve 'change' either through the modification of existing situations or creation of something new. In this context, Design can be seen as the activity of defining what a project is to deliver. Implementation can be seen as the process of producing or realising the end result, while Hand-over relates to the phase in which the finished product or service is passed from the project team to the client (sponsor) or end users.

These three inter-related phases together constitute a crucial part of the project in terms of overall impact on the realisation of the objectives. Their effective management forms the subject of this topic.

Relationship with Overall Project Management Plan

The design phase in a typical project tends to follow on from the inception or concept stage as the project manager assists the sponsor and stakeholders to clarify what the project is to deliver. In many industries, the requirements of the project are articulated into a 'brief' - a summary of the objectives, characteristics, format and other defining qualities of the proposed deliverables. The justification (why?) and the aim (what?) questions of the project need to be addressed, then all the other aspects of the project can be assembled together, i.e. time scale, resources, costs, etc. to produce a Project Management Plan. This is a comprehensive statement covering not only the questions relating to what? and why?, but also the how?, when?, by whom? and how much? of the project.

It is therefore of crucial importance that sufficient thought and analysis is put into the project design since in effect, every other stage of the work is dedicated to achieving these objectives. If the brief is wrong, then the design and hence the entire project can be a waste of effort.

Principles of Design Management

In general the design phase of projects is often a rolling process in which the project deliverables are defined in ever increasing level of detail at each iteration. For example in construction, the design phase consists of outline design, scheme design and detail design. Starting from the initial idea, the project design team addresses each aspect of the project in turn until eventually they are satisfied that when implemented, their design will satisfy the project brief.

The design phase sometimes overlaps the implementation phase. In the case of concurrent engineering, various aspects of the design and implementation may be progressed simultaneously with a view to reducing the time to market.

Assumptions made during design need to be verified and tested prior to production and successive iterations may result in design modifications. Feasibility appraisals are discussed later on.

Another fundamental aspect of the design and development phase of projects is the involvement of specialists from a variety of disciplines. In a typical organisation the design stage of many projects will involve experts from various functional departments such as sales / marketing, finance, research and development and production. Design may also involve managerial, technical and support staff and there will be the need to clarify responsibilities of team members. Adequate liaison, communication and reporting channels will need to be established.

Design strategy may be heavily influenced by customers, clients and other stakeholders who may be directly involved in the design process right from the start. This is the case in many software development projects.

The Design Brief / Scope of Work

The process of defining a project brief can also be described as Requirements Management. The client organisation or sponsor needs to be able to communicate to the project team what exactly the project is intended to accomplish including the critical success criteria. User/customer requirements, system requirements etc. all need to be articulated in a clear, unambiguous manner to increase the chances of success.

Outline and Consolidated Brief

In many cases the project brief starts as a broad outline of the requirements to be delivered. However as the requirements become more defined and detailed, the brief may be 'consolidated' into specific project deliverables which will facilitate the eventual Work or Product BreakdownStructures (WBS or PBS). Ideally the consolidated brief needs to be authorised by the project sponsor or client and used as the baseline. This will help avoid unnecessary scope creep or deviation from the original objectives such that any proposed changes can be compared with the agreed baseline.

Specifications

To facilitate implementation, the project brief needs to be translated into a WBS or PBS with specifications to cover every aspect of the work. This will include requirements for compliance with specific time, performance, cost and risk parameters.

Specifications relate to the design and may be functional or prescriptive. A functional specification defines what performance is expected from the project deliverables leaving the production team to use their skills and experience in determining how to achieve these. A prescriptive specification is more specific about what materials, components or resources must be utilised. In the latter, the production team has limited choices on how to procure the finished product or service.

Design Within the Project Context

Apart from the constraints of time, cost, performance and risk, there are a whole range of other issues to consider. These constitute the project context. Failure to properly address their impact may jeopardise the outcome of the project.

Successful management of the design and implementation phases hinges on a realistic assessment of what is achievable. Using the SMART criteria for example, project aims need to be Specific, Measurable, Achievable, Realistic and Timebound. Other aspects of the project context include, but are not limited to the following:

Stakeholder and Customer Requirements

This covers any constraint to the project (or opportunities) resulting from the prospective users and other stakeholders, e.g. shareholders in the client organisation.

Some parameters may be given higher priorities than others. In an emergency or life-threatening situation, time may become the most important element. Another point to note is that there may be multiple layers of customers for a particular product or service. These include the sponsor who pays for it, the supplier and the end user. Some projects are characterised by a fixed time frame. Examples would include sports arenas for an Olympic or Commonwealth Games, the Millennium Dome or projects to mitigate the (so called) Millennium Bug.

Budgetary/Financial issues

In addition to initial cost, project managers need to be mindful of whole life or life-cycle costs. These include operating and maintenance cost of the product or service to be delivered. The choice of a less expensive solution at the design phase may well turn out to be more expensive in the long run.

Sponsors or funding bodies may also impose a maximum budget allocation or attach certain conditions to the release of funds for a project e.g. specific cash flow sequence or particular accounting conventions. All of which may influence the way a project is designed or implemented.

Time vs Cost vs Quality

These parameters tend to be inter-related in project management. An increase in quality of a product or service would probably give rise to a corresponding increase in cost and sometimes prolong the time required. In reality, the exact relationship between these parameters would depend on a variety of circumstances and on the people involved. However, the project manager needs to be aware of how changes in any of the above parameters can affect the outcome of a project. Trade-offs may be required between each of the parameters from time to time and this may have an impact on the techniques to be adopted for the project in general and for the design and development phase in particular.

Procurement / Implementation Issues

The way a project is to be procured or brought into being may influence the way it is designed. The choice between the use of in-house expertise by the client organisation, and outsourcing or buying in external consultants is relevant to the design strategy. Also relevant are the logistics of whether to utilise products or components already available on the market.

For instance, a lot of manufacturers utilise components patented and developed by others e.g. Aircraft Companies may use Rolls Royce engines. This has the advantage of cutting down the time required for the company to develop its own engine from scratch. Concepts such as concurrent engineering, fast-track development or design and construct are utilised to enable the development of a product or service in a shorter time frame.

Level of Innovation / Technical Viability

A project that utilises well-known, tried and tested methods is much less at risk than one where there is a high level of innovation. The latter type may require more technical safeguards, a higher testing or safety regime or a substantial financial provision or contingency.

Design Within a Cultural / Socio-economic Context

Some projects relate to the softer issues of project management - people, places, attitudes and beliefs much more than the technical / technological aspects. For example, a project to relocate a Corporate Headquarters to another town will call for a far larger amount of time to work through the personnel, political and social issues such a move will raise.

Cultural differences, work ethic and varying levels of technological advancement in countries of the world imply that what is acceptable or common place in one country may not be so elsewhere. The project manager and his team need to take these issues into consideration.

Environmental Issues

There is greater awareness today about sustainable development, 'green issues' and protection of the environment. Project teams therefore need to be mindful of the possible effects of their projects on the natural environment (and vice versa). This implies that designs incorporating non-sustainable, but traditionally acceptable materials and methods may be called into question by discerning customers and clients.

Complying with National / International Standards

The design and development phase of projects may be subject to compliance with laws and regulations in force both where the project is located or where the proposed products or services are to be used.

Legislative / Statutory Requirements

The UK has a comprehensive legal framework covering a very wide range of situations including statutory consents, health and safety, contract law etc.

There is a set of 'British Standards' some of which are synchronised with European Union standards. Whilst some of these are guidelines only, there are others which are prescriptive and enforceable by national and international law. A project team should be familiar with any statutory requirements covering their area of operation. As an example, in the UK Health and Safety at work is covered by numerous regulations.

It is also noteworthy that when projects cut across international boundaries, where legal provisions may differ, advice from suitably qualified professionals can be a worthwhile or even indispensable investment, to safeguard the success of the project.

The legal restrictions on patents and copyrights are of particular relevance to the design and development phase of projects. Care needs to be taken to avoid infringing any existing copyrights or patent rights, both national and international as well as to protect any patentable concepts or products that may form part of the project deliverables.

Feasibility Appraisal

It is often quite difficult at the start to accurately forecast or envisage the implications or ramifications of the stated project objectives. So feasibility or viability assessments are usually undertaken to test or verify initial assumptions of the project concept and design before committing time and effort to its full implementation. Feasibility studies are frequently used to examine or appraise technical, logistical, financial and other aspects of a project requiring substantial financial investment. Banks and funding agencies may ask for such a study especially where the project is doubtful or risky. Financial appraisals may compare the project with industry standards or benchmarks and may include such concepts as the Internal Rate of Return on Investment, Discounted Cash Flow, Cost- Benefit Analysis etc.

Prototypes, Testing and Modelling

Assessment of technical feasibility may involve modelling or testing the design or project deliverables via small-scale models, computer simulations or virtual reality models or even through the development of prototypes. This may also involve software trials or pilot tests. In aerospace and defence industries the production and testing of prototypes is an essential part of the design and development process

Many failed projects may have had a different outcome if adequate assessments of their technical and other characteristics had been carried out prior to implementation. In the case of pharmaceutical and pharmacology projects, many years of testing are required before new drugs are licensed for public consumption in order to control and minimise risks to the users.

Nevertheless, there are situations in which an organisation may have reason to undertake a project 'at risk' even though the stakeholders are aware of the dangers e.g.

Investments in expensive sporting challenges where a competitive advantage is more of a priority.

Managing the Implementation Phase

This is the phase in which the greatest proportion of project costs are expended. The project objectives would have been crystallised into an achievable goal from previous phases and the role of the project team now switches to one of implementation or production.

The nature and length of this phase may vary considerably from one industry to another and on the nature of the project.

Keeping the Project on Track

The control functions of the project team takes on particular prominence during the implementation stage. Brilliantly devised plans and schedules can run aground if adequate attention is not given to monitoring and co-ordination of all the activities required to transform an idea into a successful outcome. Control covers the planning, measuring, monitoring and correction of these activities in line with the agreed project management plan, milestones and deliverables. It is usual to have a detailed plan for the implementation stage of a project indicating the key milestones. In Prince 2 (one of the popular project management methodologies), stage plans are mandated for each stage and these need to be agreed before that section of the work is undertaken. Regular meeting of the project team and formal reporting procedures are essential.

Change Control / Configuration Management

It is advisable to avoid unnecessary changes to the project during the implementation phase, since variations tend to be disruptive and more expensive as the project progresses. Nevertheless some measure of variation may be necessary to respond to unforeseen events, client requests or for a number of other reasons. Therefore it is good policy to establish formal Change Control and Configuration Management procedures. These will help ensure that any proposed changes are properly evaluated against the project's baseline objectives and approved before they are executed. These control procedures should be adhered to. In addition, such procedures also provide an audit trail.

Information Management

This covers the systems, activities and data that allow the substantial quantities of information generated during a project to be managed effectively. Modern web-based document management systems are now increasingly available on the market which offer a secure portal for transmitting and storing documents, drawings and other project information. Some systems keep track of when documents are posted and accessed by members of the team.

Risk Management - Coping with Contingencies

An essential element of the implementation phase is the management of risk. Since projects involve change, risks are inevitable. However, a well conceived risk analysis and management procedure introduced right from the beginning of a project, will increase the chances of success. All significant elements of risk need to be logged and analysed on the basis of probability of occurrence, potential impact and rated as high, medium or low according to weighted risk factors allocated by the project manager or designated risk manager. This needs to be followed by an action plan for the elimination, mitigation or management of the risks identified.

Keeping Track of Time / Earned Value

There are a number of tools and techniques which may be utilised to schedule and monitor the timely progress of a project. Some of the most popular are bar charts (especially the Gantt bar chart) and the network diagrams (PERT, CPM, CPA etc.) The latter are related to Critical Path Analysis. In principle, each activity in the Work or Product Breakdown Structure needs to be allocated a time duration and put into a sequence with the other activities. Actual work done can be then be compared to the planned work scheduled for that point in time according to the baseline programme or schedule. Costs (expenditure) can also be tracked by comparing actual costs with planned costs against the baseline cash-flow forecasts.

To avoid possible distortions in the assessment of progress, Earned Value Measurement can also be used. This involves representing the physical progress of the project to a cost-based measure such as money, quantity or resources utilised (e.g. man-hours) to keep track of the actual value of the work performed in a given time period.

Quality Assurance and Control (Getting it right first time?)

The ultimate goal of a project manager is to deliver his projects on time, within budget and to the agreed quality/ performance criteria. Quality Management Systems can contribute to this through the development of a structured set of operational procedures aimed at improving efficiency within an organisation. In the car manufacturing industry for instance, the adoption of 'total quality management' and 'just-in-time' techniques by some of the larger multinational firms has helped to reduce wastage of time and resources.

The UK construction industry is also making efforts to improve efficiency during production through a drive for 'zero defects' and establishment of Key Performance Indices.

It must be emphasised however that there are many industries in which the cultural norm is not for zero defects. These include Information Technology and Tele-communications where time to market is crucial and remaining at the leading edge of innovations may be more of a priority than having a defect-free product.

Managing the Hand-over Phase

A smooth hand-over from the project team to the customer is an essential part of project management. Some products or services may be highly technical and require induction and training of staff to operate and maintain the facilities. Suppliers may also be required to provide after-sales service and guarantees or warranties to cover any repairs for a specified period after completion.

Hand-over Checklists

In many industries, clients are required to formally accept or approve the end-products of a project at completion. The availability of checklists covering the various aspects of the deliverables may facilitate this signing off process.

Effects of Procurement on Hand-over

The hand-over phase of a completed project may involve the passing of authority and control from the project manager to a functional manager who will become responsible for operating the delivered project.

Depending on the nature of the project, hand-over may be a gradual process or it may be as instantaneous as handing over a set of keys. It may also happen in phases, with distinct sections of the work being handed over in sequence. In IT, construction and telecommunications the operation of the end-product may sometimes be an integral part of the project. In a recent example, a consortium was appointed to provide a new school building under a private finance initiative (PFI). At the end of the construction phase, the building was handed-over for use by the school authorities, but the consortium will retain responsibility for cleaning, maintenance and repairs to the building and its associated plant and equipment for the duration of their 25 year contract. Hence the final hand-over is not due till then. The project manager therefore needs to be aware of the various scenarios inherent in the type of project to be undertaken.

Commissioning

In some engineering projects new equipment and systems need to be tested extensively and formally commissioned at the end of their installation in order to ensure that they conform to the project specifications and are fit for their purpose. This may involve inspections by third parties such as government officials or specialist firms. Certificates may be required from the supplier or installer or approvals from the statutory authorities. Any deficiencies or anomalies need to be rectified as early as possible to ensure smooth operation.

As part of the hand-over process Operation and Maintenance Instructions need to be obtained from manufacturer's or their suppliers and such information needs to be given to the client along with any other documentation about the project.

Defect Liabilities & Warranties

In many industries the deliverables of a project (or their components) may be covered by guarantees or warranties from the manufacturers or specialist suppliers. Professionals involved in the design and development of the project deliverables may be required to have professional indemnity insurance.

Project Close-out

This refers to the point in time when a project can be regarded as complete or having reached its end. (Unfortunately, there are times when a project is stopped or aborted for various reasons prior to the intended deliverable(s) being realised).

At this stage it is useful to carry out a review exercise where the project outcomes are rated or compared to the initial project objectives. Any disparities need to be recorded and accounted for. The project manager should compile a report of the salient aspects of the project including any lessons to be learnt for future projects.

The assessment of the success or otherwise of the project can be incorporated into post project reviews which can occur shortly after hand-over and subsequently a year or more after completion. Post project review or evaluation seeks to obtain from the sponsor their views on how well the project has been delivered in relation to the 'business case'. It can also assess the project management plan, organisational structure and the performance of the project team among others. All the documentation about the project will need to be handed over to the sponsor and the project team may either be disbanded or moved on to undertake another project.

Current Developments

It has been observed that there is an increasing use of information technology and systems in almost every aspect of life and in many industries in which project management is applied. Some of the techniques being introduced into the design and development of projects include web-based software and the use of object oriented computer design techniques.

Another area of growth is the development of tools for e-Business and related technologies. These are posing a new set of challenges to project managers who are under increasing pressure to deliver projects using innovative internet technology within very limited time frames. Whilst in bio-technology, medicine and pharmaceuticals, it takes quite a while to develop and patent new procedures and drugs, the IT industry has such a fast pace of change that 'innovations' of five years ago may now be completely obsolete.

Another challenge to project managers is the growth of projects that cut across international boundaries. These require innovative strategies such as virtual teamwork, web-based communications and a flexible-working attitude. For example, inadequate telecommunications facilities and intermittent electricity supply in developing countries may limit the use of some equipment and exclude the use of certain design/development options. Similarly, user requirements may vary from one country to another hence the design of a product or service needs to be based on relevant and up to date market research.

It must be noted that the techniques and method of design, implementation and hand over management need to be applied in ways relevant to the industry in which the project is undertaken. Although the principles are the same, their applications may differ depending on the type of project. For instance, software design is different from interior design, while the design of an oil exploration platform or nuclear power plant would be much more complicated than the erection of a domestic garden shed.

41   REQUIREMENTS MANAGEMENT

Gavin Hall

"Eighty per cent of the people of Britain want more money spent on public transport in order that other people will travel on the buses so that there is more room for them to drive their cars."
John Selwyn Gummer (1939-), British politician. The Independent (October 14, 1994).

Preface

This section of the Body of Knowledge is closely related to and should be read in conjunction with the following particularly relevant subjects:

20   Project Success Criteria
30   Work Content and Scope Management
34   Change Control
50   Business Case
53   Procurement

Introduction

A project manager must have a clear understanding of the purpose of the project. This understanding must be communicated to those delivering the work so that the output the client requires is delivered on time, to budget and is fit for purpose. The requirements must be clear and comprehensive well structured, traceable and testable. The definition and ongoing management of the requirements statement is the benchmark by which project success is gauged.

In December 1997, Computer Industry Daily reported on a Sequent Computer Systems, Inc. study of 500 IT managers in the U.S. and U.K. that found 76 percent of the respondents had experienced complete project failure during their careers. The most frequently named cause of project failure was "changing user requirements." Effectively managing the recording of requirements will reduce the risk of failure. However, this effective management will lead to the generation of significant and complex documentation. Project managers and their delivery teams need to organise,

continually test and fully understand this information.
In particular requirements management is a:

♦ Methodical approach to eliciting, organizing, and documenting the project requirements; and a
♦ Process that establishes and maintains agreement between the customer and the provider including the management of any change

Requirements management is best summarised by the diagram shown in Figure 41 - 1.

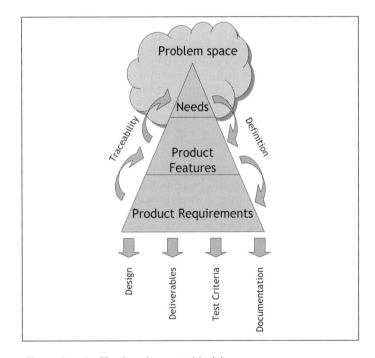

Figure 41 - 1: The Requirements Model.

Projects occupy a problem space that is ill defined and dynamic against which we attempt to define well defined, static requirements in order that potential suppliers can bid against, or project teams strive to deliver. Through a process of constant evolution, refinement and checking we can articulate the organisations needs in terms of features and requirements to inform the eventual design, build and test of the required product or service. Supporting the evolutionary definition is the captured and documented data giving the important traceability, to support constant checking and providing the necessary audit trail.

Business Context and Project Mission

Before any requirements are documented and agreed, a full and complete understanding of the business context is mandatory; this may form an integral part of the requirements document. When an organisation embarks upon a project it is usually to achieve a specific deliverable inline with the purchaser or sponsor's business objectives. The business context is therefore very relevant to the requirements statement and undertaking the management of those requirements.

The business context may be further reflected in the construction of a project mission statement. This statement expresses the customer's view of what is to be achieved and should constitute a strategic vision. This will provide a big picture perspective. It should leave no doubt about a project's long-term direction, what the project manager will deliver and its effect on the customers business and operational environment. A well conceived project mission statement is a pre-requisite to effective project leadership. A project manager cannot lead effectively without encapsulating a sound understanding of the business context, what is to be achieved, what activities to pursue and what not to pursue. This statement, combined with the business context will assist decision-making and the making of any judgement calls throughout the life of any project.

Definition and Purpose

What are Requirements?

Requirements are those externally observable characteristics of a project that a user, buyer, customer, or other stakeholder desires to have present in the deliverables.

The requirements statement must be expressed in business terms and unambiguously state not only the required deliverables but also specify the planned operational environment within which the solution is to exist.

The requirements statement is one of the earliest products of any project. For projects of significant size it is of crucial importance, not least because errors introduced at this stage tend to be the most expensive to correct later. The statement is the primary vehicle for communicating between the customer, and the contractor or internal supplier. It must be understandable to the intended user of the product, solution or service to ensure business buy-in. The statement should be free from any solution-orientated bias. The statement represents the first step towards a solution to the problem and should be based upon an abstract model but omitting any detailed design or implementation or construction bias. There may be situations when a far tighter specification can be achieved and may be wholly desirable.

Producing a requirements statement will ensure that:

1   Customers and providers have the same understanding of what is to be provided
2   All builders or developers have identical understanding of what is to be provided
3   Testers are testing for the qualities that are being provided
4   Management is applying resources to the same set of tasks that the builders or developers are performing
5   The provider can demonstrate to the customer that the original requirements have been met

The Need For Requirements Management

Requirements can change and evolve throughout the project, making it difficult to track the solution being built against an original but evolving set of requirements. Therefore, the effective management of requirements is necessary as they are:

- Not always obvious and may have many sources
- Not always easy to express clearly in words
- Of different type level of detail

- Large in number so can become unmanageable
- Related to one another and to other deliverables in concurrent projects
- Unique in their properties, being neither equally important nor equally easy to satisfy
- Generally generated from cross-functional groups of people
- Subject to change; and
- Time-sensitive

What is Requirements Management?

Requirements management is the set of activities encompassing the collection, control, analysis, filtering, documentation, dissemination and communication of the requirements of a project. It begins with the translation of a business problem into a statement and ends with the transfer of responsibility for the deliverables from the project manager to the customer. Throughout this continuum, requirements management is viewed from two perspectives: customer and provider. It is the role of the project manager to ensure that the customer and provider have a shared understanding of need, outcome and visualisation of the requirements.

The first perspective is from that of the customer. The customer sets out the business need and what is required from a project. The customer establishes a common and unambiguous definition of need that is understood by the project team, end user, and the provider. The customer is involved in base lining the requirements, continually revising the requirements as new knowledge becomes available and controlling any subsequent changes to those requirements.

The second perspective is from the provider. The requirements will form a cornerstone in some form of agreement, either a contract between two external organisations or from an internal team using a service level agreement. It leads into the specification (the characteristics of a project relating to components, capacity, size or performance) of the deliverables that may also form part of the contract or service level agreement. It is the provider's job, in conjunction with the customer to interpret the customer's needs and develop a specification that, through rational argument, can resolve the customer's problem and deliver the output required. This specification forms the basis for estimating, planning, performing and tracking the project's activities throughout the development and delivery life-cycle. It is not in the commercial interests of the supplier to have a continually changing requirements statement as the impact of accommodating change becomes increasingly more expensive the later it is introduced.

Throughout the project the project manager must continually ensure and be prepared to demonstrate that final deliverable(s) satisfy(ies) the needs of the customer and provides for easy maintenance and enhancement during the deployed lifetime.

Ideally requirements should be fixed at the outset; however, they often change and evolve throughout the production life cycle particularly as knowledge and understanding become more pervasive throughout the customer or provider's organisations. To achieve success, the project team must continually review the requirements as new information and understanding becomes available.

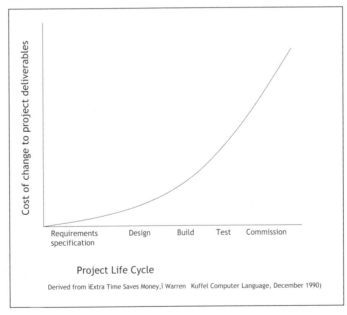

Figure 41 - 2: Increasing Cost of Change after Defining Requirements.

This new knowledge and understanding must only be accepted if tested and assessed for impact and implications. However, if requirements are identified late in the project life-cycle then costs go up exponentially as demonstrated in Figure 41 - 2 as early products are re-worked to the new requirements.

It is vital, therefore, that the project manager leads a thorough study of stakeholder and user requirements at the very beginning of the project if deliverables, satisfying the business requirements and functionality, are to be commissioned on time and to cost.

Types of Requirements

User Requirements

These relate to the requirements as expressed by a user of a system or product and focuses on attributes and outputs.

System or Technical Requirements

This is a more detailed statement of the physical or functional attributes of the deliverables from a project. A good statement will give a complete specification of the deliverables at different levels of definition and precision. A requirement with this level of detail may be incorporated within a contract and feature in contract negotiations. In this scenario the requirements may include a range of algorithms, functions, capacity and performance criteria that the provider commits to achieving in its deliverables.

Functional Requirements

These relate to the specific functions of the deliverables, e.g. the bridge must rise to let ships pass or the computer must read bar codes. The functional requirement lists the essential things the deliverables must do and which must be delivered at specific times.

Output Requirements

These requirements relate to the result of an activity or process when it is presented externally usually in a form to be used by a person. Requirements of this nature are usually used where the customer is relying on the technical expertise of the provider to select the most appropriate technology.

Outcome Requirements

Outcome requirements are of a more strategic nature and can lead to the sharing of risk between the customer and provider. Stating requirement in the form of outcomes is generally used when developing partnership deals and in the case of public sector customers may involve a PFI (Private Finance Initiative). Here the customer specifies the required outcome that typically follows from the completion of a particular process or activity. Examples of outcomes might include improvements in road safety as a result of being able to administer a vehicle test, or a means of travelling from London to Paris speedily, in comfort with minimal impact on the environment. These requirements are very strategic and often reflect the core attributes of a business or government organisation.

It is possible to build a hierarchy of different requirements specifications. An example for a computer system is set out in Figure 41 - 3.

Requirements Construction

The process of constructing a requirements statement has three stages. Each is equally important.

Requirements Elicitation

The first stage is the 'art' of understanding the needs of stakeholders, and collecting them in a repository for future analysis. Requirements elicitation will result in an unstructured set of all possible features that might be required in the product or system. This is the time to be broad and inclusive. The candidate features may come from

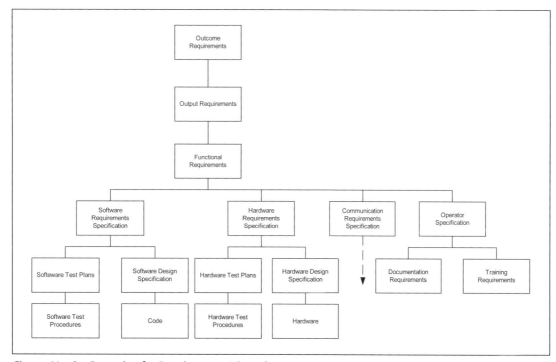

Figure 41 - 3: Example of a Requirements Hierarchy.

a variety of sources such as: potential customers, existing customers, customers of customers, marketing, sales win/loss reports, change requests, trouble reports, features rejected from earlier projects, internal development personnel, manufacturing, customer support personnel, inventors/innovators within the company or managers.

Key steps within this stage are to:

- Identify the customers' and stakeholders' strategic goals as related to the project objectives
- Verify and clarify the problem and objective statements for the project
- Agree techniques for soliciting requirements and establish a programme of work
- Implement effective fact finding processes through interviews or workshops; and identify requirements

Requirements Triage

The next stage is to decide which features are appropriate to include in the statement. It is rarely possible to include every requested feature gathered during the elicitation activity. Disparate priorities, limited resources, time-to-market demands and risk intolerance are but a few of the reasons for this.

Criteria for Inclusion

Deciding what should feature in a requirements statement is the judgement of the sponsor and users facilitated by the Project Manager using inclusion criteria to arrive at an agreed set of desired and realistic requirements. The following should help:

- Need - what is the worst thing that could happen if this requirement were not included? If there is no significant consequence, then omit the requirement
- Verification - i.e. can the requirement be verified once delivered?
- Suitability - i.e. will the requirement meet the needs of the organisation?
- Feasibility - i.e. is it both technically and financially feasible?
- Acceptability - i.e. does the requirement fit the culture of the organisation?
- Attainability - i.e. can the solution be delivered within budget, schedule, and to other constraints

Testing for a Requirement

The following simple tests will determine whether or not a statement is a requirement.

- Is it a description of an input?
- Is it the description of an output?
- Does it describe the nature of the relationship between any inputs or outputs and under what conditions will a specific input cause a specific output?

- Does the requirement specify a scenario that describes series of inputs and outputs that together perform a needed function?
- Does it set out some environment characteristics including details of how often events are expected to occur in the real world?
- Does the statement describe the variety of types of users of the project output?
- Does it indicate capacity or some form of response time which define how the end products need to perform in specific environment for each class of use?
- Does the statement define levels of reliability, adaptability, and maintainability?
- Does it describe any need expressed by the customer?

If a "requirement" is not a requirement, do not discard it! Instead just move it elsewhere. For example, descriptions of components or algorithms should be moved to a detailed specification. Timescales and milestones can be moved to other relevant project planning documents as appropriate. Information likely to be useful for the verification or testing should be moved to a draft-testing plan.

Normalising the Requirements

Discard duplication, omissions or ambiguity. Reword any that say the same thing or are more meaningful when combined or linked to others.

Test with the Customer

Check with the customer that the requirements are appropriate and that business goals will be met.

Arguments will arise concerning whether or not something is a valid requirement. Separate these into two categories: those that deal with whether or not something is a requirement, and those that deal with level of detail. Resolve the first category by applying the tests defined above. Be prepared to rationalise the reasoning for inclusion or exclusion.

Arguments of the second category are more difficult to resolve because there is no clear definition of the "right level of detail". Ask the question "Is the requirement covered by another more strategic statement" or is it implied?

Documenting The Requirement

Writing succinct, unambiguous requirements is not easy but becomes less problematic with experience. The following guidance is equally applicable to novice and experienced writers. Here are a few guidelines.

Content

The statement might open with statements regarding the business context and the problem to be overcome. The following is a checklist of requirements that typically need to be considered:

- Functionality
- Reliability
- Performance
- Maintainability
- Interfaces
- Operability
- Environmental impact
- Safety
- Facilities
- Compliance to regulation
- Transportability
- Security
- Deployment and implementation
- Privacy
- Training
- Design constraints
- Staffing needs and
- Integration

It is perfectly acceptable to reference standards that define quality in different disciplines (materials and processes) or for different projects.

Style

To see if a requirement statement is sufficiently well defined, read it from the developer's or constructor's perspective considering how the author would respond to the requirement. Use terms consistently and define them in a glossary or data dictionary.

Write requirements at a consistent level of detail throughout the document. Avoid stating the same requirement in more than one place in the document. Whilst including the same requirement in multiple places can make the document easier to read, it also makes maintenance of the document more difficult.

Requirement authors often struggle to find the right level of granularity. Avoid long narrative paragraphs that contain multiple requirements. Conjunctions like "and" and "or" in a requirement suggest that several requirements have been combined. Never use "and/or" in a requirement statement, it leads to ambiguity.

Ambiguity

Each requirement should express a single thought, be concise, and simple. It is important that requirements are not misunderstood - it must be unambiguous. Simple sentences will most often suffice for a good requirement. Write each requirement in succinct, simple, straightforward language of the sponsor or user. This natural language is highly prone to ambiguity and subjectivity so avoid the following:

- Minimise
- Maximise
- Rapid
- User-friendly
- Easy
- Sufficient
- Adequate
- Quick
- Simple
- Efficient
- Effective
- State-of-the-art and
- Improved

The words maximise and minimise cannot be verified, it is not possible to determine when it is achieved. What is user-friendly and what is rapid? These may mean one thing to the user or customer and something entirely different to a designer.

Devising approaches that test the requirement once delivered e.g. inspections or demonstrations, will assist in overcoming ambiguity.

Use of Terms

In a specification, there are terms to be avoided and terms that must be used in a very specific manner. Authors need to understand the use of shall, will, and should:

- Requirements use 'shall'
- Statements of fact use 'will', and
- Goals use 'should'

All shall statements must be verifiable, otherwise, compliance cannot be demonstrated. Written in the following way statements should be followed by 'what' the project output shall do:

- The building shall provide ....
- The system shall be capable of ....
- The Vehicle shall weigh ....

There are situations where a list is appropriate, but lists can be over-used.

Research Methods

This section briefly describes some of the common techniques for researching requirements.

Problem Analysis

Problem analysis is conducted to understand business problems, target initial stakeholder needs, and propose high-level solutions. During problem analysis, agreement is gained on a statement of the real problems and the stakeholders are identified. Initial solution boundaries and constraints are defined from both technical and business perspectives.

Stakeholder Analysis

This method involves identifying all stakeholders and then what their needs are using some of the techniques listed below. Check the validity of the work through further analysis. Reverse the process and determine the effect on stakeholders and sponsors.

Board Blasting (Brainstorming)

Board blasting is a process of gathering together all the people who have a stake in the success of a project for the purpose of soliciting and recording their needs and concerns. Most board blasting procedures have three phases. During a preparation stage, participants are invited and educated about the need for the project. During the next stage, synthesis, ideas are generated in a non-threatening manner from all parties and recorded. Special protocols are followed to keep all parties engaged; these include the disallowance of criticism, the encouragement of piggy-backing on others' ideas, and the removal of impediments to slow down the process. During an analysis stage, the board blasted ideas are organised, analysed, prioritised, and expanded for inclusion in the requirements.

Ishikawa Diagrams (Cause and Effect)

Ishikawa diagrams assist the project team to arrive at a few key sources that contribute most significantly to the problem being examined. Different names can be chosen to suit the problem in hand e.g. Materials, Machines, Manpower, and Methods (4Ms). The key is to have sufficient categories that encompass all possible influences. Board blasting is typically done to add possible causes to the main "bones". This subdivision into ever increasing specificity continues as long as the problem areas can be further subdivided. Once the entire fishbone is complete, the project team group decide what are the most likely root causes of the problem that must be overcome/satisfied by the project.

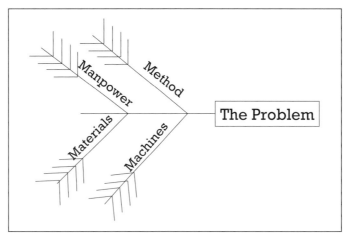

Figure 41 - 4: The Ishikawa Diagram

Affinity Diagramming

This is a group decision-making technique designed to sort a large number of ideas, process variables, concepts, and opinions into naturally related groups. Having clarified any ambiguous statements, ideas are clustered into natural groups, ensuring all the while there is maximum discussion while sorting. Aim for 5-10 groups. Groups are then given a title. If one group is much larger than others, consider splitting it.

Pareto Analysis

This analysis is based upon the concept of disproportion and often holds true in many areas. This principle of concentration, inequality, or inverse proportion can be seen in the Figure 41 - 5, where the smaller first part increases to the larger second part as shown in grey.

Examples of how this applies to a project are 20% of the time expended produces 80% of the results and 20% of the features of an application are used 80% of the time. These Pareto-type observations are helpful when planning.

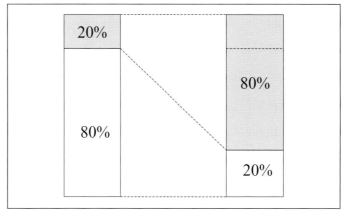

Figure 41 - 5: The Pareto Principle.

For example, if only 20% of the time spent researching requirements will identify 80% of the requirements, then that could be good for the requirement management team who can concentrate mainly on the key stakeholders. The exact values of 20 and 80 are not significant but the important thing is to notice any such disproportions, and then possibly act on such observations.

SWOT Analysis

SWOT Analysis is an effective method of analysing candidate solutions for their strengths and weaknesses and to examine the opportunities and threats faced. This technique will identify the strongest solution where there are requirements options.

Strengths

Consider what are the advantages of a particular solution? What does it do well? Consider this from different viewpoints, e.g. stakeholder, partner or user.

Weaknesses

From a different viewpoint identify what could be improved, what is done badly and what should be avoided? Do other solutions deliver a result more effectively?

Opportunities

Consider where extra value, in the eyes of the customer, might come from. Can a particular solution take advantage of things such as:

◆   Changes in technology and markets on both a broad and narrow scale
◆   Changes in government policy relevant business circumstances or
◆   Changes in social patterns, population profiles or lifestyle changes

Threats

Carrying out this analysis will often be illuminating both in terms of pointing out what needs to be done, and in putting problems into perspective. Consider what obstacles does the solution face? What is the competition doing? Are the requirements for the project, products or services changing? Is technology changing?

Matrix Diagrams (or Boston Boxes)

Aligning two criteria, one on each axis, creates a matrix diagram.   It is used to clarify problems of priority multidimensional thinking. A cost-performance matrix, for example, would chart the cost of an alternative on one axis and a measure of performance on the other axis. Placing alternatives on this matrix would show which alternatives provided the most effective performance for the least cost. An alternative high in cost and performance might be preferable to an alternative low in cost and performance.

Prioritisation

Assign a build or implementation priority to each requirement or feature to indicate how essential it is to include it in a particular product delivery. Priority is a function of the value provided to the customer, the relative cost of implementation, and the relative technical risk associated with implementation.

Traceability and Integrity

Having traceability raises stakeholder confidence and brings integrity to the Requirements Statement. Traceability is the term commonly used to refer to the collective set of relationships between requirements. Requirements may be dependent on other requirements or they may be mutually exclusive. In order for project teams to determine the impact of changes and feel confident that the project conforms to expectations, these traceability relationships must be understood, documented, and maintained.

Figure 41 - 6 shows the relationships between requirements using traceability paths.

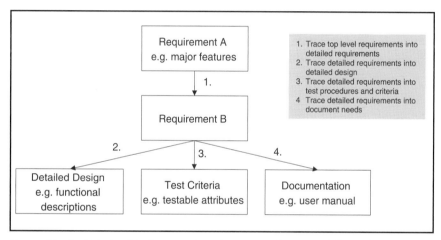

Figure 41 - 6: Relationship Between Requirements Using Traceability Paths.

There are many relationships that exist between requirements, design components and other products and processes of the project. Managing these relationships is critical to providing a comprehensive requirements management capability supporting the project.

If traceability has been consistently used throughout project life cycle it may be used to answer such questions as:

- What is the impact of changing a requirement?
- Where is a requirement implemented?
- What business goals are addressed by a requirement?

- Is this requirement necessary?
- Why is the design implemented this way and what were the alternatives?
- Is the deliverable compliant with the requirements?
- What acceptance test will be used to verify a requirement?
- How do I interpret this requirement?
- Is the project complete?

All requirements have attributes regardless of whether they are recognised. These attributes are a rich source of management information that can help the Project manager trace the requirements and plan, communicate, and track a project its lifecycle. The following attributes may be collected for each requirement:

- Date identified
- Customer benefit - why the requirement is appropriate
- Relationships to other requirements
- Estimate of effort or difficulty to achieve
- Rationale - explains the need
- Development priority (Priority communicates to the entire organisation which features will be done first, which will be implemented if time permits, and which will be postponed)
- Originator - who initially identified the requirement
- Responsible party - the person who ensures the requirement is satisfied
- Version - requirements are invariably refined
- Others might include risk, security, safety release implemented, and functional area

Quality Review

The requirements need to be formally agreed by the customer as reflecting their stated needs. The most appropriate way to do this is by adopting a formal quality review. (See Session 24). The quality review is designed to ensure the constructed Requirements Statement:

- ◆ Meets business and user requirements
- ◆ Conforms to any criteria set
- ◆ Is approved by all those with a vested interest
- ◆ Is owned and
- ◆ Establishes a baseline for future change

Configuration Management

Having created and agreed a Requirement Statement the document becomes a major project asset that needs to be managed and maintained. This is achieved through a generic project control mechanism whereby if more than one version of the document is created then these versions are managed. There are four basic functions to configuration management:

Identification: Specifying and identifying the document;

Control: The ability to freeze the requirements and only making changes with the agreement of the project authority;

Status accounting: Recording and reporting the status of the document e.g. working draft, review draft, approved etc.; and

Verification: Reviews and audits to ensure there is conformity to the standards set.

Once the Requirements Statement has been approved then that version never changes. Any succeeding version should be associated with the documentation of the changes that drive the need for the new version.

Changes to Requirements

Requirements will change. This is normal, frequent and even desirable! The only deliverables for which requirements will not change are those that have no users, no customers, and no stakeholders. The fact that requirements are changing on a project means that people care and that more is being discovered about the project deliverables that are needed.

Session 34 covers change control. The control of change means the assessment of the impact of potential changes, their importance, risk, cost and need. Creating a register of changes to the requirements and linking it to the traceability record will ensure the project deliverables are well defined and appropriate to the real needs and expectations of the customer.

Software Tools

Several specialised automated tools are emerging onto the market to support requirements management. These tools have been made possible by improvements in computer technology and that system engineering as a discipline has matured and become a definable process. These tools concentrate on capturing requirements; their relationships and attributes and managing and producing requirement specifications. Omni-Vista RM , Rational RequisitePro, QSS DOORS, and TBI Caliber are all mature products on the market.

The Problems of Requirements Management

So what might be difficult about a process intended to ensure that a project conforms to the expectations set for it? When put into practice on real projects, difficulties come to light. Figure 41 - 7 shows the results of a 1996 survey of developers, managers, and quality assurance personnel. It indicates the percentage of respondents who experienced the most frequently mentioned requirements-related problems.
Others include:

- Bad assumptions
- Implementation considerations instead of requirements
- Incorrect terms
- Missed requirements and
- Over-specification

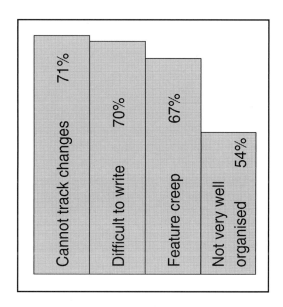

Figure 41 - 7: Most Frequently Experienced Difficulties.

References and Further Reading

Davis, Alan M., Software Requirements - Objects, Functions, and States, Prentice-Hall, Englewood Cliffs, N.J., 1993
Jones, C., Patterns of Software Systems Failure and Success, International Thomson Press, 1996.
Hooks, I.F. and Farry, K.A., Customer Centered Products - Creating Successful Products Through Smart Requirements Management; Amacom 2000.

Useful Web Sites

http://www.umlchina.com/ProjMan/apprmuc.htm
http://www2.umassd.edu/CISW3/coursepages/pages/CIS480/lab/RE/RMtop.html
http://ksi.cpsc.ucalgary.ca/articles/SE/ReqAcq/
http://www.sea.net.au/project_management/requirements/

42   ESTIMATING

Bob Saunders

"Every time I make a picture the critics' estimate of American public taste goes down ten per cent."
Cecil B. De Mille (1881-1959), U.S. film producer and director.

Preface

Thanks are due to Geoff Saunders, for his editorial input.

Introduction

Overview

My aim in this chapter is to provide a discussion platform for the topic of estimating. In the twelve years since my paper on Estimating in IJPM, I have discovered a fair-sized canon of literature, but a canon that is exemplified by confusion even 'chaos'. This confusion exists mainly in the area of language. Strategies, methods and techniques have had labels attached that, throughout the canon and over the years have exacerbated the confusion. This is because no one has taken the time and trouble to produce a lexicon of terms, and thus to standardize the language. Also, methods have been described that could be useful over the pantheon of economic sectors, but they have only applied to the author's own sector, and are thus often invisible to the other sectors. This situation is revealed in all areas of discussion, such as learned papers, articles in magazines and in books written by the gurus of project management, even where these books are said to be on generic project management. This last point is quite subtle, and bears on the cultural differences apparent at economic sector level.

This session will examine generality and also the sorts of projects that will appear in any sector. Firstly, though, I would suggest that, very broadly there are two main types of project. The first are those operating within an organisation on its structure or process, in order to clear up a problem, or to improve some aspect of that organisation.

Secondly are those undertaken by an organisation to take an opportunity of some kind. Then we have different sorts of projects, such as: research, development, introducing new product, reorganisation, and many others, all within such sectors as IT, manufacturing, banking & insurance, science, agriculture, construction, civil engineering, fashion, academia, food, pharmaceuticals and so on. Note that some of these projects have short time scales, some long. (For example, fashion: 3 months and civil engineering: 200 years! Even a military aircraft will remain in service for 40 or more years!) This time scale aspect alone means that there are many different views of estimating to take into consideration. (Would you like to estimate 200 years ahead?)

The point I am trying to make is that there is much we can learn from others. I hope this small contribution will lead to discussion and debate and possibly even some agreement on terminology. If it does no more, it will at least have moved the APM and the profession on to a new footing.

Objectives

- To provide a vehicle for the discussion of the topic of 'estimating'
- To explore different strategies, methods and techniques of estimating
- To produce a taxonomy of estimating terms, and some commonality across economic sectors
- To challenge members of the project management profession to give thought and consideration to the needs and requirements of other economic sectors than their own

Related Topics in the Body of Knowledge

23 Risk Management
30 Work Content and Scope Management
33 Budgeting and Cost Management
35 Earned Value Management
70 Communications
74 Negotiation

Why Do We Estimate, and What Goes Wrong?

Project management is, at least in the planning stage, about foretelling the future. Fortunately, we do not have to rely on tea leaves or crystal balls, though you might think that this is where most estimates come from!

Estimating, though, must be split into two segments right from the beginning. These segments are firstly, estimating material costs for the project and secondly, estimating resource costs during the life of the project. The share of each in any one project depends on the sort of project and the sort of economic sector you are engaged with, as well as all sorts of local and immediate concerns.

Material Costs

This concerns putting cost values on hardware, components or other materials, and services, but also covers rents for property, hire of transport or equipment, hiring venues for meetings or other gatherings, indeed anything that is not to do with human or other resource costs. (The Product Breakdown Structure is useful for estimating hardware and component requirements, as the name suggests.) I would suggest that, because you can get quotations for this sort of material, or work it out from price lists, that this is what could be said to be 'quantitative' and 'objective' estimating. When it comes to accuracy one would expect that it should be quite high. (+/- 5% from the outset - and note that I have quoted a range of values, both positive and negative for a percentage accuracy. (See later)). In estimating, one must always allow for the fact that we are all human, and have our own foibles, and that we deal with other humans, who will have theirs. It is never wise therefore, to suggest that any peek into the future is 100% accurate.

Resource Costs

'Resource' costs come in two types,

- The first is to do with mechanical or electronic devices to be hired for some part of the project. You could even put 'contract workers' into this area. Given rental agreements, there should be little problem with these estimates
- The second, and the much more problematic is human resource (HR for short) costs, and all that they mean in terms of expenses, and this is where the difficulties can begin. This is true 'subjective' estimating. To get +/-5% accuracy here means that the work is almost complete!

With such subjective estimating, What sort of accuracy can we expect from early, initial estimates. These are good if they get as close as +/- 30%! But why is this? Let us explore.

Given a project management software package, it seems so easy to identify an activity in the project, and to say 'This will take two people three weeks' (or whatever). You can go to the people who will be involved and ask them; they might come up with these figures. But they might also have forgotten that one of them will be on holiday for a week, that this is not quite the same as the activity that did take three weeks in the last project, that there will be an argument, and communications cut off for a few days - and so it goes on.

Let me repeat, there is no such thing as an 'accurate' initial estimate, if you are thinking of accuracy in absolute terms! We will talk more about this later; suffice it for now to recognise that there are many reasons why estimating human resource costs, depending as this does on humans and their little ways, is not an exact science. There are risks involved, (one of them being that human beings are involved!) and the best project manager will try to know something about those people who make the estimates.

The Philosophy of Estimating.

The section above has already outlined the philosophy of estimating. The philosophy, whatever your sector, has to be that we have to attempt to predict the future, that 100% accuracy is not an option, and that there are risks that have to be put into the equation. It is also true that, as a project manager you will have to depend on rather a lot of people (depending on the size of your project) for their estimates, so that you will have to have a touch of psychology at your finger- tips. You will need to explore that delicate concept 'contingencies' to cover whatever you can see may be a problem, before it becomes a problem. It is a case of uncertainties ruling a project with even the best plans, even under seemingly perfect conditions.

So, how do we estimate? Let us explore some common, well-tried strategies, methods and techniques. There are, at a basic level, four human activities that enable us to make estimates:

- Breaking down activities to basic tasks. (Work Breakdown Structure)
- Using judgement
- Using historical data
- Using standard data

But before we move on and, thinking about financial implications, it is worth considering that, in Figure 42 - 1, (taking a simple life cycle) the feasibility study will cost us 5% of our budget, but we will commit 65% of this budget at this time. The 'design' (whatever form that takes) will cost about 10% of the budget, and the commitment from that will be another 25% of it, and the implementation - furthest into the future, will cost 85% of the budget, but will only lead to another 10% budget commitment. Those figures need to be borne in mind, whatever follows!

Using these human activities means that we must also take cognisance of the possibility of error because it will happen and it does need to be factored into the equation. So let us, at last look at some reasons for error.

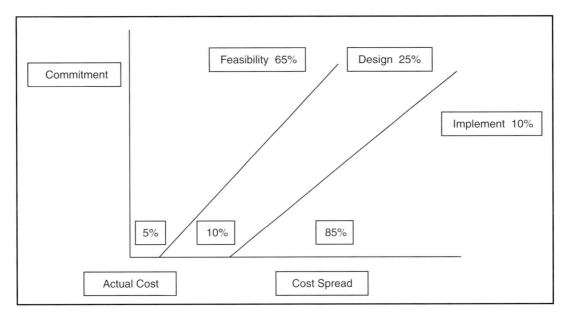

Figure 42 - 1: Budget Commitments at Key Stages.

Causes of Estimating Errors

- Psychological factors - such as optimism or pessimism. The usual bias is to be optimistic over the time it takes to do anything. But beware - a minority of people are pessimistic. Project Managers have to know their people, and themselves!
- Social and political factors - usually pressure from above, or a client, will lead to under-estimates
- Lack of estimating experience - individual training and practice help!
- Poor understanding of what an estimate requires - an organisation, as well as the people within it, needs to explore this!
- Lack of input to the estimating process - a large minimum amount of information may well be needed. (Think about tiling your kitchen floor. What do you need to know? - There is rather more than meets the eye, if you explore this)

Types of Estimating Error

a   An error in the 'Estimating' process itself
b   Departures - from the original requirements
c   Method departure, change in approach to the activity

Levels of Error

a   Soluble, certain
b   Some uncertainty
c   Total uncertainty

Having looked at the way estimating works, and the errors that can creep in, it is time that we found out something about the processes of estimating.

Estimating (Human Resource) Strategies

Drawing up a Work Breakdown Structure (WBS)

It seems to me that the first and basic strategy is to break the project down into the smallest possible parcels of work. The Work Breakdown structure can be used here. This will start life as a fairly high level structuring of the work to be done, but as you explore the work, more and more details of smaller activities will surface. I would suggest that what you are looking for here is a base level activity that takes one or two people a short/medium time to complete. It is at this level that, generally, estimates are reasonably easy to make, for all sorts of reasons, the main one being that there is a small bounded task performed by one or two people. It may well be within the experience of the task leader, but even if not, the task is 'visible'. It is at this level that 'Statements of Work' (a document for the task leader, to give details of the task required) are used. Do not forget that not only direct labour costs but also overheads, accommodation, transportation and supervision that have to be accounted for in this area - in fact anything to do with the 'human resource'. In the provision of estimates at this level, there are skills that are helpful, so let us look at those.

The Judgement of the Estimator

The estimator will hopefully be the person who will carry out the task. This is common and, given an experienced person, usually adequate, though one must remember that there are these optimists and pessimists in the world, and a good project manager will have to know the individual well enough to be aware of their perspective.

The Use of Historical Data From Other Projects

The organisation will need to have stored this information - which is not always the case - but given that it has, or the staff have good memories, and given that there is a need to update figures to take care of inflation, then, if the past and present tasks are the same or reasonably similar, a reasonably 'accurate' estimate can be made.

Using Standard Data

Different economic sectors, and indeed, companies within them have their own 'blue books' of standard data. Where available, use them! People have spent much time and resource collecting the evidence and the figures. However, do be sure to bear in mind, those occasions when your task may deviate from the standard.

These are the basic strategies, but before we look at methods of estimating, project managers need to implement an organisation so that 'estimating' can be dealt with quickly and efficiently in a controlled fashion.

Organising for Estimating

There are a number of tasks to be done: -

- Draw up a task list (WBS)
- List the non - Human Resource (HR) requirements ('Material') such as components and hardware, drawing a product breakdown structure if this is appropriate. (You might also need to think about rent on buildings or other costs if you are running - for instance - a 'move something' project. If you have employed a contract

team, then those costs could be treated as 'material', or as a fixed cost for a set of activities. If individual contract staff have been hired, it might be better to treat their costs in the same sort of way as you treat 'HR' costs, i.e. within the WBS.)

- From the WBS, which will give a list of the project tasks to be completed, arrange for estimates of the duration of the work, the numbers and types of skills required for each activity. You will then be able to calculate the estimated HR cost of each activity. (Because you have identified the people and skills required to carry out the task. Each of these will carry costs such as pay and overheads). Remember people are not productive 365 days of the year! More like 200 days, and creative for no more than 60% of this time, if you are lucky!

- Work out, for each individual, extra costs like travel and accommodation, for meetings or on-site work, and apply these costs to the activities as applicable.

- Apply this information to the WBS, and in whatever way, convert this now to a network diagram. This is where one of the project management packages comes in useful. The result will give you the overall HR budget, and the ability to spread that budget through time (the duration of the whole project) to give a view of the spend against time.

- Prepare structured cost documents to provide a view of both H.R. and material costs. Put the two together to provide the information that will be required of you by senior management. Bear in mind though, that you should be able to monitor spend on the two aspects separately because they operate differently! (HR costs give a smoothish curve, materials spend is often lumpy).

- Do remember that you will have an enormous pile of information by now. It might be useful to write yourself a checklist, to ensure that you do not miss anything.

You will be asking people to estimate progress during the life of the project. Bear in mind that what has been discussed already and what will be discussed below will be just as applicable to these estimates as they are to those you make during the planning stage. It is not a bad idea to give some thought to your project life cycle, and try to ally your estimating strategies with this. After all, as the life cycle progresses from stage to stage, as they change, the whole nature of the project will change. You will therefore need to ensure that the documentation is always up to date.

Methods of Estimating

The important thing about these methods is that they can all be used to provide a total project estimate, and it is always worthwhile to check the results obtained by one method by using another.

Non-quantitative Methods

Qualitative or Subjective

These fall within the scope of the 'Judgement' strategy. Judgement depends on experience and knowledge - and common sense. Also, of course the 'World View' of the estimator. Not only do 'optimistic' and 'pessimistic' people have to be recognised, the inconsistency between - and within - individuals has to be taken into account. The risks here are very real.

Comparative

This covers the 'history' strategy. If the past is being plumbed for 'similar' activities, unless the organisation is diligent with its collection of records, this method is likely to depend largely on the memory of the estimator. Finding a 'similarity' also requires caution. It is sometimes easy to wish the required structure onto a previous activity, thus producing a very dodgy estimate. When depending on human resource in this sort of activity, make sure that your risk analysis takes this into account.

Quantitative Methods

Parametrics

These methods are quantitative, but can be helpful nonetheless. Be warned though, figures obtained in this way are just as 'accurate' as any other estimate, and there are risks in taking them at face value, just because the numbers look pretty!

Simple Variable Formulae

This technique relates cost to a single technical or physical characteristic as a ratio (e.g. development cost against complexity, expressed as number of staff). This is a rule of thumb that can be helpful.

Parametric Estimates

This method uses multi-variable formulae obtained from analyses of data relating cost, effort or material content to performance parameters. (For example, in the aerospace industry, the cost of a wing (and of course the rest of the aircraft) can be obtained using this method. There exists a large database that consists of different wing designs against their costs.) This sort of estimating is often used in Life-Cycle Costing, a technique often used by the MOD to produce costs over the lifetime of a product. This, in the case of an aircraft can be 40-50 years so the estimating needs to be as precise as possible at the front end to (at least) minimise the inevitable drift as the years go by! As we see only too often, it does not always work!

Statistical

Successive Principle

This principle uses the starting point that planning and cost data contain statistically random uncertainties and can therefore be used as statistical variables, or as probability distributions as per Bayesian rules. The procedure is:

- Select the most important type of data. (e.g. durations)
- Split the plan into a few high level activities
- Produce an estimate of time, mean value and an uncertainty value, so that the variance can be calculated
- The variances show the crucial activities. Reduce that criticality

- ◆ Iterate, until the reliability is adequate, and all you are left with is the residual uncertainty

Three Estimate Method

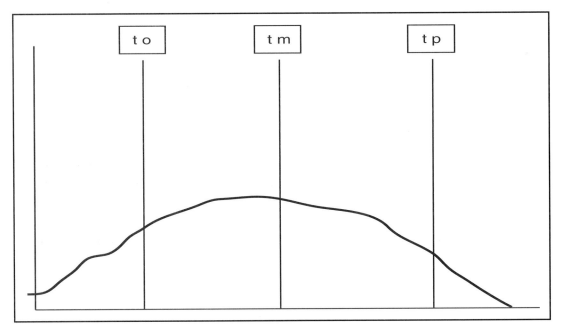

Figure 42 - 2: Pessimistic, Expected and Optimistic Estimates.
(Where t = time, o = optimistic, m = likely, p = pessimistic)

Obtain three estimates, on the lines of 'pessimistic', 'expected' and 'optimistic' for each activity. These can be used to provide a range of values either for cost or duration for the whole project and this also helps the project manager to calculate risk. This method was often used in the oil industry (in the 1970's) to provide views of the probability of meeting 'weather windows' when launching oil platforms.

Software Estimating

Of all the economic sectors, the IT sector has unique problems that need special approaches. After all, in IT, you never actually see the product, only what it does! So let us look at some of the methods used by IT estimators. (If you arefrom another sector, take note, there might well be something useful here.) They too, have little problem, we are told, with small (<10 people) projects. It is larger projects that give trouble. Remember that most estimating in IT projects will be of human resource requirements.

Delphi

Ask a number of project staff for their estimates (independently). Calculate a weighted average of these estimates and use that.

Curve Based

Depend on resource usage curves (The Rayleigh curve) where the area under the curve is the total amount of H.R. required.

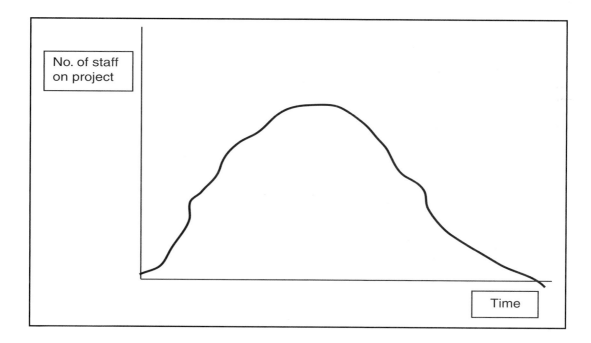

Figure 42 - 3: The Rayleigh Resource Usage Curve.

Multi-parameter Estimating

This is based on parametric principles as described elsewhere. A notable software package is COCOMO, which has four categories of factors that it considers. These are the attributes of Product, Computer, Personnel and Project. It is a successful method, given appropriate mathematical skills. It requires a large historical database.

Function Point Analysis

This is based on requirements factors. The number of functions the software delivers can provide a measure of the size of a system. In fact, counting the number of inputs, outputs, enquiries, master files and the interfaces it contains does this. These are weighted in terms of their value to clients and adjusted for other factors such as complexity. The result, when summed together gives the number of 'function points' delivered by the system, and so the size is given, and then the cost of the system can be deduced.

'Before You Leap'

This method uses mathematical methods, such as COCOMO, coupled with an Expert System (here based on fuzzy logic) to provide estimates. It gives results good to +/- 20%, so needs thought from the estimator on matters of contingenc. Nevertheless it is judged to be a very successful method.

Accuracy of Estimating

Whichever method you use, it is worth keeping the following ideas in your mind.

1   Your first 'quick look' analysis and estimates for a project are unlikely to be any better than +/- 30%. This is where there is hazy information and perhaps little in the way of a requirement specification

2   If you then carry out a feasibility study, you will likely bring that down to +/-15%. Some information on what is needed will have been obtained, the estimates will

have been checked and refined and people will be (hopefully) pulling in the same direction. It is at this level that you might have to make a fixed-price quotation on a project. (Does that idea frighten you? It certainly frightens me!)

3   Once some of the initial design work has been carried out, you should be able to come to an estimate that is +/- 5%. Bear in mind though, that as you progress, the estimates for later activities will begin to bear less and less resemblance to fact. You do have to revise estimates as you go along, just as you have to revise your network!

Contingencies

These are set when the project assesses risk, but it is worth thinking about them when estimating, because of the difficulty of predicting the future to a high degree of accuracy. It is worth applying a contingency to each estimate, after working out how accurate an individual estimate is likely to be. Some help with this is given in the text. If it is a 'ball park' estimate (+/- 20-30%) then a similar contingency could be applied, all else being equal. This will, of course depend on the circumstances.

Summary and Conclusions

So there we are, a short and partial view of 'estimating'. Partial, because although I have tried to make it as generic as I can, I have my own perspective and my own experience - as is true of all the authors in the book in which this chapter appears. 'Partial' is all we can ever be. So, forgive me if it is not what you wanted, I am afraid that there is a long way to go before a generic narrative on estimating will be possible. But, if you are interested, why not do something about it? Visit websites, get others interested, start a specific interest group, talk to me (details from APM) whatever!

What have we looked at? The overview set the scene, the objectives highlight what I wanted to achieve - and only you can tell me if I succeeded - and I gave a list of topics related to this one. Is it complete? Tell me!

I went on to discuss the philosophy; errors; estimating strategies; organisation and methods, both quantitative and qualitative. There is something on the special problems of estimating software, then a little on 'accuracy' - a loaded term when you are talking about estimating. I have talked about the spectra of values of 'accuracy' possible at different stages in the project - but please, do not become hooked on 'accuracy'. It is subjective, and largely depends on the viewpoint of the beholder! Give some thought to the proposition that you pay for 'accuracy', that demanding more and closer estimates will increase your project budget. Given what has been said above, it is worth being careful, and pragmatic in making these choices.

I think that, at the moment that is all I want to say. I hope that you have enjoyed reading it, and that it has given you something to think about. You may be disappointed, and if so, I challenge you to improve it! But remember, here I have been talking to the whole spectrum of project managers from the whole gamut of economic sectors. If this causes you to improve standards in your own sector, then I will have succeeded and I will be pleased. If it leads you to improve standards for the whole of project management then I shall be delighted!

References and Further Reading

Field & Keller, Project Management, Open University, Thomson Learning, 1998

Ince, Darren, Project Costing, Systems International, 1988

Keller, Laurie, Evaluation, Estimates & Contracts, PMT605, Open University 1987

Lock Dennis, Project Management, 7th. Edition Gower 2000

MOD (PE), Compendium of Project Management, HMSO 1978

Rook, Paul, Meeting the bottom line, VNU Publications (NK)

Saunders, R.G., Project Management in R&D, the art of estimating Development Project Activities, IJPM 1990

Swinnerton, David, Estimating techniques & their application, Project 1995

43   TECHNOLOGY MANAGEMENT

Martin Stevens

"Technology is the name we have for the stuff that doesn't work yet"
Daniel Hillis

Introduction

The management of technology is an issue that will impinge upon the activities of project and programme managers at a number of levels including:

- Management of technology at a corporate strategic level for all project stakeholders
- Management of technology used to support or manage the project and/or the project team
- Management of technology used to deliver the project
- Management of a technology related project

This session, therefore looks at technology management with reference to all of these areas and also explores the use of technology roadmaps as a methodology for aligning technological development with the needs of the organisation, be it, corporation, project team or project itself.

It should be noted that the discussion that follows is not just about "information technology", but any technology used by the corporate or project organisation.

Technology Management - A Definition

Chanaron, Jolly and Soderquist (1999) defined technology as: "the integration and employment of technology in order to leverage all functions within a company". The proposition is that any management function within the organisation (including the project organisation) will make use of technology, from which it follows that technology is an "input" that will shape the strategic vision and procedures of the organisation.

A Hierarchy of Technology

Project related organisations may be considered to have a hierarchy of technology (Figure 43 - 1) that will require management's attention. At the highest level is Business Management Technology which concerns the technology used to support the management of the business enterprise itself. This management activity will be present in all project stakeholder organisations including the sponsor's and the project manager's project management organisation.

A sub-set of this within the project management organisation will be the technology used to support the project management function itself; if you like the technology for the Project Support Office.

Outside of this "organisational technology" falls three other categories of technology: Project delivery technology (i.e. technology employed to physically deliver the project as distinct from that used to manage the process); technology as one of, or a part of, the project deliverables and finally the technology project itself.

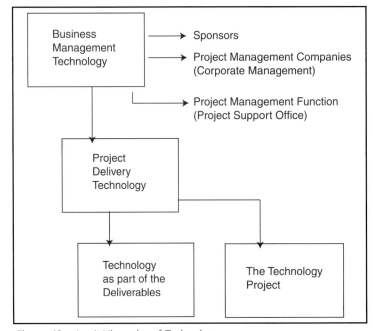

Figure 43 - 1: A Hierarchy of Technology.

Business Management Technology

Technology is both an asset and a capability within the organisation and is integral to the way in which it transacts business. As suggested above, it will affect all areas of the business and all business management disciplines.

It follows, therefore that technology and its management needs to be coherent with and compatible to the short, medium and long term needs of the business as a whole and to the needs of constituent business units.

The Open University Systems Group in "Systems Behaviour" (1988) suggested that not only is technology an essential element of any business organisation system, but that there are active links between technology and all the other elements of the system (Figure 43 - 2). Technology impacts on each business function and vice versa.

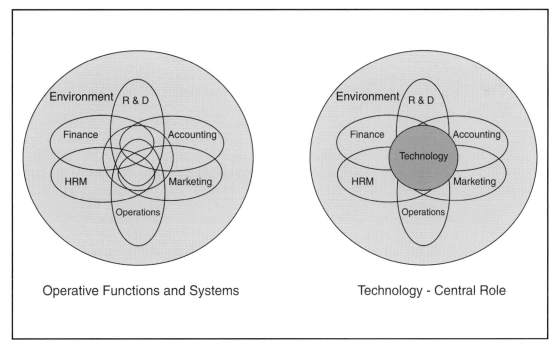

Figure 43 - 2: A Systematic Approach to Technology and the Operative Functions of a Firm.
(After Chanaron, Jolly and Soderquist)

One particular area of significant technological impact can be on the performance of people within the organisation, which can affect:

- Job design and content
- Attitudes to work
- Job satisfaction

Management generally and project managers in particular need to be alert to these matters when developing technological strategies. They may need to have regard to their own approach to communication (Session 70); leadership (Session 72); teamwork (Session 71); and personnel management (Session 75) in terms of the "soft" skills as well as organisational structure and roles (Sessions 66 and 67); project success criteria (Session 20) and strategy (Session 21).

As Peters (1997) reminds us: "technology - no matter how powerful is "merely" an enabler. You can wire yourself up until you are blue in the face (and broke) ... but in the end it's a people game."

Effective technology management is important because the rate of change of technological capability is so fast (and accelerating). The capabilities of the personal computer, launched by IBM in 1981 would have amazed Charles Babbage and yet barely a generation later pocket sized PDA's that are many times more powerful than those early desktops are commonplace and many readers will be aware that the modern car is equipped with more computing technology than Armstrong's 1969 Apollo spacecraft.

It is this rate of change that gives rise to management's dilemma (possibly alongside pressure from suppliers' marketing teams that inform you that you need the latest, fastest, glitziest gismo). When developing your management approach to technology for your business or project you need to 'pitch' your decision making within a changing technological scene. Over the course of the business or project life-cycle the technological 'norm' will have shifted. Do you elect to use tried and tested technology? Do you use recently new technology? or do you go for emergent technology that will be available by the time you have to install it?

The choice you make will depend on the nature of the business or project; the purpose of the technology; the corporation's and project sponsor's attitude to risk and so on. Decision making will be influenced by good business and project management practices and techniques espoused throughout Pathways and elsewhere, supplemented by methodologies such as technology roadmapping discussed later in this session.

Project Management Technology

For the project management organisation, project management technology is a sub-set of business management technology. Accordingly, the same disciplines as those adopted to manage technology at a business management level, should be employed at the project office level.

A key difference however, is that any technology deployed at project office level is more likely to be "mission critical" for the project office and therefore particular attention should be focussed on risk management, avoidance of single points of failure and business contingency and continuity arrangements.

A further issue at project office level is the increasing need to share information in real time with partners, collaborators and others via project intranets, hosting services etc.

Project Delivery Technology

In the context of this session, project delivery technology is that critical technology used to physically deliver the project, it concerns computer aided manufacture, computer numeric control, just in time delivery and inventory systems whose failure would have a major impact upon the success of the project.

It does not include computer aided design, simulation, modelling, project management applications and the like used to generate solutions, production information or management information.

Technology as a Project Deliverable

Projects can often have a technological 'component' as one or more of the deliverables. Examples would include building management systems in a new or refurbished building, access control systems, navigation and communication systems in an aircraft or ship; business systems in a change management project and so on.

Particular attention is required by the project management team to technology components of any project to ensure that these elements are delivered in a timely manner as required by the project plan.

The Technology Project

A technology project is, by its nature, leading (or bleeding) edge. Such projects are configured to "push" the boundaries of existing systems, equipment and methodologies by developing better, faster, more reliable, more accurate devices and systems.

It follows therefore, that not only are the deliverables of such projects more difficult to define in absolute terms, they are likely to change as the early feasibility studies and research and development inputs emerge as the project progresses. Accordingly, establishment of timelines and agreement of milestones is more difficult. Activity durations, resource requirements and attainment of key performance criteria or benchmarks are more difficult to predict.

For the successful project, therefore, the management team will need to place specific emphasis on the Strategic and Control techniques discussed in Pathways Sections 2 and 3.

Framework for Technology Planning

As previously stated, technology assets and resources and their management must be linked to corporate objectives and, therefore also linked to project objectives within project related firms. Technology is of strategic importance in delivering value and competitive advantage. It is becoming increasingly important as costs, complexity and rate of technological change increases alongside the globalisation of competition and technological sources.

"The essence of business strategy and planning is concerned with aligning the activities and resources of the firm in such a way as to generate a sustainable competitive position in the market place." (Phaal, Farrukh & Probert)

When considering technology, it is necessary to reflect upon:

◆ Internal aspects
◆ External aspects
◆ Sources of new or improved technology
◆ Strengths of competitor's technology
◆ Expectations of clients and stakeholders

Phaal, Farrukh and Probert (1999) note that, in general, an organisation's technology tends to be action-oriented and focuses on know how: "While technology is often associated with science and engineering ('hard' technology), the processes which enable its effective application are also important, for example new product and innovation processes, together with organisational structures and supporting communication/knowledge networks ('soft' aspects of technology)."

The framework for technology planning and management therefore occurs at three levels:

1 Business level
2 Product level
3 Technology level

Phaal, Farrukh and Probert note that for the effective alignment of technology with business (and therefore project) objectives, effective mechanisms are required to promote knowledge flow. Moreover, there is a need to create a balance between the "pull" of business need and the marketplace with the "push" of technological capabilities. They propose a framework for technology planning (Figure 43 - 3) which brings together the three levels referred to above with notions of knowledge management comprising 'know-why'; 'know-what'; 'know-how'; know-who' and 'know-when' (Chai et. al., 1999).

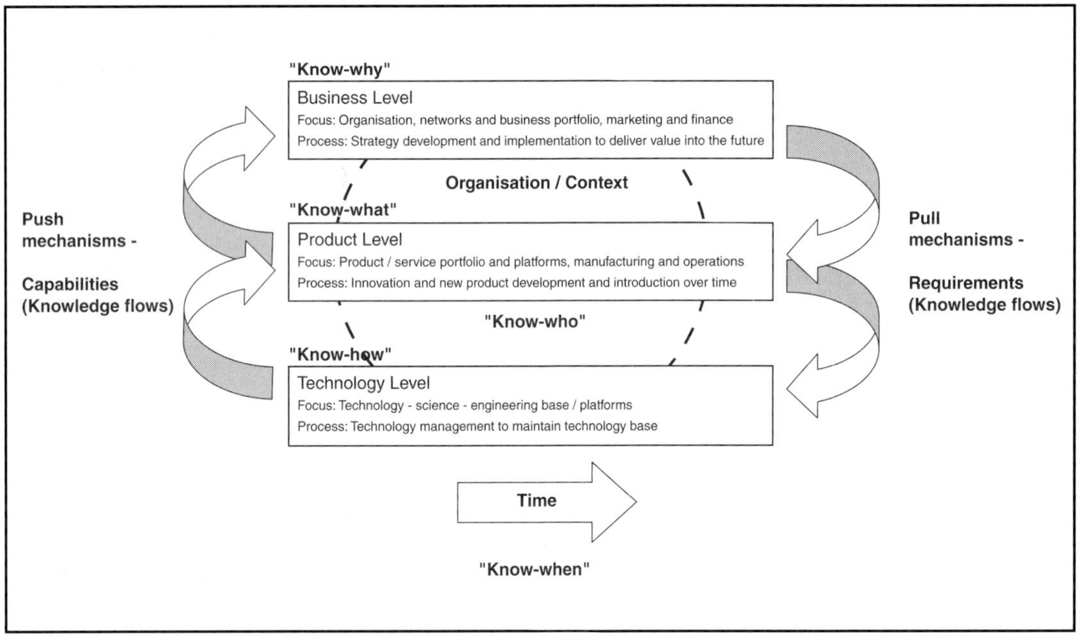

Figure 43 - 3: Technology Planning Framework (Phaal, Farrukh and Probert)

Technology Roadmapping

Technology roadmapping is a methodology to support the development of and planning for technology strategies within the organisation. It commences by developing a need for an understanding of the business environment:

- Market
- Competition
- Customers
- Collaborators
- Regulatory matters etc.

Maps may be of different forms, but generally take the form of a time-based chart that seeks to link developments in technology to future product, project and market requirements.

The primary components of the map are: technology, product, market and the time dimension. However, the process is, at least initially, exploratory and iterative in nature. Its success relies on both vision and commitment from participants to the process, although a difficulty with the process is that the resultant roadmaps can be difficult to maintain.

The Roadmap Process

Preparation of the technology roadmap centres around four key phases:

1   Market
2   Product
3   Technology
4   Roadmapping

These phases are supplemented by planning, co-ordination and implementation activities (Figure 43-4).

An effective way of undertaking the four key stages is by means of a facilitated workshop for each stage. Workshop participants should be drawn from all elements of the organisation including technical and commercial functions.

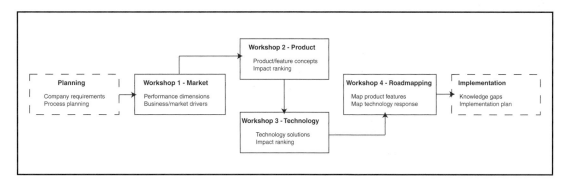

Figure 43 -4: Roadmap Process

Process Planning

A successful mapping exercise will itself require careful planning and co-ordination. The aims and objectives of the process need to be circulated and agreed (not necessarily simple to do, given that part of the purpose behind the process is "crystal ball gazing") and an individual needs to take ownership of the process and undertake the required co-ordination of activities and participants.

It is, of course, desirable that all participants will be involved at all stages. The reality however, is that some specialists may only be able to be involved in some of the workshops. The co-ordinator, therefore, has the crucial task of recording the results and outputs of each workshop so that it may be used as informed input to subsequent sessions.

Market

The purpose of this workshop is to examine the drivers for future business or project success. Matters to consider could include:

- Current business plans
- Aims and objectives of senior management
- Views of customers and clients including customer demand
- Views of the wider market place
- Views of the media
- Competitor activity
- Regulatory or legislative constraints
- Resources

Once a range of drivers has been identified, consideration should move towards evaluating the extent of the impact they may have, the time frame involved and an assessment of their priority or importance.

The output from the workshop should be a series of groups of prioritised key drivers to the business, mapped with respect to time.

Product

The product workshop seeks to determine those products that are (or will be) required to meet the drivers identified by the earlier market workshop. What will the company offer its clients and customers in response to identified drivers over the time-frame under consideration?

Identified products may either be produced 'in-house' or sought from external sources, thereby creating demand in the market place.

Bear in mind that, for the project management organisation, it is project management itself that is the 'product' and this workshop can be used to identify and develop services to be offered to clients as well as service needs from suppliers or sub-consultants.

A key remit of the product workshop should be to consider alternative strategies for meeting the business drivers identified.

The output from the workshop should be a series of products and their feature concepts ranked by the impact they may have on the market and key business drivers.

Technology

The purpose of this workshop is to identify the tools, devices and technologies required to enable the products that emerged from the product workshop to be delivered and thereby the key business and market drivers satisfied. This workshop should also consider if the required technology is available, tried and tested; available but new or expected to be available in due course.

Iteration

Clearly, the time-frames expected for key drivers to materialise as identified in the market workshop are unlikely to co-incide exactly with the timing and availability of the required technologies or products. Accordingly, there will be a degree of iteration required as the product and technology workshops moderate the outputs from the market workshop (and vice-versa).

Roadmapping

The fourth workshop's objective is to draw together the outputs from earlier workshops into a coherent form that enables the business or project to chart its forward course.

Amongst other things, the workshop should opine or make recommendations about:

- Key drivers
- Time-scales
- Milestones
- Levels of importance
- Product strategies
- Product evolution
- Technological programmes
- Priority
- Impact

Output from the workshop is likely to take the form of a report comprising both words and, importantly, time-related charts depicting the linkages between the constituent elements of the roadmap. Figure 43 - 5 provides a contents template for a roadmap report, recommended by Industry Canada, whilst Figure 44 - 6 on page 43 - 14 depicts an illustrative technology roadmap.

Roadmap Report Contents

1. **Introduction and Background**

   - Mission/vision
   - Project goals, objectives and end states
   - Scope and boundary conditions of the roadmapping effort
   - The current industry; its products, customers, suppliers and production processes
   - Market trends and projections
   - Relevant constraints (regulatory, stakeholder, budget etc.)

2. **Technical needs and capabilities**

   - Targeted products
   - Functional and performance requirements
   - Current science and technology capabilities
   - Gaps and barriers
   - Development strategy and targets

3. **Technology development strategy**

   - Evaluation and prioritisation of technologies
   - Recommended technologies
   - Decision points and schedule
   - Budget summary

4. **Conclusion**

   - Recommendations
   - Implementation plan

5. **Appendices**

   - Roadmapping process
   - Participants

Figure 43 - 5: Template for Roadmap Report Contents (After Industry Canada)

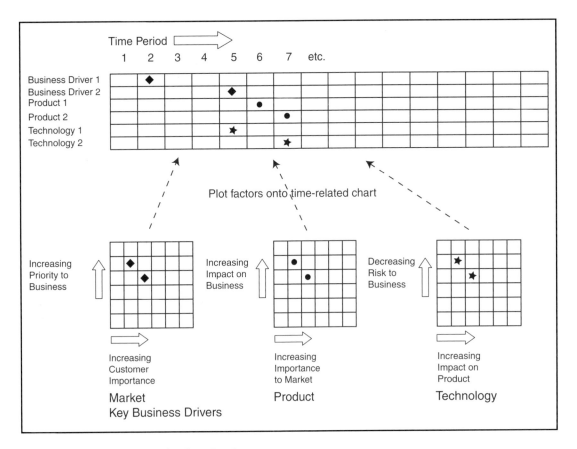

Figure 43 - 6: Illustrative Technology Roadmap

Conclusion

The impact of fast-changing technology upon project and business management is a factor that requires particular attention. Decisions concerning use and deployment of technology on a project by project basis need to balance the modernity of chosen technologies with the risks of project delays or deliverable failures. New and untested emergent technologies are clearly more risky than established ones, but may be expected to have a longer life before becoming obsolescent.

Roadmapping enables consideration of technology and technological developments and investments theirin to be linked to the product needs of the business and the demands of the market in which it operates.

"A technology roadmap does not predict future breakthroughs in science or technology; rather, it forecasts and articulates the elements required to address future technological needs. a roadmap describes a given future, based on the shared vision of the people developing the roadmap and provides a framework for making that future happen technologically" (Industry Canada).

References and Further Reading:

Cardozo, R N., "Obstacles to Growth of New Technology-Based Enterprises", Carlson School of Management, University of Minnesota.

Chai, K H, Shi, Y J, and Gregory, M J., "Bridging Islands of Knowledge: A framework of knowledge sharing in international manufacturing networks", 6th European Operations Management Annual Conference, Venice, 1999.

Chanaron, J, Jolly, D and Soderquist, K., "Technological Management: A Tentative Research Agenda", Groupe ESC, Grenoble, 1999.

Industry Canada, "Technology Roadmapping: A Guide for Government Employees", Ottawa.

Maxwell, C., "The Future of Work: Understanding the Role of Technology", Telecomunications Journal Vol 18 No. 1, British Telecommunications, 1999.

Open University Systems Group, "Systems Behaviour" 3rd Edition, Paul Chapman Publishing, London, 1988.

Peters, T J., "The Circle of Innovation. You can't shrink your way to greatness", Hodder and Stoughton, London, 1997.

Phaal, R, Farrukh, C J P, and Probert, D R., "Fast-Start Technology Roadmapping", University of Cambridge.

United States Department of Energy, "Building Envelope Technology Roadmap (Draft)", 2000.

44   VALUE ENGINEERING

Martyn Quartermain

"Intellectuals are people who believe that ideas are of more importance than values. That is to say, their own ideas and other people's values."

Gerald Brenan (1894-1987), Maltese-born writer and novelist. Thoughts in a Dry Season "Life" (1978).

Links to Other Body of Knowledge Topics

Value Engineering is a value improving technique, which can contribute significantly to the successful delivery of projects, products or services, particularly when integrated within the project management process. As such Value Engineering has logical links to several other sessions within Pathways, these are:

22   Value Management
23   Risk Management

Introduction

Definition and Link to Value Management

The terms Value Engineering, Value Management, Value Analysis and a variety of other 'Value Titles' are often used interchangeably within the context of value improving approaches. This situation has evolved from numerous value organisations and societies throughout the world, each promoting differing definitions. In a sense this confusion of definition has not helped the establishment and development of value techniques within the project management arena, interest has focussed on appropriate definition rather than the power of technique. In Europe, the publication of The European Standard on Value Management (BS EN 12973:2000) has provided clarity in that Value Management is seen in a macro sense as " a style of management aimed at maximising the overall performance of an organisation". For example Value Management would be concerned with the 'What' - What do we need to improve within our business/organisation? What cultural change is required? What project or programme of projects is required? What are the objectives? and so on. Whereas, Value Engineering focuses on the 'How' - How to deliver projects at optimum value? How to achieve desired functionality at least cost?

Value Engineering being seen as a subset of Value Management and a technique to support the overall management of value. Within this context Value Engineering may be defined as a "A systematic approach to delivering required functions (or objectives) at lowest cost without detriment to quality, performance and reliability" (Connaughton and Green, CIRIA, 1996). It is on this basis that Value Engineering is considered here, that is a technique to be used within the project life-cycle in support of delivering overall value for money.

Value Engineering in the Project Life-Cycle

Developing the above concept it can be seen that throughout the project life cycle there is an opportunity to influence value. This is illustrated in the simple model of project life cycle below.

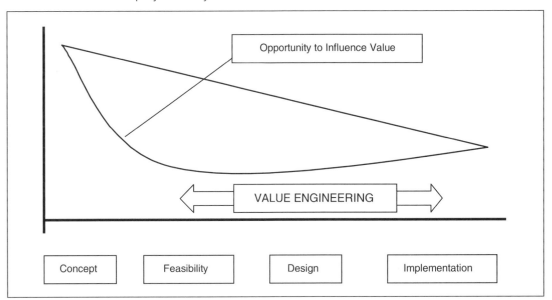

Diagram 44 - 1: Value Engineering in the Project Life Cycle

As we move through the life cycle the opportunity to influence value diminishes. This is because issues become fixed, for example elements of design may be frozen.

Value influencing opportunitites in the early stages tend to be of a macro nature, What should we be doing? Is there a project at all?, and therefore fall within the consideration of Value Management. Value influencing opportunities in the middle and latter stages, although perhaps not so large, never the less remain significant in support of the overall delivery of value. It is here influence can be applied through the use of Value Engineering.

History and Background

Development since 1940's

Before moving on to the principles and application of Value Engineering it is useful to establish the credibility of the technique. Value Engineering is by no means 'new', it is an established discipline, possessing both an extensive theoretical literature base and track record of application throughout the world. The origins can be traced back to manufacturing in the USA during the 1940s, Larry Miles of GEC being considered the father of the technique. During this period US manufacturing was running at maximum capacity in order to support World War II and was faced with a scarcity of raw materials together with rising demand for key products. Within GEC this prompted the creation of teams to address the problem, the primary difference being the teams adopted a functional approach to analysing products. For example, completed products were broken down into separate parts, the functionality of each part identified and then the question asked 'If we can't get the part (due to supply shortages of raw materials), how else can we achieve the function'. This approach resulted in the identification of alternatives which overcame the scarcity of raw materials whilst still delivering the required functionality.

In addition it was noticed, as a side effect of the process that many substitutions often resulted in reduced cost. This early work analysing products on the basis of functionality was termed Value Analysis. Over the next ten years the approach became more refined with the focus on products in design and development and the term Value Engineering adopted. Use spread throughout US manufacturing and to other parts of the world. For example, Value Engineering was adopted in Japan, being seen as an integral part of a Total Quality Management philosophy. More recently the process has evolved into Value Management with application at a macro level as referred to earlier in this chapter. This evolotion is illustrated in Figure 44 - 2.

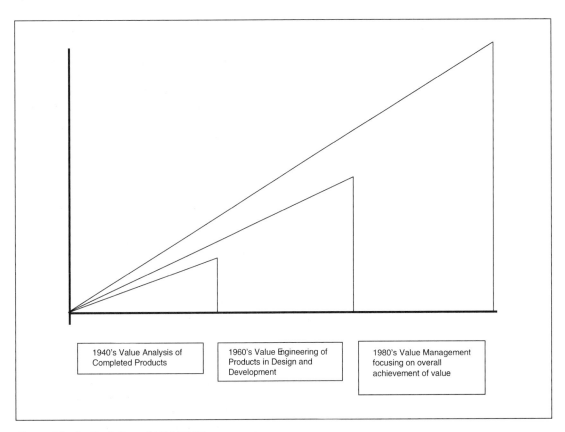

1940's Value Analysis of Completed Products

1960's Value Engineering of Products in Design and Development

1980's Value Management focusing on overall achievement of value

Figure 44 - 2: Evolution of VA/VE/VM

Principles and Tools

Concept of Value

The word value is frequently used in everday life, but often not fully understood. Dictionary definitions refer to words such as 'worth, utility, standards, benefit, desirability' and so on. Certainly value can mean different things to different people. It is worthy of note that 'quality' is frequently cited as being the same as 'value', however this can be countered by examining maufacturing products. A company may well produce products which are of best quality through control of its manufacturing processes yet still goes out of business because the products cannot be sold at a competitive price. Surely, such products are not good value to the company? It follows then value must have a dimension beyond quality. This difficulty of understanding value is addressed in Value Enginneering through the inclusion of project stakeholders. Who is better placed to determine value than the stakeholders to the project?, indeed failure to consider key stakeholders is a major cause of poor value on projects.

Value Relationship

Value Engineering seeks to address the issue of understanding value by introducing a key feature of the technique, that is the Value Relationship or Value Equation. This is typically expressed as:

$$\text{Value} = \frac{\text{Function}}{\text{Cost}}$$

Correctly speaking this is not an equation and as such should not include the equals sign. It is in fact a 'common sense relationship' which indicates value is a 'trade-off', where desired functionality is on the top and what you are prepared or able to spend on the bottom.

Accepting that this relationship has validity then its use is very powerful and forms the nucleus of the Value Engineering Technique. Firstly, it can be expressed in many different forms, for example The European Standard in Value Management uses the higher level form of:

$$Value \quad = \quad \frac{Satisfaction\ of\ Needs}{Use\ of\ Resources}$$

In this form it can be seen the relationship would apply equally to the macro consideration of value. Secondly, it acknowledges that there is a three-way relationship between function, cost and value. For example, if function is reduced as well as cost, then there is no resultant increase in value. Eliminating cost without impact on function would result in significant value improvement i.e. in the equation if cost goes down and function remains the same value increases, such cost reduction is termed 'unneccessary cost' (Green & Popper, CIOB, 1990) and would be the obvious area to examine for initial value improvement. It should also be noted that increasing cost, perhaps in particular areas of a project or process, provided that it delivers a proportionate increase in functionality would also result in an improvement in value. It is the recognition of this three-way relationship between function, cost and value which differentiates Value Engineering from other cost improvement/cost reduction approaches. Typically, raw cost reduction techniques target the easy areas of cost reduction without fully thinking through the impact on functionality.

Blanket cost reduction that impacts significantly on functionality is likely to result in diminshed value. What differentiates Value Engineering is the focus on cost reduction whilst endeavouring to protect desired functionality.

Thinking in Terms of 'Function'

Clearly then, understanding function in the value relationship is key to Value Engineering, yet it is the area typically found most difficult. Primarily because function represents a paradigm shift in thinking, most people tend to think in terms of technical solution. How many of us go out to purchase a new washing machine rather than take a step back and seek alternative ways of achieving the desired function i.e. clean clothes? Perhaps setting up a partnering arrangement with a laundry would represent improved value? A further complication is that the definition of function is always situation specific. For example, at lunchtime the main function of a glass of water may be to 'quench thirst', after two days lost in the desert the main function may be quite different, namely to 'save life'.

In essence, function is probably best defined by the following:

- What something does (or should do)
- The use or purpose of something

Function is always independent of technical solution i.e. it is a 'step back' from the solution. Once an understanding of function is achieved it is then possible to explore alternative solutions (some of which may well improve the value relationship). For example, using the glass of water anology, 'glass of water' is a solution, the desired functionality is to 'quench thirst'.

Exploring options to deliver the functionality might lead to say a "juicy orange", which on examination is found to be available at lower cost due to the abundant supply of local oranges. Therefore the desired functionality could be delivered at lower cost i.e. better value.

Function Analysis

As soon as functionality is examined on anything but the very simplest of objects then it becomes impossible to describe the functionality with one function. In the example of the glass of water, its main function is 'quench thirst', but it may well fulfil supplementary functions perhaps 'stop cough', 'create image' (mineral water) and so on.

Complex projects and products will comprise many functions, the process of identifying these functions and ranking them in a hierarchy of importance is termed function analysis. Typically this analysis is presented in the form of a function diagram as shown in Figure 44 - 4.

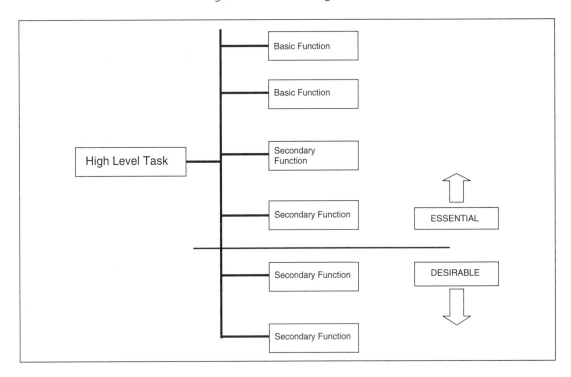

Diagram 44 - 3: Simple Function Diagram

Using this process all the functions being provided by the project can be ranked in a hierarchy of importance. Functions considered to have the highest importance being Basic Functions, the remaining functions being Secondary. At some position on the diagram it is possible to establish an 'Essential/Desirable' cut-off line, functions above the line would be protected when examining options and alternatives, whilst those below the line may be considered for trading-off.

Function Costing

A further powerful use for the function diagram is in the assignment of cost to functions. For example, a cost estimate for a project could be broken down on the basis of a proportion of cost going to each function. Using this process a table is drawn up showing functions along the top and components of the cost estimate down the side. The cost of each estimated component can then be allocated to one or more functions which it addresses. When all items have been considered an addition of values under each particular function will show the cost of that function. This information points immediately to what are termed 'Value Mismatches', these would include too much cost attributed to secondary functions and perhaps too little cost attributed to important basic functions.

FAST Diagram

The function diagram process has been taken further by a more sytematic and complex method of function analysis known as the Function Analysis System Technique (FAST). This was originally developed by Charles Bytheway of the Sperry Rand Corporation in the 1960s. FAST applies the systems approach to understanding functionality and presents functions in the form of a horizontal block diagram where reading from left to right addresses the question 'how' (How are functions to be delivered?) and reading right to left tests the logic with the question 'why' (Why are solutions proposed?). Using the FAST process is a highly effective technique for understanding what a project is trying to achieve rather than concentrating on solutions (Hayles & Simister, BRE, 2000). However, the production of a FAST diagram requires considerable experience and time. As such it is likely the full FAST process will only be applicable to large and complex projects.

Job Plan

Job Plan Stage:	Content:
Information	This stage is effectively an information gathering process. The objective being to ensure all project stakeholders share a common level of understanding Frequently poor value occurs as a result of misunderstanding or misinterpretation. This is addressed through the information stage
Analysis	This stage provides the basis for understanding the 'function' part of the value equation through the use of function analysis The advanced application of Value Engineering may also use other value related tools and techniques, for example Flow Charting and Fishbone Analysis This stage would also include Function Costing and Ranking of Functions to identify value improving opportunity areas
Speculation	This stage is concerned with generating alternative ideas to provide the identified functions. Creative thinking techniques (typically brainstorming) are used in order to identify as many ideas as possible. Initially the quality of ideas is unimportant , the objective being to break out of the normal pattern of thinking· This stage often suffers from a reluctance to consider a large number of ideas and alternatives. However, it is the generation of quantity rather quality which may well lead to the exposure of a 'winning idea' in terms of value improvement
Evaluation	During this stage of the process ideas are examined in terms of their impact on the value relationship i.e. functionality and cost. It is often neccessary to combine and consolidate ideas in order to satisfy functional requirements. The output from this stage is a 'shortlist' of worthy ideas suitable for further consideration
Development	The shortlist of ideas carried forward from the prvious atage are now subject to full development. Each proposal is examined in detail in terms of its technical validity, impact, risk and so on. Each proposal is also fully costed so that the full impact on the value equation can be assessed.· This stage often suffers from insufficient time being allocated for developmemt, leading to the robustness of Value Engineering recommendations being challenged
Implementation	In the final stage value improving proposals are action planned for implementation·This stage may also include a presentation of proposals to senior management and other interested parties· Value Engineering is often cited as having failed due to the non-implementation of proposals. The author has found use of a Value Register can assist considerably with the process of managing implementation. Each proposal is assigned a unique reference number and registered in the Value Register. Implementation actions are recorded together with responsibilities and dates. This document then provides a woking mechanism for the project manager to 'track' implementation

Figure 44 - 4: Job Plan

The definition of Value Engineering refers to a systematic (or structured) approach to analysing projects or products and achievement of value. Much of this structure is delivered through the use of a process or agenda referred to as the 'Job Plan' (Figure 44 - 4). The job plan is based on the concept that the human mind tends to jump to solutions too quickly, often before consideration of all options. The job plan process seeks to 'slow down' this thinking in a logicaland commonsense manner and comprises six stages that would form the agenda for the application of Value Engineering:

Variations in Different Industries/Countries

The power of the job plan process lies in the logical step by step approach to opening up a problem, exposing options/alternatives and finally closing down to solutions. It is worth mentioning here that different countries and industries have adapted the job plan process to suit particular needs and circumstances. Two variations which merit consideration are as follows:

7 Phase Job Plan Adopted in France (AFNOR)

- Preparation

1 Orientation Activity
2 Data Gatherring

- Analysis of Needs

3 Function and Cost Analysis

- Analysis of Solutions

4 Search for ideas and solutions
5 Study and Evaluation of Solutions

- Implementation of Recommendations

6 Anticipation of Outcomes
7 Follow-up of Implementation

10 Phase Job Plan Adopted in India (Bureau of Indian Standards):

1   Orientation
2   Project Selection
3   Information
4   Function
5   Creativity
6   Analysis
7   Evaluation
8   Recommendation
9   Implemenatation
10 Feedback

The important feature of both of these job plan variants is that they include particular focus on the implementation of proposals. In the French version emphasis is placed on anticipation of outcomes, thereby providing an opportunity to mitigate any potential implementation problems. In the Indian version a feedback stage is included allowing the later review of implementation. This focus on implementation is to be commended and both of these features merit inclusion when applying the Value Engineering process.

Whole Life Costing

The final item considered here under the heading of principles and tools is the applicability of whole life costing to Value Engineering. Generally, in developing projects it is essential that cost is considered on the basis of anticipated cost over the whole life span of a project. Typically this would include:

*   Capital costs
*   Finance costs
*   Operating costs (including staff costs, energy consumption, maintenance, cleaning, insurance and so on)
*   Residual costs (including disposal, residual value or liability, site clearance and so on)

Clearly, the value equation readily accommodates capital or whole life cost and cost used within the equation could be either. However, it is important to establish from the outset of Value Engineering the applicability of capital or whole life costing. For example, within a project for a temporary retail unit with a design life of three months then consideration is likely to be exclusively one of capital cost.

Conversely, a project for the installation of a new IT System with extensive organisational and staff changes and an overall life of ten years is likely to warrant careful whole life cost consideration. Recent developments in the UK concerning the funding of capital investment, for example the Private Finanace Initiative (PFI) and Public Private Partnerships (PPP) have also highlighted the importance of whole life costing. Within these arrangements parties contract to develop, deliver and operate facilities, often for periods in excess of twenty five years. In such arrangements there is a significant role for Value Engineering based upon whole life costing. Even the most minor of proposals when costed over twenty five years could have very significant value improving benefits.

One of the significant areas where whole costing often fails is in the adequacy of historical cost data. Typically, an abundance of sound cost data is available on capital investment, but data on operating costs and maintenance is woefully inadequate. Clearly, for Value Engineering decisions on a whole life cost basis to be robust then adequate cost data is essential. Many companies and organisations are recognising this and endeavouring to establish databases of whole life cost information. Again, this is an initiative which has been made all the more important by PFI/PPP funding approaches.

Practical Application

Workshop or Continuous Application

Turning now to the practical application of Value Engineering, four main methods are considered here:

40 Hour Workshop

This method is often referred to as the USA approach as its origins are established within the United States. Here an external team is assembled to review project proposals for value improving opportunities in an exercise lasting approxiamtely 40 hours (One week). Such an approach offers a rigorous examination, but tends to be adversarial as proposals may generate emotional responses from the existing project team. As a result this approach has found little favour in the UK and Europe.

One/Two Day Intervention Workshop

With this approach a team is established comprising existing project stakeholders led by an independent workshop facilitator. The facilitator leads the team through the job plan process to generate value improving proposals in a workshop forum, typically over a period of one to two days. This approach has proved popular in the UK and would normally comprise several workshops during the project life cycle. It is important to note that when this approach is adopted too late in the design process then abortive work enevitably occurs as design is revisited to incorporate value improving proposals.

Continuous Application Integrated into the Project Management Process

Under continuous application regular formal Value Engineering Reviews are programmed into the design management process.

The duration of each review would depend on the particular element of the project under consideration. Typically, the sessions would vary from three hours to one day. The process is iterative and particularly effective for ensuring a value culture is enshrined within the project process. However, for the approach to be effective several principles are essential:

- Reviews must be led by an independent Value Engineering Faciltator (to ensure objectivity is maintained)
- Reviews must be formal and structured to gain maximum benefit from the Value Engineering Job Plan Process
- Sessions should be separate and differentiated from other project meetings to ensure dedicated time is allocated to the Value Engineering process
- Careful selection of participants is essential to ensure 'key stakeholders' are included

This approach has the major benefit that Value Engineering is fully integrated into the project management process and not seen as an unneccessary 'add-on'.

Value Engineering Incentives / Contract Clauses

Recent devlopments in procurement approaches are leading to early appoinment of suppliers and delivery contractors to the project team. Within this environment Value Engineering Contract Clauses are particularly effective. Here a contract clause encourages suppliers, delivery contractors and the project team to work together in the identification of value improving proposals. The benefits from such proposals are then shared between the respective parties, often on an equal basis. Such clauses are an excellent vehicle for encouraging a value culture within project/delivery teams and for supporting mutual wins.

Variations on Job Plan Approach

The power of the Value Engineering Job Plan Process lies in the deliberate structure that it brings. However, this structure need not result in inflexibility. Two practical variations on use of the Job Plan are described below:

Smaller Project Value Engineering

Value Engineering is often cited as being applicable only to major projects. Flexible use of the job plan allows Value Engineering to be applied equally as effectively to smaller projects. The author has developed an approach where a limited period of time is allocated for Value Engineering review, typically three hours. The Job Plan Process is then divided into six thirty minute sessions managed by the faciltator. The duration of each session is strictly controlled with a 'guillotine mechanism' being applied at the end of the allocated time. It has been found such a process still produces effective Value Engineering results even on the smallest of projects, principally because of the deliberate and focussed structure.

Halted/Reflective Job Plan

With this variant the job plan process is adherred to, but halted at approprite points to allow reflection. For example, workshop sessions might comprise:

- Session One - Information
- Session Two - Analysis through to Evaluation
- Session Three - Development and Implementation

Each of these sessions could be separated by several days (or weeks). The author has found the break between session two and three particularly effective as it allows stakeholders time to consider/reflect on value improving proposals.

When the value engineering team reconvenes final proposals are much more robust with greater commitment to implement.

Value Engineering Facilitator

The methods described here for the implementation of Value Engineering all envisage some use of workshops or structured meetings, whether for just three hours or a full week. Within this scenario an effective workshop faciltator is essential, indeed Value Engineering often suffers (sometimes irrecoverably) from poor facilitation.

The facilitator provides the "catalyst" for effective communication within the Value Engineering team and the source of expertise for effective application of the Value Engineering tools and techniques. Such a facilitator requires a wide range of management and interpersonal skills, for example:

- Controlling team behaviour
- Planning and organising workshop style sessions
- Disciplining and monitoring team's activities
- Complete competence in the tools and Techniques of Value Engineering

A question often asked is "Can the Project Manager be a Value Engineering Faciltator?" and of course the immediate answer is yes. The management and interpersonal skills referred to above are fully within the competences of an experienced project manager, indeed it is often said project management is all about the 'facilitation' of a successful project. However, a note of caution, a principle of Value Engineering is that the project stakeholders work together to define optimum value.

Within this context the project manager is a stakeholder and as such will find it difficult to remain truly independent and objective. As a result it is recommended project managers should not fulfill the role of Value Engineering Faciltator on their own project, but appoint an independent facilitator.

Applicability, Expectations and Results

Value Engineering offers a structured and deliberate methodolgy to assist delivery of value within the project life cycle. The methodology is flexible and as such can be applied to most projects and areas of technology. However, the Value Engineering approach is particularly powerful in multi-stakeholder environments, for example complex construction and engineering projects, projects involving new technologies, those impacting across departments and organisations and so on. In fact, any situation where misunderstanding in the interpretation of value may occur.

An essential prerequisite though is the willingness of stakeholders to actively participate in the Value Engineering process. Value Engineering is often cited as the 'panacea' for addressing all project problems. This impression is ill informed and has been particularly damaging to the credibility of the technique. Management of expectation is essential, value improvements of some 5-15% are typically achievable (RICS, Improving Value for Money in Construction, 1998), but this is within the context of Value Engineering being integrated into the project management process and the implementation of proposals fully seen through.

Conclusion / Further Study

In summary, Value Engineering is a subset of Value Management used within the project life-cycle in support of delivering overall value for money. The distinctive features are:

- Difference from other cost reduction techniques in the acknowledgement of a three-way relationship between function, cost and value
- Deliberate and structured approach delivered through the use of the Job Plan
- Focus on functionality
- Recognition and involvement of stakeholders through the use of workshops/structured meetings
- Use of the Value Engineering Facilitator to apply the tools and techniques, for example Function Analysis, a technique unique to Value Engineering

When applied during the middle and latter stages of the project lifecycle the results can be significant, but implementation of these results is critical. Certainly, the author has found integration of Value Engineering into the project process rather than seeing Value Engineering as a 'stand alone' technique offers the best approach for successful application.

Within the project management arena the application and use of Value Engineering continues to evolve. Two areas of extensive development are:

1   Link to Risk Management - Clearly there are significant links between the delivery of value and management of risk.

In a practical sense it is impossible to consider the implementation of value improving proposals without assessing the risk of such proposals. Options for integrating risk identification into Value Engineering workshops are worthy of consideration provided that adequate time is allowed.

2   Training & Certification - Within the UK and Europe considerable progress has been made with the setting-up of the European Training and Certification System. This system aims at establishing value approaches within organisations and achieving levels of competence in application through the use of accredited training programmes. The system is administered in the UK through the Institute of Value Management.

References and Further Reading

For further study and reading two sources are recommended:

1   The Institute of Value Management Web Site at www.ivm.org.uk offers links to many other sources of value information
2   Value from Construction - A Comprehensive Bibliography (Hayles, Bowles and Gronqvist, BRE, Watford, 1997) offers a very complete listing of published material on value approaches from a wide range of industries and countries.

British Standards Institute, The European Standard on Value Management, BS EN 12973:2000
Connaughton J.N., Green S.D., Value Management in Construction: A Client's Guide, CIRIA, London, 1996
Green S, Popper P., Value Engineering - The Search for Unnecessary Cost, Chartered Institute of Building, Ascot, 1990
Hayles C., Simister S., The FAST Approach - Function Analysis and Diagramming Techniques, BRE, Watford, 2000
RICS, Improving Value for Money in Construction, London, 1998

45   MODELLING AND TESTING

Alan Webb

**"The Ark - designed by an amateur.
The Titanic - designed by an expert."**
Anon.

Links to Other Sessions

23   Risk Management
40   Design, Implementation and Hand-over Management
43   Technology Management
54   Legal Awareness
60   Life-cycle Design and Management
62   Design and Development

Modelling

Models have been used as a way of developing a design before materials are cut as far back as history can record. The use of physical models preceded the formalised use of drawings as a way of defining the product to those charged with making it. In the 17th and 18th century shipwright's models were essential to the process of building a new ship, they were often the only means of reference that the craftsmen could understand. In addition, models had other uses including providing the sponsor with a view of the product before work started.

A model can be defined as a device that duplicates some aspect of a system without achieving reality. Originally it meant a three dimensional representation, thus distinguishing it from a drawing, but the concept has been extended to cover behavioural aspects. Modelling is a separate process to testing as it implies some form of synthesis, which need not apply to testing, although models can be used for test purposes. The reasons for creating models can vary; often they are a design aid but there may be other commercial motives. They can be used to display certain of a product's characteristics and, if the models contain a dynamic element, they can be used to demonstrate and explore aspects of its performance.

Models can be either physical or virtual.

Physical Models

Physical models can demonstrate shape, form, spatial arrangement and in some cases operating or dynamic characteristics. They are a design aid. In some cases they are essential to the design process as some aspects of a product can never be appreciated by studying drawings, particularly where complex shapes interact or human issues such as comfort are involved. When made to represent the full size article they are often referred to as mock-ups. In the course of a development programme many mock-ups may be created to explore various aspects. James Dyson produced over 5000 mock-ups and prototypes during the development of his Cyclone vacuum cleaner. Mock-ups should not be confused with working prototypes as the latter are intended to exhibit reality rather than simulate some aspect of it.

Physical models can also be part of the test programme as some tests may be easier to perform on models than on the real thing; ship's hull design being just one example where scale modelling in a water-tank may be the only practical method of confirming the dynamic characteristics before committing the design to paper and building the actual vessel. In other cases where human interaction is involved, the testing needs to be performed on specially constructed models of some special feature before the physical design can be finalised. Escape arrangements from passenger aircraft are an example where models of the fuselage and wing are built and people are timed at getting out of the proposed plane. Practically any physical product that has a human interaction from a hand-held computer to the interior of a new car can benefit from the use of models in the design phase.

Virtual Models

Virtual models are usually based on some form of mathematical representation of certain characteristics of a product; they exist only on paper or in electronic format. The development of infinitesimal calculus in the 17th century allowed the mathematical representation of varying dynamic properties and introduced the concept of a numerical model that could describe the behaviour of objects that obeyed physical laws. For the first time, men could calculate the precise characteristics of a system once they had established the equations. They were limited in what they could model but the fundamental equations that were developed were essential to the progress of both science and engineering. Although they were mathematically dynamic representations, in operation they were static, i.e. one calculation produced one result. The advent of high speed computing changed all that. Now calculations could be performed at such speed, and in sequence, that the dynamic behaviour could actually be simulated rather than represented as a series of unique results. This process has completely changed the nature of design as now aspects of a system's behaviour can be "modelled" on the computer and investigated before any detailed design is done. For example, a "mesh" model of a proposed structure can be defined in computer code then, using the process of finite element analysis, its behaviour can be predicted when loads are applied.

Simulation modelling can be absolutely fundamental to the development of software driven systems particularly where human interaction is involved. For example, the flight control system of a combat aircraft can only be designed when the dynamic characteristics of the aircraft can be simulated together with the human inputs that represent the pilot's instructions. Ultimately all the inputs and responses must be reduced to computer code, both in the model environment and in the system that is actually installed on the real aircraft. By simulating flight conditions, aircraft behaviour and the pilot's inputs, the optimum control laws can be devised together with optimum aerodynamics. Without the modelling process this would be impossible.

Models of all types have always had a commercial and promotional aspect as well as a developmental role. The use of computerised virtual reality has allowed organisations to create images of objects and their functions that a) can be explored by potential users before a commitment is made, b) can be used for advertising or c) can raise public awareness, particularly if retaining public support is seen as essential tothe project. Examples of this are the superb animations created by NASA to explain and promote its space projects. Models are often created at an early stage in the project life-cycle for both their contribution to the design process and the promotion of the project to sponsors or prospective purchasers, they can be an essential ingredient to overall project success.

Testing

Projects exist to create something where nothing existed before; they are about change and novelty. Change and novelty bring opportunities to be exploited but they also contain risks that things will not turn out as expected. The greater the degree of novelty or complexity the greater are the chances of the unforeseen and unexpected arriving on the doorstep, bringing with them the unwelcome. It would be foolish of any project manager charged with the creation of producing something novel not to include within the project plan activities designed to test those aspects that have been newly created and for which little previous experience exists. But testing is not simply a matter of ensuring what has been created works as intended, it may be an integral part of a process of discovery that may be fundamental to the aims of the project.

In many cases testing is not a matter over which the project manager has total discretion. If the product is to have an end user then, in one way or another, that user will want to be satisfied that what he has acquired will work as intended, and it might not be just the end user involved. Society as a whole demands that products of every kind from consumer goods to railway trains and beyond are not intrinsically harmful and furthermore demands that their safety is demonstrated. Thus many projects that result in an end product or service involve some aspect of testing but the scale of the work can vary enormously. It could range from an extensive development test programme lasting many years to a straight-forward commissioning process at the end of construction. Arts, media and social projects may be somewhat different and the formalised testing associated with material products may be absent.

In some cases projects are instigated to exploit a new idea which may be unproven at the start and, an element

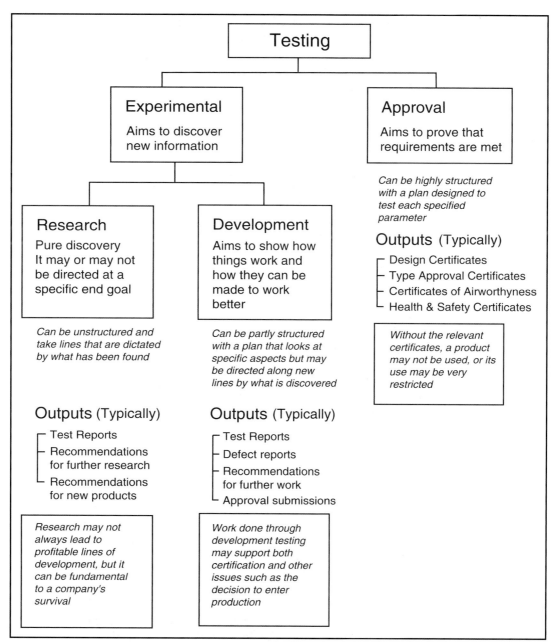

Figure 45 - 1: The Structure of Testing in Projects

of pure research may also be involved. Testing may thus be fundamental to both product acceptability and to research; from this we define the testing process as a set of activities with differing objectives and the structure is shown in Figure 45 - 1.

Structure of the Testing Process

Figure 45 - 1 shows that testing associated with projects can be broadly divided into two categories:-

+ Experimental testing
+ Approval or certification testing

Experimental testing can be further divided into:-

+ Testing for pure research
+ Testing for the purposes of development

Each of these sub-divisions has differing characteristics that govern both the nature of the tests that will be conducted and the way that they are incorporated in the project plan. It should be noted this does not cover testing associated with processes for product or quality assurance purposes, it should also be noted that testing is different from inspection.

Research

Testing for pure research purposes will be aimed at making discoveries. Those discoveries may not always be aimed directly at creating new inventions; they may be exploratory, possibly seeking to establish if a new line of technology has a worthwhile application. Much government sponsored research in the defence field is of that type. As research generally aims to find knowledge, the approach may be less structured than for other types of project as the outcome of the tests may not be clearly perceived in advance but the findings may dictate the course of future tests. A good example of this was the development of the drug Viagra which started as a research programme for a cure for angina; it was an unexpected side-effect that led to its development as an anti-impotence drug.

Most large organisations realise that research into new technologies and products is fundamental to business survival and set aside budgets specifically for this activity; how large those budgets are depends on the nature of the industry and the pace of technological advancement.

Development

Many projects are instigated to develop new products either to the requirements of a sponsor or for general sale. Where these products involve novel or advanced technology, development testing will be a major feature of the project and could absorb a significant part of the development budget. With complex high technology products this can be very extensive and cover not only performance aspects but development of the production technologies as well. The Engineering and Manufacturing Development phase of the current US Joint Strike Fighter programme is set to last 70 months. Projects for the development of new drugs can take up to 15 years. Testing in the course of product development may have less of a research element but it will have a knowledge gathering aspect. It will look at areas of design risk and aim to prove the viability of design concepts.

Development testing can and should have a structured approach; to a great extent this will be dictated by the nature of the project and the state of knowledge at the start. It can be planned in advance and should be incorporated into the project as a fundamental aspect of technical success. In this respect project managers should seek the views of those responsible for testing at an early stage in the development of the project plan and ensure that adequate provision is made in terms of cost, time and facilities. The plan should be structured so that those issues most essential to project success are explored as early as is practical and the findings used to aid the decisions that shape the future course of the project. This structured approach is used in many product development projects that pass through concept definition, prototype construction and initial testing, full-scale development, pre-production and production phases. In some cases, particularly government funded projects, this is a formalised process to which projects must conform. With the exception of the production phase, test results from earlier phases will influence what follows which could, of course, include abandoning the project if issues are discovered that are likely to render it worthless.

Development testing need not be restricted to physical or systems aspects, it could be applied to issues outside the project that could influence it in some way, public opinion surveys or market testing, for example.

Approval, Acceptance and Certification

Approval, acceptance or certification testing has the specific aim of proving a product or system can perform as specified. It has two aspects, approval by the sponsor that what has been developed meets his specific requirements and certification that it meets all statutory demands. It normally comes at or near the end of the development or construction phase but before a product is approved for production, sale to the public or use in normal service.

Sponsoring organisations will normally lay down a series of design and performance criteria in a specification or a design brief; they will also demand evidence that all these criteria have been met before accepting the final product. Project managers will be required to include these approval testing or demonstration activities in the project plan and sponsors may demand the right to approve those plans before they are put into effect. Completion of the approval test programme will result in an "approval submission" or similarly titled document. It sets out all the evidence of conformity gathered from the tests and demonstrations and seeks approval from the sponsor to accept the product for use or go to the next phase in the project, which may be to put the developed item into production.

Some aspects of a product will clearly be a direct reflection of the sponsor's wishes but other aspects may be legal requirements relating to public health and safety. Proof that these requirements have been met may be termed "Certification" testing and should be included in the project plan. Aspects of performance and conformance to legally enforceable regulations must be demonstrated as being achieved to the satisfaction of the certifying authority. The certifying authority will not only specify the requirements to be satisfied but may also specify the method of testing to be undertaken. In some cases the certification process may be left to the contractor, for example a statement of conformity may be given by the issuing of a design certificate (proof that the product conforms to its design specification and any limits that may apply). Any organisation accepting the product should be confident of its characteristics from the details contained in the specification and the design certificate. Without a design certificate the product need not be accepted. Where products are designed to conform to national or international standards, the standards bodies such as the British Standards Institution may provide a testing service as may government agencies such as the Vehicle Certification Agency.

Other examples are:- Type Approval Certificates (proof that the product has satisfactorily completed all required tests and that the "type" is approved for sale and use, first introduced for aero-engines in the 1920's but extended to cover such products as motor vehicles), Certificates of Airworthiness for aircraft and Health and Safety Certificates for public works.

The Testing Process

Product testing can be divided into three broad areas:-

- Structural and physical testing
- Functional testing
- Environmental testing

There is a fourth area that straddles both functional testing and environmental testing; it is termed Field Testing.

Physical and Structural Tests

Where products are physical, rather than software or are primarily a service, structural and physical tests may be required. Physical tests aim to discover or confirm the basic characteristics such as space envelope and dimensions, mass, centre of gravity position, moments of inertia, interface characteristics etc. These properties could be important if the item is to be a part of a larger system and conformance to requirements could be essential to acceptance. Structural testing aims to determine strength and durability; typical tests would include applying a series of loads and measuring the effects on the structure as well as subjecting the item to a vibration spectrum representative of the service environment. Where highly stressed materials are involved, fatigue testing in a manner that represents the cycle of loadings throughout the product's life will be required. It may be a long-term programme, extending beyond the development phase, but one that is designed to run ahead of any product in service and thus give early warning of a possible fatigue problem.

Functional Testing

Unless the project is to produce an inanimate object, e.g. a public work of art such as the "Angel of the North", functional testing will be a significant feature of any development project. Functional testing aims to discover or demonstrate that all required aspects of performance are achievable. In this respect functional testing is all about how things work and behave in use, aside from the physical and structural aspects. Many current products are now an amalgam of discrete systems that are all required to function together in the end product. Whereas this has always been true, at a conceptual level, for any large product, integrating those systems into the performance of the whole was largely under human control. With the advent of computer based systems, that integrating function is now passing out of human hands. With a growing dependence on software based systems in many products, functional testing has grown in importance. Functional testing used to be largely associated with establishing performance characteristics and operational aspects. Some of this work obviously fed into the development process. Now however, functional testing could incorporate systems integration testing aimed at proving that systems required to work together can do so in a satisfactory way. With increasingly complex products incorporating both hardware and software elements, integration is becoming one of the most significant aspects of the whole development process. It can also throw up many more problems than with earlier products and systems integration problems have been at the heart of many delays with advanced technology projects.

Functional tests should aim to replicate the demands on the product or system in service and discover how well or badly it performs under those circumstances. It is a well known feature that all products and services are at their most vulnerable at the extremes of the specification. The test programme should aim to explore these extremes, not just to confirm that the requirements can be met but to discover what form a failure takes should it occur. In some cases the test may seek to determine the failure characteristics and testing will continue until a failure happens, for example the load at breaking for an aircraft wing.

Besides matters of pure performance it has become popular to specify characteristics that are rather more difficult to determine at the outset, in particular reliability and maintainability. Often these are given as targets in the product specification rather than guarantees as they can be a somewhat unpredictable feature and depend, in part, on how the product is used and the environment it is subjected to. The Northrop B-2A Spirit "stealth bomber" had a target maintenance requirement of 50 man-hours per flying hour but the out-turn has been 120 man-hours per flying hour. Maintainability and reliability "demonstrations", rather than "tests", can be included in the development plan but there is no substitute for experience in service.

Environmental Testing

Environmental testing aims to demonstrate that a product can still perform under the range of environments that it is likely to be exposed to in use. Because the passage of time is also an environmental issue, environmental tests often take place over an extended period that may continue beyond the end of the normal development project. Environments to which products can be subjected include such things as:- climatic conditions (temperature, humidity etc.) electromagnetic emissions (radiation levels and frequencies), biological environments (moulds, germs etc.) abrasives (sand, dust etc.), wear and tear (transport shocks, repeated use etc.). All can be simulated in suitable test chambers. Environmental testing can be both expensive and time consuming, the amount of testing will depend on both the certification or approval requirements imposed from outside the project and commercial decisions regarding the worth of such testing. With short life consumer products it may not be deemed to be worth much but with complex equipment subject to harsh environments, such as airborne weapons, it can be an essential part of development. Extended testing beyond that required for certification and approval can build up a data bank of information that could assist product operation by:- predicting failure modes, determining component lives, assisting in developing operating and maintenance procedures and repair schemes etc.

Field Testing

An extension of both functional and environmental testing is Field Testing. The approach is to carry out tests with actual service items in the hands of the user to determine such things as user acceptability, ease of repair and maintenance etc. (In the USA this form of testing is often called Beta testing, to distinguish it from Alpha testing which is in-house work.) It could form part of the development programme where representative examples are given to potential users to assess their reactions and the findings are incorporated in the design as it evolves into its final form. Items such as new food products, children's toys and video games can be tested in this way before any decision on production is taken. Microsoft distributed over 400,000 copies of its Windows 95 operating system to software developers and end users before finalising the package that went on sale. Another form of field testing is "Clinical Trialing" adopted by the drugs industry where a new drug is administered to a selected group of patients under strict conditions. This form of testing aims to look at performance over a wide sample of the population to determine not only the effectiveness of the drug but if there are any side-effects that might affect some persons more than others. In this case the varied nature of the population means that results have to be established on a statistical basis and what is discovered will determine if the drug can go into production and wide-spread use. A failure to detect the presence of side-effects at an early stage led to the Thalidomide tragedy while a recognition of one particular effect led to Viagra. It is at the clinical trials stage that many drugs fail as their effectiveness is not established, an example being British BioTech's much publicised cancer cure.

With increasingly complex products, a more demanding public and an ever tightening regulatory framework, the role of testing and certification is growing in importance and this fact must be recognised in the development of all project plans. However, the three factors mentioned all combine to generate test programmes that are longer and more costly than ever but this has come about at a time when reducing time to market is seen as an increasingly valuable competitive weapon. Ultimately it may lead to distorted judgement and the wrong choice of action on the part of project managers.

Limitations

It must be recognised that formalised testing can never hope to discover all that can occur with any particular product or system. Test programmes are normally designed around a) the extremes of certain aspects that a product might have to perform or be subjected to and b) other aspects based on a reasoned assessment of what might occur. Failures could thus still occur if conditions arise that are outside of those considered reasonable or were not recognized as significant at the time tests were conducted

For example, when the Concorde was certified as safe for a strike on the lower wing surface, a 1kg mass of tyre was assumed but when a tyre was damaged on take off in July 2000 a 4kg mass of rubber struck the wing with disastrous results. Furthermore, the fact that the wing was full to its upper surface with fuel may also be a major contributory cause in what happened; a fact that may not have been considered significant when certification was obtained.

There has been a drive towards concurrent engineering where design, testing and initial production all overlap. Besides formalised field testing, some product testing may actually be done by releasing products onto the market and noting market reaction to faults when they arise. This can occur in situations that may be seen as too diverse to easily simulate in a test situation, an example of this is consumer software which may be expected to run on a variety of machines of varying configuration. There may be commercial and practical motives for such an approach but there are also clear dangers; products that come to be perceived as unreliable can seriously damage the reputation of the manufacturer. For example: facing a threat from Proctor and Gamble's Aerial Future washing powder in 1994, Lever Brothers decided to improve on their popular Persil brand with a new version called Persil Power. This contained a manganese "accelerator" designed to shorten washing time; despite millions spent on research the accelerator's damaging effect on clothes was not discovered until it hit the market. Following a public outcry the product was withdrawn despite Lever Brothers' insistence that its technology was "first class" and "well ahead of the market".

Equally serious can be the desire to reduce testing in an effort to shorten overall timescales particularly with complex systems, as the US General Accounting Office noted regarding US Air Force projects. "Our reviews.... have identified concurrency as one cause of cost, schedule and performance problems in system acquisition programmes..... The Pentagon is expecting to begin producing well before tests and design studies will have proven that the entire complex of hardware and software will work together." The warning is clear enough; testing is an essential element of all development projects, its importance should be recognised at the outset and an adequate test programme should be incorporated in the project plan, it should not be sacrificed for other expedients without a very clear understanding of what is being done and the risks involved.

Conclusion and Summary

Creating models that simulate some aspect of a product's appearance or behaviour are becoming an essential feature of the design process as product complexity increases. Whereas there will always be a need for physical models where physical products are involved, computer based models are now assuming growing importance in the development process. Where systems are increasingly software controlled the use of simulation models may be essential to the development of satisfactory systems, particularly where human, computer and machine interfaces are involved.

Project managers should expect to see, and be aware of the potential, for increasingly sophisticated modelling techniques in the coming decades.

All project plans must acknowledge the need for testing where areas of uncertainty exist. It should be built in from the time the plan is conceived. By building a project plan that ensures that:

a   Knowledge is gained through testing in a logical manner and
b   Design decisions are taken at one stage that are based on knowledge discovered in earlier stages, a robust and logical approach can be generated that minimises technical, cost and programme risks.

Project plans must take into account all statutory requirements for product conformity and any approval process that may be required.

46   CONFIGURATION MANAGEMENT

Rodney Turner

Mc Donald's Corollary to Murphy's Law: "In any given set of circumstances, the proper course of action is determined by subsequent events."
Anon.

Introduction

A project is ultimately judged to be successful if it satisfies the purpose for which it was undertaken, that is it solves the problem (or exploits the opportunity) intended, and thereby delivers value to the owner and sponsor, (Session20, Turner, 1999; Turner, 2000 a). To achieve this, the project's outputs, the facility delivered, need to perform required functions, the functionality. Configuration management is the process by which the project team ensure the facility has the required functionality.

In addition, there may be some uncertainty about the optimum process to deliver the facility. In a development project, for instance, the main point of the project is to find the optimum method of delivering the facility. In other projects, uncertainty in the design of the project can feed through into uncertainty in the method of delivery. And yet in other projects, uncertainties in the background information, which can only be resolved as the project progresses, will create uncertainty in the methods of project delivery that need to be managed as the project is delivered. Configuration management is the process used to manage the resolution of these uncertainties.

In my view, configuration management is one of the three or four core methodologies of project management. People talk about the golden triangle of time, cost and quality/functionality, the triple constraint. Well:

1   Critical path analysis and bar-charts are the method for managing the time-scale. (I cannot bring myself to call them Gantt charts, an unnecessary piece of jargon, which exists in a vain attempt to turn project management into rocket science)

2   Earned value analysis, (Fleming and Koppleman, 2000), is the method for managing the cost, (and, en passant, time on average)

3   Configuration management is the method for managing quality and functionality, (and, en passant, uncertainty in the process of delivery)

4   The fourth core methodology is resource histograms and smoothing, to manage people and organization, (which Kerzner, 1999, puts at the centre of the triangle)

In my books (Turner, 1999), I show a tetrahedron, scope, time, cost and quality, with organization at the centre. Configuration management addresses two corners of the tetrahedron, scope (or functionality and process) and quality. The other three methodologies manage the other two corners, time and cost, and organisation.

In this session I describe configuration management. In the next section I introduce and describe the four steps in the process, and give a simple example of its application. I then show the different emphasis of configuration management at the design and execution stages of the project. In the final section I give a brief overview of document management that various project management standards say should be used to support the process.

In Session 20 (Project Success), I give several essential definitions over and above those contained in the APM Glossary of Terms. I do not repeat those here, but refer you to Session 20.

The Configuration Management Process

There are four steps in the configuration management process:

1   Identify the configuration
2   Review the configuration
3   Control the configuration
4   Record the configuration and changes

I will discuss each step in turn, but first I will give an overview of how it works:

An Overview of the Process

Figure 46 - 1 gives an overview of the process of configuration management. The horizontal dimension represents the uncertainty in the project outcomes. The vertical dimension represents the uncertainty in the project delivery methods. At the start of the project, the team define both as well as they can. This is known as configuration identification. The configuration, as defined, is then agreed with all the stakeholders. (In Session 20: Project Success, I say it is important to agree success criteria with the stakeholders before the project starts. This is where it is done.) The configuration at its current level of definition is frozen, (baselined), and work on the project design begins.

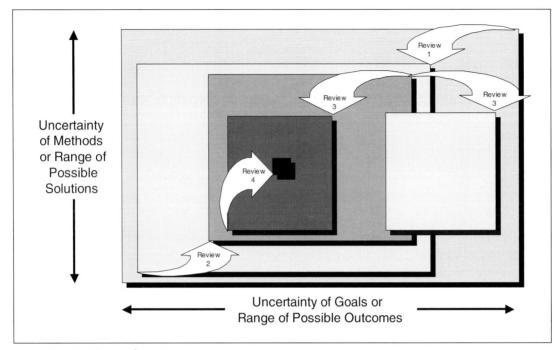

Figure 46 - 1: The Configuration Management Process

Through the design, understanding of project outcomes and work methods improves. The level of uncertainty is reduced. The project team then hold a review with the stakeholders, to agree the revised configuration. This is configuration review. Note this is hopefully a process of reducing uncertainty, narrowing the range of potential outcomes and work methods. The new configuration lies within the scope of the old. The configuration should not need to change. However, it is necessary to agree the refined configuration with the stakeholders, to agree the options taken in narrowing the range. In this way, not only does the team agree the success criteria with the stakeholders before they start, they continue to agree them throughout the project.

The process is then repeated, and (hopefully) the configuration narrowed to the eventual outcome. In the process, the project team massage the expectations of the stakeholders, so that at the end of the project they get what they are expecting, and expect what they get. However, the team also massage their own understanding of the stakeholders' requirements, so that what is delivered is what the stakeholders actually need, (it is fit for purpose), not what the project team think they need. The final configuration should also incorporate the stakeholders' desires (wants) as much as possible, so that they are delighted with what they get.

At one review one of the stakeholders may say the configuration is not what they are expecting. Then either the previous specification was wrong, or the work to reach this specification was wrong. Either the specification needs to be changed or the work needs to be repeated. Both are an anathema to traditional project managers, but the team need to know whether it is more important that the outcomes should be fit for purpose, or delivered on time and cost. (This should have been decided before the project started.) Hopefully, if the mistake is discovered early enough it will cost very little, (in time and money), to rectify. This step is known as configuration control.

Finally, if a mistake is discovered, the team need to be able to cycle back to a previous configuration, and start again from there. This will not be possible if the team have lost all memory of previous configurations. At each review, the team should record the current configuration, and the changes made since the last one, so that at anytime they can go back and start again from there. This is known as status accounting.

A Case

East Lauderdale Business School, ELBS, is revising course materials for its distance learning MBA. The materials are all fundamentally rewritten once every five years. Half the course materials are actually being written and published by a sister organization, East Lauderdale Academic Publishers, ELAP. For one course, Managing People, ELBS gives ELAP a specification, and ELAP goes off for nine months to produce a prototype for the course. They derive a contents list, and a specification of each session. They commission authors and edit their text. They desk top publish the materials and print the prototype course. They then show ELBS their handiwork. ELBS then say, "No! That is not what we were expecting the course to look like."

What has happened is that ELAP has interpreted Managing People as Personnel Management. The course is about industrial relations, employment law, selection and recruitment, appraisal and counselling. ELBS wanted about one third of the course to be about that, but about a third on Leadership and Team Building, and about a third on Organization and Work Design. There is only about one session on each of these latter two subjects. But, too late. The money has been spent, and it would be too expensive to go back and rewrite the course. ELBS used an inappropriate course for five years, (not wrong, just the wrong balance).

But it would have been so easy to avoid. All ELAP had to do was produce a contents page with word count, and go back and sign that off with ELBS. At that stage, with almost no money spent the mistake would have been found. Then, ELAP could have also asked ELBS to approve the specification for each session. For this simple project only two or three reviews would have been required. (Reviews do not serve the same purpose once design is finished and execution of the project starts, see below.)

So what are the steps of the configuration management process.

Identify the Configuration

The configuration is identified through the break down structures. The project outcomes can be defined through the product breakdown structure, PBS, and the work methods are defined through the work breakdown structure, WBS.

The refinement of understanding is usually done by breaking the PBS or WBS down to lower levels, and putting a clearer definition on the elements of the breakdown structure. Lets see how it is done using the distance course written by ELAP for ELBS as an example, see Figure 46 - 2.

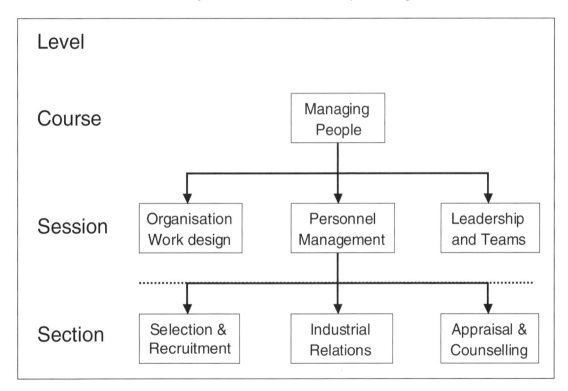

Figure 46-2: Configuration Identification for a Course.

ELBS tells ELAP that they want a course on Managing People, to cover personnel management, work and organisational design, and management, leadership and team building. ELBS and ELAP write an overall specification showing the broad content and structure of the course.

ELAP now develop a contents page, showing that the course has three parts:

1   Personnel management
2   Work and organisational design
3   Management, leadership and team building

They agree that with ELBS. ELAP then break each part into several sessions. Personnel management includes sessions on industrial relations, employment law, contracts of employment, recruitment and selection, appraisal and counselling, etc. Work and organisational design has sessions on classical management theory, Taylor and work study, Fayol and organizational structures, the theory of the firm, etc. Management, leadership and team building has sessions on the role of the manager, leadership versus management, motivation, personal development, etc. HLAP propose how many words each session should have. Perhaps the initial word count suggests a split between the three parts of 70%, 15% and 15% respectively. ELBS and ELAP work together to redefine the balance as 50%, 20% and 30% respectively.

ELAP now commission authors, and ask them to write a synopsis of their sessions, including a list of the sections, indicating how the words will be split between them. ELBS now agree that.

At this point writing will commence. As I show below, the emphasis of configuration management changes, and the configuration should now become the baseline against which delivery of the course is judged. Once work starts the team should avoid any further changes. They are really expensive from this point on. The configuration is the baseline against which delivery of each section is judged, and then delivery of each session, and then delivery of the parts and the course.

This example does not illustrate so well the development of the work breakdown structure. Writing words is writing words. However, what you can say is that each author will have their own style of writing and their own approach to the session they are commissioned to do. And their own view of the sections in their session. Thus the PBS is not resolved until the WBS is resolved, and the WBS is not resolved until the OBS (organisation breakdown structure) is resolved. In this simple example, the responsibility chart at each level, (Turner, 1999), defines the WBS and OBS, and so identifies the configuration of both.

Review the Configuration

We saw above that ELBS and ELAP met three times to agree the current baseline:

1   They agreed the broad specification of the course
2   They agreed the specification, contents page and word count of each part
3   They agreed the specification, section titles and word division of each session

ELBS will need to involve several stakeholders in these decisions:

◆   the faculty must approve content from a pedagogical perspective
◆   the course director who has to run the course, must approve studiability
◆   the marketing department, and perhaps people involved in developing company tailored programmes must approve content from a client needs perspective
◆   the finance department have to agree to the budget

By agreeing each decision point, all are involved in agreeing the final configuration. There can be no surprises.

Control the Configuration

As we have seen, it is possible that at one review, one or more of the stakeholders says that the revised configuration is not what they were expecting. In that case, one of two things has happened. Either the previous configuration was wrong, or the work to go from the previous configuration to this one was wrong.

With ELBS's distance learning course, at the second review the word count was unbalanced. ELAP had proposed that the split of words between the three parts be 70%:15%:15%. This was a wrong interpretation of the specification as agreed at the first review, and after further work a split of 50%:20%:30% is agreed. Perhaps, at the second review, one of the authors who has been given 5000 words for her session, says she needs 10,000. Either the author needs to be told to go back to revise their design, or if her argument is persuasive, the previous specification needs to be changed and 10,000 words accepted, or perhaps 8,000. We see that perhaps the work needs to be redone, or the specification changed, or perhaps some mixture of both.

Record the Configuration and Changes

At each review a careful record needs to be kept of the current components of the breakdown structure, and the specification of each, and the work methods to deliver them. This is the baseline against which to judge the configuration at the next review. Does the new configuration lie within the range of uncertainty at the previous review, in which case it can be accepted. Or has it fallen outside, in which case the specification needs to be changed or the work redone to pull it inside.

If at a review the team find they cannot make the new configuration work, they may need to go back to the previous configuration and restart from there. Sometimes they need to cycle back two or three reviews. Thus a record needs to be kept of the configuration at each review. If the team get to a subsequent review and find they cannot make the configuration work, but have lost the memory of previous configurations, then they are stuck up the creek without a paddle. It is very difficult to unpick the previous changes. Thus you can see this requires careful recording of the configuration at each review and careful accounting of the status at each review.

This is also the case if the team is developing several prototypes. They then need to record the configuration of each prototype, and how they relate.

Configuration Management and the Project Life-Cycle

We began to see above that the emphasis of configuration management changes throughout the life-cycle, Figure 46 - 3. shows the four project stages:

1   Feasibility
2   Design
3   Execution
4   Close-out

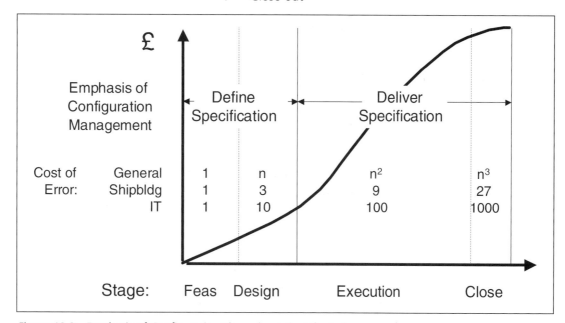

Figure 46-3: Emphasis of Configuration Throughout the Life-Cycle.

There is a rule of thumb in many industries, that for every £1 it costs to correct a mistake during the feasibility stage, it costs £n in design, $£n^2$ in execution and $£n^3$ in close-out. In shipbuilding the ratios are £1:£3:£9:£27. In IS/IT/ICT the ratios are £1:£10:£100:£1,000. The reason changes become more expensive is that the design becomes more integrated and so changes in one area lead to changes in another. Once work begins, then changes require increasing amounts of rework elsewhere and lead to delays in execution, increasing costs further and reducing benefits. The consequence is that the project team should aim to make all the changes during feasibility and design. Once execution begins, as much as possible the design should be frozen and no more changes made. Certainly during execution and close-out the team should no longer consider changes which are nice-to-have. They may be improvements on the current configuration, but they should have been identified during feasibility or design. Even if they are improvements, during execution and close-out the cost of the changes cannot possibly be justified by the benefit from the improvement (if they are nice-to-have). The only changes that should be countenanced during execution and close-out are show-stoppers, like the system will not work without this change. Then the benefit is infinite.

This means the emphasis of configuration management changes as the project moves from design to execution. During feasibility and design, when little money is being spent, the emphasis is on trying to agree the configuration with the stakeholders, and to come up with the optimum design. It is worthwhile during these stages to spend a bit longer getting the right answer. During execution and close-out, the emphasis is on using the configuration so agreed as a baseline to measure the delivery of the components of the system and then the overall system. Once the team start spending real money, they need to deliver the solution as quickly as possible to get the revenue stream to repay the money invested. I said above that once authors writing words of ELBS's distance learning course, the configuration should be used to judge the sections, sessions and parts produced.

I recently heard of the replacement of an air traffic control system in a developing country. The government wanted the new system in 18 months, and perceiving tight timescales they gave the project team just two weeks to write the statement of requirements. With only two weeks, the team did not feel they had time to talk to the operators (air traffic controllers and pilots) nor airlines. It then took them five years to deliver the new system as they corrected all the mistakes in the design during project delivery. How much better to spend three months over the writing of the statement of requirements, and gain the input of all the stakeholders, to get the design correct, and then spend just 18 months delivering it.

Document Management

We saw above that status accounting is an essential element of configuration management, and for that proper records need to be kept. There is a risk that configuration management can be turned into a bureaucratic nightmare. On simple projects it should be kept simple. It can produce powerful results, and so the project manager should avoid putting people off using it by making the process overly bureaucratic. However, on larger, more complex projects an appropriate system needs to deal with the added complexity. However, even on simple projects, there is some simple house keeping that can be applied to ensure the process delivers the required outcomes.

In this section, I describe some of the document management procedures suggested to accompany configuration management.

Operating Manuals and Documentation

We start with a simple point. The handbooks, operating manuals, maintenance procedures, etc, which tell the users how to operate the facility, should themselves be configuration items. Their design and production should be tracked throughout the project in the same way as the facility itself.

Configuration Item Forms

When describing the example of the course for ELBS, I effectively said the contents page of the course should be the Product Breakdown Structure, and that simple specification documents should be written first for the course, then the sessions and finally the sections. (That is what I do when I write a book - or even this chapter.) But on more complex projects, greater formality is required. Now, documentation such as a Configuration Identification Form is suggested. Figure 46 - 4 gives the possible contents of such a form, with explanations where necessary.

Information on the CIF	Explanation
CI Name	Unique identifier
CI Description	Simple narrative specification
CI Life-cycle	Progression through the life-cycle
CI in the WBS	Where in the WBS this CI is designed and installed
CI Parent	CI next up in the PBS
CI Children	CIs next down the PBS
Person responsible	Owner of this CI
CI Source	Supplier, (in-house or external).
Issue number	
Issue date	
Change history	

Figure 46 - 4: Contents of a Configuration Item Form

I said it above, I say it again now, and I say it again in the conclusion. Configuration management, if simply applied, can be a powerful tool. So don't introduce excessively bureaucratic tools on simple projects. But do use them on more complex ones, where the data and information management are essential.

On large complex projects, it will be necessary to have a Configuration Librarian, to own all the Configuration Item Forms.

Document Housekeeping

Finally, it is good housekeeping, to maintain track of all documents relating to the project. Every document should have some of the items of the Configuration Item Form above, including:

- Unique identifier
- Issue number
- Issue date
- Owner
- Change history

Complex projects should also maintain a record of when every document was issued or received. That should be the responsibility of a project administrator, perhaps the Configuration Librarian.

Conclusion

Configuration management is one of the three or four core methodologies of project management. It is my view that it should be used on almost every project, unlike the other two or three, critical path analysis, earned value analysis and resource scheduling, which only need to be used on more complex projects.

Configuration management can be turned into a bureaucratic nightmare. However, on simple projects, the four steps can be applied in a simple fashion, providing very powerful control of the project outcomes, refining understanding of the outcomes, and avoiding mistakes at an early stage, when they cost next to nothing to rectify. It is therefore the one of the core methodologies that does the most to ensure that the project delivers its purpose and provides value to the sponsor, and yet it is so simple to apply.

References and Further Reading

H Kerzner, 1999, Project Management: a systems approach to planning, scheduling and control, 6th edition, Wiley, New York, ISBN: 0-471-28835-7.

QW Fleming and JM Koppleman, 2000, Earned Value Project Management, 2nd edition, Project Management Institute, Sylva, NC, ISBN: 1-880410-27-3.

JR Turner, 1999, The Handbook of Project Based Management, 2nd edition, McGraw-Hill, London, ISBN: 0-07-709161-2, Hardback.

JR Turner, 2000, "Project success and strategy", in JR Turner and SJ Simister, (eds), 2000, The Gower Handbook of Project Management, 3rd edition, Gower, Aldershot, ISBN: 0-566-08138-5, Hardback, & ISBN: 0-566-08397-3, CD-ROM.

G Allan, 1997, "Configuration Management and its impact on businesses that use computer platforms", International Journal of Project Management, 15(5), 321-330.

HR Berlack, 1992, Software Configuration Management, Wiley.

CCTA, 1996, Guide to Prince 2, The Stationery Office.

ISO 10,007, 1995, Guidelines for Configuration Management, International Standards Organization, Geneva.

Section 5

Commercial

50   BUSINESS CASE

Paul Vollans

"You've got a goal, I've got a goal. Now all we need is a football team."
Groucho Marks

Introduction

A project, by definition, is a set of objectives achieved within a defined timescale. This, though, does not address the basic question of why the project is being undertaken in the first place. At first glance, this may appear obvious ("Of course we need this bridge so that we can get across the river!") but this by itself is not a valid reason. Many other issues must be taken into account. This chapter is intended to provide guidance on the reasons for doing a given project. After all, the best project management in the world is of little use if it is applied to the wrong project - taking everything into account it might have been far better to forget the bridge and build a ferry terminal!

The Business Case and The Project Management Process

The complete life-cycle of a total project goes from an initial idea (or identification of a need) through to operation, decommissioning and ultimate disposal. This life-cycle can be broken down into a series of phases that represent level 2 tasks in the work breakdown structure (see Session 30 - Work Content & Scope Management). Early on in the life-cycle, shortly after the initial idea, the nascent project must be assessed to establish whether or not it is worth doing. This is often called the concept or appraisal stage and it will include development of a business plan for the project. Sub-child tasks of the business plan might include "Definition of Objectives", "Market Survey", "Financial Appraisal" and so on. These and other components of the business plan are considered in this chapter.

Within the project management process, these tasks would be incorporated into the project plans (work breakdown, cost account, network analysis, resource analysis etc.) and would be managed just like any other task.

As the project proceeds, periodic reviews may be required by the project management process. In addition to reviewing progress of the project, the business case should also be reviewed and updated as circumstances might have changed. If the project is no longer justified because the data on which the business case was originally based has now changed (eg: new technology has appeared or sales forecasts have dipped), then serious consideration must be given to abandoning the scheme or at least significantly changing the goals. Such reviews should be tasks in the work breakdown structure and should form an integral part of the project management process.

Assessing The Project - Factors to Consider

Most projects start out as a bright idea, need, or customer enquiry. They will then enter an appraisal or concept stage in which various aspects of the project are considered and a decision made as to whether it should actually be implemented. As we have seen, it is at this stage that the business case is developed. The following sections describe some of the issues that should be included.

Outline Description of the Project

The project should be described in sufficient detail to enable the scope and overall goals of the project to be understood. Formally, this may be called a concept statement, mandate, or similar synonym, but it should be concise and clear. It is not a detailed description of the project and should focus mainly on what the project goals are rather than how those goals will be achieved. The Outline Description should include a brief background to the project.

Business Objectives

The business objectives should relate the project goals to the overall company goals and include the perceived benefits to the business that will accrue as a result of undertaking the project. For example, the project goal may be to construct a new office in Edinburgh, wheras the business goals may be to increase sales in Scotland by 50% within the next two years. Business Objectives should consider how the project in question relates to other projects currently being undertaken.

Project Objectives

The project objectives or goals should be defined quantitatively so that they can be easily measured. Ultimately, they will be used to measure the success or otherwise of the project. Thus in the Edinburgh office referred to above, the objectives might be to construct an office for up to 300 people within two years that is located no more than 10 miles from the airport.

Project Benefits

The anticipated benefits from a project should be listed as part of the business case. This may well (although not necessarily) include direct financial return (eg: income or savings), but could also include many less obvious benefits. These might include:

- Prestige
- Improved efficiency (thereby making savings in other areas)
- Publicity
- Customer satisfaction/delight
- Social benefits (eg: providing amenities)
- Environmental benefits (eg: improving waste treatment)
- Health and safety improvements
- Employee benefits (eg: provision of a creche)
- Higher reliability
- Gaining experience (eg: of new technology)

- Shareholder satisfaction
- Benefiting a subsidiary company
- Reducing risk
- Political benefits
- Increasing opportunity

It will be noted that some of these benefits are less tangible than others, for example it is probably quite difficult to quantify prestige, or social benefits. Although much project appraisal work can be carried out by scrutinising financial benefits and risks, in the final analysis there may be issues that are subjective. Decisions as to whether or not to proceed with the project may frequently be based on highly subjective and sometimes emotive views.

Key Deliverables

Key deliverables are the main items that will be created during the course of the project. In the office example, this might include the building structure, a car park, boundary fences, all services, carpets, furniture, architects drawings, instruction manuals and so on.

Performance Indicators

These are the parameters against which the success or otherwise of the project is measured. For example, typical performance indicators might include completion dates and budgets for key deliverables (see above), or quality parameters such as number of software bugs. Indicators like these are measuring the success or otherwise with which the project is being managed but say little about whether or not it is the right project. Thus the project to provide an office in Edinburgh may go brilliantly as a project, hitting all performance indicators, but experience might subsequently show that an office in Aberdeen would have been better!

Location

The geographical location of the project should be considered, with justification for the preferred choice.

Location will have a direct connection with various issues including:

- Staff availability
- Cost of property
- Transport
- Access
- Customer expectations
- Future plans
- Language
- Climate
- Culture
- Planning permission
- Political aspects
- Shareholders
- Grant availability
- Services (water etc.)
- Risk
- Local opinion
- Security
- Competition
- Health & Safety

Outline Plan

An outline plan should be developed comprising a preliminary work breakdown structure, cost account, network diagram and resource analysis (see Session 30 - Work Content & Scope Management). This should be sufficiently detailed to give at least an initial idea of likely timescale, cost and resource need. Should any of these parameters be unacceptable, then the scope of the project may need to be revised.

Technical Issues

Technical aspects of the proposed project should be considered, eg: new technology, reliability, familiarity, availability and so on. Care should be taken, however, not to constrain the project by trying to define at this stage exactly how the project goals will be achieved. The emphasis should be more about what the project has to achieve .

Safety Issues

Clearly any relevant health and safety issues relating to the project must be considered. For example, is the project in a confined space, or are any dangerous chemicals involved?

Quality / Performance Issues

Can the necessary quality/performance be achieved? See also Key Performance Indicators above.

Risk and Opportunity

A risk assessment should be carried out, seeking to identify significant risks and opportunities (see Session 23 - Risk Management). Any actions arising from this must be transferred to the outline plan and timescales and cost estimates adjusted accordingly.

Risk is particularly important in assessing the business case for a proposed project as it has a direct link with most of the other topics covered by the appraisal. As an example, consider health and safety issues referred to above. If the proposed project does involve dangerous chemicals, then the risks may be significant, thus reducing the desirability of undertaking the project in the first place. Alternatively, the measures needed to counteract the dangers may be very expensive, so rendering the project uneconomical. A sound risk assessment will investigate such issues.

One possible risk on any project is that the anticipated benefits are not realised. As risk is measured in terms of impact and probability, a natural question to ask is just how likely is it that the projected benefits will not be achieved? This must be addressed in the business case to avoid a situation where a project proceeds on the basis of significant promised benefits that in reality have little chance of being realised. An example could be a project that shows a high return on investment (thereby suggesting that it goes ahead) but the figures are based on highly optimistic sales forecasts which, through risk assessment, are revealed in their true colours.

Competition and Market Issues

Many projects, for example development of a new product or service, or opening of a new service outlet, will be driven by market demand. Conversely, any changes in the market place could directly effect the success or otherwise of the project. Thus if a competitor gets a similar product to the market first, this could seriously undermine the financial outcome of the project. As part of the project assessment, a detailed market analysis should be carried out. Specialist companies exist to do this, although it can be carried out in-house. It should address such questions as:

- What is the perceived market? Why?
- Why is the proposed product needed?
- What existing products fulfil the need?
- What will be different about the new product?
- How do we know there will be a demand?
- How could the market change to the detriment or advantage of the project?
- What additional opportunities exist?
- What are competitors doing now, or likely to do in the future?
- How will competitors respond to the new product?
- What will the price of the new product need to be?
- What is the anticipated level of sales? Over what period of time?
- What publicity/advertising will be required?

Organisational Issues

Organisational issues revolve around the framework of companies, departments, individuals, customers, consumers etc. that will participate in or have some connection with the project. Both internal and external organisations must be included. A stakeholder analysis (see below) can help define such groups. In assessing a potential project, the following questions should be considered:

- What are the organisations and who are the people involved in the project?
- How and when are they involved?
- What will the management levels be?
- How do they relate to each other?
- Who is the project champion (the advocate for the project)?
- Can each organisation or person meet the demands that the project is likely to place upon them?
- What are the organisational risks?

Ownership

The owner (or sponsor) of the project is the person or organisation for whom the project is being undertaken. Generally, the owner will be the primary risk taker and should be clearly identified at the project appraisal stage.

Financial Appraisal

A financial appraisal of the project is necessary to consider profitability, cash flow and sources of funding. These issues are considered in more detail below.

In some cases, for example social projects such as a youth theatre production, there may be little or no financial justification to proceed. However, in such projects, other benefits may play a much more dominant role than the more common aim of making money (see Project Benefits above). Here, financial appraisal may form only a small part of the business plan, although attention should still be paid to the costs and cash-flow, and how these will be funded.

Monitoring and Control

The business case should consider in a broad sense the reporting and monitoring requirements of the project. The extent of such will be dictated by various factors but generally, the more complex the project in terms of risk and value then the greater the reporting and monitoring needed. By outlining such requirements in the business plan, they can be planned for and costed. An example here might be that earned value analysis is specified as a way of tracking the project.

An important aspect of monitoring and control is the need for periodic reviews. As seen earlier in this session, such reviews should form an integral part of the project management process so that if it is found, due to changing circumstances, that the project can no longer be justified, it is either aborted or the goals are changed as appropriate.

Resources

The business case should consider what resources will be required for the project and where they will be obtained from. This will not be a detailed resource analysis, which will only be implemented later once it is decided to proceed with the project, but a high level view seeking simply to ensure that appropriate resources can be made available, or, if not, how the problem can be resolved. Particular resource needs (eg: special skills) should be high-lighted, and likely resource costs must be investigated.

The business case may also consider the organisation of resources. For example, does the project justify a dedicated team?

All key resources should be considered in the business case, both human and otherwise.

Other Issues

For a given project, there will generally be many other factors involved in assessing whether or not the project should proceed. Typically, these include environmental and social issues, but other factors are listed above under "Location".

Development of the Business Case

The Business Case will develop over a period of time for there is considerable work involved in pulling all the necessary information together. Frequently there will be pressure to minimise this time, but the importance of fully investigating and researching the proposed project cannot be over-stressed. Failure to do so will easily result in potential problems and set-backs being over-looked. Lack of clarity in the Business Case could lead to considerable scope creep later, and in the worst case, embarking on a project without adequate investigation could mean ultimate abandonment and a wasted investment.

Investment Appraisal Techniques

Many projects have the ultimate aim of making money ie: either directly or indirectly contributing to profit. Several methods exist (none of them infallible!) for financial assessment of potential projects so that contribution to profit can be quantitatively estimated:

Pay Back

A project will generally require an initial investment of money that will ultimately be recovered some time after the project is completed. For example, installation of thermal insulation may, over a period of time, save energy costs. Pay back period is a measure of how long it will be before the cost of the initial project has been recovered through income or savings achieved by the project. Thus if installation of the insulation costs £20,000 and energy savings of £5,000 per year are thereby realised, the payback period is four years. This is a simple measure, often used as a criteria for justifying improvement projects.

Return on Investment (ROI)

This parameter measures how much year-on-year financial return a given project will achieve. Suppose that a project requires an initial investment of £100,000, but the income from the completed project is £60,000 over 4 years. Then the return on the investment is given by:

$$\frac{(\text{Annual profit})}{(\text{Initial Investment})} \times 100\% = \frac{15,000 \times 100\%}{100,000} = 15\% \text{ per annum}$$

In simple terms, the return must be as high as possible. If it is close to or less than current bank base rate, it may be better to invest the money in a Building Society!

Discounted Cash Flow (DCF)

Payback period and return on investment are simple and straightforward but make no allowance for devaluation of money. Particularly in times of high inflation, what at first glance (based on payback and ROI) may appear to be a good investment will in reality see inflation eroding future income or savings so that the initial investment is wasted. Discounted Cash Flow is intended to give visibility to this risk. It does so by forecasting the likely future income or savings on the basis of current prices, then devaluing the forecasts by an amount depending on the anticipated future inflation rate and the period of time spanned by the forecasts. For example, if it is anticipated that the income from a project will be £5000 in the second year, inflation will mean that by the time year two is reached, the £5000 income will not purchase as much as it could now ie: it has devalued. Therefore at today's prices (that is, at the time when the project is being assessed), anticipated income in year two should be reduced to allow for inflation.

The general formula for discounting projected income (or savings) in this way is as follows:

$$V_n = V_f (1+r)-n$$

Where: V_n = value now, V_f = future value, r = discount rate, and n = no. of years.

To illustrate, the actual current value (V_n) of £100 in 3 years time at a discount (inflation rate) of 10% per annum is given by:

$$V_n = 100 (1+0.1) - 3 = \qquad £75$$

The process can readily be carried out using spreadsheets, as built-in financial formulae generally allow DCF.

Internal Rate of Return (IRR)

In many respects, this is just an inverted version of discounted cash flow. As we have seen, increasing the underlying discount rate will mean that DCF calculations will show a lower and lower return on the investment. The IRR is simply the theoretical inflation rate at which the DCF return on investment will be zero. If the inflation rate was expected to be around 5% over the next three years, and the IRR for a given project was calculated at 30%, this would indicate that actual inflation would have to actually rise from 5% to 30% for the investment to start making a loss. This would suggest, at least in a stable political environment, that the investment was possibly quite a good one.

Other Factors

No financial appraisal of a proposed project can guarantee success. Although various ways of assessing financial return have been described in the foregoing sections, all are based on forecasts of future income, savings and/or inflation. Such predictions may therefore carry inherent errors of optimism and political uncertainty. Furthermore, for a given set of assumptions, the financial assessment techniques considered above may not show much difference between two different projects. In considering the financial benefits of projects, therefore, other related factors must be considered:

Risk

A risk assessment may indicate that one project carries intrinsically more risk than another (for example, one project may use new, unproven technology whereas another may require only established technology that has proved itself). In such a case, a cautious approach would be to go for the low risk option even though returns may be lower. Generally speaking, the higher the risk, the greater the returns should be.

It is important to recognise that sound risk assessment also includes identification of possible opportunity. This, too, may be a deciding factor in whether or not to go for a given project.

Timescales

A bird in the bush is worth two in the hand springs to mind here. Generally speaking, a project that realises a smaller return in the near future will be lower risk than a project that promises riches a long way into the future.

Cashflow

Projects will generally require an investment of cash at the start in order to begin. This initial investment may come from a bank loan or other source, but it has a cost implication until it is paid off. As the project proceeds, there will come a time when income or savings begin to balance the initial investment, thus reducing the costs of financing the project. Ultimately, a break-even point will be reached when income/savings exactly equals investment. The difference at any time between investment and income/savings on a given project is known as the cash-flow. At the start of the project, it is likely to be well into the red (negative) but will gradually climb into the black (become positive) as income or savings from the project begin to pay off the investment.

For a given project, a forecast cash-flow can be drawn up as a graph, based on forecast income and expenditure on a month by month (or other) basis. Ideally, the cash-flow will never go negative. This may be possible, for example, if a customer agrees to pay money up front. Generally, however, it is likely that some period(s) of negative cash-flow will exist. In the worst case, large negative cash-flow will exist for long periods of time (eg: on a high-value, long-term project where the customer is paying on completion). A source of funding must be available to cover periods of negative cash-flow (part of this may be credit from suppliers).

When assessing the financial viability of a project, or comparing two projects, the cash-flow forecasts must be taken into account.

Stakeholder Analysis

Definition

A Project Stakeholder is a person or organisation that has a vested interest (negative or positive!) in the ultimate outcome of the project. Their interest may lie in one or more parts of that outcome, and not necessarily the whole thing (eg: a given stakeholder may only be interested in the environmental outcome of a road construction project).

It will be evident from this that on many projects, the list of Stakeholders may include many people with diverse interests, objectives, aspirations and influence. A stakeholder analysis is a technique to identify and assess the importance of stakeholders. It can include all stakeholders, or, in more limited form, could include a defined group, for example the project team.

Why it is Used

Generally, a stakeholder analysis would be conducted in the early assessment and planning stages of a project with a view to identifying actions to improve the quality of the project by increasing stakeholder support and reducing opposition.

Undertaking a Stakeholder Analysis

Step 1

Create a table as follows:

1. Stakeholder	2. Interest in the Project	3. Assessment of Impact	4. Actions to Increase Support	5. Actions toReduce Opposition

Then, in column 1, list all known stakeholders. A brainstorming session involving a team of relevant people can be useful here

Step 2

Consider each stakeholder and in column 2 list specific interests stakeholders have in the project. This should include benefits/disadvantages, changes that the stakeholder may have to make, income/expenditure issues, possible conflicts and support and help that the stakeholder could give. It may also be useful, if appropriate, to identify the period of time for which the stakeholders' interest will exist.

Step 3

For each stakeholder, assess the significance of their interest in the project on the basis of a scale along the following lines:

A: Vitally important (they are essential to project completion)
B: Significant importance (could significantly effect cost/timescale/quality of the project, but are unlikely to prevent the project completing
C: Some effect on cost/time/quality, but not likely to be significant
D: Little or no effect

Step 4

Finally, on the basis of information in columns 1 to 3, complete columns 4 and 5 to show actions to increase support and reduce opposition. Questions that could help identify such actions might include:

- What information will they need?
- Are any groups of stakeholders important?
- What actions can reduce their concerns?
- How can they be included in the project?
- Are there any particular relationships that can be used to advantage?
- Can one stakeholder help resolve problems of another?

All actions identified should have clear deliverables, must be incorporated into the work breakdown structure, be costed and have resources allocated, so that they ultimately become an integral part of the project planning.

Post Project Audit

Upon completion of the project (ie: when the project objectives have been achieved), an audit should be undertaken. (See Session 65) This should have two main aims:

- To assess how the project was undertaken, to learn from mistakes and introduce change (to project management procedures) on the basis of lessons learned
- To assess whether or not the business goals have been achieved (ie: was it the right project, or, with hindsight, should something else have been done instead?)

The second of these two objectives may only be partially achieved immediately following the project. It may be many months or even years before full business consequences of the project can be fully assessed.

51   MARKETING AND SALES

Michael Holton

"In the factory we make cosmetics. In the store we sell hope."
Charles Revson (1906-1975), US business tycoon (CEO of Revlon).

Introduction

It is important for Project Management professionals to understand and be able to put into practice marketing and sales strategies and approaches. Project managers will often find themselves being involved in the creation of new business and /or selling projects, project managers or project management to customers. The need to undertake marketing and sales activities as a project management professional or within the context of a project can significantly affect the way projects are conceived and managed.

The current APM definition of marketing and sales is as follows:

"Marketing is the process of matching the abilities of an organisation with the existing and future needs of its customers to the greatest benefit of both parties".

The result is an exchange in which the supplier receives income through the meeting of customer needs and the customer receives benefits that satisfy their expectations.

Sales, is the process of getting someone to buy the product or service being offered by the vendor.

The purpose of this session is to explore marketing & sales in more depth and:

- Provide project managers with a general understanding of marketing and sales
- Place marketing and sales in the context of project management
- Link marketing and sales to other related project management competencies

Further this session the aims to demonstrate:

- The difference between marketing and sales
- The place of marketing and sales in the project and project management context
- The processes of marketing
- The processes of sales
- Approaches the Project Manager should take towards marketing and sales

Links to Other Project Management Competencies

In the context of Project Management, there are clear links between marketing and sales and other project management competencies including:

20 Project Success Criteria
41 Requirements Management
50 Business Case
53 Procurement
54 Legal Awareness
70 Communication
74 Negotiation

Having an understanding of and experience in these competencies is key to the implementation of effective marketing and sales strategies.

Marketing

Marketing's purpose is simple and straightforward. Its sole function is to create and retain customers or clients. This simple purpose applies to trading and non-trading organisations and to both goods and services.

The underlying premise is that without customers there will be no business, thus organisations need to be oriented around placing its customers and their needs at the core of its business decision-making processes. Marketing, therefore:

- Involves all the actions required to fit a business, its resources, capabilities and knowledge to meeting customer needs
- Involves all the activities that identify potential

customers and the needs and wants of all customers either potential or existing

- ◆ Seeks to achieve more effective and profitable selling by looking ahead, discovering customers and their needs and wants
- ◆ Devising and producing goods and services that match customer requirements as closely as possible, including production at an affordable cost relative to the price the customer will pay or the market will stand

Sales

Selling involves the presentation of products, services and ideas to existing and potential customers. The objective of selling is to complete the exchange between the supplier and the customer. This could be a reciprocal exchange of goods and services or the exchange of goods and services for cash.

The Difference Between Marketing and Sales

Marketing is the process by which a company or organisation is organised around and focused on producing goods and services that meet customer's needs and wants.

Selling is the process by which those goods and services are demonstrated to customers and the exchange is negotiated and concluded.

However, both are related and inter-dependent, which is why they are often bracketed together in process terms and within organisational structures. Sales is a part of the overall marketing process and the sales function of an organisation is often part of the marketing department, but is not of itself involved in marketing.

Marketing and Sales in the Project Management Context

There are three key goals for the Project Manager or Project Management organisation:

- To create customers for the person or organisation providing project management products and services
- To ensure the opportunity to bid for specific projects or work is created
- To sell people, specific services or project proposals to those customers created out of the marketing approach

The project manager and/or the project management organisation need to be able to create project management services that meet the needs and wants of existing and potential customers. The project manager then needs to persuade those customers (stakeholders, clients or partners) to buy the people and services on offer, to buy additional ancillary services and/or to continue to buy people and services over a long period of time.

It is especially important, where the project manager and/or project management organisation is responding to an invitation to bid or tender, that the customer is pursuaded that the manager and the organisation is offering a product that meets the client's needs and that the 'bid', 'proposal', 'design' etc. for a specific project is the one to buy.

Marketing techniques and processes can, therefore, be applied to how individuals or organisations that provide project management services operate and present themselves.

Marketing and sales techniques can also be applied to how a project itself is designed and presented to obtain the necessary buy-in and approvals from the various stakeholder groups.

In project management, marketing and selling is often bound within communication and stakeholder management and within the production of a business case, tender documents, project definitions, designs etc. It is useful and beneficial to think about these processes from a marketing and sales perspective and to apply marketing and sales approaches within them.

Equally a project manager or project management organisation needs to take a customer oriented approach to how business is conducted. Project management is a service and the providers of this service need to market themselves in the same way as any other producer of goods and services.

The Role of the Project Manager in Marketing and Sales

The project manager has a key role in all the marketing and sales related activities within projects and project management. These will include:

◆ Ensuring that project management and the project manager is presented from the perspective of the benefits they bring to the client or customer. What needs and wants are satisfied
◆ Preparing and submitting a 'bid or 'proposal' to a client or customer
◆ Preparing the project communication plan
◆ Preparing the stakeholder management plan
◆ Ensuring that documents are written from the perspective of, or the part they play in, ensuring client or customer, stakeholder and user buy-in to the project
◆ Ensuring projects and project plans recognise and plan for marketing and sales drivers behind the project

The Marketing Process

Marketing as a process is a fundamental part of the overall business strategic and operational planning process. It is, really, a philosophy that is (or should be) an integral part of all business planning and operational processes whereby a business and its decisions should be governed by its markets (customers) rather than the facilities (production, technical etc.) it has at its disposal (Figure 51 - 1).

The process of marketing, therefore, to a large extent, is the process of business. However, marketing can be broken down into a number of steps, components or techniques that represent a process based around 7 key factors depicted in Figure 51 - 2 and the process of marketing, therefore, is involved in:

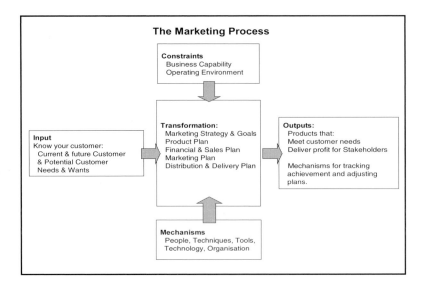

Figure 51 - 1: Marketing Process Model

Product:	What is it customers want?
Price:	What is the customer prepared to pay for the product or service?
Place:	Where are customers prepared to go to obtain the product or service?
Promotion:	How will the product or service be communicated and / or demonstrated to the customer? How will the sale of the product be promoted or incentivised with customers?
Personnel:	What is the customer experience with the staff who represent the product or service?
Physical Evidence:	What is the physical manifestation of intangible services?
Process:	How is the good or service provided or delivered?

Figure 51 - 2: The 7 P 's of Marketing

- Defining and executing all the actions required to fit a business, its resources, capabilities and knowledge to meeting customer needs
- Defining and executing the activities that identify potential customers and the needs and wants of all customers either potential or existing
- Defining and executing the activities required for achieving more effective and profitable selling
- Devising and producing goods and services that match customer requirements as closely as possible
- Production / distribution at an affordable cost relative to the price customer's will pay or the market will stand
- Delivery and distribution channels that are most convenient and accessible for customers

The marketing process is outlined in Figure 51- 3.

Know your Business What business are we in? How are we performing? Do we have capabilities we can further exploit? Do we need new capabilities?	**Areas to research** Past & Projected Performance Capabilities Resources Competencies Products/Services Distribution Technology	RESEARCH: INFORMATION GATHERING AND ANALYSIS
Know your Market What is the environment (s) within which we are operating?	**Areas to research** Competition Economy Social & Political Ethical Cultural	
Know your Customer Who are our current and future customers?	**Areas to research** Socio/demographic analysis Who buys and why are they buying (or not buying) Customer satisfaction (or otherwise) What are their needs and wants now What are their emerging needs & wants	
Define Marketing Strategy & Goals What are we going to focus our resources, facilities and capabilities on doing?	**Strategic Plan** What is the purpose, aims, objectives and targets of the business	PLANNING

Figure 51 - 3: The Marketing Process

The Sales Process

The process of selling involves the presentation of products, services and ideas to existing and potential customers (Figure 51 - 4). The objective of the sales process is to complete the exchange between the supplier and the customer. This could be a reciprocal exchange of goods and services or the exchange of goods and services for cash.

The sales process has five other components beyond its basic purpose:

◆ Persuade customers to 'trade -up'. To buy a product or service that is more expensive (or more profitable) and is of better quality than the product the customer already has or has asked for

◆ Persuade customers to buy more. At the same time as the original purchase demonstrate related products or services that will enhance the benefit, quality, utility or cachet of the basic product or service the customer has requested

◆ Cross Sell: Persuade customers to place more of their business with your organisation during the course of the relationship. Once a basic product has been purchased and a customer relationship established make further demonstrations of products to customers that they may find beneficial in their own right or that enhance the value of the other products the customer has purchased from your organisation

◆ Developing and maintain a relationship with a customer or specific customers on behalf of the organisation. This is on going and beyond the specifics of any particular sales 'event'

◆ After sales support and follow up. Making sure the customer is satisfied with the goods and services provided and the manner in which they have been provided. Making sure the customer is satisfied that the organisation is standing behind its product and/or service

The process steps, therefore, that make up the transformation process, from need to completion of the sale are, therefore as laid out in Figure 51 - 5.

Define the Products	Product Plan	PLANNING & EXECUTION
What are we going to make and sell?	What will our product mix be? What products will we continue with? What new products do we need to develop? What products can we dispense with? What products can we bundle or link together?	
Define the Price/Profit How much can/shall we charge? What return are we seeking on our investment?	**Financial & Sales Plan** Pricing policy & approach Targeted return Sales Targets	
Define Promotional Activity How are we going to communicate and demonstrate our products and services?	**Marketing Plan** Advertising strategies/channels Sales strategies/promotions Public Relations Packaging and labelling Brochures, manuals etc. Branding and Brand Values	

Define Distribution and Delivery Channels
How are we going to deliver the product and services to the customer?
	Distribution and Delivery Plan
	Supply Chain Management
	Stock and Inventory Control
	Customer delivery processes
	People: customer service standards
	Channels:
	    Multi or single channel
	    Physical or virtual	

Devise Control and Information Systems How are we going to track results against strategy/goals?		
Monitor and Feedback the Results Use the results to adjust and improve performance		

Figure 51 - 4: The Sales Process

Sales Approaches

Sales, whilst distinct from Marketing, is closely related. If marketing is the process for creating and maintaining a customer, sales is the process by which the customer actually obtains the product or service and how demand is satisfied. The prosperity of organisations and future success is based on the success the organisation has not just in marketing its products and services but selling them.

Cold Selling/Direct Selling	Communicating with potential customers either in person or via advertisement or mail shot on an 'opportunity' basis.
Warm Selling/Targeted Direct Selling	Communicating with potential customers either in person or via distribution of information, brochures etc. based on an enquiry from a customer
Demonstration	Meeting with the customer to demonstrate or present the product or service based on customer demand.
Negotiation	Negotiating the terms of sale for provision of the product or service. Seeking opportunities for trade up/bundling
Implementation/closure	Providing/implementing the product or service in the customer environment. Receiving value from the customer for the product or service provided
After-care	Follow up to ensure product meets needs customer needs. Servicing the product/product warranty. Building the customer relationship, seeking further trade up or cross sell opportunities

Figure 51 - 5: The Sales Transformation Process

Type of Product or Services	**Approach**
Basic Products: Food, fuel etc.	Delivery: Selling is a secondary matter. It is the approach to customer service which is paramount
Routine or well-established items bought for general use: tinned goods, soap, cleaning products etc.	Order Takers: Works in super markets, DIY outlets and industry where little selling is required and the 'hard-sale' discouraged. As for Delivery it is the customer service approach which is more important.
More personal or aspirational but generally simple products and services e.g. holidays, clothes	Inside Order Taker: Customers have usually made up their minds. Selling is more about suggestion and demonstration about the exact specification, style etc of product or service required.
Complex technical products and services	Demonstration: Selling is about instruction, advice and guidance on the product or service, acting as a consultant to the buying organisation to facilitate a sale
Educating the customer or potential customer on products and services available. Not product or service focused	Building Goodwill: Similar to Demonstration but focused on education and establishment of a relationship that may lead to future sales. One objective of this type of approach may be 'winning the account'
Complex, aspirational and intangible products and services. e.g. bespoke, designer or personalised products and services, financial and related services, personal computing devices (e.g. PDA's), cars etc.	Creative Selling: Approach here is to sell the benefit of the product or service or the lifestyle or personal position or cachet owning it will bring as well as providing an understanding of the technical attributes, which is secondary. The association between personal 'fulfilment' and brand values/messages is important in this context.

Figure 51 - 6: Sales Approaches

Selling when closely coupled with marketing is more effective because it is more focused on the purpose of meeting customer needs and wants rather than selling for the sake of selling or sales revenue targets. The consequence of this is a better return on investment in the process of selling. The conversion rate from sales prospect to confirmed sale is higher, thus the 'cost of sales' in terms of money and effort expended in the sales process is less. It is essential, therefore, that the 'know the customer', 'know the market', 'know the product', 'understand customer needs and wants' dictums of marketing are applied to the process of sales.

The approach taken to sales will depend on the product or service being sold, the market for that product and the distribution to that market. Some products and services may be sold 'simply' e.g. basic food-stuff at the supermarket. Other products and services require a more complex or inter-personal sales process e.g. Financial Services Products, Houses, Cars etc.

There are a number of different sales approaches that can be taken dependent on the product or service and the market. There are sales models that reflect the nature of the relationship between seller and buyer e.g. business to business or business to consumer and the nature of the product or service e.g. basic subsistence products such as food or complex and intangible products such as financial services (Figure 51 - 6).

Stakeholder Management

Stakeholder management is also a key element of the sales process. Stakeholders in the buying chain also need to be considered, given the influence they may bring to the sale completion. There will be 'initiators' who start the process by initiating a sale by expressing a need or want. There will be 'users' who will range from production managers through maintenance staff, to end users or even re-sellers. There will be 'influencers' such as finance, technical and design staff etc. There will be 'decision makers' ranging from managing directors for major items to junior staff for small or routine items. There may be 'buyers' or 'purchasers' who are responsible for ensuring an organisation obtains the goods and services it needs, 'buyers and 'purchasers' may cover all the roles above.

The main approaches to sales based on product types and sales relationships are set out in Figure 51 - 6. The following should be particularly borne in mind:

- Whilst person to person selling is important, direct channels such as the internet and telephone are increasingly being adopted by customers and consumers for a number of product & service areas, especially for basic or routine purchases.
- The use of direct channels such as internet and telephony are also becoming key elements of the business to business as well as business to consumer sales models.
- In order for sales to be targeted more closely or be more integrated with the marketing approach, creative selling in terms of personalisation or lifestyle aspiration is being increasingly applied to more routine or simple products and services.

Marketing and Selling Project Management

Marketing and sales manifests itself in a number of different ways in the project management environment and these ways can include:

- Marketing and Sales driven projects
- Marketing and Sales as a deliverable within a project
- Marketing and selling the Project
- Marketing and selling Project Management
- Marketing and selling the Project Manager

In terms of Marketing and Selling Projects and Project Management there are two conditions to consider for Project Management Professionals:

- Where the 'supply' is internal to an organisation
- Where the 'supply is external to an organisation

Each of these cases warrants a slightly different approach. In the following sub-sections marketing and sales in the project management context is explored in more depth.

Marketing and Sales Projects

The purpose of this section is to define what a marketing and sales project is and what approach the Project Manager should take to in the case of a marketing-led project.

Too often projects and project managers focus on the technical outcomes of a project e.g. the software or application etc. and lose sight of the business purpose or driver of the project. This can result in vital aspects of the project scope or design being overlooked or being given insufficient priority. It is important, therefore, for Project Managers to recognise the business drivers of a project to ensure the project scope and design are appropriate.

The following types of project are examples of Marketing and Sales driven projects:

1   New product development:
- Whether physical or intangible.
- This may also include addition to or revision of a current product.

2   New service development:
- This may also include addition to revision of a current product.

3   New channel development:
- This might also include the creation of a network of retail outlets.
- Internet or intranet delivery channels.
- New customer services roles within the physical channels.
- Branding and Packaging.

These types of project should be driven out of the Strategic Marketing plan and thus should be clearly driven on the purpose of satisfying customer needs and wants and the project scope and design should reflect this by including products and deliverables that reflect the key elements or deliverables of the marketing process.

Marketing Projects should consider as part of scoping and design the extent to which the elements of the Marketing process need to be included as deliverables and which need to be included as methods or processes employed within the project. This is to ensure that the deliverables meet the overall aims of the project and are thus fit for purpose.

Figure 51 - 7 illustrates how this approach could be used, the project objective being to create 'product 'x'.

Marketing Process / Technique	Project Deliverable	Project Technique
Product	This the primary product of the project.	• Know your customer • Know your business • Know your market Undertaking these elements of analysis within the scope of the project will enable the product specific requirements to be driven from the overall organisational level marketing strands. This analysis will lead to requirements in all other areas below.
Place	If existing 'place' is to be used it may need scaling or improving to support the new product. If the new product requires a unique 'place', then development of this needs to be within the scope of the project.	Question whether the location in which work is carried out is 'fit for purpose' in the context of the change being made.
Promotion	The launch campaign should be within the scope of the project.	Question: How are we going to launch this project: To customers? To staff of the organisation?
Price	Not necessarily a project deliverable.	Understanding the product pricing will help the project understand more about the potential size and limitations of the project as it may indicate the size of market and the rate of growth to aid capacity planning.
Personnel	If the product is to be delivered directly by staff or is an intangible product that is part manifested in people or 'physical evidence' then development of the role of staff and the process and standards they must follow should be within the scope of the project.	Question: Does the organisation have the right people with the right approach, skills and experience? Question: Does the organisation have enough people in the right place?
Physical Evidence	If the product is intangible or virtual then the 'tokens' of its existence such as packaging, brochures, instructions /help guides etc. are vital components of the customer experience and thus need to be within the scope of the project.	Question: How will the project and / or product be demonstrated?
Process	The design of the processes, by which the customer and the delivering organisations interact to deliver and support the product or service, need to be within the scope of the project. This may also include the design of a sales process to support the product.	Question: How will the product or service be delivered, maintained, sold, supported? Question: How will the customer obtain the product or service?

Figure 51 - 7: Marketing 7P Approach Applied to a New Product Development Project.

Marketing and Sales as Project Deliverables

The previous section describes marketing and sales deliverables in the context of marketing and sales led projects. This section considers whether other projects should have marketing & sales deliverables or objectives. The answer to this question is yes, but in two different ways.

In the first instance marketing and sales techniques or orientation can or should be taken to some of the key deliverables of the project. For example developing the business case and statement of requirements from a marketing perspective with customer needs and wants firmly in the forefront of thinking may help produce a more complete set of requirements and a more compelling business case. Equally taking marketing oriented approaches to project scope and design will flush out all aspects that need to be considered to make the project a success.

In the second case, the Project Manager has a job to do to ensure all stakeholders and users 'buy-in' to the project and its deliverables. One key objective of the Project Manager will be, in many cases, to change the orientation of the project from push to stakeholders/users to demand from the stakeholders/users. The role of the Project Manager is both to 'create a customer' for the project at high level and to 'sell it ' to the end users at a detailed level.

The Project Manager, therefore, has a requirement to satisfy the needs and wants of the stakeholders and users and 'sell' the project on the basis of the benefits to them. In such transactions the 'exchange' will range from budget sanction to deliver the project or the provision of resources from stakeholder areas to support the project through to positive feedbacktowards the project from the end users.

All Projects, therefore, have a range of marketing and sales oriented deliverables. These are:

- The Bid, Proposal or Tender Documents
- The Project Definition or Project Initiation Documents
- The Statement of Requirements
- The Solution or Product Descriptions
- The Business Case
- The Benefits Delivery Plan

- The Project Stakeholder Management Plan
- The Project Communications Plan.

All can and should be used to ensure a project meets the needs and wants of the stakeholder community and help create customers for the project.

All can and should be used to 'sell' the outputs of the project to the 'users' in exchange for their support and co-operation during the development and implementation of the project.

Marketing and Selling the Project

Why is there a need to market and sell a project?

It could be argued there is no need because an organisation or sponsor has requested that a project be undertaken or the project has been initiated, quite correctly, as the mechanism for implementing an agreed business strategy.

However, It is possible that the project represents an idea or opportunity that has arisen outside the normal course of business and business planning and thus is without a sponsor and/or is not part of the current strategic business plan of the organisation.

In the first case above, marketing and selling the project is important. The need for the project may well be accepted at a high level but possibly only in terms of the business problem or opportunity to be resolved or exploited. Thus, the specifics of the project, the solution (the product), how the project will be conducted (physical evidence/process), where it will be undertaken (place), how much it will cost (price), who will do the work (personnel) and the benefits of the project and when it will be delivered (promotion) need to be marketed in terms of: "is there a customer for the solution?" rather than "is there a customer for the problem or opportunity?" which is probably already well accepted and understood.

Whilst the sponsor or executives of the business may have a good understanding of the aims and outcomes of the project, it is important for the Project Manager to 'market' and 'sell' the project to the other stakeholders within the organisation. This will include all the staff of the organisation that will be affected by the change or who are users of the change; it may also include the customers of the organisation itself.

In the second case the approach to marketing and selling the project is largely the same, with two important differences:

- The project will need to be 'sold' to the executive of the organisation.
- The project will need to be marketed and sold on the basis or assumption that the organisation will have to give something else up to accommodate this project or raise more investment funding, thus the opportunity or problem must be more pressing than projects already planned or the benefits greater than for something already planned.

At a fundamental level there is no difference in approach that needs to be taken between internal projects, those being conducted by the organisation's own resource and external projects, where an outside organisation is contracted in to manage the project. However, there are some differences at a more detailed level. These differences are explored in the following sub-sections.

Internal Projects

Marketing and selling internal projects, those projects which have be initiated within an organisation and will be conducted by the staff of the organisation, is a function of stakeholder management and communication. Stakeholder management and communication should, therefore, be focused as much on ensuring the project meets the needs and wants of its customers and will be 'bought' by the stakeholders as it is on telling the stakeholders 'how are we doing'.

Commercial / External Projects

For 'external' projects, where the organisation is 'buying-in' project management expertise to run the project or out-sourcing the project to a third party, the need for marketing and sales focused stakeholder management and communication is no different from that of an internal project, once the deal is done and the consultancy or project management organisation has won the contract.

However, the external organisation or individual has some additional work, as they must assume that they are in competition with other providers both internal and external.

External organisations will need to demonstrate that the project they have put together to meet the client needs represents better value that the bids from other competitor organisations or from the sponsoring organisation itself.

Internal service providers (i.e. specialist project management functions created within an organisation to support the organisation) need to have an approach that fits within the culture of the organisation:

- They need to recognise that they will be in competition with both internal and external sources of supply
- They need to take the same commercial perspective that an external company will, especially if there is an objective of cost recovery or internal profit
- There is a requirement for the internal service provider to market and sell their 'project' to the executive and staff of the organisation they serve
- They need to ensure that the approach to marketing and sales is appropriate for how the business expects an internal supplier to act. Overt or aggressive marketing and sales may not be seen as acceptable in an internal service provider

The focus of marketing and selling the Project is clearly part of the stakeholder and communication plans, the two illustrations below demonstrate the link between marketing and sales and stakeholder management and communication:

Stakeholder Management and Marketing

The key lesson is to determine your stakeholder management and communication plan from the perspective of the stakeholder, what are their needs and wants from both the project and the project manager in terms of engaging them in the project.

First, Project Managers may wish to consider this 'old Chinese proverb' as it is very relevant to marketing and selling projects and thus also relevant in the context of stakeholder management:

Tell me and I will forget

Show me and I may remember

Involve me and I will understand

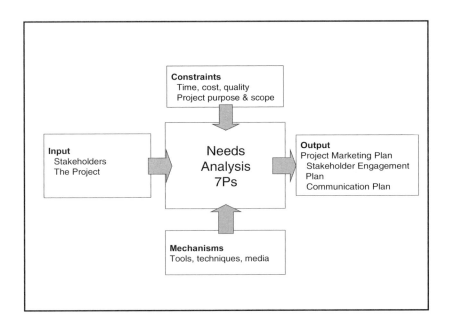

Figure 51 - 8: The Stakeholder Management Process

The stakeholder management process is concerned with identifying and analysing the stakeholders and the project with respect to the needs of the project in relation to the stakeholders and the needs of the stakeholders in relation to the project. From this a project marketing plan can be developed which includes, how and why the stakeholders will be engaged in the project and the communication plan around this.

In terms of how a Project Marketing Plan (Stakeholder Management and Communication Plan) might manifest itself, Figure 51 - 9 represents a simple illustration or example.

Marketing and Selling Project Management

Why is there a need to market and sell project management?

- The livelihood of project management professionals depends on creating and maintaining customers for project management services
- Many potential customers will be unaware or unsure of the benefits of taking a project management approach to change planning and delivery
- Many potential customers will have mis-conceptions or pre-conceptions about project management that will dissuade them from considering a project management approach

Marketing Project Management

In marketing project management, we need to understand what customers or clients needs and wants are and then apply project management to these needs and wants as a way of satisfying them.

These needs and wants can be discovered by looking at why projects succeed, why projects fail and what success and failure are attributable to. In this way the benefits of project management can be defined. This is what needs to be marketed. The benefits of taking a project management approach is the key element to be marketed not specific tools, techniques, products etc.

It is the results of the project management approach that will satisfy customer needs and wants.

Some of the key benefits of the project management approach are highlighted in Figure 51 - 10.

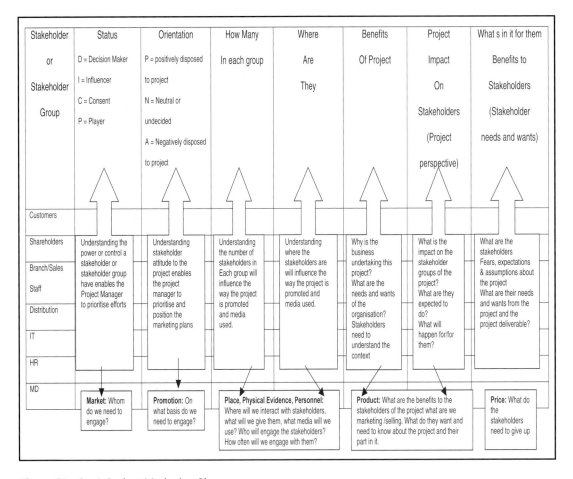

Figure 51 - 9: A Project Marketing Plan

Marketing project management should also:

- Dispel any misconceptions about project management.
- Avoid talking about proprietary products, technology and services.
- Avoid talking about the technical processes of project management.

An overall marketing plan for Project Management should follow the 7P concept.

The Benefits of the Project Management Approach.	
User and customer focused	Project Management brings structure & process to a unique or non -routine activity
Output & quality focused	Project Management controls and reduces the risks in implementing change into an organisation
Optimises the use of skills & resources across the organisation	Project Management focuses resources & controls on the project outputs across functional boundaries
Benefits Driven	Project Management increases the probability that the benefits sought from change are deliverable.
Delivery focused	Speeds up the successful delivery of change.

Figure 51 - 10: The Benefits of the Project Management Approach

Selling Project Management

Once the benefits or results of taking a project management approach have been established then the idea of products and services should be developed. Alongside the benefits of project management it is these products and services that need to be sold.

The selling of project management through products and services needs to bear in mind the need to persuade customers to 'trade up', to buy a bundle of services that together provide greater utility or value and to buy more products and services over time.

It also needs to be recognised that project management is an 'intangible' product, thus special attention needs to be placed on physical evidence, personnel and processes.

Project management should be broken down into a number of components that can either be bundled together or sold and delivered separately. This will allow the customer or client to create a solution package that best meets their needs and wants.

It should also be remembered that the products and services themselves need to be customised to meet the particular client needs which will be driven by factors such as the business the company is in and the demands placed on it by the market, its capabilities, its culture, its locations, its staff and their needs and wants.

The breaking down of project management into products and services could follow the main or principal disciplines of project management practice that can be discretely delivered. These should be further broken down into components such as: Processes, Tools and Techniques, Software to support the process etc.

A further approach might be to breakdown the delivery methods to the customer. In a broad sense these are: do it for the client; provide the clients with the tools to do it for themselves and support the client in doing it for themselves.

Marketing and Selling the Project Manager

In many respects marketing and selling the project manager is the most important part of marketing and selling project management. The project manager is the physical embodiment and representative of Project Management and, in many cases, a Project Management Organisation itself.

Project Management is an intangible product or service and customers and clients will start to form an opinion of project management and the project manager from the moment of first contact. They will make judgements on whatever physical evidence there is. This will include the Project Manager himself, how he presents himself and project management, the materials he brings with him to support the product/service and the process of project management itself.

Customers and Clients needs and wants in Project Management terms will often be formed by previous experiences with other project managers either from their own resources or from external suppliers. This may be good or bad and Project Managers need to assess and understand good and bad client experiences and address them in the way they present themselves and project management. There are clear benefits of employing a project manager for an organisation. Some of the key marketable benefits that need to be exploited are outlined below.

The Benefits of the Project Manager

In terms of Marketing the Project Manager the key is still customer needs and wants, this may be merely a 'body' to do the job, but it is more likely to be a need for:

- Knowledge of project management processes
- Experience and a track record of successfully delivering change and its benefits into organisations
- Experience. Practical hands-on experience of undertaking projects and using the methods of project management
- A track record of success in delivering a range of projects
- Knowledge and experience of the business/industry area in which the client is operating
- Filling a capability gap that does not exist in the client business or the client department
- Dedication in the role and to the project; the project manager will not be distracted from their purpose by other roles and responsibilities
- Someone the client can trust as his 'agent' in the delivery of a project
- Someone who manages the personal and business risk of the project on behalf of the client
- An agent of knowledge transfer, the project manager can increase/improve the capability of an organisation to undertake projects in the future
- A business leader and team player
- Adaptability to the needs and wants and environment of different businesses and different types of project

Figure 51 - 11 shows how project management products and services might be bundled together in the form of a product and service plan.

The product the project manager is selling to customers is The Project Manager. At a basic level it is the project manager's time that is for sale, the added value is the knowledge and experience the project manager can apply to the specific needs of the client and the project.

The 'product' also needs to be adaptable to fit within the client organisation and its culture, more importantly the

Product / Service	Resourced	D.I.Y	Supported • Application	Supported • Technology	Supported • Capability Development	Supported • Location
	Assigned Experts	Processes Guidebooks	Tools & Techniques	Software	Training Coaching Mentoring Workshops	Supplier site:- • Training and Workshops Client site or sites:- • Preferred for resource locations • Training etc. Help-desk:- • Booking training etc. • Ordering materials • Specific project problems or issues Internet/Intranet:- • Computer Based Training • Access to software • Process Manuals • Guidebooks • Tools & Techniques
General: • Project Management • Programme Management • Project Context	-	✓	-	-	Workshops	✓
Strategic: • Project Success Criteria· • Strategy / PM Plan • Value Management • Risk Management • Quality Management	✓ ✓ ✓ ✓ ✓	✓ ✓ ✓ ✓ ✓	- ✓ ✓ ✓ ✓	- - ✓ ✓ -	✓ ✓ ✓ ✓ ✓	✓ ✓ ✓ ✓ ✓
Control: • Work/Product Breakdown • Planning & Scheduling • EVA	✓ ✓ ✓	✓ ✓ ✓	✓ ✓ ✓	✓ ✓ ✓	✓ ✓ ✓	✓ ✓ ✓
Technical: • Estimating • Modelling & Testing • Configuration Management	✓ ✓ ✓	✓ ✓ ✓	✓ ✓ ✓	✓ ✓ ✓	✓ ✓ ✓	✓ ✓ ✓
Commercial: • Business Case • Procurement	✓ ✓	✓ ✓	✓ ✓	- -	✓ ✓	✓ ✓
Organisational: • Design & Development • Implementation • Hand-over • Organisation & Roles	✓ ✓ ✓ ✓	✓ ✓ ✓ ✓	✓ ✓ ✓ ✓	✓ - - -	✓ ✓ ✓ ✓	✓ ✓ ✓ ✓
People: • Communication • Teamwork • Leadership • Negotiation	✓ - - ✓	✓ - - -	✓ ✓ ✓ ✓	- - - -	✓ ✓ Coaching/Mentoring ✓	✓ ✓ 1 to 1 @ Client's Site ✓

Figure 51 - 11: A Product and Service Plan for Marketing and Selling Project Management

project manager also needs to be able to build a productive working relationship with the client. Adaptability is a marketable/saleable attribute.

Project Managers should develop a marketing plan in the same way any business needs to. Even within the context of a Project Management organisation it is as well for Project Managers to have a marketing plan as well as a curricula vitae to ensure that contracts, secondments or placements are to the mutual advantage of the client, the project management organisation and the project manager.

Marketing and selling the project manager is a very personal thing and it is down to each individual how they might approach the issue. However, each Project Manager needs to remember that they are marketing and selling themselves, so it needs to be a pro-active process. It should also be noted that marketing and selling the project manager is probably the most powerful way of marketing and selling project management and/or the products and services of a project management organisation.

Figure 51 - 12 suggests the sort of questions and answers each project manager needs to go through in creating a personal marketing plan, however, the following list of tips is also very useful when considering a personal marketing and sales approach:

- Focus on key projects and businesses: Project types and businesses that you have the knowledge and experience to make a difference in
- Don't target projects and businesses that require extensive travel and / or a long time from home if you cannot keep that sort of commitment
- Don't target projects or businesses where there are likely to be moral, ethical or cultural conflicts
- Don't target long term or full time projects if your aim is to undertake many projects or build future business in the same time frame
- Focus on a personal approach to marketing and selling. Use every opportunity and channel to meet with and communicate with clients and prospective clients
- Get your name noticed in the public domain: Write and publish articles and books, set up a web page, issue newsletters (use e-mail) or get articles in the company

newsletter. Give seminars and presentations, get involved in the community, obtain professional awards and honours

- Use advertising: Newspapers and magazines, trade directories e.g. Yellow Pages, Professional Journals, the internet etc.
- Promote yourself: Always have a business card, brochures and sales materials at the ready
- Ask and Listen: Your prime purpose is to help the client find the best solution to their needs
- Tell Clients about You: What makes you the person they are looking for or need
- Establish rapport: Be friendly, get to know the client's personality, likes and dislikes. Find a subject on which you can connect personally, e.g. a shared interest
- Target and meet the right people in the client organisation: Make sure you meet with the people who can make the decisions, sponsor the projects etc.
- Build a relationship:
  - Make and keep commitments
  - Never take on more work than you can handle, never turn down jobs because they seem too small
  - Give honest opinions
  - Keep client confidentiality
  - Never bid for or take on work you are not competent or experienced enough to handle: Suggest alternatives to meet the client's needs
  - Keep in touch and follow up on communications, meetings and actions
  - Say thank you for client time and attention
  - Don't drop a client or stop communicating if you haven't won a contract

7P	Questions/Analysis	Outputs
Product	Who are you? What is your experience and track record in Project Management? What types of project are you strong or weak in? What aspects of project management are you strong or weak in? What industries or businesses do you have knowledge and experience of? What is the market place (internal or external) for project management professionals? What have previous customers liked or disliked about the way you have managed projects or the client relationship? What elements of project management make the difference to clients and project success?	Where are you going?· Projects to target Businesses and industries to target Personal attributes to highlight Aspects of project management to focus on
Place	Where are the clients and prospective clients? Where are you based? Are you prepared to travel? Are you prepared to work at client sites? What are client preferences?	Where will I work? Proposition on working to clients
Promotion	How am I going to promote my services to clients? What media or channels do my clients and potential clients refer to when looking for project managers? Do they respond to personal approaches? Do I need to make special offers to gain business?	How will I communicate with Clients? Advertising and communication plan.
Price	How many days per year I am prepared to sell? How much do I want to earn/how much profit do I want to make? What is the cost of my time and support to the client? What is my basic rate for time? What is my premium for experience and knowledge? What is the industry norm / benchmark? What opportunities are there for a flexible approach to prices?	How much will I charge? My pricing structure.
Personnel	What do I need to do make a good impression with clients on a personal level both at first time meeting and in context of an ongoing commercial or project relationship?	How will I present myself to Clients? Personal approach, style and presentation
Physical Evidence	What tokens of evidence of knowledge, experience and capability will the clients demand to build trust and confidence in my capability?	How will I present my products, services and work to Clients? Branding and style Brochures Documents, Letterheads, Business Cards Office design
Process	What processes do I need to develop to: Manage the commercial interaction with the Client. Manage the project interaction with the client and stakeholders Manage the project.	How will I inter-act with my Clients? Simple, transparent, non-bureaucratic processes

Figure 51 - 12: A Personal Marketing Plan for the Project Manager

Key Lessons for PM Marketing and Sales

In summary a Project Manager has the following responsibilities:

- To market and sell Project Management
- To market and sell the Project Manager
- To market and sell the Project to its stakeholders and users.
- To undertake product and service development projects from a marketing and sales perspective, making sure that all the necessary marketing and sales activities are within the scope of the project.

Marketing Do's and Don'ts

Do	Don't
Do have a marketing plan for your business, your project managers, your projects	Don't ignore the need to market and sell projects, project management and project managers
Do choose your targets carefully	Don't go for business areas or projects you are not competent to undertake.
Do promote yourself and your products and services	Don't Hide your 'light under a bushel' and expect the clients to do all the work.
Do use success stories	Don't hide or gloss over situations that have not gone well
Do encourage referrals. Market via satisfied clients	Don't use un-attributable statements of satisfaction.
Do listen, listen, listen	Don't impose pre-conceived views and solutions
Do communicate, communicate, and communicate.	Don't be complacent
Do educate the clients. Ensure they know all about all the things you can do for them and the benefits for them	Don't market beyond your capacity and capability
Do look to the future Anticipate and plan for future clients and future projects and products	Don't get stuck with one client and one product. Don't take current clients for granted.
Do be open and honest about what you can do and are prepared to do	Don't waste client time.
Do recognise and act on the marketing and sales drivers within a project	Don't just focus on the outputs of a project e.g. software

Figure 51 - 13: The Do's and Don'ts of Marketing

Sales Do's and Don'ts

Do	Don't
Do remember that you set the costs, the market dictates the price	Don't under or over price
Do look for trade up opportunities	
Do look for add-on sales	
Do look for cross sales	
Do sell the benefits; demonstrate how they meet client needs and wants.	Don't sell the product or service.
Do sell your qualifications	Don't assume the client knows that you are the best for the job.
Do help the client build the proposal for the project	Don't impose your ideas or your 'standard' product or service on the client.
Do submit and discuss your proposal or project in person	Don't just send your proposal or project in by post or e-mail
Do be flexible on terms, have incentives	Don't get boxed into a rigid pricing structure
Do be patient	Don't walk away
Do be prepared	Don't try to wing it
Do leave room to negotiate	Don't get into a stand -off
Do clearly define the scope	Don't leave room for misunderstandings or interpretation
Do confirm the agreements in writing	Don't rely on verbal agreements

Figure 51 - 14: The Do's and Don'ts of Sales.

References and Further Reading

Mastering Marketing (Third Edition)
Douglas Foster with John Davis
MacMillan Master Series.

Marketing Theory & Practice (Third Edition)
Edited by Michael J Baker
MacMillan Business Series.

Consulting for Dummies
Bob Nelson & Peter Economy
IDG Books Worldwide.

Client- Centred Consulting (a Practical Guide for Internal Advisors and Trainers)
Peter Cockman, Bill Evans, Peter Reynolds
McGraw Hill Training Series.

The Project Workout (Second Edition)
Robert Butterick
Financial Times/Prentice Hall/Pearson Education.

52   FINANCIAL MANAGEMENT

Phil Fawcett

"Annual income twenty pounds, annual expenditure nineteen nineteen six, result happiness. Annual income twenty pounds, annual expenditure twenty pounds ought and six, result misery."

Charles Dickens (1812-1870), British novelist. Said by Mr. Micawber. David Copperfield (1850).

Introduction

It is usually the sponsor's responsibility to arrange financing for the project. Different sources of finance have different characteristics and the project management team must be aware of the impact of the particular requirements imposed on the project by its financing.

The type of financing depends on the size and complexity of the project. In general, there are three main options:

1   To use conventional, normal course of business sources of finance such as cashflow, free capital and overdraft

2   To use sources of finance designed for projects, such as bank loans and bonds, within the context of the sponsoring organisation

3   More complex financing structures using borrowing vehicles specific to the project. This category includes structures such as build-operate-transfer (BOT) or build-own-operate-transfer (BOOT)

The third category - using borrowing vehicles specific to the project - focuses on large-scale infrastructure projects. The term 'project finance' is often applied to this category and implies:

♦   Some reliance on project assets and cashflows without full recourse to the sponsor / borrower

♦   Specialist technical and economic evaluations of the project and its stakeholders, and on-going monitoring by the lender

- Complex loan and security documentation and innovative financing structures
- Higher margins and fees to reflect project and political risk

The cost is higher than conventional financing due to:

- The time spent on evaluating the project and negotiating the documentation
- Insurance costs - especially consequential risk and political risk insurance
- The cost of monitoring the project
- Higher charges to reflect a risk premium

The benefits include:

- Risk is shared between the stakeholders in the project
- The accounting treatment - particularly for non-recourse finance - may allow borrowings to be kept off the sponsor's balance sheet
- Restrictions on borrowing by the sponsor may be by-passed
- There may be benefits in the form of capital allowances or tax holidays

Sources of Finance

Equity

A company's equity is the money invested in the company by its shareholders. It includes the share capital - the money originally invested - and the company's reserves. Reserves are past earnings that the company has retained rather than distributed to shareholders. Shareholders expect to earn a return on their investment through dividends and increases in the share price.

Equity is usually an expensive source of funds. Share prices can go down as well as up and shareholders demand a higher rate of return to compensate for the risk. In addition, companies have to pay tax on their profits before they can pay dividends to shareholders.

Venture Capital

Venture Capital companies lend to start-ups and companies that cannot easily obtain finance from other sources. Venture Capital companies take an equity stake - share capital - in the company but they expect to earn a return when the company's shares are floated through an initial public offering (IPO) or placement of their shares. Venture Capital companies are not long-term investors but use the IPO or placement as an exit strategy.

Bank Loans

A bank loan is funding advanced by a financial institution for a specific purpose. Bank loans are for a fixed (maximum) amount and for a set duration. The bank receives interest, usually at a pre-agreed margin over a reference interest rate such as base rate or LIBOR (London Inter-Bank Offered Rate). The company will usually also have to pay a commitment fee on the part of the loan amount that has not yet been used and may have to pay other charges such as arrangement fees.

When a bank makes a loan specifically for project finance purposes, drawings against the loan (draw downs) often have a schedule that is linked to the project's planned funding requirements. The loan may also be in more than one currency, for example for projects where equipment is purchased in one country and installed in another.

Loans can be secured or unsecured. Loans for project finance purposes can be secured on the assets of the project. For example:

- Plant and machinery
- Land and buildings
- Licences and operating permits
- Rights under performance guarantee bonds or completion guarantees
- Technology and process licences
- Future production and future revenues
- Construction and supply contracts, and operating agreements

The proceeds of any insurance policies may also be assigned in favour of the lenders.

Overdrafts

An overdraft is an arrangement by which a company can draw funds from its current bank account over and above its current balance. Overdraft interest rates are higher than the interest rates charged on bank loans and rates for unauthorised overdrafts - where the company has not agreed an overdraft limit with its bankers, or has gone over the agreed limit - are very high.

Bond Finance

Companies can issue bonds. These are fixed-term debt instruments with an interest 'coupon' attached. Bonds are sold directly to investors in the (National) commercial paper markets or in the International and Eurobond markets.

Bonds may be secured on the future revenues of the project. Projects can be funded through a number of different bond issues in different currencies, and / or with different start and maturity dates. Bonds can be issued in a currency with low interest rates, swapped into the desired currency or currencies and then swapped back to allow repayment at maturity.

Bonds have particular advantages for companies with very good credit ratings and companies with poor credit ratings. If a company has a very good credit rating, bond finance will usually be cheaper than a bank loan. If a company has a very poor credit rating, it may be impossible to obtain a bank loan but it will usually be possible to issue bonds provided the interest rate is high enough - these are called 'junk bonds'.

The main disadvantage of bond finance is that individual bondholders have considerable powers to prevent any changes to the conditions of the bonds. This is a particular problem with bonds because the number of individual bondholders is large and because 'vulture funds' may buy up distressed debt (bonds the value of which has fallen) and use their holdings to try to get the best terms possible.

Other Forms of Debt Finance

Mortgage finance can be used, especially for ship financing. Ship mortgages may be secured on a long-term transportation agreement and an assignment of earnings and insurance.

Finance leases may be used, especially for ship and aircraft finance. A finance lease is a form of borrowing secured on the asset. Unlike a commercial lease, there is no provision for the borrower to end the lease and return the asset.

Leasing can allow the use of capital allowances and the lender retains ownership of the leased asset (and therefore the right to possession in the event of the project not being completed).

Cashflow

Projects financed from a company's operating cashflow are sourced from a mix of debt (loans, overdrafts and bonds) and equity. Therefore the cost of this finance is the weighted average of the cost of the two sources for the company:

Cost of capital = (cost of equity x ratio of equity) + (cost of debt x ratio of debt).

The cost of equity is the rate of return expected by the shareholders. This includes a risk premium to allow for the possibility that the share price may fall and can be shown as:

Cost of equity = risk-free rate + (b x equity risk premium).

b is the risk premium for the market as a whole. The equity risk premium is a multiplier to reflect the risk of the company - if the company has the same level of risk as the market, the equity risk premium will be 1.0.

The risk free rate is usually taken as the interest rate for short-term government securities such as Treasury Bills.

Companies pay for equity through a combination of share price appreciation and dividends. The market determines the share price, although economic theory suggests it should be the net present value of the company's expected future earnings divided by the number of shares. Therefore companies expecting faster future earnings growth will have higher market values. Companies usually try to maintain or gradually increase the value of their dividend payments.

Then the cost of debt is the interest rate at which they borrow with an allowance for the tax effects. This can be shown as:

Cost of debt   =   borrowing rate x (1 - tax rate).

Governments and Multilateral Institutions

Grants from governments or multilateral institutions - often in the form of regional development assistance - are another source of funding. Multilateral institutions may also provide loans - including 'soft loans' on concessionary terms - to projects.

The World Bank is an important multilateral lender. It lends to governments or to projects against state guarantees. The International Finance Corporation (IFC) is an arm of the World Bank. It provides finance to private sector companies on commercial terms. The IFC enters into an investment agreement with the project borrowing vehicle and enters into deposit agreements with commercial banks to refinance 80% of the loan.

There are a number of other multilateral organisations that will provide funding for infrastructure projects, including the European Bank for Reconstruction and Development (EBRD) and the Asian Development Bank (ADB).

Build-operate-transfer (BOT) agreements are used by governments to avoid direct financing for infrastructure projects. BOT is based on a concession agreement between a government or a government agency and the project borrowing vehicle for the construction and operation of the project. Project financing is secured on this agreement but there is no direct agreement between the lender and the government. BOT financing must usually include a substantial equity element, typically 10% - 30%.

Sources of Finance Compared

The advantages of equity over debt are:

- Companies do not have to pay dividends (although their share price may suffer if they do not). Interest must be paid whether or not the company is making profits.
- Equity capital does not need to be repaid. Loan capital must be repaid and the capital repayments are not tax deductible.
- Equity does not impose any restrictions on company activities, other than those laid down in the company's Memorandum and Articles of Association. Companies must enter into agreements to borrow and these may impose covenants that limit management's future activities (for example, by setting a ceiling on total borrowing).
- A high level of equity reduces the company's gearing ratio, which may make it easier and cheaper to obtain additional lending.

The advantages of debt over equity are:

- Interest payments can be claimed against tax. Dividends are paid on after tax earnings.
- Because interest payments cannot be waived, debt has a lower risk premium than equity. Therefore investors demand a lower return from interest than from dividends, making debt cheaper than equity.
- A lender has no claim on the company beyond the principal and interest. Shareholders have claims on all the income of the company.
- Debt does not dilute the rights of the owners of the company. Issuing new shares will reduce the proportion of share capital held by existing shareholders, reducing their control over the company.
- Interest and principal repayments are a known amount and can be allowed for in the company's financial plans.

There are also advantages and disadvantages in using different types of debt:

- Bonds are usually the cheapest source of debt finance for companies with good credit ratings, but they allow bondholders to prevent management from taking actions to their disadvantage.
- Bonds may be the only long-term source of debt finance for companies with poor credit ratings.
- Bank loans are cheaper than overdrafts. They can be drawn down to match the planned financial needs of the project, but it can be expensive to accommodate changes in funding requirements.
- Overdrafts are very flexible and the company only pays interest on actual borrowings, but they are expensive and the banks can demand repayment at any time.

Interest and Taxation

Interest

Interest is often the largest single cost item for a long-term project and project funding must allow for interest payments.

Bank loans may roll interest up into the loan capital. Interest and capital will be repaid when the assets created by the project start to earn income.

Bond finance may be issued at a discount to face value. The coupon (interest) rate is low or zero, but the bondholder's return comes from the difference between the issue price of the bond and the face value.

Taxation

Taxation can have a major effect on the economics of a project and is often a critical factor in investment decisions.

Capital allowances allow capital investment to be written off against tax. This reduces the cost of the investment to the company. Tax holidays on earnings resulting from the project are another type of incentive. The company may benefit from a tax-free period or a period where it pays tax at a reduced rate.

If tax holidays do not apply, tax will reduce the value to the company of the revenue from the project. It can be very complex to take this into consideration, as tax is levied on the earnings of the company as a whole and will be affected by the profitability of other operations. Withholding tax may restrict the company's ability to repatriate earnings from overseas projects.

Corporate Finance and Project Finance

The ratio of a company's debt to its equity is called its gearing ratio. If a company has a high gearing ratio - a large amount of debt relative to its equity - a large proportion of its earnings must be used to meet interest payments. During an economic downturn it may be difficult for the company to meet its debt service charges. This places a limit on the amount of debt companies can take on, as banks may be reluctant to lend if the gearing ratio is too high.

Project Investment Curve

Most projects follow a typical project investment curve (Figure 52 - 1) that includes the following stages:

1   Development: During the development stage there is a heavy demand for funds with no income. The project cashflow is strongly negative. The project expenditure follows the classical 'S-curve' pattern.
2   Operation: During operation there is a limited demand for funds through operating costs and maintenance. This is usually offset by a revenue stream from the use of the asset. The project cashflow is strongly positive, although the benefit declines over time due to increasing costs and (possibly) declining revenue.
3   Closure or decommissioning: During the decommissioning stage there may be a heavy demand for funds. There may be some income from scrap. Funding may need to be secured for reinvestment.

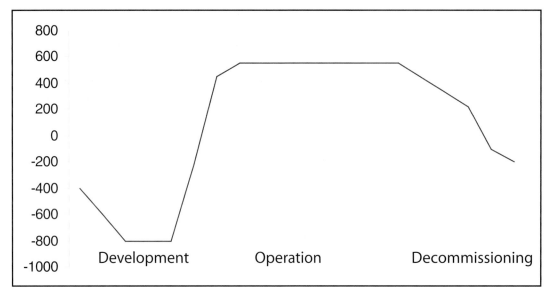

Figure 52 - 1: Typical Project Investment Curve

Approval and Drawdown

Project funding is drawn down in stages, linked to the completion of a specific stage of the project or to the production of a specific deliverable.

The approval process requires the customer to sign off that the stage has been completed or the deliverable produced. The customer may arrange for the work to be inspected before sign-off.

The drawdown process may work differently depending on whether the project is being carried out externally or in house.

- If it is being carried out externally, the contractor will issue an invoice and the customer sign-off authorises payment of the invoice.
- If it is being carried out in house, the customer sign-off will release a budget code. This will be used by the project to draw funds down as required.

All project payments and receipts should have an analysis code corresponding to the project's cost breakdown structure. This allows all project expenditure to be classified and matched to the project budget.

Payments and receipts should also be classified by income / expense type and by profit / cost centre. This allows the project accounts to be reconciled to the organisation's accounts.

There are a number of practical problems that must be considered:

1   The organisation's accounts are often finalised on a monthly basis. This allows the organisation to monitor trends but may not be sufficiently up-to-date for monitoring the project accounts

2   Analysis codes may be omitted or may be entered incorrectly

3   Entries may be passed that cover a number of different projects - for example, settlement of telephone bills. These need to be allocated between individual projects

Bid, Performance Guarantee and Retention Bonds

Bonds are used as part of the procurement process. They are usually put up by a financial institution on behalf of the bidder or supplier. The three most important types of bond are:

- Bid bonds
- Performance guarantee bonds
- Retention bonds

Bid Bonds

A bid bond is put up when the bid is made. If a bidder is awarded the contract but decides not to go ahead with the project, the bond is forfeit. Bid bonds provide the customer with assurance that the bidder is committed to proceeding if they are awarded the project, or the customer will be compensated for the costs involved if the bidder pulls out. A bid bond may typically be 1% - 5% of the contract value.

Performance Guarantee Bonds

A performance guarantee bond is part of the contract. The bidder must meet agreed standards of performance or forfeit the performance guarantee bond. Performance guarantee bonds provide the customer with assurance that the project will be completed to the agreed performance standards. A performance guarantee bond may typically be 5% - 10% of the contract value.

Retention Bonds

Retention is an amount held back by the customer from progress payments under the contract. This amount is usually retained for one year and is used to rectify any defects that are not immediately apparent. A retention bond is a guarantee and provides an alternative to the customer holding back the money. Retention and retention bonds provide the customer with assurance that any defects can be rectified without additional cost. A retention bond may typically be 5% - 10% of the contract value.

53   PROCUREMENT

Rob Blanden

"An inch of gold will not buy an inch of time".
Anon. Chinese proverb.

Introduction

Procurement is the process of acquiring new services or products. Procurement is a process that involves two or more parties with different objectives, who interact in a given market.

The procurement function of an organisation may also encompass logistics, i.e. storage, transportation, inspection, expediting, and the handling of materials and supplies. Organisations that are related though the process and activity of procurement are referred to as a supply chain. The definition of "supply chain" is a simple one: from your customer's customer to your supplier's supplier.

Good procurement practices can increase corporate profitability by taking account of quantity discounts, optimising cash flow and appointing quality suppliers. Because procurement tends to contribute so significantly to profitability, the procurement function tends to be centralised within the organisational structure of a company.

One of the most important factors in preparing a proposal and estimating the cost and profit of a project is the type of contract that will used to formalise the relationship between the parties involved in the project (typically the key project stakeholders are included in the overall contract).

In general, companies provide services or products based on the requirements of invitations for competitive bids, or the result of direct contract negotiations with the client.

Companies should be concerned when, during a competitive bidding process, one bid is much lower then the others. The client has to question the validity of this bid and decide whether the aims of the contract can be fulfilled for the low bid. In cases such as this, the client usually imposes incentive and penalty clauses in the contract for self-protection.

In this chapter, the following terms are used for consistency to define parties to a contract:

Term	Author's Definition
Company	An organisation, business or firm, and (in this chapter) the customer of a supplier or the client of a contractor, i.e. the buyer or purchaser
Customer	Refers to both customers & clients
Contract	An agreement between one or more parties enforceable by law
Project Manager	A person named under a contract who has the authority and duties to instruct and supervise a contractor
Supplier	A company that supplies products or materials and/or services to a customer as part of a contractual agreement
Contractor	A company that specifically provides resources and/or other specialist services to a client as part of a contractual agreement
Main Contractor	A contractor who manages sub-contractors on behalf of a client and reports to the Project Manager
Sub-contractor	A contractor or supplier who is party to a sub-contract agreement with a main contractor

Figure 53 - 1: Terms of Reference.

The Procurement Cycle

Requirements

The first step in the procurement process is the definition of a project, specifically the requirements. The following actions tend to be performed at this stage.

- Defining the business case for a project
- Perform a make-or-buy analysis
- Preparing initial cost estimates, including life-cycle costing analysis
- Developing the Statement of Work (SoW)
- Develop specifications
- Obtaining authorisation and approval to proceed

The SoW is a narrative description of the work to be accomplished and/or the resources to be supplied. More and more often Invitations to Tender (ITT) will require bidders to provide the resumes of the internal resources that will be committed to the project, including the percentage of their time on the project. This ensures that only suitably qualified and experienced personnel (SQUEP) resources will be utilised.

Specifications are written, pictorial or graphic information that describe, define or specify the services or items to be procured. There are three main types of specification:

1 Functional specifications - a description of how the product will be used
2 Design specifications - the detailed characteristics of the product
3 Performance specifications - measurable capabilities that the end product or service must achieve

Requisition

Once the requirements have been specified, then the requisition process can begin. This includes:

- Evaluating and confirming specifications are current and accurate
- Confirming sources of supply
- Reviewing performance of sources
- Producing a solicitation package

The solicitation package is produced during the requisition cycle, but utilised during the solicitation cycle. In most situations, the same solicitation package is issued to all potential suppliers. This is to ensure that the solicitation process is unbiased and impartial, so that hopefully the best terms for the procurement are achieved.

A typical solicitation package can include:

- Standardised bid documentation
- Listing of qualified vendors (expected to bid)
- Proposal evaluation criteria
- Process for managing change requests
- Contractual & payment terms

Bidder conferences can be used so that no single bidder has more knowledge that any other. If a potential bidder has a question regarding the solicitation package, then this can only be raised at the bidders' conference, so that all the bidders are privileged with the same information. There may be several bidders' conferences between solicitation and award. This approach is particularly common in public sector contracting, e.g. Ministry of Defence bidder conferences, where contracting firms tend to involve their project management capability at this early stage to ensure that the essence of the contractual terms and the scope of the work are clearly understood.

Solicitation

The method of acquisition is critical to the solicitation cycle and negotiation plays an important part in this process. The negotiation can be competitive or non-competitive. Non-competitive processes are termed sole-source procurement.

Customers tend to request preliminary Expressions of Interest (EOIs) from an approved vendor list by issuing a Request for Information (RFI) or a Request for Quotation (RFQ) as part of the solicitation package.

After a first round of selection, the chosen suppliers are requested to submit a detailed proposal based on a Request for Proposal (RFP) from the customer. This can be an expensive endeavour for the suppliers, since large proposals can contain separate volumes for cost, technical performance, management history, quality, subcontractor management and others.

On large contracts, the negotiation process goes well beyond negotiation about the bottom line. Separate negotiations can be made on price, quantity, quality and timing. Vendor relationships are critical during contract negotiations.

An effective process of negotiation should take into account the following guidelines:

1 Don't bargain over positions
2 Separate people from the problem
3 Focus on interests, not positions
4 Invent options for mutual gain
5 Insist on objective criteria
6 Develop your BATNA (Best Alternative to a Negotiated Agreement)

Award

The award cycle results in a signed contract. There are many types of contract and the negotiation process should include the selection of the type of contract.

The objective of the award cycle is to negotiate a contract type and price that will result in reasonable contractor risk and provide the contractor with the greatest incentive for efficient and economic performance (Kerzner, 1995).

Procurement Policies and Strategies

There are basically two procurement strategies:

1 Corporate procurement strategy: the relationship between specific procurement practices and the corporate strategy of an organisation.
2 Project procurement strategy: the relationship of specific procurement actions to the operating environment of a project.

Project procurement strategies can differ from corporate procurement strategies because of constraints, availability of critical resources and specific customer requirements. Corporate strategies might promote purchasing of small quantities from several qualified vendors, whereas project strategies may dictate sole source procurement.

A procurement strategy should be prepared very early in the project. This will often stem from a policy defined externally to the project - for example the urgency of the project. It will also often be a function of the state of the project definition, and of the supplier market.

The procurement strategy could include:

* Potential sources of supply
* Terms and types of contract/procurement
* Conditions of contract
* Type of pricing, and
* Method of supplier selection

Outsourcing

The Make or Buy Decision

Should a firm make or buy a product or service?

From a contractual point of view, it is the costs associated with the process of buying and selling that may affect a company's decision to make or buy. How procurement is organised within a firm (hierarchically) and between autonomous firms (across a market) depends on the transaction costs of each.

The major reason that firms decide to carry out activities internally or externally is largely based on the relative degree of asset specificity embedded in the relevant contractual relationship. High asset specificity is where particular skills or services are well established and 'sunk' (internalised) within the standard operating procedures of the firm. If this is the case, then the buyer and seller will have to make special efforts to design an exchange relation, i.e. contract, that has good continuity properties.

Factors involved in the make or buy decision are shown in Figure 53 - 2.

How to Organise for Outsourcing

To consider outsourcing as a form of supply naturally leads to a consideration of models of organisations that are based, in some cases very loosely, on systems theory.

Make	Buy
Less costly (but not always!)	Less costly (but not always!)
Easily integrated into existing operations	Utilise skills of suppliers
Able to utilise existing capacity	Not cost effective to produce
Maintain direct control	Having limited capacity or capability
Maintain design/production secrecy	Augment existing resources
Avoid unreliability of suppliers	Maintain multiple sources (qualified vendor list)
Stabilise existing workforce	Indirect control

Figure 53 - 2: Make or Buy Options

One extension and elaboration of the value chain model (Porter, 1985), which envisages a richer systems approach, is the value constellation (Normann and Ramirez, 1993).

This model is still based on the fundamental notion of value-adding activities, but these are not necessarily linearly related. Activities may take place simultaneously or sequentially and may be performed by one party on one occasion and another party on another occasion. Adopting the value constellation model potentially brings into question traditional organisational boundaries.

With respect to breaking down the barriers between organisations, Ashkenas et al. (1995) identify five actions that can provide ideas as to how to make inter-organisational boundaries more permeable. For example, they suggest taking customer/supplier field trips, mapping customer/supplier needs, and collecting customer/supplier data. Though these actions seem straightforward it is surprising how much new information they can provide. More than anything they provide the foundations for information and knowledge sharing networks linking employees (and organisations), that lead over time to spontaneous sharing of concerns and information, increasing levels of trust, and shared values and world-views.

Examples of Outsourcing

It is common across most types of markets for some companies to outsource entire departments to third party suppliers. The contracts that are put in place to manage these outsourcing arrangements tend to be very high value and long-term.

For example, the Department for Environment, Food and Rural Affairs (DEFRA) is to outsource its IT systems in a deal worth an estimated £65m to £80m a year. Due to be awarded in 2004, it will run for up to 10 years. The purchasing process began recently with a briefing pack being made available to potential suppliers. An invitation to tender is expected by February 2003 (Arnott, 2002).

For outsourcing arrangements to be successful, it is critical that companies take cognisance of the plethora of 'lessons learnt' information that is available. This includes establishing mechanisms that accommodate changes in requirements over the life of the contract and building in effective exit and transition strategies, so that at the end of a contract there are efficient procedures to manage through to the next one. Consistent quality of service is also very critical to the success of long-term outsourcing deals.

Outsourcing is becoming more common in the supply chain arena, where non-core functions, such as transportation and logistics, are being considered for outsourcing even though they are critical to improving supply chain management and achieving operational excellence. There are indications that companies are expanding their existing relationships with logistics providers beyond co-ordinating and tracking the movement of goods through the pipeline.

An example of this is Nortel Networks, who, in February 2002, divested its Logistics Operations Management business, which oversees global product shipments and deliveries, to a fourth-party Swiss logistics provider company. The company is now exclusively responsible for managing the performance of Nortel's multiple logistics service providers globally and executing Nortel's logistics requirements, totaling hundreds of millions of pounds annually (Shah, 2002).

This is proof that despite some major failings that have been well published in the press, outsourcing is set to remain a prominent feature on the business landscape for the foreseeable future.

Supplier Appraisal

The total control of the supplier base, source management, is a prime responsibility and task for purchasing departments, as is the need to assess the potential and actual performance of suppliers. The assessment of potential, usually done before a supplier is used, is termed supplier appraisal; performance measurement is termed vendor rating.

Although many companies do recognise the need for supplier appraisal, and go through the motions of assessing potential suppliers, in practice it too often becomes merely a routine information gathering exercise and does not constitute measurement of the suppliers' appraisal.

The question of ' does supplier X have enough potential to be considered as a supplier?' has to be preceded by 'what would make supplier X a good supplier?'. Rather than being a once-and-for-all task, supplier appraisal should be a continuing exercise whereby the understanding of suppliers and confidence in their performance increases.

Supplier Selection

Whilst the collection of the proper information and its recording to produce a comprehensive supplier data record is the bulk of the appraisal task, there should initially be an attempt to answer the key question 'can the supplier provide what we want?'. The following table gives an indication of the areas that should be investigated:

Requirement	Aspect to be Investigated
Quantity	Capacity
Quality	Technical know-how, managerial progressiveness
Reliability	Financial control, trading position, commitment
Compatibility	Management style, willingness, policies, contractual approach
Cost/Price	Efficiency, selling policy, warranty

Figure 53 - 3: Aspects of Supplier Selection.

Some of the information is factual and can be physically checked, such as equipment type and condition; but other information, such as willingness to do business requires personal judgement. The collated information is termed a supplier profile. The risk is always that the profile does not reveal latent, but potentially damaging, weaknesses. This is the main reason why prior to the collection of information, the desired profile should be prescribed, together with qualifying/disqualifying criteria for critical factors.

Sourcing Strategy

Knowledge of the overall supply market, coupled with specific assessment of the suppliers available to the buyer, permits an analysis of the risks and opportunities of the business environment. The existence of plans to phase-in/phase out certain production methods, moves for suppliers to reduce surplus capacity, cutbacks in technical personnel, and other factors should influence decisions regarding the number of suppliers to be used, make or buy, degree of contractual control, and similar strategic factors. Discovering such moves can form part of an effective supplier appraisal.

Contract Selection

Although many supplier-customer relationships seem to owe little to the terms of contract between them, it is inherent that there is a contractual relationship. Like supplier appraisal, the enquiry-quotation-order-delivery-invoice chain has become a mechanical, repetitive process in many companies. This is unfortunate, since constructive use of contract terms, especially regarding stockholding, payment, performance warranty and price variation can achieve significant advantage for both buyer and seller.

The ability and willingness of a supplier to work with the buyer in devising a workable contract becomes an important feature for the creative buyer. The prudent buyer will carefully tailor a contract to cover any potential weaknesses of a supplier. Thoughtful supplier appraisal will provide the background for this.

Control of Performance

Although it is the application of vendor rating which contributes most to measuring supplier performance, working with a supplier to achieve and maintain optimum performance requires an understanding of how the supplier functions. The aim is to be familiar with the supplier's operation and make-up in order to be able to analyse causes.

Supplier Development

Having developed a picture of the good supplier, and measured existing and potential suppliers against it, there is always the chance that no supplier, or not enough suppliers reach an adequate standard. This is where supplier development is used to work with a supplier to achieve the necessary standard. The starting point has to be clear knowledge of the standard required and the supplier's potential - the suppler appraisal.

Vendor Rating

The measurement of a supplier's performance relating to the manner in which they carry out their total obligations against a contract is an aid to understanding the total cost of doing business with a supplier.

Contracts

Definitions

What is a Contract?

A contract is an agreement between two or more parties that is enforceable at law. The rules for contracts established by law vary from country to country and a contract should state which country's law applies, which language will rule and where disputes are to be settled. Under English law an agreement to buy goods or services is a contract if:

- Intention - the parties genuinely intend to enter into a legally enforceable relationship
- Offer & acceptance - the terms of the contract are offered by one party and accepted by the other(s)
- Possibility and legality - the terms require performance of activities which are possible and legal
- Consideration - the terms include payment in money or kind in return for performance
- Capacity - the parties have the legal capacity to enter into the contract

Project management professionals will often be involved in the preparation and administration of contracts. As well as a firm understanding of the contract(s) themselves, this will involve clear definition of responsibilities and definitions of risks and their mitigation (see session 23). The world of contracts is variously described as one of planning, promise, competition, or governance.

Planning a Contract

A definitive contract tends to follow normal contracting procedures, such as the negotiation of all contractual terms, conditions, cost and schedule, prior to initiation of performance. Unfortunately, negotiating the contract and preparing it for signature may take many man-months of effort.

To be successful a contract needs to be designed to suit the objectives and priorities of the project. The ideal choice of contract terms varies from project to project, depending on the relative priorities between quality, economy, speed and flexibility, public policies, ability to perform the work and the ability of all parties to operate within the framework of the contractual agreement.

If the customer needs work to begin immediately or if actual procurement involves long lead-time items, then the customer may provide the contractor with a Letter of Intent (LOI). The LOI is a preliminary written instrument authorising the contractor to begin immediately the manufacture of supplies or the performance of services.

The final contract price may be negotiated after the performance begins, but the contractor may not exceed the limit imposed by the LOI, since, of course, the definitive contract is still to be negotiated.

Types of Contract

One Comprehensive Contract

A comprehensive or prime contract is where one supplier is responsible for everything required for a project. This means that a client has only one contractor to deal with and the client's staff can concentrate on achieving project objectives. A risk to the customer is that the entire project depends on the performance of this one supplier.

In order to obtain the desired outcome, the customer must define what the supplier has to produce ('deliverables'). Unless the work is routine and the risks are small, the responsibilities and liabilities of both parties should be defined in detail. The supplier is expected to manage all the relationships between everyone who is supplying goods and services to the project. Another risk is that the customer will have limited or only indirect ability to assess and influence the performance of the project.

Sequence of Contracts

An alternative arrangement to a prime contract is the sequential use of two or more contractors during the life-cycle of a project. For example, with public works projects, one contractor may be engaged for design and another contractor for actual construction. Starting with a contract for design and development should make it possible for options to be investigated and risks to be assessed, prior to commitment being made for more costly manufacturing or construction.

Staged contracts are logical if there is much uncertainty about what is required and/or how it will be achieved. Customers' tend to use this type of contract to limit the commitment and exposure to risks at the start of a project.

However, a sequence of contracts has the potential disadvantage that the customer's project team must plan and manage the interactions between the stages. The customer may have a less firm indication of the final cost of a project until the final contracts have been made. Also, no party can plan very far ahead.

Parallel Contracts

A set of parallel contracts is common in many industries for purchasing goods and services. Communications are directly between the customer and each specialist supplier, but this arrangement requires the customer to manage the relationships between all parties.

Separating responsibilities for stages and types of work is logical if requirements are uncertain at the start of a project, or if individual suppliers have limited capabilities or know-how relative to the amount or type of work required.

Sub-Contracts

Suppliers (or main contractors) frequently employ several sub-contractors in parallel, particularly where the project requires the input of specialised goods and services. In most contracts the customer can only communicate formally with sub-contractors through the main supplier. If much of the work for a project is sub-contracted then the customer may only have a limited ability to monitor, assess and influence progress.

Many specialist companies prefer to work directly for the ultimate user of their products and services, rather than as a sub-contractor. This provides them with a degree of continuity with customers, who deal with them directly for spares and maintenance work once the main contract is complete.

Terms of Payment

When formulating contract and procurement strategy, customers should consider what terms of payment are likely to motivate suppliers to achieve the objectives of the project. There are numerous contract payment processes that exist across most industries, so this section provides an overview of the main types:

Fixed Price Payment

Fixed price or 'lump sum' payment generally means that an agreed, fixed price is paid when the work, or stage of it, is complete. In these contracts the customer knows the total price before entering into the contract, except the cost of variations. Variations can lead to claims from suppliers for extra time and payment.

Fixed prices are preferred by many customers for prime contracts when a supplier is responsible for the complete design and supply of a project. To avoid being obliged to pay more, the customer should not enter into the contract until there is a clear and complete definition of the deliverables and liabilities. During the project, variations should be minimized and only those that are appropriate to achieving the project objectives should be allowed.

Milestone payments refer to a series of lump sums that are paid at the point a supplier completes defined stages in a project. In these contracts:

- The supplier has an incentive to offer a realistic time and cost model for the contract and there is an incentive to achieve the defined milestones
- The customer can compare the cash flow differences between bids

- The breakdown of total contract price into a series of lump sums make sit easier to predict the total cost of variations

Unit Rate-Based Payment

In these contracts payment is based on prices per unit of work done. Unit rates provide a basis for paying for quantities of work completed or resources provided. A unit-rate basis of payment is logical if the quantities of work to be undertaken or the amount of resources required is uncertain at the time of inviting priced bids.

An analysis of the rates of different suppliers can provide a basis for the detailed comparison of bids. The rates can also provide a basis for pricing small variations during the contract period.

The final quantities to be paid for may be different to those expected at the time of entering into the contract, due to errors or uncertainties. Moreover, the compilation of the bill of quantities or schedule of rates listing all the items of work, calculating the quantities, estimating the rates and measurement of the work done for payment purposes takes time and adds costs to both the bid and the project.

Cost-Reimbursement Contracts

An alternative arrangement is for the customer to pay ('reimburse') a supplier's cost in supplying people and other resources to be used as directed by the customer. In this case, more risk is allocated to the customer, but risks incur cost only if they actually affect the work being undertaken.

Suppliers are often invited to bid competitively for these contracts by being asked to state their rates per hour or per day for categories of people and other resources. Whilst this is a type of unit rate system, payment is for costs rather than performance. These contracts are frequently used in the provision of services when it is not clear at the outset what types of work will be undertaken and whether resources can be used economically.

Contract Price Adjustment (CPA)

There are potential advantages to including terms for compensating contractors for escalation of their costs due to inflation, such as contractors do not have to include in their price enough contingency if inflation is above predicted rates. Clients only have to pay for the real costs, since the contract should specify the method to calculate the effect on contract price. A disadvantage for clients is that they cannot be sure in advance what the extra costs will be.

If a contractor does not include such terms, the tender prices from contractors are likely to be higher at times of inflation, but the client knows that the total contract price is independent of inflation. The client may also expect that contractors will have an incentive to complete their work more rapidly if inflation is likely to cause their costs to rise.

Retention Money

Retention arrangements provide the customer with a fund to pay for rectifying defects or faults in the work that is completed by a supplier. Most larger contracts for engineering goods and services include a terms stating that a percentage of the payments due to a supplier as a fixed price, milestone achievement or based on unit rates will be retained by the customer until performance testing has been completed. Half of all the retention amount is then released and the remainder is then usually paid a year later if the supplier has completed all their obligations.

Liquidated Damages

Larger engineering and construction contracts in the UK have traditionally included terms for reduction of payment to the supplier if they are late in completing the work or if the equipment supplied achieves less than its specified performance. These liquidated damages agreements are intended to motivate a supplier to complete the work correctly and on time.

A liquidated damages clause in a contract can be attractive to a supplier in limiting liability for lateness. Some experienced customers prefer to include payment of a bonus for completion to quality standards and completion on time.

For the liability to pay liquidated damages to have a legal effect under English Law, the amount should be a demonstrably genuine pre-estimate of the damage likely to be suffered by the customer. Any larger sum may be construed to be a penalty and may not be payable.

Variations

Except in smaller and repeat purchases, it is rare to be able to enter into an ideal contract where one party offers goods or services which will be exactly what the other party finally wants. Market changes, competitors, new technology and unexpected problems during the contract can all make the customer want to vary what has been originally defined.

Some variations to a suppliers work may therefore be inevitable. If this is the case, then variations should be planned for in the selection of the terms and conditions of the contract and should form part of the normal managerial responsibilities of a project manager. The contract should ensure that adequate procedures exist for managing the initiation, evaluation and payment (or not) of variations.

Variations to design or other requirements can be a major threat to the success of a project. The customer and supplier should therefore have internal procedures to control all variations, such that the current and anticipated final effect of each variation on time, budget and performance is fully understood by all stakeholders.

Payment Risks

Whatever the proposed terms of payment in a contract the customer should consider risks such as insolvency of a supplier, effects of inflation and termination before inviting bids and make suitable provisions to minimise any potential impact.

Suppliers on the other hand should consider risks such as the security of payment (i.e. cash flow) and a customers ability to pay, before bidding.

Sub-contractors should be wary of contracts in which they are paid only when a main contractor has been paid by the customer. Such 'pay when paid' clauses are generally considered unlawful under UK Law.

Supply Chain Management

Notwithstanding the industry debate regarding the nature and scope of supply chain management, it is clear that it must encompass all members of a supply chain, from the supplier's suppliers' to the customer's customers'. The core operational function of an organisation, for example, needs to be supported through an efficient and effective supply chain management process.

The Value Chain

The 'value chain' (Porter, 1985) disaggregates a firm into its strategically relevant activities in order to understand the behaviour of costs and the existing and potential sources of differentiation. A firm's value chain is embedded in a larger stream of activities that Porter terms the 'value system'.

Suppliers have value chains (upstream value) that create and deliver the purchased inputs used in a firm's chain. In addition, many products pass through the value chains of channels (channel value) on their way to the buyer. A firm's product eventually becomes part of the buyer's value chain. Gaining and sustaining competitive advantage depends on understanding not only a firm's value chain but also how the firm fits into the overall value system.

Value activities can be direct, indirect or quality assurance related and every firm has direct, indirect, and quality assurance value activities. All three types are present not only among primary activities (e.g. operations), but also among support activities (e.g. procurement). In many industries, indirect activities represent a large and rapidly growing proportion of cost and can play a significant role in differentiation through their effect on direct activities.

Generally, because suppliers account for about one-half of the average company's costs, their suppliers represent one half of those costs, and so on back up the value chain (Lewis, 1995). Further, every company in the chain innovates within its scope of expertise. A customer that effectively manages all of those costs and leverages all of that creativity builds a tremendous competitive advantage for itself, compared to rivals that still regard suppliers as firms whose goods they buy through arm's-length, price-dominated transactions.

Integrated Supply Chain Management

Driven by brutal competition, supply chains in every industry are moving towards integration. For a company to deliver maximum value to its customers, it must receive maximum value from its suppliers. Moreover, no firm working alone can differentiate its products as much as is possible without suppliers' help (Lewis, 1995).

As companies start to move toward integrated procurement and supply chain management, it is becoming apparent that major changes are needed in traditional ways of looking at and solving supply problems. Most organisations need to 'get their arms around the entire supply chain'. 'Entire' usually means going out two or three levels into the end customer base or back two to four levels into the supply base.

To do this requires integration of such key information and processes as final customer needs determination, product/service development, demand planning information sharing, cost information development and reduction, performance target setting, and timing milestones. In most cases effective integration and management of the supply chain involves linking all the internal processes from new product development to customer order performance.

Innovation in Procurement

The following sections give some indication of the areas where the practice, application or understanding of procurement is breaking new ground and/or being innovatively applied.

e-Procurement

Many companies have implemented an off-the-shelf e-procurement system in an attempt to handle requisitioning more efficiently. For example, IBM (Blair, 2001) estimates that by committing to an aggressive deployment of an e-procurement solution a company can expect to save between five and fifteen percent of their total procurement spending and begin to see results in 6 to 9 months.

Much of these savings will come from controlling spending that does not leverage corporate contracts and volumes. With a balanced deployment of the right technology, re-engineered processes and effective sourcing, companies may save even more by:

- Closing the windows on procurement control and gaining compliance through easy-to-use tools
- Streamlining and speeding up the procurement process
- Reducing the number of vendors by leveraging corporate spending to renegotiate vendor agreements

Senior Management Support

Presenting management with a fully developed, concrete and reasonable ROI-based business justification helps to initiate early support. Too often companies, make huge investments without a clear view of the expected outcome, a process to measure it or the proper internal support.

Speed

Rather than asking 'how long will it take to do something?' the development and deployment methodology needs to reflect the question 'how much could be done in, say, 90 days?'. Furthermore, an '80/20' rule needs to be applied, that generally shows that a company can get 80% of the functionality or coverage in that 90-day window; the rest can be delivered later.

Supplier Enablement

A re-occurring theme throughout all e-procurement activities is that connecting with vendors electronically in order to receive content, such as catalogues, and to exchange transactions, such as purchase orders and invoices, can make or break the success of these projects. Lack of connectivity with suppliers diminishes the relative value of a solution for end users.

Integration

Legacy systems tend to house most of the important data outside of supplier content. Whether it is employee data or product information, a company needs to understand where the data is located, how to access it and in what form they need it. Unique business requirements may drive changes in other applications in order to make the data more valuable.

Processes

Although for many companies accounts payable is a separate part of the process, effective procurement depends on a coherent accounts payable process. Business rules in the procurement space need to be driving payment vehicles in the payables area. Without an efficient payment system a company looses leverage and increases costs. IBM (Blair, 2001) states that an additional 30-50% savings in accounts payable processing costs can be achieved by re-engineering and aligning payables with the procurement process.

Strategy

Without a clear objective and direction, and a strategy for streamlined processes, investments in software and other procurement tools are often wasted.

Lessons Learnt

Figure 53 - 4 indicates key lessons that should be learnt prior to embarking on an e-procurement project:

Lesson Learnt	Benefits
Gain early support from top management	• Helps organisations adapt to change more easily • Signals the need for enterprise-wide acceptance
Focus on speed - a sense of urgency	• Time efficiency presents tremendous savings opportunities • Processes that swiftly executed require fewer people & systems • Enables management to focus on prioritising requirements and driving speed
Facilitate effective supplier enablement	• Greater connectivity & access to suppliers • Leads to better spend control
Provide robust integration	• Exploits the full value of procurement data
View procurement as an end-to-end process	• Key to supplier relationships and management • Includes accounts payable
Establish a clear strategy & processes	• Drives out discussion regarding key technology decisions • Ensures existing inefficient processes are not simply automated

Figure 53 - 4: e-Procurement Lessons

Trading Exchanges - The Struggle to Build On-line Markets

Online trading exchanges are an inevitable development of the Internet. The low-cost communications infrastructure created by internet technology makes it easy and inexpensive for companies to exchange data and process transactions. In September 2000, Deloitte Research estimated that the number of online exchanges to be in excess of 1,500.

There has been significant consolidation in the sector over the last two years. Some exchanges have merged - for example Bidcom and Cephren, two exchanges in the construction sector, joined together last year to form Citadon. Some have been acquired - e-Chemicals by Aspen Technology and E-Transport by Decartes Systems Group. Some have even become "solutions" providers, selling their exchange software and services to other companies.

One reason why vertical exchanges are successful is that operators are more likely to build their exchanges around solutions to specific problems. This is an essential element in the development of online exchanges and the wider issue of re-engineering supply chains. The challenge is to move beyond providing straight transaction services and to move on to the next stage which brings in collaborative working - cutting inventory, reducing lead times and enhancing sales.

Exchanges are more likely to survive if they can offer speciality services in addition to online catalogues and transaction processing, where there is far more potential for purchasers and suppliers to work collaboratively - with the exchange providing the link.

Ultimately, the success of exchanges will depend on how well businesses can utilise the latest technologies and integrate the concept into their supply chain.

Strategic Sourcing

Many companies today are searching for ways to accelerate the changes required to achieve supply chain excellence. These efforts are not only being driven by competitive pressures, but are also related to an increasing awareness of the potential benefits associated with achieving supply chain excellence. As a result, partnerships and alliances are being formed between companies to deliver four primary benefits:

♦ A faster response to shifts in market demand, enabling an increase in market share or avoidance of obsolete inventory

♦ Improved linkages with suppliers, that result in maximum supplier added-value through the supply chain

♦ Quick response manufacturing, capable of mass-customisation if necessary and directly driven by satisfying actual customer needs

♦ An order fulfilment process that integrates all of the customer's needs and provides service levels that are a competitive strength

These attractive and competitively required opportunities are driving most companies to pursue improvement programmes that address one or more of these areas. Some companies are pursuing all these opportunities simultaneously, as an 'integrated supply-chain excellence programme'.

Supply chain improvement programmes have historically been hindered by several factors. First, the supply chain notion is a relatively new and loosely defined concept. For some senior executives it remains a buzzword that often seems to describe a problem too broad to be practically attacked. Just whose job is it to fix the supply chain anyway? The answer to this question is the second factor hindering supply chain programmes - in many companies it is either everyone's job or no one's job.

The supply chain is a process-orientated concept that does not conform to traditional organisational structures. This can easily cause conflicts with funding, leadership, and performance metric issues that can slow or derail supply chain programmes.

If purchasing resources are limited, then core competencies should be defined in order to identify strategic suppliers and allow them to assume more responsibility. Supply chain integration means the promotion of links among various members of the supply chain to create 'one-stop shopping' opportunities for an operation.

Tools

Some relevant and practical procurement tools are included in the following sections:

Tips for Contracts

Standard Terms and Conditions

Model forms of conditions of contracts are available from the Chartered Institute of Purchasing and Supply (CIPS). Email: info@cips.org

There are other models published by trade association and many sets of model terms for specialist work and sub-contracts. Guidance notes and model terms of contract are published with most the engineering institutions' model conditions of contract.

Planning	Be clear what is required. Say what is meant. Eschew obfuscation.
	Choose the terms of a contract simply and logically, depending upon factors such as: • Nature of the work • Certainty • Urgency • Motivation of project stakeholders
	Specify only what can be tested • Agree acceptance criteria for performance
	Plan how the contract will end before it starts • Be aware how the contract is created and how it can be discharged
	Anticipate what can wrong • Apply risk management • Avoid or transfer • Reduce or absorb • Allocate risks for best control
	Decide what terms of payment are most effective
	Choose suppliers and contractors who will best serve the interests of the project and contribute to its success.
Management	A contract should be a means to an end, not a playground for specialist interests.
	Establish control of the contract through a single manager who has experience of the potential conflicts of interest that can arise and the authority to deal with any issues
	Assess how much real power your contractor's manager has over resources
	Study the contract and note the rights and obligations of all parties
	Recognise that objectives and priorities can change during the lifetime of most contracts
	Control variations and take proper advantage of potential variations
	Keep records and notes of the reasons for decisions
	Distinguish between legal rights and project interests

Figure 53 - 5: Tips for Contracts

References and Further Reading

APM SIG., 1998. Contract Strategy for Successful Project Management. The Association for Project Management (APM), Specific Interest Group (SIG) on Contracts and Procurement.

Arnott, S., 2002. Defra to Award Lucrative Outsourcing Deal. Computing, Aug 22, 2002. VNU Business Publications Ltd.

Ashkenas, R., Ulrich, D., Jick, T. & Kerr, S., 1995. The Boundaryless Organisation. San Francisco: Josey-Bass.

Blair, R., 2001. e-Procurement Makes Immediate Business Sense. IBM e-Procurement Briefing Paper, July 2001.

Blanden, R.A., 1997. Searching for Synergy in Supply Chains: Can Strategic Benchmarking Alleviate 'Stickiness'? MBA Thesis, University of Durham Business School.

Dixon, M. (Ed.), 2000. The Association for Project Management (APM) Body of Knowledge (BoK), 4th Edition.

Kerzner H., 1995. Project Management: A Systems Approach to Planning, Scheduling and Controlling. 5th edition, Van Nostrand Reinhold.

Lawson, G., Wearne, S. & Iles-Smith, P. (Eds.), 1999. Project Management for the Process Industries. Institution of Chemical Engineers.

Lewis, J.D., 1995. The Connected Corporation: How Leading Companies Win Through Customer-Supplier Alliances. New York, NY: The Free Press.

Normann, R. & Rameirez, R., 1993. From Value Chain to Value Constellation: Designing Interactive Strategy. Harvard Business Review, July-August 1993.

Porter, M.E., 1985. Competitive Advantage: Creating and Maintaining Superior Performance. New York, NY: The Free Press.

Shah, J., 2002. Survey Shows Outsourcing Catches on in Supply Chain. www.ebnonline.com, Feb 06, 2002. CMP Media Inc.

54   LEGAL AWARENESS

Martin Stevens

"There's no better way of exercising the imagination than the study of law. No poet ever interpreted nature as freely as a lawyer interprets the truth."
Jean Giraudoux (1882-1944), French dramatist and writer. Tiger at the Gates (1935).

Introduction

Project management professionals should have an awareness of the relevant legal duties, rights, and processes which govern in a particular project situation. Similarly, there should be an awareness of the potential causes of disputes, liabilities, breaches of contract, means of resolving a dispute, and legal bases for industrial relations.

Further, project managers will need to have a reasonable understanding of the legal implications of their role as a manager of the project process. In addition, the project manager should be able to advise their clients of the legal consequences of decisions made and when more detailed legal advice should be sought.

The law is essentially a body of rules which everybody has to abide by. Within the UK there are two distinct bodies of law; English and Scottish. For the purposes of this Sesion we will only consider English law (which also applies to the principality of Wales). Similarities with Scottish law do exist but readers would be advised to consult alternative material with regard to the specifics of the law in Scotland and other territories.

The English Legal System

In England and Wales, the Legal system relies on a hierarchy of Courts to hear different types of cases (Figure 54 - 1). Some courts will only hear criminal matters where the issue is the establishment of guilt (or innocence); whilst others hear civil cases where the aim is to obtain compensation for a person suffering injury or damage from a transgression.

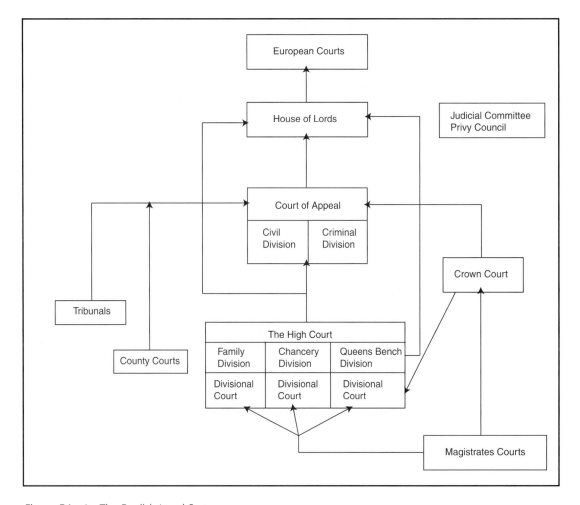

Figure 54 - 1: The English Legal System

Civil courts have a variety of remedies available to them, the award of damages being one. In some courts, there may be a financial limit on their jurisdiction.

Generally "senior" courts will hear cases considered to be more important and additionally, the senior courts will hear appeals relating to the findings of a junior court.

Magistrates' Court

Both civil and criminal cases are heard in this court. The court's jurisdiction also includes the recovery of debts including income tax and charges by statutory undertakings.

Cases are heard by Justices of the Peace who are members of the public appointed as Magistrates. Magistrates require no legal qualification and act only as decision-makers on fact as well as law. Legal advice is provided by the Clerk to the Justices. Magistrates are generally unpaid.

Magistrates Courts have limited powers and (except for breaches of the Health and Safety at Work etc. Act 1974) can impose fines of up to £5,000 and/or six months imprisonment.

County and Crown Court

There are two main civil courts in England. County Court and The High Court. The County Court is the more junior and hears only civil cases with a judge or registrar sitting. County Courts have extensive jurisdiction.

Serious criminal cases are heard in the Crown Court which also deals with those matters where either the defendant has elected for trial by jury (rather that to have the issue heard summarily by the Magistrates Court) or where the Magistrates Court have decided that the alleged offence should be tried by jury. Appeals from junior courts are also heard by the Crown Court.

The most famous (and most senior) Crown Court is the Old Bailey.

Crown Court appeals are heard by the Court of Appeal.

The High Court

All important civil cases are heard at the High Court, which is split into three divisions:

- Queens Bench Division
- Chancery Division
- Family Division

Queens Bench Division

Broadly speaking, this Division administers Common Law. It hears cases concerning contracts or civil wrongs (otherwise known as torts). It also hears those cases which cannot be brought before a County Court where claims exceed £5,000. The Division has two specialist Courts - Commercial Court and Admiralty Court.

Chancery Division

This Division administers equity and specialises in cases involving tax, trusts, bankruptcy or the Inland Revenue.

Family Division

Family Division deals with family disputes that cannot be handled at Magistrates level.

Court of Appeal

This Court also has two Divisions, one for criminal proceedings and one for civil proceedings.

The House of Lords

The House of Lords is the highest appeal body for both criminal and civil cases in England and Wales. For cases to be heard here, requires the approval of the lower court or the House of Lords appeal committee. Permission will only be given where the issue is one of "significant" importance or "in the public interest".

Exceptionally, cases can be immediately heard here without being heard in the Court of Appeal, subject to the rider that the High Court judge and the Lords must certify that there is a legal point of importance involved which may alter previous legal decisions. Judges in this Court are known as Law Lords.

Tribunals

Tribunals are created by Statute and are therefore regulated by the Statute that established them. They are not courts, but are decision-taking bodies established to administer certain areas of the law. Examples include: Industrial Tribunals for industrial disputes or Health and Safety matters and Rent Tribunals for rent disputes.

Tribunals provide an inexpensive and more informal way of solving disputes than the court system. Ultimately, tribunals are controlled by the normal court system whereby appeals against a tribunal's findings may be referred to the Divisional Court of the Queens Bench Division.

Privy Council Judicial Committee

Whilst not part of England's legal system, the Committee exerts influence over it and is the highest appeal forum for cases originating in The British Empire. It can hear cases from Commonwealth Countries, the Isle of Man and the Channel Islands. Countries that have based their legal system on English Law, generally respect decisions of the Committee.

European Context

European Court of Justice

The European Court of Justice sits in Luxembourg adjudicating upon European Union Law. By reason of the European Communities Act of 1972, the European Court's decisions are binding on British Courts. It will rule on interpretation and application of European Union Law referred to it by Member States. Judgements are binding and there is no right of appeal.

European Court of Human Rights

Sitting in Strasbourg, this Court enforces agreed standards on the protection of human rights and freedoms.

European Commission

The Commission comprises a Board of Commissioners representing each Member State. It administers EU law and proposes future legislation by means of Directives, which it sends for approval to the Council of Ministers. Such Directives define standards to be achieved by Member States, but allow those States to determine how to adopt them within their own domestic legal framework. In England, this is usually accomplished by Statutory Instrument. (i.e. a regulation made by a Secretary of State using powers granted to him by "enabling legislation").

Types of Law

Simplistically, there are two types of law - Statute and Common law. Cases are judged by the facts and the law is determined by the interpretation of the courts and announced by way of decision.

Under both statute and common law, decisions made by a senior court are binding upon a junior court. Decisions by the House of Lords are, similarly, binding on all lower courts and can only be overturned either by the House of Lords itself changing its mind or by means of an Act of Parliament.

Statute Law

Statute law is the written "law of the land" consisting of Acts of Parliament, and the rules, regulations and orders made under the powers conferred by those Acts.

Breaches of statute law are criminal offences.

Common Law

Common law enables a means of compensation for the failure of another party to comply with the requirements of statute law and, importantly, for the failure to observe any duties that have been established as owing between parties over the years by common practice.

These practices and standards, established over time fill

"the gaps" in statute law. Accumulation of common law cases has resulted in a system of precedents (i.e. decisions in previous cases) which become binding on similar future cases unless over-turned by a higher court.

Tortious Duties

Tortious Duties arise under common law. They are those obligations that one citizen owes to another or a body corporate owes to other bodies corporate or citizens. The duties and liabilities that arise are independent of any contractual relationship between the parties.

Often summarised as a "duty of care" a breach of these duties can give rise to legal action for the "Tort of Negligence".

Duty of Care

A duty of care arises under common law and is an obligation on us all. The notion is that any citizen should take reasonable care so that s/he does not adversely affect another citizen or neighbour. It should be noted that the duty of care encompasses both actions taken and actions not taken and judgements are based on "reasonableness", that is, doing things that a reasonable person would do and not doing things that a reasonable person would not do.

In the eyes of the law a "neighbour" is anyone who could be affected by an individual's acts or omissions and for whom an individual "ought reasonably to have them in contemplation".

Negligence

Negligence is a breach of a duty of care

Professional Obligations

In a professional context, the Court's assessment of "reasonableness" may take on particular importance. This is because the judgement of "reasonableness" will be moderated with regard to the level of knowledge expected of a professional person. Occupationally a professional is not just a "reasonable" person but is considered to be a "competant" person. S/he will (or should) have theoretical and practical knowledge, skills and experience beyond that expected of Ms or Mr Average. Accordingly, the Courts will ascribe to the professional a higher expectation to deploy his or her skills, to recognise the significance of acts, faults or omissions in a given set of circumstances and act appropriately.

In absolute terms therefore, project managers and other professionals can be expected, because of their specialist knowledge, to owe higher duties of care than untrained or inexperienced people.

Professional Indemnity Insurance

Also known as errors and omissions insurance, indemnity insurance policies may be written to protect practitioners against claims of negligence arising from an alleged breach of a duty of care. In this specialist area of insurance underwriting, premia will vary depending on the amount of cover required and the field of practice for which cover is sought.

Where groups of professionals are collaborating together on projects there is merit in ensuring that all participants have comparable levels of insurance cover especially when their terms of engagement impose joint and several liability.

In some project areas, an emerging practice is for the sponsor or client to arrange insurance on a project basis to cover the consequence of any errors or omisions by the project team or other project failures.

Collateral Warranties

Collateral warranties (sometimes known as duty of care letters) are used particularly in the field of construction and property development to cover a perceived void in English Law resulting from the doctrine of privity of contract.

Such warranties are intended to protect non-contracting parties who may have an interest in the development (e.g. tenants or funders) from a breach of duty by designers or others.

Essential features include:

♦ Giving rights to any person having an interest in a development but who was not a party to the contract for its design or construction

♦ Establishment of direct rights between the party suffering damage and those responsible for it (it is independent of intermediaries)

♦ The ability to tailor arrangements to match prevailing circumstances

Contracts

A contract is a formal legal relationship between two or more parties. It does not, necessarily, have to be in written form but it must comprise:

1 Offer
2 Acceptance
3 Consideration

Essentially, therefore a contract exists where one party offers to do something in return for payment (which may be in cash, goods or aid in kind) and another party accepts the offer and agrees to make the payment.

In practice contractual relationships are more complex and will require specialist legal and drafting expertise. Most significant projects will be governed by a myriad of contractual relationships between participating organisations. There will be contracts for the supply of professional services between the client and the consultant team; contracts between the client and the delivery contractor(s); contracts of supply between the delivery contractor and sub-contractors and suppliers and so on.

Standard Terms and Conditions, prepared by the professional institutions and trade organisations exist for most contractual relationships and in most business sectors. These provide a good starting point for establishing formal relationships between project participants. It is essential however that contracting parties satisfy themselves that their particular needs are met by standard documentation and that appropriate legal advice is sought if required.

Letters of Intent

Letters of intent are widely used and signify a wish by the parties to formalise a contractual relationship in due course by the execution (signing) of formal contract documents. They are often used to enable or authorise an early start to the supply of service.

Care should be taken with the wording of letters of intent so that they strictly adhere to the principle of accepting an offer to contract. Including conditions in a letter of intent that are not provided for in the anticipated contract may be construed as a counter offer and hence part of the pre-contract negotiation.

Breach of Contract

A breach of contract occurs when any contracting party fails to discharge the commitments that they have contracted to undertake. Contracts usually include clauses designed to enable breaches of the terms to be remedied. The usual scenario is that the party in default is served with a notice by the other party requiring compliance with the contract terms. A failure to comply with the notice would result in a dispute and the agrieved party may then invoke other actions, including litigation, to seek specific performance of the contract and damages for the defaulting party's failure to perform.

Potential Areas of Conflict

In a project environment, the potential areas of conflict or misunderstanding are as wide as there are types of project and sectors participating in them.

Some examples include:

- Extent of scope of work
- Late delivery
- Poor quality
- Performance benchmarks not attained
- Non-compliant components
- Shortages
- Safe working practice
- Incomplete paperwork or provenance
- Allegations of negligence
- Failure to comply with instruction(s)

Disputes and Dispute Resolution

A dispute will exist when a difference of view as to the terms of a contract emerges between the parties. Once a dispute has arisen, it may be resolved in a variety of ways ranging from negotiation to litigation.

Litigation may be regarded as the ultimate means of solving a dispute although as Street (2002) points out: "adjudicative or determinative processes are not dispute resolution processes. Judges do not resolve disputes coming before their courts; they decide disputes or adjudicate on them. Disputes are resolved through consensual interaction between the disputants."

Negotiation

Negotiation is a means of achieving a mutually agreed and acceptable resolution to a dispute, often referred to as a win/win situation. As Vollans points out in Session 74, however, a successful negotiated result does not imply that all parties will be happy with the outcome, but that the agreed outcome is sustainable and does not contribute to further conflict.

Alternative Dispute Resolution

Alternative dispute resolution (ADR) is becoming increasingly popular as a means of resolving contractual conflict. Green and Underwood (2001) noted that industry is increasingly looking towards a mediation model for dispute resolution because conceptually it is akin to partnering and supply chain management philosophies. ADR tends to be consensual in nature and undertaken in an atmosphere of openness, rather than the confrontational nature of litigation.

ADR uses a mediator to facilitate a process of open dialogue between disputing parties and the key features are:

- Any mediation is carried out "without prejudice"
- It is voluntary
- It can offer imaginative solutions unavailable to the courts
- It encourages communication between disputing parties who can thus express views and concerns in an open rather than adversarial environment
- In comparison with litigation it is quick, effective and inexpensive

Because the mediation process may take place at an early stage following the dispute, both parties have access to contemporaneous notes, records and, importantly, recollections. Alternatively, the time-lag for a dispute to reach court results in poorer recollection of events than at the time of the dispute itself and requires (expensive) legal assistance to "resurrect" that knowledge before the matter goes to court.

The objective of the facilitated process is to encourage the parties to "work through" the issues at the heart of the dispute with the objective of reaching a final conclusion, decision or action plan. A facilitator is a process manager that supports the dialogue and confronts difficulties between the parties. It is important that the facilitator anticipates the future, beyond mediation, leaving the disputees able to continue the contractual relationship with clarity and mutual respect.

Litigation

Litigation may be regarded as the final (and least desirable) option for bringing a dispute to a conclusion. The legal process can be time consuming and expensive. Moreover, as indicated above, the result is not so much a resolution of the disputed matters, but a decision and adjudication in law based on the facts of the case.

References and Further Reading

Allen, H., "Mediation techniques as a business tool", Centre for Effective Dispute Resolution, 2000.

Gatenby, J., "Plan for your dispute", Centre for Effective Dispute Resolution, 1999.

Green, P and Woodward, S., "Contracted Mediation: Dispute Resolution for Project-based Industries, Society of Construction Law, 2001.

Jensen, D. "Seven legal elements for a claim for construction acceleration," Project Management Journal, .28 (1), pages 32-44, 1997.

Ruff, A., Principles of Law for Managers, Routledge, 1995.

South, J., "The dispute resolution team: mediator and dispute resolution advisor", Centre for Effective Dispute Resolution, 2001.

Street, L., "ADR a generic, holistic concept", Centre for Effective Dispute Resolution, 2002.

Turner, J. R., The Commercial Project Manager, McGraw Hill, 1995.

Section 6

Organisational

60   LIFE CYCLE DESIGN AND MANAGEMENT

Darren Dalcher

*I would like to place this acknowledgement as a
dedication to the memory of my late father,
J N Dalcher, who passed away during the preparation
of this chapter.*

"A hen is only an egg's way of making another egg."
Samuel Butler (1612-1680), English satirist. Life and Habit (1878).

The life-cycle overlaps into most of the other sessions.
Particulary:

10	Project Management
12	Project Context
20	Project Success Criteria
22	Value Management
23	Risk Management
24	Quality Management
30	Work Content and Scope Management
31	Time Scheduling/ Phasing
32	Resource management
33	Budget and Cost Management
34	Change Control
44	Value Engineering
46	Configuration Management
53	Procurement
61	Opportunity
62	Design and Development
63	Implementation
64	Hand-over
65	[Post] Project Evaluation Review
70	Communication

The Need For Process

The skillset focusing on the life-cycle of projects is critical to both understanding and practising sound management. The life-cycle represents a path from the origin to completion of a venture. Division into phases enables managers to control and direct the activities in a disciplined, orderly and methodical way that is responsive to changes, adaptations and complications. Phases group together directly related sequences and types of activities to facilitate visibility and control thus enabling the completion of the venture. This chapter emphasises the need for such control and the practical benefits that result from its adoption.

The project life-cycle acts as a management tool focusing on the allocation of resources, the integration of activities, the support of timely decision making, the reduction of risk and the provision of control mechanisms.

The benefits of using a life-cycle approach include:

◆ Attaining visibility
◆ Breaking work into manageable chunks
◆ Identifying the tasks
◆ Providing a framework for co-ordinating and managing
◆ Controlling project finance
◆ Identifying and obtaining correct resource profiles
◆ Encouraging systematic evaluation of options and opportunities
◆ Addressing the need for stakeholder review
◆ Providing a problem solving perspective
◆ Integrating activities
◆ Encouraging continuous monitoring
◆ Managing uncertainty, and
◆ Providing a common and shared vocabulary

Variety of Life-Cycles

The technical life-cycle identifies the activities and events required to provide an effective technical solution in the most cost-efficient manner. The technical domain dictates the shape and phases included within this cycle but the main focus is on the production of a technical solution. Project management literature however, refers to a plethora of other life cycles including project life-cycles, product life-cycles, organisational life-cycles, acquisition life-cycles, implementation life-cycles, budget cycles.

The wide acceptance of the life-cycle notion has resulted in a variety of representations used by different sub-cultures. They vary greatly in their nature and encompass descriptive, prescriptive and normative variants; and are often stretched, contracted or otherwise modified to suit different organisational environments. Names and descriptions of phases differ between the various existing models. This section focuses on the variety of life cycles encountered in development and project management environments and attempts to clarify some of the distinctions.

Technical Tasks vs Management Actions

In many cases, more than one life-cycle is involved in the management of a project. The title of this section points to the division between actions and procedures required to build the system, and tasks that are essential in order to manage the project.

Project Management Life-cycles

Project management life-cycles highlight the management actions that must be taken to ensure successful completion of the project. The chief concern is with the organisation of tangible assets that enable the activities to occur and the provision of organisational structures for tasks, resources and people.

Product-Oriented Life-cycles

Building the system (or maintaining it) is underpinned by technical knowledge of the relevant domain. The technical life-cycle provides guidance in terms of the tasks (functionally oriented activities) that must be completed to ensure progression to the next stage and the ultimate delivery of a solution system; the product. The technical life-cycle can thus be viewed as a product-oriented focus on the tasks that need to be accomplished.

As discussed, a life-cycle may be conceptualised by evoking either technical design or management perspectives. The purpose of using the life-cycle determines which one is needed. Assessing technical progress on a product calls for a technical life-cycle; conversely, planning, organising and managing the effort points to a project management life-cycle.

Other Life-cycles

As well as some of the life-cycles mentioned above, project managers are also likely to encounter quality life-cycles, risk management life-cycles and a variety of supporting life-cycles. Quality life-cycles focus on documenting the implementation of quality programmes including reviews, verification and validation procedures, quality assurance mechanisms, testing cycles, evaluation and certification. Risk management life-cycles document the various stages required to identify, assess, mitigate, control and monitor risks inherent in projects. Support life-cycles address additional activities that support the technical and management action and may include configuration management. (Note that in certain industries, for example software development, project management may also fall under this heading of supporting activities).

Integrating Life-cycles

Separation between life-cycles can be hazardous. Software projects, for example, used to segregate hardware and software development life-cycles leading to problems with integration. As each stream worked in isolation, decisions about interfaces and how to structure them were often either multiplied, ignored or contradicted leading to a large number of software failures and incompatibilities. Furthermore, lack of knowledge about progress in the other stream and the decisions made there in response to problems increased the gulf in the availability of knowledge; thereby leading to additional (often insurmountable) problems with the final integration and inevitably to escalating costs and degrading schedules.

Whichever life-cycles are utilised, they need to be compatible with one another to ensure that the requirements of the different stakeholders are addressed and satisfied. Review points, gates and major decisions often provide a convenient opportunity for synchronising the activities as they offer a higher degree of visibility over attained progress and typically encompass explicit decision points. They also provide an opportunity for re-gaining control and adjusting to change.

Excellence in a single life-cycle domain does not suffice. Expertise is required in all the domains utilising life-cycles, to ensure that decisions are not biased in the direction of overcoming problems in one domain area. There is a need to integrate all relevant perspectives and ensure that optimisation at review points is based on the strengths of all areas rather than the weaknesses of some.

A Typical Life-cycle Sequence

The most important point about the standard life-cycle is that there is no uniformly standard process with universal validity. Most project management life-cycles have four or five phases, but some may have nine, ten or more. There is no agreement over terminology and the exact wording often varies between projects, industries and organisations.

The basic life-cycle follows a common generic sequence (such as the one identified in the APM's Body of Knowledge): Opportunity, Design and Development, Implementation, Hand-over and Post-Project Evaluation Review. The generic phases are individually explored in the following sessions, but just to give a flavour here, a typical sequence is likely to include tasks focusing on need or problem identification, conceptual exploration and definition, feasibility assessment and review, development of a solution strategy, architectural design, detailed technical design, execution, client hand-over and post-implementation evaluation. (Note that the phases described here and in the APM BoK emphasise the technical aspects of a project-i.e. the construction of a solution system. Managerial activities will include defining goals, conducting feasibility studies, estimating resources, appointing personnel, building the project team, allocating tasks and resources, defining the organisational approach, preparing schedules and budgets etc.)

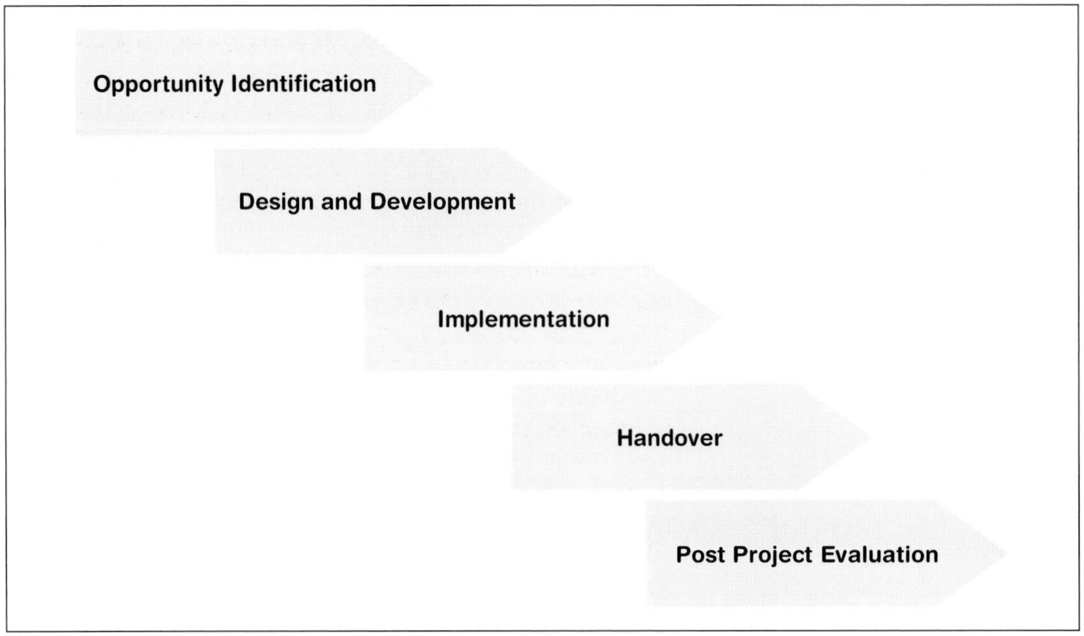

Opportunity Identification

Design and Development

Implementation

Handover

Post Project Evaluation

Figure 60 - 1: A Basic Project Life-Cycle

The Systems Approach to Projects

The concept of the life-cycle emerges from the systems approach to management as part of the attempt to reduce the inherent complexity of an undertaken task. As can be seen from the generic life-cycle described above the approach leads the manager through a basic problem solving template. This notion incorporates both the recognition that systems undergo a natural dynamic process incorporating birth, growth, maturity and death and that this can be incorporated into the planning, control and management of developed systems. The life-cycle thus allows for the concept of natural change, while encouraging a responsive approach as a result of this recognition.

Phases and Activities

Phases refer to periods of effort with an explicit time connotation. The effort is characterised by the prevalence of a specific type of activity. Phasing is therefore the division of the project timeframe into a logical collection of related activities, where each phase clearly involves different management considerations and actions to be performed. The end of a phase represents the achievement of some identified milestone or the completion of a set of tasks. Conventionally, phases take their name from the main output, activity or artefact. As a project proceeds through its life-cycle it passes through the identifiable set of steps, distinguished from each other by the type of activity characteristics of each phase and by the formal reviews, decision points, gates, milestones and baselines.

Products

Products include intermediary artefacts as well as the ultimate delivered system that emerges at the end of the life-cycle. The notion of a product extends beyond functional deliverables and includes plans, budgets, specifications, blueprints, drawings and documentation. A product is thus assumed to be any tangible, verifiable result of the work, which typically marks the completion of a phase; In short, it is any item that can be placed under configuration management.

In the UK, the government has sponsored, through the Office of Government Commerce (OGC), a set of generic project management procedures in the form of the methodology PRINCE 2. The PRINCE philosophy explicitly divides the life-cycle products into:

- Technical products which are the actual system deliverables
- Quality products used to define the required quality criteria and quality control and assurance mechanisms
- Management products required to manage the project effort

Control Gates

Control gates (also known as stage gates or decision gates) between phases provide managers with additional intermediary check-points. Their purpose is to provide early feedback on progress (or lack of) thereby enabling more intelligent, responsive and timely decision making regarding the future of the project.

Gates are used to ensure completion of activities, provide a basis for progression to the next activity and create an accountability mechanism. They thus provide the visibility needed to improve the control and monitoring of the project and to improve overall performance of the built system.

The Need For Phases

Projects can be divided into phases that must be accomplished in order to achieve the project goal. Division into phases and intermediate deliverables is useful in planning as it provides a framework for budgeting, scheduling and allocating resources as well as a mechanism for arranging milestones and project reviews. This leads to improved project communication and enhanced project manageability, resource allocation, cost control and product quality

Control is attained through the division into phases and the breaking up of work into identifiable and significant milestones and meaningful deliverables (products delivered at certain times). Partitioning activities into phases gives the impression of natural order of thought and action. The spacing of activities along a time axis suggests the mutual exclusivity of stages and the unidirectional flow of activities.

Each phase has specific content and management approaches with clearly identified decision points between them. Matching the content requires the application of an ever changing mix of resources-skills, tools, expertise, money and time. Introducing phases with formal interface points encourages the opening of a communication path and the transfer of project information through formal hand-over or technology transfer between life-cycle phases.

A clear progression mechanism supports:

- Planning for action in detail
- Tracking and assessing the degree of progress achieved
- Identifying mismatches
- Conducting trade-offs between levels of resources, attention and constraints, and
- Allocating resources to facilitate improvement and progress

Controlled Release of Funds

The introduction of phases encourages the application of responsive cost management. Rather than commit to full costs in advance for a project, organisations are able to enforce an implicit stage limited commitment within a general frame of acceptance. Release of funds thus depends on the successful achievement of intermediate targets that can be assessed at explicit milestones. The formal sign-off at the end of each major stage thus represents approval of funding for the next stage on the basis of current evidence. This enables organisations to pull the plug early and avoid unidentified and unapproved cost escalation. Furthermore, as most organisations are involved in multiple projects, it enables the organisation to maximise their portfolio on the basis of the attained visibility and the improved accountability.

Progress Review

Project management is increasingly viewed as an on-going balance between objectives, benefits, obstacles, opportunities and constraints; not the mere application of a sequence in order to attain control. Without a mechanism for assessing progress, the only point where discernible progress can be ascertained is at the hand-over point following the completion of all project activities. The introduction of phases provides the visibility mechanism for assessing progress on specific tasks at a much earlier point. Planning, as well as technical activities, can thus be re-adjusted in the light of the new information.

Different phases involve different mixes of skills, expertise and resources. These are often not identified until precursor activities have been completed. Project Management is concerned with making better use of existing resources and allowing work to flow, it is thus concerned with the overall profile of on-going work. Life-cycles encompassing project review points encourage the tracking of progress (the type of review will determine whether the work is scrutinised from a technical, management or quality perspective). Phases thereby offer a stepped mechanism for providing feedback, allocating attention, reducing the build-up of problems and maintaining organisational slack.

Decision Making

As the project life-cycle progresses the cost, time, and performance parameters must be managed. Project managers make conscious decisions about whether to proceed, to modify or to terminate a project based on progress reports, new stakeholders perceptions and environmental and organisational changes. Managing projects is thus fraught with trade-offs between characteristics, preferences and quantities. It also hinges on maintaining the on-going balance between the global parameters of cost, time, and performance (as well as expectations, perceptions, opportunities, obstacles and risks).

Risk Reduction

Complete and final understanding is seldom available at the start of any undertaking. Stage limited commitment offers a risk reduction approach to dealing with projects as the commitment to produce the next stage's end product is re-affirmed at the end of each phase. This is especially important for large projects with a rapidly changing environment where long-term estimates are inherently unreliable. Reviews and sign-offs at the end of each phase can be accompanied by estimation of the cost, time and resources required to complete the following phase enabling re-calibration based on progress to date.

Moreover, risk management operates on the premise of exposure to risk. The greater the exposure, the greater the reluctance to bear it for extended periods. Exposure thus needs to be limited to shorter time intervals. Phases reduce the total exposure into smaller chunks which are maintained for shorter periods. The net effect is of reducing both the likelihood of a (total) failure and the potential impact to smaller, more acceptable increments during which additional knowledge and confidence are acquired.

Uncertainty Management

Projects are unique undertakings involving a commitment of resources that attempt to address the complexity of a given problem, opportunity or situation. The uniqueness of each situation leads to inevitable uncertainty that must be managed. Prior to launch, project uncertainty is at its highest as little is known about the specific parameters. Division into phases helps to reduce the inherent uncertainty, limit the overall exposure and provide better visibility and management control. Milestones built into phases ensure that the readiness to tackle the next stage is assessed before progressing to that level.

Project Decisions

The life-cycle concept supports the dynamic nature of project management by providing phased opportunities for reviewing progress, adjusting resources and re-defining the balance between cost, schedule and performance. These decisions are crucial to the success and well-being of a project and they are explicitly implemented through the provision of identifiable evaluation and approval points between phases. This section reviews the mechanisms that support the provision of responsive and timely decision making, thereby offering an added rationale for adopting a pragmatic approach to process selection and application.

Reviews

Reviews are typically scheduled prior to the completion of major phases to assess progress, analyse technical approaches and quality and evaluate the encountered problems. Phase-end reviews may also be supplemented by one or more mid-phase reviews. Normally, reviews should allow time for responding to feedback through correction and re-work before the actual termination of a phase. They thus provide a basis for subsequent decisions about the future of the project as well as the potential progression to the next phase.

Reviews may focus on any combination of technical, management, quality or user related aspects by focusing on a review of deliverables or of project performance. Some of the aspects that may be assessed include conformance to requirements, technical progress, functionality, or the choice and effectiveness of adopted strategies.

Gates

Control gates were discussed earlier. Gates are the final point for important project decisions as they represent critical events in the life-cycle where the achievement of pre-determined decision criteria is measured and analysed to ensure the satisfaction of objectives. Decision points are viewed as sufficiently critical to be included in the project schedule, and often in the life-cycle model adopted for the project.

Go / No Go

Upon the completion of each phase, additional knowledge is attained. Go/No go decisions, also known as continue/cancel decisions or kill points, enable project managers to reflect upon the objectives of the overall project and the forthcoming phase on the basis of this knowledge. (This is becoming standard practice with risk management techniques and is specifically implemented in risk-driven life-cycle models such as the spiral model of software development.) The result of this reflection is an improved set of decisions about the feasibility of achieving the technical, schedule, and cost expectations and satisfying the relevant constraints.

Baseline Management and Freezing

Baselines provide the basis for future work as all major decisions are documented and their rationale is recorded and made visible to subsequent phases and additional activities such as risk management through progressive archiving of agreed baselines. The baselines represent common understanding shared between the developer and the client that defines the set of functional, performance and physical characteristics agreed at certain milestones and frozen in the agreed form. (Changes to agreed baselines are henceforth subject to special negotiation and joint action controlled by the configuration management system.)

Criteria For Success

Criteria used for judgement need to be clearly defined at the initiation stage. Criteria for success are concerned with how closely the artefact, system or project matches the original goal (or the set of revised expectation documented through intermediate decision points) within the parameters of budget, schedule, functionality technical constraints and expected quality levels.

The task of selecting one objective criteria is complex as it inevitably involves all stakeholders who maintain different criteria systems for judging value, utility and success. All views thus need to be defined and conflicting perspectives identified and resolved to secure a measurable and objective subset. This definition can be adjusted at formal decision points according to the findings of reviews, the changing expectations resulting from interaction with prototypes, the dictates of change and the identification of new opportunities.

Life-cycle Profiles

Projects do not maintain static or stable profiles. Phases represent a commitment of varied skills and resources at appropriate times. As projects pass through different phases, the tasks, people, uncertainty, risk, organisations and resource profiles change accordingly. This section provides a typical distribution of effort, resources, time and uncertainty across project phases in order to enable new managers to 'get a feel' for practical application of the life-cycle concept and to highlight their implications in practical terms.

Time Distribution of Project Effort (Staffing)

Staffing levels vary according to the relevant phase and type of activities it encompasses. Levels can be measured in terms of person-hours or resources expended per unit of time. The typical project profile for effort shows that from a slow beginning (low level of staffing), during the early stages, it progresses to a build-up of activity leading to a peak, representing the largest expenditure of effort during the execution phase. This later tails off as part of the decline in resource consumption which is eventually terminated (despite the fact that certain projects attempt to defy closure).

Time Distribution of Project Budget (Cost)

The cost profile per phase follows a similar pattern to the staffing profile (not least because staffing is a major component). However, it must be borne in mind that the accumulated profiles continue to rise (by the amount expended on each specific phase).

Risk Distribution Across Phases

The probability of completing the project is lowest at the outset, where the uncertainty and risk are greatest. The probability of successful completion increases (assuming appropriately managed decision points) as the project continues.

Uncertainty During Life-cycles

Uncertainty during the early stages precludes the possibility of obtaining definite estimates of real cost (or actual benefit) and time. This can be overcome by producing revised forecasts at certain intervals (such as end of phase or milestones). The need to address change and react to new knowledge leads to adaptations to the initial estimates in terms of ever changing levels of cost, resources, resources, time, quality and performance. Uncertainty declines as progress is made and additional information from gates, prototypes, reviews and decisions becomes available.

The area of uncertainty is thus reduced with each succeeding phase, decision point and review until the actual point of completion when costs and time are known. This underscores the criticality of early decisions. The highest degree of uncertainty is during the early stages of the life-cycle. Decisions made during the early stages have the potential to affect the overall cost, quality or schedule, as well as all subsequent decisions. The most critical decisions are the ones made when uncertainty is highest. As the project progresses through the life-cycle the relative degree of uncertainty related to the project is decreased.

Cost to Fix

Ideally all errors are corrected as early as possible where the costs of re-work and re-adjustments to other work are minimal. The later in the life-cycle an error is detected, the more expensive it is to correct (especially when the cost of re-calls, and loss of reputation is factored in for post-release discovery). This provides a justification for introducing control mechanisms, reviews and checkpoints through individual phases rather than allowing detection of errors to await for the arrival of the released final artefact.

Ability to Influence Outcome

The ability of stakeholders to influence the project parameters including cost, effort, final characteristics, and to a certain degree, uncertainty, is greatest at the beginning and gets progressively lower as the project proceeds.

Process Selection

This section provides a guide to alternative methods of carving and inter-relating activities that accounts for particular circumstances and characteristics. The choice must depend on available knowledge, learning curves and the ability to bear risk and handle uncertainty.

Sequential Approaches

Sequential approaches refer to the completion of the work within one monolithic cycle. Projects are thus sequenced into a set of steps that are completed serially and typically span from determination of user needs to validation that the given solution satisfies the user. Progress is carried out in linear fashion enabling the passing of control and information to the next phase when pre-defined milestones are reached and accomplished. This approach is highly structured, provides an idealised format for the contract and allows maximum control over the process. On the other hand, it is also resistant to change and the need for corrections and re-work.

Sequential development is also referred to as serial engineering. The serial focus ensures interaction between phases as products are fed into the next step and frozen upon completion of a milestone. This essentially represents a comparison between the input to and the output of each phase. Sequential engineering also implies a long development sequence as all planning is oriented towards a single hand-over date. Explicit linearity offers a structured approach rich in order, control, and accountability. In order to overcome the impact of a late hand-over and delayed feedback, specific decision mechanisms, review points and control gates are introduced to ensure early discovery and correction of errors and a reduced aggregate cost to fix.

Incremental Approaches

Incremental approaches emphasise phased development by offering a series of linked mini-projects (referred to as increments, releases or versions). Work on different parts and phases is allowed to overlap throughout the use of multiple mini-cycles running in parallel. Each mini-cycle adds additional functionality and capability. The approach is underpinned by the assumption that it is possible to isolate meaningful subsets that can be developed, tested and implemented independently. Delivery of increments is staggered as calendar time progresses. The first increment often acts as the core product providing the functionality to address the basic requirements. The staggered release philosophy allows for learning and feedback to alter some of the customer requirements in subsequent versions. Incremental approaches are particularly useful when the full complement of personnel required to complete the project is not available and when there is an inability to fully specify the required product or to fully formulate the set of expectations.

Evolutionary Approaches

Evolutionary approaches recognise the great degree of uncertainty embedded in certain projects and allow developers and managers to execute partial versions of the project while learning and acquiring additional information. Evolutionary projects are defined in a limited sense allowing a limited amount of work to take place before making subsequent major decisions. Projects can start with a macro estimate and general directions allowing for the fine details to be filled in in evolutionary fashion. The initial implementation benefits from exposure to user comments leading to a series of iterations. Finite goals are thus allowed to evolve based on discoveries and changed expectations along the development route. Projects in this category are likely to be characterised by a very high degree of technological risk and lack of understanding of full implications by both stakeholders and developers. It is particularly effective in change-intensive environments or where resistance to change is likely to be strong.

Prototyping Approaches

Prototyping is a rather loaded term which depends on the domain and context. It typically refers to the act of information buying through the rapid development of a model which stimulates feedback from users.

Prototypes can be utilised:

◆ During a concept exploration phase to facilitate discovery, verify a need, describe the external behaviour of the system or sample a specific approach
◆ During the design phase to test the feasibility of a solution concept, to validate the acceptability of a design solution or to investigate new options, or
◆ As an evolutionary approach to systems development by replacing the life-cycle altogether

Prototypes attempt to implement some of the key features, characteristics or technical functions. They are particularly useful in overcoming resistance, involving stakeholders and reducing the risk of failure. The value of prototyping is in proving the concept and testing its assumptions to enable the early acquisition of useful information. Rapid creation supplemented by the generation of rapid feedback deals with the instability and volatility of information needs in modern environments. It provides a shortcut to development by linking concept with implementation and problem with solution in experimental fashion that refines and improves existing concepts. Such early clarification makes prototyping suitable when the domain is too fuzzy, complex or change-ridden to afford a one step implementation.

Controlled Prototyping

Prototyping proved itself as a creative and responsive effort to address users' needs. However, once unleashed it can prove difficult to control the rate of change, the length of the effort and indirectly the cost implications. In particular it can be difficult to control the number of iterations or the length of the re-iteration phase. This has led to more structured forms of prototyping emphasising cost, time and control.

Rapid Application Development offers a more structured approach than prototyping and is focused on the need to deliver relevant working business applications quicker and cheaper. The prototyped application is thus delivered in incremental fashion. This development approach is concerned with maintaining user involvement through the application of design teams and special workshops. Projects tend to be small and limited to short delivery periods to ensure rapid completion. The management strategy utilised relies on the imposition of timeboxing, the strict delivery to target which dictates the scoping, the selection of functionality to be delivered and the adjustments to meet the deadlines. Rapid Application Development is particularly useful in environments that change regularly and impose demands of early solutions.

Other attempts to control prototyping have also been utilised in specific sectors. One such approach, the Spiral model controls the number of iterations through risk management and explicit decision making. The spiral introduces cycles of planning, risk management, prototyping and evaluation and communication stages that are repeated throughout the development effort. In effect, the spiral combines a sequential approach with prototyping and strict control driven by risk management to determine the length of the cycle.

Concurrency

In direct contrast to serial engineering, concurrent engineering (also known as simultaneous engineering or fast tracking) relies on a significant overlap between phases to shorten the time it takes to finish the product and eliminate delays and bottlenecks inherent in the sequential model. Concerns, such as faster time to market, often force the need to break down functional barriers between phases to speed up the development effort. Concurrent engineering is likely to lead to reduced time to market, greater responsiveness to the market place and improved satisfaction rates (as well as earlier break-even point, lower service cost and a longer window for profitability through an extended sales life). Furthermore, concurrent engineering ensures that considerations related to stages further downstream are raised and addressed during earlier phases as specialists from different disciplines work simultaneously. This has reportedly led to significant reduction in the number of design changes and the amount of re-work. However, it also leads to significantly increased overheads, especially in terms of planning, and intensifies the need, intensity and frequency of communication between stakeholders. The involvement of all stakeholders in tandem will often necessitate a certain degree of concurrency to enable a re-working of ideas and feedback iterations between participants. The concurrent deployment of personnel shifts the staffing peak to the early stages of the life-cycle requiring an intelligent commitment from management and the ability to see the promise of the resulting savings farther downstream.

Map or Guideline or Selection Matrix

This section introduced a number of alternative life-cycle methods. The choice of a life-cycles depends on the particular project as each project is characterised by a unique set of circumstances, constraints and pressures.

♦ The simplest life-cycles to employ are the sequential approaches. Projects amenable to this type of resolution method tend to be characterised as well-understood, structured and repeatable problems that can be specified in full, due to a low level of inherent uncertainty

♦ Incremental approaches address higher levels of uncertainty and cannot be fully specified. Despite a reasonable knowledge of the domain there is still a degree of uncertainty as to the solution mode

♦ Evolutionary approaches deal with situations characterised by a complex environment, with unidentified interactions, vague goals, frequent change and multiple participants, thus deeming anticipation inherently impossible. Knowledge is often incomplete and dispersed and discovery can be facilitated through conceptual exploration. Problems are often closely entwined with their environment which also tends to change

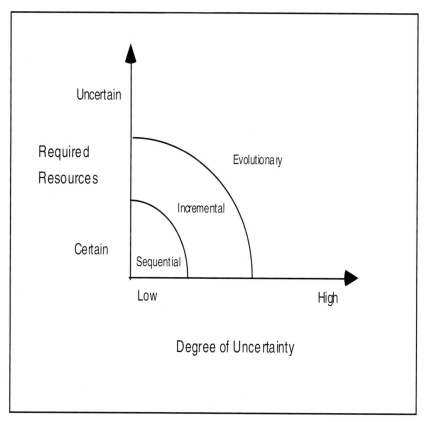

Figure 60 - 2: Selecting a Life-cycle Approach

Figure 60 - 2 acts as a useful guide for summarising the discussion and selecting an appropriate model. It illustrates the basic approaches to managing projects. When projects need to be completed rapidly there appears to be a choice between speeding up or overlapping the phases.

- Prototyping can be used to speed up the conceptual definition stages or the feedback cycles leading to the ultimate product. Prototyping can thus be used to generate understanding (more rapidly) or to speed up development.

- Rapid Application Development offers similar benefits to prototyping but in a more tightly controlled environment that focuses on delivery within certain time frames (rather than conceptual exploration)
- Concurrent engineering approaches entail shifting from a cost to a time mindset, while improving profitability and quality. Stages can be run in parallel to save time

Time to market has become a factor that distinguishes market leaders from other performers the three approaches highlighted above as well the discussion in the next section deal with urgency and speed.

Tailoring the Life-cycle

Life-cycles attempt to capture a generic rationale that applies to most projects. However, many projects have individual characteristics and special needs that require adjustments to general approaches. Some of the special characteristics may refer to the sector, where government projects, for example, may require additional regulatory cycles, or specific approval mechanisms. The driver in the need to tailor the life-cycle is often a specific constraint, such as time, or the need to complete by a certain political, marketing or business imposed date, such as a summer shutdown or an agreed deadline. Different constraints and the associated risk factors can thus play a part in introducing specific characteristics that need to be accommodated in the revised project life-cycle and negotiated in the contract. Tailoring the life-cycle may add or delete specific phases, activities, products, gates, reviews, tests or decisions. In general, risk management can play an important part in identifying such specific characteristics, devising mitigating strategies and tailoring the life-cycle.

Shortening the Cycle (and Accelerated Development)

One familiar tailorable scenario is the pressure to collapse the schedule due to the need to respond to opportunities, time-to-market demands, the need to get there before the competition or the implications of technical obsolescence. Reducing schedules is often perceived as a way of freeing up key personnel and as a cost cutting measure. Schedules can be collapsed while showing a net reduction in development costs, when operational savings and the factoring in of opportunities and market lead are taken into account.

Techniques to achieve a net reduction in time include:

- Eliminating tasks
- Shortening critical activities
- Shortening the critical path (through the combination of tasks)
- Running activities concurrently
- Re-using previously developed components, artefacts or knowledge
- Adding resources or encouraging multiple shifts and extra-time
- Using highly skilled managers or technical experts
- Skipping certain life-cycle phases or activities, and
- Using more advanced rapid technology

In all cases detailed risk assessment is required to monitor the effect on slack, the possible emergence of new critical (or near critical) paths and the overall likelihood of a successful completion.

Development in Web Time

As organisations race to ensure a functioning presence on the web, the new mode of operation is introducing additional constraints forcing new working patterns. The market is fast-moving characterised by a dynamic environment with high levels of uncertainty and risks. Customers appear more demanding and discerning expecting non-stop service around the clock. Service is being judged according to overall traffic, frequency and duration of visits and loyalty.

The rate of change endemic to this environment leads to small and quick projects with high frequency of release and smaller scope explored in each release. The scope is highly changeable over time to respond to competition and opportunities. Time is the critical factor; As the speed of release is measured by getting there before the competition, project execution is measured according to the shortest time to register a presence (often regardless of the quality). Trade-offs can often sacrifice scope, cost, expectations or quality to accelerate the speed of completion.

Most projects in this environment are new, and hence innovative and difficult to estimate and cost. The planning approach thus needs to focus on key milestones and targets, yet remain flexible enough and responsive enough to cope with changing requirements, delivery dates, release deadlines and new opportunities. Projects tend to be evolutionary and have short release cycles as they build on what already exists and are often prone to scope re-adjustments in line with shifting knowledge and expectations.

Small Projects

Smaller projects tend to be less complex and are easier to understand and manage. One way of addressing small projects is by using 'lighter' versions of the life-cycle. The reduction tends to be in the number of phases, gates, reviews and go/no go decisions, thereby speeding the process itself and utilising easier and faster transitions. Smaller projects also tend to be easier to plan and schedule as they are likely to involve fewer participants, are likely to be of shorter duration and are likely to tackle less complex issues. This enables a reduction in the amount of formal project management work that needs to be conducted. Indeed, full utilisation of formal project management mechanisms is likely to consume a larger fraction of the total project budget. However, shorter schedules, allow less time to recover and often get assigned lower priority which may also be reflected in the quality of personnel assigned to the task.

Variations on a Theme

This section addresses different terminology and standards utilised in various domains and sectors of industry.

Different Industries and Terminologies

The table (Figure 60 - 3) identifies various phase names that are commonly used in certain sectors and industries. Specific titles are likely to vary even within a specific sector or a named organisation. It is instructive however to observe the common trends in terms of the type of activities and their sequencing.

Engineering	Software Engineering	Manufacturing	Design	APM BOK
Definition	Requirements	Formation	Definition	Opportunity
Preliminary Design	Specification	Build-up	Feasibility	Design and Development
Detailed Design	Design	Production	Option Analysis	Implementation
Production	Implementation	Phase-out	Detailed Design	Hand-over
Utilisation	Testing	Final Audit	Construction	Post-Project Evaluation Review
Phase-out				

Figure 60 - 3: Typical Terminologies by Industry

Methodologies and Standards

PRINCE 2 is a government mandated project methodology in the UK. PRINCE uses the idea of stages (management stages may not necessarily map onto technical phases). At the beginning of each project a plan is created which gives the envisaged stages. A detailed stage plan need only exist for the next stage. Subsequent stages will have their plans completed shortly before they are due to commence.

The general processes encompass:

- Starting up a project
- Initiating a project
- Directing a project
- Managing stage boundaries
- Controlling a stage
- Managing product delivery
- Closing a project
- Planning

The British Standards Institution has issued a detailed project management standard BS 6079:2002 that encompasses a description of a project life-cycle comprising the following phases:

- Conceptualisation and basic ideas
- Feasibility tests for technical, commercial and financial viability
- Evaluation and application for funds and stating risks
- Authorisation and setting any conditions
- Implementation including design, procurement, fabrication, installation etc.
- Control, accountability, periodic reviews and updates
- Completion and handover to client
- Operation and inclusion in normal revenue planning/ control procedures
- Close-down and cease operations
- Termination including disposal of residual assets

Tips and Complications - A User Manual

This section offers a user manual that highlights some problematical issues emerging from the application of the life-cycle concept and highlights a number of disputed or non-conventional areas.

Overlapping and Interacting Phases

Attempts to speed up projects may force subsequent phases to start earlier. Phases may be set up in parallel so that work on one phase may begin before the previous phase is finished. Speed and modern development methods often blur conceptual distinction between phases and alter the required mix in each phase.

Activities and Phases (Activities May Extend Beyond Phases)

Activities are not exclusively limited to phases of the same name.

Phases may comprise activities that are not necessarily tied up with their logical content. Activities such as analysis or design therefore occur during a variety of phases including, but not necessarily limited to those named analysis and design. While the emphasis shifts from activity to activity as the project proceeds, most activities continue to some extent through most stages.

Evolution, Maintenance and Operation

Project life-cycles typically cover the period up to operations and maintenance. However some projects may have an extended life-cycle, which can extend to these phases or include disposal or replacement of the product or service. Equally, new versions of products may be generated during operations. Many projects have an on-going focus that continues beyond operations. If maintenance is not included it can be viewed as a project in its own right.

Contracts and Their Impact on the Life-cycle

Sequential models work well in terms of contracts as they have been optimised as output driven processes. However, this only works when the requirements are fully understood and stable prior to launch. When this luxury is not present the contract needs to be matched to what is known and to the levels of uncertainty and risk.

Moreover, even the sequential logic can fail as there is typically a need for some basic systems requirements analysis (and possibly some systems design) prior to estimating costs, committing to particular options and awarding the contract.

Project Scoping Through Life-cycle

Scope is fully known and fully understood when the project is completed. Scoping occurs throughout the phases of the life-cycle, especially in more dynamic environments. It cannot be assumed to be fully known prior to the initiation phases.

Controlling Change and Adaptation

Change and adaptation will persist throughout the life of a product (and beyond) resisting the tendency for closure.

Allowing For Life-cycle Support Activities

Facilitating processes such human resource management, risk management, communication management, configuration management and sometimes even project management are not included in technical breakdowns of tasks and may thus not be part of the WBS, effort, time and cost estimates. They need to be specifically added to the technical activities so that they can be timed and budgeted for.

Models are Abstractions

A model is an abstraction of a segment of reality with much of reality left out, thereby offering order and structure. Simplistic models are appealing to the extent that they simplify an inherently complex and pervasive process and provide an idealisation that is useful in mentally visualising a process. They remain incomplete and inherently limited with respect to other aspects of reality. In the modern environment of an ever-accelerating world, projects need to be viewed as wider issues to be understood in the context of a dynamic situation and a volatile environment. The value of models thus depends on making users aware of their limitations and linking and integrating them with other representations that cover alternative areas of concern to enable one to see the 'whole picture'.

Using Risk, Cost and Schedule to Select the Model

Risk, as well as cost, time and performance criteria should be used as the basis for selecting a life-cycle model to suit a particular project.

This session addressed the role of the life-cycle in project management and surveyed the rationale behind it and the variety of approaches for implementing it. The next five sessions delve into the specific individual phases of the life-cycle.

References and Further Reading

Forsberg K et al, Visualising Project Management, John Wiley, 1996

Kerzner H, Project Management: A Systems Approach to Planning, Scheduling and Controlling, John Wiley, New York, 2001

Turner J R, The Handbook of Project-Based Management, McGraw-Hill, 1993

61   OPPORTUNITY

Martin Stevens

"Nothing ventured, nothing gained".
Anonymous. Proverb.

Introduction

The Body of Knowledge speaks of this phase being typically split into two stages: A concept or marketing stage that "defines the opportunity", followed by a critical review stage which enables a decision to be made to proceed with or abandon the "project". In my submission however, it is appropriate to expand this further and examine opportunity in a wider context.

This session will therefore look at the ways in which projects or project opportunities arise. It will consider this in the context of the business planning and corporate governance of the firm and also in the context of project delivery organisations responding to invitations to tender or requests for proposals. From this starting point, consideration will be given to the evaluation of opportunities by means of feasibility studies or models, option analysis and critical success factors and key performance indicators. Finally it will look at accept/reject criteria.

Links to Other Topics

During the formative opportunity stages of a project, there is a particular focus on the strategic Sessions found in Section 2 of Pathways. Additionally, there are strong linkages to Sessions 50 Business Case and 51 Marketing and Sales.

Sources of Projects

It is a truism to say that there are innumerable sources of projects. For the purposes of this session, I make the distinction between projects that arise from within the business, that is business development projects that have their genesis within the business and financial planning process of the parent organisation and projects that arise as a response to a third party, by way of invitation. The latter is something that is more likely to occur within firms that deliver projects as part of their core business (e.g. consultancies, IT service providers, engineering and contracting organisations etc.)

Business Development Projects

Business development projects are projects that arise as part of the normal business management processes of the firm. They arise as a response to a variety of circumstances, issues and inputs. Such projects are about the way in which the company undertakes its business, rather than project activity being the raison d'etre of the company.

Potential projects may arise from:

- Process and procedure audits
- Problems or failures within the organisation
- Specific customer feedback
- Responses to marketing initiatives
- Feedback from clinics and workshops
- Market research
- Technology roadmaps (Session 43)
- Competitor's activity
- A need to implement new technology
- Legislation or regulation

Trading Projects

Trading projects generally concern those organisations whose core businesses activity is the delivery of projects. Such businesses would include:

- Architectural and design practices
- Software solution providers
- Management consultants and
- Contracting organisations

Projects are likely to arise from:

- Invitations to tender
- Requests for proposals
- Existing framework agreements
- Additional "sales" arising from current contracts or assignments

Opportunity Evaluation

The extent of the opportunity evaluation process will be different depending upon whether the project is a business development one or a trading one.

In the case of a business development project, both the definitional and scoping of the prospective project and the evaluation will be undertaken by the business itself. There is therefore an opportunity (indeed an imperative) for the definitional and evaluation phases to be part of an iterative process whereby the scope of the project is refined until the evaluation phase confirms an optimal output, which when implemented, will produce the maximum benefit for the firm. Further, with business development projects the potential costs and outputs can be considered over the life-cycle and a value management approach (Session 22) adopted to again optimise the outcome.

A trading project's, scope and project definition will have been undertaken by the client and his advisors and (unless the project is a partnership one) there will be limited opportunity to modify it to optimise the outcome for the client. Evaluation will therefore be undertaken by the invitee on the more parochial basis of the benefits of securing the contract for the profitability of the firm.

Business Development Projects

Prior to the evaluation of a prospective project, it will be necessary for the prospective project to be fully defined. Accordingly, the company will commence by examining the key drivers for the project in the company's business plan (Session 50). It may also develop or moderate these drivers by examining technology management disciplines and prepare a technology roadmap (Session 43) to inform the project definition.

From here it will determine requirements (Session 41), establish success criteria (Session 20) and develop a strategy and project management plan (Session 21).

Methodologies including value management (Session 22), risk management (Session 23), quality management (Session 24) and value engineering (Session 44) may also be employed to refine the project and establish a number of alternative projects to be considered for implementation.

Feasibility Studies

Feasibility studies may be commissioned to examine or determine if a project is capable of being undertaken by the company and the viability of prospective projects established. There is a clear distinction to be made here between feasibility and viability. Feasibility is a deterministic process to discover if a prospective project can be delivered technically, whereas viability is a process to discover whether the project is worth undertaking in fiscal terms i.e. will it be profitable?

Modelling and Testing

Modelling and testing of prospective projects (or elements of projects) may be carried out to help inform the definition of scope of the project; consideration of feasibility and viability and, ultimately, an accept/reject decision to implement the project (see Session 45).

Accept / Reject Decision

As Vollans explains in Session 50, the company's decision to accept or reject a prospective project for implementation will be based on the fiscal value to the firm, i.e. will it be profitable? A variety of criteria may be chosen to determine the fiscal benefit including:

- Pay back period
- Return on investment
- Discounted cash flow
- Internal rate of return
- Cost benefit analysis

Conflicting Projects

It may be the case that a company has a number of mutually exclusive projects that could be implemented. The dilemma would be which one(s) to choose? Generally speaking the "normal" choice would be to select that (or those) projects that produced the greatest fiscal contribution to the company. Where projects cannot be separated on a fiscal basis, some kind of matrix scoring needs to be devised to assess non-fiscal benefits and inform selection. Possible matters to consider could be:

- Perceived environmental benefits
- Public relations value
- Increased labour pool etc.

(Some of these factors may, in fact, have a fiscal benefit which is either hard to quantify or whose benefit may be expected to accrue outside the time frames considered in the fiscal analyses mentioned above).

Trading Projects

In the case of trading projects, it is unlikely that the invitees to undertake the project will have an opportunity to determine the scope of work, project success criteria or other benchmarks established by the client or sponsor.

The likely scenario is that the project will arise as an opportunity for the company to deliver the project in response to an invitation to tender or a request to submit a proposal from the client. Under these circumstances, consideration of the project is made on a different basis.

Deliverability / Technical Appraisal

Before the fiscal benefits of undertaking the project for the prospective client/customer can be considered, it is necessary for the project to be evaluated in terms of the company's ability to deliver the defined project:

- Does the company have the technical capability to do it?
- Does it have the resources to do it?
- Does it have the required expertise to manage it?
- Does it have the required plant and equipment to do it?

If the answer to any of these is 'no'; then the supplementary question is: "Can these services be obtained?"

If the answer remains 'no'; then the invitee will need to decline to participate. If however, the answer is now 'yes'; the next questions are:

- Can the project be delivered in the required time-frame?
- Does the company want to undertake the project?

Again, a 'no' response would lead to the invitation being declined, whilst a 'yes' response would lead to consideration of the detailed delivery and financial aspects.

Project Delivery

Prior to submitting a response to the client's invitation, the company must satisfy itself that it can deliver the project and establish the costs for doing so. This stage therefore involves the project company in developing a project strategy and project plans in sufficient detail to enable these factors to be determined. The methodologies and techniques discussed in Sections 2, 3 and 4 will be deployed, together with financial management (Session 52), procurement (Session 53) and legal awareness (Session 54).

The work breakdown structure, network analyses and delivery plans, resource schedules and procurement enquiries to sub-contractors and suppliers will develop a wealth of data that will enable the costs of delivering the project to be estimated.

Here also any opportunities to add particular value or unique expertise to the project will be identified. (This may give rise either to competitive advantage when submitting a response, or alternatively a supplementary proposal to be offered).

Financial Appraisal

From the assembled delivery data, financial evaluation of the project can be undertaken and the costs of delivering it can be estimated. Budgets and cost plans can be prepared and a build-up of cost arrived at to give a "final estimated cost" of undertaking the project. (see Session 33 Budget and Cost Management).

Once the assembled financial data is available, senior management will need to look at the financial impact of undertaking the project on the company. They will need to not only consider the level of profit they would wish to achieve, but also funding requirements, cost of capital, payment terms (both up-stream and down-stream), cash flows and the effect these will have on the companies trading position.

Sensitivity analysis should also be undertaken to gauge the impact of unexpected variation in cash flows or costs on the financial situation.

Risk

A separate assessment of the risks associated with delivering the project should be undertaken (Session 23) and both the upside and downside impacts determined. This data will both inform the financial appraisal and, in particular, sensitivity analyses, but will also will moderate decisions concerning the level of profit to be sought.

Accept / Reject Criteria

For a trading project, arriving at an accept/reject decision is a precursor to submitting a response to the participation invitation. The key determinants are likely to be:

- Can the company technically deliver the project?
- Can the risks be managed?
- Can the project be delivered at a profit?
- Is the estimated profit sufficient to make the participation desirable?

If the response to all these is 'yes'; then a bid could be submitted. A 'no' response to any of them should lead to the invitation being declined.

Opportunity Cost

The analyses undertaken so far would support a decision to bid for the work. One final consideration needs to be taken, which is to evaluate if contracting for this project would preclude the company's participation in another contemporaneous project because of capacity or resource limitations or because of (prospective) client policies not to contract with businesses who are simultaneously working for competitor companies.

Bid Submission

Once management has decided to submit a response to the invitation it only remains for the project trading company to submit the bid response or project proposal. As Holton points out in Session 51, Marketing and Sales; not only should the technical requirements of the submission be dealt with, the marketing issues should also be included. Sufficient information should be supplied (or dialogue with the client entered into) to encourage the client to contract with your organisation.

The only exception to this would be circumstances where the invitation to participate specifically prohibits canvassing during the tender action period.

Once all the data and material required to make the submission is assembled, it only remains to check that all requested information has been included and that the submission is fully compliant with any requirements set down in the invitation. Finally, a check should be made that the submission adheres to company practice and standards and that any internal QA processes have been undertaken and signed off.

Conclusion

The opportunity phase of a project is important. In the case of a business improvement project, the iterative processes of definition and evaluation will lead to the commissioning of well thought out projects that will contriute to the development and trading ability of the host firm.

Similarly, for a trading project, its successful completion will not only enhance the financial position of the delivery company, its trading position will also benefit from achieving another success on the corporate track record.

Since the objective of all project and programme management is to deliver successful projects, adoption of the processes outlined in this session and throughout Pathways can enhance the likelihood of success.

62   DESIGN AND DEVELOPMENT

Darren Dalcher

"An idea isn't responsible for the people who believe in it."
Don Maarquis.

Closely related material is covered under the heading of Life Cycle Design and Management. This phase of the life-cycle directly interfaces with the phases named Opportunity and Implementation which should be read in conjunction with this chapter.

Design means conversion of an idea (often in the form of a needs specification) into a detailed plan, specification or architecture for a product, service, process or any other system. Typically this conversion is from an abstract notion to an artefact (a product) with form and function that can be reproduced in accordance with the detailed specification. The specific output of design varies depending on the industry sector and the specific project.

Any discussion of design must focus on the interaction between concept as derived through analysis and the notion of solution offered by design. Indeed, as will be shown later design is closely intertwined with requirements. It also depends on balancing the notions of acting and discovering. The inherent tension invoked by the discussion of design revolves around the level and role of design.

Development is conventionally viewed as taking a detailed design specification and converting it into an actual product or service. This is done through the adding of features of appearance and configuration change and the creation of experimental models and production prototypes. Development thus leads to the creation of the first sample article or the full development of a service concept ready for marketing and production.

Relationship Between Design and Concept

Design is a crucial part of the life-cycle described previously (Figure 62 - 1). The act of design begins after the consolidation of the requirements, by analysts or engineers, into clearly specified client's objectives and needs.

The starting point implies that the project manager has already acquired a clear understanding of the needs and preferences of the different groups of stakeholders, including both client and user communities.

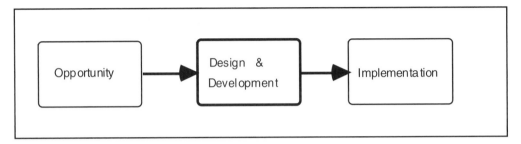

Figure 62 - 1: The Design Phase

The act of design entails imagining, specifying and verifying in the abstract, things that as yet do not exist. The activity is organised to support the making of design decisions and trade-offs and the clarification of their implications while exploring competing solution concepts. The result of this effort is the resolution and clarification of the solution concept which is refined to form a clear, unambiguous, complete and transparent solution specification. The emerging end product is sufficient to enable the fabrication of the artefact on the basis of the detailed plan. This is where the next phase, implementation, takes over.

Design as the Implementation of Project Plans?

Design makes a conscious effort at organising systems and predicting how they will fulfil the objectives. The product of the design activity is the plan to realise the goals and not the actual accomplishment of the purpose.

Designers grapple with a variety of constraints, both inherent in the environment and specific to the project, to derive a description of an artefact sufficient for its realisation.

Design appears to be ill-structured as there is no straightforward process to follow. Instead the process is transformational, involving partial and interim solutions which may ultimately play little or no role in the final design. It can thus be characterised as an exploration process in which interim responses lead to re-interpretation and re-definition of the goal. The cycles of exploration often encompass the early analysis phases so that the requirements and the design are allowed to influence one another.

Problem Changes Design

In an ideal world, the problem would be fully explored before any design decisions are attempted. This would enable designers to follow a sequential approach and deliver a simple and well-understood product. Any solution is thus determined by the definition of the problem. Designers are obliged to base decisions on current information to predict a future state that may not come about (unless their predictions are correct).

In practice, the client's statement is often insufficient to formulate a complete and definite requirements specification. As a result design problems can be viewed as ill-defined as the requirements simply do not contain enough information to enable resolution by relying on the basic set of requirements alone. Further information needs to be discovered through experimentation and interaction with the problem.

Design Changes Problem

It is often said that a problem is more fully understood only after it is solved. The act of design involves reconciling different perspectives, concepts and viewpoints. As a result design is contingent, subject to unforeseen circumstances, obstacles, interactions, relationships and influences which are uncovered as the design emerges. Indeed, changes are often brought to the surface by conditions that emerge after decisions are made.

Knowledge is generated in an on-going process. Assumptions, rationale, decisions and conclusions are being continuously challenged by new discoveries and need to be reconsidered as each step appears to create a new situation which needs to be reconciled with other knowledge. Designers work with materials, intentions and meanings;

each imposing certain constraints and complications. By testing proposed solutions, designers generate new questions via reflection and re-evaluation. Designers gain a deeper understanding of the process by gaining and dropping constraints, sampling new perspectives and exploring new avenues. In fact, improved solutions emerge over time through this trial-and-error process which entails acquiring new knowledge and making decisions that reflect the availability of new knowledge.

Design is a contingent process whose outcome cannot be deduced from the starting variables or an explicit process; but rather from a more unstructured discovery process. Tracing out intermediate steps exposes unforeseen difficulties or suggests better objectives, which may lead to the redefinition of the problem. Iteration is an essential part of the attempt to improve, co-ordinate and change previous decisions in the light of newly discovered knowledge (including new goals, functions and decisions). Taken over time, complex projects can benefit from oscillating attention between emerging requirements and the developing solution concept.

What vs How

Design means thinking before acting. Requirements are typically concerned with the formulation of the problem (the definition of the 'what needs to be done?') and possibly the formulation of the evaluation criteria. They involve cycles of interaction between analyst and stakeholder attempting to describe the proposed external behaviour of the system. The need is thus elaborated through a process of questioning the client and formulating the problem gap into a clearly understood area of agreement.

As we have seen design is aimed at generating a set of potential interpretations that address the perceived problem, selecting the best of the available representations and formulating a solution based on it (i.e. formulating the 'how to achieve the objective?'). Rather than simply act as a transition point from one type of activity to another, design is equally concerned with solving a problem and reducing uncertainty. The initial design concept starts as a vague notion shrouded in uncertainty and encompassing a host of issues and dilemmas (that can only be resolved through practical exploration).

The Transition From Selection to Design

The role of the design phase is providing the transition from a rudimentary understanding of the problem through selection of a solution to the ability to construct a product. The translation is from a systems definition to a detailed plan and architecture for the artefact. This is done by alternating attention between the problem and solution, and linking the two types of activity as decisions underlying technical choices will be partly limited by the set of constraints. Emergent understanding is gradually refined until it is sufficiently detailed to drive the construction and fabrication of a product.

Technical Problem Solving

Design is purposeful problem solving that extends beyond the issues of technical complexity. It is an iterative process that enables designers to adapt to and to learn to control their environment. Armed with past experience and knowledge, designers iterate between the present and the future by generating, gradually testing, refining and adding detail to a basic abstraction. The overall process provides an interaction between understanding (which comes before design) and creation (which follows it).

Moving From Problem to Solution

Analysis and design stages combine to convert a perceived problem into a model of the implementation of the proposed solution. The general goal is driving towards a desired state, where the problem to be solved is defined in terms of design goals (and constraints) that should be achieved by any viable solution. Analysts and designers often work together as the objectives of the problem, define the properties required in the solution. The details of the design are the designer's decisions about how to implement these properties. Design represents a detailed specification of the precise conditions for each of the characteristics of a system including its function, inputs, outputs, processing, environment, equipment and human actors. While the specification is derived through an iterative set of exploratory trade-offs, it plays a part in redefining the problem and clarifying the constraints.

Solving and Doing

In the same way that analysing and designing does not benefit from total functional separation, the acts of designing and making are equally interlined. Designers specify details and properties that must exist in the product. In order to discover the practical problems they often work with fabricators (or programmers) to discover what materials are available and what can be practically achieved in the real environment. This uncovers additional constraints that will only emerge during the doing stages, but which may require resolution further upstream, or which may challenge the client's goals or the user's expectations.

Design is therefore concerned not with attaining a perfect solution, but with finding a good enough compromise that will satisfy most stakeholders. The process itself is based on arguing towards a solution through an exploration enabled by the iterative design process and the emerging artefacts, obstacles, constraints and decisions.

The Role of Prototyping

Prototypes provide a learning medium used to verify the feasibility of a design idea, to validate the acceptability of a design notion or to investigate new options. This enables designers to sample the environment, their understanding and the fit between the two. More crucially prototypes provide a connection between the acts of planning, analysing, designing and doing. Prototypes link thinking with doing by enabling a move from concept to detail and from imagination to a tested reality. They enable designers to look ahead and retreat to evaluate, accommodate and reflect on new discoveries.

Design prototypes thus provide a facility for the proposal and validation of design options during the design activities as they enable designers to make real the conceptual nature that was specified. Indeed, many aspects of design cannot be formalised, and prototyping provides a mechanism for evaluating images and perceptions without actually building the full systems they represent.

Prototyping reduces uncertainty by working from the known towards the unknown. This enables a shift from concept to detail and from plan to implementation. Prototyping thus provides a rapid and iterative method to proposing solutions and allowing them to fail and be improved in true trial-and-error fashion. It can be used to generate experience and build that knowledge directly into subsequent models. Moreover, it provides a facility for the exploration of existing constraints and the discovery of new ones, thereby weeding out the accidental and including the essential.

The Role of Constraints

Creative activities involve a large array of potential candidates. In order to arrive at a specific product, constraints facilitate the narrowing down of this field of opportunities. The design phase, for example, attempts to derive a specification sufficient for realisation. As the process of design progresses, additional constraints emerge enabling designers to limit the possibilities and ultimately select a single course of action. Feasible solutions must take into account other constraints inherent within the environment, the process and the solution which emerge throughout the interaction with both problem and solution.

Constraints are likely to emerge at each phase of the life-cycle where additional detail is obtained (and will include cost, capability, functionality and availability concerns arising from the medium, imposed environment, methods, tools and approaches adopted, as well as the problem, the way it is perceived and the solution).

Additional constraints emerging during or following the design phase may include physical, functional, operational, support, environmental, legal, safety or human interaction issues. Downstream activities such as marketing and manufacturing are likely to add major issues that have the potential to become technical, availability, cost or timing constraints. Such new constraints need to be balanced and trade-off against other limitations and overall goals.

Levels of Design

Design and development is often said to contain three types of design activities (see references below) divided into conceptual design, preliminary design and detailed design. While this section treats design as three conceptual entities, the actual physical arrangement of these activities can carve them into two stages, or for small projects into a single design phase. The actual number of stages depends on the project, the industry and the context, but the activities described below are likely to exist in most design and development efforts. While the different design activities need to be integrated, an additional advantage in the division introduced here, is in enabling the flow of feedback between the different design activities.

As we have seen, design is not likely to be strictly sequential. As design unfolds, various choices have to be made and different paths are selected and followed as various quantities, values, risks and constraints are negotiated or traded-off.

Conceptual Design

Conceptual design, also known as functional design, design concept or concept development, represents the response to the client's project statement and to the functional requirements statement. It is often viewed as the creative part of design, as it takes design from the desired characteristics to the development of a balanced concept of solution. The first step in the design and development phase; it is concerned with evolving functional detail and design requirements with the explicit goal of achieving the proper balance among functional, operational, economic, support and logistics factors. The design itself needs to be defined in enough detail to enable the establishment of its capability to meet system level requirements.

Complex projects can lead to very different interpretations of problem statements, needs and wishes. The early activities during design are concerned with defining the boundaries within which a fruitful search for solutions can take place and breaking the problem into pieces. This can be done through the development of models, prototyping and testing and the generation of new data. Such information can be bought without the expenditure of significant resources or an unnecessary commitment to a particular approach or strategy. Accordingly, the purpose of this stage is to take general design issues into account while investigating different concepts to the point where they can be compared, assessed in terms of achievement of the objectives and used to outline different design strategies.

The establishment of performance parameters, operational requirements, environmental characteristics and design support policies evolve from a combination of needs analysis and feasibility of technology studies. The search for different design options needs to be structured to identify as many pathways as possible. During the conceptual design stage, designers identify and prepare the different design concepts offering plausible solutions. Each concept equates with a different balance between the parameters, characteristics and policies. Comparisons of different concepts require a clear evaluation criteria and sophisticated techniques for conducting trade-offs between different design objectives and the performance measures characterising them in each concept. Typically, multiple needs and preference will necessitate the development of a prioritisation mechanism prior to trade-offs. Trade-offs can then be used to balance design goals in terms of schedule, cost, performance and operational support goals.

Feasibility studies are conducted as an extension of the early definition task in order to evolve an acceptable architecture. This may be supplemented by prototypes of the concepts. Additional work will work out estimates for resources, feasibility studies and risk assessments and the implications of selecting specific options (including sensitivity and contingency analysis to determine confidence levels). This enables the marrying of technical requirements and the associated design problems with potential technologies that can be applied to them. The conceptual design provides the baseline for all subsequent design and development activities.

Preliminary Design

Preliminary design, also known as embodiment of schemes, systems design, advance development, outline design or preliminary layout, is where the proposed concepts are 'fleshed out' by adding missing attributes to obtain a detailed qualitative and quantitative design specification. Preliminary design is a more technical stage that refines the conceptual design through evaluation and ranking with reference to the original statement. In other words, this stage is concerned with a transformation; putting the pieces together in a new and meaningful way while trading-off multiple factors, values, concerns and constraints.

Preliminary design encompasses the activities of functional analysis, allocation of design requirements to each hierarchical level of the system, trading-off and optimisation and ascertaining acceptability and sensitivity of the design solution. The design process at this stage is iterative as system requirements are translated into specific design requirements and re-visited to assess the impact on the overall system. This provides the basis for the development of an architectural description of the system in terms of functions. Established requirements need to be detailed enough so that they can be allocated to lower levels when the system is broken into sub-systems and then divided into components and parts. Design requirements can subsequently be allocated to specific components within the system. The overall functionality resulting from the sub-system allocations is regularly re-visited to ensure the system is still on track to meet major reliability and quality objectives. The purpose of the allocation is to ensure that all specific requirements will be addressed by the different design components.

Trade-offs ensure the balance between specific targets such as cost, reliability or size is optimised for the system. Individual trade-offs are often used to compare different sets of parameters and their results need to be combined to view their overall effect on the system and its objectives. As a result of the studies it becomes possible to combine the sub-systems while ensuring the maximisation of the overall targets. Testing is conducted throughout this phase to ascertain the consequences of the new arrangements in a practical setting or a simulated environment. The result of this synthesis is a completed and optimised preliminary design listing physical and performance characteristics.

Detailed Design

Detailed design, also known as detailing, detail design, critical design or definitive layout, refines the choices made to a configuration ready for production or fabrication. The design product is reduced to complete descriptions so that it can be manufactured exclusively from the information produced by the design team. The design team for the detailed stage should involve representatives of the implementation, assembly or production team.

Detailed design continues to define and quantify values for lower levels sub-systems. A large part of this effort comes from continuous optimisation and trade-offs between the overall design targets (such as design for reliability versus design for economic feasibility). Refinement includes filling in specific details including physical characteristics, such as dimensions. It is currently considered good practice to specify tolerances rather than exact values. Tolerances specify the range of acceptable values or the acceptable alternatives thereby allowing some leeway for practical choices to be made downstream. (In principle, the looser the tolerances, the greater the choice and the cheaper it is to find an acceptable alternative; conversely, the stricter and more exacting, the tolerance, the more difficult it is to find the only correct component, and the more expensive the resulting effort.)

Components that must be developed from scratch are tested experimentally using models and prototypes, while products may often have a mark1 prototype ready to be tested and evaluated. The building of test articles and the set of qualification tests are likely to play a part in refining the knowledge, the understanding of the problem and the solution provision concept. Resulting detailed specifications are normally accompanied by detailed drawings that can be easily read and understood (including all important information needed in relation to drawings). This helps to build up the physical picture of what the actual system would look like by visualising shapes, sizes, dimensions and locations. Problems with the design often do not appear until the details and the visualisations are worked out. Physical design may show up logical details which are not practical and cannot be introduced in real life and hence require iterations to earlier design activities or to the initiating needs phase.

Design Communication

The results of design have to be well documented and all changes recorded to enable efficient control over revised configurations and change. However, design communication has far ranging implications; It is the key to resolving many of the issues and resolving conflicts and trade-offs and thus is central to the design process. It is also crucial to ensuring the satisfaction of targets such as design for safety or reliability. Moreover, as iterative design is knowledge driven, communication is central to defining targets and communicating decisions and rationales effectively to ensure commonality of targets.

Feedback and Iteration

The final design product is tested against the goal, client statement and client-derived criteria for acceptance, thereby completing an external feedback loop meant to validate that the design is successful. This feedback loop is placed too far down stream in the life-cycle to act as anything other than an approval mechanism. This chapter advocated that design is an iterative activity concerned with learning and generating knowledge. Frequent iteration between phases is central to capturing knowledge and improving understanding as at each level the designs must be checked back to the assumptions set back in the project strategy.

In addition, it was shown that internal feedback loops between activities, for example prototyping, support development by linking together different types of activities, such as planning, designing and doing. Results are improved by re-cycling through the problem definition, the solution identification and the evaluation stages, before the fine details are finalised. Such internal verification relies on informal feedback loops to support rapid iteration and continuous improvement. Moreover, detailed design often entails significant activity required to finalise knowledge and prepare the process for production, manufacturing or release. The division into three separate design activities thus appears to make sense in terms of making a commitment to pursuing the design prior to embarking on the detailed design and once again prior to launching into production. (Note that finite and limited resources act as a constraint that must be balanced with the wish to maintain permanent feedback and attain a perfect structure for an ideal artefact.)

Products of Design

Design leads to a number of intermediary products released at the end of internal activities. These are likely to include:

- A general design specification including a functional specification of what must be performed to meet the objectives and a performance specification that can be tested
- Conceptual specifications for different options
- A design model
- Test and evaluation results
- A detailed design specification, also known as fabrication specification, and
- (At least) the outcomes of the final design review

The main outcome that is transferred to the next phase is the detailed design specification which provides a description sufficiently contained and detailed to enable the assembly or manufacturing of the output. The specification may be augmented (or in certain cases replaced) by a configuration that can be directly produced or constructed from specifications, a set of drawings, and supporting documents.

Enabling Design

This section deals with the technical mechanisms required to enable an efficient design process.

Criteria For Success

A design effort is successful if it meets, or exceeds, the specification AND the users needs. In some cases, an explicit criteria for evaluation can be stated and applied unambiguously. In many situations specifications lose relevance during the development effort. Intermediary products such as prototyping enable stakeholders to acquire new understanding and reflect on expectations and needs providing gradual improvement and added value and relevance with respect to the emerging product.

Expanding the Design Space

Some problems have a large number of potential solutions. Many of these solutions can only be perceived when certain aspects or variables are emphasised and investigated. The design space is the intellectual space encompassing all potential solutions to a design problem. Designers need to explore the space of potential solutions and partial solutions. In fact, creativity is said to occur when a non-conventional solution (i.e. a solution that may not reside in the typical design space) is discovered.

Constraints are used to limit the size of the search (and often act as selection criteria) in the early stages of the design phase. New constraints emerging throughout design will add additional limitations with respect to materials, availability and acceptable choices. However, prior to the imposition of too many constraints it is instructive to explore the range of possibilities through the creative generation of design ideas. This can be encouraged through the canvassing of a wide range of alternative opinions, allowing ideas to diverge, remaining open to new information, building in a diversity of opinions and thinking styles, surveying the problem using different viewpoints, listing the rationale and all assumptions and using creative approaches. Creative approaches may include boundary examinations, brainstorming, group interaction techniques, literature searches in alternative domains, decision balance sheets, goalstorming, Nominal Group Techniques, lateral thinking, Kepner-Tregoe or any other technique that is likely to facilitate thinking outside standard solutions and conventional spaces. Expanding the space may often lead to the possibility of increasing the quality of the solution or the utilisation of available resources.

Recording Rationale

The numerous steps and iterations can only be traced when the developers supply detailed notes in which the rationale is recorded and the main assumptions and thoughts are clearly developed and mapped. Recording assumptions and rationale used in making a decision will enable a more objective retrospective assessment and thus underpin risk management and sound decision making practice.

Managing Trade-offs

The design phase is particularly susceptible to trade-off and balancing between values, between competing options, between design alternatives, between constraints, and between constraints, obstacles and goals. Permanent feedback and growing understanding will ensure a constant stream of competing values requiring resolution against a backdrop of limited resources, attention and patience. Trade-offs between perspectives and views must legitimately address the problem from all concerned viewpoints and strive to attain a balanced negotiated solution. The techniques used to resolve such conflicts represent standard decision making approaches such as multi-attribute utility theory and the analytic hierarchy process.

Managing Design

The issues and techniques supporting control and management during the design phase are similar to those discussed throughout this work. This section emphasises differences and specific names or actions.

Functional Concept - The Requisite Input

Design relies on the activity concerned with clarifying the client's needs and translating them into a functional statement of what is needed (i.e. a problem definition). Where this is not part of the action completed prior to the design phase, there will be a need to initiate an additional activity to focus on defining the functional statement of requirement. This functional statement represents at least a partial pre-requisite to the initiation of formal design activities. (Note that this may often be a changing or changeable input that needs to be evolved alongside the design.)

Risk Management in Design

Risk management is a central part of controlling and directing the design activity. It may indeed play a part in determining whether to continue with the development at any of the milestones, control gates or continue/cancel decision points. More crucially, it can be used to support and approve the trade-offs negotiated throughout this phase prior to progressing to the next phase. If assumptions and rationale are recorded, they can be used as a basis for intelligent decision making and reactive risk management.

Freezing Artefacts

The main output, the detailed design specification is typically frozen at the end of the design phase. Once the product is frozen, changes to design are handled via the configuration management system. This chapter supported a more iterative approach within the design phase itself. In well-understood projects it may be possible to freeze the artefacts described in 'Products of Design' (above) as individual design activities are terminated (possibly in a sequence). However, if prototyping or a more evolutionary approach is used, the design will benefit from iterations and improvement through the design activities.

Milestones and Baselines

As the design evolves further details are clarified enabling choices and trade-offs to be made. Choices will influence the desired behaviour. Milestones and baselines may thus need to be loosely defined. They are likely to include the completion of the conceptual design activity, the preliminary design activity and the detailed design activity.

Control Gates

Levels of granularity at which gates are defined, the specific project and the selected life-cycle will dictate the number and sequencing of gates. Gates are likely to match the three main design activities and possibly the deliverables and sub-tasks described above.

Cancel / Continue Decision

Decisions to continue or cancel are scheduled for critical stages. Setting a formal decision point is likely to be reflected by activities concerned with assessing the feasibility, risk, costs and schedules for the next stage. During the design phase there are likely to be at least two such major decisions. An internal decision point is located following the preliminary design when knowledge of the selected option is stable. If approved, the project will enter a more detailed (and costly) design stage. This is to allow the design to be developed in further outline before approval is given for significant resource expenditure on full design/development. (Similarly, an additional decision point may separate initial design from preliminary design.) An external decision point is normally positioned at the end of the detailed design to determine whether to progress to the implementation phase and to ensure that all preparations for the next phase are in place.

Detailed Schedule and Budget

After the completion of the detailed design, detailed schedules and budgets for operation or production can be finalised. The detailed specification can be divided into specific tasks that are required to enable the implementation, assembly or manufacturing in the next phase. The specific activities can then be scheduled and costed to produce detailed plans for the next phase with little remaining uncertainty. (This information is often fed into review and approval cycles and together with a revised cost/benefit analysis, payback schedules, monitoring reports and risk assessment may form part of the decision making process.)

Quality Design

Quality procedures applied during the design phase reflect organisational practices and the approaches described elsewhere within this volume.

Specifying Test Requirements

Specification of system level and sub-system level tests is defined at the initiation of conceptual design when the requirements are made available. The tests need to include means of verifying subsystem level specification and evaluating its correspondence to the overall systems objectives. As new needs and constraints are discovered, the overall objectives, and hence the test plans may need to be revised.

Conceptual Design Review (CDR)

CDR is utilised in order to evaluate preliminary designs and the design approach which are checked with respect to the specification requirements. It is also used to review feasibility studies, decisions, rationales, and proofs of concept (demonstrating that a new concept or configuration can be made to work). In addition, it is used to verify technical data regarding functional characteristics, operational requirements, maintenance concept demonstration tests, and design constraints. Following its completion, the CDR becomes a formalised record of early design decisions.

Preliminary Design Review (PDR)

PDR, also known as a System Design Review, is where the preliminary design is described to clients, users and stakeholders and its implications are explored and assessed. During the preliminary design phase reviews are conducted at key milestones to ensure the achievement of objectives and correspondence to the specification.

Detailed Design Review (DDR)

DDR, also referred to as Formal Design Review (FDR) or Critical Design Review (CDR), is used after the design is frozen and before assembly begins to evaluate the detailed design approach. This provides a technical and critical exploration of the design. (Note that some organisations conduct an early DDR after detailed design is complete, but prior to freezing the detailed design and the release to production and follow it with a CDR that determines progression to the next phase once the final configuration is officially approved. In fact, large projects are likely to have a series of CDR's held at strategic points during which the design is presented to a panel of experts who criticise it and approve it for the next phase or send it back for re-work.)

Design reviews can be accepted formally and signed-off by the client to indicate their satisfaction with the design and the user's approval and conformance with their taste and wishes. The timing of reviews is ideal to ensure that the results of each design phase are well-documented, that products are signed-off and placed under configuration management, that progression decisions are made and that satisfactory progress has been achieved and that design decisions have been explored and approved by technical professionals. Strategically placed reviews play a critical part in ensuring accountability and providing a mechanism for termination or correction to secure the delivery of maximum useful and usable functionality and performance.

Designing For a Purpose

Design is often conducted with a specific goal in mind (such as designing for reliability, availability, ease of use, compatibility, maintainability etc.). This affects the way decisions and trade-offs are structured and the way reviews and quality procedures are balanced. Normal projects require a careful balancing between goals and negotiation towards reaching an acceptable compromise. In this type of project, one parameter, concern or product feature becomes dominant over the others. Designers need to define such design goals from the outset of the design activity and to actively consider meeting the goals through compromises and trade-offs. (Note that the more specific design goals, the more complex the compromises and the more costly the ultimate solution.) Some examples of design goals include the following:

- Design for manufacturing-attempting to design the product while minimising cost and time to market
- Design for reliability-attempting to ensure the item functions under a set of stated conditions while taking into account susceptibility to errors and ability to operate continuously
- Design for availability-ensuring the system operates at the times when it is needed (could be on-line, intermittently, as a one-shot operation, or when called upon)
- Design for compatibility with existing system-ensuring a new design accommodates the existing system as at least a portion of the proposed system (thereby hampering top-down design)
- Design for maintainability-attempting to minimise repair and preventive maintenance costs (and time spent). Requires a true understanding of the meaning of maintenance
- Design for usability-attempting to simplify the life of users and operators by predicting and formalising their actions

Problems

This section covers some problematical issues emerging from the application and discussion of the design concept and highlights a number of disputed or non-conventional areas.

Contracts - the Constraint

Design is concerned with balancing multiple constraints. The contract however, can become an additional (and sometimes a driving) constraint on a project. The contractual approach and the expectation of proving the understanding of client needs and providing cost estimates may commit developers pre-maturely to a particular design. Commitment can be solidified and often made irreversible by binding the process to what has been agreed. Indeed, in some circumstances it may prove impossible to provide a cost estimate before considering what is to be produced and before assessing the difficulties that are likely to be encountered in attempting that production. As the overall commitment is made in advance of the process, rather than in a stage-by-stage level, the initial assessment is critical. It thus limits what can be done to what has been promised rather than to what is likely to be learned during the development process.

Design as advocated in this chapter, is an iterative approach to interacting with the problem, through the notion of a solution which clarifies the problem. Relying on overly prescriptive methods can become an obstacle and block creativity and originality, by dominating decisions and trade-offs. Contracts may become a disciplining tool when they are allowed to direct the activities within a phase. The balance needs to take into account the vagueness, rate of change, uncertainty regarding the required resources, and completeness, stability and finality of a specification as well as the risk, prevailing understanding and level of agreement before committing to an approach that may stifle technical problem solving.

Opportunities, Limits and Early Requirements

This point is really an extension of the previous issue. Design as an iterative discovery process is likely to uncover potential and opportunities that can be exploited to improve the design and utility of an artefact. This is only possible if design is allowed to iterate back to the early requirements and goal clarification stages. Both this issue and the contractual dilemma discussed previously refer to the mixing of constraints of various types. In both cases technical constraints and implications were mixed up with either budgetary constraints or time limitations (and in this case with business opportunity and potential). Some of these issues may in fact require higher level prioritisation and resolution.

Staffing the Design

Design and development work is typically multifaceted involving a range of specialists and professionals (e.g. construction projects may involve architects, interior designers, surveyors, landscape specialists, structural engineers and other specialists). Decision making at different junctures will require different usage profiles utilising the range of required specialisms. The need for staffing is dictated by the contractual relationship between the organisation and the developers. Design and development work may be performed in-house where there is sufficient internal expertise and when the bulk of the process is developed internally. Alternatively it may be contracted out to external consultants who specialise in design and development. In certain sectors, the entire life-cycle is likely to be executed and managed by external contractors who provide all the resources and specialisms needed for completing the project.

Implementation of the Plan vs Implementation as Installation

The next phase to follow design is concerned with implementation. Like design implementation is not a standard term. Implementation may refer to the execution or implementation of the specified plan. Alternatively it may refer to an installation. The type of activity that follows design needs to be reflected in the planning and budgeting that prepare the ground for that activity.

Design as a Discipline vs Design as a Stage

This session referred to design as a phase within a development life-cycle.

Design can often appear in different contexts. In particular, there is a multitude of literature on the discipline of design; A discipline that differs from science in attitude, approach and method. The design discipline views design as a third culture, separate from either science or the humanities, yet embodying scientific knowledge and principles as well as tacit knowledge and perceptions. Artefacts are viewed as a meeting point between perceptions, values and notions embodying the state of negotiation and the level of understanding and agreement. The discipline of design focuses on the evolution and growth of artefacts but from an artificial perspective.

This session described the phase of design and the main activities and techniques that are utilised during the act of design. The next chapter focuses on the next phase in the life-cycle: Implementation.

References and Further Reading

Blanchard, B S and Fabrycky W J, Systems Engineering and Analysis (second edition), Prentice Hall, 1990

Cleland D I, Project Management: Strategic Design and Implementation (third edition), McGraw-Hill, 1999

Dym C L, Engineering Design: A Project-Based Introduction, John Wiley, 2000

63   IMPLEMENTATION

Mike Bates and Paul Whitehead

"Cecil's despatch of business was extraordinary, his maxim being, 'The shortest way to do many things is to do only one thing at once.'"
Samuel Smiles (1812-1904), British writer. Self-Help (1859).

Introduction

The Body of Knowledge divides a typical Project Life-Cycle into the following phases (APM, 2000):

OPPORTUNITY IDENTIFICATION

DESIGN AND DEVELOPMENT

IMPLEMENTATION
Make, Build and Test

HAND-OVER

POST-PROJECT EVALUATION

The BoK defines Implementation as "the phase where the rate of resource expenditure is greatest. Planning should have ensured that this proceeds as efficiently as possible. There should normally be the minimum of changes in project definition at this stage". This is a statement of the obvious and it gives little insight into the complexities of this phase of the project life cycle. The Glossary of Project Management Terms in the Syllabus for the APMP Examination (APM, 2000) is more informative, defining implementation as "The project phase that develops the chosen solution into a completed deliverable". Whilst not having a specific definition, the British Standards Institution (BSI) Project Management - Part 1: Guide to project management (BSI, 2000) is more comprehensive in terms of identifying the following specific activities: Further definition; design; development; procurement; manufacture, construction or assembly;

physical completion, commissioning and acceptance testing. This sheds light on some of the activities that might occur within the phase although it is a little biased towards 'manufacturing' type projects in its terminology.

Both the BoK and the British Standard are generally in agreement that the implementation phase succeeds a process of ensuring feasibility and gaining authorisation. The BSI however, includes design and development in the implementation whereas the BoK has design as part of a phase prior to implementation. This Session adopts the BoK interpretation. Thus, whilst different documents have slightly different perspectives, the implementation phase is clearly that part of the life-cycle where the activity increases and is focussed on converting the plan into the deliverable.

In the absence of a suitable definition, the authors propose the following:

> *"Implementation is the controlled conversion of the preferred and authorised hypothetical solution into the product which will be used by the sponsor."*

With this definition in mind, this session will take a largely sequential approach to implementation; looking firstly at mobilisation, followed by communication, monitoring and control, progress review meetings, concluding with problem solving and preparing for handover. Normally a chapter on implementation would include significant coverage of topics such as change control, earned value analysis, risk and people issues. These topics will be referenced, but will receive in depth consideration elsewhere in Pathways.

Mobilisation

In amongst the excitement of actually starting the work on the project, the project manager must remember to comply with the requirements of the methodology in respect of registering and referencing the project. Appropriate authorisation following design and development enables the project to formally pass through the gate to implementation. If not already done, this transition ought to generate some formal project identification or registration number to facilitate its integration into the organisation's financial and administrative systems. An initial key process is now project mobilisation which is "The bringing together of project personnel and securing equipment and facilities" (APM b, 2000). A key early mobilisation activity, where this has not already been done, is the populating of the responsibility matrix which will have been derived from the work breakdown structure. Several of the names will almost certainly have been known for some time, but there will be other responsibilities, which have been left as departmental, or simply the name of an organisation. It is now important that these are converted to names or points of contact. In addition, there may be legal and contractual items to be dealt with, again recorded in the methodology, to avoid problems as the implementation phase unfolds.

Another significant component of early mobilisation is the delivery of a motivating project kick-off meeting where the project manager must secure the commitment of the project team. The kick-off meeting provides a key opportunity for the project manager to assert his or her style of leadership on the project; it may be first time the PM meets 'face to face' with a number of the project team. The team needs to be in no doubt as to what the project manager expects of them, both in terms of what they are to do and what they are to be responsible for. This must also provide an opportunity to communicate the main features of the project and to allow individuals to see where their contribution fits into the overall project. The relationship between the project manager and project team members can significantly impact upon the success of this key event. Lock (1997) notes that the type of organisational structure within the project will have an influence on the ease with which the meeting can be convened and conducted. For instance, a functional matrix may require "more of an invitation or persuasion rather than a direct summons", with the latter more likely to occur in a dedicated project team reporting to the project manager. This meeting must get the project off to a good start, provide a crucial forum for clarification of any issues, leave no uncertainty as to the role of the individual and instil a sense of urgency and enthusiasm.

By now, with some team members having worked together in the Design and Development phase, the project team will migrate fairly quickly through the "forming and storming" and into the "norming". As the project migrates from this phase to Implementation, the Project Team will "be in a honeymoon period". (Bee and Bee, 1997) with the excitement of being selected for this possibly prestigious project "firing members with enthusiasm and motivation for their tasks". The challenge for the project manager and the team is to sustain this high initial motivation during the whole of the Implementation Phase with Healy (1997) observing that "in the Implementation Phase, peace and stability are not on the agenda". This phase is noted for fluctuating workloads, and hence pressures on the project team, resulting from delays, changes and other unforeseen problems. This will make demands on the people management skills of the project manager who must keep the objective of the Phase in view whilst agreeing short-term goals with the team, whilst concurrently providing encouragement and handling set-backs sensitively. For more detailed coverage, the reader should seek out Sessions 71 and 72.

Finally, the importance of starting on time cannot be over-emphasised. Any delay at or near to the commencement of the project can result in an initial lack of confidence in the project and its management and may lead to reduced commitment from other contributors. The start is the first and most important opportunity to instil a sense of timeliness as part of the project culture.

Communication

An essential first step in ensuring a prompt start is the existence of a robust communication framework within the project. The lines of communication within and outwith the project will be specified within the project methodology and there should be no doubt as to "who does what when". Whilst communication is essential in all phases of the project, it takes on an increased importance during implementation due to the immediate time and cost implications if communication is not effective. Of particular concern during the implementation phase is complying with the lead in time requirements of suppliers as determined during the procurement process. Suppliers are almost always at a distance from the project and failure to secure delivery at the right time is often a frequent and costly feature of implementation. Their distance from the project can also lead to their being out of mind as well as out of sight, which can have serious repercussions when re-scheduling is being organised.

The preferred method of communication is written or written confirmation of verbal communication. Traditionally, written communication would be paper based and the use of agreed proformas ensures consistency and clarity and reduces the risk of misunderstanding. An example, the Work to List, is shown in Figure 63 - 1. A well-developed proforma, based on existing project or organisational data, ensures accuracy of information and the linking of the project to other organisational functions.

ID	Task	Scheduled Start	Scheduled Finish
1	Access	Tue 30/10/01	Tue 30/10/01
2	Start	Tue 30/10/01	Tue 30/10/01
3	Design	Tue 30/10/01	Mon 05/11/01
4	Purchase	Tue 06/11/01	Thu 08/11/01
5	Assembly	Fri 09/11/01	Wed 14/11/01
6	Accommodation	Tue 06/11/01	Mon 19/11/01
7	Installation	Tue 20/11/01	Tue 27/11/01
8	Training	Tue 06/11/01	Mon 12/11/01
9	Marketing	Tue 30/10/01	Thu 01/11/01
10	Finish	Tue 27/11/01	Tue 27/11/01
11	Handover	Tue 27/11/01	Tue 27/11/01

Figure 63 - 1: Work to List

Increasingly, communication is moving to electronic platforms with e-mail and more recently project extranets. The latter are particularly suited to projects where the team is geographically dispersed. Such advanced technology is not always appropriate and for many a simple project control file will suffice. An interesting alternative for small in-house projects has been suggested by Kliem and Luden (1993), who advocate the use of a 'Project Wall' where all of the major documents - work breakdown structure, responsibility matrix, Gantt charts and any current information is posted and made readily available to all project team members on a large project noticeboard. The method of communication should be adjusted to suit the needs of the project.

Monitoring and Control

Monitoring is the passive process of watching the project's progress. Control is the active process of implementing measures to keep the project on track; involving a subtle blend of decision making expediting and more than a little chivvying! Both monitoring and controlling will be considering time, cost and quality. Monitoring involves comparing how the progress of the project to date compares with that scheduled to have occurred in the plan. In order to undertake the comparison, it is necessary to collect progress data. It is vital that the information is accurate and gathered at regular intervals - weekly is probably reasonable for many projects. A simple way of gathering the data would be to have the 'work to' list (Figure 63 - 1) modified to allow the recording of actual progress next to the scheduled dates as shown in Figure 63 - 2. This only shows the gathering of time related data, but the same principle could be used to gather cost and quality information.

ID	Task	Scheduled Start	Scheduled Finish	Actual Start	Actual Finish	% Complete	Notes/Comments
1	Access	Tue 30/10/01	Tue 30/10/01	30th Oct 01	30th Oct 01	100%	
2	Start	Tue 30/10/01	Tue 30/10/01	30th Oct 01	30th Oct 01	100%	
3	Design	Tue 30/10/01	Mon 05/11/01	30th Oct 01	5th Nov 01	100%	
4	Purchase	Tue 06/11/01	Thu 08/11/01	6th Nov 01		60%	Slow start, but catching up!
5	Assembly	Fri 09/11/01	Wed 14/11/01			0%	
6	Accommodation	Tue 06/11/01	Mon 19/11/01			0%	Delay gaining access
7	Installation	Tue 20/11/01	Tue 27/11/01			0%	
8	Training	Tue 06/11/01	Mon 12/11/01	6th Nov 01		40%	
9	Marketing	Tue 30/10/01	Thu 01/11/01	1st Nov 01		100%	
10	Finish	Tue 27/11/01	Tue 27/11/01			0%	
11	Handover	Tue 27/11/01	Tue 27/11/01			0%	

Figure 63 - 2: Work to List with Progress Data.

The commonest way of examining actual progress with planned, or more correctly, baseline progress, is with the Gantt chart with a date line as shown in Figure 63 - 3. It provides an 'at a glance' appraisal of whether tasks are on, behind, or ahead of schedule. Project management software is now widely utilised by the majority of organisations employing a more formal project management approach. It is the view of the authors that in a lot of cases the software

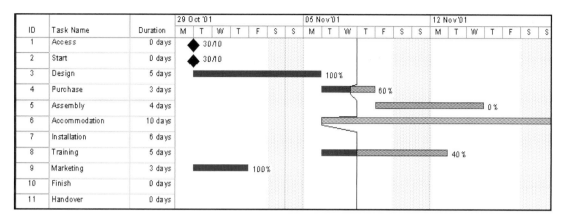

ID	Task Name	Duration	29 Oct '01							05 Nov'01							12 Nov'01						
			M	T	W	T	F	S	S	M	T	W	T	F	S	S	M	T	W	T	F	S	S
1	Access	0 days	◆ 30/10																				
2	Start	0 days	◆ 30/10																				
3	Design	5 days	100%																				
4	Purchase	3 days										60%												
5	Assembly	4 days															0%							
6	Accommodation	10 days																						
7	Installation	6 days																						
8	Training	5 days													40%									
9	Marketing	3 days	100%																				
10	Finish	0 days																						
11	Handover	0 days																						

Figure 63 - 3: Illustration of Gantt Chart with Time-line.

package is used to 'draw' Gantt charts rather than develop the project in the proper way using logic to sequence the tasks and integrating the work breakdown structure (see Session 31). If project management software is being employed then it is a relatively straightforward process to view those tasks which are critical and slippage occurring to any of them. Slippage may well need focussed additional resource allocation or sanctioned overtime work in order that project over-run is avoided. As progress is reported upwards through the project hierarchy, the amount of detail reported on the Gantt may be limited to heading level.

The benefits of clear and detailed planning have been advocated elsewhere, but the advantages in the implementation phase should not be underestimated. If the initial planning of the project was poorly detailed, as is so often the case, then the accuracy of the monitoring and subsequent control measures will be compromised. The data gathering process, as referred to earlier, needs to be very robust and the Gantt charts updated for use at subsequent progress review meetings. Any gaps in updated information must be quickly attended to.

A perennial problem with recording work done on tasks in progress is ascertaining percentage complete. This may be less of a problem in tasks where progress is easily measurable such as in construction where one can calculate the amount of wall built, but in other projects, for example a business change scheme, task progress can be much harder to measure. There is a tendency for those reporting to be overly optimistic in the early stages of the task, which leads to (apparently) very protracted progress in the latter stages. This in turn can lead to difficulty in the co-ordination of any following activities. Where planning has been undertaken in detail this should prove to be less of a problem because the task duration's will generally be shorter. Interestingly, at a recent conference two organisations suggested this was a significant problem, and were implementing project planning processes which had the project broken down into tasks of a maximum of 5 days duration and progress reporting on any task was either 'not started' or 'complete'. Both organisations reported improvements in their project monitoring processes and suggested that the system seemed to have the added advantage of motivating those involved to get tasks completed. An additional refinement is to incorporate milestone dates at key points within the programme. These are unaffected by the percent complete problem.

Whilst we would desire the project to remain on track, there are a lot of situations where, for a variety of reasons, the project runs behind time and/or over budget. In such cases, it is important to try and look for ways of remedying the situation, but it is also prudent to establish a forecast as to the time and cost implications if the project continues at the same average production rate. The use of milestones, suggested above, provides a simple forecasting tool as shown in Figure 63 - 4.

The diagram shows the reported plight of the milestone due to complete originally at week 24. The chart is plotted from left to right. At 4 weeks the milestone is still scheduled to occur on time. By week 8, a one week slippage is projected and by week 12 this has extended to two weeks. By plotting the line of best fit across to the diagonal line it can be seen that the milestone's projected completion would be week 28.

A more comprehensive technique for projecting dates and illustrating trends is that of Earned Value Analysis, recommended because of its integration of time and cost, which receives extensive coverage elsewhere. With either technique, one would not rely too much on projections in the early stages of the project because the team works towards

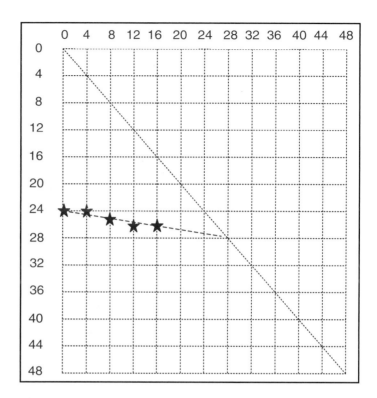

Figure 63 - 4: Forecasting Using Milestones

achieving 'norming', but certainly once 20 - 25% of the project work had been undertaken, their validity increases. Earned Value techniques, if used in combined breakdown structures as suggested by Harrison (1997), can be a particularly useful tool for comparing team performances and for providing early warnings as to out-turn. In larger projects, the Cost and Schedule Performance Indices provide a possible mechanism for empowering junior managers within the team. Values above unity suggest performance better than planned and values lower indicate performance behind schedule and over budget. One might allow a 5 or 10% buffer either side to allow managers some leeway for managing elements of the work. This is sometimes refined further to provide what is referred to as a 'red-amber-green' (RAG) mechanism, where rather than a finite 'cut off' at say 10%, there is a zone between 5 and 10%. If the indices remain within plus or minus 5% the 'performance light' remains green. If it moves into the 5-10% zone the light becomes amber which implies that senior managers have become aware and are watching! Obviously, beyond 10% usually implies the involvement of these managers.

There is a tendency to focus on slippage of projects, but lots of projects are successfully delivered ahead of schedule and under budget. When such a situation looks likely it would be prudent to check with the client that early completion can be accommodated. For instance, a building completed before the client is ready may involve the additional cost of recruiting security staff.

In and amongst expediting measures to maintain time, cost and quality objectives, the project team will be well advised to try and take a proactive approach to the monitoring of items present in the risk register, particularly those that are imminent. Similarly, health and safety issues must be managed. In industries such as construction, that have a higher risk of accidents, this will obviously receive more focussed attention and may even have to comply with specific legislation. A final function, or rather something that must not be overlooked, is quality. Most organisations have some form of quality system and each project, being unique, warrants specific consideration and ought to be a feature of the project's methodology. All three of the above will receive more detailed consideration elsewhere.

Progress Review Meetings

BS6079 rather succinctly points out the certainty in the implementation phase of costs and liabilities being incurred whilst deliverables are less certain and will generally arrive towards the end of the phase. There is a need therefore for 'competent progress reports at sensible intervals with review meetings' to ensure that the project remains directed towards meeting its time, cost and quality objectives. The frequency of review meetings is often set in relation to the client's normal business meeting cycle and may not relate to activity. Unfortunately, reporting of progress is not routinely based on data available within the project.

There may be instances where it is more efficient to manage without such meetings or to convene them when problems arise. Where projects are, say, factory based, it may be less disruptive to have nominated individuals visiting the relevant sections to gather progress information and communicate any relevant changes. In the bulk of situations however, regular review meetings are useful checking and decision-making opportunities. The frequency of such meetings is dependent upon the scale and complexity of the project and is a case of finding an acceptable balance between being often enough so that the project cannot go too far 'off track' and not being too frequent so as to disrupt those that need to report. Weekly would usually suffice for smaller schemes and monthly or bi-monthly for larger projects. Where it is felt necessary for control, it may be advisable to instigate intermediate progress review meetings attended by junior level members, the findings of which are considered at the more 'senior' review sessions.

Review meetings are often seen in a negative light as being a forum for the allocation of blame. It is incumbent on the project manager at the outset to show that their purpose is primarily proactive, rather than reactive in nature and for the benefit of the project. It is an opportunity to examine in detail what work has been completed and what is to be undertaken in the next period, with a view to ensuring that all the relevant 'ingredients' are in place and that ways of making operations proceed as smoothly as possible are considered and agreed.

In addition, it is crucial that the meetings are managed efficiently. A clear agenda should be distributed to the would be attendees well in advance of the meeting and minutes and action points with due dates and those responsible should be circulated as soon after the meeting as possible. During the meeting the PM should chair the meeting fairly and firmly, ensuring that the agenda is followed and that participants are not allowed to indulge in lengthy discussions on specifics that are of little or no interest to the rest of the gathering. Such discussions should be politely encouraged to be continued outside of the meeting.

Problem Solving, Decision Making and Change

Some sort of chaos will occur within the implementation phase. This will range from the relatively trivial requiring minor alterations to those that lead to the instigation of formal change control processes. Where possible, some form of Pareto Analysis (from brainstorming and archived records from previous projects) could be useful to determine what sort of problems are likely, ie. what are the 20% of activities that will lead to 80% of total problems, and what sort of mechanisms could be put in place in advance to deal with them? The risk analysis processes, mentioned earlier, may well lead to the identification of some of these.

As aforementioned, the implementation phase is associated with frantic work loads. When unforeseen circumstances occur, there is often a need for instant decisions; these can be derived from experience, commonsense or 'gut feeling'. Where an immediate solution is less obvious, the project team should be encouraged to at least brainstorm options and employ appropriate decision making techniques - decision trees, critical path analysis etc. - the reader should seek out the work of Maylor, (2001) for coverage of these in a project management context. The presence of a change control process should assist in at least ensuring that the suggested change is thought about.

When change is required, formal change processes have to be put in place for authorisation by a project board or similar. Assuming authorisation is given, decisions need to be made at the outset as to the appropriate rate at which to implement the change. The project manager will have to take a number of factors into consideration before coming to a decision on this. Change is often perceived as a negative and demoralising occurrence and if time and other circumstances allow, is better handled sensitively. Consider whether the change can be phased and who might be the best person to oversee the change. The authors do realise that it is often the case that the change needs to be affected immediately and a more brutal approach is all that is possible! See Session 34 for more detail.

Preparing for Handover

Handover and close out of the project are dealt with in the the following session. Nevertheless, preparation for these is an important activity as the implementation phase comes to a conclusion. Whilst there is nearly always a flurry of activity as the project nears handover to the operator, with little time for project housekeeping, it is essential that the project manager keeps the preparation for closedown in focus so that it can be achieved efficiently and quickly.

It is clearly essential that all aspects of all tasks be completed. Whilst this may seem obvious, it can prove a source of irritation to the client when the "completed" project has to be revisited to deal with minor missing or defective elements. Even at this late stage, the reputation of the project manager can be dented!

Tedious though it may be, documentation must be completed and tidied. In the excitement of finishing the project, it is possible that some administration may not have been dealt with as thoroughly as it should have been. In preparation for closing the account, all those to whom monies are owed must be encouraged to submit their invoices so that the imminent closing of the project account can be achieved in as short as time as possible.

Finally, there will be surplus items to dispose of. In the case of goods and equipment, the sale or transfer of these items needs to be dealt with. In the case of people, some will arrange to leave before taking employment elsewhere. Others may be transferred, perhaps on a part-time basis, to set off another project elsewhere. Some, hopefully Belbin's 'completer-finishers', will stay to help tie off all of the loose ends. For an effective Post Project Appraisal, it is important that items of learning do not depart with personnel and time should be set aside to gather such items from those departing early.

As people start to leave, two issues arise for the project manager. Firstly, sufficient personnel must be retained to complete the work needed to bring the project to a conclusion and, secondly, it is important to maintain the motivation of those remaining during a difficult period of change. In the midst of all of this, the project manager will also be keeping an active personal interest in the next job.

Final Reflections

There are three final reflections. Firstly, in order that the implementation phase is completed both economically and efficiently, it is important that proper planning and preparation is in place before implementation starts. Such planning and preparation may not offer the same appeal as "getting on with it" and there can be a tendency to push into the implementation phase prematurely with consequent risk of cost or time over-run as weaknesses and faults resulting from poor planning unfold.

Secondly, a sense of urgency is almost always prevalent during implementation. Higher rates of spending are being incurred and the client will have an economic need to complete quickly in order to gain benefit from using the delivered project. It may well be that the implementation of the project is affecting a business or production process and this is likely to put pressure on the project team to conclude this phase quickly to minimise disruption.

Finally, the traditional view of projects is that the implementation phase follows the design phase as considered above, but readers should be aware of concurrent engineering. This process involves the partial overlapping of the design and implementation. It is a method for reducing the delivery time of projects and is particularly suited to product development projects (Rusinko, 1997). There are obviously risks associated with embarking on implementation elements without complete design and development, but the close interaction of those involved in the two functions has been shown to provide substantial reductions in 'time to market'.

The above, given the constraints of such a text, has endeavoured to provide an overview of the important issues within the implementation phase and will, it is hoped, provide guidance and reassurance to those new to the discipline.

References and Further Reading

Association for Project Management (a) Body of Knowledge. 2000 UK, Association for Project Management

Association for Project Management (b) Syllabus for the APMP Examination. 2000 UK, Association for Project Management

British Standards Institution 2000 BS6079-1: 2000 Project management Part 1: Guide to Project Management. British Standards Institution London   CHECK THE DATE

Harrison, F.L. (1997). Advanced Project Management. Gower, London.

Healy P (1997). Project Management. Butterworth Heinemann, Australia.

Lock D (1997). Project Management. Gower, UK.

Maylor, H (2002). Project Management. Pitman UK.

Rusinko, C (1997). Design-manufacture integration to improve new product development. Project Management Journal, 28(2), 37-46.

64   HANDOVER

Peter Jones

"Never promise more than you can perform."

Publilius Syrus (lived 1st century BC), Roman playwright. Maxims (Darius Lyman (tr.); 1st century BC).

Introduction

There are many types of project and many forms of contract that govern their execution and the term 'handover' can have different implications for each of them. For the purpose of producing this session it has been assumed that the project under consideration will design, procure and construct a physical entity such as a building or a process plant. The project discussed assumes there will be a client employing a supply chain comprising a main contractor and manufacturers, suppliers and sub-contractors. Intellectual projects such as research or software development will need to be considered in a different light but the principles discussed will be applicable never the less.

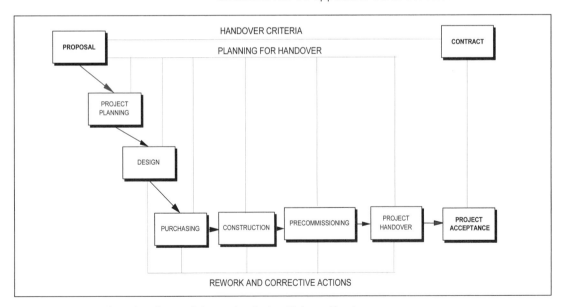

Figure 64 - 1: Project Planning and Corrective Action Links to Handover.

Successful project hand-over is dependent on effective planning and recognition of needs in the preceding phases of the project. Failure to achieve plant acceptance leads to corrective actions with risks of potential design, materials and labour costs with schedule delay and potential penalty. These linkages are illustrated in Figure 64 - 1.

Hand-over is the ultimate stage of the project's execution. It is the culmination of the efforts of all of the project stakeholders. It is where the 'product' is delivered to the client and commercial operation can begin. It is arguably a unique time where client, contractors and suppliers work closest, striving together for a quick and successful hand-over.

For the client it is the time when project costs stop and the facility goes into intended use so that benefits start to accrue to justify the investment that has been made.

For the main contractor it is the point where primary contract responsibilities cease and major liabilities for project cost, schedule and performance are removed. After a successful hand-over contingencies can be reduced or removed and profits taken.

Hand-over is also the time when judgements of success or failure are made and reputations are built or lost. This is why it is also a good time to learn from the experience gained from the undertaking.

Planning for Handover

Hand-over requirements must be reviewed and understood before entering into a contract. It is clearly the project manager's responsibility to scrutinise the bidding documents and the proposed contract to ensure that all hand-over requirements are identified and properly reflected in the plans and procedures for the project. Based on the information gathered, the project manager must closely consider the impact of hand-over requirements on each phase of the project and plan accordingly.

Proposal Phase

In the proposal or bidding phase, hand-over requirements must be reviewed with each of the key execution contributors so that their impact is properly considered in developing the scope of services to be provided and in evaluating the cost and schedule risks that ensue.

Key questions are:

- What must be done or provided to demonstrate the performance of the project 'product'.
- What must be done or provided so that the client or user can properly operate and maintain the 'product'.
- What must be done or provided to acquire supplier warranties and guarantees and transfer them to the client at the appropriate time
- What documentation must be developed and retained at each stage of the project in order to provide the client with records and other information specified in the bid document.

Many of the documentation elements to be assembled and transferred to the client at hand-over are routine and should be covered by company standard project lists detailing requirements to every discipline involved. Nevertheless the bid documents need to be scrutinised for 'special' requirements that are enforceable at project hand-over.

With the development of electronic document storage and management systems, the cost and time involved in transposing project documents into a format specified by a client to match his existing I.T. systems can be considerable and can affect all tiers of the supply chain.

Design Phase

The project design must ensure that the facility or product not only performs to requirements but can also be effectively demonstrated to do so.

There are sometimes start-up requirements that need specific 'one-off' provisions which must be included in the design to demonstrate performance at hand-over but which are redundant in normal operation.

An example could be high accuracy test instrumentation, which may have to be installed as part of the facility or must be hired at the time of demonstration of performance. Failure to include or obtain such instrumentation could lead to hand-over delay, unplanned costs and penalties if performance could not be demonstrated at the proper time.

A review of the start-up/hand-over requirements must be made and included in the design scope as necessary. Project specific start-up/hand-over check-lists for design should be developed by the disciplines involved and should include a review of the following:

- Installed components required for hand-over demonstration including equipment start-up.
- Services needed from suppliers at start-up and hand-over.
- License/patent requirements
- Technical documentation for hand-over including operating and maintenance manuals, training manuals and quality assurance records

Procurement Phase

In the procurement phase it is essential that project purchase orders and sub-contracts include all necessary requirements for suppliers and sub-contractors to furnish whatever services, special equipment, materials and documentation that will be needed to start-up and demonstrate performance of the goods or services that they are to supply. Such equipment must perform satisfactorily as an integrated part of the facility not just in isolation on an independent test.

Failure to negotiate such requirements when orders are placed is an invitation for extra cost and delay at the crucial hand-over stage.

Project specific start-up/hand-over check-lists for procurement should be developed by the disciplines involved and should include review of the following:

- Design/manufacturing documentation required from suppliers for start-up, operation and maintenance.

- Records, quality assurance documents, test certificates, warranties and guarantees required from suppliers and subcontractors for hand-over to client.
- Consumables and temporary facilities to be provided with equipment supplied.
- Supplier services needed at the project site during start-up and hand-over.

Construction Phase

In the construction phase the main contribution to hand-over is to ensure that records and quality assurance documentation for the work done at site is complete and properly controlled. Drawings and specifications should be up-dated to record 'as-built' quality information accurately and fully reflecting any changes to design or supply that may have been introduced during construction. This ensures that the correct information is available to the client and the designer should replacement be required or problems subsequently occur which need modification. The cost and resources to undertake these tasks must be included in the project estimates and plans.

Commissioning Phase

Before a project can be delivered to a client the component parts must be commissioned. In buildings this may include heating and ventilation systems, electronic and electrical systems, drainage and other utilities. It is essential to identify these elements in the proposal phase so that testing and demonstration procedures can be agreed with the client and documented in the contract unless there are industry agreed standards for acceptance which apply. Not having these procedures agreed before the hand-over phase is reached is to risk ambiguity and conflict of interest at hand-over with the client and/or the suppliers with risk to your company's interests.

The Primary Elements of Handover

The Hand-over Chain

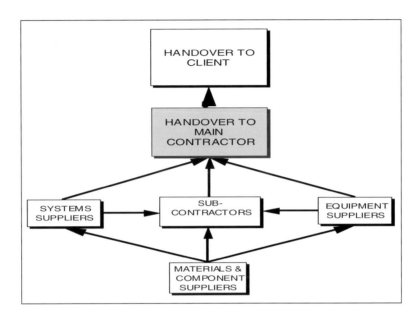

Figure 64 - 2: Handover Chain From Suppliers and Sub-Contractors

Hand-over may be a complex process involving several tiers of the supply chain. Figure 64 - 2 shows some of the different types of supplier linkages that the project manager must consider and ensure are properly managed in earlier stages of the project and which are essential in preparing for the ultimate stage of hand-over to the client. It should be noted that where direct contractual arrangements existbetween suppliers and subcontractors the subcontractors must also ensure that the necessary services and documentation are available for transfer to the client via the main contractor.

Managing Project Handover

Site Organisation

On a major project the project manager should preferably be located at the project site through the major part of the construction phase and through commissioning. This is not only to give commercial leadership and support to the construction and commissioning staff but also to prepare the way for and to co-ordinate a successful hand-over. The site organisation changes significantly as construction labour is released; supervision is no longer required and commissioning and operating staff come to the fore as systems and equipment components are commissioned and preparations for hand-over to the client are made. At this time of change the project manager must ensure the smooth transition from completion of construction to commissioning and start-up and to co-ordinate and lead the hand-over process.

Stakeholder Perceptions

It is important for the project manager to recognise the different stakeholders in the hand-over process and to be alert to their different perceptions. The client, for example, may have several stakeholder interests: the client's venture manager will be interested in finishing the project on time and under budget with a facility that meets specification and is fit for purpose. The clients 'operating' group will be more concerned with the long-term operability and maintenance aspects of the facility. The latter group may seek to delay hand-over seeking to make the facility perfect and foolproof to safeguard their particular interests.

Suppliers, manufacturers and sub-contractors may also exert pressure to get final payment and release from their contract liabilities having completed their work and obtained the main contractor's acceptance.

The project manager must handle all of these issues in the best interest of his company and the success of the project.

Pre-Hand-over Preparation

Component systems and major equipment items must be checked and tested wherever possible before the overall facility is commissioned. Checklists should be used to ensure that inspection and testing follows established practice and that the prescribed specifications are met. Punch lists should be developed to list all observed faults that are to be rectified by the supplier or subcontractor before their work can be accepted. It is important to schedule these inspections sufficiently in advance of project hand-over to the client so that defects can be rectified without delay to the overall completion of the project.

It should be verified that all necessary supplier technical documentation, safety and quality assurance records have been received. It should also be confirmed that any spare parts for operation and maintenance that were ordered have indeed been supplied.

When all of these requirements have been met the appropriate acceptance certification should be issued to the supplier. Where the performance of a component cannot be demonstrated independently prior to commissioning of the overall facility then this will occur after hand-over to the client.

In the commissioning period preceding hand-over to the client the project manager should run whatever performance tests are possible on the whole facility so that any problems are identified and if possible corrected before making any request to officially demonstrate the facility to the client.

Project Acceptance and Transfer to Client

Figure 64 - 3 shows the steps that may be involved in project hand-over and close-out.

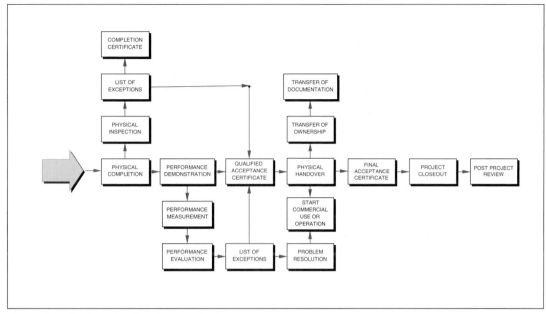

Figure 64 - 3: Steps For Handover and Close-out.

The project manager must decide when to start the hand-over process as the steps form a sequence which once started has to be followed through to the end. The project manager therefore should ensure that all elements of the work are completed, have been inspected and tested as far as possible so that the outcome of the client inspection and performance testing can be anticipated.

In the event that problems are foreseen the project manager will have to exercise judgement whether to go ahead with hand-over balancing the possible cost of delays and penalties against the cost of corrective action that will be necessary to make the facility comply with contract requirements.

Physical Completion

The client and the main contractor should make their reviews of the completed work and mutually agree the state of completion. Any items that require modification or corrective action or are incomplete or fail in any other way to meet the required specification for the satisfactory completion of the contracted work must be mutually agreed and noted on a 'List of Exceptions'. The project manager must agree with the client whether these exceptions are resolved before hand-over or negotiate a settlement whereby the contractor or the client might carry out the required work at a later time so that the facility can start commercial operation or use without further delay.

Performance Demonstration

Once the physical completion of the facility has been agree either unconditionally or with negotiated exceptions the performance demonstration can proceed.

Procedures for performance demonstration and each party's obligations to support the process must be agreed and clear to all parties.

Performance measurements must be mutually observed, agreed and documented. Any necessary calculations must also be agreed and the success or failure of the demonstration mutually concluded.

Conditional Acceptance

If the test is successful then the client should issue a 'Certificate of Acceptance' If however there are any areas of the demonstration that fail to meet the specified requirements these may be detailed in a further 'List of Exceptions'. This will make acceptance conditional upon the items on the list being corrected by the responsible parties in a timeframe which should be specified and which may require re-testing of the facility.

If the test is not successful the project manager must decide if a re-test is possible or desirable or whether liquidated damages should be accepted.

It is the responsibility of the project manager to negotiate a final settlement with the client and to obtain formal confirmation of this agreement.

Problem Management

Items, which have been put on the List of Exceptions, often require corrective work by the supplier or subcontractor responsible for that part of the work. The project manager must use the resources of his project organisation working with the involved suppliers and subcontractors to plan and implement the best approach to correcting each deficiency. Supplier's guarantees or warranties should cover equipment and materials defects and the necessary corrective actions can usually be contractually enforced.

Failure to meet performance guarantees may be more difficult to put right. It may not be possible to correct errors in design and/or major redesign may be required and modified equipment needed. Replacement of key equipment components may not be possible with the facility in operation, which has a significant effect on the client's commercial position.

The project manager must negotiate the best solution to the problem and manage the corrective actions until the intended solution is achieved. It is essential to get the highest priority from within the contractors own organisation and from suppliers in order to minimise the impact on the project re-work costs and delays.

Physical Hand-over

When the stages of Physical Completion and Performance Demonstration have been successfully completed and the facility passed into the hands of the client. Unless the defects listed on the List of Exceptions prevent successful commercial use or operation the facility can usually be transferred to the client and close-out can begin.

Final Acceptance Certificate

When the Completion Certificate has been issued; the performance demonstration has been successfully carried out; and the facility physically handed over to the client with its necessary attendant documentation, the Final Acceptance

Certificate should be issued by the client drawing the work to its contractual conclusion. The project manager can now proceed to close out the project

Project Close-out

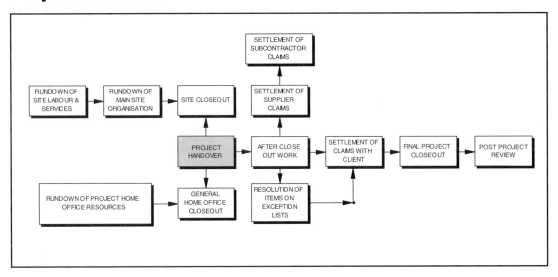

Figure 64 - 4: Elements of Project Close-out

Figure 64 - 4 shows the elements of project close-out, which precede or follow project hand-over. Close-out is not a single function but is a number of separate elements which must be dealt with at the appropriate time as the project draws to its conclusion.

At the time that project hand-over is achieved the project should have already been closed out for most home office disciplines as they finish their scheduled work and staff are released for work on other projects. Any support required to help resolve problems at site should be budgeted separately from the main project so that the cost of changes or corrective work can be identified for subsequent analysis.

Similarly the site resources will be run down and suppliers, subcontractors and staff released as their work is finished. When hand-over is complete then the site project facilities may be closed and staff released.

After Close-out Work

Work that is to be carried out to resolve claims with subcontractors, suppliers and with the client or to resolve items on the List of Exceptions should be fully defined and separately budgeted and managed to keep costs and progress under control. The project manager must ensure the project receives adequate resources and priority from all involved parties to complete after-close-out work as efficiently as possible.

Financial Close-out

When all claims are settled; all items of exception are resolved; final acceptance is formalised and all known work is finished, the project can be financially closed out. Analysis of performance against plan can then be undertaken

Legal Close-out

All documentation to be kept for legal purposes must be assembled and sent to storage and retained for the appropriate statutory period.

Preparation for Post Project Review

There is however another important part of close-out, which should be undertaken at this time - the assembly and analysis of project performance statistics and the preparation of reports to assess the successes and failures and capture the lessons learned from the project. This analysis should include every possible aspect of the project as a mechanism for correcting weaknesses in estimating and operation of the key disciplines and stakeholders on the project.

Judgements of the outcome of the project will unavoidably be made in terms of success or failure against each stakeholder's own criteria. The client will view the results in terms of the one-off business case; the contractor and the rest of the supply chain will look at profitability, resource utilisation and reputation to help win further work. It is important that everyone involved sees this exercise as an issue of organisational and personal development and a mechanism to capture and share the learning and experience in every area of the project.

Performance reports should be prepared for all assigned staff with an assessment of their work and recommendations for training and possible promotion made where warranted.

Session 65 explores project evaluation further.

65   (POST) PROJECT EVALUATION REVIEW

John Wateridge

"Apparent failure may hold in its rough shell the germs of a success that will blossom in time, and bear fruit throughout eternity."
Frances Ellen Watkins Harper (1825-1911), U.S. poet, novelist, and reformer.

Introduction

Projects (such as the Channel Tunnel, TAURUS, Millennium Dome) have a long track record for being seen as failures. They often cost more than they were originally budgeted for; the projects invariably exceed timescales by a considerable amount; the various stakeholders (customers, senior management, project managers, sponsors) are not happy with the overall process, do not assess that the project has delivered the expected benefits and are not satisfied with the product or facility. Each stakeholder has identified individual success criteria and has not appreciated other views on how success is to be measured with the consequence that the project has been aiming at quite different targets depending on each stakeholder's perception of the success criteria.

There are a number of ways in which project managers can assess whether the project came to meet the criteria identified by the various stakeholders and ensure that the project runs according to plan. At the start of the project, in the launch workshop, they can examine post-implementation reviews for previous projects to ascertain the lessons learnt and apply these lessons accordingly as appropriate. However, such reviews are rarely carried out as part of the system life cycle or are conducted in a superficial way. Perhaps most importantly of all, they can carry out Health Checks on the project to assess the performance of the project, to ensure that all the stakeholders are focusing on the same criteria, that appropriate factors, tools and techniques are being applied and that the right team skills are available.

Time, cost and specification are in many people's eyes the accepted measures of success. However, this does not go far enough in defining the success criteria. In addition, it would seem that very few projects assess the effectiveness of the product and whether the project delivered what was needed and the benefits were realised. This is rarely done after the handover of the project and seemingly never during the project. If any review is held in order to understand the project lessons, it is usually a post-implementation review which does nothing for the success of the project in hand.

This chapter describes three ways in which reviews can be conducted:

1   Post Implementation Reviews
2   Health Checks
3   Project Audits

Each can give valuable benefits to all projects - post implementation reviews to future projects, health checks and project audits to the current project.

Post Implementation Review

Organisations have often been disappointed by the returns on investment of many of their projects. This has been particularly true of Information Systems projects and their ability to deliver the benefits outlined in the investment appraisal. The reasons for these failures [unclear objectives, lack of user involvement, poor planning] have been well documented by researchers and authors over the years. One of the major reasons for such problems being repeated time and again is that organisations do not review the project after implementation to learn the lessons for future reference. They will need to assess the management of the project, whether it achieved the benefits required and what were the reasons for any non-realisation of those benefits.

If post project evaluation reviews are held, they often only examine the issues which are readily apparent. Management must look into the project deeply to find out the real reasons for failure or success. Stakeholders are liable to hide the problems experienced rather than report and analyse them. This situation can stem from organisations not wishing to make their failures public.

The review must involve all stakeholders in the project - users, sponsors, senior management, project management etc. It is important to review all aspects of the project, the successes as well as the failures. There are many different ways in which organisations respond to a failure. This depends on their acknowledgement that people are not perfect and that they can make mistakes and their fear of a failure. For organisations who do not accept these principles very often blame those people who they see are accountable. Those organisations with a high fear of failure and a desire to make people accountable for their mistakes tend to apportion blame. The outcome very often is for people to lose their jobs. However, the blame is rarely followed by a thorough evaluation of the lessons of the project. Organisations do not assess who is really accountable for the project outcome. The team members fear that they will lose their jobs after a project on which they had been working is perceived to have failed. Those organisations that have a low fear of failure tend to water down the lessons.

Organisations who accept that some projects will fail and not deliver the expected benefits and also do not look for scapegoats when a project fails are enlightened organisations who have the opportunity to learn the valuable lessons from the project. A learning organisation accepts that people make mistakes and that, if mistakes are made, there is a chance that their Information Systems projects may fail.

A post project evaluation review must look at different aspects of the project:

♦   An analysis of the lessons that can be learnt for the benefits of future projects
♦   An audit of the performance off the product

It must be a constructive review of what was good about the project as well was what was bad. It should address a number of different aspects of the project:

♦   The estimates of resources required on the project should be compared with actual effort
♦   The total overall costs of the project should be examined
♦   The reasons behind the variances between the plan and the actual spend and effort should be analysed
♦   The improvements in the conduct of the project (what would have been done differently with the benefit of hindsight) should be highlighted. This will include many aspects and factors which impacted on the project such as communication and consultation, project mission, risk management, planning and control, tools and techniques, capability of the project team, education and training

The proper post-implementation review can only take place some time after the delivery of the facility. An independent body is best placed to conduct the review so that the review itself looks objectively at the delivered product, how it has met the requirements and objectives and identifies any weaknesses in the product. When reviewing any project - for example, an Information Systems project, such areas should be examined as:

♦   The reliability of the system
♦   The adequacy of the documentation (particularly user training documentation)
♦   The responsiveness of the system
♦   The objectives of the system as against the delivered product. As user needs tend to develop over time in response to the changing business environment, the

post-implementation audit needs to take this into account by assessing the real objectives as opposed to those that may have been defined at the outset of the project

The reluctance to learn from project failures is only part of the problem. A post-implementation review will always be retrospective. It will only examine the project and indicate lessons for future projects. Every project will need to discover, as part of the project start-up process, the issues dealt with in reviews from other projects. All stakeholders will need to discuss the outcome and decide whether the procedures can be adapted for the benefit of the project. However, it does not help the project under review. There will be little or no effect on the perception of success or failure amongst the stakeholders of the project. In short, if the project is perceived to have failed, a post-implementation review will not turn it into a success.

However, if the project was subject to a continuous review process throughout its life cycle, the project manager would be able to identify areas of concern within the project team. These areas of concern will involve the critical success factors, the tools and techniques used, the skills required by the team for completing the tasks, the communication and inter-personal aspects. Most importantly, different stakeholders will have different perceptions of the success criteria and how they will measure the success of the project. The project manager may view short-term objective criteria (such as time and cost) as the important criteria; users may be looking into the long term, more subjective, criteria (such as achieving purpose, meeting quality constraints). It is exactly this lack of understanding of the aspirations of the different stakeholders which has very often led to the perception of failure, particularly in the eyes of the business community. A way of assessing the criteria is through a diagnostic tool.

Project Health Check

Organisations need to change in response to a changing business environment. If they do not develop in response to these forces, they are likely to cease to exist. To achieve this change, they undertake projects. Having undertaken a project, organisations need to make efforts to ensure that the project achieves its purpose. At the start of, and indeed during, a project, stakeholders need to understand how the project is to be perceived as a success. More importantly, the different stakeholders must be aware of the different viewpoints on the success and agree on the criteria. Health checks should address this issue and identify any misunderstandings or differences of opinion. Project managers can then take some action to overcome these problems as and when they arise. Health Checks will help project mangers and other stakeholders to focus on the problems and misunderstandings and identify improvements in the way the project is progressing.

Project managers must continually ask themselves questions such as:

- Do all the stakeholders understand and agree the direction of the project?
- Are we all moving in the direction to succeed?
- Are we employing the necessary factors to deliver the success criteria?
- Are we using appropriate tools and techniques?
- Do we have the right skills?

A Project Health Check is a simple project management tool which gives project managers answers to these questions. Many reports and statistics (such as GANTT charts, network diagrams) are delivered to project managers in order that they can assess the status of the project. However, these tools tell project managers where they are on the project and whether the project is falling behind the schedule. They do not give the answers to the questions above which should also concern project managers.

There are a number of prospective diagnostic tools available to project managers to assess the relative success of projects. They are mainly retrospective, thereby only helping future projects to learn from failure. Periodic reviews are often recommended but these reviews tend to concentrate on success factors, not on any success criteria to measure success. They generally provide little or no assistance to achieve a successful outcome for the project subject to the diagnostic process. An example of a Health Check is given in Turner, Grude and Thurloway.

This diagnostic tool:

- Provides feedback during the project on its current state
- Allows the project team to identify their important (and not so important) success criteria
- Provides feedback to the project manager on project issues and direction
- Gives an assessment of the team's views on the progress of the project
- Identifies the areas where improvements could be made before the project proceeds too far

It is necessary for the project manager to regularly review the project. The management and development process is dynamic and requires regular review in order that any change is recognised and accommodated at the earliest opportunity. The Project Health Check addresses these key issues.

The Project Health Check is based on the Project Diagnostic developed by Grude which aims to discover whether organisations are ready to achieve their objectives through projects. The Health Check specifically examines individual projects and assesses the effectiveness of the project to achieve success. It provides the project manager with the ability:

- To monitor the projects in the early stages
- To understand in outline what skills are needed on the project
- To focus on the problem areas in the project
- To anticipate problems
- To rectify any problems that may have already occurred on the project

It is a series of questions for all participants on the project to answer. The project manager and the team to identify the successful aspects of the project and recognize the areas which need improvement and change. It addresses the fundamental aspects of:

- The success criteria
- The success factors
- The methodologies, tools and techniques
- The skills required
- The project execution

Stakeholders are often pulling in different directions and not appreciating the ambitions of others. Consequently, the start point of any health check should be defining the criteria and enabling the project manager to ensure everybody agrees with the criteria. Then, and only then, can the project manager define the factors and tools and techniques to deliver success.

It will allow the project manager to evaluate and appraise the project, thereby understanding the strengths and weaknesses of the project. The Health Check needs to be completed at the start of the project and at regular intervals throughout. The project manager will need to examine the variances - where one person marks statement as 5 or 6 where another marks it as 1 or 2. The project manager will need to identify whether these variances are affecting the project. These differences of opinion must be discussed and opinions need to be brought closer together in order that all stakeholders are moving in the same direction.

The main emphasis of the Health Check is ensuring that all stakeholders agree on the success criteria and are, therefore, pulling in the same direction. Initially, it needs to identify the important project success criteria and the understanding of the general goals and objectives of the project - the project mission - and how the project fits into the overall strategy.

It also needs to examine the factors that are being used on the project to deliver the success criteria. The factors identified need to be used with the main success criteria to analyse whether the appropriate factors are being employed to deliver the success criteria. The tools, techniques and methodologies are assessed to see whether they are being used by the project team and are being applied well.

One particular problem on many projects is the lack of skills available on the part of the project manager and the team. With the emphasis on a project meeting its time and budget constraints, training is one area that is neglected [or even omitted]. The project manager needs to identify the requirement for additional skills (for organising, planning and controlling the project) which need to be acquired by the project manager and other members of the team.

Respondents are asked to rate the health check statements, identifying whether they agree or disagree with the statement. As many of the project team and stakeholders need to complete the Health Check so that the project manager can get a full picture of the project's status. Most importantly, it needs to be completed as part of a regular review process.

The project manager needs to assess the answers in a number of ways, identifying where there is disagreement and significant variation between the responses. The results must be discussed with the project team in order to overcome these problem areas.

Project Audits

Throughout the project there must be a system of controls over the whole project. Each control has a specific goal ensuring that an undesired outcome is prevented from occurring or some loss happening. The controls are:

- Deterrence and prevention: The objective of this control is to deter possible fraudulent activity (for example, financial loss) and prevent erroneous processing (for example, hardware and software errors) in project computer systems, particularly those dealing with project accounting
- Detection: Any fraud must be detected early in order that the situation can be rectified as early as possible. Very often the existence of controls simply acts as a deterrent
- Investigation: This could be both internal or external audits

These controls are directed at a number of issues. Computer systems, both hardware and software, sometimes fail but, more importantly, the weakest links in any system are the people who interface with the system. This is often apparent with intentional fraud by inaccurate data processing to gain some financial advantage. Data processing is now much faster and complex which gives workers an opportunity for embezzlement. Another fraudulent activity is the copying of data, programs or software (for example, copying company data to leak to a competitor, taking copies of word processing or accounting packages for one's own use).

Company's computers are prone to sabotage or vandalism from disgruntled or disaffected employees or external pressure groups (for example, animal rights groups). Added to this threat of sabotage is the problems of unauthorised access to computer systems usually by 'hackers' gaining access via modern telecommunications. In other cases employees may gain access to parts of the system to which he/she is not entitled. Unauthorised access has the added problem of the potential introduction of viruses. However, viruses can be introduced unintentionally by illegal copies of software being copied by employees onto company's computers.

These threats should be controlled by system audits, both internal and external. Both types are required to control and deter potential fraudulent activity. Auditors must understand system functions, document, evaluate and test the internal controls and finally report on the systems. They must be able to report on the accuracy of financial statements, the reliability of the systems that provide the information and provide advice on potential fraud and errors.

Conclusion

Many projects continue to fail. This is often caused by project managers not agreeing the measurements for success (the criteria) and then focusing on the wrong factors and/or doing them badly. Furthermore, project managers are not learning from their mistakes. What happens when the project starts to go wrong and either the system is never implemented or during operation major problems arise? What can be done to learn from these projects? Little can be done about the current project but much can be learned for the benefit of future projects. With a record of estimates and plans of previous developments, many problems can be addressed and overcome. Therefore, project reviews are a valuable source of information for the future. Projects are investments and, as such, they must provide some return on the investment. Some are critical to future operations, others improve management and performance. Whatever the nature of the project, it will need to provide benefits and those benefits need to be measured to assess the success of a project.

On projects which have spanned a long time, there will be problems in team members remembering all the issues if there is only a post-implementation review. People's memories will be selective. What is important is not simply carrying out a project review after implementation but undertaking periodic reviews and Health Checks during the project in order to detect deviations from the plans and objectives. The Project Health Check provides a useful addition to the other, more traditional, monitoring tools, with its emphasis on success criteria and the views of all stakeholders on the project. Project audits, both internal and external, are necessary to ensure that any fraudulent activity is investigated, detected and prevented.

References and Further Reading

Abdel-Hamid, TK and Madnick, SE, "The Elusive Silver Lining: How we fail to learn from software development failures", Sloan Management Review, Fall 1990, 39 - 48

DeMarco, T, Controlling Software Projects, New York:Yourdon, 1982

Hougham, M., "London Ambulance Service computer aided despatch system", International Journal of Project Management, 1996, 14(2) 103-110

Morris, PWG and Hough, GH., The Anatomy of Major Projects, John Wiley, UK, 1987

O'Connell, F., How To Run Successful Projects, Prentice-Hall, UK, 1993

Pinto, JK and Slevin DP, "The Project Implementation Profile", Project Management Institute Seminar/Symposium, Atlanta,Georgia, Oct 7-11, 1989, 174-177

Turner, JR., The Handbook of Project-based Management, McGraw-Hill, UK, 1993

Turner, JR, Grude K and Thurloway L., The Project Manager as Change Agent, McGraw-Hill, UK,1997

Turner, JR and Simister S, The Gower Handbook of Project Management, Gower, 2000

Wateridge, J., "IT Projects: A basis for success", International Journal of Project Management, 1995, 13(3) 169-172

66   ORGANISATION STRUCTURE

Dennis Lock

"I'm surprised that a government organisation could do it that quickly."
Jimmy Carter (1924-), U.S. president. During a visit to Egypt, after being told that it took twenty years to build the Great Pyramid. Time Magazine (March 1979).

An appropriate organisation is a key requirement for effective project management, yet what actually constitutes an appropriate organisation is not always clear. There might even be more than one solution. Project managers typically find themselves appointed to organisations that already exist, with no chance or authority to make any significant change. What is certain, however, is that the project manager and those who establish project organisations should know how different organisation structures can affect staff motivation, work performance, communications and, ultimately, project success.

Charting the Organisation

It has often been said that a picture is worth more than a thousand words. This is certainly true when describing organisation structures. The pictures in question are organisation charts, often called organigrams. Most organigrams conform to the conventions used in Figure 66 - 1. Each box on the chart represents a job or role in the organisation. Those at the top of the chart usually have higher status than those at the bottom, often coupled with greater authority and accountability.

Solid lines depict channels down which commands may be given. Feedback reports flow back up the same channels. Informal communication channels will usually exist between all the roles in a complex pattern but broken lines are used to emphasize communication paths of particular importance. It may be, for example, that Manager B in Figure 66 - 1 is specially authorised to communicate directly with and expect information from staff who officially report to Manager C.

Some people might report directly to a senior manager (which usually gives them some status) but have no direct line authority. These people occupy staff positions. The secretary in Figure 66 - 1 is such a person and, in project management, planners, cost engineers and specialist consultants sometimes hold staff positions.

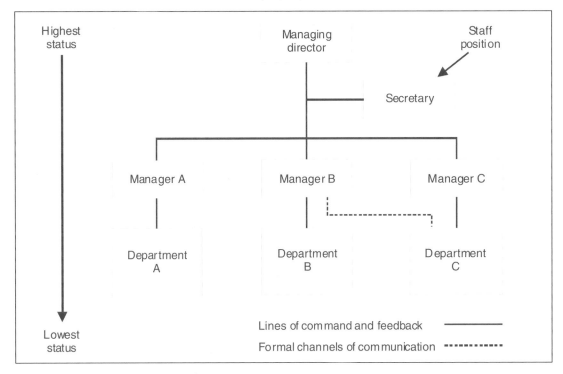

Figure 66 - 1: Organigram Conventions.

Organigrams cannot convey all the interplay and subtle influences between the various roles. This will be seen, for example, when the relative authority of the project manager in a matrix organisation is discussed later in this chapter. However, the organigram is an essential part of project management documentation. Wherever a project warrants its own project manual or handbook, organigrams should always be included to show the identities and relationships of the key internal and external roles.

Basic Project Organisation Structures

There are probably almost as many organisation structures as there are projects. Each company or business group has its own ideas and requirements, often complicated by business diversity or scattered geographical locations. Yet more variations are seen when not-for-profit and government organisations are considered. It should always be possible, however, to analyse any organisation and identify the underlying structure or structures on which it is based.

Line and Function (or Functional) Organisation

A line and function organisation is not a project management organisation but it is useful to examine this structure first. Figure 66 - 2 depicts the organisation of a company engaged in routine operations. Although the example given is a manufacturing company, a comparable chart could be drawn for any company that operates a number of specialist functions under the command of a general manager. An insurance company, for instance, might have functions for automobile policies, house and home insurance, business clients, various claims departments, assessors and so on.

All except the very smallest organisations have a set of functions that are concerned principally with the core operations of the business (carrying out those activities which fulfil the business aims of the organisation) and another set of functions that add no direct value to the operations but provide essential supporting services. In Figure 66 - 2 the fulfilment functions are shown to the left of the diagram, with the support services on the right.

Suppose that the company in question is suddenly faced with the need to carry out a project, quite different from its routine operations. For the insurance company this might be an office relocation (an example that will be visited later in this chapter), replacement of all the company's computer systems or a radical management reorganisation. In the manufacturing case, a customer might request the special design and manufacture of a product that differs substantially from any product listed in the catalogue and which must involve considerable time, expense and new design work.

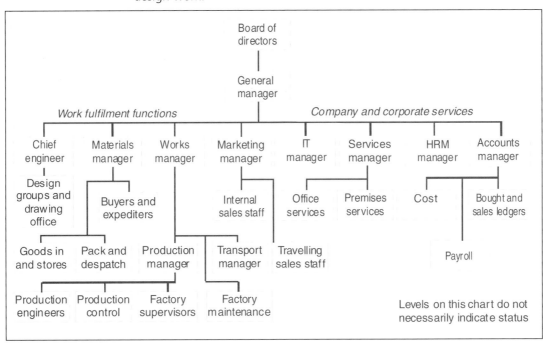

Figure 66 - 2: Line and Function Organisation for Routine Manufacturing Operations

By no means all the problems created by the arrival of a special project will be technical. Any functional organisation tends to operate as a set of isolated departments, each carrying out its daily routine tasks without the need for constant reference to other departments. A project, however, is by its nature usually multifunctional, and requires the coordinated work of several functional departments throughout its active life cycle. There is a need, therefore, unique to projects, to plan and coordinate all the activities not just within departments but also across the organisation. Someone is needed to carry out this planning and coordination role, a person whose responsibility is not simply the management of one function but delivery of the complete, successful project. That person is the project manager.

Co-ordination Matrix or Functional Matrix

In the previous section the need to appoint a project manager was seen when a functional organisation encounters a project occasionally or for the first time. A common organisational solution is shown in Figure 66 - 3, which shows a coordination matrix (known also as a functional matrix). Here a project manager has been appointed to a staff position, reporting directly to the general manager. The project manager has no personal line authority but has the task of scheduling the project and coordinating the project tasks across all the relevant functions so that the project is progressed in an holistic way.

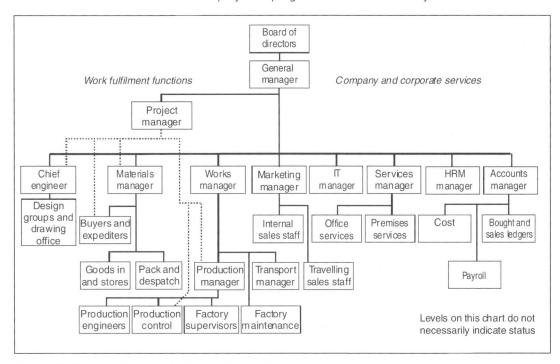

Figure 66 - 3: Co-ordination Matrix for a Single Manufacturing Project

With no direct authority, this project manager can only achieve results if the functional line managers choose to cooperate. However, the project manager should be able to rely on the backing of the general manager for enforcement, should conflict arise.

The project manager might be a professional specialist engaged for the project but could be an internal appointment. For most internal appointments the individual will probably need some training in basic project management methods. Where the project technical content has a bias towards one of the functional departments, the project manager might reside within that department and report to the department manager rather than to the general manager. It is common, for example, for the project manager of a project involving a great deal of engineering design to reside within the engineering design department and report to the chief engineer. The project manager for a replacement computer system would most likely report to the IT manager. But wherever the project manager resides, in a coordination matrix he or she will be expected to coordinate project activities across all the company's participating functions.

Matrix Structures for Multiple Projects

The coordination matrix (described above) offers an attractive solution for companies who want their routine line and function organisations to remain intact, yet be able to handle a single intrusive project.

Companies that routinely handle more than one project at a time yet still wish to maintain a stable organisation have to look for another form of matrix structure.

Balanced Matrix

Now consider those companies that regularly handle a number of medium to large sized projects, where each project must have its own project manager to drive the project to successful completion and also act as principal contact with the client. Figure 66 - 4 shows the kind of matrix organisation adopted by some heavy construction companies and those engaged in mining engineering or petrochemical plant construction.

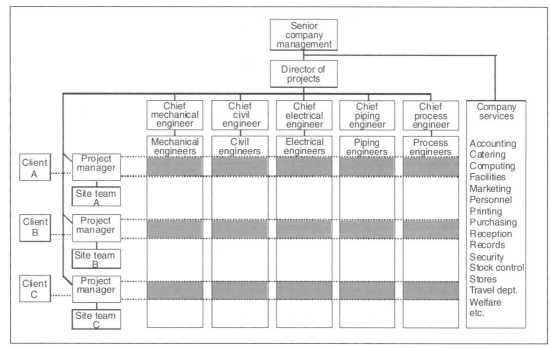

Figure 66 - 4: Matrix Organsation for Multiple Petrochemical or Mining Projects

The organisation in Figure 66 - 4 is carrying out projects for three clients (named A, B and C) but this number can be extended to many more clients and projects. Each project has its own project manager who reports (along with all the fulfilment functions) to a director of projects. Every construction site in this example has its own site manager who manages the site team and reports to the project manager. The support functions (the company services at the right of the chart) are usually outside the matrix and do not come within the jurisdiction of any project manager.

There is a balance of power between each project manager and the functional managers. When project manager B, for instance, needs a mechanical engineering task to be performed, the chief mechanical engineer will choose and assign an appropriate engineer and be responsible for supervising and progressing the work.

A balanced matrix can be attractive to companies because of the following properties:

- It provides an organisation that is likely to remain fairly stable, regardless of individual projects
- It concentrates expertise within each specialist function, giving potential for high technical quality
- Functional managers can switch their staff between projects as workload demands, providing flexible and efficient use of human resources
- Individual members of staff perceive a stable organisation, continuity of employment and opportunities for career development and promotion within their specialist function

There are some serious disadvantages with the balanced matrix. The most important of these are:

- There is no overriding reason why a functional manager should carry out a project manager's wishes to the letter. For example, a functional manager might decide to give priority to project A against the wishes of project manager B. This can lead to conflict and delayed projects
- People working in a balanced matrix have two bosses. Any person working within a functional group might receive conflicting instructions from the project manager and the functional manager. This violates the principal of unity of command and can cause confusion and discontent
- Some project work has to be conducted in a confidential, even secret environment. It is difficult to maintain confidentiality when the work of a project is spread over an organisation in which people are working on a range of other projects.
- Because people are dispersed over a number of different functions and work alongside colleagues who are engaged on tasks for other projects, all those working for any particular project may not feel part of a project team. They cannot see the whole picture or easily be motivated towards achieving the total aims of a project in which they play only a small, isolated part

At one time the balanced matrix organisation was actively promoted by those who saw its structure as the single solution to cure all ills. There are certainly many arguments in favour of this organisation but it is not the easiest form to manage and it is by no means the appropriate solution for all occasions.

Stronger Forms of the Matrix

It is of course possible for senior management to give the project managers in a matrix more power and authority (in varying degrees) than that accorded to the functional managers. Some of those options will now be described. The organisation chart remains the same as that shown in Figure 66 - 4 because organigrams generally are not able to indicate these differences in the balance of power and authority.

A matrix organisation in which the project managers are given a power advantage over functional managers is called strong matrix. In a strong matrix the project manager can demand that his or her instructions are carried out in a manner and at a time to suit the project, although the functional manager should always have a controlling voice in the technical approach.

The strongest matrix of all is the secondment matrix, in which functional managers are required to assign named members of their groups to a project manager to work on the project for as long as required. This can even mean removing people physically from their normal places of work.

The stronger forms of the matrix retain most advantages of the balanced matrix. All functional specialists should still have access to their home groups in order to seek expert advice or technical guidance, so that technical quality need not be compromised. Continuity of individual career development should not be endangered, because all participants still have a home department to which they return at the end of each project.

Project Teams

The opposite extreme of the balanced matrix is the project team. Here, the project manager heads the whole project organisation and even the functional managers report directly to him or her. An example is shown in Figure 66 - 5.

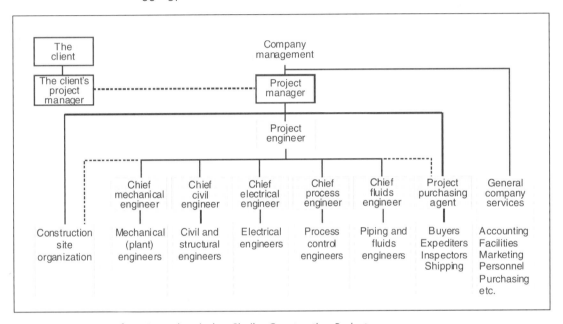

Figure 66 - 5: Team for a Petrochemical or Similar Construction Project

When all project staff are organised as a team it is far easier for them to feel part of the project. They should be motivated by general enthusiasm and team spirit, knowing that everyone in the team is working towards a common goal. This sense of motivation will be highest at the start of the project, but should be maintained throughout the early and middle stages of the project life cycle. A project team organisation is indicated for any project where completion on time is critical. A special team or task force is therefore a good choice where a project has fallen far behind schedule and has to be 'rescued'.

The team structure facilitates the maintenance of project confidentiality because, provided that the premises are suitable, team members can be located within closed boundaries that exclude unauthorized persons and prying eyes and ears. A team can even be given a 'war room' where team members can hold meetings at short notice and where drawings and schedules can be freely displayed.

Even where the main company operates as a matrix, whenever a project requires working at a remote site, particularly for construction work, a self-contained team will almost certainly be established at the site under the general control of a site manager.

A project team, however, can never be a stable organisation. Its size and composition must adapt to different phases of the project life cycle. While the team is growing this might present no problems but when the end of the project is in sight some team members might begin to wonder what lies in store for them when their job is done. This fear of the unknown can lead to slow working as the project nears it end.

After the project has been handed over to the customer and the team has been disbanded there could be potential problems in providing certain post-project services to the customer. When work has to be carried out under warranty, for example, it is important that the relevant project records and suitably qualified people are available somewhere in the organisation.

Summary of the Basic Structures

Figure 66 - 6 summarises the basic project organisation structures described above. The list is sorted in ascending order of the project manager's power and authority compared with the power and authority of functional managers.

Line and function organisation
    No project manager at all

Functional matrix (weak matrix or functional matrix)
    Project manager can only persuade or advise

Balanced matrix
    Project managers share authority equally with the functional managers

Strong matrix
    Project managers have more authority than the functional managers

Secondment matrix (or project matrix)
    Project managers have primary responsibility for meeting project objectives. Functional managers are required to assign named staff from their groups to work under the direct and full control of each project manager.

Project team or task force
    Functional managers or their delegates report to the project manager along with all project staff.

Increasing power and authority for the project manager

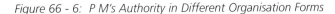

Figure 66 - 6: P M's Authority in Different Organisation Forms

Common Support Services

A misconception of some writers is always to show a company's central service departments as lying within the project organisation structure. Project managers in team or matrix organisations for the average industrial project will not usually have any authority over departments such as marketing, accounting, human resources, purchasing and general administration. These functions provide central, corporate services and will usually report directly to the company's board or senior management. They lie outside the command lines of the project team or matrix. No project manager can operate without those services but the organisational relationship is usually expected to be one of mutual cooperation and dependence.

There are, of course, exceptions to every rule. For example, it is possible that all managers and staff of a company set up specially to perform a single project would report to the project manager. The project manager of a market research project will obviously expect to have marketing personnel in the project organisation. A special staff recruitment project will most likely be based in the human resources department. A very large industrial project might need its own purchasing group, and the central purchasing department could possibly assign one or more of its people to work under the project manager. A company relocation project should include members of all departments in the team.

Project Services

Project services groups are a special common support services case. Perhaps called a 'project office' or 'programme office', a typical group will comprise one or more competent planners, estimators, cost engineers and progress clerks who provide a common service to all the organisation's project managers. Of course such a group might be formed for a single project, but when provided as a common service the group will help to ensure consistency and quality of procedures across all projects. The group should be capable not only of planning and coordinating project activities, but should also be able to collect timesheet data, carry out earned value analysis, draft progress and cost reports, and administer change control procedures.

If the organisation is using sophisticated project management software, especially if that software is being used to schedule multiproject resources, the project services group provides a possible home for the specially trained operators needed to maintain the integrity of the model.

More Complex Organisations

Hybrid Organisations

A hybrid organisation is any organisation in which two or more of the basic structures described so far are mixed.

A fairly common example is seen when a specialist project team is set up within an existing balanced matrix structure. A London mining engineering company was organized as a balanced matrix (as shown in Figure 66 - 4). One of the company's clients was a copper mining company in Zambia. Most projects for that client were for the creation or expansion of mining and ore treatment plants, in which engineers from all parts of the matrix became involved. It became necessary to carry out a special project to design and carry out pumping operations to remove slurry and reclaim a mine that had been flooded several years earlier in a tragic accident. Because this project consisted principally of pumping and piping, a dedicated project team was set up within the fluids engineering department with the chief fluids engineer as project manager. The remainder of the company (including the rest of the fluids department) continued to operate as a matrix.

Contract Matrix

Large projects are likely to involve many companies and some of those companies might appoint their own project managers or coordinators. Someone, of course, has to oversee the whole project. A project that involves large capital expenditure and heavy construction work for a client who has no in-house construction capability might result in an organisation of the type shown in Figure 66 - 7. Here the client (project owner) has engaged a managing contractor, a company with architectural and design engineering capabilities, to design and manage the project.

In the example of Figure 66 - 7 the owner has appointed an internal project manager, but that person will probably have only limited project management skills and acts principally as the contact point between the owner and other principal parties in the project organisation. It is the managing contractor who, on the owner's behalf, designs the project, carries out procurement, engages subcontractors and carries out overall project management. The site manager and his or her management team would all be direct employees of the managing contractor.

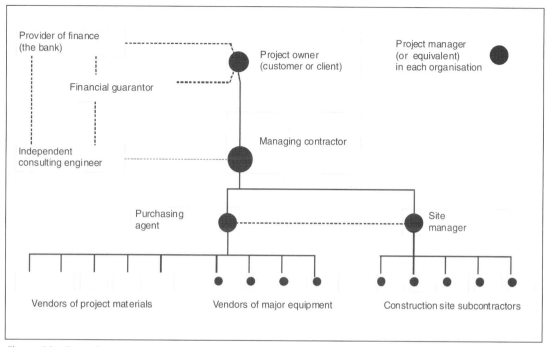

Figure 66 - 7: A Contract Matrix

The owner in this case did not have sufficient liquid funds for the project and has had to arrange a large bank loan. The bank agreed to the loan but required a guarantor to underwrite a substantial part of it. A guarantor has been found, but both the bank and the guarantor (having no technical capability of their own) have demanded the services of an independent consulting engineer, part of whose role is to certify that all invoices issued by the managing contractor are valid and reflect the amount of work actually performed.

Some of the vendors are suppliers of complex, specially designed equipment. Each of those supply contracts is a project itself, with its own organisation and project manager. Similarly, some of the subcontractors are supplying equipment and skilled workers; some of those will effectively be managing sub-projects, again each with its own project manager.

Joint Ventures and Consortia

When the capital investment, degree of risk and amount of technical expertise required for a proposed project are too great for one company to accept, two or more companies might decide to join forces and bid for the new project as a consortium. If a contract results, the contributing companies would most likely establish a private limited company as a joint venture. This allows the parent companies to pool some of their resources and skills but limits their financial liability should the project fail. All or some of the joint venture company's management committee members will probably be seconded from the parent companies. One arrangement is shown in Figure 66 - 8.

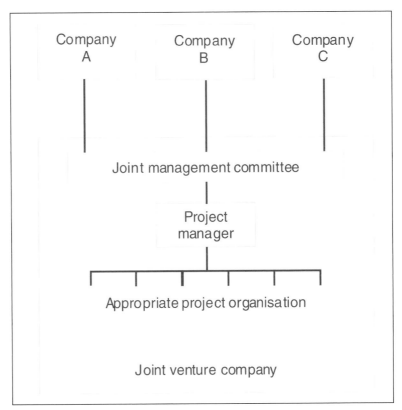

Figure 66 - 8: A Joint Venture Organisation

Occasional Management Projects

Occasional management projects (sometimes called management change projects) are projects that are conducted to achieve management, procedural or organisation changes. They might involve the installation of a new computer system, business process re-engineering or the relocation of a company. They are usually funded internally. What these projects have in common is that they do not result in a saleable product, and they can take place in a company whose core operations are routine and usually unconnected with projects of any sort. Here is a case where there might be no resident project management expertise in the company, yet the change process will be most effectively managed if it is treated as a project. This means appointing at least a project manager and establishing a project organisation of some sort.

An example is a project to plan and execute the relocation of a company from one city to another. All functions of the company will be heavily affected, with every aspect of the company and its employees' personal and family lives affected. Project activities would be far-reaching and comprehensive, starting with detailed research into a range of possible new locations and ending with implementing the move and the resumption of normal day-to-day operations. When the project is in its early stages, before relocation decisions have been made, confidentiality will be important so that rumours that might cause unfounded alarm and despondency among the staff are not started. Yet within this confidential environment every functional manager must be consulted and will be expected to contribute information and ideas if the company is to operate effectively from the start of its arrival at the new location. All of this points to the establishment of a small project team, a task force comprising delegates from all the principal functions placed under the command of a project manager. If the delegates have sufficient authority, this team will be able to make appropriate decisions and drive the project forward to a successful conclusion. A possible organisation for the relocation of an insurance company's headquarters is shown in Figure 66 - 9.

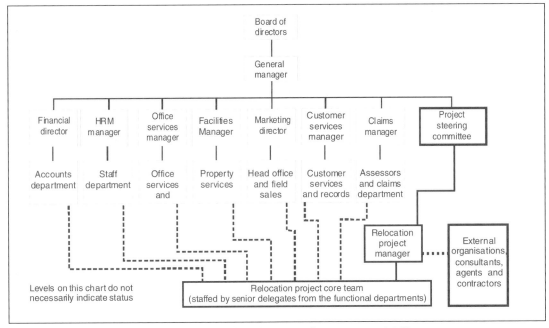

Figure 66 - 9: Possible Project Organisation for Relocation of a Group Head Office

Management Projects That Span Multinational Groups

A whole new dimension of project management is opened up when we consider projects conducted across multinational groups of companies. These projects might be concerned with marketing initiatives, global accounting procedure changes, reorganisation, mergers and acquisitions or other administrative changes. These projects often have a very high information technology content, when they will be led by IT professionals or at least will have an IT expert in a senior role. A common example occurred at the approach of the year 2000, when concern for the so-called millennium bug caused multinational groups to take seriously the possible risk to computer systems in all parts of the business, ranging across all computer-dependent procedures, technical processes and distribution logistics.

An international banking organisation might wish to change the way in which it handles customer accounts and alter its corporate reporting structures and, in the process, its customer service image. An international airline might decide to restructure its services and principal operating bases and destinations, possibly associated with the acquisition of another airline.

Group management have to make several important organisational decisions and take preliminary actions before embarking on any global project. They might, for instance, have to:

♦ Decide which member of corporate management should be responsible for supporting and guiding the project and issuing the necessary authorisations. This person might be regarded as the project champion

♦ Determine the office from which the project activities are to be coordinated and led. This might not always be group headquarters

♦ Provide the central office facilities

♦ Decide who is to lead the project (appoint a global project manager)

♦ Consider how the organisation should be set up at each regional or national centre or branch. Set up a project communication and reporting structure and name an official point of contact at each location

♦ Carry out public relations activities for internal and external stakeholders

♦ Arrange for local managers to receive training or retraining

Every regional or national centre will probably have its own project staff for the local implementation of the project. These people will perhaps be assigned on a temporary basis from the existing staff. A strong formal team might be appropriate at some locations while an informal functional matrix could be adequate for others. These projects bring problems on a new scale. There are multinational cultural issues. Much time will be spent in travel, with all its attendant fatigue and inconveniences. The project managers often have to overcome apathy, distrust or open hostility from managers or groups of people that consider themselves remote from group head office and like to maintain a semblance of independence.

Establishing Organisational Responsibilities

Before any project begins it is important to examine the work breakdown (see Session 30) and decide how work should be allocated across the organisation, determining who should bear the management responsibility for each work package or task. There are several tools that can contribute to the solution. In addition to the project organigram these include the organisation breakdown structure, linear responsibility matrix and (unless no direct labour or other resources are employed) an extension of the original time schedules to include resource scheduling.

Organisation Breakdown Structure and Information Flows

An organisation breakdown structure (OBS) is the logical way of allocating management responsibility across the organisation for all project work. An OBS also provides a basis for sorting, filtering and distributing project management information. The OBS (along with a cost breakdown structure) can be regarded as complementary to the work breakdown structure. However, defining the OBS is usually more difficult and complex because there are often several different ways of associating the organisational structure with the work to be done:

1   For a large project the organisation breakdown might be based on allocating a manager to each main work package. The organisation breakdown structure can then be arranged and coded to correspond with the work breakdown and cost breakdown structures. This is the most obvious first approach to defining the organisation breakdown structure in many cases. A railway development project, for example, might have separate managers responsible for the following work divisions:

- Surveying and route planning
- Estates and land acquisition
- Legal affairs
- Track and signalling
- Power generation and distribution

- Civil engineering, including earthmoving, bridges and tunnels
- Buildings, including passenger stations and offices
- Locomotives and rolling stock

2   A logical organisational breakdown could be made by looking at the trades or professional skills involved in the project and arranging the OBS according to the relevant functional managers.

3   Another approach is to categorise tasks by their nature, for example looking at responsibilities for approving drawings, authorising purchases and many other categories.

4   In addition to the lateral division of responsibilities between managers across the organisation (functional), there will also be a vertical structure (based on individual status). Just as the work breakdown structure is taken down in a series of levels until individual tasks are reached, so the organisation breakdown structure will have different levels of management and supervision. When taken to the limit, the lowest vertical level will contain the individuals who must actually perform the smallest day-to-day tasks.

In practice the OBS is likely to need a combination of substructures, overlaid in a complex criss-cross style that would be most difficult to chart. The first step is to analyse the organisation, consider all the substructures and decide how responsibilities should be allocated.

Then the information flows have to be considered, asking how much information each manager or supervisor needs and at what level of detail. The aim must be to filter and sort information from the masses of data available so that each manager receives only the information that he or she needs and wants to know.

Once the OBS requirements have been decided, a suitable project management computer package will be essential for processing, filtering, sorting and distributing data across the organisation breakdown structure. The related subjects of information management and communications are dealt with in Sessions 36 and 70, respectively but some of the tools can be described here.

Linear Responsibility Matrix

Matrix charts can be very useful in a number of project management applications. One, a document distribution matrix (who gets what) is illustrated and described in Lock (2000). A linear responsibility matrix chart is similar in approach to the document distribution matrix but is used for indicating those members of the organisation who have primary and secondary responsibilities for dealing with work packages or project tasks (who does what).

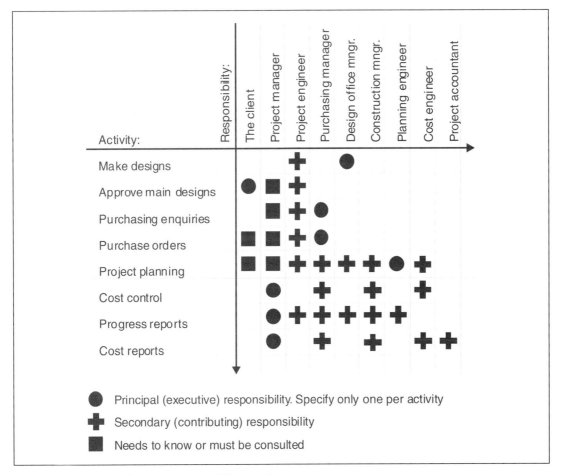

Figure 66 - 10: Part of a Linear Responsibility Matrix

Some writers tell us that the responsibility matrix chart includes all project activities. In a project with hundreds or thousands of activities the compilation of such a huge chart, not to mention keeping it up to date, would be a time-consuming, expensive, unnecessary and imprudent exercise. The chart need only list task categories, as shown in Figure 66 - 10.

Coding

All good project management software programs allow several codes to be appended to the computer record of every task in the schedule. Intelligently used, these codes allow computer reports to be filtered and sorted in a number of ways according to the information requirements of the organisation breakdown structure. Codes can be used to distinguish between the lateral form of the organisation (by selecting functional managers) and the vertical form (by directing information to people at different status levels). Some possibilities will now be described.

Resource Codes

If resource scheduling is to be used, all activities requiring resources will have resource information added to their records in the form of a short resource name or code plus the number of resource units estimated. Although the primary use of resource codes is for resource scheduling and management, those codes often align with functional departments and, with some software, can be used to filter data into sets that apply only to each relevant functional manager.

Departmental Codes

A more reliable method for filtering data according to departments is to give each departmental manager a code and add the relevant code to every task record. Most software has ample capacity for such codes.

Status Level Codes

Activity records can usually carry codes that indicate the status of the person who most needs to have information about a task. Such codes are therefore based on the organisational level for which data are to be filtered. Information can then be edited so that the most senior manager in the organisation receives summary reports containing only the most important tasks.

Milestone Reports

Activities or events designated as project milestones can be filtered exclusively for milestone reports, which is a common and reliable method for producing reports intended as summaries for senior members of the organisation.

Access Codes

When all the project data are held in the server files of an internal network, precautions have to be taken to prevent unauthorised access. This is to protect confidentiality and to prevent unauthorised tampering that might corrupt the database or the system. Again the solution is coding, but this time allocating codes or passwords to individuals in the organisation provides an answer. The project manager, for example, would probably have a code allowing free access to any information held in the system and would be allowed to enter progress data. More junior members of staff would be allowed access to information that they needed to know, and would also be given access for entering timesheet data. The project planner should have full access to the system, with freedom to change any part of the set-up.

Senior management would be allowed free read-only access to any data but would be denied freedom to make any change with one important exception. In multiproject resource models it is useful to provide a secondary file of the main model that allows senior managers to conduct what-if testing for strategic planning and testing. This is based on the assumption that senior managers will not have received the specialist training and daily use of the system that is essential if system changes are to be made without corrupting the live model. No harm can be done however if the model offered to them is a secondary file not connected to the main database, provided specifically for what-if strategic tests.

Activity or Task ID Codes

It is possible to design activity identifiers in the project critical path network diagram so that they contain coded information that can be used to sort and filter output reports according to the requirements of the OBS.

The Individual and the Organisation

The structure and behaviour of organisations makes a fascinating study that has exercised the minds of management theorists for centuries. It is a large and complex subject that cannot be covered in a single chapter. Any person faced with the task of setting up a new project organisation will probably find some difficulty in making a choice, and might receive conflicting advice. One question must always rank high in the argument, however, and that is 'How is a proposed organisation structure likely to affect and motivate the people working within it?' The answer to this question is not usually simple, not only because people themselves have different personalities, perceptions, aspirations and reactions but also because the organisation will exert different influences according to the roles that people are asked to fill.

There is, however, one piece of advice that can be offered in conclusion. That is to chart the proposed organisation and then look at the roles, one by one, imagining oneself fulfilling each of those roles. This exercise should ideally include the most important external stakeholder roles, especially the client. How would it feel, for example, to be a person working in an electrical engineering group in a balanced matrix organisation? You would be surrounded by people doing similar work on other projects, with good access to a departmental technical library, a chief engineer who can give technical advice, with prospects of promotion up the ladder to senior engineer and beyond. But you might be working on a task for one project (and one project manager) today and on a different project tomorrow.

Now switch the role to that of a project manager in the matrix. How would you view your chances of success; how easy would it be to communicate across the organisation and receive all the feedback reports that you would need? Then there are the needs of higher management, above the project organisation structure. How would you, as a general manager, feel that the proposed organisation would be likely to serve your own purposes and the corporate objectives?

References and Further Reading

Belbin, R.M., (1996) Management Teams: Why They Succeed of Fail, Butterworth-Heinemann, Oxford

Cleland, D. I., and King, W. R., (1998) Project Management Handbook, Van Nostrand Reinhold, New York

Harrison, F. L., (1992), Advanced Project Management: a Structured Approach, 3rd edn, Gower, Aldershot

Huczynski, A. and Buchanan, D.A., (2000), Organisational Behaviour: an Introductory Text, 4th edn, Prentice-Hall, Hemel Hempstead

Kerzner, H., (2000), Project Management: A Systems Approach to Planning, Scheduling and Controlling, 6th edn, Van Nostrand Reinhold, New York

Kliem, R. L. and Ludin, I. S., (1992), The People Side of Project Management, Gower, Aldershot

Meredith, J. R., and Mantel, S. J. Jnr., (1995), Project Management: a Managerial Approach, 3rd edn, Wiley, New York

Pinto, J. (ed), (1998), PMI Project Management Handbook, Jossey-Bass

Turner, J.R., Grude, K.V. and Thurloway, L., (1996), The Project Manager as Change Agent, McGraw-Hill, Maidenhead

Wearne, S., (1993), Principles of Engineering Organisation, Thomas Telford, London

67   ORGANISATION ROLES

Bill Carpenter

"A committee is a cul-de-sac down which ideas are lured and then quietly strangled."
Hilaire Belloc (1870-1953), French-born British writer. New Scientist (1973).

Introduction

This chapter describes a number of key and support roles in projects, outlining primary responsibilities and typical activities. These role descriptions should be seen as a guide, from which clear and agreed roles can be defined in general terms for an organisation and specifically for individual projects.

The chapter begins with an introduction to the reasons for the roles. This starts by looking at the cultural aspects of project management, with particular reference to issues of responsibility, authority and accountability. It then proceeds to expose a number of problems faced in projects which relate to roles.

The bulk of the chapter considers the roles of Project or Programme Sponsor, Project Manager and Project Team Member, beginning with how they integrate into a project structure. It also considers the roles of User and Stakeholder. A number of other, optional support roles are also mentioned briefly.

Context

Organisational Culture

In order to fully understand the roles and responsibilities of people involved on projects, it is first necessary to recognise the context in which they work. In particular, it should be recognised that project management involves a different culture to that associated with many 'day-job' activities. The Session on Organisational Structure has explored the cultural differences in some depth, so it is sufficient to rehearse here the aspects which have biggest impact on the roles.

Project Working is, by definition, a cross-functional team activity. This means that many of the roles must accommodate and promote this non-hierarchical 'we're all in this together' style of working.

Projects deliver change and that is not always welcomed universally. The roles major, therefore, on being catalysts for change.

Projects are subject to high levels of risk and variation. This must also be reflected in the roles.

All roles should be clearly defined. Some aspects may be generic and form a 'boiler-plate' job description. Others may vary from project to project depending on the type of work and the capabilities of the person fulfilling the role. In an ideal world we would, for instance, pick perfect project managers for all our projects and the role could be pre-defined. In the real world, we have to make adjustments to accommodate variances on a case by case basis.

As well as defining individual roles, the relationships between them also need to be established. This helps promote teamwork and ensures there are no gaps and any necessary overlaps are recognised and accepted.

Responsibility, Authority and Accountability

When discussing roles, we need to consider these three key aspects.

- Responsibility - The personal obligation taken on by someone - this implies a culture where saying "No" is acceptable
- Authority - The power someone has to make decisions and get things done. This forms part of the relationship structure which must ensure that all necessary authority is vested somewhere in the project and that the escalation routes to be used when an individual's authority runs out, are clear
- Accountability - The extent to which someone is 'held to account' for things. Sensibly, people can only be accountable for the things over which they have authority. If they can't influence it, we can't look to them if it goes wrong

Therefore, the accountability relationships are fully aligned with the authority relationship structure.

In the 'day-job' environment of largely procedural work, good job design suggests that people should be afforded a level of authority commensurate with their level of responsibility. This will basically ensure that things will get done. Therefore, aligning their accountability with their authority means that they are accountable for their entire area of responsibility.

In the project environment, people take on temporary roles and are asked to take on the responsibility for things over which they do not have full authority. This is a perfectly normal part of project working. It does however mean that they are not accountable for their full responsibility, just for their use of authority. We'll see how that works specifically when we explore the individual roles.

Problems

A focus on problems might seem to be a strange way to look at things and if I were to suggest that problems were just opportunities to develop solutions, you could be forgiven for a derisory laugh. The reality is, though, we often learn most from our mistakes and, in the true spirit of risk management, if you know what could go wrong, you can choose to take steps to avoid it (or not if it's not that big a deal).

In my many years of project management and from the many insights shared by my clients and course delegates, a number of recurrent themes arise.

Organisational Problems

Many of the problems identified to me are prefaced by, "They ...". This is a collective term for more senior people and, particularly, for strategy makers. Removing the rhetoric, we are left with some important issues:

- Insufficient organisational commitment - nobody 'owns' the project or the real 'need' for it. As a result, the project and all involved in it 'float around' at the mercy of, it seems, anyone who feels like dabbling in it
- Too many projects - projects just appear on the scene with little or no thought or justification, consuming vast quantities of time and money
- Prioritisation - two for the price of one; no prioritisation, so all projects get treated the same or prioritised on a 'who shouted loudest or last' basis; frequent priority changes, so people don't know whether they are coming or going
- Can't get the right resources - two again; everyone is too busy with their day job and the projects are treated as 'spare time' activities; the skills required by the project don't exist in the organisation

Role Problems

In many cases, the problems here stem frequently from a lack of recognition that project roles are different. This gives rise to:

- Role ambiguity - nobody is quite sure what they are doing and how that fits in with what other people are doing
- Lack of training - too many people are still given a piece of project management software (or not) and told to go and manage a project without sufficient training
- Lack of time - linked to the resource problem above, the amount of time needed to perform project management is often significantly underestimated

The Roles

Structure and Roles

All organisations need to integrate the key project management roles into their main organisational structure. How this is done will depend, to some extent, on the shape of the main structure. In all cases, the 'project' structure remains similar, as depicted in Figure 67 - 1. For all projects and programmes, a project or programme sponsor takes ownership at the strategic level and is responsible for delivering the organisational benefits. Reporting to the sponsor will be the project or programme manager, who takes responsibility for delivering the objectives. A programme manager heads up a team of project managers, one for each project. A Project Manager leads a team of experts who will support the project manager in managing and doing the project.

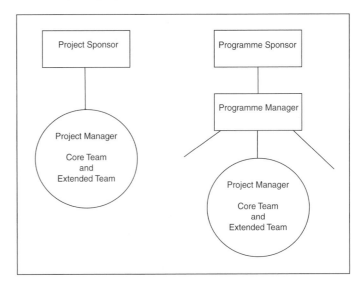

Figure 67 - 1: Project and Programme Structures

These structures ensure clear lines of authority allowing, for instance, the Project Manager to make decisions in line with clear boundaries of authority and accountability and have easy escalation to the sponsor for decisions outside those boundaries.

The programme or project sponsor serves as the direct link with the main organisational structure, at an appropriate strategic level. This linkage enables the sponsor to own the project/programme throughout the life cycle, as the change is achieved and as the benefits are delivered. The other roles in the project structure are temporary and drawn from the main structure or externally on the basis of knowledge and skill expertise. In this form of matrix, the management is 'folded back' into the main structure, ensuring that both project and 'day job' work is prioritised and supported in line with one set of consistent strategic objectives.

Different main structures will be more or less supportive of this project structure. One effect of this is in the level of authority that programme and project managers are given, typically less in role than in task cultures.

Project or Programme Sponsor

As stated above, the primary responsibility of the sponsor is to own the project or programme on behalf of the organisation and, therefore, to ensure the benefits are achieved. The sponsor thus has the authority of the organisation. The sponsor may need to engage another manager to actually get this authority enacted, but this should be largely mechanical assuming common strategic goals.

The sponsor is in a position to shape and maintain the appropriate strategic direction for the project in line with corporate needs and to identify and support its priority in the context of the overall organisational objectives.

The sponsor will select a project or programme manager in agreement with the individual and their functional manager. It is important to establish and agree levels of authority and accountability as early as possible.

During the project process, the sponsor oversees and pro-actively supports the manager, resolving escalated issues as quickly as possible. On completion of each phase of the project, the sponsor gives authorisation to proceed to the next one.

In carrying out the role the sponsor may need to refer to other people with knowledge and interest in strategic level issues. This will often be done in the context of a Steering Committee. In general, there are two common forms of this. One relates to issues mainly focused on the individual project or programme. The other relates to the integration of a number of projects and programmes sponsored from one 'strategic area' of the organisation.

For the individual project or programme, the steering committee will help the sponsor to understand a broad range of internal and/or external factors influencing the strategy of the project or programme. It is specifically not part of the project management structure.

Some organisations operate project/programme steering committees at each structural level where strategic goals reside. These committees do not form a hierarchy, but link into the main structure as described above for individual sponsors. This type of steering committee helps the sponsors ensure that projects are prioritised and maintained in alignment with strategic aims, taking customer and other contextual issues into account. They review the status of all their projects and programmes, acting as an additional level of escalation. This often enables issues to be resolved simply by considering solutions across a number of projects and programmes.

Any issue that cannot be resolved by the sponsor or steering committee is no longer a 'project' problem, but becomes a strategic problem to be resolved within the main organisational structure at whatever level necessary.

Project Manager

The primary responsibility of the Project Manager is to deliver the objectives of the project, on time and within budget. All aspects of the role must be focused on increasing the chances of that being achieved.

The first action of the project manager will be to recruit the core team. These members will assist the project manager by providing the total range of expert knowledge required to manage the project effectively. More details of this role are given in the next section.

The project manager's overall role can be divided into three main areas of focus:

1   Managing stakeholders
2   Managing the project process
3   Managing performance

Managing Stakeholders

Stakeholders are the key to a successful project. The Project Manager, assisted by the core team must first identify who they all are. Then they prioritise them by the extent to which the project is to be 'designed' to meet their particular needs. The level and method of communication will then be determined in accordance with this. The Project Manager must ensure that regular ongoing communication continues throughout the project, keeping the stakeholders informed and involved as apprpiate.

Managing the Project Process

The process used for managing projects may differ from organisation to organisation, but will generally follow an overall pattern of:

- What are we to do and why?
- How will we do it?
- Doing it
- Finishing it and learning from the experience

In the first stage, the project manager must ensure that the experts in the core team understand the needs and expectations and identify the right objective and scope. This may not be what was 'suggested' in the first instance. Even though the project manager is not responsible for delivering the benefits, it is important to support the experts in deciding on the objective and scope most likely to enable them to be achieved. During this important stage, the project manager must work to build the commitment of all involved. This stage also sees the beginning of ongoing risk management on the project.

During the 'how' stage, the project manager leads the team in compiling the work breakdown structure and project network, estimating and scheduling timings, costs and resources. It is vital to involve the extended team in this stage to continue building commitment. Next, the project manager will need to secure the budget and resources from within and outside the organisation. This may involve the team in some creative solutions to time, money and resource constraints.

Having completed this, the project manager will need to make the necessary arrangements for the project to be carried out, including establishing monitoring and control procedures and getting the sign-off for implementing the project.

While the project is under way, the project manager leads the team in monitoring the progress, costs, quality, risks and ongoing resource commitment on the project. This will enable the team to apply necessary control actions where variances require it. Current project data and action plans are used to update the plan and this forms a large part of ongoing communication with the stakeholders.

The final phase requires the project manager to make sure that handover and acceptance processes are in place and followed. Once the project is signed off, the project manager's main responsibility ends, although there will still be an involvement in tidying up loose ends (invoicing, disposal of facilities etc) and in conducting the post project evaluation. Then, of course, the team is thanked and disbanded (Party!).

Managing Performance

An important part of the project manager's role is in ensuring that everyone who has to do anything to support the project's success knows what is expected of them and carries it out to the correct quality, on time and within agreed costs. This includes all support activities as well as the tasks of the project.

This will probably require the project manager to have regular one to one reviews with the core team members and the project sponsor. In both cases, this will be a two-way process of ensuring that everyone is supporting each other in 'doing their bit' and, if anyone needs to improve their performance, there is a spirit of mutual open feedback.

Project Team Members

Project Team Members include the experts supporting the project manager in managing the project (core team) and the resources involved in conducting the tasks of the project (extended team). In both cases, the selection of team members is based mainly on the skills and knowledge required to perform the roles, not on their position in the organisation.

In many instances, the same people may perform both roles. Where this occurs, the project manager and the individual will need to make sure that both are being performed adequately. This will be greatly assisted by clear agreements of responsibilities, authority and accountability.

Core Team Members

Most of the core team will stay with the project throughout, although some may join the team only for the parts of the project in which their area of expertise is directly involved.

The core team may need to distance themselves to some extent from their 'home' departments so that they are not seen as representatives on the inside. Their primary role is to support the project manager in managing the project to meet its objectives, by providing the combined expertise to allow the project objectives and scope to be correctly identified and achieved.

Specific Core Team Member responsibilities may include:

- managing communication with some of the stakeholders
- managing sections of the work breakdown structure (identifying tasks, estimating, monitoring, problem solving, ensuring completion to quality, on time and within budget)
- managing some of the risks
- supporting the project manager and other team members in solving project-wide problems (this will include responsibility for actions from team meetings)
- contributing to the evaluation of the project at all stages

Extended Team Members

The Extended Team includes everyone who has to perform some activity on the project. Their primary responsibility is to achieve their own piece of work to the correct quality, on time and within cost. They are also members of the team and will, therefore, need to ensure that their work dovetails in with what others are doing.

In order to do this, they will need to get involved in the thinking and planning of the project; to identify work required; to clarify their input needs to the other team members who produce those inputs; to listen to the input needs of others whose work depends on their outputs. Also, during the planning, they will be required to estimate the times and costs for their work and, once overall project timing has been determined, commit to carrying out the work in agreed periods.

During the conduct of the work, extended team members will monitor and control their own work, as well as providing updates on quality, cost, time, resource and risk to the core team member responsible for their area of work. Although working nominally on their own, they need to remember they are part of a team and keep in contact with those who are affected by their activities.

On completion of work, they must inform the core team member and the user of their work outputs and together agree that the work is complete.

Extended team members will also contribute to the evaluation of the project during and at the end of the project.

Users

As the name suggests, the users are those people who are involved in the use of the project deliverables and outcomes. Their primary responsibility is in delivering the benefits of the project either to themselves or their organisation. There are broadly two categories of users to consider. First, the end users who sit at the end of the 'value chain' created by the project. They will often be members of the general public who use a product or service as customers. Second, the people who will operate and maintain the deliverables through their useful life.

The first group's responsibility is to themselves in getting benefit from the product or service provided. They may be consulted early on in the project to determine their needs and expectations, but often play little active role in the project.

The second group, on the other hand, may be very involved. As with the end users, they need to be involved in the early stages of the project to ensure that their knowledge and expertise of using what currently exists is taken into account in the formulation of the project objectives and scope. It is often they who know best what can and should be done to improve things.

During the project, the users will most probably be continuing to use what already exists. When the project starts to affect that - as changes are made or the existing is used to test out the new - they have a responsibility to support the integration of day to day operational work with the demands of the project.

Towards the end of the project, typically, there may be an extensive and intensive period of user involvement in piloting, trialling, testing and, ultimately, accepting the project outputs.

After this, their main role begins in using the project outputs to bring benefits to their organisation. At the beginning of this period they will be involved in project evaluation and again at 'Post Implementation Review' when the benefits are evaluated.

Stakeholders

As well as the most common and necessary project roles identified above and the specialised, 'as required', roles below, other stakeholders may have particular responsibilities on the project. This section does not attempt to cover these exhaustively, but to provide an indication of some that typically occur.

Provision of expert knowledge is one of the most common roles. An internal or external specialist or consultant may be called upon to advise on specific issues.

Expert skills will often be needed to carry out detailed testing.

Specialised services are sometimes required on projects. These may include training, facilitation, coaching or mentoring support, assessment and audit.

External suppliers are a common feature on projects, providing materials or additional resource.

The stakeholders whose needs are being met by the project, including the sponsor, have a particular role. They initially provide information to the team to enable them to determine the project objectives and scope. They provide approval at various stages to enable the project to proceed. They will need to accept the project once it is complete. In between times, they will need to engage with the communication process by providing feedback on the project reports and inform the project manager, in accordance with an agreed change procedure, of any project changes they require as a result of their altering circumstances.

Other Roles

This section deals with some of the other roles which may be required on projects.

Programme Manager

Where the extent of the change required is too large or dispersed to be conducted as one project, the Programme Manager role is added as shown in Figure 67 - 1. The role combines most of the facets of the Project Sponsor and Project Manager roles, providing strategic guidance for each of the individual projects and co-ordinating between those projects to ensure overall success.

Project Co-ordinator

This role basically provides support to the project manager and core team in covering those activities related to ensuring that parts of the project carried out in different areas (departments, sites, countries) are integrated properly.

Project Support Officer

I hesitate to say 'making the tea', but this is very much about supporting the project manager and core team in all sorts of ways. Some specific areas might include:

* Managing the information system
* Maintaining the project network
* Processing data to provide consolidated information
* Compiling and despatching reports

Quality Manager

Responsible for ensuring that relevant quality standards and procedures are identified and adhered to. May conduct spot checks of actual quality as part of a quality assurance process, but will reinforce the fact that quality is everyone's responsibility.

Configuration Manager

Will manage the configuration management system, ensuring that all documentation and other configuration items have been identified and are being controlled. Responsible for the upkeep of the master record index.

Resource Manager

Responsible for allocating resources (people, equipment, facilities) to projects in accordance with organisational priorities. That said, will need to be flexible in supporting the project managers in solving specific resource problems. Also maintains a shared responsibility with the project manager for managing the performance of their resources.

Procurement Manager

Ensuring that all procurement on the project is carried out in accordance with organisational and project-specific guidelines. Where this is detrimental to the success of the project, will work with the team to identify, evaluate and seek approval for alternative approaches.

Administrator

Another fairly wide-ranging role, primarily focused on keeping the team's 'wheels oiled'. This may include taking and issuing minutes of meetings, receiving, sorting and distributing incoming information.

Planner

Facilitating the team in creating the project plans at a variety of levels of detail as required by various other roles. Supporting the team with analysis of 'what if' scenarios for risk management and evaluation of problem solving options. Updating the plans based on current data and corrective action plans.

Cost Manager

Supporting the team in identifying task costs. Collating the project budget. Collating and reporting ongoing cost data. Ensuring the project is run in accordance with organisational financial rules.

Summary

It is vital, if projects are to be consistently successful, that roles and responsibilities are established at the outset. This is not least due to the many organisational and role-related problems that can occur on projects.

Exactly what these roles entail will be, to some extent, dependent on the organisation and the project. However, this chapter has outlined some of the typical key and support roles found in many instances.

For all roles, it is important to recognise the context and culture of managing projects. For instance, projects imply cross-functional team working, achievement of change and increased levels of risk.

When defining responsibilities (what the person has agreed to do), it is also important to define levels of authority (power to get things done) and accountability (extent to which use of authority must be justified). In the project environment, authority is often much less than responsibility would seem to demand. A clear structure, providing a framework for authority and accountability relationships is needed.

The Roles and Their Primary Responsibilities

- Project or Programme Sponsor - deliver the project benefits, owning it on behalf of the organisation over its entire life cycle. This includes maintaining the strategic focus, giving authorisation and resolving issues escalated by the Project Manager
- Project Manager - deliver the right project objectives to enable the benefits to be achieved. This will involve managing stakeholders, the project process and people's individual and team performance
- Project Team Members - core team members will take responsibility for managing elements of the project; extended team members will take responsibility for doing elements of the project
- Users - primarily responsible for elements of work in the phase of the project when the benefits are achieved. They will certainly be involved early on to identify their needs and may be involved later in testing and accepting the project deliverables
- Stakeholders - may perform a variety of support activities
- Other roles - a number of other support roles may be necessary, depending on the requirements of the project/programme.

Section 7

People

70   COMMUNICATIONS

Bob Saunders

"I know you believe you understand what you think I said, but I'm not sure you realise that what you heard is not what I meant."
Anon.

Preface

I am indebted to the reviewers, Dave Hawken, Dave Webster and to the APM Pathways Core Review panel and its Chair, Dennis Lock for their useful and helpful comments. I hope I have done them justice. My grateful thanks are also due for material provided by Dave Hawken.

Introduction

This chapter is aimed at promoting the idea of the importance of good communications.

The discussion is not to be taken as written on tablets of stone, but rather points to use for discussion and points to reflect upon, and to use to improve the communications in the organisation. The objectives of this chapter are to:

- To provide a vehicle for discussion of the topic of 'Communications'
- To explore different types of communications, different media, and different channels
- To produce for thought and reflection some of the problems in providing clear communications
- To provide some suggestions for improving communications
- To explore the message, the media, channels, barriers and possible 'ways ahead'

Related Topics in the BoK

- All topics are enriched by good communications
- Communications is of particular relevance to the rest of Section 7, 'People'
- There are strong and significant links with Session 36, 'Information Management'

Defining 'Communications'

'Communication' is: 'The imparting or exchange of information, ideas or feelings'. (Most dictionaries) As the 'Pathways' Glossary states - 'the transmission of information so that the recipient understands clearly what the sender intends'. At this juncture I must say that I do not disagree with the BoK authors and others, who see Information and its management as being part of communication, and therefore worthy of consideration in this chapter. I would however suggest that Information Management is an important topic of its own, and would refer readers to Session 36, and the chapter written there.

The Importance of Communications

Communications were (are or will be) always the most important part of human interaction. However we accomplish it, over whatever distance, it is communication which makes us what we are, and enables us to do the things we want or need to do to be 'human' in the sense of working together co-operatively to accomplish what we could not do on our own. For example, pre-historic men must have found it very helpful to be able to communicate with each other when they were trying to catch lunch! (Stonor &Wankel 1986)

As project managers, (1) we need to communicate in order to carry out our planning, organising, leading and controlling functions. (2) It ought to take up much of our time. (3) It ought always to be two ways. (4) People respond differently to communications, and to the forms used to communicate. Project Managers need to be aware of this! (5) A project manager needs to develop good networking skills. As the authors above suggest, communication (as they define it) gives us three essential points:

1   Understanding communication means understanding how people relate to each other
2   People have to agree on the definition of the terms they use
3   Communication is symbolic, gestures, sounds, letters,

numbers; words can only approximate and represent the ideas they are meant to communicate

The authors said that these are the most important basic facts about interpersonal communications. Everything else, although important, is secondary. Get this right; understand what is being said and communication is possible! The actuality of what is communicated depends on the objectives that someone might lay out to achieve through communicating. An example of this in the project management business could be the marketing experts 'to inform the designer of the technical specification required by a product'. Success in reaching this objective would be measured by the degree of the understanding of the designer. But, because the objective is not only to impart the information but also to motivate the designer into doing the design, the designer has to believe in and accept that specification, and to know that the specification is appropriate. If the designer gets the idea that the product is irrelevant, motivation will not occur. So, communication is also about influencing, persuading or motivating. (Brooks 1982)

The Communication Process

The simplest model is that there is a sender, which sends a message to a receiver, who feeds back a response. But reality is, as ever, rather more complex than this as can be seen in Figure 70 - 1, and below.

This diagram is deceptively simple in appearance. Firstly, it is only one way; secondly the symbols and rules are not trivial (The worlds' philosophers argue about them eternally) and thirdly, the whole communication process needs to be thought through.

Take a face-to-face situation. You as sender might want to say something. You arrange words into sentences in your mind, then you try to repeat them - your 'encoder' or 'message sender' is your mouth. Have you ever noticed that what you say is not always what you think? This is the first incidence of 'noise' or 'interference/distortion'. Then the sound travels through the air (more 'noise') to the ear of the

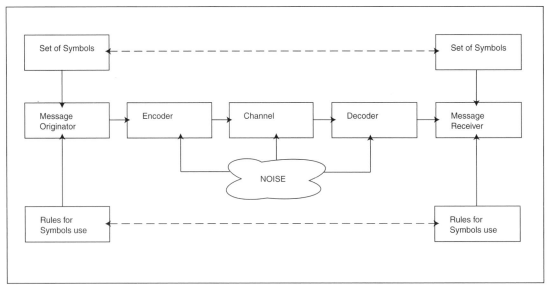

Figure 70 - 1: Model of a Generalised Communication System

receiver, his/her 'decoder' or 'message receiver' in this situation. The words are passed (and there may well be 'noise' here) to the brain, which does the 'interpreting'. Now, when you insert telephones, microphones, keyboards, screens into this process, you may well wonder how we manage to communicate at all. (In some respects, direct mind-to-mind communication or Telepathy, could be likened to the Holy Grail of communicators!)

And remember that when B becomes the source, and A the receiver, as must happen, then the whole thing is reversed. So, let us explore all this a little further.

Communications Media

There are many different media, these are the basic set:

1   Oral, using language at some level, face-to-face. This rates as the most successful form of communication. It includes meetings, seminars, debates even gossip

2   Oral, using language, through telephone or similar instruments. The telephone, (a replacement for face-to-face communication) in contrast offers only 30 per cent

of the 'communication' potential, as it lacks visual cues and the bandwidth of the speech is severely limited. Most of the missing 70 per cent represents non-verbal communication, which of course only face-to-face can provide. (Video-conferencing helps to replace some of what is missing, if not all. One can move one's eyes, but not a fixed camera!)

3   Visual, via writing or mechanical typing, memos, letters, minutes, notices, reports, or via signals such as Morse code. Also, pictures and diagrams

4   Non-verbal, a type of visual communication by body language, expression, gesture and the arrangement of visual cues (even such things as furniture arrangement)

5   Electronic, a hugely growing source of communications techniques mainly 'writing' in terms of fax or e-mail, but also via video screens, tele-conferencing, and more recently net meetings, internet and intranet. All of these can also be used for seminars, meetings, debates and gossip

6   Written, via mail, notice boards, and newsletters, printed or electronic

What to Use, and When?

What medium you use depends on circumstances:

Quicker Methods

- One-to-one - praise, blame, briefing
- Department/project meeting - briefing, again, praise or blame, generally
- Organisational meeting - often motivational
- Gossip - to get feelings, and information quickly disseminated

Any of these can be face-to-face or electronically conducted.

Slower Methods

- Letters
- Magazines

- Newsletters - to provide information and perhaps social matters
- Organisational cascaded briefings (Garrett (1973))

But the medium is far less important than the message. All of these media have but one purpose, to communicate with other people, to 'pass a message'.

Channels

All these media require 'channels' to carry the information. The channels can be formal, informal, one-to-one, network, up/down/across an organisation, or some subset of all of them. They can also be physical or structural.

A. Physical Channels

In face-to-face, the channel is the air between the respondents. In a telephone conversation, it is the instruments and the wire. With visual media, it is the air, vacuum, or wires, and then screens. So there is a multitude of channels, each with its own way of reducing 'communication' by introducing 'noise' and each needs careful use for the best results. (Hodgetts 1979) The basic rules given earlier apply in all circumstances.

B. Structural Channels

Within an organisation, another meaning of 'channels' is required, because we introduce 'direction' into the equation. We speak of communicating 'upwards' to senior management, 'across' to colleagues, 'down' to subordinates. There may be formal channels (or 'reporting chains') or less formal 'gathering around the drinks machine', or even 'gossip' (a very efficient method of communicating some sorts of information). Each of the above directions brings it's own channel and its own preferred degree of formality of communication. Daft (1995) suggests that the formal channels are: -

(i) Downward communication

This refers to messages from senior management to subordinates. These messages will usually be about:

1 Implementation of goals, strategies and objectives
2 Job instructions and reasons
3 Procedures and practices
4 Performance feedback
5 Motivation

Major problems can arise from the loss of information that occurs each time a message is passed from one person/department to another. (It is said to be about 25 per cent a time!) You may remember the old saw about the message passed from person to person, started as 'We are under fire, send reinforcements' and finished as 'We're in the custard, send 37 pence.' (Or something like that! Stand your team in a line and do a 'whisper' message passing exercise. The bigger the team, the more you will lose! It really is a fun game!)

(ii) Upward Communication

Messages flow from the lower to the higher levels. Many organisations will make efforts to facilitate communication in this direction:

1 Problems and exceptions
2 Suggestions for improvement
3 Performance and progress reports
4 Grievances and disputes
5 Financial and accounting information

(iii) Horizontal Communication.

These consist of the lateral or diagonal exchange of messages among peers or co-workers, within or across departments. They usually inform, but also solicit help, and are used to coordinate effort:

1　Intra-departmental problem solving
2　Inter-departmental co-ordination
3　Staff advice to line departments

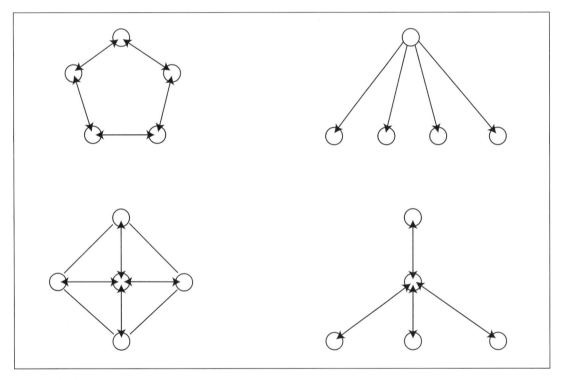

Figure 70 - 2: Communication Networks

There are other, recognised structures for communication, see Figure 70 - 2 for a few examples of different 'networks'. But, we now need to consider what humanity can do to attempt to communicate.

Communicating and its Problems

Communication is not easy. Just as there are many ways in which it can be accomplished, so there are many ways to disrupt it. I think it was Napoleon who complained about his cough ('Ma sacre toux'), and caused the death of some hundreds of people because it sounded like 'massacre tout'.

A. Abstraction

Using language to communicate is not always easy. Abstraction is what happens when a communication is shortened by leaving out a piece which is well known to the sender, and deemed to be well known by the recipient. For example, 'Come to my place, 9am tomorrow' sounds easy enough, but there are three abstractions in that statement. (1) 'at Number 9, Blob Lane' (2) 'the 3rd of June' (3) 'to collect the papers we have just discussed.' A trivial example, but it does show what can be left out of a communication.

B. Inference

Inference refers to assumptions made by a listener/receiver that may or may not be accurate. If interpretation of facts becomes necessary, inference may well appear, and this quite often causes major communications breakdown.

For example, ' Come and pick me up!' The inference here is that it is to collect the person, or to meet and move on. It could also be to physically pick up and move the person, but that is not the immediate inference. Inferences are often caused by other peoples' abstractions, of course.

C. Redundancy

Using repetitive language, repeating an instruction in a different form is a way of improving communications. Redundancy is also achieved by using multiple paths to transmit a communication. (for instance, using different media) This could be something as simple as saying 'you're a good chap' and at the same time smiling and shaking his hand. One of these communications ought to have been enough, but the use of three enhances the message and makes 'communication' of the basic point more certain.

D. Perception

Personal perception is the way one makes sense of the environment, but it is not always accurate. (Daft , 1995) We screen and select objects and stimuli which catch our attention, and organise or categorise them according to our 'frame of reference'. This is known as 'perceptual organisation'. For example, stereotyping, where one makes a generalisation about a group of people on the basis of one or few categories, for instance, race, age or occupation.

Perceptual differences and mistakes occur when people perceive objects or other stimuli in dissimilar ways. They are natural, but can cause communications to fail. An example might be sending a young accountant and a young chemist for a 'balance'. Who might return with what?

There are also non-verbal equivalents to perceptual discrepancy, through actions and behaviour, though generally, non-verbal communication is less troublesome in this respect. One can generally believe what one sees! For example. 'Well done mate, good idea' when accompanied by an unhappy expression, a red, perspiring face might well mean 'damn it all, that was my idea in the first place!'

E. Listening

Listening is actually part of communication, because communication is always a two way process. Much of the headings in this section, notice, refer to both sending and receiving. Listening is being at the receiving end, where one has to convert the symbols and messages being received into something that one understands. One can listen attentively, selectively, pretend, or ignore! Listening is a skill to be learned. Daft (1995) suggests that there are specific techniques such as asking questions, paraphrasing, not being distracted, making mental summaries, feeds back to the sender by nods, by showing interest, eye contact, judging only the content, not the delivery, and that not until the presentation is complete. All these will help to improve the listening ability.

F. Language

The language in use needs to be common to the people to be involved. But 'We all speak English, don't we?' is not an adequate approach. A major constraint on communications is difference in culture and this may mean quite simply people from different professions (as in my earlier example) where people use simple words differently, giving them different meanings. This is also relevant where different English speaking nationalities are working together. American - (versus English) - English is a case in point. One cannot take it for granted that the two nationalities understand the same things from the same words and phrases, because in many instances, they do not! Here is where differences in culture begin to make an appearance. I have mentioned it in terms of different professions and industries earlier. Here, I am thinking in terms of nationalities and Hofstede (1994) suggests that if people speak different languages entirely then even a good knowledge of -say- English is not enough to guarantee that communication occurs. The same state of affairs arises when jargon and slang raise their heads.

I had some years working in NATO. There, fourteen nations, as many languages and many different disciplines try to communicate, sometimes under stressful conditions. The need for good communications there are paramount!

G. Communications in Teams

Communicating with your team is where it becomes interesting and difficult for project managers. What is discussed here is relevant. Good communications between team members means a higher degree of synergy and it is this that drives the team towards success. If you study the other chapters of Section 7, the importance of 'good communication' will become apparent as being paramount. Try to improve your team communications. Use the ideas given later in this chapter, write an internal communications plan to go with your plan to communicate outside the project and use it, take note of the '10 Commandments' and *USE THEM*.

H. Communications in Meetings

Whether face to face or through a videoconference, meetings are where one needs to overcome some of the problems of human interaction. Different perceptions, language, 'noise', distrust and all the others detailed here. It takes some effort and planning. Rules such as 'Quaker' - no response to a statement for at least 10 seconds, to restate the previous viewpoint before moving on without evaluating it, to discuss the problem, not some one else's suggestion, to empathise, not remaining neutral, to treat people as equals, to make provisional suggestions, not arrogate certainties to one's self. (Stonor & Wankel 1986)

Good communications really depends on the Chair, mainly through ensuring clear objectives, good and thorough preparation, ensuring full participation by those present, encouraging a clash of ideas, asking senior staff to wait until the rest have their say, giving credit where it is due, summing up, setting actions in a positive way and lastly, following up. (Daft 1995) So, where the Project Manager usually chairs meetings, be aware of the ideas set out above. Good communications at meetings can contribute to project success in a very real way.

Specific Barriers to Communications

Communications is often not done very well. If you go to a lecture, you will retain about 50 per cent, but after two weeks, only 25 per cent will be left. A study of 100 US firms revealed that as information was passed from level to level, less and less of the original was recalled. At the 'shop floor (about six levels down) it stood at 20 per cent of the original. Another study suggests a 44 per cent loss at each level!

Handy (1985) has a considerable, and rich, section on this topic. He suggests that there seems to be two types of barrier. Firstly, psychological, related to the attitudes of the people involved and the personal characteristics of sender and receiver and secondly technical barriers, the way the communication process is organised and structured.

Perhaps one of the most common barriers to communication is linked with the idea that 'having information is having power.' People with information are trying, often, not to impart too much. Those without information are trying to extract the maximum. All of which depends on their worldview and perspective.

Below, I will introduce some examples of the two types of barrier, but do note that there are many others!

Psychological Barriers

I will discuss some of the very many major causes of barriers arising from our day-to-day interaction with other people. After all, when people can transmit information assertively, aggressively, passively, or in an informal manner, and be received in any of the ways discussed, how does the human race ever manage clear, good communication? This whole topic might well appear to be a minefield, and I suppose that it can be. Ways round the problems will be discussed later.

A. Perception

'Perception' has been mentioned before, but there are specific barriers to communication caused by perceptual difficulties. People tend to absorb information that is relevant to their function, and relate to it better where the implications of knowing that information are explained first. This is a perception concern, because it is the view of the people in that situation, not an external notion of what is important. For example, if a designer has a concern to produce high quality, then his/her interest might be caught if the information concerns a way of improving quality.

B. Dislike

If the receiver dislikes the sender then one is less likely to listen, or to take the sender seriously. In discussion of a particular aspect, the concern might be to score debating points, rather than making a proper case.

C. Lack of Credibility and/or Respect of the Sender

Respect for a person, and their technical expertise will engender a positive listening attitude. If we want to get people to listen, we might try to ensure that our expertise in that topic is known before the discussion.

D. Perceptual Bias

The listener hears what they want to hear. e.g. At an interview, if the interviewer likes the interviewee on first acquaintance, then the interviewer needs to be aware that this might lead to the interviewee being accepted as a 'good prospect' without the careful exploration normally applied.

E. Defensiveness

Again, defensiveness is due to perceptual bias, this time arising from people giving us information about ourselves. If the information does not accord with our own self-image, then it is likely to be rejected. From there, all sorts of problems will arise. There will be accusations of irrationality and tempers may well be raised. If the receiver gets the impression of being evaluated, judged or controlled or if the sender is perceived as having a devious stratagem, then the defensiveness will be redoubled.

G. Neutrality

A clinical, detached approach by the sender will also produce defensiveness. The receiver gets the feeling that they are a 'case', not even human!

H. Dogmatism

Being dogmatic is about not taking account of other people's opinion. Receivers will defend their own view much more strongly and an impasse will result.

J. Bad News Syndrome

No one likes bad news and receivers will resent it, especially, as is often the case, the only communication they ever receive is negative. (Quite often occurs in organisations).

Technical Barriers

Even if the psychological barriers are not there, there are purely technical reasons for communication barriers.

A. Lack of Clarity

This arises through the use of technical terms and jargon. This does not help if you are trying to communicate with people outside your project.

B. Lack of Logical Structure

This may well prevent the receiver from being able to pick out which is important from communications received.

C. Overload

This happens when too much information is sent, and the receiver is unable to pick out the most significant items. 'Overload' can be minimised where computer communications are concerned through filtering and sorting activities. Otherwise, tact and diplomacy are perhaps important.

D. In-industry 'Language'

Language difficulties are not just about speaking another tongue. This is also about the different jargon different disciplines use. As project people, working in interdisciplinary and/or international situations, we need to be sensitive to this.

Using 'industry' in the widest possible sense, each skill, discipline or trade has its own language. It is basically in English in this country, but it is often quite incomprehensible to people from outside this profession. This is of some importance in cross discipline teams, where, by their very nature, they will have members from different trades or professions. For the individual, this requires some knowledge and understanding of those working around him/her. For the project manager it means knowing the language of all the different disciplines in the team, and being able to make themselves understandable to them all. This can be difficult enough even at the language level, but there are cultural differences which cause enormous differences in viewpoint, and these have to be taken into account as well.

A prime example might be, in a manufacturing environment is mixing designers with those trying to build their design. The language/culture differences are immense. Again, as an engineering project manager, it can be very difficult to communicate with an accountant. The viewpoints are entirely different, even if the objectives are similar. (This is not necessarily the case!)

I have discussed barriers to communication, and will later provide some suggestions on how to improve matters. Firstly, I want to consider other reasons for poor communications that, in themselves may well lead to these barriers being present.

More Barriers

A. Culture

This has been mentioned already, in relation to industries, but it is worth exploring this a little further. Many of us are involved with cross-cultural projects these days, especially with the globalised organisations that now abound. Not only are we dealing with people from other countries, we often do not ever meet them face-to-face!

Hodgetts (1979) suggests that we need to be aware of customs, religious beliefs, social relationships, value systems, tastes and temperament, both in general, and where they result in specific significant elements. Stonor & Wankel (1986) talk of race and gender, values and customs in terms of socio-cultural variables and quote the French as having more formal relationships than the Americans. Their major point is that it is essential to identify the implications of all these differences. Both national and organisational cultures will affect communication, and the way it is carried out. The project manager therefore has to know what is faced in the parent organisation, and others in the project environment. Are relationships formal or informal, are the structures hierarchical or flat? Do they support communications (and feedback) well, or not?

Daft (1995) mentions that some cultures ('High context', mainly Eastern) communicate to build up personal social relationships, and that for them meaning is derived from context, setting, status and non-verbal behaviour. The group is more important than the individual. Other cultures ('low context', European and Western) use communications to exchange facts and information. The meaning is derived from the words, the individual is more important than the group.

What does this mean for the project manager? It means, as I said earlier when I was discussing cultural differences between the disciplines within an organisation, that the team and the project manager has to become aware, early on in the life of the project of the complexities of the relationships between members of his/her staff, and their relationships with the project manager. When dealing with other cultures, one cannot take an ethnocentric or monocultural stance.

B. Nationality

This is best thought of in the wider context of culture. The difference in language only covers up the more fundamental differences to be found under that heading.

C. Security

If security matters to an organisation, then communications could well be less than open or free. As a project manager, there may well be times when you are unable to communicate, as you would like. It means being aware that the situation exists and perhaps living with it is the only option. What ever you do to improve, communications needs to be acceptable to those who set the security level, so you need to communicate with them!

Good Practice - Improving Communications

Be as open and free with your communications as you can. Use multiple channels, multiple media, remember that good communications is one of the most important, indeed critical success factor. Tailor your medium and channel to the person receiving your communication we are all different! Remember to use a medium that meets the needs of the situation. An e-mail to warn of an approaching fire would not be suitable! Given below is 'The Ten Commandments of Good Communication', first proposed by Richards & Nielander, in 'Readings in Management' (1958) (See either Stoner & Wankel(1986) or Hodgetts (1979)) This list has proved to be a worthwhile checklist over the years, and is quoted by many management writers.

A. Ten Commandments for Communications

1   Clarify ideas before communicating
2   Examine the true purpose of communication.(What do you really want to say?)
3   Take the entire environment, physical and human into consideration
4   When valuable, obtain advice from others in planning reports
5   Be aware of the overtones and undertones as well as the basic content of the message. (If it is said, the receiver will be affected, not only by the words used, but by the way it is said.)
6   When possible, convey useful information. (Useful to the individual receiver)
7   Follow up on communications. (Solicit feedback)
8   Communicate with the future, as well as the present, in mind
9   Support words with deeds. (If your message is to set a time and perhaps to complain about others being late, then be there on time!)
10 Be a good listener. (As you do, your sender will have not only explicit things to say, but also implicit things. Listen for these!)

So, plan your communication, but first perhaps, for the project manager as for any manager, there ought to be a plan of your projects' communications, their channels, perhaps the media to be used and the targets for your communications. Perhaps you need to set up a proper strategy for your communications. There are many models to be used, the one given below comes with recommendations. (Do remember that your communications strategy and subsequent plan will be designed around your project, and therefore are likely to be unique to that project. (Not that you could not use it to form the basis of a new one later!)

A communications strategy will require some meetings with the team, but you might also like to consider firstly asking the team the question 'what do we want to achieve from communications?' This might well include making a list of your stakeholders, and their communications requirements. The best way of obtaining their requirements might be to send out a survey. If you choose these later ideas, then your first meeting would help to formulate your stakeholder list, and the wording for the survey. Then, to complete the strategy, with this information to hand, the structure might be: -

1   Executive Summary - What needs to be done, and why
2   Where are we now? - A summary of the present status
3   What can be done to improve? - The strategy is not a 'one-off' occasion. Repeat it once in a while, and you will find that Number 3 assumes monumental proportions of importance!
4   Who are the audiences? Your stakeholders?
5   What media should we use?   And remember the enormous choice available to you
6   How do we measure the effectiveness of our communications?

There are other questions to answer in this plan. One is 'How do we communicate the important aspects of the business case?' (A matrix is suggested, business objective against communications objective) another, 'What are the barriers and drivers to communications?' (SWOT is suggested here), and lastly 'What do we need to plan our communications?'

So, we come to the idea of a 'Communications Plan'. It is a project document like any other you will prepare, and to my mind it is as, if not more, important to the success of your project than many others. Remember that yours will be unique to your project, and may well differ from this template. This is of no consequence, as long as it does the job properly. That job is enabling you to plan the communications scenario for your project.

B. Communication Plan

Just as one would plan a schedule or resource usage, so one should plan the way one is to communicate, both within and without the project:

Figure 70 - 3 provides a useful template, but do not forget, it is not set in concrete! It can be changed to suit particular circumstances.

Communication Plan.

1. Executive Summary
2. The key messages:
   - Mission/vision
   - Business plan objectives
   - People issues
3. The audience.
   - All team members
   - Senior management
   - Other departments & sites
   - Customers
   - Contractors
4. Communications methods
   - Face-to-face.
   - Cascade briefings. (Senior manager briefs next level, which briefs next level etc.)
   - Full-team briefings.
   - Paper notices/minutes/memos
   - Electronic communications, web site, 'project notice board', e-mail.
5. Feedback routes
6. Define responsibilities
7. Define measurement system.
8. Construct timing chart.

Figure 70 - 3: Model Communication Plan

Conclusions

So, there it is. I would like to add a set of basic and general points to remember which will act towards the provision of good communication, especially about 'change'. They are very simple, and that is the way it ought to be. Keeping things simple is always a good idea.

Good Communications

A. The message

Have a clear, common message. Write it down, so that it will not change under stress. Give your people time to understand it, question it and absorb it.

B. The content

Be clear about the reasons for change and be prepared to justify it, declare a positive aim, and identify the approaches to be used to implement the change.

C. Timing

Communicate as far ahead as possible, to give people time to absorb it. If this is not possible, communicate and do it. Whichever, ensure that no one is left out.

D. The people

Ensure that the message is given in the right way, at the right level in the right language.

References and Further Reading

J Stonor & C Wankel, 'Management', Prentice Hall, New Jersey 1986 *
R Hodgetts, 'Management Theory & Process', Saunders, Philadelphia, 1979
R Daft, 'Understanding Management', Dryden Press, Orlando, 1995 *
C Handy, 'Understanding Organisations', Penguin, London 1993.
G Hofstede, 'Cultures & Organisations', Harper Collins, London 1994 *
F Brooks, 'The Mythical Man-Month' Addison Wesley, Philippines, 1982

* = major reference

Figures
1. T301, 'Complexity, Management and Change', Block 2, fig.19, Open University 1984.
2. Inspired by Exhibit 14.8,R Daft, (1995) as above.

71   TEAMWORK

Charles Egbu and Christopher Gorse

"The world is made of people who never quite get into the first team and who just miss the prizes at the flower show."
Jacob Bronowski (1908-1974), Polish-born British scientist, poet, and humanist. The Face of Violence (1954).

Introduction

Projects are becoming increasingly complex, requiring multidisciplinary teams comprising of specialists and consultants from different organisations. The management and development of project teams needs considerable thought. Managers must understand how individuals perform when they become members of teams. How the team will influence the individual and how the individual can influence the team need to be given due cognisance. Managers must recognise and understand how the nature of the task and the structure and organisation of the team can affect the performance of the group. As well as motivating the group members, using established techniques; the group's culture, cohesiveness, types and levels of conflict, leadership, structure, communication and style of management can influence the effectiveness of a team. Team members must have the capabilities, skills, knowledge, competence and social awareness that allows them to integrate their specialist attributes with others so that members complement one another. Managers must be aware of this relationship, developing and fostering an environment and culture that facilitates effective teamwork.

Other Body of Knowledge topics that cover closely related matters are Communication (70), Leadership (72), Conflict Management (73), Negotiations (74) and Human Resource Management (75)

Defining a Team

Teams usually have a specific performance objective or recognised goal that is shared by team members. The members' activities are co-ordinated, facilitated or directed by individual group members and leaders. Individual members of project teams are usually brought together because of their complimentary skills and knowledge that is required for the task.

According to Conti and Kleiner (1997), a team has "two or more people; it has a specific performance objective or recognised goal to attain; and co-ordination of activity among the members of the team is required for the attainment of the team goal".

An ideal concept of a team is that described by Ingram, et al, (1997, p.120)

"... a special sort of group which voluntarily unites the members towards mutually-held objectives ... [They are] focused groups which exhibit a unitary perspective"

Organisation and Team Performance

Teamworking is often viewed as a much favourable alternative to individuals working in isolation, teams and groups producing more and better solutions to problems (Ingram et al, 1997). Teams can achieve things that individuals can't. However, the way a group is organised and structured can have major effects on the group's performance (Shaw, 1970). Occasionally people can perform better on their own than when they are with others in a group. For many tasks, the mere presence of others stimulates levels of arousal and excitation that results in increased performance (Brotherton, 1999). When performing simple or well-learned tasks people perform better in the presence of others. The presence of others can also be a distraction, affecting concentration and reducing performance. Where tasks are difficult, but achievable by one person, and require high levels of concentration the presence of others may impair performance. The nature of each task and its demands on the group's skills, knowledge, intellectual ability and manual input must be considered in detail. A task may have different aspects requiring individuals to undertake one part in isolation and then come together as a group to perform other activities.

Problem solving is an activity that benefits from people working alone and coming together as a group

Often people come together; meeting in a group, to solve problems when the problems would be better dealt with by individuals. Many problem solving and decision making groups waste time dealing with trivial problems that can be dealt with simply by one or two members. When making decisions or solving problems different types of structural arrangement can increase the efficiency and effectiveness of the process. Research has shown that certain types of tasks are better dealt with by one person using formal channels of communication rather than openly interacting with all members of a team. When dealing with simple problems or queries it is more effective to feed the information to a single person who is responsible for a particular area allowing them to make the decisions on their own. A large number of simple requests or problems can be dealt with by one person quickly and effectively without them suffering from information overload. If occasional decisions are slightly more complex, other people can be contacted as and when necessary. However, with complex issues and problems, groups have been found to perform better when problems are openly discussed between members (Stewart, 1999; Procter & Mueller, 1999). If complex information and problems are sent through formal channels to one central person they may not have the range of knowledge, experience or skills to solve the problem. In situations where individuals deal with large quantities of complex issues they are susceptible to information overload.

Some problematic tasks are better dealt with by individuals working the task through on their own and then coming together as a team. An example of a situation where advantages are gained from individuals working through problems in isolation before coming together as a group is brainstorming (Brown, 2000). Brainstorming involves attempting to resolve a problem by listing as many solutions as possible. Although this is often carried out in groups, research shows that individuals will tend to produce more and better quality solutions when they work on their own rather than in groups.

Some individuals are reluctant communicators in the group situation, others will dominate discussion (Daly, McCroskey, Ayres, Hopf, Ayres 1997). To ensure that all parties participate and contribute, different mechanisms must be used to release knowledge. For example in brainstorming individuals can generate a list on their own. Once the list is generated these can be presented to the group, with all members contributing their ideas. An open discussion can follow individual presentations to add a level of criticism and enquiry that the individual may not have considered.

Groups may also perform differently to individuals when taking risks. Research has found that groups tend to take more risky decisions than individuals (Bem, Wallach & Kogan, 1970). However, if consequences of the decision will have a direct effect on the individual in the group, individuals become more conservative in their risk taking. It is suggested that high-risk takers may dominate the group discussion exerting disproportionate influence in the risky decision on the other members of the group (Bem, Wallach and Kogan, 1970).

Group Culture

Some groups that are cohesive have been found to outperform other groups, which exhibit high levels of conflict. Members of teams often feel greater levels of satisfaction when the group they are part of is a cohesive group. However, groups that are too cohesive can suffer from problems such as groupthink. Groupthink is a phenomenon that occurs in groups where individuals do not challenge other's opinions even though they know or believe them to be wrong.

In summary, the main perceived advantages and disadvantages of a cohesive team are presented in Figure 71-1

Team Motivation and Conflict Resolution

There is an acceptance, in many quarters, that cognitive links between people's efforts, performance and outcomes determine behaviour at work. The inference from this is that fully motivated teams would perform better than their counterparts that are less motivated. A variety of approaches and incentives exists for motivating teams. The successes of these approaches will depend on a host of factors, including the nature of the team, the tasks to be accomplished by the

```
┌─────────────────────────────────────────────────────────────────────┐
│                                                                       │
│  Cohesive Teams                                                       │
│                                                                       │
│  Advantages                                                           │
│    ◆   Improves quality, productivity and efficiency                  │
│    ◆   Encourages innovation                                          │
│    ◆   Improves employee motivation and job satisfaction - can be a rewarding experience │
│                                                                       │
│  Disadvantages                                                        │
│    ◆   Could lead to a lack of co-operation with, or opposition to, non-members │
│    ◆   Difficult to change attitudes and behaviour of a team that is fully developed and │
│        have an established culture                                     │
│    ◆   Some people might find teamwork contrary to their 'normal' style. This could lead to │
│        embarrassment and marginalisation of some member of the team   │
│                                                                       │
└─────────────────────────────────────────────────────────────────────┘
```

Figure 71 - 1: Perceived Advantages and Disadvantages of a Cohesive Team

team, the environment within which the team has to work and the team's perceived value of the incentive or reward. Two main types of incentive systems exist. They are either based on financial rewards or on non-financial rewards. Examples of the two include bonus, profit sharing, employee ownership, status recognition, personal growth, knowledge growth, career growth and job security.

The actual way the group functions, how each member is regarded and the way members interact with each other will affect the group's performance. Pressure to conform to the group behaviour may be so strong that individuals go along with the task or activity without any challenge. A member who has a high status, or is well regarded may make a weak suggestion or proposal, and other members may choose not to discuss the weakness of the statement. Such behaviour can lead to 'groupthink'; this is where individuals in a group do not wish to challenge statements because they believe all other members of the group agree with the sentiment of the statement, even though individually they suspect the statement is wrong. Many researchers believe that groupthink has been responsible for a number of disasters. Conflict that is used by members to challenge or question proposals exposing possible risks should be encouraged. Dysfunctional conflict that is used against another member because of personal dislikes must be eliminated. A supportive team environment is often encouraged as a way of managing conflict rather than avoiding it. Conflict is considered to be an unavoidable aspect of projects (Kolb ,1992).

A supportive environment offers a way of reducing organisational and personal barriers, encouraging professionals to seek help when needed. Often, because of fears of being viewed as incompetent, many professionals are reluctant to seek help from other colleagues in the same team. Where professionals experience problems and do not have a complete understanding of the situation they may be reluctant to ask for assistance because help seeking implies incompetence, showing a dependence on the other person which may result in a loss of power or status (Lee, 1997). Major projects such as the Hubble Telescope have resulted in costly mistakes due to individual and teams failing to seek help when needed (Lee, 1997). Help seeking behaviour can be encouraged by reducing perceived differences in status, and providing informal social environments.

Whilst teams should be encouraged to work closely together with members supporting each other, groups that become too cohesive may not perform at optimum levels. Maylor (1999) suggests that groups are ineffective when they work as a collection of individuals, where team members cannot agree with each other, and where the team is so integrated and cohesive that complete consensus occurs. For teams to be effective a balance has to be drawn between levels of conflict and cohesion (see Figure 71 - 2).

With new developments in technology the nature of teams is changing, it is no longer possible to consider just human interaction. Projects and contemporary organisations are becoming increasingly complex. The influx of information technology (IT) is also a contributory factor. The importance of IT in improving teamwork could increase in the future. Information technology has the potential to improve teamwork and close integration in a number of areas such as speeding up communication, getting dispersed groups to work together and speeding up decision making in teams. The impact of IT on teamworking can also be negative, especially with regard to its impact on the culture of the team and the potential reduction of tacit knowledge and experiences that could be shared through face-to face contact among team members. A balanced approach to the utilisation and exploitation of IT for teamworking is needed

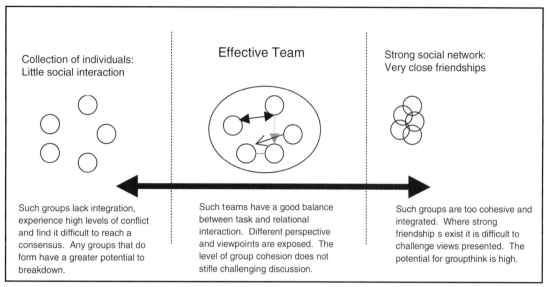

Figure 71 - 2: Cohesive and Non-cohesive Groups

(Egbu et al, 2001 a, 2001 b).

Whilst groups must build and establish networks and relationships, they need to deal with the task in hand. Many studies have shown that effective groups need to balance task and social interaction. Discussing tasks and proposed solutions in a critical way will have an emotional effect on others. This may weaken relationships. Where criticism is raised, supportive communication may need to be used to maintain the professional relationships. However, it is also difficult to criticise close friends. Where relationships become too close the functional conflict that is necessary in problem solving may be reduced.

There are many characteristics associated successful teams. These are listed in Figure 71 - 3

> - Members have a belief in shared aims and objectives
> - There is a sense of commitment by members to the group
> - Members accept team norms and values
> - Mutual trust and dependency prevails
> - Members fully participate in teamwork and use consensus in decision making
> - Members are able to express their feelings, challenge issues and offer solutions
> - Open layout - information and communications flow freely
> - Shared skills, knowledge, experience and problems
> - Self managing, self organising and self-regulating - tend to resolve conflict themselves
> - Negotiated production targets

Figure 71 - 3: Characteristics of a Successful Team

Types and Characteristics of Teams

People often use the word 'team' quite loosely. This is largely due to the fact that teams can take different forms and serve many different functions. There are also different types of teams and many possible ways of classifying teams. One classification sees teams as 'Formal' and 'Informal'. Another divide sees teams as production or service teams, action or negotiated teams, project and development teams, and advice and involvement teams. There are also permanent or temporary teams, and stable or unstable teams. Another useful classification is that of functional, project, matrix and contract teams.

- Functional team - Groups of people are divided along functional lines, people working together carryout the same or similar work
- Project team - This is a group of people who work together on a project. Where a team is successful at one project they may stay together as a group. A project manager usually leads the project team
- Matrix team - Staff report to different managers for different aspects of their work. Matrix structures are often found on projects. Members of staff are responsible to their project manager for their contrib-

ution to the project and report to their functional line manager for routine aspects including appraisals, training, general duties, and routine tasks. Matrix management is used when there are multiple customers, multiple activities and where resources are shared

- ◆ Contract team - A team is brought in from outside the organisation in order to do the project work. The responsibility lies with the project manager, the person in charge of the contract. Managers have limited direct control of sub-contracted personnel when compered to their own employees

Social Relationships and Influence

When people work together for prolonged periods of time they are likely to become a social group, they acquire a group identity.

The group's dynamics can work for and against the project. Informal groups often exist within a team. These could be a collection of friends who play sport together and enjoy working together or they could be a collection of individuals who are discontented with the management. Group dynamics that work against the project need to be recognised and dealt with. Groups will develop norms. These can encourage quality and increase quantity of performance and can also restrict the quantity and quality of performance (Brotherton, 1999). If not implemented correctly, it is common for informal group norms to restrict performance when incentive schemes are used. Groups can establish quite elaborate systems of ensuring norms are maintained that restrict performance. Such behaviour needs to be recognised and strategies need to be implemented so the group regulator framework (norms) encourages optimum performance and does not restrict it.

People do not always join a team for the same reasons. In projects, individuals are often selected because of theirspecific skills, knowledge or expertise. They may belong to different departments, organisations or groups. Their roles outside the project may be quite different and it is likely that they have different ideas on how the project will contribute to their personal and professional development.

Being part of a team has an impact on the individual. It affects their beliefs, attitude, behaviour, work and social life. If the team is to perform effectively members should share a common goal and make positive contributions towards the achievement of the goal.

Team Development: Tuckman Model - Forming, Storming, Norming and Performing

There are a number of studies that have looked at how a group develops and behaves over the project life cycle. One such study was carried out by Tuckman (1965), the research found four stages of group development. At each stage different types of group behaviour tend to emerge. The four stages identified by Tuckman were, forming, storming, norming and performing.

Forming - During this initial stage the individual members of the group start to interact. They tentatively identify the purpose of the group, and start to recognise the composition of the group.

Storming. - As the members become more familiar with each other they will put over their views and perspectives more forcefully. Disagreements may be expressed and conflict emerges. Challenges may be made on the nature of the task, organisational arrangements and responsibility for undertaking the task.

Norming - As feelings are expressed and conflict and hostility starts to be controlled by the team members, the group will establish its own norms, forming implicit and explicit guidelines. These provide a framework that regulates the members' behaviour allowing them to operate as a team.

Performing - Once the group has progressed successfully through the previous stages of development, its social structure will be more aligned and cohesive. This will allow them to work more effectively as a team. It is at this stage that the group can concentrate on the team goal and function effectively towards that goal.

Different labels have been used to describe the same process e.g:

Dependence	=	Forming
Conflict	=	Storming
Cohesion and interdependence	=	Norming and Performing

An additional label of 'mourning' can be used to describe when the team is dissolved. If a team has successfully worked on a project, its members may be reluctant to move from the team, fearing that such success will not be repeated.

Team Roles and Performance: Belbin's Team Roles

The constitution of a group is very important for group success. For teams to be effective, the individual members must have complimentary skills, knowledge and expertise and be committed to co-operating with other members working towards the achievement of the group objective. A number of tools exist for identifying individual qualities that contribute to specific roles within teams. Such tools can be used to select individuals, building a 'balanced group' or to restructure the group so that tasks are undertaken by those with the most appropriate skills. These tools can also be used by groups as a development or discussion exercise, enabling the individuals and group to recognise some of their strengths and weaknesses and discuss possible action to overcome the weakness.

Belbin (1981, 1993) devised a system for recognising and classifying specific roles within groups. One of Belbin's findings was that groups composed entirely of highly intelligent people, or people with similar personalities did not perform as well as those who had a balance of personalities and mixture of intelligence levels. Figure 71 - 4 shows the team roles produced by Belbin and the strengths and allowable weakness of each of the roles.

The role that a person undertakes is not fixed and may change depending on the context of the problem or task faced. Individuals tend to have primary and back-up roles. Those best suited to the primary role are those with the highest score in that category. If certain roles are missing from a team, the members' best equipped to fulfil that role would be those with the highest scores in that category.

Another model that identifies and groups personality traits is 'The Myers-Briggs Type indicator' (MBTI) (Briggs-Myers, 1993). The MBTI is a personality test that asks people how they feel or act in particular situations. The test 'labels' people as extroverted or introverted (E or I), sensing or intuitive (S or N), thinking or feeling (T or F), and perceiving or judging (P or J). These are then combined into sixteen personality types.

Such models are useful for creating open discussions that focus on individual and team strengths and weakness.

Group Formation and Development Teams - Cultural and Contextual Considerations

Difficulties with teams that are known to occur must be managed throughout the project life cycle.

- Networks must be quickly established during the early stages of projects
- Levels of conflict must be managed so that relationships are sufficiently maintained
- Problems must be resolved at all stages of the project

Levels of conflict are often high during early and late stages of a project. Some professionals have difficulties establishing relationships with other professionals. This can have a major impact on the start of projects. At the start of a project many of the professionals may not be familiar with other professionals, who may belong to another group or organisation. To perform effectively professionals must quickly learn how to interact with others without causing too much conflict or offending them. During early stages of socialisation mistakes are occasionally made. We may present our view, beliefs, opinions, or state how things should be done without being aware of the other person's perspective. Being aware of other people's cultures and viewpoints helps us to change our communication behaviour and interaction to ensure that the desired outcome is achieved.

Team Roles		
Team Role: Category	**Typical Feature and characteristics of the category**	**Allowable weakness associated with the category**
Plant	People who fall into this category are creative, imaginative and unorthodox. They have an ability to solve difficult problems.	Plants tend to ignore the details of procedures and tasks. Due to the amount of thought put into task they can become too preoccupied to communicate effectively.
Resource Investigator	Resource investigators are inclined to be extroverts, enthusiastic and communicative. They explore opportunities and have an ability to develop contacts.	They are often over-optimistic and tend to lose interest once initial enthusiasm has passed.
Co-ordinator	Co-ordinators are mature and confident. They have characteristics that are well suited to the role of a chairperson. They are good at delegating, clarifying roles and decision-making.	Due to their personal traits they can be seen as manipulative. They tend to delegate personal work.
Shaper	Shapers are challenging, dynamic and thrive on pressure. They have the drive and courage to overcome obstacles.	They can be provocative. They can lack sensitivity to others' feelings when discussing issues.
Monitor evaluator	The monitor evaluators are sober, strategic and discerning. They tend to look and evaluate all options.	Weaknesses include a lack of drive and ability to inspire others. They tend to be over-critical of others' work.
Team worker	Team workers are co-operative, mild, perceptive and diplomatic. They have an ability to listen to others, build relationships, avert friction, and resolve differences.	Team workers can be indecisive in crunch situations. They also have a greater tendency to be influenced by others.
Implementer	The implementers are disciplined, reliable, conservative and efficient. They are able to turn others' ideas into practical actions.	A weakness of the implementers is that they can be rather inflexible and slow to respond to new possibilities and opportunities.
Completer	Completers are extremely conscientious and anxious. They spend considerable time searching out errors and omissions. They have an ability to deliver things on time.	It is in the compeleters' nature to worry unduly. They are reluctant to delegate. Others may be irritated by the minor errors picked up or the detail of the reports.
Specialist	Specialists are single minded, self- starting and dedicated. They have specific knowledge and skills that are in short supply	Specialists contribute on specific aspects. They dwell on technicalities and details associated with their specialism and may overlook the broader issues.

Figure 71 - 4: Team Roles: Adapted from Belbin, R.M. (1993. P.23) Team roles at work.
Butterworth-Heinemann.

The amount of conflict is also said to be related to the amount of project information. As the amounts of information builds, the potential for problems to emerge between conflicting information increases. When the level of project information is about to peak, the pressures of work and stress are likely to have their greatest impact on performance. When the work demands increase, pressures are imposed on individuals and the professional relationship between members of a team. During or after demanding periods of work mechanisms for strengthening relationships should be implemented.

Many different tools and techniques can be used to overcome the difficulties outlined. However, the tools are not appropriate for all situations. For example, taking people out of the project environment for an 'away day' when a project deadline is close may heighten the levels of stress rather than reduce them. Some team building games may be seen as patronising, and activities that are related to the project may be more beneficial. The type of event selected to build, maintain or recover relationship should be suited to the situation and professionals. Examples of tools that can help build and recover professional relationships include:

- Workshops
- Away-days
- Face to face meetings
- Informal meetings in a relaxing environment
- Team building games and activities
- Presentations
- Letter of praise
- Rewards

Summary

Project teams have a good deal of potential to contribute to project success and to modern organisational life. Positive and successful teams encourage involvement, flexibility, efficiency, innovation and productivity improvements. It is however, important that necessary steps are taken for successful group work (see Figure 71 - 5).

```
┌─────────────────────────────────────────────────────────┐
│  Team Development Maintenance and Performance             │
│                                                           │
│   ◆   Understand the nature and demands of the project and tasks     │
│   ◆   Identify roles and check individual's strengths, skills, capabilities and │
│       knowledge to perform the roles                      │
│   ◆   Ensure that the team's structure and culture are suited to the project │
│       demands                                             │
│   ◆   Identify appropriate methods of developing the desired team culture e.g. │
│       away days, presentations, work shops, education, training, team building │
│       exercises, fun days, family days.                   │
│   ◆   Create a supportive culture                         │
│   ◆   Encourage members to work with one another - break down barriers │
│   ◆   Foster a 'help-seeking' and 'question-asking' culture │
│   ◆   Eradicate groupthink and also allow functional criticism │
│   ◆   After critical discussions, ensure relationships are maintained │
│   ◆   Remove dysfunctional conflict                       │
└─────────────────────────────────────────────────────────┘
```

Figure 71 - 5: Points to Consider for Effective Group Work

References and Further Reading

Belbin, R.M. (1993) Team Roles at work. London, Butterworth-Heinemann

Procter, S. and Mueller, F. (Eds.)(2000)" Teamworking". Management, work and Organisations Series. Published by Macmillan Press Ltd. ISBN: 0 333 76004 2

Stewart R. (Ed) (1999) Gower Handbook of Teamworking. Gower Publishers, Aldershot. ISBN: 0 566 07968 2

Belbin, R.M. (1981) Management Teams: Why they succeed or fail, London, Butterworth Heinemann

Bem, D.J, Wallach, M. A. and Kogan, N (1970) Group Decision Making under Risk of Aversive Consequences. In P. Smith. Group Processes Selected Readings. Middlesex, Penguin. pp 352 - 366

Briggs-Myers, I (1993) "Introduction to Type". 5th edition, Consulting Psychologists Press Inc., Palo Alto, C.A., USA.

Brotherton, C, (1999) Social Psychology and Management, Buckingham, Open University Press

Brown, R (2000) Group Process - Dynamics within and between groups, 2nd Ed. Oxford, Blackwell Publishers.

Conti, B. and Kleiner, B. H. (1997) "How to increase Teamwork in Organisations". Training for Quality, Vol. 5, No. 1, pp. 26 - 29.

Daly, J.A, McCroskey, J.C, Ayres, J, Hopf, T, and Ayres, D.M, (1997) Avoiding Communication, Shyness, Reticence and Communication Apprehension, 2nd Ed. Cresskill, NJ, Hampton Press.

Egbu, C.; Gaskell, C. and Howes, J. (2001a) "The Role of Organisational Culture and Motivation in Effective Utilisation of Information Technology for Teamworking in Construction". Proceedings of the 17th Annual Conference of the Association of Researchers in Construction Management (ARCOM). September 5th - 7th, University of Salford, England, UK

Egbu, C.; Gaskell, C. and Howes, J. (2001b) "Information Technology for Improving Teamworking in Construction: Opportunities and Challenges for Practice and for Research" Proceedings of COBRA 2001, the Construction and Building Research Conference of the RICS Foundation, 3rd -5th September, Glasgow Caledonian University, Glasgow, Scotland, UK.

Ingram, H., Teare, R., Scheuing, E. and Armistead, C. (1997) "A Systems Model of effective teamwork' The TQM Magazine, Vol. 9, No. 2, pp. 118 - 127.

Kolb, D. (1992) "Hidden Conflict in Organisations". Sage Publications, London, UK.]

Lee, F. (1997) 'When the Going Gets Tough, Do the Tough Ask for Help? Help Seeking and Power Motivation in Organisations.' Organizational Behaviour and Human Decision Processes, Vol. 72, No. 3. December, pp 336 - 363.

Maylor. H. (1999) Project Management, 2nd Ed. Harlow, Financial Times - Prentice Hall.

Procter, S. and Mueller, F. (Eds.)(2000)" Teamworking". Management, work and Organisations Series. Published by Macmillan Press Ltd. ISBN: 0 333 76004 2

Shaw, M. E. (1970) "Communication Networks" In; Smith, B. (Ed) 'Group Processes', Penguin, Middlesex, pp. 75 -96

Stewart R. (Ed) (1999) Gower Handbook of Teamworking. Gower Publishers, Aldershot. ISBN: 0 566 07968 2

Tuckman, B.W. (1965) Development Sequences in Small Groups, Psychological Bulletin, vol.63, pp 384 - 399

Williams, H (1996) The essence of managing groups and teams. Hemel. Prentice Hall

72   LEADERSHIP

Bill Carpenter

"He who would lead must be a bridge."
Translated from "a fo ben bin bont" - "The Mabinogion"

Introduction

"If you think you're leading, but nobody is following, you're just going for a walk".

I don't know where this quote came from, but it strikes me as a very good start for a chapter on leadership. It rightly focuses our attention on those we would endeavour to lead rather than on ourselves. Much of this chapter deals with how we can improve our understanding of people and teams involved in projects.

The chapter begins by looking at leadership characteristics, drawing on a number of leadership 'gurus'. This leads to a more detailed exploration of motivation, goal setting, situational leadership and morale building.

The section on motivation looks at Maslow and Herzberg's work as well as the subjects of Motivational Value Systems and Neuro-Linguistic Programming.

The importance of goal setting and the SMART acronym are covered in the next section.

The largest part of the chapter explores Hersey and Blanchard's Situational Leadership model. After a general look at the model, each of the four leadership styles are discussed, followed by methods of diagnosing which style to use for individuals and teams in which situations.

The final section focuses on how the leader can help the team achieve and maintain high levels of morale.

Leadership Skills and Attributes

What is a good leader? There are many models around which help us to answer that question. None of them, I would suggest, are complete or entirely accurate. This is partly because, as leaders, we are different and partly because our circumstances are different, particularly with regard to those we lead. That said, the models do enable us to highlight a number of key areas to consider when developing our own leadership approach. They also help us to complete one answer to the question - It depends on...

Warren Bennis, in his book, Organizing Genius, identifies a number of characteristics of great leaders:

- Must command respect and inspire trust
- Civility - not imposing your own views on others
- A pragmatic dreamer - gets things done, but with immortal longings
- Scientific minds with poetic souls
- Original vision - a dream of achievable greatness rather than a simple will to succeed
- Articulation of the vision - sharing the meaning of the goal, inspiring zeal and uniting the team
- Provider of freedom to be creative - using failure as a learning opportunity
- Willing to decide, but prefers to allow team to decide
- Protector - from undue outside influence or criticism, even enabling the team to draw strength and focus from opposition
- Passionate belief - seducing others into sharing the dream
- Facilitation rather than control
- Communicator - ensuring the right information gets to the right people
- Allowing people to discover their own greatness

His list is particularly relevant to project leadership because the book is all about leading groups of talented people in an environment of 'collaborative meritocracy', rather than in a conventional 'functional bureaucracy'.

Kouzes and Posner, in their book, The Leadership Challenge, summarise part of their research into what makes a great leader by listing the most admired characteristics of leaders in the eyes of their followers. The top four, by quite a margin, were:

1. Honest
2. Forward-looking

3. Inspiring
4. Competent

One of the classic leadership models is that developed by John Adair - Action Centred Leadership. In this model, he identifies three key areas for leadership focus:

1. Defining the task - it is not the leader's job to do the work, nor necessarily to manage it, but to ensure that everyone has a clear understanding of the objectives and scope of the project as well as their own individual roles and responsibilities. This clarity also ensures that the right objective (the one most likely to meet the needs and deliver the benefits) has been determined, based on the collective expertise of the team as well as the aspirations of the stakeholders.
2. Building the team - the project leader should be involved in selecting the team and then developing it to achieve its 'synergistic' potential.
3. Developing the individuals - the project leader should try to maximise the performance and contribution of each team member.

If the leader fails to focus sufficient time and effort into any one of these areas, the result tends towards a failure in all three.

Motivation

One of the key skills of a leader, appearing in a variety of guises in the above lists, is motivation. The skill is not, however, in motivating people. Only they can do that. The skill is in recognising what people find motivating and providing an environment in which those factors occur. In order to do that, it is useful to understand some of the things people might find motivating. As with the whole subject of leadership, motivation is served by many models.

Maslow's Hierarchy of Needs

One of the best known is Abraham Maslow's Hierarchy of Needs (Figure 72 - 1). Developed around the 1940's, this model is largely speculative and unproven by scientific research.

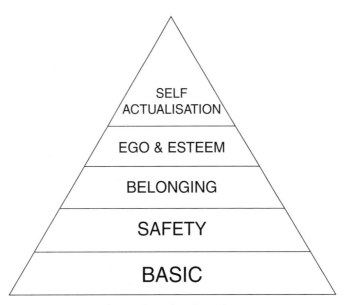

Figure 72 - 1: Maslow's Hierarchy of Needs

Maslow suggests that higher levels of motivation are achieved at higher levels of the hierarchy.

The Basic needs are those associated with survival and include a baseline standard of living - implying sufficient money, food, shelter - and the production of offspring.

The Safety needs are about protection and security, including job security.

The Belonging needs relate to social status and membership of a community. This might be a team or an organisation - a place in which relationships may be fostered.

Ego and Esteem is about having a sense of self-worth based on knowing that you can add value.

Self-actualisation means not standing still.

This motivation deals with the aesthetic and spiritual as well as the need for growth, development and moving forward to better things.

Herzberg's Factor Theory

Frederick Herzberg's work (Figure 72 - 2), based on research in the 1960s, supports Maslow's findings in terms of the types of motivator, but shows some clear differences in terms of motivational impact. Herzberg identifies "Hygiene Factors" and "Motivators" as two distinct aspects of motivation and plots the extent to which those interviewed deemed them to increase satisfaction (+) or increase dissatisfaction (-). Lack of the hygiene factors, shown in the lower part of Figure 72-2 from 'Company Policy' downwards, tends to result in demotivation and poorer performance. Positive motivation largely relies on the Motivators, from 'Personal Growth'.

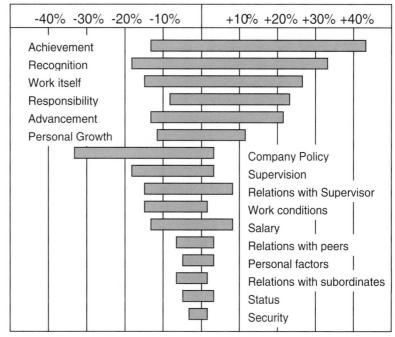

Figure 72 - 2: Herzberg's Factor Theory

Motivational Value Systems

As mentioned in the introduction to this section, motivation is personal and the project leader needs, therefore, to get to know the team members. There are many 'instruments' , psychometric and otherwise which can be used in this regard. Elias Porter, a professor in psychiatry, developed a Strength Deployment Inventory which is based on Relationship Awareness Theory. This identifies seven different Motivational Value Systems. Each system describes a set of filters through which different people interpret and understand life. These result in actions by the individual which achieve or enhance their feeling of self-worth. Providing an environment which is rewarding to a given individual's value system is likely to increase their motivation. For instance:

- An 'altruistic-nurturing' person likes to be needed by others
- An 'assertive-directing' person likes innovation and challenge
- An 'analytic-autonomising' person likes efficiency and organisation
- A 'flexible-cohering' person likes democracy and flexibility

Neuro-linguistic Programming

Joseph O'Connor and John Seymour's book, 'Introducing NLP' is sub-titled, 'The new psychology of personal excellence'. Under this broad heading, amongst other things, lies a powerful insight into motivation. People are motivated by the things they value and if the project leader can 'pace' those values by exhibiting behaviours and using words that indicate those values, rapport and motivation will be the almost inevitable result. As with many 'techniques', NLP is capable of being used to manipulate. This is a dangerous path which may well lead to a complete breakdown in the relationship. Pacing is simply about identifying with another's values and communicating from that standpoint. It's a bit like taking the time to learn and use a foreign language to improve communication when visiting another country.

Some of the 'patterns' we could look for to distinguish different forms of motivation include:

- Towards (the cool side of the room) or Away (from the fireside)
- Necessity (because I must) or Possibility (because I can)
- Self (for my benefit) or Others (for their benefit)
- Matching (like last time) or Mismatching (for a change)
- Short-term (project milestones) or Long-term (life-cycle benefits)

Goal Setting

Setting goals is another significant facet which appears in the leadership models. Without clear goals, teams and individuals can easily waste effort on irrelevant activity. It is the goal that provides the focus and the test for everything - on a project, the objective and scope statements define the project leader's 'bottom line'. Arguably, all aspects of projects - the process, the techniques, the interpersonal skills, the structures etc - are all secondary to achieving the goal. They must all be used sufficiently to maximise the likelihood of success. Under-use and over-use are as bad as each other.

In addition to providing the general focus for activity (managerial and technical), the goal also provides a specific basis for:

- Risk management - analysis of potential impact on the goal in terms of quality, cost or time
- Planning - the top of the product or work breakdown structure; the sum of the outputs of all the final tasks in the logic network
- Control - the baseline against which what actually happens is compared; impact analysis in determining the need for control actions

The project leader will need to ensure that the project goals are defined and will also need to make sure that all team and individual goals are established in alignment with the overall goals.

One of the most popular acronyms used for goal setting is SMART.

S - Specific

Firstly, it is important to ensure that any goal is clear and unambiguous. This includes making sure that it is understood in the same way by all interested parties - project stakeholders.

Secondly, the goal must be specifically the responsibility of one person and describe what they have agreed to deliver. For instance, the project goals describe the objective and deliverables of the project, but not the long-term benefits. The latter are not within the remit of the project leader even though they are part of the justification for doing the project.

M - Measurable

The measurability of goals is a vital part of ensuring that the right activities are done to the right standard. It also defines the way in which achievement of the goals can be evidenced, 'Improve output', for instance, is always and never complete. 'Improve output by 10%' is measurable and can be evidenced.

A - Achievable

At the time of setting the goal, we mustn't expect concrete confirmation of this - that comes later with detailed planning. What is needed, though, is a level of confidence that allows us to move into that planning process or, conversely, agree to stop now. Achievability is a comparison of what we need with what we've got. A high level plan of how the goal is to be achieved and what that requires in terms of money, time, resource etc is compared with any constraints on those factors. As this information is fairly inaccurate, we are only looking for them to be 'in the right ballpark'.

R - Realistic

Easily confused with achievability, some people prefer 'relevant'. This is about making sure the goal is really appropriate. Firstly, there is a need to ensure that the goal contributes to a wider need - individual goals to project goals, project goals to organisational goals. Secondly, the overall benefit must be compared with the whole life cycle costs. Using an organisational 'hurdle', which might be purely financial (eg Investment Appraisal) or include non-financial benefits, determine whether the project should be done.

T - Timebound

'As soon as possible' is a task scheduling option, not a time bound! Many goals will have a target time for achievement stated either as an end date ("Do it by Wednesday") or a maximum elapsed time ("The system upgrade must be complete within 30 minutes of starting it"). Some goals may also have a defined start time. The planning will determine how long the goal will take to achieve and solve any discrepancy with the target, so, in the absence of any constraint, set the timebound as the planned time.

Situational Leadership

The Model

The Situational Leadership model, developed by Ken Blanchard and Paul Hersey, provides a very powerful way of determining appropriate leadership behaviour, depending on the situation. It is relevant to both team and individual leadership scenarios and its simplicity makes it easy to understand and use.

In basic terms the model recognises two aspects of leadership behaviour - directive and supportive. These are combined to identify four distinctive leadership styles - structuring, coaching, encouraging and delegating (Figure 72 - 3).

The model includes a diagnostic element, enabling the project leader to identify the 'maturity' of the team or individual with regard to a particular activity and then use the appropriate leadership style. The team or individual will exhibit different levels of maturity with regard to different activities and even different aspects of the same activity. For instance, someone may be very accomplished with regard to the technical aspects of performing a task, have a reasonable degree of skill in estimating time and cost for that task, have limited knowledge with regard to setting the goal for it and have no idea where it fits into the bigger picture. Each level of maturity requires a different leadership approach, so the leader must be very flexible in the use of the styles. The diagnostics for teams and individuals are described in more detail below.

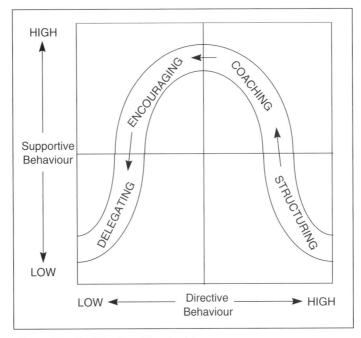

Figure 72 - 3: Situational Leadership

Hersey and Blanchard's work has shown that, as a team or individual moves through the levels of maturity, their performance increases. Situational Leadership is, therefore, also a team and personal development model, mapping the stages and, importantly, the order of those stages. It is not possible to skip a stage, although some may be passed through more quickly, depending on the people involved. Having reached a particular stage of maturity does not mean that the team or individual cannot slip back. Circumstances of crisis or change - new team members, significant problems, change of direction etc - may cause people to go back one or more stages and the leader must be ready to respond with an appropriate style. Asking the team what they think when the whole project seems to be crumbling round their ears may well be met with short shrift!

Style 1 - Structuring

Structuring is a high directive, low supportive style. This means that the leader will largely tell people what to do and sometimes even how to do it. If they don't know the latter, this style includes the use of knowledge and skills training which could be sourced from elsewhere. Goal setting is clearly an important aspect of this.

Although supportive behaviour need only be low at this stage, because the people are looking after themselves and have not yet allowed themselves to be supported by anyone else, there is a great need for motivation. People will not necessarily be 'bought in' to the goals and the leader will need to be 'selling' the ideas by linking them to appropriate motivational factors as described above.

Style 2 - Coaching

Coaching is a high directive, high supportive style. The most significant change from structuring is the way in which direction is maintained. In the structuring style, the leader largely tells people. In coaching, the leader uses questions to ascertain what the team or individual thinks and to make sure that their thinking is not only correct but correct for the right reasons. In this way the leader is more supportive of the ideas of the team and is able to help them analyse any mistakes or misconceptions, while retaining a high level of control.

This approach allows one of the most important facets of coaching to emerge. When a coach works with an athlete, it is the athlete who competes, because they are better than the coach. Coaching is about enabling people to be as good as they can be. Structuring limits people's performance to being 'almost as good as the leader'! The questioning style allows the person or team being coached to come up with ideas that may turn out to be better than the coach's ideas. This can feel quite threatening for some people and will need practice to become comfortable with it.

The coaching process is a lot like the project process. Figure 72 - 4 shows an example of what should be included.

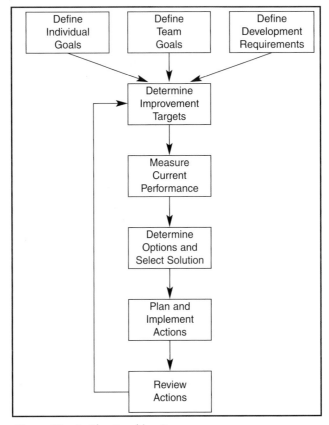

Figure 72 - 4: The Coaching Process

It is important to note that coaching takes place on the job, using people's activities and sometimes problems as an opportunity to help people learn how to learn. Briefly, the steps in the process are:

- Determine improvement targets - once overall goals have been set, the improvement targets may achieve them in one go or may need to be taken a bite at a time. It is important to make each target SMART.
- Measure current performance - as with a project it is important for people to understand where they are coming from as well as where they are going to.
- Determine options and select solution - there is an opportunity here to be creative and enable people to explore wide-ranging alternatives. This not only increases the chances of finding a good solution, but also allows the leader to understand how people assess the options and to make sure that they are making the right considerations using the correct information.
- Plan and implement actions - having defined the solution, some planning of how it will be done is required. This will include agreement of how the work is to be monitored and how much visibility the leader will have. Early on in the use of this style, the leader's monitoring will be more frequent but can reduce as everyone's confidence grows. The plan is then implemented.
- Review actions - this includes the monitoring and control done by the team or individual during implementation and the reporting back to the leader as agreed. It is also the feedback for the coaching process itself, to determine how far the performance gap has been closed, to confirm or adjust the target, reassess and celebrate improved performance, re-plan etc

Style 3 - Encouraging

Encouraging is a low directive, high supportive style. Mentoring is one form of encouraging and is a natural development of the coaching style. It aims to provide high levels of support and encouragement while gradually reducing the amount of direction given.

After the first few times through the process, the team and individuals will be able to ask themselves the coaching questions without the need to refer to the leader as often. After a few coached sessions, they will be able to complete goal setting, performance measuring, option generation, selection and planning on their own, bringing their options and preferred way forward to the leader. As their experience and the leader's confidence grow, the leader will be able to reduce the number of checkpoints and allow them to implement their own plans without seeking approval.

The leader should provide positive feedback when people have been successful. This should include:

♦   Giving praise where it is due.
♦   Explaining the reasons why their action was good.
♦   Linking back to the improvement targets by confirming achievement and reinforcing future behaviour.

The leader should also provide constructive feedback to help people identify where they could improve. This should include:

♦   Explaining what the action was, what the impact was and what the desired outcome was
♦   Asking the team or person what their opinion of this situation is and if they have any suggestions.
♦   Linking back to the improvement targets by identifying progress and confirming or modifying the target.

In the encouraging style, the leader should NEVER provide negative feedback. This only serves to put people on the defensive or, worse still, to destroy the relationship.

Style 4 - Delegating

Delegating is a low directive, low supportive style. This does not mean abdication, because the leader should always be watchful in case the maturity level slips back.

As a leadership style, delegating is about letting people get on with their own job. Delegation in its fuller sense is entrusting your powers or functions to another person, getting that person to complete tasks that you would otherwise have undertaken yourself.

It is important to recognise a few key concepts:

- Delegation is a way of fulfilling the leader's responsibility, not removing it.
- Authority needs to be agreed paying due regard to organisational constraints.
- The leader should: want to be a leader, not a doer; want to be an achiever; want to treat people well and enable their development.
- Good delegation requires practice.

Some of the signs of poor delegation are:

- Taking up a lot of time
- Burying the leader in details
- Causing conflicts
- Lack of initiative
- Too much or too little help sought
- Dissatisfaction
- Confusion
- Little flexibility, growth or development
- Poor communication

Good delegation delivers the opposite of these things. Some of the things which could be delegated are:

- Anything for which you can't think of a good reason not to!
- Routine tasks
- Necessities - as opposed to optional tasks
- Trivial tasks - but only if it really needs doing
- Specialist tasks
- Tasks you don't enjoy - someone might (for a while!)
- Projects

Don't delegate:

- Things that rely on your position for credibility
- Policy Making
- Personnel issues - evaluation, discipline, dispute resolution
- Crises
- Confidential matters

Do:	Don't:
Encourage the free flow of information	Hoard information
Focus on results	Emphasis methods
Delegate through dialogue	Do all the talking
Fix deadlines	Leave timescales uncertain
Make sure the person has all the necessary resources	Half-delegate by giving an assignment without the tools
Delegate the entire task to one person	Delegate half a task
Give advice without interfering	Fail to point out pitfalls
Build in controls	Impose controls, particularly as an afterthought
Back up delegatees in disputes	Leave people to fight their own battles
Give the delegatee full credit	Hog the glory or look for scapegoats

Figure 72 - 5: Do's and Don'ts of Delegation

Diagnosis

For Individuals

Maturity of individuals is diagnosed in relation to a specific task and has two parts:

- ◆ Psychological maturity - Their self-confidence, ability and readiness to accept responsibility.
- ◆ Job maturity - Their relevant skills and technical knowledge

Four levels of maturity, M1 to M4, relate to styles 1 to 4 respectively.

M1 Psychological: Moderately eager; high expectations; anxious about role and expectations; testing the situation and other people, dependent on authority and hierarchy; needing to find a place to fit.
Job: Lacking basic skills and knowledge

M2 Psychological: Experiencing discrepancy between hopes and reality; dissatisfied with dependence on authority; frustrated with goals, tasks and action plans; feeling incompetent and confused; reacts negatively towards leader and others; competing for power and attention.
Job: Basic skills but lacking flexibility; basic knowledge

M3 Psychological: Resolving discrepancies between hopes and reality; dissatisfaction decreasing; developing harmony, trust, support and respect; developing self-esteem and confidence; more open; willing to share responsibility

Job: Good skills and experience of a number of applications; good knowledge and ability to relate it to new circumstances

M4 Psychological: Enthusiastic; working collaboratively; highly confident; sharing in leadership; positive about success; constructive about mistakes

Job: Performing well, even in new situations; teaching others

For Teams

The diagnosis of the four levels of team maturity is provided by Tuckman's team development model. This comprises four stages - Forming, Storming, Norming and Performing which map directly to leadership styles 1 to 4 respectively. Typical characteristics displayed at each stage are as follows.

Forming

- Polite
- Dependence on leader
- Guarding
- Watchful
- Impersonal
- No conflicts
- Need for group identity is low
- Concern for structure, methods, etc.
- Hidden agendas stay hidden

Storming

- Cliques start to have influence
- Conflicts occur
- People confronted
- Hidden Agendas begin to be raised
- Struggle for leadership by cliques
- Opting out
- Feeling stuck
- Own positions rationalised
- Lack of listening

Norming

- Procedures developed
- Issues confronted
- More open exchanges of ideas and views
- Cliques dissolved
- Leadership shared
- More listening and co-operation
- Giving feedback
- Pre-conceived ideas are changed
- Creativity high

Performing

- Resourcefulness
- Creativity
- Flexibility
- Openness
- Effectiveness
- Close and supportive
- Settled interdependence
- High group morale
- Warmth/closeness of members
- Empathy
- High level of problem-solving behaviour

Morale

Morale, as distinct from motivation, is a more team-centred concept. The dictionary definition is 'Conduct and behaviour of a group with respect to confidence, hope, zeal, submission to discipline.'

The final stage of the Tuckman model, 'Performing', lists high morale as a characteristic. The implication of this is that morale is largely related to a level of team maturity which the leader can achieve by seeking to develop as many aspects of the team's work into that stage.

This, however is not the whole story. The team does not operate in a vacuum and its morale will be influenced greatly by the support and encouragement they receive not just from the leader, but from other project stakeholders. This is particularly true of the project sponsor. The sponsor and the project leader will, therefore, need to work together to ensure that organisational support is given. Nowhere is this more relevant than in the securing of project resources. If the team have to battle for people to do tasks or to retain their budget, morale will be severely dented as the team begin to ask themselves how seriously the organisation really takes this project.

Other stakeholders may also need to be influenced to be positive about the project, especially if they are initially negative and quite powerful. Again, the sponsor and the project leader will need to, at best, get these people on side or, at least, protect the team from their interference. If the project is constantly at the mercy of powerful stakeholders, the team will quickly lose confidence in the leader and the sponsor, lose hope in achieving a successful outcome, lose their zeal to drive the project forward and, ultimately, become undisciplined in their work,

Summary

This session on project leadership has identified from a number of sources, a variety of characteristics of good leadership. They are:

- Respect and trust - Honest
- Civility
- A pragmatic dreamer
- Scientific minds with poetic souls
- Original vision - Forward-looking
- Articulation of the vision - Defining the task
- Provider of freedom to be creative
- Willing to decide, but prefers to allow team to decide
- Protector
- Passionate belief - Inspiring
- Facilitation rather than control
- Communicator
- Allowing people to discover their own greatness - Developing the individuals
- Competent
- Building the team

Motivation is an important aspect of these characteristics. Maslow and Herzberg's work give us some important factors in motivation:

- Basic Needs - Salary
- Safety - Company Policy, Work, Work conditions, Supervision, Security
- Belonging - Relationships
- Ego and Esteem - Achievement, Recognition, Responsibility, Status
- Self-actualisation - Advancement and Personal Growth

It is important to recognise that everyone is different and motivated in different ways. Motivational Value Systems and Neuro-Linguistic Programming provide ways of understanding people and determining what kind of behaviour and communication are most likely to create a motivating environment.

Goal setting is vital to ensure that people know what they are doing and also as a basis against which to judge risk, plans, control actions etc. The SMART acronym serves as a reminder that goals should be:

- Specific - unambiguous and owned by a named individual
- Measurable - so that achievement can be evidenced
- Achievable - we can think of a way of doing it that fits the constraints
- Realistic - it provides benefit to a 'bigger picture' which is appropriate to the investment to be put into it
- Timebound - time limits are clear

Hersey and Blanchard's Situational Leadership model defines four styles of leadership which are used in relation to different levels of individual and team maturity, as follows:

Structuring - a high directive, low supportive style appropriate for teams in the Forming stage and individuals with low levels of skill and dependence on the leader.

Coaching - a high directive, high supportive style, appropriate for teams in the Storming stage and individuals with basic skills who are becoming frustrated. The coaching process, carried out on the job, helps people learn how to learn.

Encouraging - a low directive, high supportive style, appropriate for teams in the Norming stage and individuals with a broadening range of experience and developing in confidence. Mentoring and giving feedback are key skills for the leader at this stage.

Delegating - a low directive, low supportive style, appropriate for teams in the Performing stage and individuals working collaboratively with high levels of transferable skill and enthusiasm. Delegation in its fuller sense means that people do aspects of the leader's work.

Morale is about the conduct and behaviour of the group. High morale is one of the characteristics of a team in the Performing stage. It is also very dependent on the level of support and encouragement given to the team by the project sponsor and other significant stakeholders.

References and Further Reading

Organizing Genius - Warren Bennis - Nicholas Brealey Publishing

The Leadership Challenge - Kouzes and Posner - Jossey-Bass Publishers

Work and the nature of man - Frederick Herzberg - Granada Publishing Ltd

The one minute manager builds high performing teams - P. Hersey and K. Blanchard - Fontana

Introducing NLP - J. O'Connor and J. Seymour - Mandala, Harper Collins

Don't do, delegate - J. Jenks and J. Kelly - Kogan Page

73   CONFLICT MANAGEMENT

Peter O'Neill

"Nothing is more frustrating than to win the argument and lose the decision."

John Davies. (The Rt Hon John Davies PC, MP, former Secretary of State for Trade and Industry and former President of the Board of Trade.)

Links to other topics

The nature of the majority of projects is for them to include the potential for conflicts of interest or value. The project manager has a key role to play in identifying, reducing and managing conflicts in order to achieve project success. Conflict management skills are therefore relevant to many aspects of project management - in particular there will be strong links to the following topics:

20   Project Success Criteria
23   Risk Management
25   Health, Safety & Environment
30   Work Content & Scope Management
32   Resource Management
34   Change Control
53   Procurement
64   Hand-Over
71   Teamwork
74   Negotiation

The Nature and Impact of Conflict

Conflict as a Natural and Productive Aspect of Project Activity

As stated in the introduction, projects have considerable potential to generate conflict. The range of people involved as stakeholders in a large project will almost certainly mean differences of objectives, viewpoints, styles and attitudes. Cross functional, or cross cultural teams will generate similar differences. It is important for two reasons not to see conflict as such in purely negative terms. Firstly, it is often a natural and predictable result of attempting to work jointly between people, teams and organisations. Secondly, conflict itself can have many positive effects if well handled:

- A wider range of views can generate better strategies and solutions
- Challenging views and assumptions can ensure they are well thought through and may identify shortcomings
- Facing up to a conflict may result in the identification of a more sustainable agreement rather than one which causes later problems
- Relationships between individuals, groups, organisations and cultures can be enhanced by fully understanding and respecting the other party as a result of a resolved conflict
- Positive competitiveness can increase commitment and effort

Conflict as an Unnecessary and Unproductive Aspect of Project Activity

Nevertheless, if conflict is not addressed positively, it has the potential to cause many problems for the project manager. The failure to identify potential conflict or the lack of constructive approaches to conflict may significantly impact on project cost, timescale or likelihood of success. Indicators and results of unproductive conflict may include:

- Conflicts of interest deteriorate into personal conflict
- Conflicts are increased rather than reduced by contact between the parties
- Communication becomes increasingly one way
- Positions become entrenched, with the formation of factions within the stakeholder group
- Attempts to resolve conflict delay progress and / or increase cost on the project

Conflicts of Interest, Value and Personality

A conflict of interest occurs when a decision or action within the project is seen as having a negative impact on the circumstances of one or more of the stakeholders. Examples might include an increase in workload for a team member which they perceive as unreasonable, or a department resisting a system installation project which they believe will result in job losses. Although such conflicts can be serious, they are nevertheless focussed on tangible, and possibly, negotiable issues.

A conflict of value occurs when a decision or action within the project is seen as morally wrong by one or more of the stakeholders. Examples could include protestors resisting a road development, or a team member objecting to a marketing proposal on the grounds of sexism. These conflicts can be more difficult to resolve as they relate to principles which can be perceived completely differently by the participants.

A conflict of personality occurs when two or more participants in a project find that their style, motivation, background or world view clash in a way which makes communication or co-operation difficult. These conflicts can range from minor irritations to a refusal to work together.

The Project Manager's Role in Conflict Management

The project manager needs to carry out 3 major functions in relation to conflict:

1   Conflict identification - activities aimed at recognising the potential for conflict which may impact on the project
2   Conflict avoidance - activities aimed at reducing the likelihood or potential impact of conflicts identified
3   Conflict resolution or reduction - activities aimed at handling a conflict which has occurred

Experienced project managers will recognise the similarities with Risk Management, and this illustrates the value of recognising conflict as one of the common risks associated with project activity.

Identifying Sources of Conflict

Sources of Conflict Among Project Stakeholders

Stakeholder mapping - a process of identifying stakeholders in the widest sense and evaluating their attitude to the project, can be of assistance here. A stakeholder can be regarded for this purpose as any individual or group who may impact on or be impacted by the project. By investing time in investigating and considering the interests and values of these stakeholders, it may be possible to identify clear areas of likely conflict.

The potential conflicts may be associated with a number of issues:

- The purpose of the project - most projects generate change to some degree, and change may be perceived negatively by some of those involved. It is good practice for the project manager to consider as objectively as possible the potentially different viewpoints of other parties in regard to the project's purpose. Discussions with stakeholders or their representatives are likely to be valuable in this regard, and the project manager may find it necessary to facilitate discussion to clarify the project objectives across the group.
- The method of the project - even where there is agreement on purpose, conflict may arise from differences of view on how to achieve it. Here, the project manager should consider how much consensus there may be for key decisions on how the project is implemented. Often decisions will be seen to favour one group at the expense of another, or there may be technical disagreements on how to proceed.
- The participants in the project - some individuals, groups or organisations may have a history of conflict, or their nature may indicate its potential. Knowledge of the participants will assist the project manager in predicting which may be likely to generate conflict with each other.
- Differing styles and preferences in communication - particularly between separate organisations in the

stakeholder group. Miscommunication is often a starting point for conflict and the project manager should pay particular attention to the interfaces between organisations.

Sources of Conflict Within the Project Team

Given the increasing use of cross-functional and other mixed teams, it cannot even be taken for granted that the team members will all agree on the purpose for the project. Certainly there is usually plenty of scope for conflict in relation to the method and between the participants. Although cross-functional teams have many potential benefits in a project environment, by their nature they also create a higher likelihood of conflict. Apart from the issues listed for the larger stakeholder group, common causes of conflict within the project team can include:

- Departmental interests or loyalties in competition with team interests or loyalties
- Members competing negatively for resources, control or recognition
- Lack of understanding or respect for other functions or expertise
- Differences in work pressure between departments or individuals
- Differences in commitment, style or personality

Conflict and the Project Life-cycle

The progression through the project lifecycle also provides an insight into possible causes of conflict. Common issues may include:

Project Selection:

- Differences of view about the need for a project
- Competition between sponsors of competing projects

Project Planning:

- Differences of view about the objective(s) of the project
- Differences of view about the scope of the project
- Disagreements about task or project requirements in terms of time, resources or specification

Project Implementation:

- Conflict resulting from miscommunication between participants on responsibility, task hand-over, support, timescale, cost, payment arrangements
- Changes in the project will often generate conflict in relation to their justification, approval and implications

Project Termination:

- Differences in view on the extent to which the project deliverables have been achieved
- Disagreements about the stage at which responsibility is transferred from the project team
- Conflict within the project team arising from uncertainty or apprehension about the effect of the project ending

Avoiding Conflict

Project Management Tools Which Can Reduce Unproductive Conflict

As mentioned in section 2.1 above, good stakeholder mapping can be a positive aid to the reduction of conflict. Many aspects of good practice in project selection and planning will also reduce the likelihood or impact of unproductive conflict. In particular, attention should be paid to:

- Project selection: poor processes here can led to a lack of agreement or commitment to projects. It is important for the organisation to take on the appropriate number and type of projects which can be supported and resourced. Taking on too many projects will increase the probability of negative competition for resources and attention. The use of agreed and objective processes will reduce this problem.

- Project definition: A poorly defined project will be likely to generate excessive conflict in relation to scoping and content disagreements. These may be focussed internally in the project team or externally with other stakeholders. Tools such as Project Initiation Documents, including requirements for a clear and confirmed Project Brief are needed.

- Project Team Selection: As well as the common criteria of expertise and availability, it will help if some thought is given to the overall mix of styles and personalities within the team. For a key project, it may be worthwhile using profiling tools such as Belbin's Team Role Preferences, or the Myers-Briggs Type Indicator. While these are unlikely to be used as the definitive selection indicator, they can at least be used to avoid (or give the project leader advanced warning of) major potential conflicts.

- Responsibility Matrices will often assist in the reduction of conflict around the issue of resourcing. These should include reference to, or sign-off by, relevant functional managers to reduce problems of divided loyalties in cross-functional teams.

- Duration and effort estimates for work packages or phases should include input from the likely participants. This may seem to be common sense, but many organisations generate unproductive conflict by poor estimating processes driven more by the preferences of senior staff than the experience of practitioners.

The Role of Communication Processes in Avoiding Conflict

Most projects rely heavily on good communication processes for success. Even in a relatively small project involving 10 people within the stakeholder group, there are (n(n-1)/2) or 45 potential communication channels. Managing communication successfully is often a trade-off between allowing (even encouraging) easy and informal communication, and controlling essential communication to avoid missing key occurrences. While this can sometimes lead to detailed and all-encompassing processes, it is important to remember that communication overload can also be a cause of conflict.

Points which project managers should focus on include:

- Following organisational procedures. While these may not be seen as ideal, particularly if they are generated by other organisations within the stakeholder group, they have the benefit of being agreed and traceable. Often the project manager can act as a facilitator here to balance the communication preferences of project team members with the need for a standardised set of communication procedures.

- Managing shortfalls in established procedures. The fact that a procedure is in place does not mean that it will be exactly right for any given project. The project manager should assess the need for, and if necessary develop, additional processes. Good practice may include the drafting of a Communication Matrix - a definition of the when, who and how of communications within the project. This draft can be circulated within the stakeholder group and amended to generate a suitable and supported approach.

- Managing communication outside the formal procedures. A competent project manager will constantly be aware of the need for informal, exploratory or conciliatory communication. This may be seen as 'keeping in touch' or MBWA (Managing by Wandering Around) and can consist mainly of informal contacts. Encouraging these contacts in larger or geographically disbursed stakeholder groups may be equally important, where the potential communication is too much for the project manager alone. The key is to ensure that everyone understands when the content of an informal communication crosses the dividing line and needs to be included in the formal processes. A good example of where this can be a 'grey area' is in design modification, where good definition of work package specification, inputs and outputs will also help to avoid the recriminations often associated with "I'm sure I mentioned this at the time".

Early Indicators of Conflict

A project manager who does not keep in close contact with members of the stakeholder group may not be aware of conflicts until they have become serious. Under these circumstances, the conflict may have escalated to a stage which will require far more work to resolve. The project manager can encourage contact by formal and informal contacts as discussed above, and by ensuring that stakeholders have easy access to them - an 'open door' approach. However, not all participants will be comfortable to express conflict either informally or objectively, so the project manger should be aware of other indicators:

- Reductions in communication - individuals who are uncomfortable with conflict may try to avoid it by not communicating in the area of conflict.
- Irritation or aggressiveness without an apparent focus - again individuals may display their lack of comfort by 'signals'. Unfortunately, these can be hard to read, so good practice in the face of unexpected negative behaviour should be to openly and calmly offer opportunities to raise the 'real' issue.
- 'Opting out' at project meetings - either by non-attendance or again by 'signals' such as non-contribution, negative body language or obstructive behaviour.
- Interpersonal comments which exhibit on the surface as humorous, but which have an undertone of intent to criticise or contradict.

There are many ways in which the early signs of conflict may manifest. The project manager is most likely to be aware of the signs by maintaining contact with the stakeholder group, and by being sensitive to changes in behaviour and mood. This can be much more difficult in situations where the stakeholders are from different cultural backgrounds.

Methods of Resolving Conflict

Even in the best managed projects, it is still likely that conflict will occur. Some of this may be positive conflict which can potentially enhance project success, where the role is to prevent it deteriorating. In other cases, negative conflict may arise and need to be addressed.

Options for Conflict Management - Assertiveness vs. Co-operativeness

A useful model for considering the options available in situations of conflict was developed by Thomas and Kilman. Their model maps 2 elements in the style of the person facing conflict. The first is Assertiveness - the ability and intent to achieve an outcome suitable to our own needs. The second is Co-operativeness - the ability and intent to achieve an outcome suitable to the needs of the other party. These can be mapped to generate 5 options: (Figure 73 - 1)

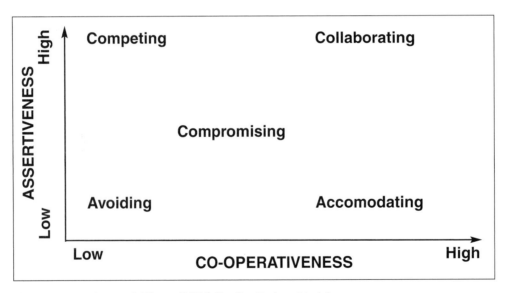

Figure 73 - 1: Thomas & Kilman (1974) Conflict Options Model

It is an important aspect of the model that each option can be a valid choice, depending on the circumstances surrounding the conflict. A project manager with only one

Project Management Pathways

conflict style may sometimes be successful, but also runs the risk of increasing rather than reducing the level of conflict overall. It should also be recognised that the project manager's preferred choice may be constrained by the attitude of the parties in conflict - particularly where the project manager is representing another parties views in the conflict. As the English churchman Dean Inge (1860-1954) said, "It takes in reality only one to make a quarrel. It is useless for the sheep to pass resolutions in favour of vegetarianism while the wolf remains of a different opinion".

The options, and their implications, are:

1   Avoiding (low assertiveness, low co-operativeness).
     It is sometimes possible and desirable to simply ignore or retreat from a conflict situation. Although this may not be seen as fulfilling the project manager's responsibilities, it may be appropriate when the conflict is:

♦   Minor and unlikely to escalate
♦   Personal in nature and where discontinuing the contact is feasible
♦   Escalating and some or all parties need a temporary respite to reduce the level of emotion
♦   Best resolved by an arbitrator or other 3rd party

2   Competing (high assertiveness, low co-operativeness)
     This option is to insist on only a resolution meeting one's own needs. Although this may be seen as aggressive or likely to escalate the conflict, it can be appropriate when:

♦   The project manager or the party they represent has much higher power or authority, or much more to lose, than the other party
♦   The conflict relates to an issue of safety or other legal responsibility
♦   The approach is being used as a considered negotiating tactic
♦   There appears to be only a win / lose solution available

3   Accommodating (low assertiveness, high co-operativeness) In some cases, it may be appropriate to accede to the other parties view in the conflict. Although this may run the risk of being seen as an 'easy touch', or of giving away power or influence from the project manager's role, it may be appropriate when:

- The other party clearly makes a better case for their preferred resolution
- The other party has much more power, authority or expertise
- It can be seen as building a relationship or generating an obligation for a future accommodation by the other party
- The issue is minor, unlikely to escalate or may take an unacceptable timescale to achieve a better result

4   Compromising (medium assertiveness, medium co-operativeness) This is often seen as the 'negotiated' solution, where each party will concede some aspect of their needs in order to reach agreement. It is frequently and appropriately used in conflict management in the project environment. It does incur risks of accepting a sub-optimal solution, and of failing to satisfy any party fully, but will often be accepted as the expected approach for the project manager. It is particularly relevant in situations where:

- It is important for all parties to 'save face'
- There are a range of issues across which compromises can be 'traded'
- It is a conflict of interests in which no party expects to get entirely their own way
- Power is evenly balanced between the parties

5   Collaborating (high assertiveness, high co-operativeness): An option where a solution is sought which meets all parties needs to a large extent. Because of the nature of conflict, this solution may not always exist, or may need considerable inventiveness or willingness to operate outside normal practice. For this reason, the potential disadvantage of the option can be

that it is time consuming and may not generate a truly collaborative outcome. However, it can be appropriate when:

- The issue is of high importance to all parties
- Other options threaten the project's success
- There is considerable scope and approval for new initiatives
- The situation is unfamiliar to all parties

Resolving Conflicts of Interest

All of the options above are likely to be valid choices, under appropriate circumstances, for conflicts of interest. Of them all, compromising (or negotiating) will be the most common choice and therefore project managers should develop skills in this area (see session 74 - Negotiation). In a large organisation, there may well be specialist staff to deal with major negotiations - purchasing or sales based, perhaps - but many conflicts of interests may arise outside the mainstream issues. In a less structured environment, it may be that arranging for the parties to meet - on neutral ground and with an agenda focussed on clarifying issues and concerns - may be enough to allow the process to move forward positively into negotiation.

Resolving Conflicts of Value

In a conflict of value, it may not be possible to negotiate an acceptable resolution for all parties as strongly held beliefs may be opposed. Where power is unequally distributed among the parties, competing or accommodating may result in the best achievable outcome, even though one or more parties may see it as win / lose. Arbitration by a 3rd party such as ACAS may be an option, but only if agreement can be reached to accept this as a way forward. A number of arbitration services are available across a range of subjects and industries and the project manager should be aware of the appropriate ones for a given project environment. Before using arbitration, the project manager should check with relevant stakeholders that the outcome will be supported, and should take advice on the best approach to putting forward their case.

Again, the process of meeting to clarify concerns may assist the process, but it is advisable to work in advance to develop an agenda acceptable to all parties and to agree ground rules aimed at avoiding escalation. Emotions can run high in conflicts of value and care needs to be taken with face-to-face meetings. Particular care should be exercised where one of the parties is applying pressure by using public opinion. Activities such as protests or other public expressions of conflict are popular with the media and the project manager may find that stakeholder support drops away under these circumstances.

Dealing With Inter-personal Conflict

At its simplest, inter-personal conflict within the project team can be treated as a performance issue, using the Competing approach. Team members in conflict should be given clear guidelines. The basic rule is that while liking each other is optional in the project, behaving professionally is not. Project managers should not accept negative behaviour from team members as a result of conflict. Apart from the immediate problem, such behaviour is likely to impact on morale and may result in the formation of 'sides' or cliques within the team.

Inter-personal conflict is more difficult when it appears between stakeholders outside the project team, where the project manager has little authority to intervene. Here the role is more likely to be facilitating, advising or acting as an intermediary. It is important not to underestimate the potential of inter-personal conflict, which has been known to cause the failure of major projects. Acting early and positively may be uncomfortable, but may also avoid significant future problems if the conflict escalates.

Skills Required in Conflict Management - Facilitation, Arbitration & Assertiveness

In serious situations it may be desirable, to bring in professional assistance to deal with conflict. However, the project manager will often find themselves fulfilling the role and should develop at least the basic skills in this area:

Facilitation

Assisting the processes of listening, understanding and exchanging information and views.

Wherever possible, the project manger should focus effort on being seen as objectively seeking solutions. Where the project manager is a party to the conflict (for example, in a dispute with a sub-contractor), the objectivity may be less accepted. In all cases, however, the problem solving focus is likely to be helpful.

Facilitation will often consist in guiding communication by:

- Questioning - using open questions (How, Why, etc.) to explore issues, and closed or specific questions (What day was that? Did you see this?) to check facts or details
- Encouraging - bringing relevant or reluctant participants into the discussion
- Controlling - limiting or closing the contribution of participants who are dominating the discussion
- Summarising - pointing out what has been addressed and any actions, and identifying issues that are still outstanding

Facilitation may also involve processes such as empathy building (asking participants to list reasons to support the other parties view, or for counter arguments to their own), but these should be used with caution by an inexperienced facilitator.

It needs to be noted that in situations of geographic disbursement, facilitation can be much more difficult. This is mainly due to the reduced information available, both on content and intention, where communication does not take place face-to face. Technologies such as video conferencing can improve the process, but even with experienced users will still be likely to reduce the overall effectiveness of communication in a conflict situation. Occasionally, distance may reduce emotional engagement, but this is by no means guaranteed.

Arbitration

Proposing or deciding a solution to a conflict between other parties. Mention has been made of using formal arbitration, but sometimes the project manager may find themselves given this role between stakeholders in conflict. Arbitration has most chance of success when the arbitrator:

- Is seen to listen objectively and equally to all parties
- Tests the willingness of the parties to support the eventual decision
- Is seen to give an appropriate amount of consideration before making a decision
- Explains the basis of a decision before announcing the decision itself
- Acknowledges the problems or concerns related to the decision
- Proposes a timescale for the implementation of the decision

When acting as an arbitrator, it is important the decision does not become simply an opportunity for another argument between the parties - if this happens, it implies that the situation was not suitable for arbitration.

Assertiveness

Standing up for one's own rights while acknowledging the rights of others. Assertiveness is a vital characteristic in project managers, particularly in situations where they have little formal authority. It is as much a state of mind as a technique, and is based on high self esteem coupled with a positive attitude towards others. One of the basic tools of assertiveness which can be useful in conflicts consists of 3 linked steps:

1   Showing acknowledgement for the other person's situation or view - not just the throwaway 'I hear what you say', but active listening followed by a brief summary or check question. This builds empathy and helps the other person to be receptive

2   Explaining one's own situation or view - done briefly and objectively, this helps the other person to understand the context and nature of the potential conflict

3   Proposing a positive way forward - this is important as it focuses on the solution rather than the problem.

An example would be:

- "I understand that you're annoyed that you hadn't heard earlier about the change in design"
- "The customer didn't confirm it until yesterday and I felt that you wouldn't want it raised with your staff unless it was definite"
- "Let's discuss how to get the design adapted now, and later we can look at preventing this happening again"

Ensuring That Solutions Continue to Work

One risk in managing conflict can be that an apparent resolution only deals with a symptom of the conflict rather than its cause. If this is the case, it is likely that the conflict will continue to generate problems. Project managers should keep resolved conflicts under observation and check that solutions are being successfully applied before assuming the situation is closed.

Cross-cultural Conflict

In international projects, or others involving the potential for conflict between representatives of different cultures, the situation is complicated by differing approaches to conflict across cultures. While this is a major subject in it's own right, there are some potential differences which it is useful to bear in mind:

- Degree of openness. Some cultures are more, and some less, comfortable to express concerns, disagreements or dislikes. The less open the culture, the more likely conflicts may not be apparent without a local adviser

- Importance of 'face'. Face is a concept of importance in many cultures, related to the impact of being seen to lose, to be insulted or to be wrong. The more important that face is, the more likely that conflicts will arise if the issue is not appreciated
- Potential for offending or insulting participants inadvertently. Many organisations which are used to doing business internationally will be tolerant of foreigners who are unaware of cultural issues. In a situation of conflict, however, this tolerance may be less reliable. It is worth remembering that the casual use of gestures, body language or comments and queries can result in giving offence in many cultures different from our own
- Language problems. In conflict, understanding can be of vital importance. It may be advisable in these circumstances, to use an interpreter even though the participants language ability is suitable for 'normal' situations

Finally, in important cross-cultural situations, get advice. The book by Morrison, et al. is a useful basic source, or organisations may have specialists or provide local agents or advisers. Embassies or overseas trade organisations are also a good source of information.

References and Further Reading

Parker, Glenn M., "Cross functional teams - working with allies, enemies and other strangers", Jossey-Bass Publishers, 1994

Gillen, T., "Assertiveness", Chartered Institute of Personnel Development, 1998

Morrison, Conaway & Borden, "Kiss, Bow or Shake Hands - How to do business in 60 countries", Adams Media Corporation, 1997

Thomas, Kenneth W., and Ralph H. Kilmann, Thomas-Kilmann Conflict Mode Instrument (Tuxedo, N.Y.: Xicom, 1974)

74 NEGOTIATION

Paul Vollans

"You cannot shake hands with a clenched fist."

Indira Gandhi (1917-1984), Indian stateswoman.
Remark, press conference, New Delhi (October 19, 1971).

Links to other topics

In the reality of project management, negotiation is an essential requirement. A key role for the project manager is to facilitate communication and interaction between project stakeholders - and these stakeholders will often have conflicting interests and requirements. It is important to see negotiation as an integral part of many of the processes of project management - in particular there will be strong links to the following topics:

20   Project Success Criteria
23   Risk Management
25   Health, Safety & Environment
30   Work Content & Scope Management
31   Time Scheduling/Phasing
32   Resource Management
33   Budget and Cost Management
34   Change Control
53   Procurement
64   Hand-Over
71   Teamwork
73   Conflict Management

The Need for Negotiation

The Project Context

Negotiation is one of the most common processes by which people in the project environment attempt to reach agreement. As mentioned above, the nature of most groups of stakeholders will involve differences in objectives, requirements, interests and values. The project manager will often play a key role in attempting to reconcile these differences to facilitate project success. Common examples of the need for negotiation include:

- Agreement of the project objectives and scope
- Agreement on the financial, staff and other resources required to achieve the project
- Agreement on the processes and activities required within the project
- Agreement on the responsibilities and commitment of key contributors
- Agreement on pricing and other issues with suppliers and sub-contractors
- Agreement on changes or differences of interpretation which arise as the project progresses
- Agreement on the completion and acceptability of the project

Dependent on the nature of the project, negotiation skills may be anything from a useful additional competency, to an essential requirement for project approval, implementation and success. Negotiation may be occasional and informal, or continuous and highly formal. It may involve one-to-one discussion or the interaction of teams from several stakeholders. It is therefore important for project managers to have a wide understanding of the nature and components of negotiation.

Reducing Unnecessary Negotiation

Whilst some negotiation may be a necessary part of project management, it is important to avoid using it as a substitute for good practice in other activities. Tools and approaches which have the potential to reduce the need for unnecessary or unproductive negotiation include:

- Using SMART (Specific, Measurable, Agreed, Realistic and Time-based) objectives both at the project and task levels
- Using Stakeholder Mapping to identify the full group of project participants and their aims and concerns
- Consulting widely when estimating task requirements in terms of resource, duration, effort and cost

- Putting in place agreed procedures for communication and change management
- Applying risk management techniques to reduce, or plan for, potential areas of disagreement

Outcomes of Negotiation

The intention of most negotiation is to achieve an acceptable and agreed outcome for all participants - this is sometimes referred to as a Win / Win result. It does not imply that all parties will be equally happy with the result, but the key factors are that the outcome is sustainable and does not contribute to further conflict. The other combinations for an outcome are:

- Lose / Lose - no party achieves an acceptable result. This may simply be a case where the parties objectives were mutually exclusive, as in the case of price negotiations where one party declines to take on potentially unprofitable business. However, it can also result from poor negotiation technique from one or more parties, where a suitable outcome potentially existed but was not achieved
- Lose / Win - the party which sees itself as the loser may have accepted an outcome which will not be sustainable for them in the longer term. This is often due to poor preparation and lack of a minimum target for the result. Low negotiating strength may require a low target, but this should not be seen as 'losing'
- Win / Lose - Although a party which sees itself as the winner my be happy with the outcome, attention should be paid to the problems outlined above. Using organisational authority to 'force' a project team member to accept an unrealistic task timescale can be a source of more serious problems later in the project

In general terms, Win / Win should be the preferred outcome in the project environment, using good negotiation technique to maximise the benefit to the organisation, while avoiding unprofitable or unsustainable agreements.

Developing Negotiation Objectives

A key element in being 'successful' in negotiation is the investment of initial time in defining how success is to be measured.

Liaison With Stakeholders

Unless the project manager is negotiating solely on their own behalf and fully within their authority limits, it is important to agree objectives with the other stakeholders being represented. While the objectives should allow for flexibility in negotiation, they should also set clear limits to what outcomes are, and are not, acceptable to the stakeholder. Consultation should identify the range of important issues, such as the inclusion of batch size and delivery timescale as well as cost in a negotiation for a component supply. This process of consultation can be time-consuming when representing multiple parties, but should be seen as an investment in avoiding later delay, dissatisfaction and/or renegotiations.

Establishing Authority and Limits

In order to balance flexibility and measurability, it will be useful for objectives for each of the key issues in the negotiation to expressed in terms of:

- Definition of negotiating purpose - for example, 'To agree a percentage allocation of technical staff effort which will allow the design phase to be completed within the planned duration and without serious disruption from other concurrent projects'. This can help to remind the negotiator of the larger picture thereby avoiding the risk of focussing only on the 'numbers' and increasing openness to creative solutions
- Target outcome (or Most Favoured Position)- for example, 'A total of 150% allocated, from 2 named technicians beginning 5th May'. This may not be the figure used as an 'opening position', but should be the best anticipated result

- Lower limit to agreement (or Least Favoured Position) - for example, 'Not less than 120% allocated with 75% or more contributed by a named technician, beginning 12th May'. This is a vital point and should be regarded as the stage at which the negotiator would be prepared to 'walk away' from the negotiation. In a complex negotiation, lower limits on different issues may be connected

- Strategy in the event of lower limit not being achieved - for example, 'Inform resource manager that the work will have to be outsourced'. It is important to consider the issue of non-agreement and decide what alternative will be applied. If there appears to be no alternative, the lower limit should be reviewed as it may be that the alternative would need to be applied at a more strategic level - i.e. renegotiation of project timescale, which might be beyond the negotiator's authority

Preparation Phase

Agreeing negotiating objectives allows the negotiator to start the detailed preparation. Skilled negotiators will see this the most important phase in contributing to their likelihood of success. Although the activities are described separately, in complex negotiations they will often involve overlap and perhaps several iterations. The phase may also overlap with the initial 'Discussion' phase when the negotiating parties are in contact. Obviously the amount of time invested in preparation should be dependent on the value and complexity of the negotiation, however all of the content below should be included to some degree.

Developing the Negotiator's Situation Map

Using the issues, objectives and limits outlined above, the negotiator can now map out their parties situation. This will consist of an overall objective, supplemented by a list of major and minor issues. The major issues will have an MFP / LFP as outlined in Figure 74 - 1.

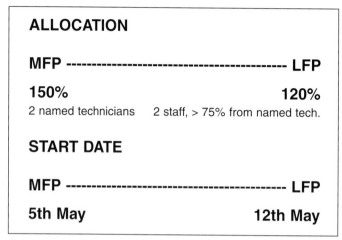

Figure 74 - 1: Negotiator's Situation Map.

In complex negotiations, or when negotiating on behalf of more than one party, notes will be added to indicate the interrelationship or ability to 'trade off' one issue against another.

Researching the Other Parties Situation

It is essential to invest time during preparation to investigating, or at least estimating, what the objectives, issues and MFP / LFP ranges of the other party will be. Without this, it will be difficult to develop an appropriate strategy for the negotiation or to decide on suitable opening positions on issues. A simple example would be developing an understanding of the current order book and utilisation targets of a production department before approaching them to schedule a series of large-scale production trials needed by an NPI project.

In negotiations with cultures that the negotiator is not familiar with, the research should include an appreciation of cultural issues.

Information about the other party can be obtained in a number of ways:

- Informal preliminary discussions - this is particularly suitable for internal or non-confrontational situations. In other cases, it may run the risk of allowing an opportunity for negotiations to begin before the negotiator is fully prepared
- Publicly available information - company accounts, price lists, terms and conditions, newsletters or press comment can all be potentially useful sources
- Third party advice - shared suppliers or customers may be a source, but should be used with caution as they may inform the other party of your approach. In major negotiations, it might be worth using professional advisors

In the absence of available information, it will still be worth developing a 'best guess' which can be updated as the situation becomes clearer once negotiations begin. The aim is to approximate the planning information which would be prepared by a good negotiator representing the other party.

Evaluating the Balance of Power

Research on the other party should help to clarify the relative value to each side of the issues to be negotiated. This is an important consideration, as it will impact on negotiating strategy and flexibility. The general rule is that 'the party that wants the deal the most has the least power'. While this is a simplification, it illustrates the value of not always sharing the information on the value of reaching agreement. Other relevant factors include:

- The existence of laws or regulations supporting either parties position
- The relative size or strength of the organisations or departments represented
- The relative value of the issue to the organisation as a whole
- Time pressure on one or more parties to resolve an issue
- Public or moral support for either parties position
- The experience of the parties in dealing with the type of issue

Comparing Positions

It is now possible to map one set of MFP / LFP against another for each major issue (including those which emerge as important to the other party) as shown in Figure 74 - 2:

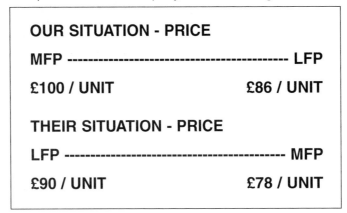

Figure 74 - 2: Comparative Issue Map 1

Obviously, the other parties MFP is more easily accessible information than their LFP. However, this diagram provides an indication of the probable area for an agreement (£86 - £90 per unit) and allows a review of the suitability of the negotiator's MFP as an opening position. Other situations which might be mapped are: shown in Figure 74 - 3.

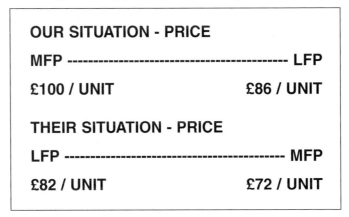

Figure 74 - 3: Comparative Issue Map 2

This implies that there may (remembering that this is an estimate) not be the potential for agreement. Further investigation may be advisable, or a review of the negotiator's LFP, or it may be feasible to 'package' better terms on other issues in order to gain agreement to a higher unit price. If the negotiator is fairly confident of the predicted figure for the other parties LFP and has little flexibility in his or her own, it may indicate that there is little point in continuing to pursue this negotiation.

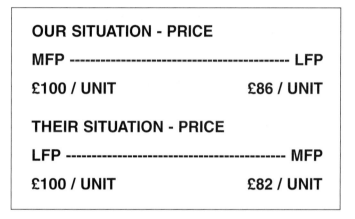

Figure 74 - 4: Comparative Issue Map 3

In this case depicted in Figure 74 - 4, researching the other party indicates that an outcome around the negotiator's MFP is possible. Given the uncertainty of the other parties LFP, it might be the case that the negotiator's MFP is too low. Certainly it indicates that an opening position above this figure would be advisable. Additionally, this diagram illustrates the danger of being too quick to quote an opening position in an uncertain negotiating situation, as it may in fact be an unnecessary concession.

Developing a Strategy for the Negotiation

Given the above preparation, the negotiator should be able to decide on their initial approach. This should cover areas including:

◆ The style of relationship to be fostered. This might range from informal and friendly in internal, low con-frontation situations, to an aggressive approach in a situation where this is appropriate and the other party has little power

◆ The probable timescale and format for the negotiation. In simple cases, it may be realistic to expect completion within a single, short meeting. In larger, more complex situations, or where multiple parties have to be consulted during the process, negotiation may consist of a number of discussions over a period of weeks

◆ The opening position. Commonly, the negotiator will encourage the other party to state their opening position first, as it often provides or confirms information. At some stage the negotiator will be required to make a proposal and this should usually consist of linked requirements some degree above the MFP for each key issue. In general, opening positions should indicate realism and imply some calculation rather than appear to be simply an optimistic 'first try'

◆ The issues which will be used to move the negotiation forward. Most negotiation will consist of exchanging movements on one issue for a movement on another by the other party

Negotiating With Teams

In some cases, the project manager may be part of a team negotiating with either an individual or one or more other teams. It is essential under these circumstances, to clearly agree in advance the roles and responsibilities of all team members. Failure to do this will leave the team open to problems such as:

◆ Disagreements within the team become apparent to the other party
◆ There is inconsistency between proposals or responses from team members
◆ Failure to accurately record the progress of the negotiation
◆ Valuable information is given away by team members

Key issues to be agreed are the responsibility for 'leading' the team, the contribution expected from each member, the process for recording progress and the arrangements for consultation within the team during negotiation.

The Stages of Negotiation

It is useful to recognise that effective negotiation usually progresses through four stages - Discussing, Proposing, Bargaining and Agreeing. The time allocated to each will vary depending on the nature (and cultural setting) of the negotiation. Each has important purposes and it will be of benefit to the negotiator to steer or influence the progression through the stages.

Stage 1 - Discussing

Although there may have been contact between the parties during preparation, this stage is usually seen as the start of the negotiation process itself. In most cases, parties will meet face to face, although telephone or videoconferencing are also options. The experienced negotiator will use this stage for 3 main purposes:

- Establishing rapport. Greeting, hospitality, general conversation, links to shared acquaintances are all part of this process. If the strategy is for formality or an aggressive approach, this initial contact will be adapted accordingly
- Clarifying the purpose and agenda. If this has not been established previously, it is important to outline the intention and scope of the meeting and to check that this is similar to the perception of the other party. In any case, it is often useful to set the current discussion in the context of the larger picture - project success, customer value, future business, etc. It will also be useful to informally explore the range of issues being considered and their relative importance

- Seeking or checking information. The experienced negotiator will realise that information is often easier to obtain in this initial stage than when bargaining is under way and perhaps conflicts have surfaced

Stage 2 - Proposing

This is when opening positions begin to emerge and indications are given as to their potential flexibility. In many cases, as discussed earlier, the negotiator will encourage the other party to begin this process, often by simply asking for their proposal. In some cases the negotiator may decide to state their sides opening position as a starting point - alternatively it may be stated as a counter proposal. It is important to pay attention to identifying and providing signals here without making commitments or concessions. Some examples of phrasing will illustrate this:

- "So we are looking for agreement to reduce the timescale of the development phase by 6 weeks, and of course we would not expect any significant increase in the cost." This states the opening position on timescale, and indicates a small potential flexibility in cost as a bargaining area
- "I can see no way of freeing more programming staff for your project, considering your requirement for at least 6 months experience in HTML work" Again the opening position is stated, while indicating a possible approach for resolving the problem
- "We'd be happy to discuss ways to help your accountants in structuring your payments, but the bottom line is that we have a binding contract for the payment to be made in this financial year." An indication of what is, and what is not (at least as an opening position) negotiable

General advice on responding to the other parties proposal would be to respond in a way that does not immediately indicate the negotiators view of positive elements, while clearly signalling disapproval of negative elements.

Stage 3 - Bargaining

Although this stage is often seen as the core aspect of negotiation, it is important to recognise that the activities of preparation, discussion and setting out the opening positions will usually have more potential to impact on success. The practical bargaining stage should be seen as reliant on good preparation, not as a substitute for it.

Critical to successful bargaining is an understanding that negotiation is very difficult when the focus is on only a single issue. Consider a situation where only timescale is at issue. Negotiator A states an opening position of 10 weeks. Negotiator B responds by stating that only 6 weeks would be acceptable. How can either party progress the negotiation? It is tempting to see the next step as one party moving a little closer - for example A could suggest that they might consider 9 weeks. What A is hoping for is that B will 'play the game' and move a little in exchange. While this may be acceptable in simple, less important situations, an experienced negotiator will recognise that A has in fact made a concession and gained nothing in return. The range has moved from 10 weeks / 6 weeks to 9 weeks / 6 weeks. In fact A's behaviour may signal a lack of power and encourage B to become firmer in their position in the expectation of further concessions.

In the majority of cases, good bargaining will consist of linking a movement on one issue to a reciprocal movement on another. In the example above, an option for A might be a response of: "If you would be prepared to discuss reducing the requirement for full certification, then it might be possible to reduce the testing period from 10 weeks." As bargaining progresses, the suggestions become more specific. "So let's be clear on this - would you guarantee certification in no more than 9 weeks and cover the costs of re-testing, if we agree to an extension of initial testing to 8 weeks and ensure that all samples are with you at the start of the period?" The balance of power between parties will often dictate the relative size of movements being exchanged.

The phrasing of "If you.... Then we..." is important. It avoids the problems of making concessions and clearly indicates the proposed way forward. By selecting issues of different values to each party, it is often the best way towards the 'Win/Win' outcome that we are aiming for.

Agreeing

Providing the negotiation can be resolved, it will be important to end the process by a review of exactly what has been agreed. A common problem where this is not done, is for parties to have different views on the outcome - resulting in later problems, recriminations and possible re-negotiation. In complex negotiations, this process should be made easier by regularly summarising what has been agreed and which issues are currently outstanding. In an important negotiation, it will be common to draft a written agreement at this stage. If the agreement is complex, legal advisers may well be involved. In less formal situations where a written agreement would be seen as inappropriate, it would still be good practice for the negotiator to send a confirming letter or email shortly afterwards to ensure that a record exists.

Of course, many negotiations will be more complicated than this and may involve a range of tactics, including pressure, aggression and threats to 'walk out', but the basic principle is usually the same.

The experienced negotiator will remember that their aim is to reach agreement somewhere between their MFP and LFP on the key issues and will strive to achieve this for as long as is appropriate.

Using and Recognising Strategies and Tactics

The Use and Effect of Tactics

'Tactics' loosely describes the wide range of embellishments available to the basic process described above. Generally, it is best for less experienced negotiators to treat tactics with caution as they have the potential to confuse the situation and to generate negative responses. It is, however, important to recognise tactics being applied by the other parties. A negotiator should develop a view on what is, and is not, acceptable in balancing the need to get the best outcome for his or her stakeholders, with the need to behave in a professional and acceptable manner.

Some Examples of Tactics

- "I'll have to ask my boss (or our accountants, etc.)" - creates delay and allows a further contact of "I'm sorry, but my boss says..."
- "You'll have to do better than that" - a statement that often gets a result
- Assumed Close - "Good, shall we sort out the paperwork?"
- "I know you're halfway through making our order now, but I need to discuss payments...." - waiting for committed cost to exert pressure
- Cherrypicking - (to X) "Y will do it in 3 weeks, can you match that?" (not mentioning Y charge double for this)

Responding to Unprofessional Tactics

While it can be tempting to respond in kind when a negotiator feels badly treated by the other party, it is usually best to either ignore or directly confront negative tactics.

Cross Cultural Implications for Negotiation

Negotiation style can vary widely between cultures. While globalisation of many businesses has reduced the impact of this, it is still essential for negotiators to be aware of the cultural issues affecting a specific negotiation.

The Range of Cultural Approaches to Negotiation

While the scope of this subject is very wide, there are a number of basic negotiation issues which will vary between cultures. As indicated above, the degree of cultural influence will often be mitigated by the individual's experience doing business internationally. ·

- Timescale for negotiation. This can vary from the tendency of Western cultures (particularly Americans) to 'get down to business' rapidly, to a much slower pace common in many other societies. In some cultures it will be considered inappropriate to discuss business at all in the first meeting between participants

- Basis for decision making. While Western cultures often emphasise individuality, facts and the 'bottom line', other cultures may be more influenced by collective values, beliefs or personal relationships in judging the value of a proposal

- Openness and confrontation. Some cultures are very open, and comfortable to display a range of emotions, while others regard this as naïve or inappropriate. In some countries, aggressive confrontation can simply be an expected tactic, in others it might be seen as rude or would imply a very severe problem

General Guidelines for Cross-cultural Negotiation

- Do research other cultures before engaging in important negotiations with their representatives. Recognise that serious errors can be made from ignorance that may jeopardise not only the current, but also future business

- Do identify those countries where it will be difficult, if not impossible, to negotiate successfully without a local agent or sponsor

- Do pay attention to details - in some cultures it is possible to offer serious insult by comments, questions, gestures or even a choice of gift, that our own culture would see as acceptable. While the host may make allowances for ignorance, the overall impression created will still be negative

- Don't apply the standards of one culture in judging another. Punctuality, formality, even the expectation of personal monetary benefit in a business negotiation, are valued differently across cultures

Managing the Agreement

In addition to reaching agreement, it is important to manage it.

Reviewing the Outcome with Stakeholders

Once negotiation appears to be complete, it is advisable to review the agreement to ensure that all parties are clear on what has been agreed. If the project manager is negotiating on behalf of other parties, they should also be consulted for approval.

Dealing with the Paperwork

Depending on the formality of the agreement, this might be anything from a legally binding document prepared by both parties' legal advisers, to an e-mail confirming the outcome of a verbal discussion. Unless everyone is very sure of the sustainability of the outcome, some form of written agreement is advisable to prevent later problems of interpretation or a change of view.

Merging the Outcome into the Project Plan

Where the agreement impacts the project plan, as in the case of resourcing or a change of timescale, it should be clearly updated, referring to the negotiation and following good practice in recording the reasons and date.

References and Further Reading

Fisher R, Or W & Patton B., Getting to Yes: Negotiating Agreement Without Giving In, Penguin, 1991.

Obeng, E., "All Change - The Project Manager's Secret Handbook", Financial Times Management, 1996

Morrison, Conaway & Borden, "Kiss, Bow or Shake Hands - How to do business in 60 countries", Adams Media Corporation, 1997

75 HUMAN RESOURCE MANAGEMENT

Anne Keegan

"A man's greatest battles are the ones he fights within himself."
Ben Okri (1959-), Nigerian novelist and poet. Flowers and Shadows (1980).

Managing Human Resources in Project Based Firms: Conventional Wisdom and Unconventional Challenges

Abstract

In this session, we will examine core issues in managing human resources in project based firms. In our introduction, a brief discussion of labour market trends sets the scene for examining staffing strategy in project based firms. We will examine how project based firms find the right people, select them and assess their performance at work. We will look briefly at evidence that the day to day work of personnel is an important determinant in job satisfaction, and explore the options project based firms have in designing jobs and roles. Career management in project based firms is also discussed. An important aspect of this session is critical assessment of the usefulness of traditional Human Resource Management tools and techniques within the context of project based organising. Throughout this session, reference is made at appropriate points to primary research on HRM in project based firms (Keegan & Turner 2000). Core trends in HRM in project based firms are signalled, and current thinking is explicated. References are provided throughout for further reading and in-depth treatment of all the issues that are discussed.

Abbreviations

HRM	Human Resource Management
HRP	Human Resource Planning

Other Relevant Topic Areas:

Introduction

Labour Market Trends and Project Based Firms

Labour market commentators and business experts are making one thing clear: the employment relationship has changed in fundamental ways. The traditional model of long-term commitment to a firm, reciprocated by long-term job security and slow and steady career progress, has been gradually eroded. In place of job security, the new discourse emphasises employability and marketability of employee knowledge and skills as the key to their own personal security in labour market terms. This is evident from the fact that even though 1999 was one of the best business years in corporate America, more workers were laid off by US companies than had been laid off during the recession years (Gomez-Mejia et al 2001:1). This new flexibility in employer-employee relations is not confined to the US. Far from it! According to leading European commentator on labour market trends, Chris Brewster, employment in Europe is becoming more and more flexible. Flexibility encompasses different types of practices including part-time work, sub-contracting, and the use of non-permanent work.

Capelli (2000) has analysed changes in labour markets and coins the phrase "the new deal" to refer to the shift from expectations of long term employment, and long-term employee loyalty, towards a market based perspective on the employment relationship. He cites evidence that employers and employees are increasingly approaching the employment relationship in a transactional way, committed only for as long as it is mutually profitable. This is supported by research into project based firms carried out by Arthur, Claman and DeFillippi (1995: 9) who state:

> "The 'excellent' firms of the past proved unable to live up to their employment promises. Because of their inability to predict the future, firms have been typically unable to predict the future of their employee's careers. Even the most enduring employer-employee relationships will be best served by regular renegotiations of contracts and of associated terms and inducements"

That mainstream industry and service sector firms have experienced profound shifts in the employment relationship in the last twenty years cannot be denied. Legge (1998) summarises evidence of a general decline of permanent, long-term employment in the UK, citing as follows:

- The fall in the proportion of the working population in full-time employment from 55.5% in 1975 to 35.9% in 1995
- The doubling of the number of part-time male employees between 1984 and 1995
- An increase in the number of temporary jobs of 31% between 1984 and 1998, compared to an increase of merely 0.5% in the number of permanent jobs

Project based firms are among the firms that have most experience with atypical forms of employment - and the difficulties they face reflect changes that are taking place in the labour force in general. Some estimates say contract labour can, for example, account for up to 80% of labour on a project (Keegan & Turner 2000).

Consequences of Labour Market Trends for HRM in Project Based Firms

The increase in flexible forms of labour, declining employee loyalty to organisations, and the tight labour market that exists for some categories of skills - notably managerial and IT skills - all suggest that project based firms need to consider their approach to managing human resources. How are they going to attract and keep the kind of people necessary for successful management of projects? Who are these people likely to be, and where are they likely to come from? What kind of relationship do they want to forge with people who are hired on part-time, temporary and flexible contracts? If these people play a crucial role, how can they be encouraged to stick with the organisation - despite more attractive options in the open market - for the duration of the project or crucial phases of it?

The changing nature of the employment relationship has rendered conventional approaches to HRM incomplete and inadequate to the challenge of managing people in project based firms. A good deal of writing in HRM assumes that the firm has a majority of regular, long-term, permanent employees. As Brewster (1998: 257) points out, the relevance of conventional HRM may therefore be called into question.

> "Like the texts written on personnel management, the literature on HRM tends to continue to be written as if all or most of the organisations human resources are found among employees on standard (long-term, full-time) employment contracts. As long as this remains the focus, the literature, like the profession, will be doomed to discussing an ever-smaller proportion of the way work is done."

The relevance of this comment for project based firms is clear. Many, if not all projects, are carried out with the aid and assistance of people who are not directly employed by the project based firm. When project-based firms consider their human resources therefore, they may benefit - at least during crucial projects - from considering the impact of human resources they do not directly employee. They may also benefit from considering HR practices in a fluid and evolving way. This perspective, often missing in conventional HRM writing, is explicitly drawn into the picture. In this chapter, these labour market trends and trends in the employment relationship provide a backdrop for discussing HRM in project based firms. We will examine issues including:

- Planning for employment in project based firms
- Recruiting personnel for the project based firm
- Selecting personnel for the project based firm
- Job and role design in project based firms
- Rewards in project based firms
- Performance management and project based firms
- Careers in project based firms
- Information management and human resources

Planning for Employment in Project Based Firms

To respond to labour market trends and changes in markets, technologies and competitive conditions, project based firms can look to the future, consider the changes likely to have the most impact on them, and how they are going to respond to these changes. How they do this is the subject matter of Human Resource Planning. The illustration below sketches a typical approach to Human Resource Planning.

Almost every HR textbook on the market has a similar schematic representation of HR planning depicting five basic elements:

1 Activities to analyse changes in *the environment.*
Assessing possible changes in:

- social developments
- demographic developments
- technological developments

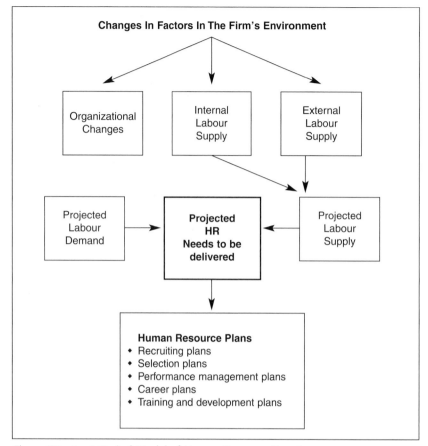

Figure 75 - 1: A Typical Model of Human Resource Planning

* industry developments
* market developments
* competitor developments
* legislative developments
* political developments

An example of how this is relevant for the project-based firm is illustrated below:

A recent development is the increasing incidence of dual career families. Companies are finding that it is more difficult to get employees to accept overseas postings because of the potential conflict with the career of one of the dual earners. Project based firms with extensive overseas activities and the need for flexibility in posting staff overseas can benefit from being aware of social changes of this nature and their potential impact on international staffing arrangements. They may, for example, need to build factors such as employment search programmes for spouses into their overseas postings activities.

2   Activities to analyse changes in *organisational objectives and strategies.*
Assessing possible changes in:

* Organisation structure
* Workforce composition
* Developments in labour representation
* Organisational strategy re clients, competitors, etc.

Planned changes in organisation structure can have profound consequences on people's lives and livelihoods. Information technology is enabling firms to flatten their hierarchies and remove layers of middle management. Changes to organisation structure of this type impact on how human resources are organised. Self-managed teams need to be facilitated and trained in these flattened hierarchies. Those formerly in middle management roles may need to be redeployed or fired - as has been the case in many US and European firms throughout the 1990s. Planned changes in organisation structure can have profound consequences on people's lives and livelihoods. Not all these changes are pleasant, and many have both legal and moral implications that should be considered when formulating HR plans.

3   Activities to forecast labour demand including:

* One year, three year and five year forecasts
* Judgmental forecasts
* Expert panel forecasts
* Managerial estimates
* Statistical projections
* Trade union projections based on labour market intelligence and research

4   Activities to forecast of labour supply - Internal:

- Replacement planning (short-term) and Succession planning (long-term) = Creating overview of names of current and potential occupants of positions
Potential promotions are estimated based on performance assessments of those in current positions, and their developmental needs. Charts usually show both incumbents as well as potential successors
- Analyses of staff leaving the organisation in different segments of the labour pool
- Retention profile of specified groups e.g. all those who remained from the employees hired within a specific year

External:

- Estimating the number of new graduates expected to come onto the labour market in a given field in a given year

5   Activities to reconcile these forecasts through HR plans:

- Hiring plans
- Development and training plans
- Reward plans
- Performance management plans
- Employee utilisation plans
- Employee relations plans
- Communications plans
- Knowledge management plans
- Learning plans
- Firing plans

Planning can be formal and informal, qualitative and quantitative. Planning can achieve a number of different things. Firstly, plans help project based firms to operationalise the ideas they have about where they are going. By planning, the consequences of ideas outlined, discussed, probed, debated, and changed in light of what is possible, probable and feasible. Planning helps to explicate assumptions held by organisational members about where the organisation is going and how it can get there. Planning is also a way of increasing communication within the project based organisation about what strategies are already in place. Sometimes several different types of strategy are in operation and when plans are made, the opportunity is presented for members to explicate and clarify the kinds of strategies they have in place. The strengths and weaknesses of different prevailing approaches can be explored in the planning process. The planning process can also be seen as a process for providing organisational members with ideas. Opening up the debate about the kind of markets in which a firm is involved and projects it carries out can yield surprising information previously held by diffuse organisational members.

HR Planning and Project Based Firms: Issues to Consider

Although the schema presented in Figure 75 - 1 may suggest that planning is a neat solution to the problems of how project based firms should approach their HR needs, most project managers probably know that this schema is a highly simplified version of the thorny reality they work within. The feasibility of planning and the relevance of plans always mediate the potential value of planning for HR needs. This is especially true in the case of project based firms.

Underlying the planning process is the assumption that future events can be anticipated, and that these events will unfold - perhaps not exactly - but with reasonable proximity to what has been anticipated. Project based firms undertaking unique novel and transient work for different clients face uncertainty about the kinds of projects they will undertake in the near and distant future. Projects themselves, even those secured, can change substantially during their lifecycle in terms of the kinds of HR demands placed on the firm. More importantly (HR) planning may contribute to the creation of a mindset within project-based firms that the future is certain, stable, and under control. Planning may help to create the illusion that future needs have been understood, anticipated and controlled by management and may in the process absolve each individual person of responsibility for sensing and responding to changes.

Experts argue that firms operating in uncertain and rapidly changing markets should avoid heavy reliance on formal planning (Arthur, Claman and DeFillippi 1995; Mintzberg 1979). Low emphasis on formal planning, and high emphasis on searching, scanning and reacting to changes in people management, encourages the development of a culture in which each and every member of the firm feels responsible for sensing and responding to changes in the market place. Creating a culture where everyone feels responsible for monitoring and responding to changes, and everyone knows how their own work fits into the overall work of the organisation, is seen as more valuable than carrying out formal (HR) planning.

Added to the uncertainty that project based firms face in their markets is the inherent uncertainty of planning for HR needs. In work on corporate planning Hussey (1999) argues that planning for human resources is more complex than planning for financial resources. This is because of the difficulties of moving people around (internal rigidities, legislative restrictions, the human desire for stable sets of tasks, colleagues), the high costs of overstaffing, the importance of treating people with respect and recognising they are not simply another (inanimate) resource, and the power of individual needs and motivations as an input to how work is actually performed - often in spite of plans.

In the absence of extensive planning practices project based firms can create a culture in which project managers, line managers and other personnel continually search and scan the labour market for potential employees. A study by Keegan (1998) of knowledge intensive firms reveals that a core role played by managers in advertising agencies is to stay in touch with movements on the talent market - both of established people and of newcomers. They do this by attending industry events, maintaining informal contact with peers in other agencies, and by encouraging newcomers to the industry to engage in projects, trials and work experiences.

Why then, given these caveats, should we even consider planning as a useful process? The answer lies in the fact that different firms face different conditions in their internal and external environment in ways that impact on the efficacy of planning. Planning, per se, is neither a good nor a bad thing. It is neither effective nor ineffective. It depends entirely on how the firm positions itself with respect to its environment (e.g. a reactive posture, favouring stable markets or a prospector posture, favouring the exploitation of new, uncharted market territories). Project based firms need to examine the efficacy of planning in their own context which in turn is driven by the choices they make in terms of the kind of markets and strategies they are willing and able to pursue. Where conditions are fairly stable, and changes are easy to anticipate, planning can help to increase the effectiveness of human resource activities.

However, where project based firms face an uncertain environment, with volatile product-market-client characteristics, high magnitude of change and high levels of flexibility, they should attempt to instil in every worker a sense of responsibility for sensing and responding to changes and understanding the place of their own work and contribution within the overall scheme of things (Gomez-Meija & Balkin 1999; Burns & Stalker 1961). In these circumstances, highly formalised planing should give way to active development of a culture where everyone is encouraged to recognise their role in the total work of the organisation, and their responsibility of sensing, interpreting and communicating changes they detect in carrying out their work. Whatever the situation, careful consideration of the kind of HR environment - internal and external - and how sensibly to respond to it, can be of great value to project based firms.

Recruitment

Recruitment is the process of generating a pool of potential job applicants. Recruitment practices can be formal or informal. Formal recruitment practices are often, if not always, based on job analysis . The main goal of job analysis is the development of a normative statement of how a job should be performed to realise strategic objectives. A classic HRM tool, job analysis is used to produce job descriptions as templates to which people are then hired. These job descriptions generally emphasise the actual behaviours jobholders should exhibit in order to perform their jobs in ways that achieve strategic goals. There are many ways of performing job analysis, and tools and techniques that can be used (Torrington, Hall & Taylor 2002).

Before we proceed, it is important to note here that we encounter the same problems with job analysis in the context of project based firms as we encounter when discussing HR planning. From a conceptual perspective, job analysis assumes that firms can accurately predict changes, translate these into strategic objectives, and further translate these - using job analysis - into relevant, accurate descriptions of what jobs will be and how they should be performed to achieve effective, strategic job performance. This assumption is increasingly viewed as untenable in the light of increasing boundarylessness of new forms of organising (Barnes-Nelson 1997).

Project based firms operating in volatile, fast-moving environments, producing customised offerings for clients, may well find that job analysis has limited efficacy. Job analysis assumes jobs to be discrete bundles of tasks. In project based firms, jobs evolve as projects evolve, mapping themselves to the contours of the project and the unique novel and transient aspects of the client, technology, and project team members. Job descriptions, if in fact they are used at all, should probably be seen as a basis for beginning the search for personnel, but not as a template predicting a tight fit. Flexibility is a core issue in staffing projects.

Perhaps because of the difficulties of predicting future needs of jobholders in a specific way, project based firms undertake a lot of informal hiring (Keegan and Turner 2000). Informal hiring and a "buy" skills strategy are both linked to high levels of change in a firm's environment (Gomez-Meija & Balkin 1992).

A list of recruiting methods - formal and informal - is ste out in Figure 75 - 2.

Recruiting Methods:

Employee Referrals
Walk-in applicants
Advertising in Newspapers
Advertising in Journals/Magazines
Advertising in Direct Mail
Advertising in Radio/Television Media
Government employment service
Private employment agencies
Internet
Colleges/Universities
Technical/Vocational schools
Trade Unions
Careers Fairs
Open House
Head-hunters
Informal soliciting of identified persons - directly or through intermediaries

---

Figure 75 - 2: Recruiting Methods

Informal hiring practices include:

- Headhunting
- Employee referrals

Headhunting - based on formal and informal labour market intelligence - is a core form of recruitment for KIFs (Knowledge Intensive Firms) in general, and project based firms (Keegan 1998; Keegan & Turner 2000). Employee referrals are also becoming more common as a way of identifying potential new recruits. This may be linked to changes in the labour market and the declining expectation that employee's will have a job for life (Capelli 2000). Using employee referral highlights social ties development at the pre-employment stage.

Employee referral programmes can be informal (project managers asking around among their team about potential recruits from among family, friends, former workmates, former classmates etc.) or formal (employees are rewarded for referring successful applicants). In the case of formal employee referral schemes, rewards can vary from as little as several pounds to as much as several thousand pounds. In many formal schemes, conditions are attached to payout, for example that the referred employee must complete a certain period of employment, a certain project, etc. One aspect of employee referral programmes often cited is that referred employees have a more realistic view of the job and organisation than non-referred employees, and that this reduces risks of turnover. One problematic aspect of employee referral programmes is that people tend to recommend people like them, especially in terms of cultural background. Over-reliance on employee referrals may lead to a largely homogeneous workforce and may be detrimental in terms of equal employment opportunity obligations. Developing links with educational establishments is a common recruiting method among project based firms (Keegan & Turner 2000).

Selection

Having identified potential hires, project based firms have to select from among them. Common selection methods are shown in Figure 75 - 3.

Employment interviews are the most common form of selection tool used in both the United States and Europe. Employment interviews are very well accepted by candidates, even though their validity in terms of predicting job success is low . All of the project based firms studied by Keegan and Turner (2000) and Keegan (1998) use employment interviews. Graphology - handwriting analysis - is not a common form of selection, although it is commonly used in France. Projects, trials and work experiences are very popular as a way of selecting personnel in project based firms and knowledge intensive firms. Exceptional expertise in particular fields is important, but the capacity to function well within

Selection Methods:

Employment interviews
Medical and physical tests
Reference and background checks
Work simulations
Ability, personality and interest tests
CV checking
Application forms
Assessment centres
In-Tray exercises
Graphology (hand-writing analysis)
Projects, trials, work experience
Headhunting

Figure 75 - 3: Selection Methods

a project-based environment is crucial. Project workers interact with members of a variety of functions and disciplines, and with different kinds of clients. Project managers claim that when hiring personnel, the most important issues are whether or not the person can tolerate ambiguity, shifting project conditions, instability, and movements in (key) personnel within the life-cycle of the project. These questions are very important, but difficult to answer. Many selection models in HRM are premised on go-no go decisions based on HR planning, job analysis and selection tools like interviews, assessment centres and selection tests. Project based firms may benefit from a more fluid and continuous form of selection that allows first hand observation of how potential hires cope with the nature of project work. Hiring a person on trial, or for a particular project, allows first hand observation of how the person copes with the nature of project work, and with the kind of projects and clients the firm is handling. This may explain why qualitative research indicates that project, trails and work experience, and hiring from pre-selected pools of candidates, is especially popular in project based firms (Keegan 1997; Keegan & Turner 2000).

Searching and scanning the labour market for appropriate people is a core tool in responding to uncertainty in the management of human resources in project based firms. Project managers and their human resource personnel should act as talent scouts, aware of the staffing challenges for project based firms and responsive to opportunities - such as student internships - that arise and that offer potential candidates far more lasting employment relationships. The searching and scanning process can never be too broad for project based firms. They deal with a wide range of actors - formal employees, clients, contractors, free-lance agents, etc. - and encounter talent, skill and expertise in a variety of ways. The labour pools for potential organisational members are therefore constantly evolving and emerging.

Finally, whereas selection is traditionally seen as something that takes place at the beginning of a career, project based firms encourage us to see selection as something that occurs throughout careers. People are selected for particular project teams, new free-lancers and sub-contractors are selected for new projects, and personnel are selected to suit new clients. This places new pressures on organisations to constantly revisit their talent pool in light of new clients and projects. It also places pressure on employees who are frequently evaluated and scrutinised in terms of what challenges they will be offered, and in what order. Undoubtedly, as this mind-set becomes more common, employees also select and de-select their employers more consciously and more often, placing pressure on project based firms to provide an employment experience attractive to current as well as prospective organisational members.

Job Satisfaction and Project Based Firms: The Problems of Role Ambiguity and Role Conflict

Once employees are hired, the way the organisation designs its work has a key impact on whether or not new hires will stay and how they will perform. Research on job satisfaction reveals that factors relating to the work situation are very important in retaining employees. Core factors in job satisfaction include those relating to tasks. There are many studies relating task characteristics to worker reactions and job satisfaction. Task characteristics that influence job satisfaction include the number of tasks a worker must perform; the responsibility a worker has for carrying out their tasks; how physically demanding tasks are; how meaningful tasks are to the person; the quality of feedback given to the worker; whether or not the tasks are valued by the worker; etc.

Job satisfaction is also strongly related to roles. The person's role in the organisation can be defined as the set of expected behaviours that both the person and other people who make up the social environment have for that person in that job (Noe et al 2000). Role design is particularly important in project based firms. Project based organising has particular consequences for roles, and in particular the potential for role ambiguity. Role ambiguity refers to the level of uncertainty about what the organisation expects from the employee in terms of what to do and how to do it. The most problematic form of ambiguity in terms of predicting job satisfaction is ambiguity related to performance criteria. This is important in project based firms because of the frequent overlapping of roles that occurs when people work for project teams and are also working within a functional or departmental context. The performance criteria from the project side can clash with performance criteria from the functional side. Matrix management can also contribute to role ambiguity, because project managers and line managers have different expectations of workers. Since studies suggest that employees have strong needs to know how they are going to be evaluated on the job, it is not unreasonable to suggest that problems may arise for employees in project based firms if they are (formally and/or informally) evaluated by both functional managers and project managers. In the extreme, when working on more than one project, employees face the potential of ambiguity arising from having at least three people who assess their performance, on different projects, and according to different criteria. Under these circumstances, it is hardly surprising if role ambiguity arises and leads to job dissatisfaction.

Another important source of job dissatisfaction that project based firms should be aware of is role conflict. Role conflict arises when an employee is faced with incompatible or contradictory demands. Noe et al (2000) specifically cite members of cross-functional project teams as an example where role conflict might be expected to occur.

To minimise role ambiguity and role conflict, managers in project based organisations should be aware of how roles in their organisations are designed whether deliberately or as a result of loosely connected historical decisions. Where it appears that role ambiguity and role conflict are a source of job dissatisfaction for employees in project based firms, one useful and relatively simple technique is for the organisation to perform a role analysis. To do this, managers should identify those people - which we shall refer to as role occupants - they suspect may experience problems with role ambiguity and role conflict. Each role occupant and each member of the role occupant's role set (e.g. supervisors, co-workers, subordinates, and clients) are asked to write down their expectations for the role occupant. A meeting of the role occupant and members of the role set is called during which all of the expectations are discussed, and ambiguities and conflicts are identified. The group resolves important sources of role ambiguity and role conflict so that more balanced roles can be developed.

Performance Management

The management of individual performance is one of the biggest challenges facing project-based firms. Torrington, Hall and Taylor (2002: 298) envisage individual performance management of a simple cycle, a version of which is depicted in Figure 75 - 4.

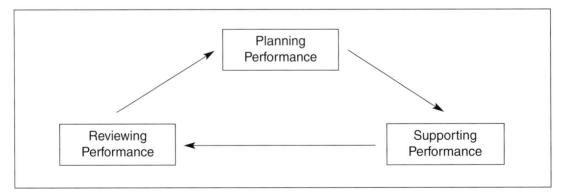

Figure 75 - 4: Performance Management Cycle

Even though difficult to measure, performance differences between individuals may have an impact on overall performance of a project team, or an organisation. This is the assumption underpinning performance management. Performance management includes practices for:

Planning Performance

When planning performance, project based firms face different challenges in terms of regular employees and those members of the project team or broader environment that substantially impact on performance.

In the case of regular employees, most experts agree that both employee and employer should draw up performance plans. Plans drawn up by the employer and given to the employee to carry out may be greeted with hostility, disillusionment and suspicion. Where employees are genuinely involved in planning for their own performance, they can inform employers of what is realistic and desirable. They can also try to influence the plans to support their own personal development and career goals. Excluding the employee from the planning process is unlikely to stop them from pursuing their own goals. If these goals motivate employees, it is better to use that energy and try to achieve some sort of agreement with employees about their own goals and those perceived as important by employers. In terms of content, plans are often drawn up to include generic objectives with open timeframes as well as specific goals with specific deadlines. When both employee and employer are involved in drawing up plans, there is a greater likelihood that the employee will understand the goals and that the goals will be realistic and achievable. In the face of other people who substantially affect performance on a project, the project based firm can try to work closely with clients, free-lance agents, sub-contractors and others to plan performance and try to develop a shared view of what is important. This requires a mind-set that embraces a whole range of human resources, and not just those within real or imaginary organisational "walls". Joint problem solving teams, brain-storming sessions and informal contacts may help to surface performance assumptions, and reveal bottlenecks or conflicting performance plans. However, this will only be seen as useful if the project-based firm embraces the idea that managing performance is a challenge that goes beyond its immediate, identifiable employees. Barriers to such initiatives can include, for example, a conventional view of performance management as involving only direct employees, and also historical mistrust between clients and contractors.

Supporting Performance

Project based firms can, through their managers and the provision of resources, enable workers to achieve performance plans. Support can include anything from off the job training, coaching, mentoring, to manager's simply being available and accessible to help employee's overcome organisational or personal barriers to achieving their plans.

Reviewing Performance

In project based firms, review of performance is vital. Regular, informal review is necessary to monitor employee performance and ensure that employee's are receiving all the support they need to achieve the objectives set in the planning phase. However, because project based firms operate in a volatile and rapidly changing environment, regular review also provides an opportunity for managers to communicate changes in - for example - project objectives, client demands, market or technological changes, etc, that impact on employee performance objectives.

Many companies formalise the review stage of the performance management cycle with performance appraisal systems. Appraisal systems of a formalised nature are usually centralised in the HR department, and require line managers to carry out formal appraisal interviews at regular intervals - annually, six-monthly, quarterly, etc. Appraisal forms are often used to record the outcomes. Performance appraisal systems can serve several often conflicting - ends. Appraisal interviews can be used to determine a person's potential, or to decide on their compensation, or to set performance goals and objectives. This means that the appraiser can be called on to simultaneously 'judge' and 'help' the employee.

Difficulties arise for both the employee being appraised and the appraiser. For example, the employee may withhold vital information that could help them to perform better because they fear it will reduce the rewards attached to the appraisal process. The appraiser may find it hard to maintain trust and confidentiality as a 'helper' if they are placed in a position where the 'judgement' they levy as a result of the appraisal process is harsh.

These difficulties are compounded by the simple fact that appraisal, which involves judging others, is a subjective and frequently highly political process. The appraiser has power over the appraisee, and may return judgements that serve their own ends, for example having someone they dislike removed from a project; overrating someone they feel is essential to a project in order to gain extra resources even though the person's performance is actually poor, etc. Project based firms must consider and allow for this political side of performance management, as it cannot be eliminated.

Performance management systems - including performance appraisal - can be used for a variety of purposes as summarised below:

Uses of Performance Management (incorporating performance appraisal):

Compensation decisions
Improvement of performance
Feedback, counselling and mentoring
Documentation for legal purposes
Promotion Decisions
Transfer decisions
Training and development
Discharge decisions
Redundancy decisions
Selection procedure validation
Human Resource Planning

Figure 75 - 5: Uses of Performance Management

Performance Management and the Project Based Firm

No performance management system is perfect, and many see performance appraisal as a waste of time and a mere paper-pushing exercise. For performance management to be successful, it should be embedded within the organisation and suited to the type of work and type of people employed. This is particularly true of a formal appraisal system. In project based firms for example, it is likely that successful performance appraisal, in a multi-disciplinary environment where there are many teams and many clients, will benefit from multiple inputs for appraisal. This is necessary to ensure that employees working on different projects, or working for both project managers and functional line managers, have a chance for their over-all performance to be taken into account. The development of a performance appraisal system that takes into account the many "views" of a person's performance that exist within the project based firm can help to tackle problems of role ambiguity and conflict discussed in the last section. Faced with the problem of managing career development in a context where personnel have multiple overlapping roles in different projects, some project-based firms appoint managers whose role it is to focus specifically on the development of personnel in their charge (Keegan & Turner 2000). These managers play a key role in gathering information and assimilating feedback on the performance of those personnel.

Where possible, input from clients with whom the employee closely works can also be useful. Peer appraisal may also be beneficial to building a sense of teamwork and team based performance. Perhaps most importantly, the multi-team multi-disciplinary nature of most project work calls for customised appraisal processes for people, rather than uniform procedures more suited to highly bureaucratised firms in stable environments (Gomez-Mejia 2000). In advertising agencies for example, regular daily feedback is vital to the progress of creative work on campaigns. The idea of feedback at once-yearly intervals, during an appraisal process, is blatantly unsuitable in such a context. In this situation a culture of frequent, informal appraisal should be built into any attempts to formalise the system. Furthermore, formalisation should not de-prioritise the kind of appraisal and feedback that occurs during the natural workflow of the project process.

Rewards

Rewards are an important aspect of managing people in project based firms. Even though a lot of factors work towards a situation in which a person is satisfied or dissatisfied at work, rewards play a key role because for most people, a job is their primary source of income and financial support. Rewards are a powerful symbol and are strongly linked to social status.

In recent years, there has been increasing flexibility in reward systems. Performance related pay has become the norm in many industries, and increasingly firms are adopting flexible cafeteria style rewards to cater for the different things people value at different stages in their careers. Another aspect of rewards is how very difficult it is to get it right. HRM literature is replete with examples of how to manage rewards effectively. The following principles are advocated:

Process is Crucial

The reward design process is crucial in winning acceptability and gaining legitimacy. If employees understand how rewards are decided upon, they are more likely to support the outcomes.

Flexibility

Not everyone values the same outcomes. It is becoming more common that firms design flexibility into reward systems so that people can choose those options best suited to their career stage.

Emphasise Total Rewards

When communicating about rewards, it is valuable to take an overall perspective including base pay, variable pay, medical plans, pension contributions, etc. Many people do not know the total value of their reward package, and many companies do not take the time or resources to communicate total rewards. Many firms offer family friendly time and work scheduling, but fail to let people know. Many more offer generous tuition reimbursement, but again fail to let people know.

Be Fair

If employees feel they are being unfairly rewarded - comparing their situation internally or externally - they can be strongly de-motivated. Sources of unfairness can derive from the way the reward process is perceived -leading to feelings of procedural injustice - and also with the way it is perceived that rewards are shared in an absolute sense - leading to feelings of distributive injustice. Regular internal and external salary surveys can be used to detect misalignments within the internal situation and with the external marketplace. It is always important to be aware of the company's responsibilities under relevant equal pay legislation. Because fairness is something people perceive, it is vital that communication about rewards - how they are determined and what the outcomes are - is very high and very clear.

Be Realistic About What Monetary Rewards Can Achieve

There is strong evidence that the motivating potential of financial rewards may be short-lived. Remember that if people are attracted to your company because of money, they can easily be 'bought' by a competitor. Gold handcuffs are easily unlocked with golden handshakes.

Communicate the Value of Non-monetary Rewards

Surveys suggest that people are attracted to firms because of the growth potential of the work on offer. It is important therefore to emphasise the growth potential in the projects you have, the clients you deal with, etc. Sveiby (1997) argues that in order to motivate and retain talented employees in knowledge based project work, the right projects and clients are important, and matching personnel to these projects and clients is critical to growth.

> **Reward Checklist:**
>
> Internally, is the process of deciding rewards understood within the company?
>
> - Is it based on principles of procedural justice?
> - Are the principles well understood by organisational members?
> - Is it based on principles of distributive justice?
> - Does it support business strategy?
> - Do key stakeholders, e.g. trade unions, support the process?
>
> Externally, are you making efforts to gain knowledge of what competitor firms are offering?
>
> - Do you use industry surveys?
> - Do you use personal contacts?
> - What kind of reward strategy do you want to have vis a vis competitors?
>
> When you think rewards, are you thinking total rewards?
>
> - Are you communicating the value of total rewards?
> - Are you emphasising the value of non-monetary rewards?

Figure 75 - 6: Reward checklist

Careers in Project Based Firms

It is tempting to view project based firms as an answer to the problems of the traditional, functional hierarchy. Project based firms are more flexible, they work in a more customer focussed way, and they deliver unique answers to one-off problems. Despite its drawbacks however, the traditional functional hierarchy has one strong benefit: it provides a conduit for people to have stable, predictable careers. The hierarchy allows people to develop 'upward' careers. Functions themselves act as training grounds, allowing people to specialise and develop expertise in specific fields. Project based organisations of today are increasingly 'flatter', stripping out layers of management and emphasising the importance of multi-disciplinary teams as a core governance structure. In so-called new forms of organising that emphasise multidisciplinary project teams as a core building block - including boundaryless firms, virtual organisations, network firms, etc. the nature of careers is changing.

As we discussed in the section under labour market trends, the employer employee relationship is changing. This has direct implications for the management of careers in project based firms. Arthur, Claman and DeFillippi (1995) explain how employees (career actors) and managers can rethink popular employment practices to prepare for a "new career world" in which commitment to specific projects is more important than commitment to broader corporate policy. In this view, project outcomes dominate and career success is directly linked to project success. From a career perspective, it is more important to achieve project success (over and over) than to be seen as "a good solider" regardless of results.

In research by Keegan and Turner (2000) the spiral staircase is the image that best suits career development in project based firms. Spiral staircases sweep upward rather than ascending in a narrow, ladder-like way. The sweeping element reflects the breadth of experience, skills and knowledge required in a multi-disciplinary project environment that people acquire from different project experiences and opportunities. Non-employee members of project teams may also be developing their careers while working on projects. Supporting them can help to engender loyalty over the longer term and a propensity to respond positively to future overtures made by the project based firms when new project opportunities arise.

Career development in project based firms can be reformulated to reflect the importance of a wide variety of different experiences, some of which do not yield immediate advance in an upwards manner. The spiral staircase career places emphasis on slow and gradual development of knowledge and skills, and draws emphasis away from seniority and management of increasingly large numbers of subordinates as the measure of career success. In flatter organisations, there are simply fewer points in the hierarchy for people to ascend to. Careers are therefore differently predicated. Success is interpreted differently.

The management of careers in project based firms is inextricably linked with the management of career expectations. The signals of career success are blurred, the rewards from hard work and long service are by no means guaranteed. Although exciting, challenging places within which to work, new flatter flexible organisations are also rife with insecurity and competition for scarce status symbols. Arthur, Claman and DeFillippi (1995:19) caution that managing careers in new flatter, flexible project oriented companies as though they are still tall, functional hierarchies with many separate levels of hierarchy, and the ability of offer rewards for long service and employment security, is bound to lead to clashes in the employment system.

Finally, the role of managers in supporting career development and expectations is very important. Survey after survey reveals the importance of management to how satisfied workers are, and whether or not they intend to stay with a company. The quality of managers is crucial in creating a culture where people can develop and grow. In project based firms, supporting the career development of individuals means developing a culture where project pressures are balanced against the necessity to release talented people for vital opportunities. In some companies, an overarching framework for monitoring career development, learning and individual growth opportunities may be necessary to ensure that career development is a strong factor in attracting and retaining talented personnel.

Information Management

All of the areas of HRM we have discussed need to be underpinned by an effective information management system. HRIS (Human Resource Information Systems) are often developed to meet this need. The HRIS should be designed to provide information gathering, sorting and disseminating support in areas such as recruitment, performance management, etc. One of the most important functions is the support it gives to internal and external corporate communications about human resources. As more and more companies are adding Human Resource Management Sections to their corporate branding, communications and annual reports, HRIS can provide up-to-date information. In addition, HRIS can provide information required for legislative purposes in terms of health and safety, selection, discipline, etc. The degree of sophistication of such a system will depend on many contextual factors including the size of the company, number of projects or functions in place, and the presence of skilled personnel to manage the system. For further information on detailed design issues in establishing and managing HRIS, see Torrginton and Hall (2002) and Noe et al (2000).

Areas of Interest Not Covered in This Chapter

HRM in an extensive area of management. Some aspects of managing people are governed by legislation and guidelines that project based firms should be aware of. These include health and safety, grievance and discipline, etc. For information on these topics - which are too extensive to be covered in this chapter - there are many excellent standard HRM textbooks. For example, please refer to Torrington and Hall (2002)for treatment and also further references. Local government agencies in the area of health and safety and employment can also provide information.

Conclusion

This chapter has dealt with topics such as planning, recruitment, performance management and rewards from the perspective of the project based firm. For managers of projects and project personnel, the challenges of HRM derive from the evolving, changing and volatile nature of project work. HRM must be adapted to that reality. Project based firms have to seek out, find, select, motivate and reward personnel in situations that change on a continuous basis. This requires a flexible approach, also capable of adapting and evolving in line with developments in the project based firms. Conventional wisdom in HRM literature provides strong guidelines as to what aspects of the employment relationship are of enduring interest and importance. However, it is important that this conventional wisdom be continually scrutinised, and where necessary adapted, in the light of unconventional pressures in project based organisations.

References and Further Reading

Core References

1. Keegan, A. and Turner, J.R. (2000) "Managing Human Resources in the Project-Based Organisation", Chapter 38 in Turner, J.R. and Simister, S. Gower Handbook of Project Management, 3rd Edition, pp 693-708.
2. R. Noe, J. Hollenbeck, B. Gerhart and P. Wright Human Resource Management Gaining a Competitive Edge, 3rd Edition, Irwin MacGraw-Hill, 2000 pp352-384.
3. Torrington, D., Hall, L. and Taylor, S. (2002) Human Resource Management, 5th Edition, Pearson Education.

Further References

Arthur, M., Claman, P., and DeFillippi, R. (1995) Intelligent Enterprise, intelligent careers, Academy of Management Executive, Volume 9, Number 4, pp7-20.

Barnes Nelson J. (1997) "The Boundaryless Organisation: Implications for Job Analysis, Recruitment and Selection", Human Resource Planning, Volume 20, Number 4, pp. 39-49.

Brewster, C. (1998) "Flexible Working in Europe: extent, growth and challenge for HRM", Chapter 16 in Sparrow, P. and Marchington, M. Human Resource Management: The New Agenda, Pitman Publishing, pp 245-258.

Burns, T. and Stalker, G.M. (1961) The Management of Innovation, Tavistock Press.

Capelli, P. (2000) "A market-driven approach to retaining talent", Harvard Business Review. January/February.

Gomez-Meija, L., Balkin, D. and Cardy, R. (2001) Managing Human Resources, 3rd Edition, Prentice-Hall.

Sveiby, K. (1997) The New Organizational Wealth: managing and measuring knowledge based assets, Berrett-Koehler.

Hussey, D. (1999) Strategy and Planning: A Manager's Guide, John Wiley & Sons.

Keegan, A. (1998) "Management Practices in Knowledge Intensive Firms (KIFs): The Future of HRM in the Knowledge Era", RIBES (Rotterdam Institute for Business Economic Studies) Research Paper 9846, ISBN 90-5086-302-7), Rotterdam.

Legge, K. (1998) "Flexibility: the gift-wrapping of employment degradation", Chapter 19 in Sparrow, P. and Marchington, M. Human Resource Management: The New Agenda, Pitman Publishing, 286-295.Mintzberg, H. (1979) The Structuring of Organisations: A synthesis of Research, Prentice-Hall.

GLOSSARY OF TERMS

Note: Terms defined in the British Standard (BS 6079) are denoted by an asterisk *.

A

Abstract Resource*
Imaginary resource introduced so that its availability and activity requirement gives an extra means of control. (For example, two jobs not being worked upon simultaneously in order to obviate an accident hazard.)

Acceptance
The formal process of accepting delivery of a product or a deliverable.

Acceptance Criteria*
Performance requirements and essential conditions that have to be achieved before project deliverables are accepted.

Acceptance Test*
Formal, pre-defined test conducted to determine the compliance of the deliverable item(s) with the acceptance criteria.

Accrued Costs*
Costs that are earmarked for the project and for which payment is due, but has not been made.

Acquisition Strategy
Determining the most appropriate means of procuring the component parts or services of a project.

Activity*
Task, job, operation or process consuming time and possibly other resources. (The smallest self-contained unit of work used to define the logic of a project. In general, activities share the following characteristics: a definite duration, logic relationships to other activities in a project, use resources such as people, materials or facilities, and have an associated cost. They should be defined in terms of start and end dates and the person or organisation responsible for their completion.)

Activity Definition
Identifies the specific activities that must be performed in order to produce project deliverables.

Activity Duration
Activity duration specifies the length of time (hours, days, weeks, months) that it takes to complete an activity.

Activity File
A file containing all data related to the definition of activities on a particular project.

Activity ID
A unique code identifying each activity in a project.

Activity-on-Arrow Network*
Arrow diagram, Network in which the arrows symbolise the activities.

Activity on Node Network*
Precedence diagram, a network in which the nodes symbolise the activities.

Activity Status
The state of completion of an activity. A planned activity has not yet started. A started activity is in progress. A finished activity is complete.

Actual Cost*
Incurred costs that are charged to the project budget and for which payment has been made, or accrued.

Actual Cost of Work Performed (ACWP)*
Cumulative cost of work accrued on the project in a specific period or up to a specific stage. Note: for some purposes cost may be measured in labour hours rather than money.

Actual Dates
Actual dates are entered as the project progresses. These are the dates that activities really started and finished as opposed to planned or projected dates.

Actual Direct Costs
Those costs specifically identified with a contract or project. (See also Direct Costs)

Actual Finish
Date on which an activity was completed.

Actual Start
Date on which an activity was started.

Adjourning
The last stage of team building where the team disbands.

Advanced Material Release
A document used by organisations to initiate the purchase of long-lead-time or time-critical materials prior to the final release of a design.

AND Relationship*
Logical relationship between two or more activities that converge on or diverge from an event. Note: The AND relationship indicates that every one of the activities has to be undertaken.

Application Area
A category of projects that have common elements not present in all projects. Application areas are usually defined in terms of the product of the project (i.e. by similar technologies or industry sectors) or the type of customer.

Approval
The term used when an individual accepts a deliverable as fit for purpose so that the project can continue.

Approval to Proceed
Approval given to the project at initiation or prior to the beginning of the next stage.

Arrow*
Directed connecting line between two nodes in a network.
Note 1:   It symbolises an activity in 'activity-on-arrow'.
Note 2:   It symbolises a dependency relationship in 'activity-on-node' Arrow Diagram* (See 'activity-on-arrow network')

Arrow Diagram Method
One of two conventions used to represent an activity in a project. Also known as Activity-on-Arrow or i/j method.

As-Late-As-Possible (ALAP)
An activity for which the early start date is set late as possible without delaying the early dates of any successor.

Associated Revenue*
That part of a project cost that is of a revenue nature and therefore charged as incurred to the profit and loss account. Note: Associated revenue differs from the capital element of the project in that the capital element is taken as an asset to the balance sheet and depreciated over future accounting periods.

As-Soon-As-Possible (ASAP)
An activity for which the early start date is set to be as soon as possible. This is the default activity type in most project management systems.

Assumptions
Statements taken for granted or truth.

Audit*
Systematic retrospective examination of the whole, or part, of a project or function to measure conformance with pre-determined standards. Note: Audit is usually qualified, for example financial audit, quality audit, design audit, project audit, health and safety audit.

Authorisation
The decision that triggers the allocation of funding needed to carry on the project.

Authorised Un-priced Work
Any scope change for which authorisation to proceed has been given, but for which the estimated costs are not yet settled.

Authorised Work
The effort which has been defined, plus that work for which authorisation has been given, but for which defined contract costs have not been agreed upon.

Automatic Decision Event*
Decision event where the decision depends only on the outcome of the preceding activities and that can be programmed or made automatic.

B

Backward Pass*
Procedure whereby the latest event times or the latest finish and start times for the activities of a network are calculated.

Balanced Matrix
An organisational matrix where functions and projects have the same priority.

Bar Chart*
Chart on which activities and their durations are represented by lines drawn to a common time scale.
Note 1: A Gantt chart is a specific type of bar chart and should not be used as a synonym for bar chart.
Note 2: See also 'cascade chart'.

Baseline*
Reference levels against which the project is monitored and controlled.

Baseline Cost
The amount of money an activity was intended to cost when the schedule was baselined.

Baseline Dates
Original planned start and finished dates for an activity. Used to compare with current planned dates to determine any delays. Also used to calculate budgeted cost of work scheduled for earned valued analysis.

Baseline Review
A customer review conducted to determine that a contractor is continuing to use the previously accepted performance system and is properly implementing a baseline on the contract or option under review.

Baseline Schedule
The baseline schedule is a fixed project schedule. It is the standard by which project performance is measured. The current schedule is copied into the baseline schedule which remains frozen until it is reset. Resetting the baseline is done when the scope of the project has been changed significantly, for example after a negotiated change. At that point, the original or current baseline becomes invalid and should not be compared with the current schedule.

Benefits
The enhanced efficiency, economy and effectiveness of future business or other operations to be delivered by a project or programme.

Benefits Framework
An outline of the expected benefits of the project or programme, the business operations affected and current and target performance measures.

Benefits Management
Combined with project or programme management, Benefits Management is the process for planning, managing, delivering and measuring the project or programme benefits.

Benefits Management Plan
Specifies who is responsible for achieving the benefits set out in the benefit profiles and how achievement of the benefits is to be measured, managed and monitored.

Bid
A tender, quotation or any offer to enter into a contract

Bid Analysis
An analysis of bids or tenders.

Bottom Up Cost Estimating
This is the method of making estimates for every activity in the work breakdown structure and summarising them to provide a total project cost estimate.

Brainstorming
The unstructured generation of ideas by a group of people.

Branching Logic*
Conditional logic. Alternative paths in a probabilistic network.

Breakdown Structure
A hierarchical structure by which project elements are broken down, or decomposed. (See also Product Breakdown Structure (PBS), Organisational Breakdown Structure (OBS) and Work Breakdown Structure (WBS))

Budget*
Quantification of resources needed to achieve a task by a set time, within which the task owners are required to work. Note: A budget consists of a financial and/or quantitative statement, prepared and approved prior to a defined period, for the purpose of attaining a given objective for that period. (The planned cost for an activity or project.)

Budgetary Control*
System of creating budgets, monitoring progress and taking appropriate action to achieve budgeted performance. Note: A budget should provide the information necessary to enable approval, authorisation and policy-making bodies to assess a project proposal and reach a rational decision.

Budget Cost
The cost anticipated at the start of a project.

Budget at Completion (BAC)
The sum total of the time-phased budgets. (The projected total cost of the project when done).

Budgeted Cost of Work Performed (BCWP)
The planned cost of work completed to date. BCWP is also the 'earned value.' of work completed to date.

Budgeted Cost of Work Scheduled (BCWS)
The planned cost of work that should have been achieved according to the project baseline dates.

Budget Element
Budget elements are the same as resources - the people, materials, or other entities needed to do the work Budget elements can be validated against a Resource Breakdown Structure (RBS). They are typically assigned to a work package, but can also be defined at the cost account level.

Budget Estimate
An approximate estimate prepared in the early stages of a project to establish financial viability or secure resources.

Budgeting
Time phased financial requirements.

Budget Unit
The budget unit is the base unit for the calculation. For example, the Engineer budget element might have a budget unit of hours. Since budget units are user defined, they can be any appropriate unit of measure. For example, a budget unit might be hours, pounds sterling, linear metres, or tons.

Burden
Overhead expenses distributed over appropriate direct labour and/or material base.

Business Case*
Information necessary to enable approval, authorisation and policy making bodies to assess a project proposal and reach a reasoned decision.

C

Calendars
A project calendar lists time intervals in which activities or resources can or cannot be scheduled. A project usually has one default calendar for the normal work week (Monday through Friday for example), but may have other calendars as well. Each calendar can be customised with its own holidays and extra work days. Resources and activities can be attached to any of the calendars that are defined.

Capital Cost*
The carrying cost in a balance sheet of acquiring an asset and bringing it to the condition where it is capable of performing its intended function over a future series of periods. (See also 'revenue cost')

Capital Employed*
Amount of investment in an organisation or project, normally the sum of fixed and current assets, less current liabilities at a particular date.

Cascade Chart*
Bar chart on which the vertical order of activities is such that each activity is dependent only on activities higher in the list.

Cash Flow*
Cash receipts and payments in a specified period.

Cash Flow, Nett*
Difference between cash received and payments made during a specific period.

Champion
An end user representative, often seconded into a project team. Someone who acts as an advocate for a proposal or project.

Change Log
A record of all project changes, proposed, authorised or rejected.

Change Management
The formal process through which changes to the project plan are approved and introduced.

Change Control*
Process that ensures potential changes to the deliverables of a project or the sequence of work in a project, are recorded, evaluated, authorised and managed.

Change Control Board
A formally constituted group of stakeholders responsible for approving or rejecting changes to the project baselines.

Change Request
A request needed to obtain formal approval for changes to the scope, design, methods, costs or planned aspects of a project. Change requests may arise through changes in the business or issues in the project. Change requests should be logged, assessed and agreed on before a change to the project can be made.

Child Activity*
Subordinate task belonging to a 'parent' task existing at a higher level in the Work Breakdown Structure.

Client
The party to a contract who commissions the work and pays for it on completion.

Close Out
The completion of work on a project.

Closure
The formal end point of a project, either because it has been completed or because it has been terminated early.

Code of Accounts
Any numbering system, usually based on corporate code of accounts of the primary performing organisation, used to monitor project costs by category.

Commissioning*
Advancement of an installation from the stage of static completion to full working order and achievement of the specified operational requirements.

Commitment
A binding financial obligation, typically in the form of a purchase order or contract.

Committed Costs*
Costs that are legally committed even if delivery has not taken place with invoices neither raised nor paid.

Communication
The transmission of information so that the recipient understands clearly what the sender intends.

Communications Planning
Determining project stakeholders' communication and information needs.

Completion Date
The date calculated by which the project could finish following careful estimating.

Compound Risk
A risk made up of a number of inter-related risks.

Conception Phase*
The phase that triggers and captures new ideas or opportunities and identifies potential candidates for further development in the feasibility phase.

Concurrent Engineering
The systematic approach to the simultaneous, integrated design of products and their related processes, such as manufacturing, testing and supporting.

Configuration*
Functional and physical characteristics of a product as defined in technical documents and achieved in the product. Note: In a project this should contain all items that can be identified as being relevant to the project and that should only be modified after authorisation by the relevant manager. (Includes documentation)

Configuration Audit
A check to ensure that all deliverable items on a project conform with one another and to the current specification. It ensures that relevant quality assurance procedures have been implemented and that there is consistency throughout project documentation.

Configuration Control
A system through which changes may be made to configuration items.

Configuration Identification
Identifies uniquely all items within the configuration.

Configuration Item

A part of a configuration that has a set function and is designated for configuration management. It identifies uniquely all items within the configuration.

Configuration Management*

Technical and administrative activities comprising: conguration identification, configuration control, configuration status accounting, configuration auditing. Note: See BS EN ISO 10007: 1997 for guidance on configuration management, including specialist terminology.

Configuration Status Accounting

Records and reports the current status and history of all changes to the configuration. Provides a complete record of what happened to the configuration to date.

Conflict Management

The ability to manage conflict creatively and effectively. Constraints Applicable restrictions that will affect the scope of the project or the sequence of project activities.

Consumable Resource

A type of resource that only remains available until consumed (for example, a material).

Contingency

A Contingency is the planned allotment of time and cost or other resources for unforeseeable elements within a project.

Contingency Plan*

Mitigation plan. Alternative course(s) of action devised to cope with project risks. Note: See risk plan.

Contingency Planning

The development of a management plan that uses alternative strategies to minimise or negate the adverse effects of a risk, should it occur.

Contract

A mutually binding agreement in which the contractor is obligated to provide services or products and the buyer is obligated to provide payment for them. Contracts fall into three main categories: fixed price, cost reimbursable or unit price but may contain elements from each.

Contract Administration

Managing the relationship with the seller.

Contract Budget Base

The negotiated contract cost value plus the estimated value of authorised but un-priced work.

Contract Close-out

Settlement of a contract.

Contractor

A person, company or firm who holds a contract for carrying out the works and/or the supply of goods in connection with the Project.

Contract Target Cost

The negotiated costs for the original defined contract and all contractual changes that have been agreed and approved, but excluding the estimated cost of any authorised, un-priced changes. The contract target cost equals the value of the budget at completion plus management or contingency reserve.

Contract Target Price

The negotiated estimated costs plus profit or fee.

Control
Control is the process of developing targets and plans; measuring actual performance, comparing it against planned performance and taking effective action to correct the situation.

Control Charts
Control charts display the results, over time, of a process. They are used to determine if the process is in need of adjustment.

Co-ordination
Co-ordination is the act of ensuring that work carried out by different organisations and in different places fits together effectively. It involves technical matters, time, content and cost in order to achieve the project objectives effectively.

Co-ordinated Matrix
An organisational structure where the project leader reports to the functional manager and doesn't have authority over team members from other departments.

Corrective Action
Changes made to bring future project performance back into line with the plan.

Cost Account
A cost account defines what work is to be performed, who will perform it and who is to pay for it. Cost accounts are the focal point for the integration of scope, cost, and schedule. Another term for Cost Account is Control Account.

Cost Account Manager
A member of a functional organisation responsible for cost account performance, and for the management of resources to accomplish such tasks.

Cost Benefit Analysis *
An analysis of the relationship between the costs of undertaking a task or project, initial and recurrent, and the benefits likely to arise from the changed situation, initially and recurrently. Note: The hard tangible, readily measurable benefits may sometimes be accompanied by soft benefits which may be real but difficult to isolate, measure and value. (Allows comparison of the returns from alternative forms of investment.)

Cost Breakdown Structure*
Hierarchical breakdown of a project into cost elements.

Cost Budgeting
Allocating cost estimates to individual project components.

Cost Centre*
Location, person, activity or project in respect of which costs may be ascertained and related to cost units.

Cost Code*
Unique identity for a specified element of work. (Code assigned to activities that allow costs to be consolidated according to the elements of a code structure.)

Cost Control Point
The point within a programme at which costs are entered and controlled. Frequently, the cost control point for a project is either the cost account or the work package.

Cost Control System
Any system of keeping costs within the bounds of budgets or standards based upon work actually performed.

Cost Curve
A graph plotted against a horizontal time scale and cumulative cost vertical scale.

Cost Element
A unit of costs to perform a task or to acquire an item. The cost estimated may be a single value or a range of values.

Cost Estimating
The process of predicting the costs of a project.

Cost Incurred
Costs identified through the use of the accrued method of accounting or costs actually paid. Costs include direct labour, direct materials, and all allowable indirect costs.

Cost Management
The effective financial control of the project through evaluating, estimating, budgeting, monitoring, analysing, forecasting and reporting the cost information.

Cost Overrun
The amount by which a contractor exceeds or expects to exceed the estimated costs, and/or the final limitations (the ceiling) of a contract.

Cost Performance Index (CPI)*
A measure, expressed as a percentage or other ratio of actual cost to budget plan. (Ratio of work accomplished versus work cost incurred for a specified time period. The CPI is an efficiency rating for work accomplished for resources expended.)

Cost Performance Report
A regular cost report to reflect cost and schedule status information for management.

Cost Plan
A budget which shows the amounts and expected dates of incurring costs on the project or on a contract.

Cost Plus Fixed Fee Contract
A type of contract where the buyer reimburses the seller for the seller's allowable costs plus a fixed fee.

Cost Plus Incentive Fee Contract (CPIFC)
A type of Contract where the buyer reimburses the seller for the seller's allowable costs and the seller earns a profit if defined criteria are met.

Cost Reimbursement Type Contracts
A category of contracts based on payments to a contractor for allowable estimated costs, normally requiring only a 'best efforts' performance standard from the contractor. Risk for all growth over the estimated value rests with the project owner.

Cost/Schedule Planning and Control Specification (C/SPCS)
The United States Air Force initiative in the mid-1960's which later resulted in the C/SCSC.

Cost-Time Resource sheet (CTR)
A document that describes each major element in the WBS, including a Statement of Work (SOW) describing the work content, resources required, the time frame of the work element and a cost estimate.

Cost Variance*
The difference (positive or negative) between the actual expenditure and the planned/budgeted expenditure.

Credited Resource*
Resource that is created by an activity or event and can then be used by the project.

Critical Activity
An activity is termed critical when it has zero or negative float.

Criticality Index
Used in risk analysis, the criticality index represents the percentage of simulation trails that resulted in the activity being placed on the critical path.

Critical Path*
Sequence of activities through a project network from start to finish, the sum of whose durations determines the overall project duration. Note: There may be more than one such path. (The path through a series of activities, taking into account interdependencies, in which the late completion of activities will have an impact on the project end date or delay a key milestone.)

Critical Path Analysis*
Procedure for calculating the critical path and floats in a network.

Critical Path Method (CPM)
A technique used to predict project duration by analysing which sequence of activities has the least amount of scheduling flexibility. The Critical Path Method is a modelling process that defines all the project's critical activities that must be completed on time. The start and finish dates of activities in the project are calculated in two passes. The first pass calculates early start and finish dates from the earliest start date forward. The second pass calculates the late start and finish activities from the latest finish date backwards. The difference between the pairs of start and finish dates for each task is the float or slack time for the task (see Float). Slack is the amount of time a task can be delayed without delaying the project completion date. By experimenting with different logical sequences and/or durations the optimal project schedule can be determined.

Critical Performance Indicator
A critical factor against which aspects of project performance may be assessed.

Critical Success Factor
A factor considered to be most conducive to the achievement of a successful project.

Customer
Any person who defines needs or wants, justifies or pays for part or the entire project, or evaluates or uses the results. Could be the project promoter, client, owner or employer.

Cut-off Date
The ending date of a reporting period.

D

Dangle
An activity or network which has either no predecessors or no successors. If neither, it is referred to as an isolated activity.

Decision Event*
State in the progress of a project when a decision is required before the start of any succeeding activity. Note: The decision determines which of a number of alternative paths is to be followed.

Delaying Resource
In resource scheduling, inadequate availability of one or more resources may require that the completion of an activity be delayed beyond the date on which it could otherwise be completed. The delaying resource is the first resource on an activity that causes the activity to be delayed.

Delegation
The practice of getting others to perform work effectively which one chooses not to do oneself. The process by which authority and responsibility is distributed from Project Manager to subordinates.

Deliberate Decision Event*

Decision event where the decision is made as a result of the outcomes of the preceding activities and possibly other information but it cannot be made automatically.

Deliverables*

End products of a project or the measurable results of intermediate activities within the project organisation. Note: Deliverables may be in the form of hardware, software, services, processes, documents or any combination thereof.

Delphi Technique

A process where a consensus view is reached by consultation with experts. Often used as an estimating technique.

Dependency*

Precedence relationship. Restriction that one activity has to precede, either in part or in total, another activity. (Dependencies are relationships between products or tasks. For example, one product may be made up of several other 'dependent' products or a task may not begin until a 'dependent' task is complete. See also logical relationship.)

Dependency Arrow*

A link arrow used in an activity on node network to represent the interrelationships of activities in a project.

Design Authority

The person or organisation with overall design responsibility for the products of the project.

Design and Development Phase

The time period in which production process and facility and production processes are developed and designed.

Deterministic Network*

Network containing paths, all of which have to be followed and whose durations are fixed. Note: Deterministic network is a term used to distinguish traditional networking from probabilistic networking.

Direct Costs*

Costs that are specifically attributable to an activity or group of activities without apportionment. (Direct costs are best contrasted with indirect costs that cannot be identified to a specific project.)

Discounted Cash Flow (DCF)*

Concept of relating future cash inflows and outflows over the life of a project or operation to a common base value, thereby allowing more validity to comparison of projects with different durations and rates of cash flow.

Discrete Milestone

A milestone that has a definite scheduled occurrence in time. Logical link that may require time but no other resource.

Dummy activity in activity on arrow network*

An activity representing no actual work to be done but required for reasons of logic or nomenclature. Note: There are three uses for a dummy activity in 'activity-on-arrow network'. (a) logic; (b) time delay and (c) uniqueness.

Duration

Duration is the length of time needed to complete an activity.

Duration Compression

Often resulting in an increase in cost, duration compression is the shortening of a project schedule without reducing the project scope.

E

Earliest Feasible Date
The earliest date on which the activity could be scheduled to start based on the scheduled dates of all its predecessors, but in the absence of any resource constraints on the activity itself. This date is calculated by resource scheduling.

Early Dates
Calculated in the forward pass of time analysis, early dates are the earliest dates on which an activity can start and finish.

Earliest Finish Time*
Earliest possible time by which an activity can finish within the logical and imposed constraints of the network. (The Early Finish date is defined as the earliest calculated date on which an activity can end. It is based on the activity's Early Start which depends on the finish of predecessor activities and the activity's duration).

Early Start Time*
Earliest possible time by which an activity can start within the logical and imposed constraints of the network.

Earned Hours
The time in standard hours credited as a result of the completion of a given task or a group of tasks.

Earned Value*
The value of the useful work done at any given point in a project. Note: The budget may be expressed in cost or labour hours.

Earned Value Analysis
Analysis of project progress where the actual money, hours (or other measure) budgeted and spent is compared to the value of the work achieved.

Earned Value Cost Control
The quantification of the overall progress of a project in financial terms so as to provide a realistic yardstick against which to compare the actual cost to date.

Earned Value Management*
Earned value analysis Technique for assessing whether the earned value in relation to the amount of work completed, is ahead, on, or behind plan.

Effort
The number of labour units necessary to complete the work. Effort is usually expressed in staff-hours, staff-days or staff-weeks and should not be confused with duration.

Effort-Driven Activity
An activity whose duration is governed by resource usage and availability. The resource requiring the greatest time to complete the specified amount of work on the activity will determine its duration.

Effort Remaining
The estimate of effort remaining to complete an activity.

Elapsed Time
Elapsed time is the total number of calendar days (excluding non-work days such as weekends or holidays) that is needed to complete an activity. It gives a realistic view of how long an activity is scheduled to take for completion.

End Activity
An activity with no logical successors.

End Event (of a project)*
Event with preceding, but no succeeding activities. Note: There may be more than one end event.

Environmental Factoring*
Use of data relating to an external factor (such as the weather) to modify or bias the value of parameters concerned.

Equivalent Activity*
Activity that is equivalent, in the probabilistic sense, to any combination of series and parallel activities.

Estimate
A quantified assessment of the resources required to complete part or all of a project. The prediction of the quantitative result. It is usually applied to project costs, resources and durations.

Estimate At Completion (EAC)
A value expressed in either money and/or hours, to represent the projected final costs of work when completed. The EAC is calculated as ETC + ACWP.

Estimate To Complete (ETC)
The value expressed in either money or hours developed to represent the cost of the work required to complete a task.

Estimating
The act of combining the results of post project reviews, metrics, consultation and informed assessment to arrive at time and resource requirements for an activity.

Event *
State in the progress of a project after the completion of all preceding activities, but before the start of any succeeding activity. (A defined point that is the beginning or end of an activity).

Event on Node
A network technique in which events are represented by boxes (or nodes) connected by arrows to show the sequence in which the events are to occur.

Exception Report*
Focused report drawing attention to instances where planned and actual results are expected to be, or are already, significantly different. Note: An exception report is usually triggered when actual values are expected to cross a predetermined threshold that is set with reference to the project plan. The actual values may be trending better or worse than plan.

Exclusive OR Relationship*
Logical relationship indicating that only one of the possible activities can be undertaken.

Execution phase
The phase of a project in which work towards direct achievement of the project's objectives and the production of the project's deliverables occurs. Sometimes called the implementation phase.

Expected Monetary Value
The product of an event's probability of occurrence and the (financial) gain or loss that will result. Hence if there is a 50% probability of rain and the rain will result in a £1000 increase in cost, the EPV will be 0.5 x 1000 or £500.

Expenditure
A charge against available funds, evidenced by a voucher, claim, or other documents. Expenditures represent the actual payment of funds.

Exceptions
Exceptions are occurrences that cause deviation from a plan, such as issues, change requests and risks. Exceptions can also refer to items where the cost variance and schedule variance exceed predefined thresholds.

External Constraint
A constraint from outside the project network.

F

Fast -Tracking*
Reducing the duration of a project usually by overlapping phases or activities that were originally planned to be done sequentially. (The process of reducing the number of sequential relationships and replacing them typically with parallel relationships (usually to achieve shorter overall durations but often with increased risk))

Fallback plan
A plan for an alternative course of action that can be adopted to overcome the consequences of a risk, should it occur (including carrying out any advance activities that may be required to render the plan practical)

Feasibility Phase*
The project phase that demonstrates that the client's requirement can be achieved and identifies and evaluates the options to determine the one preferred solution.

Feasibility Study*
Analysis to determine if a course of action is possible within the terms of reference of the project.

Feasible schedule*
Any schedule capable of implementation within the externally determined constraints of time and/or resource limits.

Final Report*
Post-implementation report. Normally a retrospective report that formally closes the project having handed over the project deliverables for operational use. Note: The report should draw attention to experiences that may be of benefit to future projects and may form part of the accountability of the project team.

Finish Date
The actual or estimated time associated with an activity's completion.

Finishing Activity
A finishing activity is the last activity that must be completed before a project can be considered finished. This activity is not a predecessor to any other activity - it has no successors.

Finish-To-Finish Lag
The finish-to-finish lag is the minimum amount of time that must pass between the finish of one activity and the finish of its successor(s).

Finish-To-Start Lag
The finish-to-start lag is the minimum amount of time that must pass between the finish of one activity and the start of its successor(s). The default finish-to-start lag is zero.

Firm Fixed Price Contract
A contract where the buyer pays a set amount to the seller regardless of that seller's cost to complete the contract.

Fixed Date
A calendar date (associated with a plan) that cannot be moved or changed during the schedule.

Fixed-Duration Scheduling
A scheduling method in which, regardless of the number of resources assigned to the task, the duration remains the same.

Fixed Finish
See Imposed Finish.

Fixed Price Contracts
A generic category of contracts based on the establishment of firm legal commitments to complete the required work. A performing contractor is legally obligated to finish the job, no matter how much it costs to complete. Risks of all cost growth rest on the performing contractor.

Fixed Start
See Imposed Start.

Float*
Time available for an activity or path in addition to its planned duration. (Float is the amount of time that an activity can slip past its earliest completion date without delaying the rest of the project. The calculation depends on the float type. See start float, finish float, free float, positive float, and negative float)

Forecast At Completion
Scheduled cost for a task.

Forecast Final Cost
See Estimate at Completion.

Forward Pass*
A procedure whereby the earliest event times or the earliest start and finish times for the activities of a network are calculated.

Free Float*
Time by which an activity may be delayed or extended without affecting the start of any succeeding activity. Note: Free float can never be negative.

Functional Manager
The person responsible for the business and technical management of a functional group.

Functional Matrix
An organisation type where the project has a team leader in each functional department and the products are passed from one team to the next.

Functional Organisation
A functional management structure where specific functions of a business are grouped into specialist departments that provide a dedicated service to the whole of the organisation e.g. accounts department, production department, drawing office.

Functional Specification
A document specifying in some detail the functions that are required of a system and the constraints that will apply.

Funding Profile
An estimate of funding requirements over time.

G

Gantt Chart*
Particular type of bar chart showing planned activity against time. Note: 'Gantt Chart', although named for a particular type of bar chart, is in current usage as a name for bar charts in general. (A Gantt chart is a time-phased graphic display of activity durations. Activities are listed with other tabular information on the left side with time intervals over the bars. Activity durations are shown in the form of horizontal bars.)

Goal
A one-sentence definition of specifically what will be accomplished, while incorporating an event signifying completion.

Graphical Evaluation and Review Technique (GERT)
A network technique that allows for conditional and probabilistic treatment of logical relationships (i.e. some activities may not be performed).

H

Hammock*
Activity, joining two specified points, that span two or more activities.
Note: Its duration is initially unspecified and is only determined by the durations of the specified activities.
Note: Hammocks are usually used to collect timedependent information, e.g. overheads. (A group of activities, milestones, or other hammocks aggregated together for analysis or reporting purposes. Sometimes used to describe an activity such as management support that has no duration of its own but derives one from the time difference between the two points to which it is connected.)

Hand-over
The formal process of transferring responsibility for and ownership of the products of a project to the operator or owner.

Hierarchical Coding Structure
A coding system that can be represented as a multi-level tree structure in which every code except those at the top of the tree has a parent code.

Hierarchy of Networks*
Range of networks at different levels of detail, from summary down to working levels, showing the relationships between those networks.

Histogram
A graphic display of planned and or actual resource usage over a period of time. It is in the form of a vertical bar chart, the height of each bar representing the quantity of resource usage in a given time unit. Bars may be single, multiple or show stacked resources.

Holiday
An otherwise valid working day that has been designated as exempt from work.

Host Organisation*
Organisation that provides the administrative and logistical support for the project.

Hypercritical Activities
Activities on the critical path with negative float.

I

Impact
The assessment of the adverse effects of an occurring risk.

Impact Analysis
Assessing the merits of pursuing a particular course of action.

Implementation
The controlled conversion of the preferred solution into the product which will be used by the sponsor.

Implementation Phase*
The project phase that develops the chosen solution into a completed deliverable.
Note: Realisation is the internationally accepted and preferred term for implementation.

Imposed Date*
Point in time determined by circumstances outside the network. Note: A symbol is inserted immediately above the event concerned on activity on arrow networks or adjacent and connected to the appropriate corner of the node on activity on node networks.

Imposed Finish
A finished date imposed on an activity by external constraints.

Imposed Start
A start date imposed on an activity by external constraints.

Inclusive OR relationship*
Logical relationship indicating that at least one but not necessarily all of the activities have to be undertaken.

INCOTERMS
A set of international terms defining conditions for delivery and shipping of equipment and materials.

Incurred Costs*
Sum of actual and committed costs, whether invoiced/paid or not, at a specified time.

Indirect Cost*
Costs associated with a project that cannot be directly attributed to an activity or group of activities. (Resources expended which are not directly identified to any specific contract, project, product or service, such as overheads and general administration.)

In-house Project
A project commissioned and carried out entirely within a single organisation.

Initiation
Committing the organisation to begin a project.

In Progress
An activity that has been started, but not yet completed.

Integrated Logistics Support*
Disciplined approach to activities necessary to (a) cause support considerations to be integrated into product design; (b) develop support arrangements that are consistently related to design and to each other and (c) provide the necessary support at the beginning and during customer use at optimum cost.

Integration
The process of bringing people, activities and other things together to perform effectively.

Internal Rate of Return (IRR)*
Discount rate at which the net present value of a future cash flow is zero. Note: IRR is a special case of the 'discounted cash flow' procedures.

Inverted Matrix
A project oriented organisation structure that employs permanent specialists to support projects.

Issue
An immediate problem requiring resolution.

J

Joint Venture
A joint ownership of a firm by two or more persons or other firms or
A partnership between two or more companies mutually engaged in a particular venture such as a major project. In this case the venture exists for a specific purpose for a limited time.

Judicial
Belonging to a branch of Government responsible for the administration of justice.

Jurisdiction
The extent of territory over which legal or other power extends, e.g. authority to interpret and apply the law.

Just In Time (JIT)
A philosophy in which goods, servicesor actions are provided on demand as needed and without waiting, queuing or staorage.
A "pull" system driven by actual demand. The goal is to produce, provide or deliver parts or supplies just in time for the next operation. The approach reduces stock inventories or storage costs but leaves no room for error. As much a managerial philosophy as it is an inventory system.

K

Key Events
Major events the achievement of which are deemed to be critical to the execution of the project.

Key Events Schedule
See Master Schedule.

Key Performance Indicators (KPI)
Measurable indicators that will be used to report progress that is chosen to reflect the critical success factors of the project.

L

Labour Rate Variances
Difference between planned labour rates and actual labour rates.

Ladder*
Device for representing a set of overlapping activities in a network diagram. Note: The start and finish of each succeeding activity are linked only to the start and finish of the preceding activity by lead and lag activities, which consume only time.

Lag*
(a) In a network diagram, the minimum necessary lapse of time between the finish of one activity and the finish of an overlapping activity.
(b) Delay incurred between two specified activities.

Late Dates
Calculated in the backward pass of time analysis, late dates are the latest dates by which an activity can be allowed to start or finish.

Latest Event Time*
Latest time by which an event has to occur within the logical and imposed constraints of the network, without affecting the total project duration.

Late Event Date
Calculated from backward pass, it is the latest date an event can occur.

Latest Finish Time*
The latest possible time by which an activity has to finish within the logical activity and imposed constraints of the network, without affecting the total project duration.

Latest Start Time*
Latest possible time by which an activity has to start within the logical and imposed constraints of the network, without affecting the total project duration.

Lead*
In a network diagram, the minimum necessary lapse of time between the start of one activity and the start of an overlapping activity.

Lead Contractor
The contractor who has responsibility for overall project management and quality assurance

Leadership
Getting others to follow.

Letter of Intent
A letter indicating an intent to sign a contract, usually so that work can commence prior to signing that contract.

Levelling
See Resource Levelling.

Life Cycle
A sequence of defined stages over the full duration of a project.

Life-Cycle Costing
When evaluating alternatives, Life-Cycle Costing is the concept of including acquisition, operating and disposal costs.

Likelihood
Assessment of the probability that a risk will occur.

Line Manager
The manager of any group that makes a product or performs a service.

Linked Bar Chart
A bar chart that shows the dependency links between activities.

Logic
See Network Logic.

Logic Diagram
A diagram that displays the logical relationships between project activities.

Logical Relationship
A logical relationship is based on the dependency between two project activities or between a project activity and a milestone.

Loop*
An error in a network which results in a later activity imposing a logical restraint on an earlier activity.

M

Management by Project
A term used to describe normal management processes that are being project managed.

Management Development
All aspects of staff planning, recruitment, development, training and assessment.

Management Reserve*
A central contingency pool. Sum of money held as an overall contingency to cover the cost impact of some unexpected event occurring. Note: This is self-insurance.

Master Network*
Network showing the complete project, from which more detailed networks are derived.

Master Schedule
A high level summary project schedule that identifies major activities and milestones.

Material
Property which may be incorporated into or attached to an end item to be delivered under a contract or which may be consumed or expended in the performance of a contract. It includes, but is not limited to raw and processed material, parts, components, assemblies, fuels and lubricants, and small tools and supplies which may be consumed in normal use in the performance of a contract.

Matrix Organisation
A structure in which individuals, groups and managers continue to work within their specialist functional departments, but are assigned to work full-time or part-time under the direction of a project manager who is not their line manager. Note: Such assignees are usually responsible to the project manager for their project work and to their functional manager for other activities.

Methodology
A documented process for management of projects that contains procedures, definitions and roles and responsibilities.

Mid-Stage Assessment
An assessment in the middle of a project that can be held for several reasons:
(1) at the request of the project board; (2) to authorise work on the next stage before the current one is completed; (3) to allow for a formal review in the middle of a long project; or (4) to review exception plans.

Milestone*
A key event. An event selected for its importance in the project. Note: Milestones are commonly used in relation to progress. (A milestone is often chosen to represent the start of a new phase or completion of a major deliverable. They are used to monitor progress at summary level. Milestones are activities of zero duration.)

Milestone Plan
A plan containing only milestones which highlight key points of the project.

Milestone Schedule
A schedule that identifies the major milestones. See also Master Schedule.

Mission Statement
Brief summary, approximately one or two sentences, that sums up the background, purposes and benefits of the project.

Mitigation
Working to reduce risk by lowering its chances of occurring or by reducing its effect if it occurs.

Mobilisation
The bringing together of project personnel and securing equipment and facilities. Carried out during project start-up phases.

Monitoring
Monitoring is the recording, analysing and reporting of project performance as compared to the plan.

Monte Carlo Simulation
A technique used to estimate the likely range of outcomes from a complex process by simulating the process under randomly selected conditions a large number of times.

Multi-Project
A project consisting of multiple sub-projects.

Multi-Project Analysis
Multi-project analysis is used to analyse the impact and interaction of activities and resources whose progress affects the progress of a group of projects or for projects with shared resources or both. Multi-project analysis can also be used for composite reporting on projects having no dependencies or resources in common.

Multi-Project Management
Managing multiple projects that are interconnected either logically or by shared resources.

Multi-Project Scheduling*
Use of the techniques of resource allocation to schedule more than one project concurrently.

N

Near-Critical Activity
A low total float activity.

Negative Total Float*
Time by which the duration of an activity or path has to be reduced in order to permit a limiting imposed date to be achieved.

Negotiated Contract Cost
The estimated cost negotiated in a Cost-Plus-Fixed-Fee Contract or the negotiated contract target cost in either a Fixed Price-Incentive Contract or a Cost-Plus-Incentive-Fee Contract. See also Contract Target Cost.

Negotiation
The art of satisfying needs by reaching agreement or compromise with other parties.

Net Present Value* (NPV)
Aggregate of future net cash flows discounted back to a common base date, usually the present.

Network
A pictorial presentation of project data in which the project logic is the main determinant of the placements of the activities in the drawing. Frequently called a flowchart, PERT chart, logic drawing, or logic diagram.

Network Analysis*
Method used for calculating a project's critical path and activity times and floats. Note: See also critical path analysis, project network techniques.

Network Interface*
Activity or event common to two or more network diagrams.

Network Logic
The collection of activity dependencies that make up a project network.

Network Path
A series of connected activities in a project network.

Nodes*
Points in a network at which arrows start and finish.

Non-recurring Costs
Expenditures against specific tasks that are expected to occur only once on a given project.

Non-splittable Activity*
An activity that, once started, has to be completed to plan without interruption. Note: Resources should not be diverted from a non-splittable activity to another activity.

Not Earlier Than
A restriction on an activity that indicates that it may not start or end earlier than a specified date.

Not Later Than
A restriction on an activity that indicates that it may not start or end later than a specified date.

O

Objectives
Predetermined results toward which effort is directed.

Operation Phase*
Period when the completed deliverable is used and maintained in service for its intended purpose.

Opportunity
The opposite of a risk. The chance to enhance the project benefits.

Order of Magnitude Estimate
An estimate carried out to give very approximate indication of likely out-turn costs.

Organisation Design
The design of the most appropriate organisational design for a project.

Organisational Breakdown Structure (OBS)*
Hierarchical way in which the organisation may be divided into management levels and groups, for planning and control purposes.

Organisational Planning
The process of identifying, assigning and documenting project responsibilities and relationships.

Original Budget
The initial budget established at or near the time a contract was signed or a project authorised, based on the negotiated contract cost or management's authorisation.

Original Duration
The duration of activities or groups of activities as recorded in the Baseline Schedule.

Other Direct Costs (ODC)
A group of accounting elements which can be isolated to specific tasks, other than labour and material. Included in ODC are such items as travel, computer time, and services.

Out-of-Sequence Progress
Progress that has been reported even though activities that have been deemed predecessors in project logic have not been completed.

Output Format
Information that governs the final appearance of a report or drawing. (Usually refers to computer-generated documents)

Outsourcing*
Contracting-out, buying in facilities or work (as opposed to using in-house resources)

Overall Change Control
Co-ordinating and controlling changes across an entire project.

Overhead
Costs incurred in the operation of a business that cannot be directly related to the individual products or services being produced. See also 'Indirect Cost.'

Overrun

Costs incurred in excess of the contract target costs on an incentive type contract or the estimated costs on a fixed fee contract. An overrun is that value of costs which are needed to complete a project, over that value originally authorised by management.

P

Parallel Activities

Parallel activities are two or more activities than can be done at the same time. This allows a project to be completed faster than if the activities were arranged serially.

Parametric Estimating

An estimating technique that uses a statistical relationship between historic data and other variables (e.g. square metreage in construction, lines of code in software development) to calculate an estimate.

Parent Activity*

Task within the work breakdown structure that embodies several subordinate 'child' tasks.

Pareto Diagram

A histogram, ordered by frequency of occurrence, that shows how many results were generated by each identified cause.

Parties (to a contract)

The persons or companies who sign a contract with one another.

Path*

Activity or an unbroken sequence of activities in a project network. (Refer to critical path method for information on critical and non-critical paths.)

Percent Complete

A measure of the completion status of a partially completed activity. May be aggregated to sections of a project or the whole project.

Performance Measurement Techniques

Performance measurement techniques are the methods used to estimate earned value. Different methods are appropriate to different work packages, either due to the nature of the work or to the planned duration of the work package.

Performance Specification*

Statement of the totality of needs expressed by the benefits, features, characteristics, process conditions, boundaries and constraints that together define the expected performance of a deliverable. Note: A performance specification should provide for innovation and alternative solutions, by not defining or unduly constraining the technical attributes of the intended deliverable.

Performing

A team building stage where the emphasis is on the work currently being performed.

Phase (of a project)*

That part of a project during which a set of related and interlinked activities are performed. Note: A project consists of a series of phases that together constitute the whole project life cycle.

Physical Percent Complete

The percentage of the work content of an activity that has been achieved.

Pilot
A form of testing a new development and its implementation prior to committing to its full release.

Plan
A plan is an intended future course of action. It is owned by the project manager, it is the basis of the project controls and includes the 'what', the 'how', the 'when', and the 'who'.

Planned Activity
An activity not yet started.

Planned Cost*
Estimated cost of achieving a specified objective.

Planning
The process of identifying the means, resources and actions necessary to accomplish an objective.

Planning Stage
The stage prior to the implementation stage when product activity, resource and quality plans are produced.

Planner
A member of a project team or project support office with the responsibility for planning, scheduling and tracking of projects. They are often primarily concerned with schedule, progress and manpower resources.

Portfolio
A grouping or bundle of projects, collected together for management convenience. They may or may not have a common objective, they are often related only by the use of common resources.

Portfolio Management
The management of a number of projects that do not share a common objective.

Positive Float
Positive float is defined as the amount of time that an activity's start can be delayed without affecting the project completion date. An activity with positive float is not on the critical path and is called a non-critical activity. The difference between early and late dates (start or finish) determines the amount of float.

Post Implementation Review
A review between 6-12 months after a system in a project has met its objectives to verify that it continues to meet user requirements.

Post Project Appraisal
An evaluation that provides feedback in order to learn for the future.

Precedence Diagram Method
One of the two methods of representing project as networks, in which the activities are represented by nodes and the relationships between them by arrows.

Precedence Network*
A multiple dependency network. An activity-on-node network in which a sequence arrow represents one of four forms of precedence relationship, depending on the positioning of the head and the tail of the sequence arrow.
The relationships are:
(a) Start of activity depends on finish of preceding activity, either immediately or after a lapse of time.
(b) Finish of activity depends on finish of preceding activity, either immediately or after a lapse of time.
(c) Start of activity depends on start of preceding activity, either immediately or after a lapse of time.
(d) Finish of activity depends on start of preceding activity, either immediately or after a lapse of time.

Preceding Event*
In an activity-on-arrow network, an event at the beginning of an activity.

Pre-commissioning
That work which is carried out prior to commissioning in order to demonstrate that commissioning may be safely undertaken.

Predecessor
An activity that must be completed (or be partially completed) before a specified activity can begin.

Predecessor Activity
In the precedence diagramming method this is an activity which logically precedes the current activity.

Prime or Lead Contractor
A main supplier who has a contract for much or all of the work on a contract.

Probabilistic Network*
Network containing alternative paths with which probabilities are associated.

Probability
Likelihood of a risk occurring.

Process*
Set of interrelated resources and activities which transform inputs into outputs.

Procurement
The securing of goods or services.

Procurement Planning
Determining what to procure and when.

Product Breakdown Structure
A hierarchy of deliverable products which are required to be produced on the project. It forms the base document from which the execution strategy and product-based work breakdown structure may be derived. It provides a guide for Configuration Control documentation.

Product Description
The description of the purpose form and components of a product. It should always be used as a basis for acceptance of the product by the customer.

Product Flow Diagram
Represents how the products are produced by identifying their derivation and the dependencies between them.

Programme
A broad effort encompassing a number of projects and/or functional activities with a common purpose.

Programme Benefits Review
A review to assess if targets have been reached and to measure the performance levels in the resulting business operations.

Programme Director
The senior manager with the responsibility for the overall success of the programme.

Programme Directorate
A committee that directs the programme when circumstances arise where there is no individual to direct the programme.

Programme Evaluation and Review Technique (PERT)

PERT is a project management technique for determining how much time a project needs before it is completed. Each activity is assigned a best, worst, and most probable completion time estimate. These estimates are used to determine the average completion time. The average times are used to calculate the critical path and the standard deviation of completion times for the entire project.

Programme Management

The effective management of several individual but related projects or functional activities in order to produce an overall system that works effectively.

Programme Management Office

The office responsible for the business and technical management of a specific contract or programme.

Programme Manager*

Individual or body with responsibility for managing a group of related projects.

Programme Support Office

A group that gives administrative support to the programme manager and the programme executive.

Progress

The partial completion of a project, or a measure of the same.

Progress Payments

Payments made to a contractor during the life of a fixed-price type contract, on the basis of some agreed-to formula, for example, Budget Cost of Work Performed or simply costs incurred.

Progress Report

A regular report to senior personnel, sponsors or stakeholders summarising the progress of a project including key events, milestones, costs and other issues.

Project*

A unique process, consisting of a set of co-ordinated and controlled activities, with start and finish dates, undertaken to achieve an objective conforming to specific requirements, including the constraints of time, cost and resources.
Note: An individual project may form part of a larger project structure. In some projects the objective(s) is (are) refined and the product characteristics defined progressively as the project proceeeds. The outcome of the project may be one or several units of product. The organisation is temporary and established for the lifetime of the project. The interactions among project activities may be complex.
(See also BS ISO 10006: 1997.) (Alternative definition: An endeavour in which human, material and financial resources are organised in a novel way to deliver a unique scope of work of given specification, often within constraints of cost and time, and to achieve beneficial change defined by quantitative and qualitative objectives.)

Project Appraisal

The discipline of calculating the viability of a project.

Project Base Date*

Reference date used as a basis for the start of a project calendar.

Project Board

A project board is the body to which the Project Manager is accountable for achieving the project objectives.

Project Brief *

Statement that describes the purpose, cost, time and performance requirements/constraints for a project. (A statement of reference terms for a project. A written statement of the Client's goals and requirements in relation to the project.)

Project Calendar

A calendar that defines global project working and non-working periods.

Project Co-ordination*

Communication linking various areas of a project to ensure the transfer of information or hardware at interface points at the appropriate times and identification of any further necessary resources.

Project Co-ordination Procedure

Defines the parties relevant to the project and the approved means of communicating between them.

Project Champion*

Person within the parent organisation who promotes and defends a project.

Project Closure*

Formal termination of a project at any point during its life.

Project Cost Management

A subset of project management that includes resource planning, cost estimating, cost control and cost budgeting in an effort to complete the project within its approved budget.

Project Culture

The general attitude toward projects within the business.

Project Definition

A report that defines a project i.e. why it is required, what will be done, how when and where it will be delivered, the organisation and resources required, the standards and procedures to be followed.

Project Director

The manager of a very large project that demands senior level responsibility or the person at the board level in an organisation who has the overall responsibility for project management.

Project Environment

The project environment is the context within which the project is formulated, assessed and realised. This includes all external factors that have an impact on the project.

Project Evaluation

A documented review of the project's performance, produced at project closure. It ensures that the experience of the project is recorded for the benefit of others.

Project File

A file containing the overall plans of a project and any other important documents.

Project Initiation

The beginning of a project at which point certain management activities are required to ensure that the project is established with clear reference terms and adequate management structure.

Project Initiation Document

A document approved by the project board at project initiation that defines the terms of reference for the project.

Project Issue Report

A report that raises either technical or managerial issues in a project.

Project Life-Cycle*

All phases or stages between a project's conception and its termination. Note: The project life cycle may include the operation and disposal of project deliverables. This is usually known as an 'extended life cycle'.

Project Life Cycle Cost*

Cumulative cost of a project over its whole life cycle.

Project Log*
A project diary. A chronological record of significant occurrences throughout the project.

Project Logic
The relationships between the various activities in a project.

Project Logic Drawing
A representation of the logical relationships of a project.

Project Management*
Planning, monitoring and control of all aspects of a project and the motivation of all those involved in it to achieve the project objectives on time and to the specified cost, quality and performance. (Alternative definition: The controlled implementation of defined change.)

Project Management Activity (PMA)*
An operation within a work package of a work breakdown structure (WBS), that is a specific action to be completed to aid fulfilment of the project as a whole.

Project Management Body of Knowledge
This is an inclusive term that describes the sum of knowledge within the profession of project (and programme) management. As with other professions, such as law and medicine, the body of knowledge rests with the practitioners and academics that apply and advance it.

Project Management Plan*
A plan for carrying out a project, to meet specific objectives, that is prepared by or for the project manager.

Project Management Software
Computer application software designed to help with planning and controlling resources, costs and schedules of a project. It may also provide facilities for documentation management, risk analysis etc.

Project Management Team
Members of the project team who are directly involved in its management.

Project Manager*
Individual or body with authority, accountability and responsibility for managing a project to achieve specific objectives.

Project Matrix
An organisation matrix that is project based in which the functional structures are duplicated in each project.

Project Monitoring*
Comparison of current project status with what was planned to be done to identify and report any deviations.

Project Network*
Representation of activities and/or events with their inter-relationships and dependencies.

Project Network Techniques*
Group of techniques that, for the description, analysis, planning and control of projects, considers the logical inter relationships of all project activities. The group includes techniques concerned with time, resources, costs and other influencing factors, e.g. uncertainty. Note: The terms 'program evaluation and review technique' (PERT) 'critical path analysis' (CPA), 'critical path method' (CPM) and 'precedence method' refer to particular techniques and should not be used as synonyms for project network.

Project Organisation*
Structure that is created or evolves to serve the project and its participants. (A term which refers to the structure, roles and responsibilities of the project team and its interfaces to the outside world.)

Project Phase*
Part of a project during which consistent activities are performed to attain a designated objective. One of a series of distinct steps in carrying out a project that together constitute the project life-cycle.

Project Plan
A document for management purposes that gives the basics of a project in terms of its objectives, justification, and how the objectives are to be achieved. This document is used as a record of decisions and a means of communication among stakeholders. It gives the supporting detail to the project definition which details the schedule, resource and costs for the project.

Project Planning
Developing and maintaining a project plan.

Project Portfolio
The constituent projects within a programme.

Project Procedures Manual
A collected set of the management and administrative procedures needed for the project.

Project Procurement Management
A subset of project management that includes procurement planning, source selection, enquiry, tender assessment, placement of purchase orders and contracts for goods and services, contract and purchase order administration and close-out in an effort to obtain goods and services from outside organisations.

Project Progress Report*
Formal statement that compares the project progress, achievements and expectations with the project plan.

Project Quality Management
A subset of project management that includes quality planning, quality assurance and quality control to satisfy the needs and purpose of the project.

Project Review Calendar*
Calendar of project review dates, meetings and issues of reports set against project week numbers or dates.

Project Risk Management
A subset of project management that includes risk identification, risk quantification, risk response development and risk response control in an effort to identify, analyse and respond to project risks.

Project Schedule*
Project programme (Planned dates for starting and completing activities and milestones.)

Project Scope Management
A subset of project management that includes initiation, scope planning, scope definition, scope verification and scope change control in an effort to ensure that the project has all of the necessary work required to complete it.

Project Sponsor
(1)   The individual or body for whom the project is undertaken, the primary risk taker
(2)   The individual representing the sponsoring body and to whom the project manager reports
A person or organisation providing funds for the project.

Project Start-up
The creation of the project team.

Project Status Report
A report on the status of accomplishments and any variances to spending and schedule plans.

Project Strategy
A comprehensive definition of how a project will be developed and managed.

Project Success/Failure Criteria
The criteria by which the success or failure of a project may be judged.

Project Support Office
The central location of planning and project support functions. Often provides personnel and facilities for centralised planning, cost management, estimating, documentation control and sometimes procurement to a number of projects.

Project Team*
Set of individuals, groups and/or organisations that are responsible to the project manager for undertaking project tasks. (Includes all contractors and consultants.)

Project Technical Plan
A plan produced at the beginning of a project that addresses technical issues and strategic issues related to quality control and configuration management.

Project Time Management
A subset of project management that includes activity definition, activity sequencing, activity duration estimating, schedule development and schedule control in order to complete the project on time.

Public Relations
An activity meant to improve the project organisation's environment in order to improve project performance and reception.

Q

Qualitative Risk Analysis
A generic term for subjective methods of assessing risks.

Quality
A trait or characteristic used to measure the degree of excellence of a product or service. Meeting customer's needs.

Quality Assurance (QA)
The process of evaluating overall project performance on a regular basis to provide confidence that the project will satisfy the relevant quality standards.

Quality Assurance Plan
A plan that guarantees a quality approach and conformance to all customer requirements for all activities in a project.

Quality Audit
An official examination to determine whether practices conform to specified standards or a critical analysis of whether a deliverable meets quality criteria.

Quality Control (QC)
The process of monitoring specific project results to determine if they comply with relevant standards and identifying ways to eliminate causes of unsatisfactory performance.

Quality Criteria
The characteristics of a product that determines whether it meets certain requirements.

Quality Guide
The quality guide describes quality and configuration management procedures and is aimed at people directly involved with quality reviews, configuration management and technical exceptions.

Quality Plan (for a project)*
That part of the project plan that concerns quality management and quality assurance strategies (see also ISO 10006)

Quality Planning
Determining which quality standards are necessary and how to apply them.

Quality Review
A review of a product against an established set of quality criteria.

R

Recurring Costs
Expenditures against specific tasks that would occur on a repetitive basis. Examples are hire of computer equipment, tool maintenance, etc.

Relationship
A logical connection between two activities.

Remaining Duration
Time needed to complete the remainder of an activity or project.

Request for Change
A proposal by the project manager for a change to the project as a result of a project issue report.

Request for Proposal
A bid document used to request proposals from prospective sellers of products or services.

Request for Quotation
Equivalent to a Request for Proposal but with more specific application areas.

Requirements
A negotiated set of measurable customer wants and needs.

Requirements Definition*
Statement of the needs that a project has to satisfy.

Reserve
See Contingency.

Resource*
Any variable capable of definition that is required for the completion of an activity and may constrain the project.
Note 1: A resource may be non-storable so that its availability has to be renewed for each time period (even if it was not utilised in previous time periods).
Note 2: A resource may be storable so that it remains available unless depleted by usage. Such a resource may also be replenished by activities producing credited and storable resource. (Resources can be people, equipment, facilities, funding or anything else needed to perform the work of a project.)

Resource Aggregation*

Summation of the requirements for each resource, and for each time period. Note: Where the earliest start time of an activity is used alone, it is often termed an 'early start' aggregation. Similarly a 'late start' aggregation uses the latest start times.

Resource Allocation*

Scheduling of activities and the resources required by those activities, so that predetermined constraints of resource availability and/or project time are not exceeded.

Resource Analysis

The process of analysing and optimising the use of resources on a project. Often uses resource levelling and resource smoothing techniques.

Resource Assignment

The work on an activity related to a specific resource.

Resource Availability

The level of availability of a resource, which may vary over time.

Resource Breakdown Structure

A hierarchical structure of resources that enables scheduling at the detailed requirements level, and roll up of both requirements and availabilities to a higher level.

Resource Calendar

A calendar that defines the working and non-working patterns for specific resources.

Resource Constraint*

Limitation due to the availability of a resource.

Resource Cumulation*

Process of accumulating the requirements for each resource to give the total required to date at all times throughout the project.

Resource Driven Task Durations

Task durations that are driven by the need for scarce resources.

Resource Histogram

A view of project data in which resource requirements, usage, and availability are shown using vertical bars against a horizontal time scale.

Resource Level

A specified level of resource units required by an activity per time unit.

Resource Levelling

See resource limited scheduling.

Resource Limited Scheduling*

Scheduling of activities, so that predetermined resource levels are never exceeded. Note: This may cause the minimum overall or specified project duration to be exceeded.

Resource Optimisation

A term for resource levelling and resource smoothing.

Resource Plan

Part of the definition statement stating how the programme will be resource loaded and what supporting services, infrastructure and third party services are required.

Resource Planning
Evaluating what resources are needed to complete a project and determining the quantity needed.

Resource Requirement
The requirement for a particular resource by a particular activity.

Resource Scheduling
The process of determining dates on which activities should be performed in order to smooth the demand for resources, or to avoid exceeding stated constraints on these restraints.

Resource Smoothing*
Scheduling of activities, within the limits of their float, so that fluctuations in individual resource requirements are minimised. (In smoothing, as opposed to resource levelling, the project completion date may not be delayed.

Responsibility Matrix
A document correlating the work required by a Work Breakdown Structure element to the functional organisations responsible for accomplishing the assigned tasks.

Responsible Organisation
A defined unit within the organisation structure which is assigned responsibility for accomplishing specific tasks, or cost accounts.

Retention
A part of payment withheld until the project is completed in order to ensure satisfactory performance or completion of contract terms.

Revenue Cost*
Expenditure charged to the profit and loss account as incurred or accrued due.

Risk*
Combination of the probability or frequency of occurrence of a defined threat or opportunity and the magnitude of the consequences of the occurrence. Note: Combination of the likelihood of occurrence of a specified event and its consequences. (Potential occurrences or threats that would jeopardise the success of a project. The probability of an undesirable outcome.)

Risk Analysis*
Systematic use of available information to determine how often specified events may occur and the magnitude of their likely consequences. (A technique designed to quantify the impact of uncertainty.)

Risk Assessment
The process of identifying potential risks, quantifying their likelihood of occurrence and assessing their likely impact on the project.

Risk Avoidance
Planning activities to avoid risks that have been identified.

Risk Event
A discrete occurrence that effects a project.

Risk Evaluation*
Process used to determine risk management priorities.

Risk Identification*
Process of determining what could pose a risk.

Risk Management*

Systematic application of policies, procedures, methods and practices to the tasks of identifying, analysing, evaluating, treating and monitoring risk. (The process whereby decisions are made to accept known or assessed risks and/or the implementation of actions to reduce the consequences or probability of occurrence.)

Risk Management Plan

A document defining how Project Risk Analysis and Management is to be implemented in the context of a particular project.

Risk Matrix

A matrix with risks located in rows, and with impact and likelihood in columns.

Risk Prioritising

Ordering of risks according first to their risk value, and then by which risks need to be considered for risk reduction, risk avoidance, and risk transfer.

Risk Quantification*

Process of applying values to the various aspects of a risk. (Evaluating the probability of risk event effect and occurrence.)

Risk Ranking

Allocating a classification to the impact and likelihood of a risk.

Risk Reduction

Action taken to reduce the likelihood and impact of a risk.

Risk Register*

Formal record of identified risks. (A body of information listing all the risks identified for the project, explaining the nature of each risk and recording information relevant to its assessment and management.)

Risk Response*

Contingency plans to manage a risk should it materialise. (Action to reduce the probability of the risk arising, or to reduce the significance of its detrimental impact if it does arise).

Risk, Secondary*

Risk that can occur as a result of treating a risk.

Risk Sharing*

Diminution of a risk by sharing it with others, usually for some consideration.

Risk Transfer

A contractual arrangement between two parties for delivery and acceptance of a product where the liability for the costs of a risk is transferred from one party to the other.

Risk Treatment*

Selection and implementation of appropriate options for dealing with risk.

S

Safety Plan
The standards and methods which minimise to an acceptable level the likelihood of accident or damage to people or equipment.

Schedule
A Schedule is the timetable for a project. It shows how project tasks and milestones are planned out over a period of time.

Schedule Control
Controlling schedule changes.

Schedule Dates
Start and finish dates calculated with regard to resource or external constraints as well as project logic.

Schedule Performance Index (SPI)
Ratio of work accomplished versus work planned, for a specified time period. The SPI is an efficiency rating for work accomplishment, comparing work accomplished to what should have been accomplished.

Schedule Variance (cost)
The difference between the budgeted cost of work performed and the budgeted cost of work scheduled at any point in time.

Scheduled Finish
The earliest date on which an activity can finish, having regard to resource or external constraints as well as project logic.

Scheduled Start
The earliest date on which an activity can start, having regard to resource or external constraints as well as project logic.

Scheduling
Scheduling is the process of determining when project activities will take place depending on defined durations and precedent activities. Schedule constraints specify when an activity should start or end based on duration, predecessors, external predecessor relationships, resource availability, or target dates.

Scope
The scope is the sum of work content of a project.

Scope Change
Any change in a project scope that requires a change in the project's cost or schedule.

Scope Change Control
Controlling changes to the scope.

Scope Verification
Ensuring all identified project deliverables have been completed satisfactorily.

Scope of Work
A description of the work to be accomplished or resources to be supplied.

Secondary Risk
The risk that may occur as a result of invoking a risk response or fallback plan.

Secondment Matrix

An organisational structure whereby team members are seconded from their respective departments to the project and are responsible to the project manager.

S-Curve

A display of cumulative costs, labour hours or other quantities plotted against time.

Sequence

Sequence is the order in which activities will occur with respect to one another.

Slack*

Calculated time span within which an event has to occur within the logical and imposed constraints of the network, without affecting the total project duration.

Note 1:   It may be made negative by an imposed date.
Note 2:   The term slack is used as referring only to an event.

Slip Chart

A pictorial representation of the predicted completion dates of milestones (also referred to as Trend Chart).

Slippage

The amount of slack or float time used up by the current activity due to a delayed start or increased duration.

Soft Project

A project that is intended to bring about change and does not have a physical end product.

Soft Skills

Soft skills include team building, conflict management and negotiation.

Source Selection

Choosing from potential contractors.

Splittable Activity*

Activity that can be interrupted in order to allow its resources to be transferred temporarily to another activity.

Sponsor*

Individual or body for whom the project is undertaken and who is the primary risk taker.

Stage

A natural high level subsection of a project that has its own organisational structure, life span and manager.

Stage Payment*

Payment part way through a project at some predetermined milestone.

Stakeholder*

A person or group of people who have a vested interest in the success of an organisation and the environment in which the organisation operates. (Project stakeholders are people or organisations who have a vested interest in the environment, performance and/or outcome of the project.)

Start Event of a Project*

Event with succeeding, but no preceding activities. Note: There may be more than one start event.

Start-To-Start Lag

Start-to-start lag is the minimum amount of time that must pass between the start of one activity and the start of its successor(s). This may be expressed in terms of duration or percentage.

Starting Activity
A starting activity has no predecessors. It does not have to wait for any other activity to start.

Statement of Work*
A document stating the requirements for a given project task.

Status Reports
Written reports given to both the project team and to a responsible person on a regular basis stating the status of an activity, work package, or whole project. Status Reports should be used to control the project and to keep management informed of project status.

Steering Group
A body established to monitor the project and give guidance to the project sponsor or project manager.

Subcontract
A contractual document which legally transfers the responsibility and effort of providing goods, services, data, or other hardware, from one firm to another.

Subcontractor
An organisation that supplies goods or services to a supplier.

Subnet or Subnetwork
A division of a project network diagram representing a subproject.

Sub-project
A group activities represented as a single activity in a higher level of the same.

Success Criteria
Criteria to be used for judging if the project is successful.

Success factors
Critical factors that will ensure achievement of success criteria.

Successor
A successor is an activity whose start or finish depends on the start or finish of a predecessor activity.

Sunk Costs
Unavoidable costs (even if the project were to be terminated).

Super-Critical Activity
An activity that is behind schedule is considered to be super-critical. if it has been delayed to a point where its float is calculated to be a negative value.

Supplier
Includes contractors, consultants and any organisation that supplies services or goods to the customer.

System
The complete technical output of the project including technical products.

Systems and Procedures
Systems and procedure detail the standard methods, practices and procedures of handling frequently occurring events within the project.

Systems Management

Management that includes the prime activities of systems analysis, systems design and engineering and systems development.

T

Target Completion Date

A date which contractors strive toward for completion of the activity.

Target Date

Date imposed on an activity or project by the user. There are two types of target dates; target start dates, and target finish dates.

Target Finish - Activity

Target Finish is the user's imposed finish date for an activity. A Target Finish date is used if there are pre-defined commitment dates.

Target Finish Date

The date planned to finish work on an activity.

Target Finish - Project

A user's Target Finish date can be imposed on a project as a whole. A Target Finish date is used if there is a pre-defined completion date.

Target Start - Activity

Target Start is an imposed starting date on an activity.

Target Start Date

The date planned to start work on an activity.

Task

The smallest indivisible part of an activity when it is broken down to a level best understood and performed by a specific person or organisation.

Team

A team is made up of two or more people working interdependently toward a common goal and a shared reward.

Team Building

The ability to gather the right people to join a project team and get them working together for the benefit of a project.

Team Development

Developing skills, as a group and individually, that enhance project performance.

Team Leader

Person responsible for leading a team.

Technical Assurance

The monitoring of the technical integrity of products.

Technical Guide

A document that guides managers, team leaders and technical assurance co-ordinators on planning the production of products.

Technical Products
Products produced by a project for an end user.

Tender
A document proposing to meet a specification in a certain way and at a stated price (or on a particular financial basis), an offer of price and conditions under which the tenderer is willing to undertake work for the client.

Termination*
Completion of the project, either upon formal acceptance of its deliverables by the client and/or the disposal of such deliverables at the end of their life.

Terms of Reference
A specification of a team member's responsibilities and authorities within the project.

Tied Activities*
Activities that have to be performed sequentially or within a predetermined time of each other.

Time Analysis
The process of calculating the early and late dates for each activity on a project, based on the duration of the activities and the logical relations between them.

Time Based Network*
A linked bar chart, a bar chart that shows the logical and time relationships between activities.

Time Limited Scheduling*
Scheduling of activities, so that the specified project duration, or any imposed dates are not exceeded. Note: This may cause the envisaged resource levels to be exceeded.

Time-Limited Resource Scheduling
The production of scheduled dates in which resource constraints may be relaxed in order to avoid any delay in project completion.

Time Now*
Specified date from which the forward analysis is deemed to commence. (The date to which current progress is reported. Sometimes referred to as the status date because all progress information entered for a project should be correct as of this date.)

Time Recording
The recording of effort expended on each activity in order to update a project plan.

Time-Scaled Logic Drawing
A drawing that displays the logical connection between activities in the context of a time scale in which each horizontal position represents a point in time.

Time-Scaled Network Diagram
A project network diagram drawn so that the positioning of the activity represents schedule.

Time Sheet
A means of recording the actual effort expended against project and non-project activities.

Top Down Cost Estimating
The total project cost is estimated based on historical costs and other project variables and then subdivided down to individual activities.

Total Float*
Time by which an activity may be delayed or extended without affecting the total project duration (or violating a target finish date.)

Total Quality Management (TQM)
A strategic, integrated management system for customer satisfaction that guides all employees in every aspect of their work.

Transit Time*
Dependency link that requires time and no other resources. It may be a negative time.

Turnaround Report
A report created especially for the various responsible managers to enter their progress status against a list of activities that are scheduled to be in progress during a particular time window.

U

Undistributed Budgets
Budget applicable to contract effort which has not yet been identified to specific cost accounts or work packages.

Unlimited Schedule*
Infinite schedule, schedule produced without resource constraint.

User Requirements
The requirements governing the project's deliverables or products as expressed by the user.
What the user needs expressed in user terminology.

User Requirements Statement
A document that defines the user's needs in user terminology from the user's perspective.

Users
The group of people who are intended to benefit from the project.

V

Value
A standard, principle or quality considered worthwhile or desirable.

Value Management
A structured means of improving business effectiveness that includes the use of management techniques such as value engineering and value analysis.

Value Engineering
A technique for analysing qualitative and quantitative costs and benefits of component parts of a proposed system.

Value Planning
A technique for assessing, before significant investment is made, the desirability of a proposal based on the value that will accrue to the organisation from that proposal.

Variance
A discrepancy between the actual and planned performance on a project, either in terms of schedule or cost.

Variance at Completion
The difference between Budget at Complete and Estimate at Complete.

Variation
A change in scope or timing of work which a supplier is obliged to do under a contract.

Variation Order
The document authorising an approved technical change or variation.

Variations Management*
Monitoring, recording and assessing of variations to the scope or timing of a project, irrespective of who generated the change. The objective is to make all parties fully aware of the cost, time and quality implications of implementing such changes.

W

What-If Analysis
The process if evaluating alternative strategies.

What-if Simulation*
Changing the value of the parameters of the project network to study its behaviour under various conditions of its operation.

Work
The total number of hours, people or effort required to complete a task.

Workaround
Response to a negative risk event. Distinguished from contingency plan in that a workaround is not planned in advance of the occurrence of the risk event i.e. it is reactive.

Work Breakdown Code
A code that represents the 'family tree' of an element in a work breakdown structure.

Work Breakdown Structure*
Way in which a project may be divided by level into discrete groups for programming, cost planning and control purposes. Note: see also 'work package'. (The WBS is a tool for defining the hierarchical breakdown of work required to deliver the products of a project. Major categories are broken down into smaller components. These are sub-divided until the lowest required level of detail is established. The lowest units of the WBS become the activities in a project. The WBS defines the total work to be undertaken on the project and provides a structure for all project control systems.)

Work Load
Work load is the amount of work units assigned to a resource over a period of time.

Work Package*
A group of related tasks that are defined at the same level within a work breakdown structure. (In traditional cost schedule systems, the criteria for defining work packages are as follows: (1) Each work package is clearly distinguishable from all other work packages in the programme. (2) Each work package has a scheduled start and finish date. (3) Each work package has an assigned budget that is time-phased over the duration of the work package. (4) Each work package either has a relatively short duration, or can be divided into a series of milestones whose status can be objectively measured. (5) Each work package has a schedule that is integrated with higher-level schedules.)

Work Units
Work units provide the measurement units for resources. For example, people as a resource can be measured by the number of hours they work.

X

No Terms Defined

Y

Yield
The return (%) on an investment.

Z

Zero Float
Zero float is a condition where there is no excess time between activities. An activity with zero float is considered a critical activity.

Further Reading

Readers may also care to consult the Wideman Comparative Glossary of Common Project Management Terms to be found at: http://www.pmforum.org/library/glossary/index.htm.

BIBLIOGRAPHY

A

Abdel-Hamid, TK and Madnick, SE, "The Elusive Silver Lining: How we fail to learn from software development failures", Sloan Management Review, Fall 1990, 39 - 48

DeMarco, T, "Controlling Software Projects", New York:Yourdon, 1982

AIIM ARP1-2001 - "Implementation Guidelines and Standards for Web-Based Document Management Systems", Association for Information and Image Management International (USA). 9th March 2001.

Allan, G., "Configuration Management and its impact on businesses that use computer platforms", International Journal of Project Management, 15(5) 1997.

Allen, H., "Mediation techniques as a business tool", Centre for Effective Dispute Resolution, 2000.

Andersen, E S, Grude, K V, Haug, T and Turner, J R., "Goal Directed Project Management", Kogan Page/Coopers & Lybrand, London, 1987.

Ansoff, H.I., "Corporate Strategy",. Pelican, 1988.

Arthur, M., Claman, P., and DeFillippi, R. "Intelligent Enterprise, intelligent careers", Academy of Management Executive, Volume 9, Number 4, 1995.

Arnott, S., "Defra to Award Lucrative Outsourcing Deal", Computing, VNU Business Publications Ltd, Aug 22, 2002.

Ashkenas, R., Ulrich, D., Jick, T. & Kerr, S., "The Boundaryless Organisation", San Francisco: Josey-Bass, 1995.

ASTM Subcommittee E-06.81 on Building Economics, "Standard Practice for Performing Value Analysis (VA) of Buildings and Building Systems", Standard Designation: E 1699-95, ASTM, Philadelphia, Pa, July 1995

APM, "Contract Strategy for Successful Project Management", The Association for Project Management (APM), Specific Interest Group (SIG) on Contracts and Procurement, 1998.

B

Backhouse, C J. and Brookes, N., (eds), "Concurrent Engineering", Aldershot, Gower, 1996

Baker, M J., (ed), "Marketing Theory & Practice" (Third Edition) MacMillan Business Series.

Baker, B N, Murphey, P C and Fisher, D., "Factors affecting project success".

Barnes, N J., "The Boundaryless Organisation: Implications for Job Analysis, Recruitment and Selection", Human Resource Planning, Volume 20, No. 4, 1997.

Belbin, R M. "Team Roles at work", London, Butterworth-Heinemann, 1993.

Belbin, R M., "Management Teams: Why They Succeed of Fail", Butterworth-Heinemann, Oxford, 1996.

Bem, D. J, Wallach, M. A. and Kogan, N., "Group Decision Making under Risk or Aversive Consequences", in Smith, P., Group Processes Selected Readings, Penguin,Middlesex, 1970.

Bennis, W., "Organizing Genius", Nicholas Brealey Publishing.

Berlack, H R., "Software Configuration Management", Wiley, 1992.

Blair, R., "e-Procurement Makes Immediate Business Sense", IBM e-Procurement Briefing Paper, July 2001.

Blanden, R.A., "Searching for Synergy in Supply Chains: Can Strategic Benchmarking Alleviate 'Stickiness'?" MBA Thesis, University of Durham Business School, 1997

Blanchard, B S and Fabrycky W J, "Systems Engineering and Analysis" (second edition), Prentice Hall, 1990.

Brewster, C. "Flexible Working in Europe: extent, growth and challenge for HRM", in Sparrow, P. and Marchington, M. Human Resource Management: The New Agenda, Pitman Publishing, 1998.

Briggs-Myers, I "Introduction to Type". 5th edition, Consulting Psychologists Press Inc., Palo Alto, C.A., USA, 1993.

British Standards Institution, BS 6079-1: 2000 Project Management Part 1: Guide to Project Management. British Standards Institution, London, 2002

British Standards Institution, BS 6079-2: 2000 Project Management Part 2: Vocabulary, British Standards Institution, London, 2002

British Standards Institution, BS 10005: 1995,Quality management - Guidelines for Quality Plans.

British Standards Institution, BS 10006, 1997 Quality management - Guidelines to Quality in Project Management.

British Standards Institution, BS EN ISO 14001:1996 Environmental Management Systmes - Specification with guidance for use.

British Standards Institution Technical Committee DS/1 (BSI), PD 6663: Guidelines to BS EN 12973: Value management- Practical guidance to its use and intent, British Standards Institution, Chiswick, June 2000

British Standards Institution Technical Committee CEN/TC 279, Value Management, BS EN 12973:2000, European Committee for Standardization (CEN)- British Standards Institution (BSI) Technical Committee DS/1, Apr. 2000

British Standards Institution Technical Committee CEN/TC 279, Value Management, value analysis, functional analysis vocabulary BS EN 1325-1:1997, European Committee for Standardization (CEN)- British Standards Institution (BSI) Technical Committee DS/1, Jan. 1997

British Standards Institution, BS ISO 15489-1:2001 Information and Documentation - Records Management - Part 1: General

British Standards Institution, BS ISO/TR 15489-2:2001(E) Technical Report. Information and Documentation - Records Management - Part 2: Guidelines.

British Standards Institution, BS 7799-1:1999 Information Security Management - Part 1: Code of Practice for Information Security Management

British Standards Institution, DISC PD 3002:1998 Guide to BS 7799 risk assessment and risk management

British Standards Institution, DISC PD 0008:1999 Code of Practice for Legal Admissibility and Evidential Weight of Information Stored Electronically.

British Standards Institution, DISC PD 0009:1999 Compliance workbook for use with PD 0008:1999. Code of practice for legal admissibility and evidential weight of information stored electronically.

British Standards Institution, DISC PD 3004:1999 Guide to BS 7799 auditing.

British Standards Institution, BS 7799-2:1999 Information Security Management - Part 2: Specification for Information Security Management Systems.

British Standards Institute, The European Standard on Value Management, BS EN 12973:2000.

Becker, M. "Project or Program Management?, PM Network, PMI Communications, Drexel Hill, PA, Vol.13- No.10, 1999.

Brooks, F., 'The Mythical Man-Month' Addison Wesley, Philippines, 1982.

Brotherton, C, "Social Psychology and Management", Open University Press, 1999.

Brown, R "Group Process - Dynamics within and between groups", 2nd Edition. Oxford, Blackwell Publishers,2000.

Burke, Rory, "Project Management: Planning and Control", 3rd edn. Wiley, Chichester, 1999.

Burns, T. and Stalker, G.M. "The Management of Innovation", Tavistock Press, 1961.

Butterick, R., "The Interactive Project Workout" (Second Edition) Financial Times/Prentice Hall/Pearson Education, 2000.

C

Capelli, P. "A market-driven approach to retaining talent", Harvard Business Review. January/February, 2000.

Cardozo, R N., "Obstacles to Growth of New Technology-Based Enterprises", Carlson School of Management, University of Minnesota.

Central Computer and Telecommunications Agency (CCTA), "Managing Successful Programmes", Stationery Office, London, 1999.

Central Computer and Telecommunications Agency (CCTA), "Programme Management Case Studies: Volume 1", Stationery Office, London, 1994.

Central Computer and Telecommunications Agency (CCTA), "Guide to Prince 2", The Stationery Office, London, 1996.
(Note: CCTA is now part of The Office for Government Commerce).
Central Unit on Procurement, "CUP Guidance Note 54", H M Treasury, 1996.
Chai, K H, Shi, Y J, and Gregory, M J., "Bridging Islands of Knowledge: A framework of knowledge sharing in international manufacturing networks", 6th European Operations Management Annual Conference, Venice, 1999.
Chanaron, J, Jolly, D and Soderquist, K., "Technological Management: A Tentative Research Agenda", Groupe ESC, Grenoble, 1999.
CIRIA, "Value Management in Construction: A Client's Guide", Special Publication 129, (CIRIA), 1996.
Cleland D I, "Project Management: Strategic Design and Implementation", (third edition), McGraw-Hill, 1999
Cleland D I and King W R., "Project Management Handbook", 2nd edition, Van Nostrand Reinhold, 1988.
Cockman, P, Evans, B and Reynolds, P., "Client- Centred Consulting (a Practical Guide for Internal Advisors and Trainers)" McGraw Hill Training Series.
Connaughton J N., Green S D., "Value Management in Construction: A Client's Guide", CIRIA, London, 1996.
Conti, B, and Kleiner, B H., "How to increase Teamwork in Organisations". Training for Quality, Vol. 5, No. 1, 1997.
Crawford, L., "Project Management Competence: the value of standards", DBA Thesis, Henley Management College, Henley-on-Thames, 2001.

D

Daly, J.A, McCroskey, J.C, Ayres, J, Hopf, T, and Ayres, D.M, "Avoiding Communication, Shyness, Reticence and Communication Apprehension", 2nd Ed. , Hampton Press, Cresskill, NJ, 1997.
Daft, R., "Understanding Management", Dryden Press, Orlando, 1995.
Davis, A M., "Software Requirements - Objects, Functions, and States", Prentice-Hall, Englewood Cliffs, N.J, 1993.
Devaux, S. A., "Total Project Control: a Manager's Guide to Integrated Project Planning, Measurement and Tracking", New York, Wiley, 1999.
Dixon, M. (Ed.), "The Association for Project Management (APM) Body of Knowledge (BoK)", 4th Edition, APM, High Wycombe, 2000.
Drucker, P., "Managing for Results", Heinemann Professional, 1989.
Dym C L., "Engineering Design: A Project-Based Introduction", John Wiley, 2000.

E

EFQM, (European Foundation for Quality Management), "The EFQM Excellence Model", EFQM Publications, Brussels, 1999.

EFQM, (European Foundation for Quality Management), "Assessing for Excellence - A Practical Guide for Self-Assessment", EFQM Publications, Brussels, 1999.

Egbu, C, Gaskell, C and Howes, J., "The Role of Organisational Culture and Motivation in Effective Utilisation of Information Technology for Teamworking in Construction". Proceedings of the 17th Annual Conference of the Association of Researchers in Construction Management, University of Salford, England, UK, 2001.

Egbu, C, Gaskell, C and Howes, J., "Information Technology for Improving Teamworking in Construction: Opportunities and Challenges for Practice and for Research" Proceedings of the Construction and Building Research Conference of the RICS Foundation, Glasgow Caledonian University, Glasgow, Scotland, UK, 2001.

F

Field, M. and Keller, L., "Project Management", The Open University, Milton Keynes, 1998.

Fleming, Q W and Koppleman, J M., "Earned Value Project Management", 2nd edition, Project Management Institute, Sylva, NC, 2000.

Fisher R, Or W and Patton B., "Getting to Yes: Negotiating Agreement Without Giving In", Penguin, 1991.

Forsberg K et al, "Visualising Project Management", John Wiley, 1996.

Foster, D and Davis, J., "Mastering Marketing" (3rd Edition) MacMillan.

G

Gareis, R., "Managing the project start", in Turner, J R and Simister, S J., (eds), The Gower Handbook of Project Management, 3rd edition, Gower, Aldershot, 2000.

Gatenby, J., "Plan for your dispute", Centre for Effective Dispute Resolution, 1999.

Gillen, T., "Assertiveness", Chartered Institute of Personnel Development, 1998.

Gomez-Meija, L., Balkin, D and Cardy, R., "Managing Human Resources", 3rd Edition, Prentice-Hall,2001.

Görög, M. and Smith, N., "Project Management for Managers", Project Management Institute, Sylva, NC, 1999.

Gray, C F and Larson, E W., "Project Management: the Managerial Process", Irwin/McGraw-Hill, Singapore, 2000.

Green, P and Woodward, S., "Contracted Mediation: Dispute Resolution for Project-based Industries, Society of Construction Law, 2001.

Green S, Popper P., "Value Engineering - The Search for Unnecessary Cost", Chartered Institute of Building, Ascot, 1990.

Green, S. D. "A Reinterpretation of Value Management", CIB W-65, Organisation and Management of Construction - The Way forward, (ed. Lewis, T. M.), Trinidad, W. I., 1993.

Green, S D., "A Kuhnian crisis in value management?" Value World. Vol. 20 (3), 1997.

Grundy, T., "Strategy implementation and project management", International Journal of Project Management, Elsevier Science Ltd. and IPMA. 16, 1997.

H

Hamilton, A., "Managing for Value: Achieving high quality at low cost", Oak Tree Press, Dublin, 1999.

Hamilton, A., "Management by Projects: Achieving Success in a Changing World", Thomas Telford, London, 1997.

Handy, C., "Understanding Organisations", Penguin, London, 1993.

Harbison, J. and Pekar, P., "Smart Alliances", Jossey-Bass, San Francisco, 1998.

Harpham, A., "Political, economic, social and technical influences - PEST", in Turner, J R and Simister, S J., (eds), The Gower Handbook of Project Management, 3rd edition, Gower, Aldershot, 2000.

Harris, P R and Moran, R T., "Managing Cultural Differences", Gulf Publishing, 1996

Harrison, F L., "Advanced Project Management: A Structured Approach", 3rd edition, Gower, Aldershot, 1992.

Hayles C and Simister S., "The FAST Approach - Function Analysis and Diagramming Techniques", BRE, Watford, 2000.

Healy P., "Project Management", Butterworth Heinemann, Australia, 1997.

Hersey, P., "The Situational Leader", Center for Leadership Studies, Escondido, CA., 1997.

Hersey, P and Blanchard K., "The one minute manager builds high performing teams", Fontana.

Herzberg, F., "Work and the nature of man", Granada Publishing Ltd.

Hobbs, B, Ménard, P, Laliberté, M and Coulombe, R., "A Project Office Maturity Model", Project Management Institute 30th Annual Seminars & Symposium Proceedings, PMI Communications, Drexel Hill, PA., 1999.

Hodgetts, R., "Management Theory & Process", Saunders, Philadelphia, 1979.

Hofstede, G., "Cultures & Organisations", Harper Collins, London, 1994.

Holt, A., Principles of Health and Safety at Work, 4th Edition, IOSH Publishing, 1999..

Hooks, I F. and Farry, K A., "Customer Centered Products - Creating Successful Products Through Smart Requirements Management", Amacom, 2000.

Hougham, M., "Association for Project Management Syllabus for the APMP Examination", Association for Project Management, High Wycombe, 2000.

Hougham, M., "London Ambulance Service computer aided despatch system", International Journal of Project Management, 14(2), 1996.

Huczynski, A. and Buchanan, D A., "Organisational Behaviour: an Introductory Text", 4th edition, Prentice-Hall, Hemel Hempstead, 2000.

Hussey, D., "Strategy and Planning: A Manager's Guide", John Wiley & Sons, 1999.

I

ICA Internal Control - A Guidance for Directors on the Combined Code, The Institute of Chartered Accountants in England & Wales, 1999.

IEC 61508 Symposium Proceedings, "IEC 61508 Explained", The Institute of Measurement and Control, 1999.

Ince, D., "Project Costing", Systems International, 1988.

Industry Canada, "Technology Roadmapping: A Guide for Government Employees", Ottawa.

Ingram, H, Teare, R., Scheuing, E and Armistead, C., "A Systems Model of effective teamwork" The TQM Magazine, Vol. 9, No. 2, 1997.

ISO 10007, "Guidelines for Configuration Management", International Standards Organization, Geneva, 1995.

J

Jenks, J and Kelly, J., "Don't do, delegate", Kogan Page.

Jensen, D. "Seven legal elements for a claim for construction acceleration," Project Management Journal, .28 (1), pages 32-44, 1997.

Johnson, G. and Scholes, K., "Exploring Corporate Strategy", 4th edition, Hemel Hempstead, Prentice Hall Europe, 1997.

Jones, C., "Patterns of Software Systems Failure and Success", International Thomson Press, 1996.

K

Kaplan, R S and Norton, D P., "Using the Balanced Scorecard as a Strategic Management System", Harvard Business Review, Harvard College, Jan.-Feb, 1996.

Kaufman, J J., "Value Engineering for the Practitioner", NCS University, NC., 1985.

Kaufman, J J., "Value Management: Creating Competitive Advantage", Crisp Publications, 1998.

Keegan, A., "Management Practices in Knowledge Intensive Firms (KIFs): The Future of HRM in the Knowledge Era", Rotterdam Institute for Business Economic Studies Research Paper 9846, Rotterdam, 1998.

Keegan, A. and Turner, J R., "Managing Human Resources in the Project-Based Organisation", in Turner, J R and Simister, S J., (eds) Gower Handbook of Project Management, 3rd Edition, 2000.

Keller, L., "Evaluation, Estimates & Contracts", PMT605, Open University, 1987.

Kelly, J and Male, S., "Value Management in design and construction (The economic management of projects)", E & FN Spon, Chapman and Hall, London, 1993.

Kerzner, H., "Project Management: A Systems Approach to Planning, Scheduling and Controlling", 6th edn, Van Nostrand Reinhold, New York, 2000.

Kerzner, H., "In Search of Excellence in Project Management: Successful Practices in High Performance Organisations", Van Nostrand Reinhold, New York, 1998.

Kliem, R L and Ludin, I S., "The People Side of Project Management", Gower, Aldershot, 1992.

Kolb, D., "Hidden Conflict in Organisations". Sage Publications, London, 1992.

Kouzes and Posner, "The Leadership Challenge", Jossey-Bass Publishers.

L

Lawson, G, Wearne, S and Iles-Smith, P., (eds.), "Project Management for the Process Industries", Institution of Chemical Engineers, 1999.

Lee, F., 'When the Going Gets Tough, Do the Tough Ask for Help? Help Seeking and Power Motivation in Organisations", Organizational Behaviour and Human Decision Processes, Vol. 72, No. 3. December, 1997.

Legge, K., "Flexibility: the gift-wrapping of employment degradation", in Sparrow, P. and Marchington, M., Human Resource Management: The New Agenda, Pitman Publishing, 1998.

Lester, A., "Project Planning and Control", 2nd edition, Oxford, Butterworth-Heinemann, 1991.

Levy, D., "Chaos Theory and Strategy: Theory, Management and Managerial Implications", Strategic Management Journal, 15, 1994.

Lewis, J D., "The Connected Corporation: How Leading Companies Win Through Customer-Supplier Alliances", The Free Press, New York, NY., 1995.

Lock, D., "Project Management", 7th edition, Gower, Aldershot, 2000.

Locke, E A and Latham, G., "A Theory of Goal Setting and Task Performance", Prentice-Hall, London, 1990.

Lockyer, K G and Gordon, J., "Project Management and Project Network Techniques", 6th edition, Financial Times/Pitman Publising, London, 1996.

M

Male, S, Kelly, J, Fernie, S, Grönqvist, M and Bowles, G., "The value management benchmark: A good practice framework for clients and practitioners", Thomas Telford Publishing, London, 1998.

Marion, E D and Remine, E W., "Natural Networks-A different approach." Project Management Institute 28th Annual Seminars & Symposium Proceedings, PMI Communications, Drexel Hill, PA., 1997.

Maylor, H., Project Management, Pitman, 2002.

Maxwell, C., "The Future of Work: Understanding the Role of Technology", Telecomunications Journal Vol 18 No. 1, British Telecommunications, 1999.

McElroy, W and Mills, C., "Managing stakeholders", in Turner, J R and Simister, S J., (eds), The Gower Handbook of Project Management, 3rd edition, Gower, Aldershot, 2000.

Meredith, J R and Mantel, S J Jr., "Project Management: A Managerial Approach", 4th edition, Wiley, New York, 2000.

Miles, L D., "Techniques of Value Analysis and Engineering", 3rd Edition, McGraw-Hill Book Company, New-York, NY., 1972.

Mintzberg, H and Waters, J A., "Of Strategies, Deliberate and Emergent", Strategic Management Journal, Vol. 6, No. 3, 1985.

Mintzberg, H., "The Structuring of Organisations: A synthesis of Research", Prentice-Hall, 1979.

MOD (PE), "Compendium of Project Management", HMSO, 1978.

Morris, P. W. G., "The Management of Projects", Thomas Telford, London, 1997.

Morris, P W G., "Managing project interfaces", in Cleland, D I and King, W R., (eds), Project Management Handbook, 2nd edition, Van Nostrand Reinhold, New York, 1988.

Morris, P W G and Hough, G., "The Anatomy of Major Projects: a study of the reality of project management", Wiley, Cichester, 1987.

Morrison, Conaway and Borden, "Kiss, Bow or Shake Hands - How to do business in 60 countries", Adams Media Corporation, 1997.

Murray-Webster, R. and Thiry, M., "Managing Programmes of Projects" in Turner, J R and Simister, S J., (Eds), Gower Handbook of Project Management, 3rd edition, Gower, Aldershot, 2000.

N

Nelson, R and Economy, P., "Consulting for Dummies", IDG Books Worldwide.

Nevis, E. DiBella, A and Gould, J., "Understanding Organizations as Learning Systems", The Society for Organizational Learning, Massachusetts Institute of Technology, 1997.

Noe, R, Hollenbeck, J, Gerhart, B and Wright, P., "Human Resource Management Gaining a Competitive Edge", 3rd Edition, Irwin MacGraw-Hill, 2000.

Normann, R and Rameirez, R., "From Value Chain to Value Constellation: Designing Interactive Strategy", Harvard Business Review, July-August 1993.

O

O'Connell, F., "How To Run Successful Projects", Prentice-Hall, UK, 1993.

O'Connor, J and Seymour-Mandala, J., "Introducing NLP", Harper Collins.

O'Neil, J., "Short-Staffed? Maximise Scarce Resources with Knowledge Resource Planning." PM Network, Project Management Institute, February 1999.

Obeng, E., "All Change - The Project Manager's Secret Handbook", Financial Times Management, 1996.

Obeng, E., "Putting Strategy to Work. The blueprint for transforming ideas into action", Pitman, London, 1996.

Open University Systems Group, "Systems Behaviour" 3rd Edition, Paul Chapman Publishing, London, 1988.

P

Parker, Glenn M., "Cross functional teams - working with allies, enemies and other strangers", Jossey-Bass Publishers, 1994.

Partington, D. "Implementing strategy through programmes of projects" in Turner, J R and Simister, S J., (Eds), Gower Handbook of Project Management, 3rd edition, Gower, Aldershot, 2000.

Pellegrinelli, S and Bowman, C., "Implementing Strategy Through Projects", Long Range Planning Vol 27 No.4, 1994.

Pellegrinelli, S., "Programme management: organising project-based change", International Journal of Project Management, Elsevier Science and IPMA. 15, 1997.

Peters, T J., "The Circle of Innovation. You can't shrink your way to greatness", Hodder and Stoughton, London, 1997.

Phaal, R, Farrukh, C J P, and Probert, D R., "Fast-Start Technology Roadmapping", University of Cambridge.

Pinto, J K., (ed), "The Project Management Institute: Project Management Handbook", Jossey Bass, 1998.

Pinto, J K and Slevin D P., "The Project Implementation Profile", Project Management Institute Seminar/Symposium, Atlanta, Georgia, 1989.

Pinto, J K and Slevin, D P., "Critical success factors in effective project implementation", in Cleland, D I and King, W R., (eds), Project Management Handbook, 2nd edition, Van Nostrand Reinhold, New York, 1988.

Porter, M E., "Competitive Advantage: Creating and Maintaining Superior Performance", The Free Press, New York, NY., 1985.

Procter, S and Mueller, F., (Eds), "Teamworking", Management, work and Organisations Series, Macmillan Press, 2000.

Q

Quinn, J B., "Strategic change: logical incrementalism". Sloane Management Review, 1978.

Quinn, J.B., "Strategies for Change", Irwin, 1980.

R

Rea, P J and Kerzner, H., "Strategic Planning: A Practical Guide", Van Nostrand Reinhold, New-York, NY., 1997.

Reason, J., "Human Error", Cambridge University Press, 1990.

Rees, D., "Managing Culture" in Turner, J R and Simister, S J., (eds), The Gower Handbook of Project Management, 3rd edition, Gower, Aldershot, 2000.

Reiss, G., "Project Management Demystified: Today's Tools and Techniques", 2nd edition, Spon, London, 1995.

Reiss, G., "Programme Management Demystified: Managing Multiple Projects Successfully", Spon, London, 1996.

RICS, "Improving Value for Money in Construction", London, 1998.

Rook, P., "Meeting the bottom line", VNU Publications (NK).

Ruff, A., Principles of Law for Managers, Routledge, 1995.

S

Saunders, R.G., "Project Management in R&D, the art of estimating Development Project Activities", International Journal of Project Management, 1990.

SAVE International, "Value Methodology Standard", Save International, 1997.

Sawacha, E, Naoum, S and Fong, D., "Factors Affecting Safety Performance on Construction Sites". International Journal of Project Management, Vol. 17, No. 5, 1999.

Shah, J., "Survey Shows Outsourcing Catches on in Supply Chain", CMP Media Inc., 2002.

Shaw, M E., "Communication Networks" in; Smith, B., (Ed) 'Group Processes', Penguin, Middlesex, 1970.

Simister, S J., "Managing scope - functionality and value", in Turner, J R and Simister, S J., (eds), The Gower Handbook of Project Management, 3rd edition, Gower, Aldershot, 2000.

Simon, P, Hillson, D and Newland, K., "Project Risk Analysis and Management Guide", Association for Project Management / APM Group Limited, Norwich, 1997.

South, J., "The dispute resolution team: mediator and dispute resolution advisor", Centre for Effective Dispute Resolution, 2001.

Stacey, R D., "Strategic Management and Organizational Dynamics", Pitman, London, 1993.

Stewart, R., (Ed), "Gower Handbook of Teamworking", Gower, Aldershot, 1999.

Stonor, J and Wankel, C., "Management", Prentice Hall, New Jersey, 1986.

Street, L., "ADR a generic, holistic concept", Centre for Effective Dispute Resolution, 2002.

Sveiby, K., "The New Organizational Wealth: managing and measuring knowledge based assets", Berrett-Koehler, 1997.

Swinnerton, D., "Estimating techniques & their application", 'Project' the Magazine of the Association for Project Management, 1995.

T

Thiry, M., "The benefits of value management through the project life cycle". 'Project' the Magazine of the Association for Project Management, Vol.10-9,1998.

Thiry, M., "Would you tell me please which way I ought to go from here?" Is Change a Threat or an Opportunity? Proceedings of the 30th PMI Seminars and Symposium, Philadelphia, PA., 1999.

Thiry, M,. "Sensemaking in Value Management Practice" International Journal of Project Management, Elseveir Science, Oxford, 2001.

Thiry, M., "Combining value and project management into an effective programme management model", Proceedings of the 4th Annual PMI-Europe Conference, London, 2001.

Thiry, M., "The European VM Standard; will it change the way we practice VM?" Proceedings of the 4th Annual PMI-Europe Conference, London, 2001.

Thiry, M., "Value Management Practice", Sylva NC., Project Management Institute, 1997.

Thiry, M., "The Emergent Organisation", Proceedings of the 3rd PMI Europe Conference, Jerusalem, 2000.

Thiry, M., "A Learning Loop for Successful Program Management", Proceedings of the 31st PMI Seminars and Symposium, PMI, Newton Square, PA., 2000.

Thiry, M., "Successfully integrating value & project management into a complete strategic decision making-implementing cycle", Proceedings of the 'International Business and Corporate Planning and Strategy Congress 2000', Amsterdam, 2000.

Thomas, K W and Kilmann, R H., "Thomas-Kilmann Conflict Mode Instrument" Xicom, Tuxedo, N.Y., 1974.

Torrington, D, Hall, L and Taylor, S., "Human Resource Management", 5th Edition, Pearson Education, 2002.

Tsuchiya, S., "Simulation/Gaming, An Effective Tool for Project Management", Project Management Institute 28th Annual Seminars & Symposium Proceedings, PMI Communications, Drexel Hill, PA., 1997.

Tuckman, B W., "Development Sequences in Small Groups", Psychological Bulletin, vol.63, 1965.

Turner, J R, Grude, K V and Thurloway, L., "The Project Manager as Change Agent", McGraw-Hill, Maidenhead, 1996.

Turner, J R and Simister, S J., "The Gower Handbook of Project Management", 3rd edition, Gower, Aldershot, 2000.

Turner, J R., "The Handbook of Project-Based Management", 2nd edition, McGraw-Hill, Maidenhead, 1999.

Turner, J R., "The Commercial Project Manger", McGraw Hill, 1995.

Turner, J R., "Project success and strategy", in Turner, J R and Simister, S J., (eds), The Gower Handbook of Project Management, 3rd edition, Gower, Aldershot, 2000.

Turner, J R and Keegan, A E., "Mechanisms of Governance in the Project-based Organization: a transaction cost perspective", European Management Journal, 19(3), 2001.

Turner, J R., and Simister, S J., "Project contract management: a transaction cost perspective", in Proceedings of PMI Europe 2001, 'A Project Management Odyssey', London, ed TM Williams, Marlow Events, Marlow, UK, June 2001.

U

United States Department of Energy, "Building Envelope Technology Roadmap (Draft)", 2000.

W

Ward, J and Murray, P, "Benefits Management: Best Practice Guidelines", The Information Systems Research Centre, Cranfield School of Management, Cranfield, UK., 1997.

Wake , S., "E.V.A. in the UK", Fifth Edition, London 2001.

Wake, et. al. "Earned Value Manangement - APM Guideline for the UK", First Edition, Association for Project Management, High Wycombe, 2002.

Wateridge, J., "IT Projects: A basis for success", International Journal of Project Management, 13(3), 1995,

Wateridge, J F., "Project health checks", in Turner, J R and Simister, S J., (eds), The Gower Handbook of Project Management, 3rd edition, Gower, Aldershot, 2000.

Wearne, S., "Principles of Engineering Organisation", Thomas Telford, London, 1993.

Westerveld, E and Walters, D G., "Op weg naar project excellence", Samson/Kluwer, 2001.

Williams, H., "The essence of managing groups and teams", Prentice Hall, 1996.

Winch, G., Usmani, A. and Edkins, A., "Towards total project quality: a gap analysis approach", Construction Management and Economics, Vol 16, 1998.

Z

Zimmerman L W, Hart, G D., "Value engineering (A practical approach for owners, designers and contractors)", Van Nostrand Reinhold, New York, NY., 1982.

CONTRIBUTOR PROFILES

Authors:

In addition to writing individual sessions, a number of authors also contributed by reviewing one or more sessions written by colleagues.

Michael Bates

Mike Bates is a Senior Lecturer within the Centre for Project Management at Leeds Metropolitan University. Alongside his undergraduate and postgraduate teaching commitments, he undertakes consultancy work with companies implementing Project Management methodologies.

Mike initially worked on medical projects before migrating into construction, largely in the house building sector. In the early 90's, lecturing changed from being a part time 'hobby' into a full time commitment.

His specific interests are the use of ICT in project management and the assessment of the benefits of project management education and training.

Rob Blanden

Rob Blanden is a Chartered Engineer who holds a Bachelor degree in Mechanical Engineering from The University of Leeds and an MBA from Durham. He has a background in mining, process engineering and operations management, and specialises in knowledge transfer and the utilisation of technology in strategic supply chain management.

Currently, he is a project manager within the Retail Bank IT division of HBOS and is also a part time Associate Lecturer for the Open University Business School.

Terry Brennand

Terry Brennand has an extensive background as a project manager and team leader having been involved in the construction, operational management and decommissioning of gas fired and nuclear power generating and transmission plant.

Exposure to the demands of quality assurance in his sector led Terry to develop his interest and skill in effective leadership, quality management and continuous improvement systems.

He is a qualified EFQM and ISO 9000 Assessor and currently acts as a QA consultant and business mentor. His clients include The Princes Trust, National Utilities Companies and Local Authorities.

Bill Carpenter

Bill is a Mechanical Engineering graduate of the Royal Naval Engineering College in Plymouth and also holds a Certified Diploma in Accounting and Finance. In 1991, he graduated from the University of Bath Executive MBA programme where his final thesis was an investigation into the management of collaborative projects.

For a number of years Bill worked for Westland Helicopters as Project Manager on the EH101 helicopter development programme, leading multi-disciplinary teams on this high technology, bi-national project.

He now works as an Organisation, Management and Leadership Development Consultant, specialising in Culture Change, Business Process Re-engineering, Project Management, Team Development and Leadership.

Darren Dalcher

Darren specialises in systems forensics and project failures and is Director of the Centre for Systems Forensics and Capability (CSFC) at Middlesex University and a senior tutor at the Open University

His Doctoral thesis, at King's College London, focused on life cycles and the need for a dynamic and adaptive perspective. In 1992 he founded, and has subsequently continued as chairman of, the Forensics Working Group of the IEEE Technical Committee on the Engineering of Computer-Based Systems (ECBS). The group comprises academic and industrial participants, correspondents and subscribers world-wide, with the purpose of sharing information and developing expertise in analysing and deriving lessons from failures.

He is an External Examiner for the Association's APMP examination.

Karl Davey

Karl is an experienced risk management consultant specialising in active risk management with Strategic Thought Limited.

He has undertaken many risk management assignments, in both the public and private sectors including major projects for various Government Departments including the Ministry of Defence, Utilities Companies and major Corporations.

Additionally, Karl is involved in preparing and delivering a range of risk management training courses, covering the full breadth of risk management practice and is a regular contributor to risk management seminars, and publications.

Charles Egbu

Originally trained as a Quantity Surveyor, Charles obtained his PhD, in Construction Management (Specialising in Refurbishment Management) from the University of Salford in 1994.

He worked as a Senior Research Fellow and a Lecturer at University College London before joining the Building Research Establishment as a Project Manager and Senior Consultant and subsequently Leeds Metropolitan University before being appointed Professor at the School of the Built and Natural Environment, Glasgow Caledonian University, Scotland.

Charles is a corporate member of the Chartered Institute of Building and APM.

Contributing widely to international journals and conferences in the areas of Refurbishment Management, Construction Procurement Methods, Project Management Methodologies, Risk Management, Quality Management, Value Management, Decision-Making, Innovation and Knowledge Management; Professor Egbu is actively involved in research in these areas within the construction, shipping, finance and aerospace industries.

He is visiting Fellow to the Management, Knowledge and Innovation Research Unit (MKIRU) of the Open University Business School.

Christopher Gorse

Christopher is a senior lecturer and researcher in the Centre for Project Management at Leeds Metropolitan University where he teaches on a variety of vocationally directed and generic project management courses at both undergraduate and postgraduate level.

Prior to his involvement with academia, he worked in a number of industries including transportation and engineering in a professional management role.

Christopher is an active researcher with over twenty publications in international journals and conference proceedings. Research interests include group work and performance, group interaction and communication, group decision making, meetings, and project culture.

In addition to his teaching and research activities, he undertakes consultancy work for a number of regional and national companies.

Gavin Hall

Gavin Hall, a managing consultant with 20 years experience of information systems and technology, specialises in knowledge management with a particular emphasis on corporate knowledge management and information management strategies.

His experience in this arena includes strategy development, feasibility studies, risk analysis, business process re-design, organisation design, project formulation and contract design.

Gavin's expertise embraces the development and implementation of strategies for sourcing IT services and supplier management and his procurement experience includes procurement strategy and planning, negotiation and management of the procurement process. Gavin has led PFI and Joint Venture projects.

Working for the last 10 years in the public sector Gavin has experienced and contributed to the restructuring of public sector businesses; and is now delivering solutions for the 'modernising government' agenda by helping to define 'joined up solutions' for major Government Departments.

Michael Holton

A senior Business Project Manager with the Royal Bank of Scotland, Michael has 15 years Project Management experience within the Financial Services industry.

Currently responsible for major business integration projects; he was, prior to the take over of National Westminster Bank by the Royal Bank of Scotland, Head of NatWest Project Services; An internal professional project management practice responsible for project delivery, project manager development and project management practice development.

His responsibilities extend beyond the delivery of major business projects to the development of project management best practice including project & programme management guides and project competency based master-classes.

Mike is a member of both APM and PMI

Peter Jones

An apprentice trained engineer and a past Fellow of the Institute of Mechanical Engineers, Peter has over 30 years experience with major international contractors in the Oil and Petrochemical Industry engaged in designing and constructing refineries and chemical plant.

He has worked as Project Manager and later as Senior Project Manager on various projects in Europe, the Middle East and South America. More recently, Peter managed a department of over 250 professional engineers providing staff resources and services to multiple projects undertaken world-wide. In this capacity he led the introduction of pioneering 2D and 3D computer-aided design on projects and the development of quality management in a project based organisation achieving ISO 9001 accreditation for the organisation.

Peter is now an occasional lecturer at Cranfield School of Management and undertakes a number of consultancy assignments.

Anne Keegan

Anne Keegan is a Post-Doctoral Researcher at the Rotterdam Institute of Business Economic Studies and lecturer in the Department of Business and Organisation in the Faculty of Economics of Erasmus University, Rotterdam.

She undertakes research in the fields of human resource management and organisation theory, concentrating on project-based organisations and knowledge intensive and professional firms. A regular presenter at conferences on HRM, knowledge intensive firms and project management, Anne has also taught management, industrial relations, innovation and international business at Trinity College, Dublin where she studied management and business and completed her doctorate on the topic of 'Management Practices in Knowledge Intensive Firms'. She has also worked as a consultant in the area of human resource management and organisational change to firms in the computer, food, export and voluntary sectors in Ireland.

Dennis Lock

Dennis Lock is a freelance writer. His early career began as an electronics engineer with the General Electric Company. His subsequent management experience has been successful, and exceptionally wide, in industries ranging from electronics to heavy machine tools and mining engineering. He is a Fellow of the Institute of Management Services, Fellow of the Association for Project Management and a Member of the Institute of Management.

Denis carries out lecturing and consultancy assignments in the UK and overseas, lecturing on masters' programmes at Southampton and Surrey Universities, and has written or edited many successful management books.

Akin Oluwatudimu

Following graduation with bachelor and masters degrees in architecture from the University of Ife (now Obafemi Awolowo University), Nigeria; Akin studied in Trieste, Italy and obtained a Doctorate in Building and Settlement Engineering in 1991.

A full member of the Architecture and Surveying Institute and APM, Dr. Oluwatudimu also holds the APMP qualification and the RIBA Certificate in Project Management and has worked in architectural and interior design practices in the United Kingdom for the past 8 years, successfully completing numerous fast-track developments for Blue Chip clients.

Currently, a project manager in the Estates Division of the Imperial College of Science, Technology and Medicine, London, he has published a number of technical papers and contributed to books on various aspects of the Built Environment.

Peter O'Neill

A graduate of the Open University with a degree in Technology and Systems, and an MBA from Warwick Business School, Peter is a member of both the Association for Project Management and the Institute of Personnel Development.

Previously Course Director at the British Steel Management College, he now combines public and in-company training and consultancy, delivering project management, project leadership and negotiation programmes to a range of top UK companies, with tutoring in Organisational Behaviour on the Warwick Business School's MBA programme.

Peter's project and leadership experience is extensive, beginning as a farm labourer and developing through foremanship to contract management and project leadership. He has led projects for the Manpower Services Commission, contributed to a European Parliament IT project and been responsible for marketing and developing products for a national team of field staff.

His practical experience in negotiation includes 2 years as a Group Chairman within the ASTMS union and face to face negotiation in Industrial Relations, Sales and Purchasing.

Martyn Quarterman

Martyn Quarterman is a Chartered Surveyor, Project Manager and recognised industry specialist in the field of Value Management.

He is currently the Director responsible for Value Management, Risk Management and Training Services with Appleyards. Prior to this he was Head of Value Management for BAA plc responsible for the implementation of Value Management on capital projects undertaken at all BAA's airports including Heathrow and Gatwick. Martyn specialises in training and implementation of Value Management in organisations and is currently assisting a number of major clients in this area. During his career Martyn has utilised Value Management and Value Engineering on well over 100 projects.

Martyn has an MBA (Project Management) from Henley Management College and lectures at several colleges and universities. He is a former member of the Executive Committee of the UK Institute of Value Management and a fully qualified European Trainer in VM (TVM).

Bob Saunders

Bob Saunders has been in the RAF, the Defence industry, and presently is an Associate Lecturer with the Open University, working on project management and systems management courses.

Bob has been involved with 'Systems Thinking' for 15 years, and uses the concepts and methods to inform his work.

Recent research has been into communications, chaos, complexity, and the effects of post-modernism on the world of project mangers. He also lectures in these areas.

Bob is also involved with the Association for Project Management in the Development and Education arena, where he is leading a project to introduce systems of higher education qualifications in project management.

Martin Stevens

Martin has extensive experience as a designer, strategist and project manager over a period of 25 years. With a bachelor degree in architecture and a masters degree in project management, he has worked in both public and private sector organisations in consulting and contracting roles. He now practices as a project management consultant and has undertaken assignments for both central and local government and retail, construction and banking sector clients. He is particularly experienced in the configuration and management of joint venture projects involving public and private sector participants and also the management of business change to enable corporations to capitalise on their project investments. Additionally, he is an occasional tutor at the London Management Centre. A member of the Association for Project Management since 1989, he is a former Branch Chairman and Council member. Martin is also a member of The Chartered Management Institute.

Michel Thiry

Michel Thiry is an organisational consultant and President of the European Governing Board for Value Management Certification and Training and is certified in both project management and value management in the USA and the UK.

A regular speaker and writer on project and value management at an international level, he is author of the book Value Management Practice. Michel has delivered numerous training sessions in project and value management, both in Canada and in Europe following more than twenty-five years professional experience in projects, gained on 'both sides of the pond'.

Following a fruitful career in construction, Michel has now focused on strategic management consultancy; specifically change, value and programme management, as well as the management of strategic training programmes.

In addition to his professional experience, Michel has participated in the translation of the PMI-PMBoK into French and was also professional coordinator for the development of the 'Project Management Step-by-Step'© CD-Rom.

Rodney Turner

Rodney Turner is Professor of Project Management in the Department of Business and Organisation of the Faculty of Economic Sciences, Erasmus University, Rotterdam, and a founding director of EuroProjex, the European Centre for Project Excellence. He is also a member of the associate faculty at Henley Management College.

After leaving Oxford University, where he undertook work leading to a doctorate and was a post-doctoral research fellow at Brasenose College, he spent several years with ICI working on engineering design, construction and maintenance projects in the petrochemical industry. He also worked as a consultant in project management with Coopers and Lybrand before joining Henley Management College. He has been with Erasmus University since 1997.

Professor Turner works as a project management consultant, lectures worldwide and has published several books and papers on project management, including the best-selling Handbook of Project-based Management. He edits the International Journal of Project Management, is Vice-President and past Chairman of the Association for Project Management and past President of the International Project Management Association.

Paul Vollans

A Chartered Electrical Engineer by profession, Paul has been responsible for the management of many projects, including redevelopment of the Port of Sudan, the control system for the London Water Ring-Main and construction of a major dry-dock in India. For several years, Paul was Principle M & E Engineer with a major water utility and has worked at senior level for contractors, manufacturers and consultants. He was also Operations Director of a small M & E contracting organisation, developing the business from scratch to a half million pound turnover company.

Whilst working in industry, Paul took a considerable interest in training, and lectured in management topics at the University of Central England.

Joining Smallpeice Enterprises Limited in 1997, he developed and presented courses in Project Management and related topics, including risk, finance, assertiveness and negotiation. He also developed bespoke Program Management training for an international supplier to the car industry and a telecommunications company; presenting the material across Europe and North America.

Recently, to further his interest in the provision of help, advice and facilitation in the introduction of project management to client organisations, Paul joined Interserve Engineering Services where his role is to identify business improvement needs and address those issues through training, coaching and other initiatives. His knowledge of industry combined with his training experience enables effective new ideas and techniques to be introduced into the business.

Steve Wake

Steve Wake is a leading Earned Value champion. A business graduate with a Master's degree in Manpower studies, Steve has planned, managed, consulted and trained in a variety of industries: Aerospace, Defence, Construction, Transport, Automotive, Engineering, FMCG manufacturing and software development. He has written popular and highly regarded books on Earned Value, Integrated Programme Management and Enterprise Resource Planning. He plays an active part in promoting and lobbying for Earned Value with an annual conference now a permanent fixture as well as speaking engagements with official bodies. He is Chair of the Association's Specific Interest Group on Earned Value which published a Guideline for Earned Value Management in the UK in May 2002.

John Wateridge

John Wateridge is a senior lecturer at Bournemouth University. He has been lecturing in information systems, systems analysis and IS/IT project management for ten years. He received his Ph.D. in 1997. Before joining Bournemouth University, he worked for ten years in industry as a computer programmer, systems analyst and project manager.

Alan Webb

Over the last twenty five years Alan Webb has worked at every level in manufacturing industry from shop floor supervisor to senior project manager and much of that has been at the sharpest end:- aerospace development work. During his time as a practising project manager he has managed the development of various advanced technology products.

He formed his own consultancy in 1991 providing services to industry and education in the field of project management, particularly in the area of innovative development work. He has provided consultancy to a variety of well-established organisations including: the UK Civil Aviation Authority, The GEC Group, Flight Refuelling Limited, MoD Procurement Executive and Rolls-Royce.

Additionally Alan has lectured at Master's degree level in project management at home and abroad and has been an examiner at four universities. He is an established author, having written "Managing Innovative Projects", and "Project Management for Successful Product Innovation" and numerous articles on all aspects of project management. He is a member of APM and a member of the British Standards Institution having contributed to the production of a variety of recent standards.

Paul Whitehead

Paul Whitehead is a Senior Lecturer at Leeds Metropolitan University's Centre for Project Management where he undertakes significant consultancy work with companies implementing Project Management systems in addition to his undergraduate and postgraduate teaching commitments.

Paul's background is in Highway Engineering having spent several years with South Yorkshire Highways Department before moving into education. His specific interests include project control and implementing project management techniques within organisations.

Bob Wiggins

Bob Wiggins is a highly experienced information professional and a Fellow of Chartered Institute of Library and Information Professionals and the Institute of Management Consultancy.

Having been responsible for corporate information and data services in major organisations he established his own consultancy company in 1995. (www.curaconsortium.co.uk) He consults at both tactical and strategic levels, in the areas of business/process analysis, change management, quality management, auditing, requirements specification, tender preparation, supplier selection, planning, project support, programme or project management or system implementation.

He is the author of 3 books on document management - the latest being "Effective Document Management - Unlocking Corporate Knowledge", published by Gower 2000.

Core Review Panel

The Core Review Panel comprised:

Steve Armstrong	**Martin Hamilton**
Nadine Honeybone	**Bill Johnson**
Dennis Lock	**Des Mc Carthy**
Pippa Newman	**Bob Saunders**
Martin Stevens	

Topic Reviewers

The following individuals have also contributed to Pathways by acting as topic reviewers:

Chris Chilton	**Owen Davies**
Martin Graham	**David Hawken**
Nick Johns	**Norman Price**
Elizabeth Randall	**Geoff Reiss**
Geoff Saunders	**Mike Sherwood**
Simon Springate	**Mark Tomlinson**
Dave Webster	

INDEX

A

acceptance testing 63-2
accountability 13-6
Action Centred Leadership 72-3
action plans 67-9, 67-15
activity ID codes / numbers 31-17, 32-23
activity-on-arrow 31-7, 31-8
activity-on-node 31-8, 9, 31-12
(ACWP) actual cost of work performed 33-10, 35-8
Admiralty Court 54-4
ambiguity 41-11/13, 41-14
appraisal 12-4, 20-7, 8, 30-8
appraisal interviews 75-20
approval cycles 62-18
Approved Codes of Practice 25-1, 25-4
Arbitration 73-13/16
as-built 64-5
Assertiveness 73-10/16, 73-18
assessment 67-13
audit 25-10, 25-14
audit trail 36-13, 36-18, 19, 67-13

B

balance sheet 52-2
balanced matrix / organisation 66-6/10, 66-14, 66-25
Balanced Scorecard 22-3, 22-15
bar chart 31-3/6, 46-2
Bargaining 74-11/13
base rate 52-3
baselined 46-3
benchmarks 24-2, 24-6, 40-8, 41-1
benefits 22-1, 22-4/6, 22-8, 22-10, 22-13/16, 22-18, 19
Best Available Techniques Not Entailing Excessive Costs (BATNEEC) 25-9
Best Practicable Environmental Option (PBEO) 25-9
Bidder conferences 53-4
biological environments 45-12
Board blasting 41-15
bonds 12-5, 52-1/5, 52-8, 52-11, 12
Boston Boxes 41-18
boundaryless firms 75-25
brainstorming 22-11/13, 23-6, 7, 41-15, 71-3, 4
Branding 51-9, 51-14, 51-29
breach of contract 54-10
British Quality Foundation 24-14, 24-17
budget 20-5, 20-8, 21-7, 21-14, 42-5, 42-6, 42-9, 42-16
build-operate-transfer 52-1, 52-6
Build-up 20-9/11
Business Case 10-6/9, 10-27, 12-4, 5, 24-2, 24-7, 24-12/16, 40-1, 40-13, 51-2, 51-4, 51-16, 51-26, 53-2
business context 41-3, 41-12

D

G

H

M

N

O

P

Q

R

S

T

NOTES